In part 2, the contributors examine the effects of
jurisdictional shifts from a variety of vantage points,
including the levels of punishment associated with
different types of legislation, the ethical and jurisprudential issues arising from them, and their racial
dimensions and impacts. The section concludes with
a review of current practices in the assessment of
adolescents for *fitness* for the court and the clinical
dimensions of the boundaries of the juvenile court.

The final section of the book offers insight into
the developmental and psychological aspects of
current and future reform, as well as the editors'
synthesis of the policy implications drawn from the
earlier analysis.

JEFFREY FAGAN is professor of public health and director
of the Center for Violence Research and Prevention at the
Joseph L. Mailman School of Public Health at Columbia
University. FRANKLIN E. ZIMRING is William G. Simon
Professor of Law and director of the Earl Warren Legal
Institute at the University of California at Berkeley.

Contributors: *Donna Bishop, Richard J. Bonnie,
M. A. Bortner, Elizabeth Cauffman, Linda Frost Clausel,
Robert O. Dawson, Jeffrey Fagan, Barry C. Feld,
Charles Frazier, Thomas Grisso, Darnell Hawkins,
James C. Howell, Akiva Liberman, Richard Redding,
Simon Singer, Laurence Steinberg, David Tanenhaus,
Marjorie Zatz, Franklin E. Zimring*

THE CHANGING BORDERS

OF JUVENILE JUSTICE

The John D. and Catherine T. MacArthur Foundation
Series on Mental Health and Development

Research Network on Adolescent Development
and Juvenile Justice

Also in the series

*Youth on Trial: A Developmental Perspective on
Juvenile Justice,* edited by Thomas Grisso and
Robert G. Schwartz

THE CHANGING BORDERS
OF JUVENILE JUSTICE

*Transfer of Adolescents
to the Criminal Court*

Edited by
JEFFREY FAGAN AND
FRANKLIN E. ZIMRING

THE UNIVERSITY OF CHICAGO PRESS / CHICAGO AND LONDON

Jeffrey Fagan is professor of public health and director of the Center for Violence Research and Prevention at the Joseph L. Mailman School of Public Health at Columbia
University. Franklin E. Zimring is director of the Earl Warren Legal Institute at the University of California, Berkeley.

The changing borders of
juvenile justice

The University of Chicago Press, Chicago 60637
The University of Chicago Press, Ltd., London
© 2000 by The University of Chicago
All rights reserved. Published 2000
Printed in the United States of America
09 08 07 06 05 04 03 02 01 00   1 2 3 4 5
ISBN: 0-226-23380-4 (cloth)

The University of Chicago Press gratefully acknowledges a subvention from the John D.
and Catherine T. MacArthur Foundation in partial support of production of this volume.

Library of Congress Cataloging-in-Publication Data.

The changing borders of juvenile justice : transfer of adolescents to the criminal court /
edited by Jeffrey Fagan and Franklin E. Zimring.
    p. cm. — (The John D. and Catherine T. MacArthur Foundation series on mental health
and development)
    Includes bibliographical references and index
    ISBN 0-226-23380-4 (cloth : acid-free paper)
    1. Juvenile justice, Administration of—United States.   1. Extenuating circum-
stances—United States.   3. Transfer of cause—United States.   4. Criminal courts—
United States.   I. Fagan, Jeffrey.   II. Zimring, Franklin E.   III. Series.
KF9779.C435   2000
364.36'0973—dc21   99-045190

For Francis Allen, Intellectual Pioneer

CONTENTS

The Changing Borders of Juvenile Justice: Transfer of Adolescents to the Criminal Court

FRANCIS A. ALLEN

Issues of when and under what circumstances cases of juvenile delinquency and criminality should be transferred from juvenile courts to adult courts for adjudication may at first sight appear to involve technical operational concerns of little broad social significance. In fact, as even brief scrutiny of the papers that follow will reveal, the waiver decision gives rise to a plethora of such basic concerns as the definition of childhood and adolescence in modern American society, the public safety, the definition of proper roles for state power in the lives of individual members of our society. Unhappily, the tendency of much modern legislation to view expansion of the waiver device as a sovereign remedy for the problems of juvenile justice in these times has obstructed thoughtful public consideration of what juvenile policy consists of, and by ignoring basic considerations threatens basic values.

It can hardly be expected that these brief prefatory remarks will add importantly to the impressive analyses and marshaling of data in the other contributions to this volume. No such attempt will be made. Instead, these comments will attempt to identify a few pervasive and recurring issues that emerge from close consideration of juvenile justice, issues likely to persist whatever courses reforms of juvenile justice may take. Attention will be directed primarily to the notion of culpability in the adjudication of juvenile offenses and to the phenomenon of official discretion in the administration of juvenile justice, and its persistence and regulation.

Perhaps the beginning of wisdom when considering these issues is to note that they are by no means confined to juvenile justice but arise whenever efforts are made by the state to penalize and contain proscribed behavior of offenders of any age. The traditional literature of the juvenile court displays a strong tendency to view the problems of juvenile justice as things separate from the general issues of criminal justice administration. The aspiration of the juvenile court's founders was to establish an institution wholly distinct from criminal courts in form, procedures, and purposes. It can hardly be doubted that courts dealing almost exclusively with the behavior of children and adolescents are confronted regularly by a range of considerations in some measure peculiar to those age groups. Although reasoned cases for the abolition of the juvenile court are being advanced in these times, many observers retain the belief that the juvenile court is best equipped to deal with an important range of concerns involving children and adolescents, and are hopeful that its functioning may be rendered more effective.

Yet it has always proved impossible to isolate the administration of juvenile justice from broader concerns of penal policy. From the beginning, juvenile court operations embraced punitive objectives—deterrent, incapacitative, and perhaps retributive. This being true, the question of what elements are relevant to the culpability of juvenile offenders was always present, however much ignored in the classical juvenile court literature. In 1967 the Supreme Court of the United States in the well-known *Gault* decision gave constitutional recognition to the reality that the juvenile courts are engaged, among other things, in the dispensation of penal sanctions. Accordingly, the juvenile proceeded against in a delinquency hearing is entitled to many of the basic procedural protections mandated in adult proceedings.

Recognition by the Supreme Court of the penal nature of juvenile delinquency proceedings was an event of great importance, but the insight was one that had been familiar to observers of the juvenile courts long before the *Gault* decision. These critics had noted, for instance, the confinement of serious juvenile offenders in institutions that, whatever sobriquet is attached, are in fact youth prisons, and sometimes among the least progressive prisons in their jurisdictions.

The critique of some observers in the pre-*Gault* era, however, went well beyond such obvious pursuits of punitive objectives in the juvenile courts, and asserted that judicially authorized treatments of juveniles motivated by rehabilitative purposes and aspirations must be seen as encompassing inescapably punitive elements when the courses of treatment entail significant intrusions into the lives and liberties of the affected children.

Today issues of penal culpability have emerged undisguised throughout the administration of juvenile justice. At present no informed observer of juvenile justice is able to view the waiver decision as one simply involving a choice between rehabilitative treatment in the juvenile court and punishment in the adult penal system. Often the issue posed is whether the penal measures available to the juvenile court under state law are adequate and appropriate to the case at hand. Culpability issues today receive overt consideration in the adjudication of delinquency cases in juvenile courts and in hearings to transfer adjudication of such cases to adult courts. When transfer is granted the culpability issues persist in the criminal proceedings.

Since at least the eighteenth-century Enlightenment, theories of penal culpability in liberal societies have encompassed the principle of penal proportionality: penalties imposed on offenders by the state should be proportional to the blameworthiness of the offender. The principle not only represents an expression of a basic moral intuition, it also sets limits on the exercise of the penal powers of government. To say that criminal sanctions are to be limited by the notion of proportionality is not to deny that penal treatment may also aspire to other purposes—deterrent, rehabilitative, or incapacitative. It is to say that in pursuit of these objectives punishments must or should be commensurate to the offender's blameworthiness. By providing a theory of limitation of state powers in the penal areas, the proportionality principle performs functions analogous to the restraints on governmental authority contained in the Bill of Rights of the federal Constitution. Indeed, in a number of state constitutions the proportionality principle has been given explicit expression. Like the bill-of-rights immunities, applications of the proportionality principle may often conflict with the immediate wishes and expectations of public opinion. The insecurities generated in these times by instances of extreme juvenile violence tend to submerge culpability considerations in demands for prompt incapacitative and deterrent outcomes. That the principle of penal proportion is important to the survival of basic political values may be inferred from the history of twentieth-century totalitarian regimes. The ideology and practices of these societies demanded that in the penal process concerns with the culpability of accused individuals be regularly sacrificed in the interests of internal security and conformity. It was precisely such assaults on the claims of individual autonomy that evoked the strongest repugnance of those who in the recent past opposed the aggressions of the totalitarian regimes.

Application of the proportionality principle entails calculations of degrees of offenders' blameworthiness, an activity hardly tending to scientific exactness. On the other hand, one may doubt that estimates of the deterrent capacity of penal measures or of the efficiency of contemplated programs of rehabilitative treatment are any more certain. At present the primary source of conflict in applying the proportionality principle resides in the determination of what elements are to be taken into account in calculating the degree of culpability of the individual offender and what weights and priorities are to be assigned to the various factors identified. Penal dispositions may violate the proportionality principle by being disproportionately lenient as well as disproportionately severe. The present legislative surge toward limiting the jurisdiction of juvenile courts in cases of juvenile violence often reflects a strong public perception of the inadequacy and hence the disproportionality of penal sanctions available to juvenile courts. In many instances the perception may be accurate and defensible. What has been lost in the legislative initiatives is a concept of proportionality that gives sober weight to factors relevant to the blameworthiness of individual offenders. Thus issues of degrees of culpability of the juvenile offender are slighted or ignored when focus is directed almost wholly on the losses of life and limb sustained by victims of juvenile violence and on retributive and incapacitative demands.

When confronting behavioral problems of children and adolescents it has long been the policy of American law to attribute a large significance to the factors of age and immaturity. The central importance of these factors is an underlying assumption of the juvenile court movement. Youth policy both limits the privilege of the young and also affords them special protections in recognition of their limited life experiences, undeveloped cognitive skills, and often limited capacities for self-discipline and control. Such attributes seem highly relevant to application of the principle of penal proportion in cases involving juvenile misconduct. As stated in a plurality opinion of the United States Supreme Court: "The reason why juveniles are not trusted with the privileges and responsibilities of an adult also explains why their irresponsible conduct is not as morally reprehensible as that of an adult."

Despite the critical importance of issues of age and immaturity in waiver decisions and determinations of culpability of young offenders in both juvenile and adult courts, American law remains strikingly inarticulate in relating immaturity to culpability in the various contexts in which determining degrees of blameworthiness of offenders is of the essence. The substantive criminal law denies criminal capacity to children of tender years, but for older children doctrines of diminished responsibility on grounds of age and immaturity are largely lacking. Instead, such issues are typically related to judicial discretion when waiver decisions are made or penal sanctions imposed, a discretion largely unsupervised and unguided by communicable principles. It is here that social-science research has an important role to play. Although modern research does not speak with one voice on questions of age and immaturity, it contains the potential for more equitable and accountable resolutions of culpability issues in the administration of American juvenile justice.

Analysis of the culpability concept leads almost inevitably to the phenomena of official discretion in the administration of juvenile justice. Discretionary decisions of judges, prosecutors, and staff functionaries abound in virtually all aspects of juvenile court operations, and when cases are transferred to the adult courts, dispositions often reflect the broad sentencing discretion of trial judges. The importance of official discretion and the problems associated with it, however, are not confined to juvenile justice administration, but characterize the entire range of penal operations, adult as well as juvenile. Thousands of discretionary decisions profoundly affecting the lives and liberties of individuals are made each day by judges, prosecutors, police officers, and correctional officials. A great many such decisions are guided by no articulated legal norms. The consequences of the pervading normlessness (or perhaps anarchy of competing unexpressed values) is often caprice, inequity, and a paucity of principles and procedures to test official performance and enforce accountability on the system of criminal justice. More effective measures to guide and contain official discretion is thus one of the pressing needs of juvenile justice, and in this respect reflects problems that are common to the entire apparatus of penal justice operations.

Broad consideration of problems associated with official discretion can perhaps best be directed to three basic queries: (1) Which decisions should be relegated to the exercise of official discretion and which should be governed by preexisting provisions of statutes or administrative regulations?; (2) in those instances in which discretion must or can best be exercised, where should the locus of discretion be lodged, and which officials should be granted discretionary powers?; and (3) when discretion is to be exercised, what measures or techniques are available to guide discretion toward a fuller realization of basic values and of a more rational systemic performance?

In response to the first inquiry it may be said that no comprehensive efforts have been made to identify which of the myriad issues encountered in criminal justice administration are appropriate for discretionary decision making. Discretion abounds throughout the system, but for the most part its prevalence is not the product of conscious and rational choice. It cannot be doubted that many decisions that today are the product of unguided official discretion could feasibly be made the subject of rules of law to the great advantage of the fairness and effectiveness of the system. One reason for the preference shown discretionary decisions in the operation of the system is that they provide escape from consideration of difficult issues of policy not so easily evaded when efforts are made to govern decision making through statutory mandates. Yet recent years have provided examples of significant improvements in the quality of justice achieved by subjecting areas formerly left to official discretion to governance by preexisting legal rules. Thus contemporary efforts to recodify the substantive criminal law have in many areas replaced unguided judicial sentencing discretion with articulate and considered provisions governing a multitude of critical distinctions. This experience demonstrates that a fuller statutory articulation of basic principles is often entirely feasible and may result in a penal law more fully expressive of basic values.

Yet experience has shown that many vital decisions require intelligent exercise of discretionary authority by public officials. The problem posed by this necessity is not to be solved by futile attempts to eliminate discretion from the system's operations, but rather by efforts to come to terms with discretionary authority in ways that advance as far as possible basic political and cultural values. Discretionary authority is particularly required in situations in which there is a multiplicity of factors to be taken into account in decisions to be made, many of which factors are peculiar to the particular case under consideration. The waiver decision in the juvenile court provides a prime example of such situations. Attempts to govern outcomes in such cases by statutory mandates produce unfortunate results because of the inability of legislation to anticipate and enumerate all factors relevant to intelligent decision making and because generality of application can be achieved only by ignoring elements essential to equitable and rational outcomes. Much recent legislation in the areas of juvenile justice illustrates these phenomena.

If it is assumed in a given area of operations that discretionary decision making is desirable or required, the second inquiry stated above often arises: Where and with which officials should discretionary authority be lodged? These questions pervade the entire system of penal justice. Thus, should each individual police patrolman be conceded the power of decision when participating in certain specified operations, or should patrolmen's performance reflect a broad departmental policy? To what extent should prosecutorial discretion represent the judgment of an individual official rather than a systemwide practice established by some supervisory authority such as the state attorney general? Frequently centralizing discretionary authority may advance the objectives of consistency and accountability in the system's operations.

In the areas of juvenile justice, the question of locus of discretionary authority may be of large importance; thus, should the burden of decision in waiver cases be placed wholly or largely with the juvenile court judge, or should a legislative judgment be made to avoid discretionary decisions altogether in certain categories of cases and require that they automatically be removed from the juvenile to the adult courts? The tendency of statutory law has been for some considerable time to erode the authority of juvenile court judges and enhance that of prosecutors. A full discussion of the issue will not be attempted here. It can be said, however, that the waiver decision, involving as it does the weighing of multiple competing considerations of individual equity and social interests, is of the sort that experienced judges are most familiar with. One may fairly expect, therefore, that informed and unpartisan decisions are most likely to result from the exercise of judicial discretion.

Efforts through legislation, such as some modern waiver statutes, to control discretion by eliminating it create consequences that are, again, akin to those experienced elsewhere in the penal system. The history of sentencing guidelines in the federal courts provides a striking example. While limiting the sentencing discretion of federal judges, the guidelines have significantly expanded the discretion of federal prosecutors, a discretion less open and less supervised than that exercised in judicial sentencing. Legislative efforts to eliminate discretionary waiver in juvenile courts by mandating automatic transfers to adult courts in certain categories of cases may produce the unforeseen consequence of enlarging prosecutorial authority in transfer cases. Since the prosecutor possesses the authority to select the offense on which the juvenile will be tried, he may charge an offense not included within the automatic transfer statute, thereby gaining final authority over the waiver decision.

The third inquiry is perhaps the most important. Given the inevitability of discretionary authority throughout our public life, what can be done to monitor, direct, and contain it? The issue is critical, for unguided discretion often produces capricious institutional performance resulting in inequities and unfairness to the individuals affected. It is an obstacle to rational and consistent policy, and thereby weakens the effectiveness of governmental action. It enhances the difficulties of imposing accountability on public officials for their performances in office. It is, in short, a threat to the values summarized in the concept of the rule of law.

Issues of directing and containing discretionary authority are particularly acute in the administration of juvenile justice. They are by no means limited to the waiver decision, but the transfer cases illustrate the problems and the importance of devising solutions. If it is assumed that in the future juvenile court judges will play an important role in waiver decisions, what devices and procedures can be employed to guide and assist exercise of judicial discretion? The first requirement is the formulation of more considered and articulate guidelines for waiver adjudication. Some juvenile courts have adopted the formulation advanced in the appendix to the *Kent* case in the United States Supreme Court. The factors mentioned in that statement are no doubt relevant to waiver decisions, but they afford little assistance to judges considering what weights and priorities should be given to the factors enumerated in particular cases. The task of formulating modern guidelines in waiver cases can hardly be left to legislative action, but must be delegated to commissions operating on a systemwide or local basis. Certain measures internal to the court may prove useful. In large juvenile courts collegial consultation among judges in which particular cases before the court are considered could result in fuller deliberation and more consistent outcomes. A larger role for appellate courts in reviewing waiver decisions could result in the evolution of principles providing guidance now lacking in waiver decision making. Perhaps more important than any particular suggestion for guidance of discretion in these cases is promoting an awareness of the significance of the problems of accommodating discretionary authority to the ends and values of our political society.

It has been suggested in these remarks that many of the pervasive and overarching issues of juvenile justice are common to the broader penal justice system, and that in some measure these issues emerge in areas of social concern far removed from the administration of penal sanctions. In confronting the urgent contemporary problems of juvenile delinquency and crime it may prove useful to consult this broader experience. It may also prove true that intelligent thought and action directed to the problems of juvenile justice may find application in broader arenas of social action. In the meantime there is clear danger that the greatest long-term losses resulting from the social malfunctions confronted by juvenile justice today may be those stemming from measures intended to cure these ills. An important contribution of intelligent scholarship in these times is its effort to reduce that danger.

ACKNOWLEDGMENTS

The cast of characters that launched and supported the venture that led to this book was a large one. The John P. and Catherine T. MacArthur Foundation Research Network on Adolescent Development and Juvenile Justice commissioned the book project and provided generous financial support to the venture. Laurence Steinberg, the head of the network, initiated this project and Lynn Boyter, the network administrator, coordinated and sustained the planning and execution of the project.

Once draft papers had been prepared, the project organized a meeting and retained nine distinguished experts in juvenile justice to review each chapter and suggest revisions. Shay Bilchik, Barbara Boland, Martin Guggenheim, Julie Horney, Richard Kempert, Tracey Meares, Steven Z. Perren, Ruth Peterson, Michael Smith, Michael Tonry, and Michael Wald served as reviewers and greatly improved the chapters in this book. Erik Carlson gracefully shepherded the book through its production.

The staff support at two research institutes that the house the editors of this volume was exemplary as usual: Karen Chin and Toni Mendicino of the Earl Warren legal Institute and Carol Huezo of the Center for Violence Research and Prevention at Columbia University.

JEFFREY FAGAN AND FRANKLIN E. ZIMRING

The most serious juvenile crimes have always been the political Achilles' heel of the American juvenile court. Even when public opinion is tolerant of juvenile delinquency, the teen killer is the nightmare case for the juvenile justice system. In an age where the phrase *juvenile superpredator* is often heard in the federal congress and state legislatures, the deep-end adolescent offender is a particular threat to public acceptance of the mission and objectives of juvenile justice. If the court as a whole is politically vulnerable in such circumstances, the cases and procedures concerned with transfer to criminal court are doubly vulnerable. It is little wonder, then, that legislation concerning transfer is a near-universal feature of the politics of juvenile justice.

This volume is one of two initial ventures to launch a cross-disciplinary research project in adolescent development and its implications for juvenile justice policy. A companion volume addresses key terms in the legal and behavioral descriptions of adolescent development, terms such as "capacity" and "culpability" that are of general importance across the range of ages and jurisdictions of American juvenile courts. The topic of this volume—standards for transferring young offenders out of juvenile court—might seem both peripheral and parochial by comparison to the general themes engaged by the other inaugural venture of the MacArthur Research Program on Adolescent Development and Juvenile Justice.

Waiver might seem a peripheral issue because it is not about the bulk of cases and kids processed by juvenile courts, but only the few older and more serious offenders pushed onto the criminal court. It might seem a parochial topic by contrast to general concerns like culpability, because transfer does not appear to involve basic questions about adolescent development so much as it simply decides which of two courts should hear a case. Why should such an isolated issue have implications for other domains of juvenile justice?

This book is intended to be not only a detailed study of procedures of great practical importance to a second century of American juvenile justice, but also a study of policy issues that should force observers to confront fundamental questions about the functions and limits of the juvenile courts. We argue that the view from the backdoor of American juvenile justice must provide a clear picture of the rationale of juvenile justice if waiver policy itself is to be rational and appropriately invoked.

1. Transfer Policy in Practice and Theory

No American doubts the practical importance of transfer-related issues to the operation of juvenile courts and to the political viability of juvenile justice. When very serious crimes by youth are a focus of public concern, laws about transfer to criminal court jurisdiction are the most likely legislative response to that concern. Between 1990 and 1996, no fewer than forty of the fifty states passed legislation creating new standards for transfer decisions (Griffin, Torbet, and Szymanski 1998). Without exception, these new laws were designed to expand the number and kind of cases where transfer occurs, but this expansive objective was pursued using a wide variety of tactics.

The political importance of transfer[1] policy is as a safety valve for the juvenile courts, a way to provide for punitive treatment of adolescents but still preserve the programs and policies of the juvenile court intact. The different ways this safety valve procedure can be designed will have very different impacts on both juvenile and criminal justice systems. Should transfer standards be designed to facilitate a small number of cases—twenty to one hundred in a state system per year—or to produce two to three thousand? Both types of systems have been constructed. Should decisions be made principally on the juvenile's current charge, or on his prior record? Should general standards for transfer be made in legislation or should discretion be delegated to judges or prosecutors? If discretion becomes the key to transfer decisions, who should be trusted with the power to decide? And on what basis? And what is the significance of the decision in the constitutional framework of juvenile justice? These are very important issues, not frequently discussed in the ad hoc atmosphere of legislative response to public concerns about youth crime.

While the practical importance of transfer standards is acknowledged, the theoretical significance of transfer standards is not widely known or mentioned. It turns out, however, that the principles that govern transfer out of juvenile court are one defining element of a theory of juvenile justice. One can't know why juvenile court is the appropriate place for the hundreds of thousands of accused delinquents that the court sees without knowing what sorts of otherwise eligible cases are transferred out of the court's jurisdiction, and why. To test theories of why the court is appropriate for adolescents only against the cases the juvenile court retains is to risk false generalizations if cases transferred share the characteristics emphasized. In an important sense, one can't know why a juvenile court keeps cases until one knows why other cases are excluded from juvenile justice, and what happens to them in other courts.

The standards used in transfer decisions are thus a test of the content and coherence of a theory of juvenile justice. At the same time, it is important to use a theory of juvenile justice as one important test of whether particular proposals for transfer rules make sense. It should be necessary to compare the kids and events that are nominated for transfer with the larger rationales for a juvenile court as one test of the quality of a transfer policy.

But that's the role that theory should play in transfer policy. The reality is that most decisions about transfer standards are made on an ad hoc basis without any reference to general notions about the competence or limits of juvenile courts. Decisions are made as an aspect of policy toward crime, but not as a self-conscious act of constructing or elaborating a theory of juvenile justice. One of the major ambitions of this volume is to reverse this process, to make the consideration of transfer standards an important part of the theoretical work of defining the scope and content of juvenile justice.

There is an even broader canvas on which decisions about transfer should have theoretical significance, and that is on the legal theory of adolescent status. Are the youngsters transferred to criminal courts no longer children in the eyes of the law as a result of that decision?[2] If so, why? If not, how should the continuity of childhood status be acknowledged in the criminal court? And should childhood status be decided on theoretical bases separate from culpability for criminal behavior? These turn out to be important questions about the boundaries of American adolescence. A juvenile court for the adjudication of delinquency has become a standard feature of the legal construction of the first half of adolescence all over the developed world. The exceptions to that practice should help us to discern not only the prevailing theories of juvenile justice but also the theories of adolescence that form its larger context.

With all this theoretical import inherent in the subject, two aspects of the debate about transfer policy are very discouraging. The first is the paucity of careful attention to matters of theory when discussing transfer policy. The second is the extraordinary distortion of the one theoretical construct that has been widely used in the discussion of transfer policy in juvenile justice. A central term that governs judicial waiver tests in juvenile justice is "amenability to treatment." The way in which the contextual pressures of waiver decisions distort the term "amenability" is a cautionary tale for those who wish to promote a theoretical dimension to discussions of transfer outcomes.

2. Amenability: When Words Lose Their Meaning[3]

The official theory that launched the American juvenile court in its policy toward delinquency was that the sole basis for juvenile court intervention was to help the development of a child found delinquent, and the mechanism for delivering that help was to require treatment of youths and their families either in the community or in special institutions. The reach of authority was substantial, but the justification for the use of state power was one-dimensional: the policy of the court was only to help.

This is why children who had not violated any laws could be found delinquent and treated in the same manner as children who had violated laws. Blameworthy conduct was unnecessary because punishment wasn't a part of the court's response to delinquents. Being in the company of bad companions, or being in danger of leading an immoral or dissolute life, or any other sign that help was needed was a sufficient predicate for court intervention.

If status offenses were not the delinquent's fault, what of acts that would be criminal if committed by adults? Judge Julian Mack's classic statement of the original theory of the juvenile court suggested that he thought blameworthiness was not significant here, as well. The function of the court was "not so much to punish as to reform, not to degrade but to uplift, not to crush but to develop, not to make [the delinquent] an offender but a worthy citizen."[4] The object for uncomplimentary comparison with the juvenile court in the Mack rhetoric was obviously the criminal court.

Now here is the problem. If some youths under the maximum jurisdictional age were to be pushed out of the juvenile court and into the jurisdiction of the disfavored criminal courts, what could justify the rejection? If fault was irrelevant to the definition and treatment of delinquency, how could fault be an important distinguishing characteristic for waiver? And if juveniles are never at fault, why should they ever be subject to transfer to criminal courts?

Two approaches were possible, and both can be found in the juvenile court's performance. The first is a form of doublespeak where fault is not referred to in the *juvenile* court, but once the decision has been made to transfer an accused, the blameworthiness of the offense and the offender can appropriately be the subject of comment.

Here is the juvenile court of Cook County Annual Report for 1907:

> All right-minded people are willing to have boys and girls have chances to do the right thing, but after they persistently throw chances away the same people would have a right to insist that

these young people be really controlled, even if it takes the criminal court process to do it.[5]

This is one of the earliest documents in the administration of American juvenile justice, and the vocabulary of blame is already a major element in the operational rhetoric of the court in waiver cases.

The second approach is to leave undisturbed the analytic framework that created the status of delinquency, but to define a second status that would not be consistent with treating an adolescent as a delinquent. This status designation was usually described as a finding that a particular youth "was not a fit subject for the juvenile court."[6] But what could render a fourteen-year-old not a fit subject for the juvenile court?

If the sole function of the juvenile court was treatment, the one characteristic that would clash with this treatment function was the failure to be treatable. Here was the critical role of a finding that a youth was not amenable to treatment—it put that young offender beyond the single aim of the juvenile justice system. If the ideology of the juvenile court was treatment, the lack of amenability to that single tool was the sole theoretically justified ground for expulsion from the system dedicated to treat delinquent youth.

In this sense, the dominant theory of the juvenile court, need for treatment as the defining feature of the court's caseload, implied the basic rationale for waiving juveniles: a finding that the youth in question would likely not respond to treatment. This is in one sense an exemplary illustration of theory-based rules for the operation of juvenile justice. The problem with it, from early on, was that a huge gap between theory and practice within the juvenile court doomed the attempt to explain waiver solely in terms of amenability to treatment.

The motives for juvenile court action were always a spectacular mix of the punitive, the authoritarian, and the mentorly. Very serious offenses put pressure on the juvenile court to waive a youth if he was fifteen or sixteen. Of course, one could construct an amenability-to-treatment argument out of the accusation of a serious crime by suggesting that to commit the offense was inconsistent with the type of responsiveness to treatment that makes youngsters appropriate subjects for juvenile court treatment. To similar effect, a history of frequent offending could be read as evidence that the youth in question was not amenable to any treatment in the arsenal of juvenile justice. Indeed, a rebellious attitude, an inappropriate haircut, or anything else that provokes a negative response from a juvenile court judge can be marshaled as evidence that treatment won't work. Everything can be grist for the theoretical mill of finding a youth not amenable to treatment if the term acquires a sufficiently loose meaning and standardless practice.

The two problems with this approach are that it is disingenuous and distortive. It often misstates the real reasons why decisions to transfer are made, the motives that have produced the decision to transfer well before the nonamenability label has been pasted on the defendant. And it assembles under the umbrella category of nonamenability a miscellaneous collection of situations that do not fit a single meaning. The precedents that accumulate under the heading of nonamenability will give ample authority for application of the label (and achievement of the waiver result) in future cases. But the word has lost any distinctive conceptual meaning. The label will be applied whenever the result must be achieved. There is no value added by the labored transformation of the diverse motives for waiver into a distended amenability category. What the process loses is candor and clarity.

3. Dimensions of Transfer

Some mechanism for transfer of juveniles to criminal court has been a feature of juvenile justice systems from the beginning. But the law and practice relating to transfer has also been changing in recent years, creating a diversity of systems with new complexities that are a formidable challenge to the student of comparative juvenile justice. By way of introduction to these complexities, consider four basic dimensions of transfer processes in a jurisdiction.

1. *Mechanisms of transfer.* There are now at least three distinct methods the law can provide for transfer of juveniles to criminal court. Traditional waiver systems would place a juvenile at risk for criminal prosecution only if a juvenile court judge had "waived" that court's jurisdiction over a minor. Legislation can provide, however, for the exclusion by law of minors over a certain age or charged with certain crimes from juvenile court, so that criminal court becomes an automatic consequence of a covered criminal charge. Legislation can provide also for concurrent jurisdiction in both juvenile and criminal court for some charges and minors with the choice of court at the discretion of the prosecutor. In systems with legislative exclusions or concurrent jurisdiction, the law may provide for criminal court judges to refer selected minors back to juvenile court, a process usually called "reverse waiver." These different mechanisms may exist alone or in combination, so that a single jurisdiction has different modes of transfer. Or one form of mechanism may be exclusive or at least dominant.

2. *Standards for transfer.* What factors in the offense or the minor should be decisive in determining which court should hear a case? The mechanism used to decide on transfer may influence the substantive standards used, but the same legislative technique or judicial power can be used to administer systems that depend on very different criteria. Whether explicit or implicit, most transfer decisions are based on some substantive standard. In jurisdictions with multiple mechanisms, however, the different decision makers may be using different substantive standards.

3. *Rates of transfer.* The number of minors transferred and the proportion of juveniles charged with crimes who are transferred are the two best measures of the rate of transfer to criminal court. This significant dimension of transfer policy may be largely independent of the mechanisms of transfer available in a particular jurisdiction and the substantive criteria emphasized by the decision maker. Rates of transfer may be low or high in a legislative exclusion system depending on the breadth of the exclusion. Also, two jurisdictions that concur in emphasizing offense seriousness as the dominant influence on transfer policy may differ on the degree of severity that produces transfer and thus might produce greatly different rates of transfer. One set of interesting questions concerns the variations over time and among American jurisdictions in rates of transfer. A second set of important issues concerns the relationship between the mechanisms and standards used for transfer and the rate of transfer that is likely to result.

4. *Consequences of Transfer.* What are the legal provisions for treatment of juveniles who are transferred from juvenile to criminal courts? Are there any restrictions on punishment in the criminal court? Are there special provisions on sentencing in the criminal court that are either mandatory or available at the discretion of criminal court judges or prosecutors? In some jurisdictions, special provisions were inserted in legislation along with the reforms transferring classes of juveniles to criminal courts (e.g., New York). In other jurisdictions, special provisions for young offenders in criminal court were provided by court case or legislation independent of changes in transfer mechanisms or standards.

As new layers of legislation are added onto established frameworks of transfer, the interaction between new mechanisms and old can produce systems that are difficult to comprehend and outcomes that are not easy to predict. If the policy analysis of juvenile court reform was ever an easy task, that day has long passed into history.

4. Overview of the Volume

The first two sections of this essay each illustrated a shortcoming of traditional discourse about transfer from juvenile court that this book has been organized to avoid. In the first section, we referred to the lack of theoretical content in contemporary analyses of transfer issues and practice. In the second section, we complained about how a unitary theory of juvenile justice created misleading labels and results in waiver decision making. The lessons from these two cautionary tales are complementary. First, theory counts. Observers of transfer policy debates must pay close attention to the theoretical implications of transfer policy choices for the legal framework of the court and the legal theory of adolescence.

But theory can rarely be imposed by force on contrary practice. What distorted the one-dimensional treatment theory of juvenile justice, and the nonamenability rationale for waiver that was its mirror image, was that it provided a counterfeit account of the real reasons for transfer decisions. Thus, the second lesson: the problem with phony accounts of the reasons for transfer is the reality of transfer motives. This is the necessary starting point for realistic proposals for reform.

The first task in constructing this volume was to prepare a principled table of contents, to subdivide the mass of materials and topics into a set of important issues that could be addressed by separate chapters in an edited volume. The three parts of the book illustrate this progression of emphases. Part 1 is concerned with the basic structures and concepts that have grown up around the practice of transfer from juvenile to criminal court. David Tanenhaus launches this enterprise by narrating the evolution of transfer as a practice and an issue in the early days of juvenile court operations in Chicago. Robert Dawson analyzes the traditionally dominant mode of judicial waiver decisions in juvenile court in chapter 2. In chapter 3, Barry Feld addresses the proliferation of legislative mandates for transfer of offense categories and age-offense combinations. Richard Redding and James C. Howell discuss the variety of ways in which juvenile courts have been given expanded punishment powers in modes of "blended jurisdiction" and the justification that can be put forward for these hybrid systems in chapter 4. In chapter 5, Lynda Frost Clausel and Richard Bonnie analyze appellate review of transfer decisions that are made in differently configured systems. Franklin Zimring argues in chapter 6 that waiver by judicial decision is a structural necessity in a juvenile court system committed to protect its subjects from disfiguring punishments.

Part 2 shifts attention from the structure of transfer to some of the organizational and behavioral effects of transfer. Donna Bishop and Charles Frazier report in chapter 7 on the consequences of transfer for the later behavior of transferred youths. M. A. Bortner, Marjorie Zatz, and Darnell Hawkins focus on the racial consequences of the sorting and allocation processes that characterize transfer in chapter 8. Thomas Grisso describes and critiques the forensic assessment processes that judicial waiver has generated in chapter 9. Simon Singer, Jeffrey Fagan, and Akiva Liberman report on the systemic lessons of the wholesale shifts of jurisdiction to criminal courts in New York, a type of transfer not of subjects but of an entire subject matter from family to criminal court.

The final section of the volume addresses the policy significance of current knowledge. In chapter 11, Laurence Steinberg and Elizabeth Cauffman are concerned with what developmental psychology can teach about the appropriate directions of transfer policy. In the final chapter, the editors provide a synthesis of the transfer policy implications drawn from the common themes found throughout the volume.

For those who worry that the topical subdivisions in this volume might emphasize the trees to the detriment of the forest, we recommend a careful reading of the foreword by Francis Allen, which provides as good a statement of the context of transfer decisions as we have yet seen.

References

Conrad, John P. 1981. "Crime and the Child." In *Major Issues in Juvenile Justice Information and Training: Readings in Public Policy.* Edited by John C. Hall, Donna M. Hamparian, John M. Pettibone, and Joseph L. White. Columbus, Ohio: Academy for Contemporary Problems.

Griffin, Patrick, Patricia Torbet, and Linda Szymanski. 1998. *Trying Juveniles in Adult Court: An Analysis of State Transfer Provisions.* Washington: Office of Juvenile Justice and Delinquency Prevention, Office of Justice Programs, U.S. Department of Justice.

Mack, Julian. 1909. "The Juvenile Court." *Harvard Law Review* 23:104.

Tuthill, Richard. 1907. *Report of the Cook County Juvenile Court.* Chicago: Cook County Juvenile Court.

White, James B. 1978. *When Words Lose Their Meaning.* Chicago: University of Chicago Press.

Notes

1. We use the term "waiver" to denote judicial prerogative to transfer a case from juvenile to adult court jurisdiction and "transfer" as the universal term that embraces legislative, executive, and judicial mechanisms to transfer jurisdiction.

2. Cf. Conrad 1981.

3. Cf. White 1978.

4. Mack 1909, 107.

5. Tuthill 1907, 123.

6. The language of "fit and proper" subject recurs through California Welfare and Institutions Code, § 707. For example, in 707(a), "the juvenile court may find that the minor is not a fit and proper subject to be dealt with under the juvenile court law if it concludes that the minor would not be amenable to the care, treatment, and training programs." In 707(b), (c), (d), etc., the statute uses various offense criteria to create presumptions that the "minor shall be presumed to be not a fit and proper subject to be dealt with under the juvenile court law unless the juvenile court concludes, based upon evidence, which evidence may be of extenuating or mitigating circumstances, that the minor would be amenable to the care, treatment. . . ."

Part One

The Evolution of Intercourt Transfer

Chapter One

The Evolution of Transfer out of the Juvenile Court

David S. Tanenhaus

A child, a boy especially, sometimes becomes so thoroughly vicious and is so repeatedly an offender that it would not be fair to the other children in a delinquent institution who have not arrived at his age of depravity and delinquency to have to associate with him. On very rare and special occasions, therefore, children are held over on a *mittimus* to the criminal court.

Judge Merritt Pinckney, Cook County Juvenile Court, 1911

We do not consider whether, on the merits, Kent should have been transferred; but there is no place in our system of law for reaching a result of such tremendous consequences without ceremony— without hearing, without effective assistance of counsel, without a statement of reasons. It is inconceivable that a court of justice dealing with adults, with respect to a similar issue, would proceed in this manner. It would be extraordinary if society's special concern for children, as reflected in the District of Columbia's Juvenile Court Act, permitted this procedure. We hold that it does not.

Justice Abe Fortas, United States Supreme Court, 1966

Anglo-American courts from at least the fourteenth century have used chronological age as an approximate measuring stick to distinguish children from adults in determining their culpability for crime (Platt and Diamond 1966, 1233–34). According to Sir William Blackstone's famous *Commentaries on the Laws of England* ([1769] 1979, 4:22–24), a tripartite schema for handling the cases of infants (i.e., persons under twenty-one) accused of committing "serious offenses" evolved over the centuries. Under this system the common law made its clearest distinction with respect to age and discretion in capital cases, a category that Parliament broadly expanded during the eighteenth century to cover increasing numbers of property offenses (Hay 1975, Beattie 1986, Lieberman 1989). Children under seven were immune from prosecution in these cases because they were considered incapable by nature of having "felonious discretion." From seven to fourteen, children were presumed to be incapable of having the necessary intent to commit a serious crime, but this presumption could be rebutted and children could be tried as adults. Finally, once children reached fourteen years of age, they were tried as adults.[1] Remarkably, the outlines of this ancient classification system have shown tremendous resiliency despite revolutionary attempts, especially during the last hundred years, to redefine the relationship of the child to the state. If present trends continue, there is a distinct possibility that twenty-first-century juvenile justice will mirror its common law past.

Before looking to an uncertain future we must first come to terms with a forgotten past. Many of today's seemingly unprecedented problems in the theory and practice of juvenile justice, such as the transfer of adolescents from juvenile court to criminal court, have histories that can offer useful perspectives on present concerns.[2] In this chapter, I will demonstrate that the history of transfer reveals a diversity of practices, which emerged in the years between the establishment of the nation's first juvenile court in 1899 and the Supreme Court's pronouncements about the constitutionality of transfer in *Kent v. United States* (383 U.S. 541 [1966]). In this sixty-seven year period, social workers, probation officers, lawyers, and judges handled "hard cases" that raised fundamental questions about the nature of children and how they should be treated at law. These cases helped to define the scope of juvenile justice by establishing jurisdictional boundaries, the limits of childhood, and the amenability of children to reform *within* these systems.

Recovering this lost history of intercourt transfers also helps to test the new master narrative of twentieth-century juvenile justice that Barry Feld (1984, 1987, 1993, 1997), most notably, has helped to develop in a series of landmark articles.[3] This narrative begins at the turn of the century with the creation of the juvenile court as a social welfare institution whose mission was to protect the best interests of children, particularly the poor children of immigrants growing up in congested urban areas. However, by creating a court to deliver social services to needy children, the progressives "situated the juvenile court on a number of cultural and criminological fault-lines" (Feld 1997, 72).[4] On one side stood the juvenile court with its mission of rehabilitation, benevolent rhetoric, and informal procedures. The criminal justice system stood on the other side with its traditional emphasis on punishment, adversarial practices, and procedural safeguards.

Once in place, according to the narrative, this dual system of justice remained fairly stable until after World War II. A declining faith in "the rehabilitative ideal" after the war began to spell trouble for the juvenile court and then, in the late 1960s, beginning with *In re Gault* (387 U.S. 1, 87 S. Ct 1428, 18 L. Ed. 2d 527 [1967]), its conceptual foundations were shaken by the Supreme Court.[5] This decision not only granted limited due process rights to children in juvenile courts, but also questioned whether the reality of juvenile justice matched its benevolent rhetoric. The Supreme Court's "constitutional domestication" of the juvenile court thus changed its focus "from paternalistic assessments of youth's 'real needs' to proof of commission of a crime" (Feld 1997, 73). This change blurred the conceptual lines established by the progressives between juvenile and criminal courts and cleared the way for state legislatures to criminalize juvenile justice in the following decades. By the 1990s, as Feld and others have argued, the juvenile court had become a second-rate criminal court for children where young people receive "neither positive treatment nor criminal procedural justice," and, accordingly, the court should be abolished (Feld 1997, 90).[6]

Although this new master narrative offers a compelling account of the major structural transformations of juvenile justice over the course of the twentieth century, it obscures the diversity of practices, procedures, and controversies that have characterized American juvenile justice since the early 1900s. Despite the numerous warnings about the danger of casting the juvenile court as an "ideal type," scholars, and journalists to a larger degree, still choose to describe the first half-century of juvenile justice in such artificial terms.[7] This approach encourages policy makers as well as the public to think that the past was simpler, static, and somehow irrelevant. It also discourages further historical analysis.[8]

Such presentism is dangerous because it unnecessarily distances us from earlier generations and their experiences with the problem of serious youth crime. Not only can we learn from their approaches, but we must also avoid their proclivity to make such difficult cases disappear from view. From the 1910s to the 1960s, for example, appellate court judges creatively read statutes in order to allow for criminal courts to try the cases of serious adolescent offenders, who were technically under the *exclusive* jurisdiction of a juvenile court. Once these adolescents were out of the juvenile court system, they ceased to be counted as children and were forgotten. Clearly, we need to know what has happened with past juvenile legislation before we can construct a theory of transfer for the future.

This chapter begins with a prehistory of the juvenile court that examines the radical reconstruction of the relationship between the child and the state in the late nineteenth century, which laid the conceptual foundation for modern juvenile justice in this country as well as abroad (Abbott 1925; Lou [1927] 1972, 23–25). It then examines the period from roughly 1900 to 1920, focusing primarily on America's model court in Chicago, in order to learn how early officials handled hard cases involving juvenile offenders accused of serious crimes.[9] These findings, supplemented by exploratory forays into less well studied regions, suggest that the landscape of Progressive Era juvenile justice needs to be mapped more carefully because its boundaries were in constant flux due to lingering constitutional concerns about jurisdiction, the development of diverse transfer procedures, and the lack of an official theory of waiver. As a result, it is instructive to conceive of juvenile courts as works in progress that adapted to changing social conditions and, I would argue, continue to do so.

The chapter then explores how in the 1920s and 1930s, supporters of besieged juvenile courts articulated a theory of judicial waiver to defend them against mounting criticism. In these years, public concerns about modern youth and crime waves produced harsh critiques of court systems as inefficient and ineffectual. The theory of judicial waiver helped to shield juvenile courts against these charges by asserting that the juvenile court judge's expertise made him or her a qualified state actor to protect the community against dangerous youth. Accordingly, the judge should have the discretion to decide how individual cases should be handled. He or she could transfer individual cases to protect the safety of the community, while retaining the majority of children in the juvenile justice system, which was equipped to meet their special needs. This defense of judicial waiver, which made the case for judicial discretion, set the terms for subsequent debates over the boundaries of juvenile justice that developed after World War II.

After the war, renewed public concerns about youth crime and the beginning of sustained critiques of juvenile justice by the legal community focused attention on procedural matters, including whether children should have the constitutional right to due process in juvenile court. By the early 1960s, there were concerted attempts by scholars to discover how practices like transfer worked and efforts to define how they should work. *Kent* was decided in this context of rethinking the basic assumptions of juvenile justice. The decision, however, clouded the issue of transfer by helping to establish the appearance of uniformity in how the nation's juvenile courts exercised this procedure, while at the same time insulating the practice from appellate review on due process grounds. Moreover, the changing political landscape of the 1970s would leave *Kent* standing as a monument of a passing era instead of a symbol of a new age.

1. The Prehistory of the Juvenile Court

The juvenile court movement, which began in the 1890s in Illinois and spread both nationally and internationally, called for the creation of specialized courts to hear the cases of all children, including adolescents, because they were understood to be qualitatively different from adults. The movement's remarkable success in the United States benefited from the infectious nature of "progressivism," which, as Arthur Link and Richard McCormick have noted, was "the only reform movement ever experienced by the whole American nation" (1983, 9). Individuals joining to form interest groups with the goal of enacting innovative public policies defined this period of frenzied reform that began in the 1890s and fizzled out after World War I (Rodgers 1982, Pegram 1992). The juvenile court movement in Illinois epitomized this process of interest group politics as social reformers, including the first generation of college-educated women, formed coalitions with philanthropists, social workers, and leaders in the legal profession in order to win political and legal acceptance for the idea of a juvenile court (Tanenhaus 1997, 1:73–136).

Two interrelated developments in late nineteenth- and early twentieth-century social thought—the inventions of "childhood" and a "social" conception of law—served as the conceptual cornerstones of the juvenile court. Although the idea that children were by nature different from adults and should be treated differently by the law was not new (Schlossman 1977, 49–54), it achieved a new stature due to the child study movement of the late nineteenth century and became the first principle of modern juvenile justice (Ainsworth 1991, 1085–101). In addition, as Janet Ainsworth has argued, the new science of child development successfully made the case that adolescents were "more like infants in their nature and needs than they were like adults" and should be treated like children at law (1991, 1101).

The moral crusaders for the juvenile court, once they had established that all children belonged to a separate class, invoked a new social conception of law to support their efforts to expand state power.[10] This theory of socialized law contended that the law must adapt to rapidly changing social conditions produced by large-scale industrialization, mass immigration, and explosive urban growth (Willrich 1998). These seismic changes made traditional ideas about individual responsibility seem antiquated in the "modern" world (Pound 1913).[11] Societal conditions, according to this theory, produced environments that encouraged criminal behavior. Thus, the power of the state had to be extended to police those social conditions that caused disorder.

Ironically, the inventors of the juvenile court turned to the medieval

English doctrine of *parens patriae* (literally "the father of the country") to build their "new piece of social machinery" (Tanenhaus 1997, 1:140). In the United States, beginning in the early nineteenth century, states began to use this paternalistic doctrine, which gave the king power to protect his dependent subjects, to justify intervention in the lives of neglected children (Rendleman 1971; Pisciotta 1982; Grossberg 1996, 74–75). The creators of the juvenile court used the doctrine of *parens patriae* to argue that benevolent state treatment of children was in their best interest. The juvenile court, they argued, would act as a chancery court, not a criminal court, and seek to rehabilitate, not punish, children. As Jane Addams, who helped to establish the world's first juvenile court, later explained:

> There was almost a change in *mores* when the Juvenile Court was established. The child was brought before the judge with no one to prosecute him and with no one to defend him—the judge and all concerned were merely trying to find out what could be done on his behalf. The element of conflict was absolutely eliminated and with it, all notion of punishment as such with its curiously belated connotation. (1935, 137)

Yet the idealized juvenile court that Addams and other leaders in the juvenile court movement spoke about so glowingly never actually existed. Even in Chicago's model court, conflicts erupted from the beginning. These conflicts ranged from individual disputes, such as a rheumatic mother writing the governor asking him to persuade the juvenile court to free her incarcerated son, to political mobilization, such as that of Catholics to remove a Jewish juvenile court judge who they argued had interfered in their community's affairs (Tanenhaus 1997, 1:198–208). These critics of the court, whether outraged parents or an organized ethnic community, were challenging the underlying assumption that the interests of the child and the state were the same and questioned the progressives' motives for wanting to help *their* children. There is a growing historiography that examines how competing conceptions of childhood exposed tensions between democratic notions and the authority of experts in this period, provoking intense social conflict (Moran 1996).

The enormous diversity among juvenile courts within states as well as across the nation also complicates the history of juvenile justice. This diversity, of course, stems from the fact that American juvenile courts are statutory creations and, as David Rothman has observed "practically no two courtrooms (let alone any two states) followed identical procedures. It is far more appropriate to think not of *the* juvenile court, but of many juvenile courts" (1980, 236). In New York State, for example, children's courts were part of the criminal justice system until 1924 and continued to use more formal procedures into the 1930s (Tappan 1949, 177; Sobie 1987, 125–55). Racial considerations could also play a role. Under a 1934 Tennessee law, for instance, in some counties the juvenile court had the power to transfer "incorrigibles" for felonies or misdemeanors, and "colored" girls in any case (Ludwig 1955, 35). Such differences meant that there would not be a single history or evolution of transfer in the twentieth century, but rather that multiple local cultures of intercourt transfer would develop.[12]

2. Transfers, Commitments, and "No" Theory in the Progressive Era

When writing about the history of juvenile justice, scholars generally differentiate between its theory and its practice.[13] The titles of classic accounts, such as Ellen Ryerson's *The Best Laid Plans* (1978) and David Rothman's *Conscience and Convenience* (1980), suggest that the administration of juvenile justice represented a fall from grace or at least from high foundational principles. Given the American tendency to weave legal theory from the worn cloth of experience, the idea that theory preceded practice and practice departed from theory may be the wrong approach, especially in the case of procedures like transfer, where diverse practices developed before a coherent theory was articulated.[14] Accordingly, I offer a different perspective that treats the juvenile court in the early twentieth century as a work in progress and argues that the practice of transferring hard cases was an important part of its larger process of self-definition.

Essential to the success of these courts at the turn of the century was defining which children they could best serve. The debate about the future of the juvenile court, which began almost immediately after its creation, centered on the question of which children belonged in juvenile court.[15] In Chicago, for example, almost from the beginning, the number of delinquency cases overwhelmed the nation's first juvenile court. The judge and chief probation officer had to find ways to control an overwhelming caseload for practical as well as political reasons. They tried to keep younger children out of court because their cases clogged the court's calendar and did not appear serious enough to merit a judge's attention. Less serious cases also diverted the court's attention from recidivists, whose lack of amenability to reform threatened the court's legitimacy. At stake was the future of this new experiment in local governance (Tanenhaus 1997, 1:136–208).

During the Progressive Era, juvenile court judges in Chicago feared that the Illinois Supreme Court would declare the state's pioneering juvenile law unconstitutional.[16] Because of lingering constitutional concerns, court officials did not always assert the original and exclusive jurisdiction granted them by a 1905 revision of the state's juvenile law.[17] Instead, these officials allowed for an informal system of concurrent jurisdiction to develop by not challenging the state's attorney's decisions to prosecute adolescent offenders accused of serious crimes in the criminal courts. Thus, the state's attorney could prosecute any child over the state's age of criminal responsibility, which was set at ten. In 1921, for example, regarding a case involving a sixteen-year-old boy who had stolen seven hundred thousand dollars in bonds from a bank, the state's attorney declared: "This is a criminal case, and the boy will be tried in criminal court, regardless of his age. And I believe in speedy trials, too" (quoted in Jeter 1922, 14). The juvenile court judge did not press his court's jurisdictional claims over the child because he believed the Illinois Supreme Court would hold that the juvenile court had only concurrent jurisdiction, not exclusive and original jurisdiction, over children, despite the 1905 revision of the law.[18] Such a decision would have given the state's attorney the express authority to prosecute any child offender, ten or older, as an adult (Jeter 1922, 15).

The Chicago Juvenile Court also opted not to exercise its jurisdictional claims in the cases of older children who committed crimes while on probation.[19] Under the state's juvenile law, the court had jurisdiction over the case of a child already in the juvenile court system until he turned twenty-one, but did not have jurisdiction over first offenders between seventeen and twenty-one. A citizens' committee investigating the court in the early 1910s had urged that the state raise the age of jurisdiction of the juvenile court to cover all minors to avoid this "anomalous situation." Their report pointed out that a nineteen-year-old boy "who [had] never been brought before the juvenile court" could be "arrested and forced to associate in the police courts with the worst criminals in the community, while a boy with a long record in the juvenile court evades police jurisdiction by virtue of this court record. In other words a premium is placed on getting a juvenile court record" (quoted in Jeter 1922, 15). In practice, the juvenile court prevented this anomalous situation by declining to exercise its jurisdiction in the cases of recidivists over seventeen years of age because "the officers of the court [were] of the opinion that if probation under juvenile-court officers [had] not been effective when the boy was younger, it is not likely to be effective as the boy grows older" (Jeter 1922, 15). The city's Boy's Court, a branch of the Municipal Court, or the Criminal Court of Cook County heard these cases.

By not pressing its jurisdictional claims over these cases of serious offenders and older recidivists, the juvenile court allowed for the transfer of children under its jurisdiction out of the juvenile justice system. It is not entirely clear why these boys who violated the law while on probation could not be institutionalized in a reform school. The answer most likely would have been that these older boys were considered to be a threat to younger ones in the state's juvenile reformatories. Thus, judges, by not fighting to keep these children in the juvenile justice system, were using a form of "passive transfer." By doing nothing the judge, in effect, allowed for a child to be tried as an adult.

The first state juvenile laws also shielded juvenile courts from at least some potentially volatile cases. Jurisdictional upper age limits, excluded offenses, and transfer mechanisms reduced the likelihood of juvenile court judges hearing cases involving adolescent offenders charged with serious crimes. In 1910, for instance, out of the thirty-two states with juvenile laws that set explicit age limits, only Louisiana, Nebraska, and Oregon established eighteen years as the upper age limit for children of both sexes, and Utah used nineteen, which was the highest limit in the nation.[20] The other states limited their courts' jurisdiction to children who were sixteen or seventeen (Hart 1910). In addition, states such as Indiana, Kentucky, and Michigan excluded certain children charged with felonies (Hart 1910). Almost every state's law also permitted the juvenile court to transfer cases to the criminal justice system. The option of transferring cases to the criminal justice system served as a built-in safety valve, which a judge could use to relieve political pressure on his court by expelling a controversial case (Sargent and Gordon 1963, 121–28; Feld 1978, 518–19). Thus, limited jurisdiction kept older children out of the juvenile justice system, while offense exclusions and the transfer option made it possible to remove those accused of the most serious crimes.[21]

The law-in-action, of course, often varies from the law-on-the-books, and more historical research into the everyday operations of juvenile courts in the early twentieth century is required before a comprehensive history of transfer can be written. Yet, contemporary studies conducted by the United States Children's Bureau that lamented the diversity of juvenile court practices, combined with the agency's repeated attempts in the 1920s to create uniform standards, suggest that individual judges and courts were constructing their own procedural cultures (Lenroot and Lundberg [1925] 1975). For example, Oklahoma judges might have incorporated procedures laid out by the state's Criminal Court of Appeals in *Ex parte Powell* (6 Ok. Cr. 495, 120 Pacific 1022 [1912]). According to *Powell,* one of the earliest discussions of transfer in the case law, the juvenile court had to determine in serious cases whether there was evidence that the child had committed the alleged crime and also whether the child understood the "wrongfulness" of the act. "[S]hould the court find affirmatively," *Powell* stated, the judge had the "discretion, under the law, to hold such child to be proceeded with in the manner provided by law in a court having competent jurisdiction of the offense committed, certifying to such court both its finding as to probable cause, and that the child *knew* the *wrongfulness* thereof" (120 Pacific 1027 [italics in original]). Whether this dual requirement of supplying evidence about probable cause and the child's competence was actually used by courts will require further historical research.

In Chicago, Judge Tuthill helped to construct a local culture of transfer by exercising this option in cases of criminally "experienced" boys near the outer age limit of the court's jurisdiction. Originally, the age limit for boys was set by the legislature at sixteen years, but was later raised to seventeen. Tuthill was skeptical about whether these older and more experienced boys were amenable to reform and considered them a threat to the other children in the system.[22] However, a number of the early state juvenile laws, including that of Illinois, stated that juvenile courts could commit children only to "some detention school or House of Reform or to any institution willing to receive [them] and having for its object the care of delinquent children" (Hart 1910, 134). This meant that courts in many states could not commit juvenile offenders to institutions that housed adult convicts. Thus, if a judge believed that committing a criminally experienced offender to a juvenile institution threatened the safety of the other children, he or she faced a dilemma.

The solution, which Chicago judges used sparingly in the first two decades of the twentieth century, was to dismiss the delinquent petition and remand the case to a grand jury. In his 1904 testimony before the International Prison Commission about the Chicago Juvenile Court, Judge Tuthill spoke about these hard cases, albeit in the passive voice. At the beginning of his testimony in support of the juvenile court, he declared that "the basic principle of the [juvenile court] law is this: That *no child under 16 years of age shall be considered or be treated as a criminal; that a child under that age shall not be arrested, indicted, convicted, imprisoned, or punished as a criminal*" (Tuthill [1904] 1973, 2 [italics in the original]). Yet, in closing, he added that during the past year 17 out of the 1,301 cases of delinquent boys adjudicated by the court "because of their age and confirmed criminal characteristics, were transferred to the criminal court, in order that they might be sent to the State Reform School" (Tuthill [1904] 1973, 6). Tuthill's use of the passive voice did not change the fact that he had actively triggered the waiver process by signing the orders to transfer these boys into the criminal justice system, which had the power to commit them to the State Reform School in Pontiac. Originally, Pontiac housed older adolescents, but by the end of the 1910s it also incarcerated select adult convicts.

Tuthill assumed that the boys he sent to the grand jury would be indicted, tried, found guilty, and sent to Pontiac. Unfortunately, it is difficult to know whether this assumption was accurate. The juvenile court's founders had, for example, expressed concern about whether grand juries would indict minors. Moreover, the literature about the treatment of children transferred into criminal court in the late twentieth century has shown that criminal courts often treated adolescents more leniently than did juvenile courts (Greenwood, Abrahamse, and Zimring 1984). These studies suggest that this practice in the early twentieth century needs to be studied more carefully.

Throughout the Progressive Era, judges serving on the Chicago Juvenile Court continued the practices of both passively and actively transferring serious adolescent offenders because of concerns about the safety of other children. Helen Jeter, who was commissioned in the early 1920s by the United States Children's Bureau to write a report on the nation's oldest juvenile court, calculated that the percentage of boys transferred by the juvenile court judge was usually less than 1 percent. She reported that between 1915 and 1919 the court had transferred only 70 out of 11,799 cases, or 0.6 percent.[23] All of these boys were at least sixteen years of age, "many had been tried on probation or had been at one time committed to institutions for delinquent boys," and the few who were first offenders were close to seventeen years of age. Their crimes included "daring holdups, carrying guns, thefts of considerable amounts, and rape" (Jeter 1922, 89).

By the late 1920s, it appears that a local culture of waiver had developed in Chicago. Judges continued to acquiesce in the informal system of concurrent jurisdiction and still explained the active transfer decision as a means of protecting children housed in reform schools. Concerns about the manageability of older adolescents in the state's juvenile reform schools, which were designed for malleable delinquents, not hardened criminals, triggered the transfer decision. The judges believed that they had to transfer these hard cases out of the juvenile justice system because they still lacked the authority under the state's juvenile law to commit these experienced children to the State Reform School.[24]

The Chicago experience was not representative of how serious young offenders were treated nationwide in the Progressive Era for three important reasons. First, not all juvenile courts were based on the Chicago chancery model, which formally separated them from the criminal justice system. In New York, for example, juvenile courts continued to use the principles of criminal jurisprudence until the 1930s and did not have the option of transferring cases (Sobie 1987; Singer 1996, 35). Under New York law, judges could not find children under sixteen, except in cases punishable by life imprisonment or death, guilty of committing a crime; they could only be found "delinquent" (Sobie 1987, 126–27). Moreover, judges were not permitted to commit "juvenile delinquents" to either the state penitentiary or a county jail. Thus, in New York procedures in juvenile court were more like criminal courts', but transfer was not an option.

Second, juvenile courts, like other progressive social welfare programs, did not always exist in the same form in rural areas. In fact, in Illinois, due to the lack of probation officers in rural areas, courts institutionalized children at higher rates than in Chicago. In addition, these children were often younger and had committed less serious crimes than their urban counterparts (Gittens 1994, 134–42). The problem of different standards within the same state or "justice by geography" continues in the administration of juvenile justice to this day and complicates any analysis of American juvenile justice (Feld 1993, 218).

Third, the informality of juvenile court procedures in the courts using the chancery model contributed to diverse practices and thwarted progressive reformers in their quest to make juvenile justice more uniform. The diverse set of courts produced numerous procedures to try juvenile offenders accused of crimes in criminal court rather than juvenile court (Lou [1927] 1972, 38–41). In Texas and Tennessee, for example, a child had the right of "self-transfer." He or she could request to be tried in criminal court. This option has been traditionally used in vice cases, where criminal courts have often been more lenient than juvenile ones (Zimring 1998, 108). Other states, such as Wisconsin, allowed an examining magistrate to make the determination about which court should hear the cases involving children near the juvenile court's upper age limit. States also divided over how to calculate a child's age for jurisdictional purposes. In Texas, for instance, the age at the time of trial, instead of at the commission of the alleged crime, was controlling (Flexner and Oppenheimer 1923, 76).

The question of what to do about children whose cases technically should have been heard in juvenile court, but had been tried and convicted in criminal court, raised additional problems. Controversial appellate court decisions in Texas and California allowed the convictions to stand, even though, due to age considerations, the cases should have been heard in juvenile court. The appellate courts in both cases declared that the failure of the child to bring up the question of his or her age in a criminal proceeding validated the conviction (Flexner and Oppenheimer 1923, 76). In a study of "The Legal Aspect of the Juvenile Court" prepared for the United States Children's Bureau, Bernard Flexner and Reuben Oppenheimer noted that "these cases consider the juvenile-court laws as though they were designed only to give the accused the advantage of another technicality; the interest of the state, in not having children tried as criminals, is entirely disregarded" (1923, 76).

Despite the diversity of intercourt transfer procedures in the Progressive Era, the contemporary literature by juvenile justice experts often condemned the practice. The political scientist Henry Lou, for instance, declared that "waiver of jurisdiction and transfer of cases whether by the juvenile court, the examining magistrate, the prosecuting authority or the child himself, though seldom exercised, is objectionable in principle" (Lou [1927] 1972, 40). Along similar lines, the final committee report on juvenile court standards, produced in 1923 by the National Probation Association and the United States Children's Bureau, rejected a transfer proposal that resembled the Chicago practice of dismissing the delinquent petition and waiving jurisdiction.[25] Instead, the committee called for exclusive juvenile court jurisdiction for all children eighteen and under and stated unequivocally that "the juvenile court should not have the power to waive jurisdiction and certify cases for trial in another court" (United States Children's Bureau 1923, 1).

The efforts of progressive child advocates, including the National Probation Association and the United States Children's Bureau, did not abolish transfers, but by 1930 they did prompt the majority of states to raise the maximum age of jurisdiction of their juvenile courts to eighteen and Arkansas, California, Colorado, Iowa, and Wyoming to raise theirs to twenty-one (Van Waters [1931] 1968, 156). However, at the same time state legislatures raised jurisdictional age limits, they also began to exclude serious offenses, generally murder and other crimes punishable by death or life imprisonment, from the jurisdiction of their juvenile courts (Van Waters [1931] 1968, 158–72). This combination of higher upper age limits and legislatively excluded offenses would remain fairly stable in most states, with some exceptions, until the early 1970s.[26]

Thus, in the Progressive Era, practice produced transfers, but not an official endorsement or coherent theory. The lack of attention to transferred children also meant that, uncharacteristically, the progressives did not compile detailed statistical reports about these children. Once transferred, whether passively, actively, or legislatively, a child disappeared because he or she literally did not count in the official tabulation of "children in the courts" (United States Children's Bureau 1940).[27]

3. The Defense of Judicial Waiver

Constitutional concerns about jurisdiction, the diversity of transfer practices, and the lack of an official theory of waiver suggest that early twentieth-century judges either had to develop a local culture of waiver as they did in Chicago or perhaps look to law reviews and case law as a guide. If a judge kept up with law reviews and case law, he would have found beginning in the mid-1920s the outlines of a theory of waiver that challenged the condemnation of intercourt transfers and championed judicial discretion in hard cases. In 1929, for example, *The St. Louis Law Review* published a note on the prosecution of delinquents under criminal statutes, which quoted Henry Lou's criticism that judicial waiver was "objectionable and subject to abuse." But it added: "Such discretionary power, however, should not be objectionable. Doubtless cases are presented where moral decadence has reached such an advanced stage that efforts at reformation would be fruitless" (C.R.S. 1929, 431). In this section I argue that in the 1920s and 1930s supporters of juvenile justice used the idea of judicial waiver as a defense against charges that juvenile courts either were ineffective, abused their vast discretion, or coddled criminals. In the process, they helped to establish the terms for subsequent debates over transfer.

Evidence of the desire to make judicial waiver a more prominent part of the juvenile court can be seen in the Standard Juvenile-Court Law, adopted by the National Probation Association in June 1925. Apparently, the framers of the model law rejected the committee's recommendation to ban transfers and instead included a section entitled "waiver of jurisdiction" (Lou [1927] 1972, 237). This section granted a judge the power to transfer a child over sixteen years of age charged with a felony, but only "after [a] full investigation" had convinced him that transfer was "for the best interests of the child and the state" (Lou [1927] 1972, 237–38). The act did not define what constituted a "full investigation," but this requirement implied that at least some procedural integrity was necessary because of the gravity of the decision.

Defenders of juvenile justice could hold up the full-investigation requirement to counter charges of procedural arbitrariness, which had plagued the court from its beginning, but gained momentum in the 1920s (Waite 1921; Ryerson 1978, 93–98). In fact, when Congress updated the District of Columbia's juvenile justice system in 1938, it included this procedural requirement in the new law. That law would be the one tested almost thirty years later in *Kent*. Thus, by the late 1930s specialists contended that juvenile laws should not only include judicial waiver, but should also have some procedural guidelines regulating it.

In the 1920s and 1930s, the charge that juvenile courts coddled criminals was a much greater threat to the legitimacy of these courts than scattered procedural critiques by academics and judges. The "soft on crime" argument was dangerous because it threatened devastating political consequences. In planning a Chicago conference to commemorate the first quarter century of juvenile justice, the philanthropist Ethel Sturges Dummer informed a fellow organizer: "We must plan cautiously lest our conference meet with antagonism and ridicule. People are considering the juvenile court somewhat sentimental and are taking boys of 16 and 17 to the police stations and the criminal courts" (Dummer 1924). The hostile local climate resulted, in part, from the sensational trial in Chicago of the "boy-murderers," Richard Loeb and Nathan Leopold, whom Clarence Darrow had defended that past summer, but also reflected a growing mistrust of modern youth that had begun to take hold in many nations after World War I.[28]

In Chicago during the Great Depression, the treatment of youthful offenders became more punitive as the city's political machine seized control of the juvenile court and blocked reforms, including reformers' efforts to raise its jurisdictional age limit (Dodge 1998, 6). Moreover, in the wake of a number of sensational cases, the chief justice of the Cook County Criminal Court launched a campaign to amend the juvenile court law in order to strip the Chicago court of its jurisdiction in the cases of children over ten years of age (Alper 1941, 230). He declared: "The outdated Juvenile Court Act permits highly dangerous gunmen and thieves, or even murderers, to be accorded leniency intended only for bad boys or bad girls who have committed no serious crime and who are not habitual offenders. The act is clearly in conflict with the legal rights of the Criminal Court" (quoted in Dodge 1998, 6).

The legislative attempt to amend the juvenile law did not pass during this period of concerns about youth crime, but the Illinois Supreme Court did restrict the jurisdiction of the nation's model court. *People v. Fitzgerald* (322 Ill. 54 [1926]) and *People v. Bruno* (346 Ill. 449 [1931]) gave the state's attorney the power to determine whether a child would be brought to juvenile court or criminal court, and then *People v. Lattimore* (362 Ill. 206, 199 N.E. 275 [1935]) stripped the juvenile court of its exclusive jurisdiction over children already in the juvenile justice system (Gittens 1994, 131–34).[29] At issue in *Lattimore* was whether the criminal court had the jurisdiction to try the case of fifteen-year-old Susie Lattimore, a ward of the juvenile court, accused of murdering another girl in a bar fight. The criminal court convicted Lattimore, but in appeal her lawyers argued that she could not be tried by the criminal court without having been first transferred by the juvenile court (Gittens 1994, 133;

Dodge 1998, 7). The Illinois Supreme Court rejected the argument and declared that the juvenile court did not have original jurisdiction, in part, because:

> [i]t was not intended by the legislature that the juvenile court should be made a haven of refuge where a delinquent child of the age recognized by law as capable of committing a crime should be immune from punishment for violation of the criminal laws of the state committed by such child subsequent to his or her being declared a delinquent child. (199 N.E. at 275)

Clearly, this opinion reflected the mounting contempt for the juvenile court's ability to handle the cases of serious offenders. Moreover, this ruling remained in force through the mid-1960s.

It was in this troubling climate of the 1920s and 1930s that advocates of the juvenile court turned to judicial waiver as a defense against the charge that it was "soft on crime." In the *Illinois Bar Journal,* John Dickinson responded to *Lattimore* with a classic defense of judicial waiver. He argued that the juvenile justice system would not become "a veritable haven of refuge" for dangerous offenders because juvenile court judges were capable of exercising the necessary discretion to transfer appropriate cases to the criminal court (Dickinson 1936, 78). "It would seem," he added, "that the benefits to be gained from having first offenders of low age dealt with apart from the criminal courts would outweigh the rarely possible exercise of poor judgment by a juvenile court judge in not turning over to the criminal courts an offender" (Dickinson 1936, 79). Apparently, the state's attorney agreed with Dickinson. His office continued to prosecute only the most serious crimes by adolescent offenders (Gross 1946; Gittens 1994, 134; Dodge 1998, 8).

In the mid-1930s, the Court of Errors and Appeals of New Jersey also affirmed the convictions of juvenile murderers in criminal proceedings in much the same language as *Lattimore.* In *Ex parte Daniecki,* for example, the court declared that "it is inconceivable that the Legislature intended to make the juvenile court a sanctuary for juvenile felons" (117 N.J. Eq. 527, 177 Atl. 91, 92 [1935]). Two years later, the court expanded upon its earlier reasoning to explain why murder, unlike other offenses, could not be legislatively transformed into a noncriminal act, which, if committed by a child, could be placed under the juvenile court's jurisdiction. "We think," Justice Case stated,

> that a charge which is in effect that of murder cuts so deeply into human emotions, collides so violently with life's experiences and fair expectations, and is so horrible in fact and in the contemplation of society, that it remains a crime within the purview of the

Constitution, whatever name and whatever treatment may be appended to it by the Legislature. (*Ex parte Mei,* 122 N.J. Eq. 125, 192 Atl. 81, 83 [1937])

Joseph Siegler, judge of the Juvenile and Domestic Relations Court of Essex County, New Jersey, offered a strong defense of the principles of the progressive ideal and responded to the attempt "to emasculate the juvenile court" (Siegler 1939, 1). His impassioned call, however, for exclusive jurisdiction for the juvenile court in cases of all children under sixteen "*regardless of offense*" was not heeded (Siegler 1939, 2 [emphasis in original]).

By the late 1930s, supporters of juvenile justice, despite frustrations over decisions like *Lattimore* and *Mei,* had at least made the case that judicial waiver should remain as an essential part of juvenile justice that could be used to remove select cases from within the system. Although this theory of judicial waiver encouraged procedural regularity through a "full investigation," it is unclear how seriously this charge was taken. The waiver of jurisdiction continued the practice initiated by the first juvenile court judges of transferring a few children in order to save the majority.

There was, however, a major change in the rhetoric of waiver. The early judges, at least in Chicago, had discussed waiver as something they were forced to do to ensure the safety of children in reform schools. Now the proponents of judicial waiver openly acknowledged the active participation of judges in transferring hard cases. This frank acknowledgment of intercourt transfer suggested that they also accepted the existence of a class of children who were not amenable to reform within juvenile justice. The threat to public safety, no longer the safety of children in reform schools, had become the justification for waiver.

4. Rethinking Juvenile Justice

After World War II, public fears about a juvenile crime wave, fueled by the statistics published in the FBI's *Uniform Crime Reports* and the televised Kefauver hearings on juvenile delinquency, focused attention on the state of American youth (Gilbert 1986). At the same time, a new generation of legal scholars charged that the nation's juvenile justice system was largely ineffective and its rehabilitative claims were overstated. Such shortcomings, these critics argued, raised troubling questions about why these courts should be allowed so much procedural informality. By the late 1950s, as Christopher Manfredi has demonstrated, public fears about juvenile crime coupled with professional concerns about the juvenile court prompted a systematic rethinking of progressive assumptions about discretionary justice and the rehabilitative ideal (Tappan 1949; Rosenheim 1962; Allen 1964; Manfredi 1998, 32–45). It was not surprising, given this reevaluation of juvenile justice, that the intercourt transfer of hard cases would be scrutinized.

The proliferation of law review articles about juvenile justice represented a virtual rediscovery of the juvenile court by the legal community as delinquency caseloads rose nationwide and juvenile courts became more punitive (Dodge 1998, 9).[30] This body of scholarship was primarily concerned with the restructuring of juvenile justice to include more procedural safeguards for children, including legal representation in court, and a reconsideration of exactly which children belonged in court (Rubin 1952). This reassessment of juvenile justice paved the way for subsequent campaigns, which gained momentum in the post-*Gault* years, to remove both the least serious cases of "status offenders" as well as offenders accused of the most serious crimes from the juvenile court (Feld 1993, 227–43).

Initially, intercourt transfer was only a minor current in this larger discourse about justice for the child. Commentators did point out, however, that intercourt transfer was ideologically inconsistent with the mission of juvenile justice as well as theories of child development. In his article "Homicide among Children" in *Federal Probation* (1947), Dr. Ralph S. Banay laid out the conceptual problem. He stated:

> The apparent philosophy behind statutes concerning juvenile offenders is that a child has not reached a degree of intellectual and emotional development that would qualify him as fully responsible for his acts. The laws, however, embody an obvious contradiction; for when the offense is too obnoxious or repugnant, complete responsibility is placed upon the child and he must face the full weight of the law. (Banay 1947, 13)

This argument that a violent act does not transform a child into a rational adult would gain a following in the coming decades.

Legal writers followed up on this argument by criticizing appellate courts for not taking seriously the conceptual problem of treating a child as an adult. They accused courts of intentionally misreading statutes, much like the Illinois Supreme Court had in *Lattimore,* to determine that legislatures could never have intended for juvenile felons to be coddled by juvenile courts (Herman 1958, 602; Problem of Age 1966, 843–44). One such critic, Stephen Herman, again focused attention on the questionable practice of affirming the conviction of a child who had failed to bring up his or her age during a criminal proceeding (Herman 1958, 601–2). He also condemned the practice of using the child's age at the time of the trial, rather than at the time of the offense, to determine jurisdiction.

The question of when a child ceases to be a child had been debated since the creation of the juvenile court, especially at the local level, in the cases of heinous crimes such as the Leopold-Loeb murder of Bobby Franks in 1924 (Fass 1993). However, now in an era of public fears about a youth crime wave and professional criticism of juvenile justice, transfer finally received sustained attention from legal writers, who argued that this issue was part of the larger project of reconstructing juvenile justice. Forging a consensus about the proper minimum age at which a child could be transferred and establishing the criteria that should be used in making this decision proved difficult. The Standard Juvenile Court Act of 1959, for example, set sixteen as the minimum age for transfer, but the National Council of Juvenile Court Judges recommended fourteen as more appropriate (Standard juvenile court act 1959, 353–54).

In the early 1960s, as part of the reevaluation of juvenile justice, *Crime and Delinquency* published a study by the Advisory Council of Judges of the National Council on Crime and Delinquency, which criticized the nation's juvenile courts for failing to base transfer decisions on the best interest of the child (Transfer of Cases 1962).[31] The council employed a survey to determine "how effectively courts are using such transfers." It then used the results to develop a policy statement about how the transfer procedure should work (Transfer of Cases 1962, 3). The report also stressed that under the emerging case law some elements of due process, including parental notification and a thorough social investigation, were required.

The council revealed that most judges strongly supported exclusive original jurisdiction for juvenile courts in children's cases along with the "initiation and control of the transfer procedure," but that they rarely exercised this option. The problem, according to the council, was that four of the five major factors that judges used to make transfer decisions conflicted with the juvenile court's philosophy. It turned out that judges transferred cases because "issues of contestable facts indicate that the hearing in the juvenile court will be prolonged"; "the offense, occurring after correctional treatment for a previous offense, is serious"; "the case is hopeless"; or "the child needs to be punished for his attitude." The only acceptable criterion used, according to the advisory council, was transferring a child because of "the advantage in resources for treatment and public safety lies with the criminal court rather than the juvenile court" (Transfer of Cases 1962, 5).

The council declared that transfer was absolutely necessary in some cases, but that judges must use criteria consistent with the juvenile court's mission of rehabilitation. It recommended that judges consider "(1) the prior record and character of the minor, his physical and mental maturity, and his pattern of living; (2) the type of offense—whether it demonstrated viciousness or involved force or violence; and (3) the comparable adequacy and suitability of facilities available to the juvenile and criminal courts" (Transfer of Cases 1962, 7). Thus, by the early 1960s, a juvenile court judge searching for the proper grounds upon which to transfer a child could now at least refer to a policy statement and an expanding literature addressing this question.

The judge could also refer to a recent series of federal district court decisions that collectively defined waiver (Manfredi 1998, 57). The court first equated waiver hearings with hearings to determine probable cause (*Green v. United States*, 308 F.2d 303 [D.C. Cir. 1962]), then announced that waiver was "a judicial determination that the child is beyond the rehabilitative philosophy" of the juvenile court (*Watkins v. United States*, 343 F.2d 278 [D.C. Cir. 1964]) and, finally, declared that waiver was a "critically important" decision in the life of a juvenile (*Black v. United States*, 355 F.2d 104 [D.C. Cir. 1965]). The transfer decision, in other words, determined whether a child would cross the fault lines separating the juvenile court from the world of criminal justice.

5. The Significance of *Kent*

Given the scant attention paid to transfer during the early twentieth century, it is remarkable that the first case that the United States Supreme Court heard focusing on juvenile justice involved such a decision. That case, *Kent v. United States* (1966), examined the transfer by the District of Columbia's juvenile court of sixteen-year-old Morris Kent Jr. He had been denied a waiver hearing and the opportunity for his attorney to examine his case file. His case became the first of a trilogy of decisions that challenged the foundations of the juvenile court.[32]

The significance of *Kent*, which was written by Justice Abe Fortas, is threefold. First, the justices, by attaching an appendix of "determinative factors" to be considered in potential transfer cases, provided broad new guidelines that the majority of state legislatures incorporated into their own juvenile laws (Feld 1987, 505–7).[33] The adoption of the *Kent* criteria provided at least the appearance of uniformity in American juvenile justice, but also had the unintended consequence of insulating transfer decisions from appellate review on due process grounds because of the subjective nature of the standards (Feld 1987, 491–92).

Second, the endorsement in *Kent* of the concept of *judicial* waiver and attempt to fuse the goals of paternalism and procedural fairness in the juvenile court occurred at a volatile moment in American history. Calls for "law and order" from the right and for the end of "social control" from the left were eroding the rehabilitative ideal (Allen 1981, Beckett 1997). In the 1970s, as youth crime rates increased, the philosophy of "just deserts" replaced "justice for the child" as the rallying cry of reformers, and state legislatures began passing mandatory transfer laws that transformed children who committed serious offenses into automatic adults. This loss of faith in the juvenile court and turn toward the punitive may help to explain why legislatures opted for offense exclusion statutes instead of relying upon traditional and thus suspect approaches to serious youth crime, such as judicial waiver and concurrent jurisdiction (Manfredi 1998, 171–75).[34] Thus, *Kent* marked the beginning of the end of an era characterized by the incorporation of procedural safeguards into *parens patriae*.

Finally, *Kent* focused attention on intercourt transfer and encouraged criminologists to study how these decisions were made, which children were transferred, and what the consequences for them were. These children would now be counted. Yet it remains unclear what this recognition means in a society moving away from the fundamental assumption that the law should treat children differently from adults. The modern idea of childhood, which had grown up with the juvenile court, appears to be vanishing as the first century of juvenile justice comes to a close.

Acknowledgments

I would like to thank the editors, Jeffrey Fagan and Franklin Zimring; the reviewers, Tracey Meares and Michael Smith; as well as Joseph A. Fry, Chris Rasmussen, and Paul Werth; and Margaret Rosenheim for their valuable comments on drafts of this chapter. I also owe a special debt to Jenifer Stenfors for her research assistance and editorial suggestions.

References
Cases Cited

Black v. United States, 355 F.2d 104 (D.C. Cir. 1965).
Ex parte Daniecki, 117 N.J. Eq. 527, 177 Atl. 91, 92 (1935).
Ex parte Mei, 122 N.J. Eq. 125, 192 Atl. 81, 83 (1937).
Ex parte Powell (6 Ok. Cr. 495, 120 Pacific 1022 (1912).
Green v. United States, 308 F.2d 303 (D.C. Cir. 1962).
In re Gault, 387 U.S. 1, 87 S. Ct 1428, 18 L. Ed. 2d 527 (1967).
Kent v. United States, 383 U.S. 541 (1966).
People v. Bruno, 346 Ill. 449 (1931).

People v. Fitzgerald, 322 Ill. 54 (1926).
People v. Lattimore, 362 Ill. 206, 199 N.E. 275 (1935).
Watkins v. United States, 343 F.2d 278 (D.C. Cir. 1964).

Other References

Abbott, Grace. 1925. "History of the Juvenile-Court Movement throughout the World." In *The Child, the Clinic, and the Court.* Edited by Jane Addams. New York: New Republic.

Addams, Jane, ed. 1925. *The Child, the Clinic, and the Court.* New York: New Republic.

———. 1935. *My Friend Julia Lathrop.* New York: Macmillan.

Ainsworth, Janet E. 1991. "Re-imagining Childhood and Reconstructing the Legal Order: The Case for Abolishing the Juvenile Court." *North Carolina Law Review* 69:1083.

Allen, Francis A. 1964. *The Borderland of Criminal Justice: Essays in Law and Criminology.* Chicago: University of Chicago Press.

———. 1981. *The Decline of the Rehabilitative Ideal: Penal Policy and Social Purpose.* New Haven: Yale University Press, 1981.

Alper, Benedict S. 1941. "Forty Years of the Juvenile Court." *American Sociological Review* 6:230.

Bailyn, Bernard. 1992. *The Ideological Origins of the American Revolution.* Enlarged ed. Cambridge: Harvard University Press.

Banay, Ralph S. 1947. "Homicide among children." *Federal Probation* 11:11.

Beattie, J. M. 1986. *Crime and the Courts in England, 1660–1800.* Princeton: Princeton University Press.

Beckett, Katherine. 1997. *Making Crime Pay: Law and Order in Contemporary American Politics.* New York: Oxford University Press.

Blackstone, William. [1769] 1979. *Commentaries on the Laws of England.* Vol. 4. Reprint, with an introduction by Thomas A. Green, Chicago: University of Chicago Press.

Burke, Dorothy Williams. 1930. *Youth and Crime: A Study of the Prevalence and Treatment of Delinquency among Boys over Juvenile-Court Age in Chicago.* Washington: Government Printing Office.

C.R.S. 1929. "Juvenile Courts: Prosecution of Delinquents under Criminal Statutes." *St. Louis Law Review* 14:429.

Cloud, John. 1998. "For They Know Not What They Do?" *Time,* August 24, 64.

Cmiel, Kenneth. 1993. "Destiny and Amnesia: The Vision of Modernity in Robert Wiebe's *The Search for Order.*" *Reviews in American History* 21:352.

Dickinson, John. 1936. "Juvenile Court: Statute Giving It Discretion." *Illinois Bar Journal* 25:77.

Dodge, Mara. 1998. "Legitimization Struggles and Legal Challenges: The Cook County Juvenile Court, 1899–1999, a Historical Overview." Paper presented at twenty-third annual meeting of the Social Science History Association.

Dummer, Ethel Sturges. 1924. Letter to W. I. Thomas, December 14. Dummer Papers. Schlesinger Library, Radcliffe College.

Dunn, Harriette N. 1912. *Infamous Juvenile Law: Crimes against Children under the Cloak of Charity.* Chicago: privately published.

Eliot, Thomas D. 1914. *The Juvenile Court and the Community.* New York: Macmillan.

Fass, Paula S. 1993. "Making and Remaking an Event: The Leopold and Loeb Case in American Culture." *Journal of American History* 80:919.

Feld, Barry C. 1978. "Reference of Juvenile Offenders for Adult Prosecution: The Legislative Alternative to Asking Unanswerable Questions." *Minnesota Law Review* 62:515.

———. 1984. "Criminalizing Juvenile Justice: Rules of Procedure for the Juvenile Court." *Minnesota Law Review* 69:141.

———. 1987. "The Juvenile Court Meets the Principle of the Offense: Legislative Changes in Juvenile Waiver Statutes." *Journal of Criminal Law and Criminology* 78:471.

———. 1993. "Criminalizing the American Juvenile Court." In *Crime and Justice: A Review of Research.* Vol 17. Edited by Michael Tonry. Chicago: University of Chicago Press.

———. 1997. "Abolish the Juvenile Court: Youthfulness, Criminal Responsibility, and Sentencing Policy." *Journal of Criminal Law and Criminology* 88:68.

Flexner, Bernard, and Roger N. Baldwin. 1914. *Juvenile Courts and Probation.* New York: Century.

Flexner, Bernard, and Reuben Oppenheimer. 1923. "The Legal Aspect of the Juvenile Court." *American Law Review* 57:65.

Fox, Sanford J. 1970. "Responsibility in the Juvenile Court." *William and Mary Law Review* 11:659.

Gilbert, James. 1986. *America's Reaction to the Juvenile Delinquent in the 1950s.* New York: Oxford University Press.

Gittens, Joan. 1994. *Poor Relations: The Children of the State in Illinois, 1818–1990.* Urbana: University of Illinois Press.

Goldman, Wendy Z. 1993. *Women, the State, and Revolution.* New York: Cambridge University Press.

Green, Thomas A. 1995. "Freedom and Criminal Responsibility in the Age of Pound: An Essay on Criminal Justice." *Michigan Law Review* 93:1915.

Greenwood, Peter, Allan Abrahamse, and Franklin E. Zimring. 1984. *Factors Affecting Sentence Severity for Young Adult Offenders.* Santa Monica: RAND.

Gross, Fred. 1946. *Detention and Prosecution of Children: Jail Detention and Criminal Prosecution of Children of Juvenile Court Age in Cook County, 1938–1942.* Chicago: Central Howard Association.

Grossberg, Michael. 1996. *A Judgment for Solomon: The D'Hauteville Case and Legal Experience in Antebellum America.* New York: Cambridge University Press.

Hart, Hastings H., ed. 1910. *Juvenile Court Laws in the United States Summarized.* New York: Russell Sage Foundation.

Hay, Douglas. 1975. "Property, Authority, and the Criminal Law." In *Albion's Fatal Tree: Crime and Society in Eighteenth-Century England.* Edited by Douglas Hay, Peter Linebaugh, John G. Rule, E. P. Thompson, and Carl Williams. New York: Pantheon Books.

Herman, Stephen M. 1958. "Scope and Purposes of Juvenile Court Jurisdiction." *Journal of Criminal Law, Criminology, and Police Science* 48:590.

Jeter, Helen Rankin. 1922. *The Chicago Juvenile Court.* Washington: Government Printing Office.

Kett, Joseph F. 1977. *Rites of Passage: Adolescence in America 1790 to the Present.* New York: Basic Books.

Laws of the State of Illinois. 1905. Springfield: Illinois State Journal.

Lenroot, Katherine, and Emma O. Lundberg. [1925] 1975. *Juvenile Courts at Work: A Study of the Organization and Methods of Ten Courts.* Reprint, New York: AMS Press.

Lieberman, David. 1989. *The Province of Legislation Determined: Legal Theory in Eighteenth-Century Britain.* New York: Cambridge University Press.

Lindsey, Ben B., and Wainwright Evans. 1925. *The Revolt of Modern Youth.* New York: Boni and Liveright.

Link, Arthur S., and Richard L. McCormick. 1983. *Progressivism.* Arlington Heights, Ill.: Harlan Davidson.

Lou, Henry H. [1927] 1972. *Juvenile Courts in the United States.* Reprint, New York: Arno Press.

Ludwig, Frederick J. 1955. *Youth and the Law: Handbook on Laws Affecting Youth.* Brooklyn: Foundation Press.

Mack, Julian W. 1909. "The Juvenile Court." *Harvard Law Review* 23:104.

Manfredi, Christopher P. 1998. *The Supreme Court and Juvenile Justice.* Lawrence: University of Kansas Press.

Mennel, Robert. 1973. *Thorns and Thistles: Juvenile Delinquency in the United States, 1824–1940.* Hanover, N.H.: University Press of New England.

Moran, Jeffrey P. 1996. "'Modernism Gone Mad': Sex Education Comes to Chicago, 1913." *Journal of American History* 83:481.

Odem, Mary E. 1995. *Delinquent Daughters: Protecting and Policing Adolescent Female Sexuality in the United States, 1885–1920.* Chapel Hill: University of North Carolina Press.

Olney, Jesse. 1938. "The Juvenile Courts—Abolish Them." *State Bar Journal of the State Bar of California* 13:1.

Pegram, Thomas R. 1992. *Partisans and Progressives: Private Interest and Public Policy in Illinois, 1870–1922.* Urbana: University of Illinois Press.

Peukert, Detlev J. 1987. *The Weimar Republic.* New York: Hill and Wang.

Pisciotta, Alexander W. 1982. "Saving the Children: The Promise and Practice of Parens Patriae, 1838–1898." *Crime and Delinquency* 28:410.

Platt, Anthony M. [1969] 1977. *The Child Savers: The Invention of Delinquency.* 2d ed. Chicago: University of Chicago Press.

Platt, Anthony M., and Bernard L. Diamond. 1966. "The Origins of the 'Right and Wrong' Test of Criminal Responsibility and Its Subsequent Development in the United States: An Historical Survey." *California Law Review* 54:1227.

Pound, Roscoe. 1913. "The Administration of Justice in the Modern City." *Harvard Law Review* 26:302.

"Problem of Age and Jurisdiction in the Juvenile Court." 1966. *Vanderbilt Law Review* 19:833.

Rendleman, Douglas R. 1971. "*Parens Patriae:* From Chancery to the Juvenile Court." *South Carolina Law Review* 23:205.

Rodgers, Daniel R. 1982. "In Search of Progressivism." *Reviews in American History* 10:113.

Rosenheim, Margaret Keeney, ed. 1962. *Justice for the Child: The Juvenile Court in Transition.* New York: Free Press.

Ross, Dorothy. 1991. *The Origins of American Social Science.* New York: Cambridge University Press.

Rothman, David J. 1971. *The Discovery of the Asylum: Social Order and Disorder in the New Republic.* Boston: Little, Brown and Co.

———. 1980. *Conscience and Convenience: The Asylum and Its Alternatives in Progressive America.* Boston: Little, Brown and Co.

Rubin, Sol. 1952. "Protecting the Child in the Juvenile Court." *Journal of Criminal Law, Criminology, and Police Science* 43:425.

Ryerson, Ellen. 1978. *Best-Laid Plans: America's Juvenile Court Experiment.* New York: Hill and Wang.

Sargent, Douglas A., and Donald H. Gordon. 1963. "Waiver of Jurisdiction: An Evaluation of the Process in the Juvenile Court." *Crime and Delinquency* 9: 121.

Schlossman, Steven L. 1977. *Love and the American Delinquent: The Theory and Practice of "Progressive" Juvenile Justice, 1825–1920.* Chicago: University of Chicago Press.

Siegler, Joseph. 1939. "Exclusive Jurisdiction in the Juvenile Court." *New Jersey Law Journal* 62 (August 17): 1.

Singer, Simon I. 1996. *Recriminalizing Delinquency: Violent Juvenile Crime and Juvenile Justice Reform.* New York: Cambridge University Press.

Sobie, Merril. 1987. *The Creation of Juvenile Justice: A History of New York's Children's Laws.* Albany: New York Bar Association.

"Standard Juvenile Court Act." 1959. *Crime and Delinquency* 5:323.

Streib, Victor L. 1983. "Death Penalty for Children." *Oklahoma Law Review* 36: 613.

Tanenhaus, David Spinoza. 1997. "Policing the Child: Juvenile Justice in Chicago, 1870–1925." 2 vols. Ph.D. diss. University of Chicago.

Tappan, Paul W. 1949. *Juvenile Delinquency.* New York: McGraw-Hill.

"Transfer of Cases between Juvenile and Criminal Courts: A Policy Statement." 1962. *Crime and Delinquency* 8:3.

Tuthill, Richard S. [1904] 1973. "History of the Children's Court in Chicago." In *Children's Courts in the U.S.: Their Origin, Development, and Results.* Reprint, New York: AMS Press.

United States Children's Bureau. 1923. *Juvenile-Court Standards: Report of the*

Committee Appointed by the Children's Bureau, August, 1921, to Formulate Juvenile Court-Standards, Adopted by a Conference Held under the Auspices of the Children's Bureau and the National Probation Association, Washington, D.C., May 18, 1923. Publication no. 121. Washington: Government Printing Office.

———. 1940. *Children in the Courts: Juvenile-Court Statistics.* Washington: Government Printing Office.

Van Waters, Miriam. [1931] 1968. *Report on the Child Offender in the Federal System of Justice.* Reprint, Montclair, New Jersey: Patterson Smith.

Waite, Edward F. 1921. "How Far Can Court Procedure Be Socialized without Impairing Individual Rights?" *Journal of Criminal Law and Criminology* 12:339.

Willrich, Michael. 1997. "City of Courts: Crime, Law, and Social Policy in Chicago, 1880–1930." 2 vols. Ph.D. diss. University of Chicago.

———. 1998. "The Two Percent Solution: Eugenic Jurisprudence and the Socialization of American Law, 1900–1930." *Law and History Review* 16:63.

Wolfgang, Marvin E. 1982. "Abolish the Juvenile Court System." *California Lawyer.* November, 12.

Young, Pauline V. 1937. *Social Treatment in Probation and Delinquency: Treatise and Casebook for Court Workers, Probation Officers, and Other Child Welfare Workers.* New York: McGraw-Hill.

Zimring, Franklin E. 1991. "The Treatment of Hard Cases in American Juvenile Justice: In Defense of Discretionary Waiver." *Notre Dame Journal of Law, Ethics, and Public Policy* 5:267.

———. 1998. *American Youth Violence.* New York: Oxford University Press.

Notes

1. Platt and Diamond (1966) have analyzed the American replication of this English system in the nineteenth century, and Fox (1970, 659–84) has examined the subsequent attempts to remove "the infancy defense" from American law in the late nineteenth and early twentieth centuries.

2. Victor Streib (1983) has made a similar argument about the forgotten executions of children in America from colonial times to the present.

3. This new master narrative of juvenile justice has become the third major interpretive wave in a well-developed literature. The progressives produced the first one, known as the "humanitarian" interpretation, which described the creation of the juvenile court as a benevolent innovation that promoted the best interests of children. Classic accounts in this tradition include Mack 1909; Addams 1925, 1935; and Lou [1927] 1972. The second wave or "critical" tradition began approximately at the time of *In re Gault* (387 U.S. 1 [1967]) and encompasses a spectrum of works ranging from outright indictments of the juvenile court as an instrument of social control to more balanced accounts that see juvenile justice as a mixed blessing. Although there are great differences among these works (Platt [1969] 1977, Mennel 1973, Schlossman 1977, Ryerson 1978,

Rothman 1980, Odem 1995), they all focus almost exclusively on "progressive" juvenile justice. The new master narrative or third wave of interpretation draws upon the insights of the critical tradition and extends this analysis by incorporating the post-*Gault* years into the history of the first century of juvenile justice. Christopher Manfredi (1998), for example, has applied this new master narrative to frame his history of the Supreme Court and American juvenile justice.

4. Historians have begun to explore the similarities and interconnections between early welfare programs and criminal justice reform in the early twentieth century, including the problem that middle-class experts who designed these programs often worked from troubling assumptions about race, class, gender, and sexuality. Mary Odem (1995) provides a useful introduction to this literature.

5. In his dissent in *Gault,* Justice Stewart predicted the decision might have this effect on juvenile justice. 387 U.S. at 379.

6. There have been periodic calls for the abolition of the juvenile court since the early twentieth century (Dunn 1912, Eliot 1914, Olney 1938, Wolfgang 1982, Ainsworth 1991, Feld 1997).

7. Pauline Young (1937, 182) offered a classic presentation of the conceptual differences between juvenile justice and criminal justice, but acknowledged that "it may be argued that the comparison is made on the basis of the procedure in a traditional court with that of an ideal juvenile court." Paul Tappan (1949, 179–80) also cautioned against the "tendency to exaggerate the contrasts between juvenile court procedures, pictured in most glowing terms, and those of the criminal court system, viewed in a worst possible and quite inaccurate light." For a particularly egregious example of a journalist romanticizing the past, see Cloud 1998. Thomas Green (1995) offers a provocative analysis of jurisprudential thought in this period, which demonstrates that the ideals of socialized justice were being applied to criminal justice.

8. Ross 1991 examines this tendency of American social science to avoid deep historical analysis.

9. By 1910, twenty-two states plus the District of Columbia had juvenile laws modeled on Illinois's act: Alabama, California, Colorado, Georgia, Idaho, Indiana, Iowa, Kansas, Kentucky, Louisiana, Massachusetts, Michigan, Minnesota, Nebraska, Ohio, Oregon, Pennsylvania, Tennessee, Texas, Utah, Washington, and Wisconsin (Hart 1910, 122).

10. These concerns about children and social disorder were also not new. Beginning in the 1820s, a number of states had built houses of refuge to separate incarcerated children from adult convicts. This segregation of children was part of the larger nineteenth-century project of segregating people by characteristics such as age, gender, race, religion, and mental condition (Rothman 1971). On the discovery of adolescence, see Kett 1977.

11. Narratives about "modernity" are characterized by their assertion that a dramatic break with the past has occurred (Cmiel 1993).

12. As Feld (1993, 209) has noted, this diversity of practices is still a prominent feature of late twentieth-century juvenile justice: "As a consequence of variations in legislative definitions, juvenile courts in different jurisdictions may confront widely divergent clientele. While it is possible to generalize about juvenile courts,

analyses of juvenile justice administration necessarily must be qualified by specific references to each state's legislative nuances and judicial opinions."

13. Justice Abe Fortas's opinion in *In re Gault* is a classic example of this narrative structure.

14. The colonists' justification for the American Revolution is a famous example of this phenomenon of creating a legal theory to explain why things should be the way that they already are. As Bernard Bailyn observed (1992, 204), "The arguments the colonists put forward against Parliament's claims to the right to exercise sovereign power in America were efforts to express in logical form, to state in the language of constitutional theory, the truth of the world they knew."

15. Thomas Eliot (1914) provided the best early account of the controversial nature of the juvenile court during its first decade of existence. He noted "[that] not only the Denver and Chicago courts, conspicuous because of their positions as pioneers, but those in Boston, New York, Philadelphia, Baltimore, Washington, Pittsburgh, Buffalo, Columbus, Cincinnati, Louisville, Indianapolis, Milwaukee, Salt Lake City, and other localities have undergone criticism ranging from serious disapproval among local social workers to open attack" (1914, ix).

16. Constitutional concerns had also troubled the draftsmen of the juvenile law. They had to fit the juvenile court into a complex preexisting system of justices of the peace, police magistrates, criminal and superior courts, and public and private institutions. They had to negotiate jurisdictional claims to avoid political opposition as well as constitutional obstacles (Tanenhaus 1997, 1:117–35). As a result of compromises, the nation's first juvenile court did not even have *original* jurisdiction over children's cases. Before its first session, Richard S. Tuthill, the presiding judge, had to meet with the city's justices of the peace and magistrates, who handled the vast majority of the city's civil and criminal cases, to urge them to transfer children's cases to the new juvenile court (Tanenhaus 1997, 1:144). Justices of the peace and police magistrates had identical jurisdiction over "all minor civil cases and criminal cases in which the value of property to be recovered or the fine to be levied did not exceed $200" (Willrich 1997, 1: 33). In 1905, the Illinois General Assembly revised the juvenile law to give the court original and exclusive jurisdiction over children who were not inmates of state institutions.

17. Section 1 of the 1905 Revised Juvenile Act defined which children fell under the court's jurisdiction. The definition was extremely broad:

> The words delinquent child shall include any male child under the age of seventeen years or any female child under the age of eighteen years who violates any law of this State or any city or village ordinance; or who is incorrigible; or who knowingly associates with thieves, vicious or immoral persons; or, who, without just cause and without the consent of its parents or custodian, absents itself from its home or place of abode, or who is growing up in idleness or crime; or who knowingly frequents a house of ill-repute; or who knowingly frequents any policy shop or place where any gaming device is operated; or who frequents any

saloon or dram shop where intoxicating liquors are sold; or who patronizes or visits any public pool room or bucket shop; or wanders about the streets in the night time without being on any lawful business or occupation; or who habitually wanders about any railroad yards or tracks or jumps or attempts to jump onto any moving train; or enters any car or engine without lawful authority; or who habitually uses vile, obscene, vulgar, profane or indecent language; or who is guilty of immoral conduct in any public place or about any school house. Any child committing any of the acts herein mentioned shall be deemed a delinquent child and shall be proceeded against as such in the manner hereinafter provided. (*Laws of the state of Illinois* 1905, 153)

18. The Illinois Constitution of 1870 granted criminal courts jurisdiction over criminal cases, including misdemeanors (Gittens 1994, 133).

19. I will use the common designation, the Chicago Juvenile Court, to refer to what is technically the Cook County Juvenile Court.

20. These figures are calculated from Hart 1910. Illinois and Kentucky established eighteen as the upper limit for girls, but used seventeen for boys' cases. Indiana also had different limits for boys (sixteen) and girls (seventeen). Eleven states—California, Georgia, Iowa, Kansas, Maine, Maryland, New Jersey, New York, Pennsylvania, Rhode Island, and Texas—all set sixteen as the upper limit. Fourteen states—Alabama, Colorado, Idaho, Massachusetts, Michigan, Minnesota, Missouri, Montana, New Hampshire, Ohio, Oklahoma, Tennessee, Washington, and Wisconsin—as well as the District of Columbia used seventeen. On the critical importance of age limits in juvenile justice, see Zimring 1991, 272–73.

21. In California, after a rehearing the court could even transfer "incorrigible or not amenable" children from a reform school to the state penitentiary (Hart 1910, 11).

22. These early transfer cases all appeared to involve boys, but often judges would use "the masculine pronoun" to describe girls' as well as boys' as cases (Tuthill [1904] 1973, 2).

23. Juvenile court statistics are based on the number of cases a court heard, not the number of children who appeared before it.

24. Although the rhetoric of transfer remained the same, a child's experience at Pontiac may have changed dramatically because the institution now housed inmates from sixteen to twenty-six. A 1919 change in the law gave the criminal courts the authority to commit children to Saint Charles Reformatory, a school for juvenile delinquents (Jeter 1922, 89; Gittens 1994, 137).

25. The 1914 model juvenile court statute put out by the National Probation Association had included a section on transfer. Section 17 (Discretion of Court with Reference to Criminal Law) stated:

The court may, in its discretion, in any case of a delinquent child brought before it as herein provided permit such child to be proceeded against in accordance with the laws that may be in force in this State governing the commission of crimes, and in such case the petition, if any, filed under this act, shall be dismissed and the child shall be transferred to the court having jurisdiction of the offense. (reprinted in Flexner and Baldwin 1914, 264).

26. More research needs to be done into the question of how many children's cases were actually legislatively excluded from juvenile courts in this period. By 1930, for example, twenty state legislatures had excluded at least some offenses. They included: capital crimes (California [if eighteen to twenty-one], Delaware, and Vermont); crimes punishable by death or life imprisonment (Georgia, Indiana, Iowa, Massachusetts, Montana, and New York [except Chautauqua County]); murder (New Jersey and Pennsylvania); and felonies (Idaho and Utah). The other states' excluded offenses did not fit into the above categories. In Florida, rape, murder, manslaughter, robbery, arson, burglary, and attempts to commit one of these crimes were excluded. Louisiana excluded capital crimes as well as attempted rape, but only capital crimes were excluded in the Orleans Parish. New Hampshire excluded capital and certain other offenses. In North and South Carolina, any felony punishable by ten or more years' imprisonment was excluded. Rhode Island excluded murder as well as manslaughter. In Tennessee, crimes punishable by life imprisonment or death were excluded, but in some counties only murder and rape were excluded. This list is compiled from Van Waters [1931] 1968, 158–72.

27. The Children's Bureau did commission a study of "the prevalence and treatment of delinquency among boys over juvenile-court age in Chicago" (Burke 1930).

28. The Leopold-Loeb case raised questions about youth and challenged notions about class and crime (Lindsey and Evans 1925, 104–10; Fass 1993). The aftermath of World War I posed particular problems for European and Russian youth. Detlev Peukert (1987, 86–95) provides an excellent analysis of the difficulties facing youth in Weimar Germany, and Wendy Goldman (1993, 317–27) offers a grim picture of Soviet youth policy, especially in the early 1930s.

29. The court reaffirmed *Lattimore* in *People ex rel. Malec v. Lewis* (362 Ill. 229 [1935]).

30. As Manfredi noted:

Between 1926 and 1952 the *Index to Legal Periodicals* listed on average only seventeen articles per year in the categories of "Juvenile Courts," "Juvenile Offenders," and "Juvenile Delinquency." Over the next fifteen years (1952–1967), however, the average number of annual entries in these categories was fifty-two, and between 1964 and 1967 the average reached seventy-five per year. (1998, 37)

31. The following year Sargent and Gordon 1963 called for the elimination of waiver because the practice represented the abandonment of children in need of help.

32. *Kent,* unlike *Gault,* involved statutory interpretation and applied only to the District of Columbia.

33. The *Kent* criteria, which would be inscribed into states' laws, came from a policy memorandum prepared in 1959 by the chief judge of the District of Columbia's juvenile court. It read:

1. The seriousness of the alleged offense to the community and whether the protection of the community requires waiver.

2. Whether the alleged offense was committed in an aggressive, violent, premeditated or willful manner.

3. Whether the alleged offense was against persons or against property, greater weight being given to offenses against persons especially if personal injury resulted.

4. The protective merit of the complaint, i.e., whether there is evidence upon which a Grand Jury may be expected to return an indictment (to be determined by consultation with the United States Attorney).

5. The desirability of trial and disposition of the entire offense in one court when the juvenile's associates in the alleged offense are adults who will be charged with a crime in the U.S. District Court for the District of Columbia.

6. The sophistication and maturity of the Juvenile as determined by consideration of his home, environmental situation, emotional attitude and pattern of living.

7. The record and previous history of the juvenile, including previous contacts with the Youth Aid Division, other law enforcement agencies, juvenile courts and other jurisdictions, prior periods of probation to this Court, or prior commitments to juvenile institutions.

8. The prospects for adequate protection of the public and the likelihood of reasonable rehabilitation of the juvenile (if he is found to have committed the alleged offense) by the use of procedures, services, and facilities currently available to the Juvenile Court (383 U.S. 565–66).

34. Another possible explanation, given the history of transfer, is that appellate courts generally have created concurrent jurisdiction, while legislatures have preferred to pass exclusionary laws. More research, however, into the legislative history of the 1970s is required to answer this question.

Chapter Two

Judicial Waiver in Theory and Practice

Robert O. Dawson

Almost all American states make judicial waiver of jurisdiction to criminal court available within their juvenile justice systems. After notice and opportunity to be heard, a juvenile court judge decides whether there is probable cause to believe a juvenile respondent committed a serious offense and, if so, whether the interest of the community would be served by the prosecution of that offense in criminal court rather than juvenile court.

The traditionally stated purpose of judicial waiver is to permit individualization of the decision whether a particular person is capable of being rehabilitated in the juvenile system—the amenability decision (Feld 1987). In addition, the judicial waiver procedure provides a safety valve for the juvenile system to exclude children who commit offenses that are believed to require the imposition of sanctions that are beyond the capacity of the juvenile system to provide (Dawson 1992). Some form of judicial waiver—or a substitute safety valve—is necessary in order to preserve the juvenile justice system politically within the context of modern penological expectations.

Traditionally, judicial waiver was the sole or virtually the sole method of making the amenability or safety valve decision. However, legislatures have increasingly created alternatives to judicial waiver. In some instances, legislatures have excluded certain offenses from the jurisdiction of the juvenile court for respondents of certain ages. In other instances, legislatures have given prosecutors the discretionary power to file certain offenses against juveniles of certain ages directly in criminal court without prior juvenile court approval. Finally, legislatures have created systems of blended jurisdiction in which juvenile cases in certain circumstances can carry sanctions of criminal severity.

It is difficult empirically to evaluate the contemporary role of judicial waiver in the overall context of procedures intended to sort out which cases should be filed and processed in the juvenile system and which in the criminal. While the General Accounting Office estimated that "in most prosecutorial offices, judicial waivers accounted for a higher percentage of juveniles arriving in criminal court than direct filings or statutory exclusions" (U.S. General Accounting Office 1995), that estimate was made in 1995 and does not include those cases in which there were juvenile court dispositions that included criminal sentencing sanctions (one form of blended sentencing).

In addition to providing alternatives to judicial waiver, legislatures have amended judicial waiver provisions to encourage or mandate the efficient handling of more juvenile cases through judicial waiver. In certain instances, legislatures have mandated waiver, while in others they have merely created a presumption of waiver in certain cases or eased the prosecutor's procedural burdens.

This chapter first briefly examines judicial waivers in the context of competing sorting mechanisms. Next, it examines judicial waiver itself to assess its functioning, particularly in light of recent substantial changes in legal provisions controlling its use. Then, it deals with various empirical questions, such as who gets waived and for what conduct. Finally, this chapter attempts to answer the question, How, if at all, have the functions served by judicial waiver been affected by the creation or expansion of competing transfer mechanisms?

1. Judicial Waiver in Context

Judicial waiver is important in the process of sorting which criminal charges will be processed in the juvenile system and which in the criminal justice system. However, it is not the only sorting mechanism in contemporary use, nor is it the most important in terms of the number of cases handled.

Boundary Ages

Selecting and defining the boundary age is the most important sorting mechanism for determining in which system criminal charges—including serious criminal charges—will be processed. The National Center for Juvenile Justice estimated that in 1991 up to 176,000 juveniles below the age of eighteen were handled in criminal courts because they were in the small number of states that set a boundary age of sixteen or seventeen. By contrast, in 1991, juvenile courts waived only an estimated 9,700 cases to criminal court (Snyder and Sickmund 1995). The boundary age is selected by the legislature.

Virtually all states select seventeen or eighteen as the boundary age. As of 1996, about three-fourths (thirty eight of fifty-one) of American jurisdictions fixed the boundary age at eighteen. Ten jurisdictions selected seventeen, while only three chose sixteen (Szymanski 1997a).

An offense committed by a person who has achieved the boundary age at the time of the offense is processed in criminal court without prior juvenile court involvement. Such a person is fully an "adult" for criminal law purposes.

Most states define their boundary ages in terms of age at the time the offense was committed. In those states, if the offense was committed by a person who has not yet achieved the boundary age, the case must be handled, initially at least, in the juvenile justice system.

A few states define their boundary ages as referring to age at the time of court proceedings. In those states, even if the offense was committed by a person who has not yet achieved the boundary age, prosecution of that offense can be handled in the criminal courts if juvenile proceedings are delayed and the attachment of juvenile court jeopardy is postponed until the person reaches the boundary age. See *Hughes v. State,* 653 A.2d 241 (Del. 1994) (holding unconstitutional a provision requiring transfer to criminal court when a respondent who is charged with a juvenile felony becomes eighteen before the adjudication hearing is held).

Obviously, boundary ages that are defined in terms of age at the time of the proceedings potentially capture more cases for the criminal system than the same boundary age defined in terms of age at the time the offense was committed. In addition, boundary ages defined in terms of age at the time of the proceedings permit prosecutors unilaterally to individualize the sorting decision by delaying the onset of juvenile court jeopardy until the boundary age has been achieved and charges can be filed directly in criminal court. The availability of this procedure enables prosecutors to avoid judicial waiver requirements in those cases in which the respondent is close enough to the boundary age to permit judicially tolerated delay in the disposition of the juvenile case. This procedure also gives such prosecutors enhanced plea negotiation powers in those cases in which the juvenile committed the offense while approaching the boundary age.

Given the frenzy with which legislatures in virtually all states have approached juvenile justice public protection issues in recent years, it is notable that boundary ages have been lowered in only three states. In 1995, New Hampshire and Wisconsin lowered the boundary age from eighteen to seventeen, while in 1993 Wyoming changed its age from nineteen to eighteen (Torbet et al. 1996, 3).

That single action would divert more cases from the juvenile to the criminal system than any other could. Lowering a boundary age from eighteen to seventeen, for example, would probably reduce the flow of cases in the juvenile system by as much as one-fourth. In 1996, according to FBI numbers, seventeen-year-olds accounted for over 24 percent of all arrests of persons under eighteen years of age and 27 percent of all such arrests for murder, forcible rape, robbery and aggravated assault (U.S. Dept. of Justice 1997).

The fact that lowering of boundary ages has not occurred in more states signals that legislative concern is focused particularly on serious offenses by juveniles and not upon a supposed rise in juvenile crime "in general." Legislatively, lowering the boundary age in those states in which that action was taken was probably intended to send a "get tough" message to teenagers rather than to be a vote of no confidence in the juvenile justice system.

Statutory Exclusions

A boundary age operates with respect to all criminal offenses to define which cases are to be handled in which system. In addition, legislatures have, increasingly in recent years, created different boundary-type ages for different offenses. Thus, the boundary age may be age eighteen, except that for certain very serious offenses, it may be several years lower. Sometimes, the legislative exclusion is premised on prior adjudications as well as charge seriousness and age of the actor. The Office of Juvenile Justice and Delinquency Prevention reported that in 1997 twenty-eight states had statutory exclusions based on charge seriousness, age, and/or prior adjudications (Torbet and Szymanski 1998, 4).

Such exclusions have the effect of lowering the boundary age but only for specified categories of offenses. These enactments reflect the legislative judgment that seriousness of the offense and chronological age of the person charged (sometimes with prior adjudications as well) are suitable as the only criteria for making the sorting decision.

Unlike the offense seriousness decisions that are made in the context of judicial waiver, these legislative seriousness decisions are categorical and absolute. They lack, in theory, any elements of individualization of the sorting decision. In reality, individualization is permissible, but only in factually limited circumstances. A prosecutor might exercise discretion in a case in which conduct might or might not be excluded from juvenile court jurisdiction to charge the conduct as a juvenile jurisdiction offense rather than a criminal jurisdiction offense. Such a prosecutor might do so by bringing charges for a lesser included offense or a less serious offense related to an excluded offense.

How many juvenile cases are filed in criminal court because of legislative exclusions? The General Accounting Office was unable to estimate the number of juveniles who are prosecuted in criminal court because of legislative exclusions (U.S. General Accounting Office 1995). The exclusion volume is likely quite limited in many jurisdictions that exclude only a short list of very serious charges. In other jurisdictions, a longer list of not-so-serious offenses is excluded, but only when committed by an older juvenile, typically sixteen or older. Those laws are discussed later in this chapter.

Direct Filing

As of 1997, in fifteen jurisdictions, legislatures have authorized prosecutors to make the waiver decisions for certain offenses and respondents in certain age categories (Torbet and Szymanski 1998, 4). Such provisions typically provide for concurrent jurisdiction between criminal and juvenile courts and permit the prosecutor to file a case in either system. For example, in the District of Columbia, prosecutorial direct filing is available for a child who is sixteen or seventeen years of age and charged with murder, first-degree sexual abuse, burglary in the first degree, robbery while armed, or assault with intent to commit any of those offenses. *D.C. Code* § 16-2301(3) (1998). This provision coexists with the District of Columbia judicial waiver provision permitting waiver for any felony committed by a juvenile fifteen or older. *D.C. Code* § 16-2307(a).

To the extent cases are filed directly in criminal court under such schemes, the juvenile judiciary is totally excluded from participating in the decision-making process. In addition, the child and defense counsel have no right to participate in the process.

The validity and procedural details of these provisions are discussed in Barry Feld's contribution to this volume.

There are no reliable figures on the number of cases diverted to the criminal system by prosecutorial discretionary direct filing mechanisms. The General Accounting Office in 1995 estimated the number of filings in the then eleven direct filing jurisdictions as ranging from a low of four cases to a high of over seven thousand cases (U.S. General Accounting Office 1995). Its study showed a significant number of direct filings only in Arkansas (1,327 direct filings out of 10,004 juvenile cases [13.3 percent]) and Florida (7,232 direct filings out of 75,976 juvenile cases [9.5 percent]).

The Congress of the United States has weighed in to favor statutory exclusions and prosecutorial direct filing over judicial waiver by providing in appropriations bills for fiscal 1998 and 1999 that block grants to the states through the Office of Juvenile Justice and Delinquency Prevention are to be conditioned upon states having enacted, enacting, or considering enacting legislative exclusions or prosecutorial direct filing mechanisms for juveniles fifteen or older charged with murder, aggravated sexual assault, or assault with a firearm.

The basis of this policy preference must be a critique of judicial waiver. The congressional purpose must be to supplant judicial waiver with one or more of these more efficient mechanisms or, at the least, to reduce the use of judicial waivers by making these other procedures available. OJJDP guidelines state that judicial waiver mechanisms do not satisfy congressional requirements, while at least some juvenile court–based blended sentencing systems would. To the extent this congressional strategy is successful in making alternative transfer means available in state juvenile systems, it will probably result in a slight decrease in the use of judicial waiver and an increase in the number of serious juvenile cases that are transferred to criminal court. (See http://ncjrs.org/ojjdp/jaibg/sect-2.html for OJJDP guidelines.)

Reverse Judicial Waiver

By 1997, in twenty-three jurisdictions, legislatures provided that some cases that begin as criminal cases can be waived to the juvenile court by a criminal court judge (Torbet and Szymanski 1998, 4). Ordinarily, these are cases that are in criminal court under direct filing or statutory exclusion provisions. About 40 percent of the jurisdictions that provide for direct filing or legislative exclusion have reverse judicial waiver provisions (Torbet and Szymanski 1998, 4).

Reverse judicial waiver is a way of introducing individualization into the sorting process. In theory, it has the same potential for individualization as juvenile court judicial waiver. In actuality, because the burden of persuasion is upon the defendant to show the criminal court judge that the case should be sent to juvenile court, the volume of reverse waivers would be expected to be much more limited. No accurate estimates exist as to the extent to which these provisions are used.

Blended Systems

In nine jurisdictions, legislatures have created alternatives to the waiver process in the form of blended systems in which the juvenile court disposition includes elements of juvenile and criminal dispositions (Torbet et al. 1996; Torbet and Szymanski 1998, 6–7). These provisions often enable to the juvenile to be retained in the juvenile system and to avoid being handled in the criminal system altogether. For example, under the

Texas blended system, about one-half of the juveniles sentenced historically have not been transferred to the adult correctional system.

In other jurisdictions, a criminal court sentence for a transferred juvenile may include juvenile placements or elements. These provisions permit amelioration in the disposition of a transferred (waived, direct-filed, or statutorily excluded) case.

When compared with judicial waiver, blended systems that are juvenile court based postpone the sorting decision. One form enables the respondent to receive a juvenile disposition with a suspended criminal sentence that becomes operational only upon violation of the terms of the juvenile disposition, while another form provides for a later reevaluation of the need for transfer to the criminal correctional system following a period of incarceration and programming in the juvenile correctional system. In either form, blended systems are intended to give juveniles who commit serious offenses a final opportunity to avoid the severity of criminal sanctions.

Extending Maximum Control Age

Many juvenile systems have a maximum control age that is higher than the boundary age. Twenty-one is the typical maximum control age (Torbet et al. 1996, 15). At this age, the offender is released from the juvenile justice system—community supervision or correctional facility—and has discharged his or her legal obligation. In 1996, OJJDP reported that eleven states and the District of Columbia extended their maximum control ages since 1992 (Torbet et al. 1996, 15).

In a few jurisdictions, the maximum control age extends beyond age twenty-one. In California, Oregon, and Wisconsin it extends to age twenty-five (Torbet et al. 1996, 15).

Extending the maximum control age beyond the boundary age does not address the most serious of the cases of concern. Adding a few years to the maximum control age will not address community and political concerns over the most serious of juvenile offenses. At the margins, such extensions might induce some judges or prosecutors not to transfer cases to criminal court. Such age increases seem designed to deal not with the most serious cases but with more routine juvenile cases.

2. The Changing Characteristics of Judicial Waiver

No state's judicial waiver legislation is the same as any other state's. The same political pressures that have resulted in excluding more offenses from juvenile jurisdiction and in increasing the use of prosecutorial direct filings have impacted judicial waiver. In recent years, legislatures have modified judicial waiver statutes to make waivers quicker, cheaper, easier, and more frequent than before.

Because modern judicial waiver schemes trace their legal ancestry to a common source—*Kent v. United States,* 383 U.S. 541 (1996)—many have certain features in common: (1) an age bracket within which the actor must have committed the offense; (2) standards of charge seriousness—usually felonies or listed felonies—that must be met before waiver is permitted; (3) prosecutorial initial selection of cases in which to seek waiver from among the flow of eligible cases; (4) a requirement of an administrative investigation and report into the circumstances of the offense and background of the respondent coupled with a psychiatric and/or psychological evaluation of the respondent; (5) a requirement of a hearing before a judge of the juvenile court; (6) minimum proof requirements, such as probable cause to believe the offense alleged was committed by the respondent and/or a showing that waiver is necessary to protect the public; and (7) judicial discretion, if the minimum structural and proof requirements are satisfied, to waive or refuse to waive jurisdiction, usually to be exercised under the guidance of statutory waiver criteria.

In recent years, legislatures have modified almost all of these features in order to require or encourage the shifting of more cases from juvenile to criminal court. For example, in recent years there has been increasing legislative use of (8) presumptions of waiver to criminal court and (9) mandatory judicial waiver provisions.

Age Bracket

Traditionally, legislatures have created an age bracket, usually a two- or three-year period, just below the boundary age and have restricted the availability of judicial waiver to juveniles believed to have committed offenses while within that age bracket. The minimum age for judicial waiver is a particularly important age because it can exclude from criminal court handling some very serious offenses committed by very young children. Thus, it becomes the prime candidate for legislative "reform" when a particularly serious offense is committed by a juvenile under that age.

As of 1996, in all but one jurisdiction, juveniles who commit specified felonies at age fifteen or older may be transferred to criminal court for prosecution as an adult. The transfer might be made by judicial waiver, legislative offense-specific exclusion, or prosecutorial direct filing (Szymanski 1997b). In twelve of those jurisdictions, juveniles who commit specified felonies at age fourteen may be transferred by judicial waiver (Szymanski 1997b).

Within the past ten years, several states have lowered their minimum waiver ages. In some instances, lower ages were added but only for some of the offenses for which waiver had been available. For example, in 1995 Texas lowered its minimum waiver age, which had been fifteen for any felony, down to age fourteen but only for the most serious categories of felonies. *Tex. Fam. Code Ann.* § 54.02 (West 1998).

In addition to lowering minimum waiver ages, legislatures have created multiple age brackets for judicial waiver. For example, in California, waiver is permitted for any criminal offense committed by a juvenile sixteen or older, waiver is presumed for any offense from a list of twenty-nine serious offenses committed by a juvenile sixteen or older, waiver is permitted for any offense from a similar list of offenses committed by a juvenile fourteen or older, and waiver is presumed for some murder offenses committed by a juvenile fourteen or older. *Cal. Wel. & Inst. Code* § 707 (West 1998).

As a result of legislative activity, it is unusual today to find a jurisdiction with just a single waiver age bracket. Most have two or more age brackets related to different offenses or adjudication histories.

Standards of Charge Seriousness

Legislation sometimes permits waiver for any offense, but often provides that the offense charged in juvenile court must be a felony to be eligible for waiver to criminal court. In some jurisdictions, only some felonies qualify; in others, only some felonies qualify for some age groups.

Even in a circumstance in which any felony is eligible for waiver, waiver ordinarily is initiated only for serious, violent felonies or for a property offender who is a seriously repeat offender (Dawson 1992).

Statutory exclusions or direct filing provisions tend to be more restrictive than judicial waiver in terms of charge seriousness. These provisions typically authorize transfer only for serious violent felonies. Statutory exclusion and direct filing are discussed later in this chapter.

Prosecutorial Selection

The major sorting event in the process of judicial waiver occurs in the prosecutor's office, not the courtroom. It is the selection decision made by the prosecutor to seek waiver for this case from among all the cases eligible for selection. Probably on average fewer than 5 percent of eligible cases are actually selected by a prosecutor for judicial waiver proceedings. The selection is made without prior or concurrent procedures. Negative decisions are not subject to review, while positive decisions receive review in the form of a judicial hearing and the exercise of juvenile court discretion.

Partly because of this great selectivity, the rate at which prosecutorial waiver efforts are successful is high (Dawson 1992). Of course, the juvenile court judge influences the process of selection by approving or disapproving of selections in particular cases. Prosecutors practicing before a juvenile court judge soon learn which cases are likely to be approved by that judge and which are not. That informs future prosecutorial selections.

Prosecutors appear to select a very small percentage of eligible cases for judicial waiver. In Texas, in 1996, there were 18,012 referrals to the juvenile courts of fifteen- and sixteen-year-olds for felonies, the major group eligible for waiver, but the juvenile courts waived only 589, or 3.3 percent, to the criminal courts (Texas Juvenile Probation Commission 1997, 19). In 1997, there were 16,164 such referrals with only 467, or 2.9 percent, waived to criminal court (Texas Juvenile Probation Commission 1998, 19). Of course, there were more attempts to waive than successful waivers, but it would be safe to assert on those numbers that prosecutors initiate judicial waiver in less than 5 percent of the eligible cases.

Investigation and Diagnostic Study

Many jurisdictions require an administrative investigation into the circumstances of the offense and the characteristics of the juvenile prior to the waiver hearing. That report is admitted into evidence at the waiver hearing. The purpose of the report is to ensure that the maximum amount of information about the offense and the juvenile reaches the judge. However, this process also has the effect of short-circuiting the normal method by which evidence is adduced in an adversarial system—by examinations of witnesses with direct knowledge of the facts about which they are testifying. To that extent, use of the investigation, like use of a presentence investigation report in criminal sentencing proceedings, may permit the decision to be based on more, but less reliable, information than if all the evidence were required to be presented from the witness stand. The requirement of disclosure of the report to the juvenile and his or her attorney is some check on the reliability of the information it contains.

The psychiatric and psychological report requirements are premised on the notion of determining whether the juvenile is amenable to rehabilitation in the juvenile justice system and whether the juvenile poses a danger to society. The reports are intended to be diagnostic tools, but it is unclear how important a role they play in a system in which offense seriousness by itself appears to dominate the decision-making process. See Thomas Grisso's contribution to this volume for a discussion of the influence of such reports on the waiver decision.

The investigative/diagnostic requirements, particularly the diagnostic requirements, serve the unintended purpose of making the judicial waiver process more time-consuming and expensive and thus restricting the number of cases in which it is attempted. Indeed, that may in part account for the increasing use of alternative sorting devices—all of which are more "efficient" than traditional judicial waiver—in recent years.

Judicial Hearing

Because of the magnitude of the stakes at issue in a waiver proceeding, the judicial hearing can be lengthy and hard-fought. Under those circumstances, such hearings are the "capital cases" of the juvenile justice system in the sense that they are the proceeding with the most serious consequences in the system.

Because the proceeding is before a judge without a jury and because it has characteristics of a sentencing or dispositional proceeding in the sense that it does not address guilt/innocence issues but "only" the question of in which system those issues will be litigated, some courts have permitted evidence to be used without adhering to ordinary rules of exclusion. See *In the Matter of P.A.C.*, 562 S.W.2d 913 (Tex. Civ. App.— Amarillo 1978) (approving of the use of witness affidavits). This has the effect, of course, of lessening both the difficulties of proof for the state and the length of the hearing itself.

The requirement of a judicial hearing in which the respondent and defense counsel participate is one of the major ways in which judicial waiver differs from statutory exclusion or direct filing transfer mechanisms. The hearing requirement permits the juvenile to participate in the transfer decision by seeking to influence the discretionary decision of the juvenile court judge.

The requirement of a hearing gives the respondent bargaining leverage with the prosecutor. Sometimes, that leverage is used to negotiate a disposition of the case that involves an agreed sentence in postwaiver criminal proceedings or an agreed disposition in juvenile court proceedings. In such an event, the hearing has served a major function even though it was waived or conducted in a drastically shortened form.

Minimum Proof Requirements

Although the judicial waiver decision is discretionary with the juvenile court judge, there are ordinarily minimum proof requirements. The age of the respondent, probable cause to believe the offense charged (or a lesser waivable offense) was committed by the respondent, and that the offense was committed within the legislative age bracket must be shown.

Often, statutes require bifurcation of the hearing and that the juvenile court make a probable cause finding before evidence relevant to the exercise of discretion to waive is received. See, e.g., *Mich. Comp. Laws Ann.* § 712A.4(3), (4) (West 1998). In addition, statutes often provide that the juvenile may testify at the waiver hearing and that his or her testimony may not be used against the juvenile in subsequent proceedings. See, e.g., *N.J. Stat. Ann.* § 2A:4A-29 (West 1998).

In addition to a requirement of probable cause, proof must be provided that it is in the interest of the public for waiver to occur. See, e.g., *Tex. Fam. Code Ann.* § 54.02(a)(3) (West 1998). This standard is so vague as to impose no significant restriction on the discretion of the juvenile court.

Judicial Discretion Exercised under Statutory Guidelines

The United States Supreme Court published the District of Columbia Juvenile Court's criteria for waiver in the appendix to *Kent v. United States,* 383 U.S. at 566–67. The criteria announced by the juvenile court were (1) seriousness of the offense charged, (2) whether the offense was committed in an aggressive, violent, premeditated, or willful manner, (3) whether it was against person or property, (4) the prosecutive merits of the case, (5) whether the offense was committed with adult coactors, (6) the sophistication and maturity of the juvenile, (7) the juvenile's prior record, and (8) the prospects for adequate protection of the public and the likelihood of reasonable rehabilitation of the juvenile by the use of procedures, services, and facilities currently available to the juvenile court.

About three-fourths of the states have enacted by statute or adopted by court decision sets of criteria quite similar to those published in the *Kent* opinion (Feld 1987). The *Kent* criteria are of three different types—relating to the offense, the respondent, and the system. Four criteria—seriousness of the offense, whether it is an offense against the person, whether it was committed in an aggressive manner, and whether there is evidence to prosecute—relate to the offense itself. Two criteria—sophistication of the respondent and previous record—relate to the respondent. Two criteria—the ability of the juvenile system to protect the public and to rehabilitate the respondent and the desirability of disposing of cases of coactors in the same system—deal with system concerns, including how the system can serve the needs of society in dealing with this particular respondent.

These criteria are intended merely to guide juvenile court discretion in deciding upon waiver. They are not intended to be controlling or preclusive. At most, state law might require evidence in the record that the judge considered these as well as other factors in making the waiver decision. See, e.g., *In the Matter of J.R.C.*, 551 S.W.2d 748 (Tex. Civ. App. — Texarkana 1977).

Presumptions of Waiver

In an ordinary waiver proceeding, the burden is upon the government to convince the juvenile court judge that waiver is appropriate. The prosecutor would be expected to adduce evidence concerning the applicable criteria and to argue the case in terms of having met the burden of persuasion.

In certain situations, legislatures have intervened in this balance to alter the burdens. In about fifteen jurisdictions, they have created presumptions in certain kinds of cases that the juvenile court judge should waive jurisdiction unless the respondent is able to persuade otherwise (Torbet and Szymanski 1998, 4). California, for example, presumes waiver when a juvenile fourteen or older is charged with direct participation in murder. See *Hicks v. Superior Court,* 36 Cal. App. 4th 1649, 43 Cal. Rptr. 2d 269 (Cal. App. 1995) (upholding constitutionality of presumption). Minnesota presumes waiver when a juvenile sixteen or older is charged with an offense that would carry a presumptive commitment to prison for an adult under sentencing guidelines or with committing any felony while armed with a firearm. See *In the Matter of L.J.S. and J.T.K.,* 539 N.W.2d 408 (Minn. App. 1995) (upholding constitutionality of presumption). And New Jersey presumes waiver when a juvenile fourteen or older is charged with homicide, robbery, sexual assault, aggravated assault, kidnapping, or aggravated arson. See *State in the Interest of A.L.,* 271 N.J. Super. 192, 638 A.2d 814 (N.J. Super. 1994) (upholding constitutionality of presumption).

Presumption-creating provisions do not necessarily speed up waiver proceedings since the respondent can be expected to exercise the right to introduce evidence to rebut the presumption. They do not even necessarily increase the number of cases waived to criminal court, since the juvenile court is free to find that the presumption has been rebutted and to refuse waiver on that ground. They simply tip the balance in favor of the prosecution. Such statutes represent a further reflection of offense/age categorical decision making rather than individualization in situations in which the legislature, for whatever reasons, was unwilling to impose mandatory waiver, statutory exclusion or direct filing.

Mandatory Judicial Waiver

In some jurisdictions, legislatures have made waiver mandatory. One such mandatory provision is "Once an adult/always an adult." As of 1997, such provisions existed in thirty-one jurisdictions (Torbet and Szymanski 1998, 4). If the respondent has previously been waived to criminal court or has been proceeded against in criminal court by direct filing or legislative exclusion and is subsequently charged in juvenile court with an offense, the juvenile court, upon prosecutorial request, is required to waive the subsequent charge to criminal court.

This type of waiver provision should be evaluated differently from the others because unlike the others it does not increase the number of juveniles who will be waived to criminal court, but merely increases the number of cases that will be transferred concerning those juveniles already waived. These provisions are designed to prevent jurisdictional conflicts between the juvenile and criminal systems as to waived juveniles who commit new offenses before achieving the boundary age rather than to express public policy as to which system cases should be prosecuted in.

A second type of mandatory waiver is a close cousin to prosecutorial waiver by direct filing. Under these provisions, the role of the juvenile court judge is to determine whether the case fits within the statuary mandatory waiver category and whether there is probable cause to believe the respondent committed a covered offense. The only difference from direct filing is that the prosecutor must obtain a juvenile court waiver order in the mandatory waiver, while no such permission is needed to file criminal charges in the prosecutorial waiver or statutory exclusion circumstances. As of 1997, mandatory waiver provisions existed in fourteen jurisdictions (Torbet and Szymanski 1998, 4).

As subsequent discussion in this chapter makes clear, these provisions are often quite narrow in the list of offenses reached and the number of cases that fall within their scope. But they are important because they reflect legislative willingness to eliminate juvenile court discretion in the waiver system. In that respect, they resemble statutory exclusion and prosecutorial direct filing.

3. Judicial Waiver in the Real World of the Last Ten Years

From 1966, when *Kent* was decided, until the middle of the 1980s, judicial waiver was largely ignored by legislatures. It existed, was necessary to take care of the occasional horrendous juvenile case and then returned to legal oblivion. Then urban gangs, crack cocaine, and acts of extreme violence captured the attention of the public and the imagination of the press. Legislators began to view juvenile justice as a politically fruitful area for exploration.

The focus was upon violent offenses, and the political slogan of "Do an adult crime, do adult time" filled the airwaves and print media.

While the focus of legislative concern was frequently upon streamlining the judicial waiver process to enable more cases to be sent from the juvenile to the criminal system, legislatures also created or expanded competing methods of accomplishing similar objectives: lowering boundary ages, creating blended systems, providing for prosecutorial waiver, and providing for legislative jurisdictional exclusions.

The focus here is upon cases handled by judicial waiver, particularly, who gets waived, for what conduct, and whether that has changed any in recent years.

The Numbers

In terms of absolute numbers, there has been a dramatic increase in judicial waivers to criminal court. In 1985, about 7,200 cases were judicially waived, while in 1994 that number had risen to about 12,300 — an increase of 70.8 percent (Butts 1997) However, that number dropped to about 9,700 in 1995 — an increase from 1985 of about 34.7 percent (Sickmund et al. 1998, 13).

Does that increase reflect a rise in referrals to the juvenile system or a change (toughening) of attitude on the part of juvenile officials toward the waiver question? Measured against the flow of cases formally charged in the juvenile courts, the cases judicially waived to criminal court maintained a steady 1.4 percent from 1985 to 1994 (Butts 1997).

However, a higher percentage of juvenile referrals was formally handled in 1994 than in 1985. In 1994, about 850,000 of the 1.5 million delinquency referrals (56.7 percent) were handled by formal court proceedings, while in 1985 only about 46 percent of referrals were handled in that fashion (Snyder, Sickmund, and Poe-Yamagata 1996). Thus, the increase in the number of waivers — even though constant as a percentage of the number of formally processed cases — may reflect a change in attitude by juvenile officials toward those cases that should be formally processed. However, one would expect that at least the most serious of the cases waived would always have been handled formally.

There is also evidence of a change in official attitudes toward the "waivability" of formally prosecuted cases. Between 1989 and 1993, the number of cases of offenses against the person formally processed by juvenile courts increased by 58 percent while there was a 115 percent increase in judicial waivers of those cases (Snyder, Sickmund, and Poe-Yamagata 1996, 28).

The Offenses

There also appears to be a change in the type of offense for which judicial waiver will be used. Prior to 1991, more offenses against property were waived than offenses against the person. However, by 1994, offenses against the person outnumbered offenses against property. Waivers for offenses against property and drug offenses declined in absolute numbers from 1991 to 1994 (Snyder, Sickmund, and Poe-Yamagata 1996, 28).

These numbers are consistent with a focus of attention by the media, political leaders, and, ultimately, juvenile justice officials upon serious violent conduct for waiver to criminal court.

Prior Record

The *Kent* criteria, and many adopted in states using the *Kent* model, regard prior record as a factor to be used in making the waiver decision. How important is that consideration? One study suggests that prior record by itself does not seem to relate to willingness by juvenile court judges to waive cases to criminal court—in fact it is related inversely to willingness to waive (Dawson 1992, 1018). That anomaly is accounted for when seriousness of the offense is factored in. The more serious the offense charged the less likely it is that the juvenile has a prior record when a prosecutor seeks waiver. For the less serious offenses—particularly property offenses—prior record was always present (Dawson 1992, 1020–22).

Therefore, prior record has an effect that is secondary to seriousness of the offense. For the most serious offenses, waiver does not depend upon whether there is a prior record. For less serious offenses, prior record becomes important in making the waiver decision. For the least serious offenses, it is the motivating reason for the prosecutor seeking waiver and, presumably, for the judge granting it.

The General Accounting Office in a study of five states concluded that prior referrals to the juvenile system were positively related to waiver decisions and that the impact of prior referrals appeared greatest when offenses against property were charged (U.S. General Accounting Office 1995).

Age

A priori, one would suppose a straight-line relation between age of the juvenile respondent and likelihood of transfer to criminal court. A Texas study shows a positive, significant relationship between the age of the respondent at the time of the offense and the likelihood that a prosecutor will select the case for handling through judicial waiver. This relationship becomes particularly strong at the upper end of the statutory waiver eligibility bracket so that at the very top of the bracket prosecutors appear to be employing a concept of an "almost adult" in selecting cases for waiver consideration. However, this same study fails to show any significant relationship between age at the time of the offense or at the time of court proceedings and judicial willingness to waive jurisdiction (Dawson 1992, 1015–17).

The lower the minimum waiver age, the more problems are posed for a prosecutor in successfully seeking waiver to and prosecution in criminal courts. There is some evidence of resistance to waiver by juvenile prosecutors and juvenile court judges for particularly young respondents. However, there is evidence that once waiver occurs, criminal courts are more likely to accept full prosecution and punishment of the waived juvenile for younger than for older offenders. This can be explained because for a prosecutor to seek and a juvenile court judge to waive jurisdiction over a very young juvenile, the offense must be particularly serious. For example, younger respondents in waiver proceedings were significantly more likely to be charged with homicides than older respondents (Dawson 1992, 1035–37). That fact overrides any concern about the youthfulness of the offender in the processing and punishment of the case in the criminal system.

So, if one compared ages by offenses within the waiver bracket, one would expect to find that for those children at the lower part of the range, the offenses would be more serious than average, while for children at the upper end, they would be somewhat less serious.

The General Accounting Office reports that in a six-state study it conducted, "juveniles 16 years or older were more likely to have their cases waived" than juveniles under age 16 for all offense categories studied (U.S. General Accounting Office 1995, 12).

Gender/Race/Ethnicity

Virtually all respondents waived from juvenile to criminal court are male. In the Texas study, 98.2 percent (110 of 112) of prosecutorial motions for waiver were filed against males. No females were waived while 79.1 percent (87 of 110) of the males were waived (Dawson 1992, 1001, 1024).

The General Accounting Office study of six states reports, "Males were more likely than females to have their cases waived within each offense type . . . we analyzed" (U.S. General Accounting Office 1995, 12). The extent of likelihood varied by state: "males charged with violent offenses were 42 times more likely to have their cases waived than females [charged with violent offenses] in Arizona, while such males were 17 times more likely to have their cases waived than [such] females in California" (U.S. General Accounting Office 1995, 59).

Explanations for this disparity are elusive. Perhaps the seriousness of violent offenses committed by males is greater than by females. Perhaps females tend to commit such offenses in the company of males and have a more peripheral involvement in the violence of the offense than their male companions. Or perhaps the officials who operate the juvenile justice system tend to be more protective of females than of males even when responsibility for a violent offense is implicated.

The data as to the effect of race/ethnicity upon judicial waiver decisions are mixed. The entire subject of race and transfer to criminal court is discussed in the contribution to this volume by Bortner, Hawkins, and Zatz.

State and Local Differences

Whether one's case is handled in the juvenile justice system or the criminal justice system depends upon many factors, but an important one is the place where the offense was committed. State to state and locality to locality, variations play an important role in the waiver lottery that is current reality.

Of course, state-to-state differences are inevitable in a federal system of government in which fifty state governments are given substantial autonomy over such matters as juvenile and criminal justice policies. Differences among localities within the same state present more difficult circumstances.

The General Accounting Office study showed major differences in waiver rates across states by age. For example, juveniles sixteen or older in Arizona were thirty-nine times more likely to be waived than younger juveniles while only five times more likely in Florida (U.S. General Accounting Office 1995, 58).

The GAO also reported differences across states by race. For drug offenses, in California black juveniles were half as likely as white juveniles to have their cases waived, while in Pennsylvania black juveniles were more than twice as likely as whites to have their cases waived (U.S. General Accounting Office 1995, 59).

Such state-to-state differences may reflect differences in culture, laws, or state policies. There is, in general, no legal requirement that persons be treated the same in the same circumstances from one state to another. That is a consequence of federalism.

Unexplained differences within the same state, by contrast, are more troublesome because they cannot be placed at the feet of federalism and because at some level these differences may offend constitutional guarantees of equal protection of the laws or similar provisions of state law.

The General Accounting Office study noted some differences in waiver rates within states by localities. For example, in Missouri waiver rates in metropolitan areas were higher for violent and drug offenses but lower for property offenses than in nonmetropolitan areas (U.S. General Accounting Office 1995, 59).

The Texas study showed major differences in motion filing and waiver of jurisdiction by county. In particular one county—Dallas County—stood out as different from other metropolitan counties in the aggressiveness with which it pursued waiver cases. Prosecutors in Dallas County were much more likely to file a waiver motion in a case than were prosecutors in three other metropolitan counties (Dawson 1992, 1047-51). This held whether one compared filing rates with county population, county juvenile-age population, or county referral rates. The more aggressive Dallas County policy manifested itself particularly in willingness to file robbery and burglary cases.

At the judicial level, however, Dallas County waived a significantly lower percentage of cases filed than did the other three metropolitan counties. The more aggressive filing policy resulted in a lower in-court success rate, which should not surprise any criminal lawyer.

Can such major differences among counties by justified? Can they be eliminated? The answer to the second question is probably no unless one attempts to eliminate all prosecutorial discretion and local budgeting constraints on prosecution offices. Each community is given a certain amount of freedom to development its own enforcement policies to meet its own perceived needs. While that is a desirable measure of local control, the price that must be paid for it is that the decision making may depend more on where the decision is made than upon the case being decided.

4. The Functions of Judicial Waiver in a Changing Transfer Environment

Legislatures have changed the characteristics of judicial waiver and the context in which it operates. The changes in characteristics make judicial waiver a more efficient process for moving juvenile cases to the criminal justice system. Judicial waiver is more efficient in the sense that it moves more cases to the criminal system than before and probably also moves each case with fewer resources expended than before.

In addition, legislatures have created or expanded three alternatives to judicial waiver—legislative exclusion, direct filing, and blended sentencing. Almost always, these alternatives were enacted to function in a transfer environment that continues to make discretionary judicial waiver available. In 1997, discretionary judicial waiver in some form was available in forty-six of the fifty-one jurisdictions (Torbet and Szymanski 1998, 4).

What effects have there been on the functions served by judicial waiver as a result of changes in the environment in which it operates?

Judicial Waiver as the Only Transfer Process

In seventeen of fifty-one jurisdictions (one-third) judicial waiver continues to operate in an environment in which legislative exclusion and direct filing are not available. However, in three of those seventeen jurisdictions (Kansas, Rhode Island, and Texas), a form of blended sentencing in which the juvenile court retains jurisdiction but can impose an adult sanction is available in some cases in which discretionary judicial waiver is also available. In those states, juvenile court–blended sentencing, like statutory exclusion and direct filing, competes with discretionary judicial waiver for the handling of serious violent offenses.

In an additional three jurisdictions of the seventeen (California, Missouri, and West Virginia), criminal court–based blended sentencing is available. Because that disposition is available only after the juvenile has been transferred to criminal court by discretionary judicial waiver, it does not compete with judicial waiver and thus does not preclude including those states in the category of "pure" judicial waiver jurisdictions.

Thus, in fourteen of fifty-one jurisdictions (27.5 percent), discretionary judicial waiver operates in an environment without competition from statutory exclusion, direct filing, or juvenile court–blended sentencing. Those fourteen jurisdictions might be regarded as the most traditional ones in the sense that their continuing exclusive reliance on discretionary judicial waiver shows a reluctance to innovate in transfer policy.

Of the fourteen states in this category, five (Hawaii, Maine, Missouri, South Dakota, and Tennessee) retain the traditional discretionary judicial waiver process as the exclusive means of transfer and have not enacted presumptive or mandatory embellishments. In another three states (California, New Hampshire, and New Jersey), discretionary waiver is available but has been replaced by presumptive judicial waiver in some subcategories of cases eligible for discretionary waiver. In five states (Kentucky, North Carolina, Ohio, South Carolina, and West Virginia), discretionary judicial waiver remains available, but has been supplanted by mandatory judicial waiver for certain subcategories of offenses. And in one state (North Dakota), discretionary, presumptive, and mandatory judicial waiver are all available for certain offenses (Torbet and Szymanski 1998, 4).

Of these fourteen states, there is a major difference between the eight that rely upon discretionary or discretionary-presumptive provisions and the six that include mandatory provisions for certain subcategories of offenses. In the eight states without mandatory waiver, the judiciary retains absolute control over which cases are waived. That remains true whether the burden is upon the government to make a case for waiver under a traditional waiver statute or is on the juvenile to make a case against waiver in a presumed waiver case.

In the six states that have enacted mandatory waiver provisions, the discretion of the judiciary is replaced by conditional legislative exclusion for the offenses/ages/histories covered by the mandatory provisions. Unlike legislative exclusion, mandatory waiver is conditional because it is available only if requested by the prosecutor in the exercise of prosecutorial discretion by filing a waiver petition or motion. It is also conditional in the sense that the mandatory provisions apply only if the juvenile court judge finds that the case circumstances (charge, age, history) fall within the scope of the mandatory waiver statute and finds probable cause to believe the juvenile committed an offense covered by the legislation. Even in a mandatory waiver circumstance, the judiciary still retains some limited control over the waiver process. In addition, because a judicial hearing is required before waiver can be ordered under mandatory waiver provisions, the respondent has some leverage to negotiate a hearing-free disposition that may avoid waiver altogether. Such an opportunity is not as easily available in cases of legislative exclusion.

How extensive are the mandatory waiver provisions? In the six states of immediate concern, they are quite narrow. For example, in Kentucky, mandatory waiver applies only to a child fourteen or older who commits a felony with a firearm. *Ky. Rev. Stat.* § 635.020(4) (West 1998). In North Carolina, waiver is mandatory only for a class A felony committed by child thirteen or older. *N.C. Gen. Stat.* § 7A-608 (Michie 1997). North Dakota mandates waiver for a child fourteen or older who there is probable cause to believe committed or attempted to commit murder, committed or attempted to commit gross sexual imposition by force or threat, or manufactured or delivered certain controlled substances. *N.D. Cent. Code* § 27-30-34.1 (Michie 1997). In Ohio, waiver is mandatory for a child sixteen or older committing or attempting to commit murder or aggravated murder, for a child of any age committing or attempting to commit those offenses with a prior adjudication for such an offense, or for a child any age committing or attempting to commit those offenses with a prior training school commitment for a serious felony. Waiver is also mandatory for a child sixteen or older charged with voluntary manslaughter, rape, aggravated arson, aggravated robbery, aggravated burglary, or first-degree felony involuntary manslaughter who was either previously committed to training school for a serious felony or who used or exhibited a firearm during the commission of the offense. *Ohio Rev. Code Ann.* § 2151.26 (West 1997). South Carolina mandates waiver for a child fourteen or older who commits a felony punishable by ten years or more who has two prior adjudications for such offenses. *S.C. Code Ann.* § 20-7-7605(10) (1997). West Virginia mandates waiver for a juvenile of fourteen or older in three circumstances: if such a juvenile is charged with treason, murder, armed robbery, kidnapping, first-degree arson, or first-degree sexual assault; if such a juvenile is charged with a violent felony with a prior adjudication; or if such a juvenile is charged with any felony with two prior felony adjudications. *W.V. Code* § 49-5-10(d) (Lexis 1998).

Each of these six states describes a serious but relatively narrow category of conduct for compulsory waiver. In many of those cases, a juvenile charged with such an offense would likely have been waived under discretionary provisions. Mandatory waiver is a subset that isolates more serious offenses, older offenders, or offenders with more extensive juvenile histories than does discretionary waiver. Probably most, if not all, of the real safety valve cases would be covered by these mandatory waiver provisions. That would not preclude discretionary waiver in other circumstances.

In general, one would expect that when a legislature creates a mandatory waiver provision, the effect on discretionary waiver would be to shift its primary functions from safety valve to amenability.

In jurisdictions without mandatory provisions, because of the absence of competing transfer procedures, one would expect to find all of the pressures on discretionary and presumptive decision making that have traditionally been part of the waiver process. Dual waiver objectives of providing a safety valve for the system in very serious cases and making an amenability decision in repeat offender cases will likely continue to be present and exert influences on judicial decision making.

Judicial Waiver and Legislative Exclusions

Forty-six of fifty-one jurisdictions have discretionary judicial waiver as a transfer procedure. Twenty-five of those forty-six jurisdictions also have legislative exclusions (Torbet and Szymanski 1998, 4). Like mandatory judicial waiver, legislative exclusions focus on three factors—offense, age, and history. Legislative exclusions tend to be more absolute in their effects than are mandatory judicial waiver provisions. There is room, but less room, for prosecutorial or judicial control over the process.

Prosecutors have some power to charge facts as an offense covered or not covered by statutory exclusion provisions. For example, if armed robbery is excluded but unarmed robbery is not, a prosecutor may choose to charge the robbery but omit charging that it was committed with a weapon. The prosecutor may do so unilaterally from a perception that criminal proceedings would be inappropriate on the facts of the case (perhaps because of the age of the respondent or the respondent's minor role in the commission of the offense). The prosecutor may also undercharge as part of a disposition agreement with the defense resulting in an uncontested juvenile resolution of the case. Statutory language identifies excluded offenses in terms of offenses charged. Even if the facts could be charged as a more serious (and excluded) offense, a prosecutor who elects to undercharge the offense exercises discretion typically permitted in the criminal or juvenile justice system.

The role of the judiciary is after the fact. The juvenile court judge has no role in legislative exclusion of a case from the juvenile system other than the role that may be played in the initial handling of the case (such as conducting detention hearings) until the prosecutor charges the excluded offense. That role is likely to have little impact on whether the case is ultimately excluded from the juvenile system.

After the case is excluded and filed in criminal court, the criminal court judge may have a substantial role in the process. Of the twenty-five jurisdictions that have both judicial waiver and statutory exclusion, fifteen have provisions for reverse waiver under which the judge of the criminal court may remand the case to the juvenile court (Torbet and Szymanski 1998, 4). Reverse waiver is discussed in Barry Feld's contribution to this volume.

While reverse waiver is important as a way of interjecting discretion into a process of statutory exclusion that may be intended to work mechanically, it functions after the fact, which limits its importance. The child has already been filed on in criminal court under the exclusion provision and then faces the task of persuading a criminal court judge to take seriously his or her claim to be remanded to the juvenile system. That seems a daunting task.

The legislative exclusions in the twenty-five jurisdictions with judicial waiver tend to fall into three different categories, which I call the "superserious short list," the "older juvenile long list," and the "younger juvenile long list." The "list" refers to the legislative list of excluded offenses. The "superserious" offenses are murder, rape, kidnapping, and sometimes robbery, arson, assault, and various aggravated drug offenses. The older juvenile long list is a much more extensive list of serious offenses committed by a juvenile while at least sixteen years of age. The younger juvenile long list consists of the same list of offenses when charged against juveniles who are younger than sixteen. In addition, the long list for the older juveniles sometimes includes juvenile history, requiring proof of prior juvenile adjudications or even correctional facility commitments to trip the exclusion. Of the twenty-five jurisdictions with both exclusion and judicial waiver, ten fit the superserious short list definition, eleven the older juvenile long list, and four the younger juvenile long list.

Superserious Short List

Of the ten superserious short list jurisdictions, Minnesota is the most restrictive because it excludes only a charge of first-degree murder committed by a juvenile sixteen or older. *Minn. Stat. Ann.* 260.015, subd. 5(b) (West 1998). Montana mandates filing a criminal information for a seventeen-year-old who is charged with intentional murder, forcible rape, or attempted murder. The criminal court judge may refuse to accept the filing in a manner similar to a reverse waiver procedure. *Mont. Code Ann.* § 41-5-206(2). By constitutional amendment, Arizona excludes juveniles fifteen or older charged with murder, forcible sexual assault, armed robbery, or a violent felony or as a chronic felony offender as defined by statute. *Ariz. Const.* art. IV, § 22 (West 1998). Delaware excludes, without imposing a minimum age, juveniles who are charged with murder, rape, kidnapping, or an attempt to commit those offenses. *10 Del. Code Ann.*§ 921(2)(a). Georgia excludes a juvenile thirteen or older charged with murder or voluntary manslaughter, rape, aggravated sodomy, aggravated child molestation, aggravated sexual battery, or robbery with a firearm. *Ga. Code*§ 15-11-5(b)(2)(A) (1998). Illinois excludes a juvenile fifteen or older charged with first-degree murder, aggravated sexual assault, robbery with a firearm, aggravated vehicular hijacking with a firearm, or certain controlled-substance offenses on school property. *Ill. Comp. Stat. Ann.* § 405/5-130(1)(a), (2)(a) (West 1998). Under Louisiana law, juvenile court jurisdiction over a child fifteen or older charged with first- or second-degree murder, aggravated rape, or aggravated kidnapping is automatically divested once the juvenile court judge makes a finding of probable cause in a detention hearing. *La. Stat. Ann.* tit. III, ch. 4, art. 305.A (West 1998). Mississippi provides without specifying a minimum age that a juvenile charged with an offense carrying death or life imprisonment or any felony committed with a deadly weapon is excluded from juvenile court jurisdiction. *Miss. Code Ann.* § 43-21-151(1) (1998). South Carolina provides that a juvenile fourteen or older charged with a felony that carries punishment of ten years or longer who has before been twice adjudicated or convicted of such a felony is excluded from the jurisdiction of the juvenile court. *S.C. Code Ann.* § 20-7-7605(10) (1997). (The South Carolina provision can be regarded either as a statutory exclusion or as a mandatory judicial waiver provision and is treated as both.) Wisconsin provides that a juvenile charged with first-degree intentional murder or who has been adjudicated delinquent and is charged with injury or threat to an employee of a secure correctional or detention facility or probation or parole officer is excluded from juvenile court jurisdiction. *Wis. Stat. Ann.* § 938.183(1) (West 1998).

In each of these ten jurisdictions, the exclusions are for a short list of very serious offenses. Although each of these cases is important, statistically they are insignificant in their impact on judicial waiver. In total, these cases remove some of the most severe safety valve problems from the juvenile system without removing a large number of juveniles to the criminal system.

Older Juvenile Long List

In eleven jurisdictions with judicial waiver, there are legislative exclusions for a longer list of offenses but only for older juveniles. Sixteen is the minimum age in all of these jurisdictions. In three of them (Maryland, Nevada, and Oklahoma) exclusions for juveniles under sixteen years old exist for superserious short list offenses in addition to the long list offenses for those sixteen or older.

The long list may be extremely long. For example, Indiana excludes fourteen different charged offenses, which involve violence, threatened violence, gang activity, weapons possession or use, and drug dealing. *Ind. Code* § 31-30-1-4(a) (West 1998). Alabama excludes charges of a capital offense, a class A felony, any felony with a deadly weapon element, any felony with causing death or serious physical injury as an element, any felony involving the use of a dangerous instrument against a long list of public employees such as law enforcement officers, court and correctional officials, and school teachers, and trafficking in drugs. *Ala. Code* § 12-15-34.1(a) (1998). Alaska excludes any unclassified felony, any class A felony against the person, first-degree arson, any class B felony against the person committed with a deadly weapon by one with a prior adjudication for an offense against the person involving the use of a deadly weapon. *Alas. Stat.* § 47.12.030(a) (1998). Florida mandates filing a charge in criminal court against a sixteen-year-old or older juvenile charged with a violent crime against the person who has a prior adjudication for murder, sexual battery, armed or strong-armed robbery, carjacking, home-invasion robbery, aggravated battery, or aggravated assault. Florida also mandates filing a criminal charge regardless of the child's age if the juvenile has three or more felony adjudications with three or more residential commitments. *Fla. Stat. Ann.* § 985.227(2) (West 1998). Iowa excludes charges of certain drug offenses committed with firearms, criminal street gang weapons offenses, felony weapon offenses, and any forcible felony. *Ia. Code Ann.* § 232.8.1.c (West 1998). South Dakota excludes sixteen-year-old or older juveniles charged with any offense carrying life imprisonment or a sentence of at least twenty-five years. *S.D. Cod. Laws* § 26-11-3.1 (1998). Utah excludes a sixteen-year-old or older juvenile charged with murder or any felony if the juvenile was previously committed to a secure juvenile correctional facility. *Utah Code* § 78-3a-601(1) (Lexis 1998). Washington excludes charges of murder, manslaughter, assault, kidnapping, rape, assault on a child, or attempt to commit those offenses, first-degree robbery, rape of a child in the first degree, drive-by shooting, or any violent offense with a firearm and excludes other offenses against the person such as taking indecent liberties with a child, drunk driving with injuries or death, burglary, or any class A felony if the juvenile has an adjudication history. *Wash. Rev. Code Ann.* §12.04.030(1)(e)(v) (West 1998).

In addition to the superserious short list, Oklahoma excludes sixteen-year-old or older juveniles charged with murder, kidnapping, robbery with a weapon or injury, rape, use of a firearm in commission of a felony, first-degree arson, burglary with explosives, first- or second-degree burglary after three adjudications for the same offense, shooting with intent to kill, discharging a weapon from a vehicle, intimidating a witness, manslaughter in the first degree, sodomy, trafficking in illegal drugs, or assault and battery with a deadly weapon. *Okla. Stat. Ann.* § 7306-1.1 (West 1998). In addition to the superserious short list, Nevada excludes the older juvenile charged with sexual assault who has a prior felony adjudication or charged with any offense involving the use of a firearm who has a prior felony adjudication. *Nev. Rev. Stat.* § 62.040 (1997). In addition to the superserious short list, Maryland excludes a sixteen-year-old or older juvenile charged with abduction, kidnapping, second-degree murder, voluntary manslaughter, second-degree rape, robbery with a weapon, second- or third-degree sexual assault, carrying a firearm, carjacking, first-degree assault, or attempted murder, rape, or robbery. *Md. Ann. Code* tit. 8, § 3-804(e)(4) (Michie 1997).

There are discernible themes to this aggregation of offenses. First, serious violent offenses are named in most of these schemes. These offenses are less serious as a group than the superserious short list offenses, but still quite serious. Second, provisions in many of these jurisdictions focus on any offenses committed with a deadly weapon, particularly a firearm. Third, offenses believed to be typical of those committed by gang members are the focus of many of these provisions. Fourth, a history of prior felony adjudications or adjudications with residential commitment describe the focus of other provisions. Violence, guns, gangs, and history are the focal points of these provisions.

These provisions will have a significant impact on the functions of judicial waiver with which they coexist. The offenses named by legislation are aimed at a politically sensitive point of the juvenile justice system. Because the juvenile must be sixteen or older at the time of the offense, there is limited time available within the traditional limitations of the juvenile justice system to deal with the case. That magnifies pressure to move the case to the criminal system.

The precise impact of these provisions on judicial waiver practices will depend upon the legal culture in which they operate. In many places, the effects of lengthy exclusions will be to eliminate judicial waiver for offenders sixteen or older and to confine it to juveniles under that age. The extent to which judicial waiver will be used for under-sixteen juveniles will depend upon legal availability and upon the customs of local prosecutorial and judicial authorities. In almost any legal culture, the effect of these provisions on judicial waiver will be palpable.

Younger Juvenile Long List

Four jurisdictions have applied the long list to juveniles younger than sixteen years old. Oregon and Pennsylvania apply the long list to juveniles aged fifteen or older, while Idaho and Vermont apply it to juveniles aged fourteen or older.

Oregon excludes the following from juvenile court jurisdiction when committed by a juvenile fifteen or older: aggravated murder, murder, attempt or conspiracy to commit murder or aggravated murder, first- or second-degree manslaughter, first- or second-degree assault, first- or second-degree kidnapping, first- or second-degree rape, first- or second-degree sodomy, first- or second-degree unlawful sexual penetration, first-degree sexual abuse, first- or second-degree robbery, first-degree arson, using a child in a display of sexually explicit conduct, or compelling prostitution. *Ore. Rev. Stat.* § 137.707 (1997).

Pennsylvania has a complicated exclusion scheme that includes murder with no separate minimum age and any of the following offenses by a juvenile fifteen or older if committed with a deadly weapon: rape, involuntary deviate sexual intercourse, aggravated assault, robbery, robbery of motor vehicle, aggravated indecent assault, kidnapping, voluntary manslaughter, or an attempt, conspiracy, or solicitation to commit any of those offenses. In addition, Pennsylvania statutes exclude any of the offenses on the same list if the juvenile of age fifteen or older was previously adjudicated for any of the same offenses. *Penn. Stat. Ann.* § 6302 (West 1998).

Idaho law excludes the following offenses when committed by a juvenile fourteen or older: murder, robbery, rape, forcible sexual penetration by a foreign object, infamous crimes against nature, mayhem, assault or battery with intent to commit any of the previous offenses, controlled substance violations on school grounds, or arson. *Id. Code* § 20-509 (Michie 1997).

Vermont law excludes the following offenses when committed by a juvenile fourteen or older: arson causing death, robbery with a dangerous weapon or causing bodily injury, aggravated assault, murder, manslaughter, kidnapping, maiming, sexual assault, aggravated sexual assault, or burglary of sleeping apartments in the nighttime. *Vt. Stat. Ann.* § 5506 (1997).

Except in Pennsylvania, the offenses on the young juvenile long list are different from those on the older juvenile long list by the absence of provisions requiring a showing of adjudication history to be invoked and by the absence of provisions explicitly dealing with firearms. All four jurisdictions differ by the absence of provisions explicitly dealing with street gangs. The offenses are almost all serious violent offenses. Because the minimum age is lower than for the older juvenile long list, this list is shorter and covers only those offenses that would be regarded as the most dangerous from among those on the other long list.

Judicial Waiver and Direct Filing

Of the 46 jurisdictions that use judicial waiver, in 13 (28.3 percent) prosecutorial direct filing in criminal court is also permitted. (Torbet and Szymanski 1998, 4). Overlaying direct filing onto judicial waiver can have a significant impact on the waiver process. That action almost certainly displaces more potential waiver proceedings than do statutory exclusions because the scope of cases eligible for direct filing is so much broader than for exclusions.

Of the thirteen jurisdictions of interest here, seven permit direct filing in criminal court against juveniles as young as fourteen for long lists of offenses. In addition, one jurisdiction (Georgia) permits direct filing from a superserious short list with no minimum age and one (Montana) from a superserious short list for twelve-year-olds. Fifteen is the minimum direct filing age in two jurisdictions (Louisiana and Oklahoma) and sixteen is the minimum in two (District of Columbia and Vermont). By contrast, statutory exclusions for long lists of offenses tend to have a minimum age of sixteen, which leaves judicial waiver room to function for juveniles younger than sixteen. Very few juveniles are judicially waived to criminal courts for offenses committed before age fourteen.

The lists of offenses for which direct filing is available at age fourteen tend to be even longer than the long lists of exclusions for older juveniles. For example, Arizona permits direct filing with a minimum age of fourteen for a long list of serious felonies and for other felonies involving intentional infliction of serious physical injury or use of a deadly weapon or any felony committed by a chronic felony offender. *Ariz. Rev. Stat. Ann.* § 13-501.B (West 1998). Arkansas permits direct filing with a minimum age of fourteen for a list of eighteen different felonies. *Ark. Code 1987 Ann.* 9-27-318(b)(2) (1997). Colorado has a complicated scheme permitting direct filing with a minimum age of fourteen for a long list of offenses, including any felony committed with a deadly weapon and any felony committed by a habitual juvenile offender. *Colo. Rev. Stat. Ann.* § 19-2-517(1)(a)(II)(III)(V) (West 1998). Florida permits direct filing with a minimum age of fourteen for a list of fifteen offenses. *Fla. Stat. Ann.* 985.227(1)(a) (West 1998). Michigan permits direct filing with a minimum age of fourteen for a long list of offenses. *Mich. Comp. Laws Ann.* § 712A.2(a)(1). Virginia permits direct filing with a minimum age of fourteen for a long list with a required juvenile court finding of probable cause. *Va. Code* § 16.1-269.1.C (Michie 1998). Wyoming permits direct filing with a minimum age of fourteen for any felony by a juvenile with two prior felony adjudications or for any violent felony (murder, manslaughter, kidnapping, first- or second-degree sexual assault, robbery, aggravated assault, aircraft hijacking, first- or second-degree arson, or aggravated burglary). *Wyo. Stat.* § 14-6-203(f) (1998).

Two jurisdictions permit direct filing for juveniles under fourteen for a superserious short list of offenses. Georgia permits direct filing for felonies punishable by death or life imprisonment with no minimum age specified. *Ga. Code* § 15-11-5(b)(1) (1998). Montana permits direct filing for a superserious short list with a minimum age of twelve and for a long list with a minimum age of sixteen. *Mont. Code Ann.* § 51-5-206(1) (1997).

In long-list jurisdictions with a minimum age of fourteen, judicial waiver is probably displaced almost totally. While some jurisdictions would permit judicial waiver proceedings for an offense committed before fourteen, those are rare occurrences. The long-list offenses include almost all offenses that would be likely subjects of waiver proceedings.

Are there situations in which a prosecutor might forgo direct filing in criminal court in favor of judicial waiver proceedings? There are some cases in which a prosecutor may feel pressure for criminal proceedings, but believe them to be inappropriate. Such a prosecutor may prefer to have the juvenile court judge make the decision not to transfer the case to criminal court rather than to assume full responsibility for it by declining direct filing. Occasionally, criminal prosecutors use grand juries for similar purposes.

However, if a prosecutor has decided that criminal proceedings are appropriate, there is no advantage to seeking judicial waiver when direct filing is also available. But there are disadvantages. Judicial waiver consumes more of the prosecutor's resources, is less certain in outcome, and provides the defense with additional discovery of the state's evidence.

Because the minimum age for direct filing often is low—around fourteen—and because the list of eligible offenses usually is long—including lower-level felonies committed with weapons or by habitual offenders—direct filing has a more dramatic impact on judicial waiver procedures than does legislative exclusion. A prosecutor is unlikely to forgo direct filing but pursue judicial waiver. In a situation in which both are available, a prosecutor will almost always choose direct filing. Providing for direct filing with a minimum age of fourteen or lower and a long list of offenses would be expected to displace judicial waiver almost totally.

Judicial Waiver and Blended Sentencing Systems

Blended sentencing provisions and practices are discussed in Richard Redding and James C. Howell's contribution to this volume. Here, our concern is restricted to the impact on judicial waiver that should be expected when some form of blended sentencing is enacted.

By 1997, there were nineteen jurisdictions with some form of blended sentencing system in place. However, in ten of those jurisdictions, the blended sentencing system becomes available only after a juvenile case has been transferred to criminal court and a conviction has occurred (Torbet et al. 1996, 13; Torbet and Szymanski 1998, 6–7).

Blended sentencing based in criminal court will have some, but small, effects on judicial waiver. Criminal blended sentencing does not compete directly with judicial waiver because transfer by judicial waiver or some other mechanism has already occurred. It may have some gravitational pull on the exercise of discretion by a juvenile court judge in a judicial waiver proceeding because it holds out the possibility of less-than-full-adult sanctions by the criminal courts if jurisdiction is waived. In a close case, that may induce a reluctant juvenile court judge to waive jurisdiction.

In nine of the nineteen blended sentence jurisdictions, the blended sentencing system is operated initially by the juvenile court. In two of those nine jurisdictions (Massachusetts and New Mexico), there is no judicial waiver available for any offenses. In the remaining seven, the blended sentencing system competes to some extent with the judicial waiver system because they are alternative routes to a similar destination. In those jurisdictions, what effects will blended sentencing have on the practical use of judicial waiver? Will blended sentencing displace judicial waiver (like direct filing would be expected to do) in those cases of overlap? Or will there still be use of each in certain kinds of cases?

Many blended sentencing alternatives were enacted defensively. They were enacted to provide an alternative to expansion of other means of transfer to criminal court because they were believed to provide a better response. A legitimate question is, therefore, whether, compared to judicial waiver at least, systems of blended sentencing capture cases that would not have been waived to criminal court and, therefore, widen the extended control net over juvenile offenders. The answer to the net-widening question is made more difficult because one does not know what expansions in the scope of judicial waiver or other transfer mechanisms would have been made had not blended sentencing been defensively enacted.

The seven jurisdictions in which blended sentencing competes directly with judicial waiver are based on two models. In one model (Connecticut, Kansas, Minnesota, and Montana), the juvenile court imposes a juvenile disposition and an adult disposition. However, the adult disposition is suspended and is not made effective unless the juvenile violates a term of the juvenile disposition or commits a new offense. In that event, after a hearing the juvenile court is empowered to "revoke" the juvenile disposition and order execution of the adult sentence. In the other model (Colorado, Rhode Island, and Texas), a juvenile disposition is ordered that can extend beyond the ordinary upper age limits of the juvenile system (usually twenty-one). Whether the juvenile is later incarcerated in an adult prison for the offense depends upon an evaluation of his or her progress under the juvenile disposition.

The four jurisdictions in the first model are quite similar and are based on the Minnesota statute. Under Minnesota law, judicial waiver to criminal court is permitted for any felony committed by a juvenile fourteen or older. *Minn. Stat. Ann.* § 260.125, subd. 1 (West 1998). Waiver is presumed if the juvenile was sixteen or seventeen at the time of the offense and the offense carries a presumptive commitment to prison under criminal sentencing guidelines and statutes or was committed with a firearm. *Minn. Stat. Ann.* § 260.125, subd. 2a (West 1998). Minnesota law provides for extended jurisdiction juvenile prosecutions for three categories of cases. First, the juvenile court judge can designate a case against a fourteen-year-old or older juvenile as extended jurisdiction if a waiver hearing was held but the judge declined to waive. Second, the prosecutor may designate a case against a sixteen- or seventeen-year-old as extended jurisdiction if waiver would have been presumed had it been sought. Third, the judge may, after hearing and on motion of the prosecutor, designate a case against a juvenile fourteen or older for any felony. *Minn. Stat. Ann.* § 260.126, subd. 1 (West 1998). First-degree murder committed by a sixteen-year-old is excluded from this scheme. *Minn. Stat. Ann.* § 260.126, subd. 6 (West 1998). Upon adjudication of an extended jurisdiction offense, the juvenile court may impose any authorized juvenile disposition and an adult criminal sentence, the execution of which must be stayed. *Minn. Stat. Ann.* § 260.126, subd. 4 (West 1998). Unless the juvenile violates a term of the juvenile disposition or commits a new offense, the adult sentence will never be executed and the juvenile will never enter the adult system.

The Montana provisions are very similar to Minnesota's. A juvenile court may, after hearing on motion of the prosecutor, designate a case as an extended-jurisdiction juvenile prosecution if the juvenile was fourteen or older and charged with a felony. *Mont. Code Ann.* § 41-5-1602(1)(a) (1998). The court may also designate a case for extended jurisdiction if it has declined waiver after a hearing. *Mont. Code Ann.* § 41-5-1602(1)(c). The prosecutor may designate a case for extended jurisdiction treatment if the case could have been filed directly in the criminal court (twelve or older for superserious short list or sixteen or older for long list) or was any felony committed with a firearm by a juvenile twelve or older. *Mont. Code Ann.* § 41-5-1602(1)(b). If the juvenile violates a condition of the juvenile disposition, the juvenile court may order the adult sentence to be executed. *Mont. Code Ann.* § 41-5-1605 (1998).

Kansas provisions, also based on the Minnesota model, permit the prosecutor to move for and the juvenile court to grant extended jurisdiction status for any offense at any age. *Kan. Stat. Ann.* § 38-1636 (a)(3) (1997). If the juvenile was fourteen or older and charged from a long list of felony offenses or committed the offense with a firearm or is charged with a felony with a prior felony adjudication then the burden is on the respondent to rebut a presumption the case should be so designated. *Kan. Stat. Ann.* § 38-1636(a)(3) (1997). These provisions track Kansas provisions defining the scope of judicial waiver. *Kan. Stat. Ann.* § 38-1636(a)(1), (2) (1997). Upon adjudication in an extended-jurisdiction proceeding, the court imposes a juvenile disposition with a stayed criminal sentence on the Minnesota model.

Connecticut provisions are the most narrow, applying only to a fourteen- or fifteen-year-old juvenile charged with his or her third felony offense. *Conn. Gen. Stat. Ann.* §§ 46b-133c(a), 46b-120(13) (West 1998). This provision operates in an environment in which there is mandatory criminal court jurisdiction for a juvenile fourteen or older charged with capital murder or a class A or B felony. *Conn. Gen. Stat. Ann.* § 46b-127(a) (West 1998). Obviously, the target of the Connecticut provision is the repeat offender, not the superserious offense. A respondent may be designated a serious juvenile repeat offender by the court after a hearing. *Conn. Gen. Stat. Ann.* § 46b-133c(b) (West 1998). Upon adjudication, a juvenile disposition with a stayed adult sentence is imposed. *Conn. Gen. Stat. Ann.* § 46b-133c(c) (West 1998).

The second model is based on the Texas provisions. As originally enacted, these provisions permitted a sentence of up to thirty years (later increased to forty) for a superserious short list of offenses (capital murder, murder, attempted capital murder, aggravated kidnapping, and aggravated sexual assault) committed by a juvenile ten or older. *Tex. Fam. Code Ann.* §§ 53.045, 54.04 (West 1998). Probation was available. If a sentence was imposed, the juvenile was incarcerated in the state juvenile correctional facility until age eighteen, at which time the committing juvenile court conducted a hearing to determine whether to convert the sentence to an indeterminate juvenile commitment expiring at age twenty-one or to transfer the juvenile to the adult prison for service of sentence under adult law. *Tex. Fam. Code Ann* § 54.11 (West 1998). From the inception of this program in 1987 through September 1998, about half of the six-hundred-plus cases in which the up-or-out decision was made resulted in transfer to prison and in half the sentence expired before age eighteen or the judge converted the criminal sentence to a juvenile commitment.

The system was changed in 1995 to increase greatly the number of offenses covered from five to almost thirty. Now sentences of up to forty, twenty, or ten years may be imposed, depending upon the penalty category of the offense under adult law. The sentence is started in the state juvenile correctional facility. There is no longer an up-or-out decision made by the committing juvenile court judge when the offender is eighteen. The juvenile facility can parole the juvenile without judicial approval after a statutory minimum length of stay of one, two, or three years has been served. With judicial approval after a hearing, the juvenile facility can transfer the juvenile to adult prison after he or she becomes sixteen years of age. If the juvenile is paroled and is still on parole at age twenty-one, he or she is administratively transferred to adult parole supervision, where if parole is revoked he or she enters adult prison through revocation proceedings. Most of the offenses covered under the expanded law are offenses that would carry a punishment of life imprisonment for an adult. Juvenile waiver statutes permit waiver for any fifteen- or sixteen-year-old for any felony and of a fourteen-year-old for a felony carrying life imprisonment.

Colorado has an aggravated juvenile offender proceeding that has some similarities to the Texas system. Any offense punishable by life imprisonment or by a presumptive sentence of eight to twenty-four years or any juvenile who has a previous felony adjudication followed by an adjudication for a crime of violence or has been adjudicated delinquent for felonious unlawful sexual behavior, incest, or aggravated incest is eligible. *Col. Rev. Stat. Ann.* § 19-2-516(4) (West 1998). Upon adjudication for an offense carrying life, the juvenile court is required to impose a sentence of seven years; for an offense carrying a presumptive sentence of eight to twenty-four years for an adult, the court must impose a sentence of five years; and the court may impose a sentence of as long as five years for any other offense. *Col. Rev. Stat. Ann.* § 19-2-601(5) (West 1998). The training school must petition the juvenile court for authorization to parole the juvenile. Anytime after the juvenile reaches age eighteen, the juvenile training school agency may petition the juvenile court for a hearing asking for permission to transfer him or her to prison. As age twenty-one approaches, the training school must petition the juvenile court for a decision whether to transfer the juvenile to the adult prison or to permit the sentence to expire. *Col. Rev. Stat. Ann.* § 19-2-601(5) (West 1998).

The third jurisdiction using this model is Rhode Island. The procedure, called certification, is available for a juvenile of any age charged with any felony upon motion of the prosecutor and juvenile court hearing. *R.I. Gen. Laws Ann.* §§ 14-1-7(c), 14-1-7-2 (1997). Upon adjudication for a certified offense, the juvenile court may impose the sentence authorized by law for an adult. Service begins in the training school facility, where parole requires judicial approval. A hearing is conducted at age eighteen to determine whether the juvenile should be transferred to prison to serve the rest of his or her sentence under adult law. *R.I. Gen. Laws Ann.* § 14-1-42 (1997).

The first model contemplates there will be no consideration of adult sanctions unless the juvenile violates a term of the juvenile disposition, while in the second model adult sentences are possible even without conduct by the juvenile that can be said to have violated a term of the juvenile disposition. Because under the first model there is a guarantee of only a juvenile disposition unless the juvenile violates a dispositional term, those provisions would be expected to compete primarily with the less serious offense segment of cases that would be in the normal range of offenses subject to judicial waiver provisions. In other words, officials must be willing to accept at the outset that despite the imposition of an adult sanction the juvenile disposition will be the only disposition unless the juvenile violates it. There is no such guarantee in the second model, so one would expect it might compete more fully over the entire range of offenses subject to judicial waiver up to and including capital murder offenses. Certainly, the Texas provisions are aimed primarily at the super-serious offenses. The Rhode Island provisions cover the entire felony range of offenses.

In both models, there is competition between the alternatives of blended sentencing and judicial waiver. In the first model, the focus of the competition is at the lower end of the range of offense seriousness, while in the second model the competition is focused on the upper end of the range.

5. Conclusions

Fifteen years ago, discretionary judicial waiver was virtually the only way of dealing with the occasional difficult juvenile case without stressing the system or the public's confidence in it. Today, the system has a variety of ways of dealing with such cases.

The absolute number of cases subjected to judicial waiver has increased over the past decade, but so have the absolute number of cases processed by the juvenile courts and the absolute number of persons of juvenile age. Judicial waiver is not as important to the juvenile system as it was formerly. Legislatures have used three other mechanisms to achieve many of the same objectives: legislative exclusions, prosecutorial transfer, and blended sentencing systems.

We have relatively good numbers concerning the cases handled by judicial waiver. However, we have much less reliable information about the number of cases that are excluded from juvenile court jurisdiction because of age and offense category and the number of cases transferred by exclusive prosecutorial decision. We have somewhat more reliable information about the extent of use of blended sentencing systems.

Because of the lack of reliable information, it is difficult to assess the relative importance of judicial waiver today as a mechanism for sorting criminal from juvenile cases. In jurisdictions with extensive direct filing systems, one would expect that judicial waiver, while still on the books, would fall into disuse. In jurisdictions with juvenile court–based blended systems, one would expect some less significant competition with judicial waiver. Under the suspended criminal sanction model (Minnesota) of blended sentencing, one would expect the primary competition with judicial waiver to be in the lower range of offense seriousness, while in the model involving a reassessment of sanction later in the process of juvenile disposition (Texas) one would expect primary competition to be at the upper end of offense severity. Statutory exclusions compete with judicial waiver only for the most serious offenses or for a longer list of offenses committed by older juveniles.

Ironically, in jurisdictions with both statutory exclusions and judicial waiver, the legal primacy of exclusion would be expected to have one of two effects: either to displace entirely the use of judicial waiver reducing it to theoretical availability only or to redefine its use along amenability lines. Under the second possibility, if a legislature enacts a statutory exclusion scheme for a list of offenses that previously had been the subject of safety valve waivers, excluding such cases from the waiver process might focus the attention of officials on the use of judicial waiver along classic amenability lines—the repeat offender who has proven himself or herself to be impervious to the operation of the juvenile system.

References
Cases Cited

Hicks v. Superior Court, 36 Cal. App. 4th 1649, 43 Cal. Rptr. 2d 269 (Cal. App. 1995).
Hughes v. State, 653 A.2d 241 (Del. 1994).
In the Matter of J.R.C., 551 S.W.2d 748 (Tex. Civ. App.—Texarkana 1977).
In the Matter of L.J.S. and J.T.K., 539 N.W.2d 408 (Minn. App. 1995).
In the Matter of P.A.C., 562 S.W.2d 913 (Tex. Civ. App.—Amarillo 1978).
Kent v. United States, 383 U.S. 541 (1996).
State in the Interest of A.L., 271 N.J. Super. 192, 638 A.2d 814 (N.J. Super. 1994)

Other References

Butts, Jeffrey A. 1997. *Delinquency Cases Waived to Criminal Court, 1985–1994: Fact Sheet # 52.* Washington: Office of Juvenile Justice and Delinquency Prevention.
Dawson, Robert O. 1992. "An Empirical Study of *Kent* Style Juvenile Transfers to Criminal Court." *St. Mary's Law Journal* 23:975.
Feld, Barry C. 1987. "The Juvenile Court Meets the Principle of the Offense: Legislative Changes in Juvenile Waiver Statutes." *Journal of Criminal Law and Criminology* 78:471.
Sickmund, Melissa, Anne L. Stahl, Terrence A. Finnegan, Howard N. Snyder, Rowen S. Poole, and Jeffrey A. Butts. 1998. *Juvenile Court Statistics 1995.* Washington: Office of Juvenile Justice and Delinquency Prevention.
Snyder, Howard N., and Melissa Sickmund. 1995. *Juvenile Offenders and Victims: A National Report.* Washington: Office of Juvenile Justice and Delinquency Prevention.

Snyder, Howard N., Melissa Sickmund, and Eileen Poe-Yamagata. 1996. *Juvenile Offenders and Victims: 1996 Update on Violence.* Washington: Office of Juvenile Justice and Delinquency Prevention.

Szymanski, Linda. 1997a. *State Variations in Age Restrictions for Trying Juveniles in Criminal Court: NCJJ Snapshot.* Pittsburgh: National Center for Juvenile Justice.

———. 1997b. *Prosecuting 15-Year-Olds in Criminal Court: NCJJ Snapshot.* Pittsburgh: National Center for Juvenile Justice.

Texas Juvenile Probation Commission. 1997. *Statistical Report Calendar Year 1996.* Austin: Texas Juvenile Probation Commission.

———. 1998. *Statistical Report Calendar Year 1997.* Austin: Texas Juvenile Probation Commission.

Torbet, Patricia, Richard Gable, Hunter Hurst IV, Imogene Montgomery, Linda Szymanski, Douglas Thomas. 1996. *State Responses to Serious and Violent Juvenile Crime.* Washington: Office of Juvenile Justice and Delinquency Prevention.

Torbet, Patricia, and Linda Szymanski. 1998. *State Legislative Responses to Violent Juvenile Crime: 1996–97 Update.* Washington: Office of Juvenile Justice and Delinquency Prevention.

United States Department of Justice, Federal Bureau of Investigation. 1997. *Crime in the United States: 1996.* Washington: U.S. Department of Justice.

United States General Accounting Office. 1995. *Juveniles Processed in Criminal Court and Case Dispositions.* Washington: U.S. General Accounting Office.

Chapter Three

Legislative Exclusion of Offenses from Juvenile Court Jurisdiction: A History and Critique

Barry C. Feld

Transfer of juvenile offenders for adult prosecution is at the nexus between the more deterministic and rehabilitative premises of the juvenile court and the free-will and punishment assumptions of the adult criminal justice system. Although juvenile courts theoretically attempt to rehabilitate young offenders, a small but significant proportion of miscreant youths resist their benevolent efforts. These are typically older delinquents nearing the maximum jurisdictional age and often recidivists who have not responded to prior intervention and for whom successful treatment may not be feasible during the time remaining to the juvenile court (Podkopacz and Feld 1995, 1996; U.S. General Accounting Office 1995). Politicians and the public perceive these youth as mature and sophisticated offenders. Moreover, these young career offenders may account for a disproportionate amount of all juvenile crime and violence. Highly visible, serious, and violent offenses evoke community outrage or fear that politicians believe only punitive adult sanctions can mollify. Mechanisms to prosecute some juveniles as adults provide a safety valve that permits the expiatory sacrifice of some youths, quiet political and public clamor, and enable legislators to avoid otherwise irresistible pressures further to lower the maximum age of juvenile court jurisdiction (Feld 1978).

Jurisdictional waiver represents a type of *sentencing* decision. Juvenile courts traditionally assigned primary importance to rehabilitation and attempted to individualize treatment. Criminal courts accorded greater significance to the seriousness of the offense committed and attempted to proportion punishment accordingly. All of the theoretical differences between juvenile and criminal courts' sentencing philosophies emerge in the debates about transfer policies. Transfer laws simultaneously attempt to resolve both fundamental crime control issues and the ambivalence embedded in our cultural construction of youth. The jurisprudential conflicts reflect current sentencing policy debates: the tensions between rehabilitation and incapacitation or retribution, between decisions based on characteristics of the offender and on the seriousness of the offense, between discretion and rules, and between indeterminacy and determinacy. Waiver laws attempt to reconcile the conflicted impulses engendered when the child is a criminal and the criminal is a child and the cultural contradictions between adolescent immaturity and criminal responsibility. What processes best enable us to choose between competing conceptions of youths as responsible and culpable offenders and as immature and salvageable children? In the early stages of a criminal career and prospectively, what criteria can best differentiate between adolescent-only offenders and life-course persistent offenders? Which justice system actors possess the greatest institutional competence to make these difficult decisions?

Every jurisdiction uses one or more statutory approaches to prosecute some juveniles as adults. Although the technical and administrative details of states' transfer legislation vary considerably, judicial waiver, legislative offense exclusion, and prosecutorial choice of forum represent the three generic approaches (Feld 1987; Fritsch and Hemmens 1995; Snyder and Sickmund 1995; U.S. General Accounting Office 1995). They represent different ways to identify which serious young offenders to try as adults, emphasize a different balance of sentencing policy values, rely upon different organizational actors or administrative processes, and elicit different information to determine whether to try and sentence particular young offenders as adults or as children. These strategies allocate to different branches of government—judicial, executive, and legislative—the decision whether to prosecute a youth as a criminal or as a delinquent. Each reflect different ways of asking and answering similar questions: who are the serious offenders?; by what criteria should a state identify them?; which branch of government can best make these decisions?; and how should the juvenile and adult systems respond to them?

Judicial waiver represents the most common transfer strategy. A juvenile court judge may waive jurisdiction on a discretionary basis after conducting a hearing to determine whether a youth is "amenable to treatment" or poses a threat to the public. These assessments reflect the traditional individualized sentencing discretion characteristic of juvenile courts (Feld 1987).

Legislative offense exclusion frequently supplements judicial waiver provisions. This approach emphasizes the seriousness of the offense and reflects the retributive values of the criminal law (Feld 1987; Snyder and Sickmund 1995). Because legislatures create juvenile courts, they freely can define their jurisdiction to exclude youths from juvenile court based on their age and offenses. A number of states, for example, exclude youths sixteen or older and charged with first-degree murder from juvenile court jurisdiction (Sanborn 1996). Legislative line drawing that sets the maximum age of juvenile court jurisdiction at fifteen or sixteen years of age, below the general eighteen-year-old age of majority, results in the adult criminal prosecution of the largest numbers of chronological juveniles (U.S. General Accounting Office 1995). In 1991, this type of line drawing resulted in the criminal prosecution of 176,000 youths below the age of eighteen (Snyder and Sickmund 1995, 88). Two states, Wisconsin and New Hampshire, recently lowered their maximum age of juvenile court jurisdiction from seventeen to sixteen and criminalized large numbers of youths on a wholesale, rather than a retail, basis.

Prosecutorial waiver or "direct file" constitutes the third method by which about ten states remove some young offenders from the juvenile justice system. With this strategy, juvenile and criminal courts share concurrent jurisdiction over certain ages and offenses, typically older youths and serious crimes. For example, prosecutors may exercise their discretion to select juvenile or criminal processing for youths sixteen or older and charged with murder (McCarthy 1994; Snyder and Sickmund 1995). To the extent that a prosecutor's decision to charge a case in criminal court rather than juvenile court determines the jurisdiction, prosecutorial waiver constitutes a form of offense-based decision making like legislative offense exclusion (Thomas and Bilchik 1985).

Within the past decade, public frustration with crime, fear of the recent rise in youth violence, and the racial characteristics of violent young offenders have fueled the desire to "get tough" and provided political impetus to prosecute larger numbers of youths as adults. Some of these initiatives simplify transfer of young offenders to criminal courts by excluding categories of offenses from juvenile court jurisdiction or by allowing prosecutors to "direct file" and charge youths as adults. Both offense exclusion and direct-file approaches deemphasize rehabilitation and individualized consideration of the offender, and instead stress the youth's age and offenses, personal and justice system accountability, and punishment. They base a youth's adult criminal status on various combinations of age, the seriousness of the present offense and prior record, and prosecutor's charging decisions.

This chapter critically analyzes the legal history, jurisprudential theory, sentencing policy, and implementation of legislative offense exclusion and prosecutorial waiver laws over the past quarter-century. Historically, a few states always have excluded certain very serious crimes from juvenile court jurisdiction, for example, capital offenses (Feld 1987). The offense exclusion strategy gained political popularity in the early 1970s following the United States Supreme Court's decision in *Kent v. United States,* 383 U.S. 541 (1966). *Kent* required juvenile courts to provide procedural due process in judicial waiver hearings, appended substantive criteria to guide judges' waiver decisions, and thereby encumbered the informality, flexibility, and ease of judges' transfer decisions. Offense exclusion and prosecutor direct-file laws evolved and expanded in direct reaction to the procedural formality mandated by *Kent* as lawmakers sought simple and expedient alternatives to discretionary judicial waiver hearings. The "just deserts" sentencing movement of the 1970s, which advocated determinate and presumptive offense-based sentences as a conceptual alternative to judicial discretion and legal indeterminacy, provided a jurisprudential rationale for legislative offense exclusion. Research on the development of delinquent and criminal careers in the 1970s, which initially promised empirically grounded selective incapacitation sentencing strategies, provided another conceptual foundation for offense-based waiver legislation that emphasized youths' prior records. Although just deserts provided a theoretical justification and "criminal careers" research provided an empirical foundation, offense exclusion also provided a politically attractive strategy for get-tough officials who proposed to "crack down" on "baby boom" increases in youth crime that peaked in the late 1970s. A decade later, in reaction to escalating youth homicide rates in the late 1980s and early 1990s (Blumstein 1995), get-tough legislators greatly augmented the lists of excluded offenses, lowered the ages at which states could prosecute youths as adults, and expanded prosecutors' direct-file discretion (Snyder and Sickmund 1995; Torbet et al. 1996). The jurisprudential shift in sentencing emphases from considerations of the offender to characteristics of the offense concomitantly transferred discretionary authority from judges to prosecutors. By the early 1990s, as a result of political crackdowns on youth crime, the scope of excluded-offense legislation increased substantially, became overly inclusive and excessively rigid, and exhibited many of the negative features associated with mandatory sentencing laws. Prosecutors also direct file many youths in an idiosyncratic, geographically variable, and overly inclusive fashion. Consequently, many states recognized the need for greater flexibility to accommodate the increased numbers of younger offenders in the criminal justice system. About half the states allow criminal court judges either to "transfer back" or to "reverse waive" some youths whose excluded offenses place them originally in the criminal process or to sentence them as "youthful offenders" instead of sending them to prison like adult offenders. Ironically, although the procedural requirements and substantive criteria announced in *Kent* provided the initial impetus for legislators to exclude offenses from juvenile court jurisdiction, many states now use those same *Kent* procedures and criteria to guide criminal court judges' transfer-back and youthful offender sentencing decisions. Thus, somewhere in the justice process, judges still make some type of "amenability" decision as a prerequisite to sentencing young offenders. As a result, one fairly may ask what the last three decades of legislative offense exclusion and prosecutorial waiver laws have accomplished.

1. Judicial Waiver and Individualized Sentencing: The Impetus for Alternatives

From the juvenile court's inception, judges could deny some young offenders its protective jurisdiction and transfer them to adult courts (Rothman 1980). Judicial waiver reflects juvenile courts' traditional individualized, offender-oriented approach to decide whether a youth should be treated as a juvenile or punished as an adult (Zimring 1981, 1991). In *Kent,* the United States Supreme Court formalized the waiver process and required juvenile courts to provide some procedural protections (Feld 1978). *Kent* concluded that the loss of juvenile court protections through a waiver decision was a "critically important" action that required a hearing, assistance of counsel, access to social investigations and other records, and written findings and conclusions capable of review by a higher court. "[T]here is no place in our system of law for reaching a result of such tremendous consequences without ceremony—without hearing, without effective assistance of counsel, without a statement of reasons" (*Kent,* 383 U.S. at 554). Although the Court decided *Kent* in the context of a federal statute adopted by Congress for the District of Columbia, its language suggested an underlying constitutional basis for requiring procedural due process in any judicial waiver decision. *Kent*'s procedural requirements anticipated many of the same safeguards that the Court later required in delinquency adjudications in *In re Gault,* 387 U.S. 1, 87 S. Ct 1428, 18 L. Ed. 2d 527 (1967). Subsequently, in *Breed v. Jones,* 421 U.S. 519 (1975), the Court applied the double-jeopardy clause of the fifth amendment to delinquency convictions and required states to decide whether to try and sentence a youth as a juvenile or as an adult before proceeding to trial on the merits of the charge.

   Kent and *Breed* provided the formal procedural framework within which judges make waiver sentencing decisions. But the substantive bases of waiver decisions pose the principal difficulty. Until recent amendments, most states' waiver statutes allowed judges to transfer jurisdiction based on their discretionary assessment of subjective clinical factors such as a youth's "amenability to treatment." The Court in *Kent,* 383 U.S. at 566–67, for example, appended to its opinion a list of substantive criteria that juvenile court judges should consider.

> An offense falling within the statutory limitations . . . will be waived if it has prosecutive merit and if it is heinous or of an aggravated character, or—even though less serious—if it represents a pattern of repeated offenses which indicate that the juvenile may be beyond rehabilitation under Juvenile Court procedures, or if the public needs the protection afforded by such action.
>
> The determinative factors which will be considered by the Judge in deciding whether the Juvenile Court's jurisdiction over such offenses will be waived are the following:
>
> 1. The seriousness of the alleged offense to the community and whether the protection of the community requires waiver.
>
> 2. Whether the alleged offense was committed in an aggressive, violent, premeditated or willful manner.
>
> 3. Whether the alleged offense was against persons or against property, greater weight being given to offenses against persons especially if personal injury resulted.
>
> 4. The prosecutive merit of the complaint, i.e., whether there is evidence upon which a Grand Jury may be expected to return an indictment . . .
>
> 5. The desirability of trial and disposition of the entire offense in one court when the juvenile's associates in the alleged offense are adults . . .
>
> 6. The sophistication and maturity of the juvenile as determined by consideration of his home, environmental situation, emotional attitude and pattern of living.
>
> 7. The record and previous history of the juvenile, including previous contacts with the Youth Aid Division, other law enforcement agencies, juvenile courts and other jurisdictions, prior periods of probation to this Court, or prior commitments to juvenile institutions.
>
> 8. The prospects for adequate protection of the public and the likelihood of reasonable rehabilitation of the juvenile (if he is found to have committed the alleged offense) by the use of procedures, services and facilities currently available to the Juvenile Court.

States' judicial decisions and waiver statutes specify amenability criteria with varying degrees of precision, and frequently incorporate the general and contradictory list of *Kent* factors. Although some states limit judicial waiver to felony offenses and establish a minimum age for adult prosecutions, typically sixteen, fifteen, or fourteen, others provide neither offense nor minimum age restrictions and remit the adulthood determination to each juvenile court judge's discretion (Feld 1987; Snyder and Sickmund 1995).

In practice, judges appear to assess a youth's amenability to treatment and dangerousness by focusing on three sets of variables. The first consists of a youth's age and the length of time remaining within juvenile court jurisdiction. Juvenile court judges waive older youths more readily than younger offenders (Fagan and Deschenes 1990; Podkopacz and Feld 1995, 1996; U.S. General Accounting Office 1995). A youth's age in relation to the maximum dispositional jurisdiction limits a juvenile court's sanctioning powers, and provides the impetus to waive older juveniles if the seriousness of their offense deserves a longer sentence than those available in juvenile court. A second constellation of amenability factors includes a youth's treatment prognosis as reflected in clinical evaluations and prior correctional interventions. Once a youth exhausts available juvenile correctional resources, transfer becomes increasingly likely (Podkopacz and Feld 1995, 1996). Finally, judges assess a youth's dangerousness based on the seriousness of the present offense, whether the youth used a weapon, and the length of the prior record (Fagan and Deschenes 1990; Podkopacz and Feld 1995, 1996; Howell 1996). Balancing these dangerousness factors entails a trade-off between offense seriousness and offender persistence.

Waiver laws that require a judge to decide a youth's amenability to treatment or dangerousness implicate some of the most fundamental issues of juvenile jurisprudence (Feld 1978). Legislation mandating an amenability or dangerousness inquiry assumes that effective treatment programs exist for at least some serious or chronic young offenders, presumes that classification systems exist with which to differentiate among youths' treatment potential or dangerousness, and supposes that clinicians or judges possess valid and reliable diagnostic tools with which to determine the appropriate disposition for a particular youth. Evaluation research challenges these legislative presuppositions, questions whether intervention systematically reduces recidivism among chronic or violent young offenders, and disputes whether judges or clinicians accurately can identify and classify those who will or will not respond to treatment (Feld 1978, 1983, 1987; Sechrest 1987; Lab and Whitehead 1988, 1990). Similarly, statutes authorize judges to waive jurisdiction based on a prediction of a youth's future dangerousness, even though clinicians and jurists lack the technical capacity validly and reliably to predict low-base-rate serious criminal behavior (Monahan 1981; Morris and Miller 1985; Fagan and Guggenheim 1996).

Judicial waiver criteria framed in terms of amenability to treatment or dangerousness give judges broad, standardless discretion. Lists of substantive factors such as those appended in *Kent* do not provide adequate guidance. Rather, catalogues of contradictory factors reinforce judges' discretion and allow them selectively to emphasize one variable or another to justify any decision. Zimring (1981) describes typical judicial waiver laws as the juvenile equivalents of the standardless capital punishment statutes condemned by the Supreme Court in *Furman v. Georgia*, 408 U.S. 238 (1972).

The subjective nature of waiver decisions, the absence of effective guidelines to determine outcomes, and the lack of objective indicators or scientific tools with which to classify youths allow judges to make unequal and disparate rulings without any effective procedural or appellate checks. Empirical evaluations provide compelling evidence that judges apply waiver statutes in an arbitrary, capricious, and even discriminatory manner (Hamparian et al. 1982; Fagan and Deschenes 1990; Feld 1990). Different states' rates of judicial waiver for similar types of offenders vary considerably (Hamparian et al. 1982; U.S. General Accounting Office 1995). Even within a single jurisdiction, judges do not administer, interpret, or apply waiver statutes consistently from county to county or from court to court. Research in several states reports a contextual pattern of "justice by geography" in which where youths lived, rather than what they did, determined their juvenile or adult status (Hamparian et al. 1982; Heuser 1985). In some states, for example, rural judges waive jurisdiction more readily than do urban judges over youths facing similar charges (Feld 1990; Lemmon, Sontheimer, and Saylor 1991; Poulos and Orchowsky 1994). Even within a single urban county, various judges in the same court decide cases of similarly situated offenders differently (Podkopacz and Feld 1995, 1996). These differences influence both the characteristics of youths waived and the subsequent criminal sentences they receive. A youth's race also may affect waiver decisions. Minority juveniles experience greater risk of transfer than do similarly situated white offenders (Eigen 1981a, 1981b; Hamparian et al. 1982; Fagan, Forst, and Vivona 1987; U.S. General Accounting Office 1995). Thus, differences in judicial philosophies, the location of a waiver hearing, a youth's race, or organizational politics may explain as much about judges' transfer decisions as do a youth's offense or personal characteristics. Judges make individualized assessments of a youth's amenability to treatment and dangerousness even though they cannot make those decisions with any degree of accuracy, consistency, or uniformity. Because the

answers to questions of amenability or dangerousness are so indeterminate, appellate courts grant juvenile court judges' discretionary decisions
enormous deference, which, in turn, creates further potential for abuse,
inequality, and discrimination. In short, judicial waiver exhibits many of
the defects commonly associated with discretionary, indeterminate sentencing regimes.

2. Legislative Offense Exclusion and Prosecutors' Choices: "Adulthood" without a Hearing

Legislative offense exclusion simply removes from juvenile court jurisdiction youths charged with certain offenses or in conjunction with a
prior record, and provides the primary conceptual alternative to judicial
waiver (Feld 1987). Concurrent jurisdiction direct-file laws grant to prosecutors the power to choose whether to charge a youth in juvenile or
criminal court without justifying that decision in a judicial hearing or with
a formal record (Bishop and Frazier 1991; McCarthy 1994). Youths have
no constitutional right to a juvenile court. State legislatures create juvenile
courts by statute and define their jurisdiction, powers, and purposes in
many different ways. What they create, they also may modify or take away.
For example, states currently set juvenile courts' maximum age jurisdiction at seventeen, sixteen, or fifteen years old as a matter of state policy
and without any constitutional infirmity (Snyder and Sickmund 1995). If
a legislature defines juvenile court jurisdiction to include only those persons below a jurisdictional age and whom prosecutors charge with a nonexcluded offense, then, by statutory definition, all other chronological
juveniles are "adult" criminal defendants.

Analysts long have criticized statutes that mandate adult prosecution
on the basis of the offense charged rather than the characteristics of the
offender or that give prosecutors authority to choose the jurisdictional
forum because they conflict with the rehabilitative philosophy of the juvenile court (Mylniec 1976; Zimring 1981, 1991; Fagan 1990; Guttman
1995; Sabo 1996; Klein 1998). Similarly, excluded youths tried in criminal
courts have challenged their "automatic adulthood" as a denial of due
process because they do not receive the procedural safeguards required
by *Kent*, and as a violation of equal protection because exclusion on the
basis of the alleged offense constitutes an arbitrary legislative classification.[1] These youths direct their due-process claims at the lack of judicial
review of prosecutors' discretionary charging decisions that result in their
removal to criminal court. Their equal protection claims question the rationality of the legislative decision to classify youths charged with certain
offenses as adults rather than as juveniles.

Constitutional Validity of Legislative Offense Exclusion

Recall that *Kent* involved the Supreme Court's interpretation of a federal statute for the District of Columbia. Following the *Kent* decision, the United States Congress held hearings, amended the D.C. Juvenile Code waiver provision, and excluded from juvenile court jurisdiction youths sixteen years of age or older and charged with certain violent offenses, for example, murder and armed robbery. *D.C. Code* § 16-2031(3)(A) (Supp. 1970). In *Pendergrast v. United States,* 332 A.2d 919, 923 (D.C. Cir. 1975), the District of Columbia Court of Appeals described the nature of the changes to the D.C. Juvenile Court Act.

> Prior to 1970, the Juvenile Court automatically acquired jurisdiction over anyone under 18 charged with an offense, since the term "child" then was defined simply as "a person under 18 years of age." . . .
>
> In 1970, Congress enacted the District of Columbia Court Reorganization Act, which in part amended [the Juvenile Court Act]. The amendment changed the definition of a "child" and, derivatively, altered the scope of Family Division jurisdiction. [The act] now states:
>
>> The term "child" means an individual who is under 18 years of age, except that the term "child" does not include an individual who is *sixteen years of age or older* and (A) *charged* by the United States attorney *with (i) murder, forcible rape, burglary in the first degree, robbery while armed, or assault with intent to commit any such offense* . . . (emphasis supplied)

In *United States v. Bland,* 472 F.2d 1329 (D.C. Cir. 1972), *cert. denied,* 412 U.S. 909 (1973), the leading case on the validity of legislative offense exclusion statutes, the prosecutor charged the sixteen-year-old Bland with armed robbery, an "excluded offense" that mandated his prosecution as an adult in criminal court. Bland asserted that because of the critical differences between juvenile and criminal prosecution, he should receive *Kent* procedural safeguards as a prerequisite to waiver. Bland claimed he deserved a hearing because the ultimate result is the same whether a judge waives jurisdiction or a legislature excludes and a prosecutor charges a youth in criminal court.

Judge J. Skelly Wright's *Bland* dissent strongly endorsed the argument for procedural parity. Judge Wright contended that "the test for when the Constitution demands a hearing depends not on which government official makes the decision, but rather on the importance of that decision to the individual affected. The extent to which procedural due process must be afforded . . . is influenced by the extent to which [an individual] may be 'condemned to suffer grievous loss.'" *Bland,* 472 F.2d at 1345. Judge Wright decried the statute that excluded Bland from the juvenile court as a transparent effort to evade the procedural requirements of *Kent.* "This blatant attempt to evade the force of the *Kent* decision should not be permitted to succeed" (472 F.2d at 1341). Judge Wright lamented that unlike the requirements of *Kent,* offense exclusion allowed the prosecutor to waive a juvenile "without the encumbrance of a hearing, the requirement that he state reasons, the inconvenience of bearing the burden of proof, or the necessity of appointing counsel for the accused." *Bland,* 472 F.2d at 1341. Accordingly, he urged the court to subject prosecutors' charging-waiver decisions to the same fitness hearing that it required of judges.

Judge Wright's argument that the comparable consequences flowing from legislative or prosecutorial waivers necessitate comparable procedural safeguards did not persuade the majority of the *Bland* court to impose procedural requirements or to review prosecutors' charging decisions. The *Bland* majority relied on the well-established doctrine that judges do not review exercises of prosecutorial discretion except under manifestly discriminatory circumstances. In a similar challenge to a "pure" prosecutorial waiver statute, the court in *Cox v. United States,* 473 F.2d 334 (4th Cir.), *cert. denied,* 414 U.S. 909 (1973), specifically rejected procedural safeguards as a precondition to the exercise of prosecutorial discretion:

> Judicial proceedings must be clothed in the raiment of due process, while the processes of prosecutorial decision-making wear very different garb. It is one thing to hold, as we have, that when a state makes waiver of a juvenile court's jurisdiction a judicial function, the judge must cast about the defendant all of the trappings of due process, but it does not necessarily follow that a state or the United States may not constitutionally treat the basic question as a prosecutorial function, making a highly placed, supervisory prosecutor responsible for deciding whether to proceed against a juvenile as an adult. If it does, as the United States has, the character of the proceeding, rather than its consequences to the accused, are largely determinative of his rights. (473 F.2d at 336)

Courts typically decline to review prosecutorial decisions because the constitutional doctrine of separation of powers denies the judicial branch the power to compel or control the executive branch in essentially discretionary matters. In the absence of invidious discrimination on the basis of race, religion, or the like, a prosecutor's decisions about whether and whom to charge and with what remain beyond judicial review. See, e.g.,

Oyler v. Boles, 368 U.S. 448, 466 (1962); *Wayte v. United States,* 470 U.S. 598 (1985); *United States v. Armstrong,* 517 U.S. 456 (1996). Judicial reluctance to encumber prosecutors' discretion stems from a fear of intruding on sensitive legal and policy judgments. "Such factors as the strength of the case, the prosecution's general deterrence value, the Government's enforcement priorities, and the case's relationship to the Government's overall enforcement plan are not readily susceptible to the kind of analysis the courts are competent to undertake." *Wayte,* 470 U.S. at 607. Apart from separation-of-powers considerations, if judicial review entails the power to compel prosecutors to present or dismiss a case, then a judge could prevent prosecutors from maximizing enforcement effectiveness through selective prosecution and force them to misallocate resources. Courts also decline to review prosecutors' decisions because of the need to maintain secrecy during an investigation. A fitness hearing prior to the filing of charges could divulge confidential sources. Additionally, the factors that influence prosecutors' decisions—legal evaluations of evidence and guilt, resource allocation, and other law enforcement policies and priorities—seldom provide a written record in a form that permits meaningful pretrial judicial review.

The Supreme Court consistently reaffirms prosecutors' freedom from judicial review. In *Bordenkircher v. Hayes,* 434 U.S. 557 (1978), the Court noted that

> so long as the prosecutor has probable cause to believe that the accused committed an offense defined by statute, the decision whether or not to prosecute, and what charge to file or bring before a grand jury, generally rests entirely in his discretion. Within the limits set by the legislature's constitutionally valid definition of chargeable offenses, "the conscious exercise of some selectivity in enforcement is not in itself a federal constitutional violation" so long as "the selection was [not] deliberately based upon an unjustifiable standard such as race, religion, or other arbitrary classification." (434 U.S. at 564)

More recently, in *United States v. Armstrong,* 517 U.S. 456 (1996), the Court reiterated that prosecutors possess "broad discretion" to enforce criminal laws, a strong "presumption of regularity supports their prosecutorial decisions," and the defendant bears the burden to rebut that strong presumption of administrative regularity. *Armstrong,* 517 U.S. at 464. Courts will review claims of selective or discriminatory enforcement decisions by prosecutors only when the defendant can present clear evidence of an equal-protection violation, for example, prosecution of some defendants and nonprosecution of other similarly situated offenders on the basis of race. Even then, in order to prevail, the defendant must demonstrate both that the "prosecutorial policy had a discriminatory effect and that it was *motivated by a discriminatory purpose.*" *Armstrong,* 517 U.S. at 465 (emphasis added). Thus, defendants must establish that charging decisions have an invidious impact *and* an improper motive. Under the rationale of *Armstrong,* a youth prosecuted in criminal court for an excluded offense would have to demonstrate that the prosecutor intentionally charged him *because* of his race and declined to prosecute as adults other youths of different races who committed the same offense, an almost insuperable burden in an individual case.

Although Judge Wright's *Bland* dissent argued that the comparable consequences of judicial waiver and legislative offense exclusion required *Kent* procedures in both contexts, he misconceived the basic legal issue. The question whether or not judges should review prosecutors' charging decisions does not turn on the seriousness of the consequences to the defendant of being tried as an adult rather than as a juvenile. Many prosecutorial decisions have great consequences for defendants—the decision not to charge, the decision to charge conduct as a misdemeanor rather than a felony, the decision to invoke any one of several applicable statutes. As the *Bland* majority noted, due process never has required "an adversary hearing before the prosecutor can exercise his age-old function of deciding what charge to bring against whom" (472 F.2d at 1337).

The requirement of a hearing depends upon the legal question asked, and in the context of waiver decisions, whether characteristics of the offender or the nature of the offense determine the outcome. Judge Wright's *Bland* dissent objected that a prosecutor's charging decision foreclosed any subsequent consideration of a youth's amenability to juvenile treatment. " '[W]here governmental action seriously injures an individual, and the reasonableness of the action depends on *fact findings,* the evidence used to prove the Government's case must be disclosed to the individual so that he has an opportunity to show that it is untrue (*Bland,* 472 F.2d at 1346)' (emphasis added)." Judge Wright insisted that the same amenability issues should arise when a prosecutor charges a youth as an adult or when a judge decides whether to waive jurisdiction. According to Judge Wright, "a 'guilty' child may, under certain circumstances, have a right to be charged as a juvenile" (*Bland,* 472 F.2d at 1348). Whether that right exists in any given case, however, can be decided only after a factual determination of factors such as "the maturity of the child and his susceptibility to rehabilitation" (*id.*).

Judge Wright's desire to extend *Kent*'s procedural requirements to prosecutors' charging decisions stemmed from his misconstruing what prosecutors decide under an offense exclusion statute. The only factual issues involved in a charging decision relate to the nature of the offense, probable cause, and provable legal guilt. A criminal trial provides the most rigorous review of a prosecutor's initial factual determinations, proof of legally relevant facts beyond a reasonable doubt. The issue of amenability to treatment that Judge Wright sought to resolve in an adversary proceeding prior to trial simply is not a factor in the factual accuracy of a prosecutor's charging decision. No factual dispute about a youth's amenability remains to be resolved because the statutory definition that excludes certain offenses from juvenile court jurisdiction has obviated such an inquiry. Offense exclusion legislation accords conclusive primacy to the offense charged rather than to aspects of the offender.

No per se right exists to be treated as a delinquent rather than as a criminal. Such rights exist solely because legislatures create them, and what they create, they can take away. "[T]he legislature could ... withhold the protection of the doctrine of *parens patriae* from all juveniles exceeding fifteen years of age. What the legislature may do absolutely, it may do conditionally." *State v. Green,* 218 Kan. 438, 442, 544 P.2d 356, 361 (1975). The *Bland* dissent evinced a fundamental unwillingness to recognize that juvenile courts are purely statutory entities, that legislatures can modify or abolish their jurisdiction, and they may subordinate individualized, offender-oriented treatment values to other, offense-based considerations such as public safety or simply retribution. If the legislature defines juvenile court jurisdiction to include only those persons below a jurisdictional age and whom prosecutors charge with a nonexcluded offense, then all other persons are *by definition* adults. While offense exclusion laws repudiate traditional individualized examinations of the offender, the juvenile court's "rehabilitative ideal" is written neither in stone nor in the Constitution.

> While there would probably be almost universal agreement that it is desirable for a State to maintain a juvenile court and to establish special facilities for the treatment of a separate category of "juvenile delinquents," we are aware of nothing in the constitution of the United States or of this State that requires a State to do so. (*People v. Jiles,* 43 Ill. 2d 145, 148, 251 N.E.2d 529, 531 [Il. 1969])

In addition to challenges based on the absence of procedural safeguards associated with prosecutors' charging decisions, youths have argued that offense exclusion laws violate equal protection because they create an arbitrary and irrational statutory distinction—criminal or delinquent status—based on serious or minor offenses. Courts uniformly reject such claims, noting that classification on the basis of offenses involves neither an inherently suspect class nor an invidious discrimination, and the loss of juvenile court treatment does not infringe upon a fundamental right or "preferred liberty" that require strict judicial scrutiny. The *Bland* court noted that "[s]everal states have similarly excluded certain crimes in defining the jurisdiction of their respective systems of juvenile justice." 472 F.2d at 1334. Courts give statutes a strong presumption of constitutional validity to deal with a problem uniquely within the legislature's purview and invalidate them only if no rational basis exists to justify the classification:

> It is a salutary principle of judicial decision, long emphasized and followed by this Court, that the burden of establishing the unconstitutionality of a statute rests on him who assails it, and that courts may not declare a legislative discrimination invalid unless, *viewed in the light of facts made known or generally assumed,* it is of such a character as to preclude the assumption that the classification rests upon some rational basis within the knowledge and experience of the legislators. (*Bland,* 472 F.2d at 1334 [emphasis supplied])

Any court faced with a challenge to a legislative waiver statute confronts the question whether *"facts known or generally assumed"* provide a "rational basis" for the legislature to treat serious offenders differently from minor offenders. Because a youth challenging the statute bears the heavy burden of showing that a classification based on the seriousness of the offense is arbitrary and irrational, these equal-protection challenges uniformly have failed. Courts sustain a statute that distinguishes between serious and minor offenses if it comports with a generally held societal belief that serious offenders ought to be treated differently because, as a class, they are not amenable to treatment, they are too dangerous, it would be too expensive to attempt to rehabilitate them, their presence within the juvenile justice system would be detrimental to the rehabilitation of other more amenable youths, or simply because they deserve more severe punishment for their offenses. Although "rehabilitative" juvenile courts assume that all offenders differ and no direct relationship exists between their offenses and their "real needs," legislators appear to presume and courts to accept without further elaboration that youths who commit serious crimes differ from minor offenders. In adopting the District of Columbia statute considered in *Bland,* for example, the congressional legislative history included findings that offenders between the ages of sixteen and eighteen who committed certain serious crimes were "beyond rehabilitation in the juvenile justice system," "too well formed or sophisticated for . . . mere juvenile therapy," and different from "first offenders charged with minor offenses . . . [because] in certain crime categories, juvenile treatment is unworkable." *Bland,* 472 F.2d at 1332–33. In short, a court would not find that a legislature acted irrationally if it predicted amenability or recidivism based on the seriousness of the offense rather than on the characteristics of the offender.

Concurrent Jurisdiction and Direct-File Prosecutorial Waiver

"Pure" prosecutorial waiver statutes create concurrent jurisdiction in juvenile and criminal courts for certain offenses and give prosecutors discretion to direct file or charge youths of certain ages with the same offense in either forum. Direct-file legislation gives prosecutors greater discretionary authority to choose the forum than does offense exclusion, where charges only for certain offenses can result in criminal prosecution. For example, in Arkansas, juvenile and criminal courts share concurrent jurisdiction over youths sixteen years or older who commit *any felony,* and over youths fourteen years of age or older who commit one of eighteen enumerated violent crimes or who have three prior felony convictions. A prosecutor can choose to charge a youth with the same offense in either justice system. *Ark. Code Ann.* § 9-27-318(b) (Michie 1997). Similarly, in Florida, the state attorney may direct file a criminal information against any youth sixteen or seventeen years of age who committed *any felony* as well as against any youth fourteen or fifteen years of age who committed one of fifteen enumerated offenses, including murder, robbery, and sexual battery, "when in the state attorney's *judgment and discretion the public interest* requires that adult sanctions be considered or imposed." *Fla. Stat. Ann.* § 985.227(1)(a)–(b) (West 1997). Essentially, the prosecutor makes two types of decisions: whether probable cause exists to believe that the youth committed a particular offense and, if that offense is one for which concurrent jurisdiction exists, whether to charge the youth in juvenile or criminal court. While prosecutors possess expertise to evaluate the sufficiency of evidence and to select charges, they do not bring any professional insight to the forum selection decision whether to try a youth as a juvenile or as an adult (Sabo 1996).

About ten states have adopted some version of prosecutorial waiver statutes and allow prosecutors to charge youths of certain ages and offenses in either justice system (McCarthy 1994; Snyder and Sickmund 1995; U.S. General Accounting Office 1995).[2] Unlike legislative offense exclusion, in which the actual offense alleged determines juvenile or criminal jurisdiction, direct-file laws allow the prosecutor to select the forum without engaging in any charging subterfuges. In most pure or direct-file states, the statute provide no guidelines, standards, or criteria to control the prosecutors' choice of forum. Two states that purport to guide prosecutors' jurisdictional selection discretion only instruct them to consider *Kent*-like statutory criteria. *See Neb. Rev. Stat.* 43-276 (1997); *Wyo. Stat. Ann.* § 14-6-273(b)(i)–(vii) (1997). Unlike a judge, who has the benefit of judicial waiver hearings, however, where clinicians and court services personnel can provide information about a youth's maturity, sophistication, or amenability to treatment based on clinical evaluations, social service reports, interviews, and the like, prosecutors typically lack access to such personal information.

Although most states' direct-file statutes do not provide any formal criteria, prosecutors could adopt informal administrative guidelines. However, interviews with prosecutors revealed that relatively few did so, and the informal guidelines of those who adopted them provided minimal practical control over jurisdictional selection decisions (Bishop and Frazier 1991). For example, variations in prosecutors' juvenile justice philosophy—just deserts, public safety, rehabilitation—had very little impact on their charging or waiver practices; most youths whom they transferred were not especially violent or dangerous. "[Y]ouths transferred via prosecutorial waiver are seldom the serious and chronic offenders for whom prosecution and punishment in criminal court are arguably justified" (Bishop and Frazier 1991, 297)." The failure to provide any review procedures or to specify the waiver criteria results almost inevitably in arbitrary, idiosyncratic, and inconsistent decisions.

Although youths have challenged the validity of direct-file laws that delegate to prosecutors untrammeled discretion to choose a youth's juvenile or criminal status, appellate courts invoke the rationale of *Bland* and reject their claims. In upholding Florida's direct-file law, for example, the Florida Supreme Court noted that "prosecutorial discretion is itself an incident of the constitutional separation of powers, and that as a result the courts are not to interfere with the free exercise of the discretionary powers of the prosecutor in his control over criminal prosecutions." *State v. Cain,* 381 So.2d 1361 (Fla. Sup. Ct. 1975). Similarly, in *Jahnke v. State,* 692 P.2d 911 (Wyo. Sup. Ct. 1984), the Wyoming Supreme Court asserted that

> The discretion which is vested in the prosecutor by our statute to proceed against a juvenile in either the juvenile court or as an adult in the district court does not violate any constitutional requirements. There is no constitutional right to be tried as a juvenile. Any decision to initiate criminal proceedings is vested in the prosecuting attorney, and the decision is discretionary. Since

one does not have an inherent right to be prosecuted as a juvenile but that is a privilege granted by the legislature, the legislature can restrict or qualify the privilege as it sees fit, so long as there is not involved any arbitrary or discriminatory classification . . . [I]in the absence of such suspect factors as race, religion or other arbitrary classification, the exercise of discretion by the prosecutor in deciding whether to charge as a juvenile or adult involves no violation of due process or equal protection of the law.

Based on *Bland*'s separation of powers rationale, courts uphold prosecutorial waiver statutes with virtual unanimity.[3]

The singular deviation from appellate approval of prosecutorial waiver occurred in *State v. Mohi,* 901 P.2d 991 (Utah 1995), where the Utah Supreme Court struck down the state's direct-file provisions because they denied waived juveniles the uniform operation of state laws. The prosecutor charged Mohi as an adult in criminal court with intentional or reckless homicide with a firearm. The defendants in *Mohi* and in two companion cases argued that the direct-file law violated the Utah constitution, which provides that "[a]ll laws of a general nature shall have uniform operation." Mohi argued that the direct-file provision created a statutory scheme that treated one class of persons charged with a particular crime differently than another class of persons charged with the same crime.

The Utah direct-file statute, like those in every other "concurrent" jurisdiction, allowed prosecutors to charge some youths with serious offenses in juvenile court while prosecuting other youths charged with identical offenses in criminal court. Mohi argued that the legislation created an unreasonable and arbitrary classification because it did not provide any reasons to permit similarly situated youths to receive such disparate consequences. The *Mohi* court construed the "uniform" application of laws provision to require treating similarly situated offenders similarly, unless the differences in treatment reasonably tended to further the statutory objectives. Because the statute contained no criteria or rationale, however, the court could discern no reasons to justify why prosecutors charged some youths as adults in criminal court while other youths of the same age and charged with the same offenses remained in juvenile court. "Therefore, the statute permits two identically situated juveniles, even co-conspirators or co-participants in the same crime, to face radically different penalties and consequences without any statutory guidelines for distinguishing between them. This amounts to unequal treatment." *Mohi,* 901 P.2d at 999.

The *Mohi* court criticized the law because it provided no guidelines or rationale to regulate prosecutors' exercise of discretion when they classified youths as delinquents or criminals.

> [T]he statute does not require the prosecutor to have any reason, legitimate or otherwise, to support his or her decision of who stays in juvenile jurisdiction and who does not . . . The total absence of such standards makes the Utah statute unique among those of all other states employing any type of adult prosecution of juvenile offenders . . . While not dispositive, the fact that no other state has, at present, undertaken a process as arbitrary and unbridled as Utah's contributes significantly to our conclusion that the statute goes too far. There is no rational connection between the legislature's objective of balancing the needs of children with public protection and its decision to allow prosecutors total discretion in deciding which members of a potential class of juvenile offenders to single out for adult treatment. Such unguided discretion opens the door to abuse without any criteria for review or for insuring evenhanded decision making. No checks exist in this scheme to prevent such acts as a prosecutor's singling out members of certain unpopular groups for harsher treatment in the adult system while protecting equally culpable juveniles to whom a particular prosecutor may feel some cultural loyalty or for whom there may be broader public sympathy. (*Mohi,* 901 P.2d at 1002)

Although the court conceded the legislature's broad authority to create classes of youths for adult prosecution—for example, serious offenders, repeat offenders, or those who used guns—the court insisted that the lawmakers specify relevant criteria and "not create a scheme which permits the random and unsupervised separation of all such violent juveniles into a relatively privileged group on the one hand and a relatively burdened group on the other." *Mohi,* 901 P.2d at 1003.

3. Offense Exclusion Jurisprudence and Sentencing Policy

While appellate courts consistently uphold offense exclusion and concurrent jurisdiction statutes against youths' due-process and equal-protection challenges, as the *Mohi* court noted, lawmakers typically fail to articulate their sentencing policy rationale or to prescribe relevant criteria. Significantly, the increased adoption of offense exclusion laws coincided with several other jurisprudential and criminological developments that occurred during the 1970s. The renaissance of retribution and "just deserts" sentencing and criminological research on the development of criminal careers provided jurisprudential rationale and intellectual legitimacy for offense exclusion laws. Baby boom increases in youth crime during the 1970s provided a political impetus to crack down on young offenders.

Within the past two decades, offense-based determinate and proportional sentencing statutes increasingly have superseded indeterminate offender-oriented sentencing laws for adult offenders (Cullen and Gilbert 1982; Tonry 1996). The just deserts rationale for determinate sentencing laws affected juvenile court waiver and sentencing laws and practices as well (Feld 1987, 1988, 1998; Sheffer 1995). Simultaneously, empirical research on delinquent and criminal careers offered the prospect that decision makers could predict recidivism or selectively incapacitate "chronic" offenders on the basis of their persistence or seriousness of offending rather than on individualized assessments of personal characteristics (Wolfgang, Figlio, and Sellin 1972). Finally, the increases in youth crime in the late 1970s provided politicians with a strong incentive to demagogue on crime as a symbolic issue to garner public support (Beckett 1997).

Just Deserts Sentencing

During the 1970s, the Progressives' optimistic assumptions about human malleability and the efficacy of rehabilitation foundered on empirical evaluation studies that questioned both the effectiveness of rehabilitative programs and the scientific expertise of those who administered the enterprise (Allen 1981). In the 1970s, determinate sentences based on present offense and prior record increasingly supplanted indeterminate sentences for adults as just deserts and retribution displaced rehabilitation as the underlying rationale for criminal sentencing. By the mid-1980s, about half the states had enacted determinate sentencing laws, ten eliminated parole boards, and many more used guidelines to structure sentence length and in/out confinement decisions, levels of supervision for probationers, and parole release decisions (Tonry 1996).

Proponents of just deserts reject rehabilitation as a justification for sentencing because criminal justice practitioners lack the technical ability either to implement the treatment model successfully and consistently or to predict recidivism accurately and reliably (American Friends Service Committee 1971; von Hirsch 1976, 1986). Indeterminate sentences vest too much discretionary power in presumed clinical experts who cannot justify their differential treatment of similarly situated offenders based on either validated classification schemes with objective indicators or consistently successful outcomes. Therapeutically individualized sentences result in inequalities and racial disparities among those who commit the same offenses. Individualized and disparate sentences for similarly situated offenders violate fundamental norms of distributive justice and penal proportionality. Just deserts sentencing, with its strong retributive foundation, punishes offenders according to their past behavior rather than on the basis of who they are or whom clinicians predict they may become. Determinate and presumptive sentencing laws define and sanction similarly situated offenders based on relatively objective and legally relevant characteristics such as seriousness of offense, culpability, or prior criminal history.

Similar jurisprudential changes occurred in sentencing and waiving delinquents, as just deserts concerns spilled over into the juvenile justice system as well. In the context of waiver decisions, assessments of individual offenders' amenability to treatment or dangerousness historically predominated (Feld 1987, 1998). Judges and clinicians used indeterminate and discretionary processes to make predictions about offenders' future life course and criminal propensity. By contrast, legislative offense exclusion reflects a more retributive, offense-based just deserts framework. Waiver statutes embody and attempt to resolve the same tensions between individualized evaluations of the offender and more mechanical dispositions based on the offense that animate sentencing policy debates (Feld 1998). Proponents of just deserts contend that juvenile court judges lack valid or reliable bases upon which to make accurate determinations of amenability or dangerousness and that standardless discretion results in inconsistent and discriminatory decisions (Feld 1978, 1995). Legislative offense exclusion laws that define chronological juveniles as adults on the basis of a serious offense reflect a retributive, just deserts alternative to individualized, rehabilitative juvenile justice jurisprudence.

Delinquent and Criminal Careers

The publication of the seminal *Delinquency in a Birth Cohort* (Wolfgang, Figlio, and Sellin 1972) and subsequent research on the development of delinquent and criminal careers constituted a second criminological development that provided impetus and intellectual legitimacy for certain forms of excluded-offense legislation (Blumstein et al. 1986). While legislation based on a just deserts rationale could exclude an older youth who committed a particularly heinous offense simply because he *deserved* to be treated as an adult, a legislature seeking to selectively incapacitate high-base-rate career offenders would redefine juvenile court jurisdiction based on a prior record of chronic and persistent offending rather than simply the seriousness of the present offense.

Beginning in the 1970s, longitudinal research on delinquent and criminal careers reported that young offenders did not specialize in any particular types of crime, that serious and violent crime occurred within an essentially random pattern of persistent delinquent behavior, and that a small number of chronic delinquents committed many of the offenses and most of the serious and violent crimes perpetrated by juveniles. Serious offenders are persistent offenders who add violent crimes to their diverse repertoire of chronic law breaking. Although the seriousness of a youth's initial or current offense provides little basis on which to distinguish those who will or will not recidivate, an extensive prior record of offending provides the best indicator of future criminal behavior. Research on the development of delinquent and criminal careers indicates that many youths engage simultaneously in both trivial and serious law violations. Police arrest and process youths primarily as a function of the frequency, rather than the seriousness, of their delinquency (Wolfgang, Figlio, and Sellin 1972; Hamparian et al. 1978; Strasburg 1978). Career offenders do not specialize in particular types of crime; serious crime occurs within an essentially random pattern of delinquent behavior (Petersilia 1980). However, the small group of chronic offenders commit many of the offenses and most of the violent crimes perpetrated by juveniles.

For virtually all purposes, most of the significant differences in frequency and seriousness of delinquency occur between those juveniles with one or two delinquent contacts and those with five or more offenses. For example, while over one-third (34.9 percent) of all of the boys in the 1945 Philadelphia cohort recorded at least one delinquency, nearly half (46.4 percent) desisted after their initial experience and had no further contact with the police (Wolfgang, Figlio, and Sellin 1972, 159–60). Of those offenders who committed a second delinquency, over an additional one-third (34.9 percent) desisted from further offending. Youths who initially committed a violent crime desisted after one offense (43 percent) at about the same rate as did other types of offenders. The most significant differences occurred between juveniles who committed only one or two delinquencies and those whom police arrested five or more times. Chronic offenders' probabilities of subsequent criminal activity remained quite high and continued into adulthood. Although the likelihood remained low that any given delinquent event would be a serious or violent offense, the small group of chronic offenders accounted for a disproportionately large amount of the total volume of serious crime. The chronic offenders constituted 6 percent of their birth cohort and 18 percent of all delinquents, but committed more than half (52 percent) of the total delinquencies, two-thirds or more of all of the violent offenses, and all of the homicides. Moreover, their pattern of offending continued into adulthood; as they aged, chronic offenders accounted for an increasingly larger proportion of the total and violent crimes committed by their birth cohort (Wolfgang, Figlio, and Sellin 1972, 163).

A number of subsequent longitudinal cohort studies confirm the relationships between chronic, serious, and life-course persistent career offending (Petersilia 1980; Blumstein et al. 1986). A study of the delinquent careers of a second Philadelphia cohort born in 1958 again reported that about one-third of youths had only one delinquent contact, and youths with one or two offenses exhibited similar patterns of desistance as in the earlier cohort (Tracy, Wolfgang, and Figlio 1990, 15–17). However, a somewhat larger proportion of youths became chronic offenders (7 percent of all boys and 23 percent of all delinquents), and these youths accounted for an even larger proportion of all of the delinquencies committed by their cohort (61 percent), including more than two-thirds of all violent offenses. A study of violent juvenile offenders in Columbus, Ohio, reported that of those juveniles with at least one arrest for a violent crime, police rearrested about one-third (36 percent) by age twenty-five, compared with 62 percent of those with two to four juvenile arrests, and more than three-quarters (78 percent) of those with five or more juvenile arrests (Hamparian et al. 1978). Other research on criminal careers reports that while most youths desist after one or two contacts, chronic offenders exhibit a substantial probability (between .70 and .80) of continuing to commit crimes into adulthood. These studies suggest that sentencing policies can better identify serious offenders by their cumulative persistence rather than by the nature of their initial offense; the number of contacts a youth has with the justice system provides the most reliable indicator of future criminality.

Age of onset of delinquency provides another important indicator of career criminality and a strong predictor of recidivism (Farrington 1986, 1998; Greenwood 1986). Youths whose delinquent careers begin early and who become chronic offenders as juveniles are more likely to continue serious and violent offending into adulthood. Regardless of the nature of the original offense, youths first convicted of delinquency between ages ten and thirteen became chronic offenders at significantly higher rates than did those convicted later (Blumstein, Farrington, and Moitra 1985; Farrington 1998). An analytical review of criminal career research reports that the age at which youths recorded their initial police contact provided a powerful predictor of the length and seriousness of their criminal careers (Petersilia 1980).

The criminal career research initially offered the prospect that sentencing policies might significantly reduce or prevent crime through selective incapacitation of the most active career offenders (Blumstein et al. 1986). Unfortunately, selective incapacitation strategies founder on the inability prospectively to predict who the high-base-rate offenders are (Cohen 1983; Chaiken, Chaiken, and Rhodes 1994). Although longitudinal studies can identify career offenders retrospectively within the heterogeneous mass of young offenders based on their persistence, we lack the indicators or ability to predict in advance which youths will become career criminals. Moreover, given the likelihood of errors, overprediction, and "false positives," to preventively incarcerate people on the basis of what they might do in the future rather than for what they already have done poses extraordinary ethical and legal problems (Zimring and Hawkins 1995). Moreover, the best indicator of future criminality, an extensive prior record, provides an imperfect indicator of active criminality because only a small proportion of actual crimes result in arrest and conviction. Finally, young career offenders require time to accumulate an extensive prior record and thereby to distinguish themselves from their desisting contemporaries, a criminological luxury seldom available to judges and prosecutors.

Waiver statutes and youth sentencing policies unsystematically attempt to differentiate between adolescent-limited offenders and life-course persistent offenders, but confront an immediate and frustrating trade-off between serious and chronic offenders. For virtually all purposes, the most significant differences in the development of delinquent careers occur between those juveniles who engage in "normal" delinquency as adolescents and desist after one or two contacts, and chronic offenders who typically begin earlier, record five or more justice system contacts, and persist in criminality into adulthood. Legislative offense exclusion that focuses primarily on the seriousness of the present offense rather than on chronic offending fosters an over- and underinclusive response to the problems posed by young career criminals. Such a policy punishes severely one youth's serious, albeit isolated act of violence, while nominally sanctioning less severely a chronic offender's current, less serious property crime.

Despite the research on criminal careers, juvenile and criminal courts' sentencing practices often work at cross-purposes and frustrate rather than harmonize the social control of serious and chronic young offenders as they move between the two systems. Until the recent amendments of waiver laws, criminal courts typically sentenced chronic younger offenders whose rate of criminal activity was increasing or at its peak more leniently than they did older offenders because of the latter's cumulative adult prior records. The lenient responses to many young career offenders when they first appear in criminal courts occur because the criteria for removal from juvenile court and adult criminal sentencing practices often lack congruence. Several studies of the criminal sentences imposed on judicially waived juveniles report a "lack of fit" between waiver decisions and criminal sentencing practices (Feld 1987, 1995). The "punishment gap" allows chronic and active young offenders to fall between the cracks of the two justice systems (Podkopacz and Feld 1995, 1996). The punishment gap occurs because waiver decisions involve two somewhat different but overlapping populations of young offenders—older chronic offenders currently charged with a property crime *and* violent youths, some of whom also are persistent offenders.

Criminal courts respond differently to chronic offenders currently charged with a property crimes and those charged with violence because of the seriousness of their present offense. Prior to 1993, juvenile court judges transferred the largest plurality of youths for property offenses (45 percent), rather than for crimes against the person (34 percent) (Snyder and Sickmund 1995; Sickmund, Snyder, and Poe-Yamagata 1996, 31). The nature of the offenses for which juvenile courts transferred juveniles and their relative youthfulness compared with adult defendants affected their first criminal court sentences. Although studies of dispositions of youths tried as adults in several jurisdictions report substantial variation in sentencing practices, a policy of leniency often prevails. Earlier studies reported that urban criminal courts incarcerated younger offenders at a lower rate than they did older offenders, youthful violent offenders received shorter sentences than did older violent offenders, and for about two years after becoming adults, youths benefited from informal, lenient sentencing policies in criminal courts (Greenwood, Abrahamse, and Zimring 1984). Although the seriousness of a youth's present offense primarily influenced the severity of the adult sentence imposed, "youth, at least through the first two years of criminal court jurisdiction, is a perceptible mitigating factor" (Twentieth Century Fund 1978, 63). A nationwide study of judicially waived youths sentenced as adults found that criminal courts fined or placed the majority (54 percent) of transferred juveniles on probation. Even among those confined, 40 percent received maximum sentences of one year or less and only about one-quarter (28 percent) received sentences of five years or more (Hamparian et al. 1982, 106–9). More recent research reports that juvenile court judges continue to waive primarily older chronic offenders charged with a property crime like burglary rather than with a violent crime, and criminal courts subsequently fined or placed on probation most juveniles judicially transferred (Gillespie and Norman 1984; Heuser

1985; Feld 1995). Moreover, criminal court judges typically sentenced chronic property offenders convicted as adult first-time offenders more leniently than comparable adults. Several studies report that criminal court judges imprisoned transferred youths at lower rates than they did adults convicted of comparable offenses, and many incarcerated juveniles received sentences of one year or less, shorter than the sentences juvenile court judges could impose on them as "deep-end" delinquents. (Gillespie and Norman 1984; Heuser 1985; Bortner 1986). For example, criminal courts in Minnesota imprisoned waived juvenile property offenders at lower rates than they did adults convicted of comparable offenses (Feld 1995).

Baby Boom Increases in Youth Crime, the Crack Cocaine Youth Homicide Epidemic, and the Seduction of Get-Tough Politics

The baby boom escalation in youth crime that began in the mid-1960s and peaked in the late 1970s provided a strong political impetus for get-tough criminal sentencing and waiver policies (Zimring 1998a). Beginning in the 1970s, juvenile waiver policies began to shift from rehabilitation to retribution, from offender to offense, from amenability to public safety, and from the judicial to the legislative or executive branches. These statutory changes coincided with escalating youth crime rates and violence in the late 1970s and again in the late 1980s and early 1990s, and with public and political perception of youth crime primarily as an urban black male phenomenon (Feld 1999).

The Federal Bureau of Investigation's index crime rates, juvenile crime rates, and violent juvenile crime rates followed roughly similar patterns — increasing from the mid-1960s until 1980, declining during the mid-1980s, and then rebounding to another peak in the early 1990s, since which time they have declined again (Zimring 1998a; Feld 1999). Between 1965 and 1980, the overall juvenile index violent crime and homicide rates doubled, followed by a second, sharp upsurge between 1986 and 1994 (Feld 1999). The rapid escalation in juvenile violence in the late 1970s, and especially since the late 1980s, the arrests of increasingly younger juveniles for violence, and the dramatic rise in homicide arrests provide the backdrop for public and political concerns about youth crime (Blumstein 1995).

Two aspects of youth crime and violence have special relevance for understanding legislative changes in juvenile waiver policies during this period. Differences in arrest rates for violent crimes committed by juveniles of difference races and the unique role of guns in the dramatic surge in homicides since the late 1980s account for most of the changes in patterns of youth crime and violence during the past decades. Since the mid-1960s, police have arrested black juveniles under the age of eighteen years of age for all violent offenses—murder, rape, robbery, and assault—at a rate about five times as great as that of white youths, and for homicide at a rate more than seven times as great as that of white youths (Maguire and Pastore 1994, 447). Thus, any sentencing policy that targets violent offenders inevitably will have a racially disparate impact on minority youths. Beginning in 1986, when the youth homicide rates began to escalate sharply again, arrests of black and white juveniles diverged abruptly. Between 1986 and 1993, arrests of white juveniles for homicide increased by about 40 percent, while those of black youths jumped by 278 percent (Sickmund, Snyder, and Poe-Yamagata 1996, 13). Second, while the number of homicide deaths that juveniles caused by means other than firearms fluctuated within a "normal range" of about 10 percent during this period, the number of deaths that juveniles caused with firearms quadrupled (Zimring 1996; Zimring and Hawkins 1997; Feld 1999, 204–6). Because of the disproportionate involvement of black youths in violence and homicide, both as perpetrators and as victims, almost all of these "excess" homicides involving guns occurred within the urban, young black male population (Blumstein 1995; Blumstein and Cork 1996; Cook and Laub 1998, 46–47). The intersection of race, guns, and homicide fanned the public "panic" and political crackdown that, in turn, led to the recent get-tough reformulation of juvenile waiver policies.

The prevalence of guns in the hands of children, the apparent randomness of gang violence and drive-by shootings, the disproportionate racial minority involvement in homicides, and media depictions of callous youths' gratuitous violence have inflamed public fear. Politicians have promoted and exploited those fears for electoral advantage, decried a coming generation of "superpredators" suffering from "moral poverty," and demonized young people in order to muster support for policies to transfer youths to criminal court and to incarcerate them. Some analysts predict a demographic "time bomb" of youth crime in the near future to which minority juveniles will contribute disproportionately (Fox 1996; Zimring 1998a). Thus, the increase in gun homicide by young black males in the late 1980s provided a broader political impetus to crack down on young offenders in general and violent minority youths in particular.

The crackdown on youth crime of the early 1990s represents the culmination of the politicization of crime and waiver policies that actually began several decades earlier. In the 1960s, the civil rights movement created divisions within the Democratic Party between racial and social policy liberals and conservatives, northerners and southerners. Republican politicians seized crime control, affirmative action, and public welfare as racially tinged "wedge issues" with which to distinguish themselves from Democrats in order to woo southern white voters; crime policies for the first time became a central issue in partisan politics (Beckett 1997). During the 1960s, conservative Republicans decried "crime in the streets," advocated "law and order," supported a "war on crime," and favored repression over rehabilitation in response to rising baby boom crime rates, civil rights marches, students' protests against the war in Vietnam, and urban and campus turmoil. As a result of "sound bite" politics, symbols and rhetoric have shaped penal policies more than knowledge, social science research, or substance. Since the 1960s, politicians' fear of being labeled "soft on crime" has led to a constant ratcheting-up of punitiveness. Efforts to get tough have supported a succession of "wars" on crime and later on drugs, longer criminal sentences, increased prison populations, and disproportional incarceration of racial minority offenders (Tonry 1995; Feld 1999). As a result of demagogic appeals, no candidate dares to run on a platform that her opponent can characterize as soft on crime, and politicians avoid thoughtful discussions of complex crime policy issues in an era of thirty-second commercials (Beckett 1997). The mass media depict and the public perceive the crime problem and juvenile courts' clientele primarily as poor, urban black males. Politicians have manipulated and exploited these racially tinged perceptions for political advantage with demagogic pledges to get tough and crack down on youth crime, which has become a code word for young black males (Beckett 1997).

4. Recent Changes in Excluded-Offense and Prosecutor Direct-File Laws

A "rational" legislature could draw on just deserts jurisprudence and criminal career research to specify which serious offenses, offense histories, and offenders states should prosecute in criminal court. Several commentators contend that the primary occasion to waive youths is when their serious or persistent offenses require minimum lengths of confinement in excess of the maximum sanctions available in juvenile courts (Zimring 1991; Feld 1995).

> [T]he justification for waiver is singular: transfer to criminal court is necessary when the maximum punishment available in juvenile court is clearly inadequate . . . [T]he standard for mak-

> ing a waiver decision is a determination that the maximum social
> control available in juvenile court falls far short of the minimum
> social control necessary if a particular offender is guilty of the
> serious crime he is charged with. (Zimring 1981, 201)

If minimum sentences substantially in excess of juvenile courts' maximum sanctions provide the jurisprudential justification for adult prosecution, then retribution and incapacitation provide the rationale to define waiver criteria (Packer 1968; Morris 1974; Frase 1997). Retribution limits severe sanctions to the most culpable and blameworthy, imposes a degree of proportionality and determinacy on decisions, and restricts eligibility for waiver only to the most serious crimes. However, a retributive rationale alone may be overly inclusive and inflict penal harm without any offsetting utilitarian gain, because violent offenders desist at about the same rate as do other youths. The small group of chronic offenders also may deserve or require longer minimum sentences than the maximum sanctions available in juvenile court because of their persistent offending. Identifying chronic offenders based on past conduct rather than as a prediction about future criminality avoids legitimate civil liberties objections to overprediction, false positives, and preventive incarceration (Zimring and Hawkins 1995).

Selecting waiver criteria entails both empirical and value choices. The empirical judgment involves selecting present offense and prior record criteria that differentiate between the relatively few persistent and serious young offenders whom states should prosecute as adults and the vast majority of youths who should remain in the juvenile court. The seriousness of the offense and the length of the prior record constitute the most reliable and relevant criteria upon which to base these judgments. The principal values of waiver are enhanced community protection through the longer sentences and more secure facilities available in the adult system, increased general prevention though greater certainty and visibility of consequences, incapacitation of chronic offenders, and reaffirmation of fundamental norms. Most offenders do not require incarceration, and waiver policies should focus only on those most serious offenses and prior records that justify confinement for much longer term than juvenile courts can impose.

Because the question of waiver arises primarily in the context of a concern for public safety, transfer criteria should focus directly on the present offense and record of recidivism rather than on amorphous factors like amenability to treatment or dangerousness. Retributive criteria would identify older youths who commit very serious offenses, such as intentional homicide, rape, armed robbery, or assault with a firearm or with substantial injury to the victim. Preventive or incapacitative waiver criteria would focus on an extensive record of offending rather than an isolated serious offense. The trade-off between seriousness and persistence requires an explicit policy choice. A legislature also must prescribe a minimum age of eligibility for criminal prosecution—sixteen, fifteen, or fourteen years of age. At what age should states hold youths who commit serious crimes responsible for their offenses as adults and to what degree? Because "adult crime, adult time" does not constitute a sufficiently nuanced policy, sentencing laws should formally recognize youthfulness as a mitigating factor when judges sentence young offenders in criminal court (Feld 1997). If the rationale for waiver is that youths who commit certain serious offenses *deserve* longer or more severe punishment than delinquents, then regardless of the prosecutor's initial charge, if a judge or jury ultimately finds that the youth did not commit one of those serious offenses, then the criminal court should return the youth to juvenile court for sentencing. Although *Bland* declined to review a prosecutor's charging decision before a trial, nothing precludes reassessing jurisdictional divestiture after a trial at which the fact finder determines that the prosecutor's charging decision was erroneous. In the absence of some "transfer-back" provision, offense-based waiver criteria lend themselves to prosecutorial abuse via overcharging. A legislature can adequately consider these sentencing policy issues—seriousness, persistence, age of criminal responsibility, youthfulness as a mitigating factor, and transfer back—when it uses offense criteria presumptively to define the outer limits of juvenile court jurisdiction. Ultimately, a legislature must work backward from the probable sentence a criminal court judge would impose on a young offender convicted of a serious crime and with a particular prior record.

In short, just deserts jurisprudence and criminal career research provide rationale with which a legislature sensibly could define presumptive waiver criteria. Unfortunately, in an era of get-tough politics and sound bite proposals, rationality does not readily characterize legislatures' waiver or criminal sentencing policies. Although judicial waiver historically focused on amenability to treatment, more than half the states have rejected the traditional offender-oriented juvenile court sentencing philosophy, at least in part, and incorporated some offense-based retributive or incapacitative sentencing policies via legislative offense exclusion or prosecutor's choice among concurrent jurisdictions. Prosecutors dominate these waiver processes either by charging youths with excluded offenses or by directly selecting the juvenile or criminal forum. These strategies reflect a fundamental shift of sentencing discretion from the judicial to the executive branch.

Legislative Trends to Exclude Offenses or Direct File

States made relatively limited use of offense-based strategies until *Kent* provided the impetus for offense exclusion and prosecutorial direct-file laws. A few states long had excluded from their juvenile courts older youths charged with capital offenses or crimes punishable by life imprisonment, such as murder. Some states also excluded youths charged with other serious crimes such as criminal sexual conduct or armed robbery, or those who had repeat offenses. But reflecting the influences of just deserts jurisprudence, criminal career research, and get-tough politics, two distinct legislative trends have emerged during the past quarter-century. First, more states have excluded at least some offenses from their juvenile courts' jurisdiction, lowered the ages of juveniles' eligibility for criminal prosecution, and then increased the numbers of offenses for which states may prosecute youths as adults (Fritsch and Hemmens 1995; U.S. General Accounting Office 1995; Torbet et al. 1996). Second, the number of states that allow prosecutors, rather than judges, to make forum selection decisions via concurrent jurisdiction also has increased, as has the range of offenses for which they may transfer youths (Snyder and Sickmund 1995; Fritsch and Hemmens 1995). This section summarizes and analyzes these two recent legislative trends.

A compilation and analysis of states' waiver laws in 1986 reported that eighteen states excluded at least some offenses from their juvenile courts' jurisdiction (Feld 1987). Capital crimes or murder by youths sixteen or older constituted the most common form of excluded-offense legislation, although a few states had adopted more extensive lists. Six of those states excluded youths on the basis of a prior felony conviction coupled with a serious present crime. Although six states had excluded capital and life sentence offenses for more than half a century, the other dozen states adopted or expanded their offense exclusion laws only in the decade after *Kent.* In 1970 in response to *Kent,* Congress excluded murder, rape, and robbery by youths sixteen or older from the jurisdiction of the juvenile courts of the District of Columbia. By 1975, four other states followed suit, and, by 1980, nine more states excluded some serious offenses from juvenile court jurisdiction (Feld 1987). The legislative trend to excise the most serious young offenders from juvenile court jurisdiction that began in the 1970s accelerated during the 1980s.

One statutory compilation a decade later reported that twenty-six states excluded some offenses from their juvenile courts' jurisdiction, a 45 percent increase in less than a decade (Snyder and Sickmund 1995, 88–89). A second statutory compilation that also included judicially waived youths previously convicted as adults in its excluded-offense

classification reported that thirty-eight states excluded at least some offenders from juvenile court jurisdiction (U.S. General Accounting Office
1995). A third compilation that compared waiver statutes in 1979 with
those in 1995 reported that during that period, one state repealed its offense exclusion provisions, while twenty-three states excluded some offenses, including eight additional states that joined the excluded-offense
ranks during that period, a 35 percent increase (Fritsch and Hemmens
1995). During the 1979–95 period, almost half of the states also lowered
the age of eligibility for adult prosecution, increased the catalogues of
excluded offenses, or included provisions for exclusion on the basis of
prior offenses. Still another statutory survey reported that simply between 1992 and 1995, twenty-four states added some crimes to their lists
of excluded offenses and six states lowered the minimum ages for some
or all of their excluded offenses (Torbet et al. 1996). Thus, by any measure, the rate and scope of legislative offense exclusion amendments continued and expanded.

A brief review of a few states' statutory amendments will convey the
nature and expansion of legislative offense exclusion and prosecutorial
discretion. For example, in 1989 in Arkansas, prosecutors had discretion
to direct file in criminal court juveniles charged with murder, kidnapping,
armed robbery, or rape. *Ark. Code Ann.* § 9-27-318 (1989). The Arkansas
legislature amended its prosecutorial statute in 1991 to add first-degree
battery, in 1993 to add possession of a handgun on school property and
assault with a deadly weapon, in 1994 to add six additional offenses including second-degree battery, aggravated assault, soliciting a minor to
join a street gang, or conspiracy or attempts to commit the original listed
crimes, and in 1997 to include escape from a correctional institution and
attempted battery. *Ark. Code Ann.* § 9-27-318 (1998). In 1989, Indiana
excluded from its juvenile court jurisdiction youths sixteen years of age
or older and charged with one of five offenses—murder, kidnapping,
rape, armed robbery, and dealing in a sawed-off shotgun. *Ind. Stat. Ann.*
§ 31-6-2-1.1(d) (1989). The Indiana legislature amended the statute in
1993 to exclude any offense by a youth previously waived and convicted
as an adult, in 1994 to exclude carjacking, in 1995 to add four additional
offenses including criminal gang activity and carrying a handgun, in 1996
to add criminal deviate conduct, and in 1997 to add dealing in cocaine or
other controlled substances. *Ind. Stat. Ann.* § 31-30-1-4(a) (1997). In half
a decade, annual legislative tinkering expanded a modest list of five very
serious offenses to include fourteen crimes. Louisiana statutorily excludes from juvenile court jurisdiction youths fifteen years of age or older
and charged with murder, rape, or kidnapping, and gave prosecutors authority to charge and try other offenses, such as manslaughter, armed

robbery, and aggravated burglary, in criminal court as well. *La. Ch. C.* art. 305(B) (1991). The Louisiana legislature in 1994 lowered from sixteen to fifteen the age at which juveniles could be direct filed by prosecutors into criminal court and added attempted murder, lesser degrees of rape and robbery, and second and subsequent charges of battery, burglary, and drug offenses to the discretionary list. Amendments in 1995 added aggravated burglary, oral sexual battery, and battery with a firearm to the list of offenses that prosecutors could elect to charge in criminal court. *La. Ch. C.* art. 305(B)(2) (1996). Thus, in five years, prosecutors' authority to direct file included a larger cohort of younger youths and a list of offenses that increased from three to fourteen crimes. In 1979, Maryland excluded from juvenile court jurisdiction youths fourteen years of age or older charged with capital and life imprisonment offenses, and those sixteen years of age or older charged with armed robbery (Feld 1987). By 1994, the list of excluded offenses for sixteen-year-olds had expanded to include fourteen crimes, including kidnapping, manslaughter, mayhem, assault, carjacking, and drug and firearms violations. *Md. Code* § 3-804 (1994). The legislature added to its list of excluded offenses attempted armed robbery in 1995, and attempted murder, rape, or assault in 1996. *Md. Code* § 3-804(e)(4) (1997).

Often, a single highly visible case inflames public fears and political passions and provides the impetus to exclude offenses or to lower the age of eligibility for exclusion. The most dramatic example of a single case that produced an extensive excluded-offense law occurred in New York (Butterfield 1995; Singer 1996). Prior to 1978, New York's family court jurisdiction ended at sixteen years of age and no method existed to transfer younger offenders to adult criminal court. Fifteen-year-old Willie Bosket robbed and murdered two subway passengers within months of his release from a secure juvenile facility. Even under a newly strengthened 1976 young offender (YO) law for sentencing youths sixteen to eighteen years of age, the judge could impose only a maximum placement with the Division for Youth until Bosket's twenty-first birthday, i.e., a five-year maximum sentence. Less than two weeks after the juvenile court judge sentenced Bosket, New York governor Hugh Carey, a liberal Democrat whom his opponent attacked as soft on crime, called a special legislative session that quickly adopted the Juvenile Offender Act (JOA) (Butterfield 1995; Singer 1996). The "Willie Bosket Law" excluded "juvenile offenders" (JOs) as young as thirteen years of age charged with murder and those fourteen years of age charged with rape, robbery, assault, and violent burglaries (*N.Y. Crim. Proc. Law* § 1.20(42) [McKinney 1992]; Butterfield 1995). Under the JOA, prosecutors and criminal court judges retain some discretion to transfer JOs back to family court. The

1978 New York excluded-offense law provided a model that other states subsequently followed to simplify the process of trying juveniles as adults.

In Minnesota in 1988, sixteen-year-old David Brom ax-murdered his mother, father, sister, and brother. After a judicial waiver hearing, the juvenile court judge concluded that Brom, a B+ student with no prior delinquency history and whom clinicians testified suffered from a treatable depression, was amenable to treatment within the two-and-one-half years remaining of juvenile court jurisdiction (Feld 1990, 57–69). In separate decisions, the court of appeals, in *In re D.F.B.,* 430 N.W.2d 475 (Minn. Ct. App. 1988), and the Minnesota Supreme Court, in *In re D.F.B.,* 433 N.W.2d 79 (Minn. 1988), reversed the trial judge's decision to retain Brom in juvenile court and ordered him tried as an adult. Following his criminal conviction, the judge sentenced him to three consecutive life sentences, a minimum of 52½ years (Feld 1990, 101). Despite the ultimate resolution of that case, several years later and in explicit reaction to the trial judge's original ruling in *In re D.F.B.,* the Minnesota legislature excluded from juvenile court jurisdiction youths sixteen years of age or older whom prosecutors charged with first-degree murder (*Minn. Stat. Ann.* § 260.015 Subd. 5[b] [West 1995]; Feld 1995, 1051–57). Similarly, in Oregon in 1985, the legislature lowered the age of eligibility for judicial transfer from sixteen to fifteen years of age after a highly publicized murder of an eleven-year-old girl committed by a fifteen-year-old youth (Buckingham 1993).

Appendix 3.1 summarizes the range of offenses that states excluded from their juvenile courts' jurisdiction in 1997. Thirty-four of the states and the District of Columbia exclude youths charged with murder—variously defined as a capital offense, first-degree murder, second-degree murder, murder, or homicide—from juvenile court jurisdiction. Several states impose no minimum age restrictions or exclude juveniles as young as ten or thirteen years of age whom prosecutors charge with murder from the jurisdiction of their juvenile courts. About half of the states also exclude youths who attempt to commit murder. Half of the states exclude from juvenile court jurisdiction youths charged with rape or other sexual offenses. More than one-third of states exclude youths charged with kidnapping or aggravated robbery, and about a dozen exclude youths for arson, for aggravated burglary, or for assault or battery. A somewhat smaller number of states also exclude youths charged with gang offenses, drug offenses, carjacking, or other categories of felonies. Finally, ten states exclude youths on the basis of their prior record of convictions or of convictions for certain types of offenses in conjunction with a specified present offense.

Appendix 3.2 summarizes the range of offenses over which juvenile and criminal courts share concurrent jurisdiction in prosecutor direct-file states. Prosecutors in virtually every direct-file jurisdiction have discretionary authority to charge youths either as delinquents or criminals for murder, criminal sexual conduct, kidnapping, and aggravated robbery. Prosecutors in half or more of the concurrent jurisdiction states enjoy complete discretion to direct file into criminal court youths charged with aggravated burglary or assault and battery. Finally, prosecutors in Nebraska have complete discretion to try any youth of any age charged with a felony either as a delinquent or criminal, as do those in Arkansas and Florida for youths sixteen years of age or older. Recall, too, that the legislation in the concurrent jurisdiction states provide virtually no guidance to prosecutors in the exercise of their forum selection discretion.

Federal legislative proposals by congressional Republicans in 1997 reflect an even more extreme politically motivated policy to shift jurisdictional discretion from judges to prosecutors (Klein 1998). The proposed federal "Juvenile Crime Control Act of 1997" would have excluded from federal juvenile court jurisdiction youths fourteen years of age or older and charged with a long list of violent or drug offenses, would have given federal prosecutors greater discretion to try even younger juveniles as adults, and would have required states to adopt excluded-offense or prosecutor direct-file laws as a condition of receiving federal block grant money (Klein 1998). The proposed law, for example, would have required the states to adopt waiver laws that

> ensure that juveniles who commit an act after attaining fifteen years of age that would be a serious violent crime if committed by an adult are treated as adults for purposes of prosecution as a matter of law, or that the prosecutor has the authority to determine whether or not to prosecute such juveniles as adults. (*H.R.3,* § 302, 143 *Cong. Rec.* H2397-98 [daily ed. May 10, 1997])

Efforts to obtain political advantage through get-tough posturing, rather than sound youth sentencing policies, seem to animate such proposals.

Offense Heterogeneity and Prosecutorial Discretion

State laws that exclude long lists of offenses from juvenile courts or that give prosecutors greater authority to direct file charges in either juvenile or criminal court simply shift sentencing discretion from judges in a waiver hearing to prosecutors in their offices. Because offense categories are necessarily crude and imprecise indicators of the "real" seriousness of any particular offense, prosecutors inevitably exercise enormous sentencing discretion when they decide whether to charge a youth with an excluded offense rather than a lesser included offense, or to select the forum in a direct-file jurisdiction. Despite the extensive lists of excluded offenses and the ascendance of get-tough policies, it seems unlikely that state legislators intend prosecutors to charge every theoretically eligible youth in criminal court. "Assaults and robberies vary tremendously in seriousness. These two offenses account for 94 percent of all youth violence arrests. Categorical generalizations are therefore a poor basis for policy in a great majority of cases" (Zimring 1998b, 494). Even among the serious crimes contained in the catalogues listed in appendixes 3.1 and 3.2, the heterogeneity of offenses within each category requires some decision maker, either a judge or a prosecutor, qualitatively to evaluate both the specific seriousness of that crime and the nature of the individual actor's participation. For example, aggravated assaults may range from a bloody nose to a severe beating to a grievous wounding with a firearm. "[U]ndifferentiated measures of aggravated assault will be rendered opaque by the mixture of serious and less serious events agglomerated in the overall pattern" (Zimring 1979, 83). Similarly, armed robberies may run the gamut from appropriation of lunch money in a school yard while holding a screwdriver to dispossession at the point of a gun in a life-threatening confrontation.

Youths' degrees of participation in crimes vary as much as do offenses within the generic legal categories. Young offenders commit crimes in groups to a much greater extent than do adults (Zimring 1981, 1998a; Snyder and Sickmund 1995). While the criminal law treats all participants as equally responsible and may sentence principals and accessories alike, young people's susceptibility to peer group influences requires some individualized assessment of their degree of participation, personal responsibility, and culpability. The presence of a social audience of peers may induce youths to participate in criminal behavior that they would not engage in if alone. Although the criminal law treats all accomplices as equally guilty as a matter of law, they all may not be equally responsible for the actual harm inflicted.

Because of the heterogeneity of offenses and variations in degrees of participation, some individualized differentiation necessarily and inevitably occurs in the course of charging and waiving young offenders. A study of prosecutorial charging practices in filing waiver motions in Texas illustrates the magnitude of the discretionary selection process (Dawson 1992). Under the Texas law applicable in 1988, juvenile court judges used *Kent* criteria to decide whether to waive youths fifteen or sixteen years of age charged with *any felony* and against whom prosecutors filed a waiver motion. During the period of the study, juvenile courts received 14,150 felony referrals against youths aged fifteen and sixteen, but prosecutors filed transfer motions against only 112 youths. As would be expected, prosecutors focused on more serious offenses, comparable to those listed in most excluded-offense and direct-file statutes. Significantly, however, prosecutors filed transfer motions against fewer than 2 percent of felony offenders, including only 31 percent of those eligible youths referred for homicide, only 3 percent of those charged with sexual assault, only 6 percent of those charged with robbery, and only 0.5 percent of those charged with aggravated assault (Dawson 1992, 988). While prosecutors filed nearly two-thirds of all the waiver motions they made against youths charged with murder, robbery, and rape, they refrained from filing transfer motions against the vast majority of youths referred to juvenile court for those offenses. This confirms that even within most serious offense categories, prosecutors individualize and differentiate on some basis. Moreover, the study reported county-by-county variations; geographic context also influenced the types of differentiation that prosecutors made (Dawson 1992, 1024–26). The heterogeneity of offenses, the variability of youths' participation in crimes, and the idiosyncrasies of prosecutors have important implications for the implementation of offense exclusion and direct-file laws. Such statutes enable prosecutors covertly to manipulate charges or to select a juvenile or criminal forum in a low-visibility, discretionary setting with minimal information or record, and without any form of legal accountability or review. As a matter of sentencing policy, the question recurs whether prosecutors will make better-informed and more appropriate decisions under such circumstances than would judges in an adversarial waiver hearing guided by appropriate waiver criteria.

5. Reverse Waiver, Transfer Back, and Sentencing "Adults" as "Juveniles"

Progressive reformers created separate juvenile courts and correctional institutions in part to avoid confining vulnerable youths in prisons with adults (Schlossman 1977; Rothman 1980). Legislative policies to transfer more and younger juveniles to criminal courts also expose more youths to adult correctional consequences. Because many excluded offenses also carry mandatory minimum criminal sentences, juveniles charged and convicted as adults also face greater prospects of incarceration (Feld 1998). Juveniles confined in adult facilities are more likely to be victims of violent attacks, to experience sexual assaults, and to commit suicide that those confined in juvenile facilities (Fagan, Forst, and Vivona 1989; Klein 1998). And despite the legislative desire to increase the sentences imposed on juveniles tried as adults, many youths receive shorter sentences as adults than juvenile court judges could have imposed on them as delinquents (Noon 1994; Podkopacz and Feld 1995, 1996).

In order to restore some flexibility to a prosecutor-dominated waiver process and to allow for appropriate dispositions of some amenable younger offenders, many states allow judges to "reverse waive" or "transfer back" to juvenile court cases that originated in criminal court either as a result of excluded-offense or prosecutorial direct-file decisions (see, e.g., *N.Y. Crim. Proc. Law* § 725.10 [McKinney 1992]; U.S. General Accounting Office 1995; Sabo 1996). About half of the prosecutor direct-file[4] and excluded-offense[5] jurisdictions allow a criminal court judge either to return a youth to juvenile court for trial or sentencing or to impose a juvenile or youthful offender sentence in lieu of an adult criminal sentence (U.S. General Accounting Office 1995). In some states, offense exclusion or direct-file laws that place a youth initially in criminal court create a presumption of "unfitness" and shift the burden of proof to the juvenile to demonstrate why he should be returned to juvenile court for trial or disposition. See, e.g., *Walker v. State,* 803 S.W.2d 502 (Ark. 1991); *State v. Buelow,* 587 A.2d 948 (Vt. 1990); *Wyo. Stat. Ann.* § 14-6-237(g) (Supp. 1995). In other excluded-offense jurisdictions, the prosecutor may make a reverse waiver decision. In Georgia, for example, the criminal court has exclusive jurisdiction over youths thirteen to seventeen years of age and charged with murder, rape, or armed robbery, but the district attorney "may, after investigation and for extraordinary cause," prosecute the youth in juvenile court instead. *Ga. Code Ann.* § 15-11-5(2)(C) (1997). In most states, however, a criminal court judge makes the reverse waiver, transfer back, or juvenile sentencing decisions under provisions that re-create the *Kent*-style proceedings that originally impelled states to adopt offense exclusion and direct-file laws.

In Florida, prosecutors direct file about 10 percent of juveniles into criminal court for prosecution as adults (Bishop, Frazier, and Henretta 1989; Noon 1994). Except for juveniles convicted of offenses punishable by death or life imprisonment, *Fla. Stat. Ann.* § 985.225 (West 1997), criminal court judges retain the option to sentence youths convicted as adults "to the department for treatment in an appropriate program for children outside the adult correctional system or be placed in a community control program for juveniles." *Fla. Stat. Ann.* § 985.233(1)(a) (West 1997). When deciding whether to impose juvenile or adult sanctions, the statute requires judges to review a presentence investigation report, to conduct a sentencing hearing, and to base the decision on eight enumerated criteria—including the seriousness of the offense, prior record, sophistication and maturity, previous correctional dispositions—that very closely mirror those appended in *Kent.* In short, the Florida statute mandates the equivalent of a discretionary judicial waiver hearing with written findings and conclusions of law, albeit in the context of an adult criminal sentencing decision rather than a juvenile court hearing. In *Troutman v. State,* 630 So.2d 528, 531 (Fla. 1993), the Florida Supreme Court held that juveniles convicted in criminal court may still receive special treatment as juveniles and required sentencing judges specifically to decide a youth's suitability for juvenile or adult sanctions and provide written findings to support its conclusions. "[A] trial court must consider each of the criteria . . . before determining the suitability of adult sanctions. In so doing, the trial court must give an *individualized evaluation* of how a particular juvenile fits within the criteria. Mere conclusory language that tracks the statutory criteria is insufficient." Just as Judge Wright's dissent in *Bland* argued for an assessment of "the maturity of the child and his susceptibility to rehabilitation," *Troutman* emphasized that a criminal sentencing hearing provided the only opportunity to consider a youth's "suitability for treatment."

> Strict adherence to the [statutory] provisions . . . is especially important in cases involving the direct filing of criminal charges in adult court because the provisions provide the only formal means of ensuring that the juvenile is being properly treated as an adult. Unlike most situations in which a child is waived into adult court, direct file cases do not involve an initial hearing and determination by the trial judge that transfer of the case to adult court is appropriate. (*Troutman,* 630 So.2d at 531 n. 5)

Effectively, Florida's prosecutorial direct-file system simply shifts the amenability decision from an initial judicial determination of jurisdiction as in *Kent,* to a postconviction sentencing decision (Noon 1994). The statutory criteria, procedural safeguards, and appellate review mirror the *Kent* judicial waiver process albeit at a different stage of the proceedings, in a different forum, and before a different judge. Unlike youths tried in juvenile courts, those tried as adults enjoy the right to a jury trial with the additional procedural barriers that such safeguards may erect to successful prosecution. Thus, a process originally created to avoid the strictures of *Kent* actually enhances them. We have no evidence that criminal court judges possess any greater expertise with which to decide whether a youth is "suitable for treatment" as a juvenile than a juvenile court judge does to decide that a juvenile is not "amenable to treatment."

A similar procedure exists in Arkansas, where juvenile and criminal courts share concurrent jurisdiction over certain ages and offenses, and the prosecutor elects in which forum to try the case. *Ark. Code Ann.* § 9-27-318 (Michie 1997). A youth charged in criminal court may request the judge to conduct a transfer hearing at which the court will consider "the seriousness of the offense," whether the juvenile is "beyond rehabilitation under existing rehabilitation programs," and the prior record, "character traits, mental maturity, and any other factor which reflects upon the juvenile's prospects for rehabilitation." *Ark. Code Ann.* § 9-27-318(e) (Michie 1997). Using these *Kent*-like criteria, the court must find that the juvenile should be tried as an adult "by clear and convincing evidence," *Ark. Code Ann.* § 9-27-318(f), a higher standard of proof than required in many states' judicial waiver proceedings (Feld 1987, 1995). However, in *Walker v. State,* 304 Ark. 393, 803 S.W.2d 502 (Ark. 1991), the Arkansas Supreme Court held that a youth who sought to transfer the case from criminal to juvenile court was the moving party and bore the burden of proof. Moreover, as long as the trial court at least "considered" all of the statutory criteria, nothing required the judge to give equal weight to all factors. It would not constitute an "abuse of discretion" for a trial judge to place greater emphasis on the seriousness and violence of the offense than on the other "rehabilitation" factors, or to base its assessment of the nature of the offense primarily on the prosecutor's charging documents. *Walker,* 803 S.W.2d 502. Because criminal court judges often may lack "knowledge of juvenile justice" and are predisposed "to the policies of retribution and punitive treatment," their decisions typically tend to ratify those of prosecutors (Boyce 1994, 1002). Analysts of judicial waiver practices have observed a similar proclivity of juvenile court judges to ratify prosecutors' transfer motions rather than to make independent evaluations of a case (Dawson 1992).

In reaction to Willie Bosket's crime spree (Butterfield 1995; Singer 1996), in 1978 New York passed its Juvenile Offender Act, characterized as "among the most severe in the country" (Roysher and Edelman 1981, 265). The JOA excluded youths thirteen years of age or older and charged with murder, and those fourteen or fifteen years of age and charged with kidnapping, arson, assault, manslaughter, rape, burglary, or robbery. *N.Y. Crim. Proc. L.* § 1.20(42) (1997). Although JO cases originate in criminal court, the district attorney may remove a JO case to the family court in lieu of indicting and prosecuting the youth as a JO (Roysher and Edelman 1981; Singer 1996). In addition, prosecutors may charge youths thirteen to fifteen years of age with a "designated felony" in family court, *N.Y. Fam. Ct.* § 301.2(8) (1997). The list of designated felonies mirrors those crimes and ages statutorily excluded from family court jurisdiction. Youths convicted of designated felonies are subject to special sentencing procedures and placement in secure juvenile facilities for terms up to five years. *N.Y. Fam. Ct.* § 353.5 (1997). A criminal court judge also may remove a JO's case to family court. *N.Y. Crim. P. L.* §§ 725.00 et seq. (1997). Finally, if a JO case remains in criminal court, the judge may sentence the JO under the "youthful offender" (YO) statute that provides shorter sentences, placement in youth facilities rather than prison, and a sealed record if the court finds "mitigating circumstances" or that the youth's participation in the crime was "relatively minor." *N.Y. Crim. P. L.* §§ 720.10 et seq. (1997). The statute's practice commentary explains that

> the circumstances of criminal responsibility are infinitely protean in ways not accounted for by formal statutory elements, [and] the Legislature sought to eliminate unwarranted harsh effects of criminal conviction and punishment for this younger group by permitting discretionary removal to Family Court at each juncture of the criminal proceeding, if factors that became apparent at that time merit less severe treatment. (*N.Y. Crim. Proc. L.* § 725.00 [1997])

In *Recriminalizing Delinquency* (1996), Singer analyzed the genesis and implementation of the New York YO and JO laws and concluded that the JO excluded-offenses and prosecutorial and judicial transfer back provisions simply shifted discretion rather than eliminated it.

> The opportunity to reduce the offense charges to non-JO offenses or to invoke a reverse waiver procedure are the unique legal avenues in which the discretion of juvenile justice officials can be replaced with that of criminal justice officials. If legislative waiver procedures merely shift the official sources of discretion, then there is little that is automatic about the initial exclusion of juveniles based on offense categories from the initial jurisdiction of juvenile court. In states with legislative waiver, criminal justice officials may be just as arbitrary in their determination of criminal responsibility for juveniles as juvenile justice officials in states with judicial waiver. (Singer 1996, 83)

The factors that motivate prosecutors to remove JOs' cases to family court rather than to seek indictment and prosecution in criminal court— a juvenile's race, age, family structure, prior arrest record, and geographic and contextual variables—are similar to those that juvenile court judges apply when they transfer youths to criminal court (Dawson 1992; Podkopacz and Feld 1996; Singer 1996). As a result of the exercise of prosecutorial and judicial discretion in the criminal justice system, "[o]nly 25 percent of juveniles arrested as [juvenile] offenders are ultimately convicted in criminal court. If those convicted in criminal court [and sentenced] with YO status are eliminated, then only 10 percent are convicted strictly as juvenile offenders" (Singer 1996, 132)." Thus, criminal justice personnel apply the excluded-offense law to only a small fraction of those youths eligible for its provisions and do so on a subjective, haphazard, and idiosyncratic basis.

Maryland excludes from its juvenile court jurisdiction youths fourteen year of age or older and charged with murder, and those sixteen years or older and charged with any of fourteen offenses, including manslaughter, kidnapping, rape, armed robbery, and certain criminal attempts. *Md. Code* § 3-804(e)(4) (1997). However, upon motion of a party, the criminal court may conduct a reverse waiver hearing for any excluded youth, except those sixteen years of age or older and charged with murder, and transfer the case back to juvenile court "if a waiver is believed to be in the interests of the child or society." *Md. Code* art. 27 § 594A(a) (Michie 1997). In deciding whether or not to waive criminal court jurisdiction, the judge considers the youth's age, mental and physical condition, the nature of the offense, "the child's amenability to treatment," and "public safety." *Id.* at § 594A(c). The procedures and criteria for criminal court reverse waiver hearings mirror juvenile courts' judicial waiver process for nonexcluded youths, except that the youth bears the burden to prove why the case should be remanded to juvenile court. *Md. Code* § 3-817 (Michie 1997); *In re Ricky B.,* 43 Md. App. 645, 406 A.2d 690 (1979). An evaluation of Maryland juvenile and criminal court waiver decisions analyzed the factors that led juvenile court judges to relinquish jurisdiction over nonexcluded youths and criminal court judges to remand to juvenile court those youths whose cases originated in criminal court (Winokur 1996). Criminal court judges granted nearly half (45 percent) of the excluded juveniles' reverse waiver motions and transferred back significantly more younger offenders and those whom clinicians identified as amenable to treatment. Within the group of serious excluded offenses, these reverse-waived youths also had fewer prior convictions and less previous exposure to juvenile correctional services than did those youths over whom criminal court judges retained jurisdiction (Winokur 1996). These findings correspond to comparable research on judicial waiver decision making. Controlling for offense variables, juvenile court judges typically transferred older youths, those with prior juvenile correctional experiences, and those whom clinicians deemed unamenable to treatment (Podkopacz and Feld 1995, 1996). In short, the limited evidence on reverse waiver policy and practice suggests that it closely replicates juvenile court judicial waiver.

Conclusion

Excluded-offense and direct-file laws suffer from the rigidity, inflexibility, political vulnerability, and overinclusiveness characteristic of mandatory sentencing statutes (Zimring 1991; Tonry 1996). In practice, excluded-offense laws transfer discretion from juvenile court judges in a waiver hearing to prosecutors who determine a youth's delinquent or criminal status by manipulating their charging decisions. The concurrent jurisdiction direct-file strategy simply makes explicit the allocation of power and sentencing authority from the judicial to the executive branch. While a rule-of-law approach that uses present offense and prior record criteria as presumptive sentencing guidelines can improve upon juvenile judges' discretionary decisions (Feld 1995), most states' offense exclusion and direct-file laws do not provide either a jurisprudentially satisfactory or principled legal answer to the question of which youths states should prosecute as adults. Rather, such laws prescribe a simplistic, politically attractive sound bite solution for a complex problem, curtail judicial discretion and juvenile courts' clientele, and obscure the bases and processes of "adulthood" decisions.

Proponents of offense exclusion strategies favor just deserts sentencing, advocate sanctions based on relatively objective factors such as offense seriousness, culpability, and criminal history, and value consistent, uniform, and equal handling of similarly situated offenders (Feld 1981, 1983). While offense criteria provide a principled basis for sorting offenders, critics question whether legislators can remove discretion without making the process excessively rigid and overinclusive (Zimring 1981). As the review of states' amendments of excluded-offense laws indicates, politicians in a get-tough climate experience considerable difficulty resisting their own impulses to adopt expansive lists of excluded "crimes de jour" (Zimring 1991). Once legislators enact an excluded-offense statute, the list of offenses often lengthens quickly and can result in criminal trials of far more youths than would occur under a more flexible, discretionary judicial waiver system (Feld 1995). Moreover, when legislators adopt get-tough exclusion laws, they seldom consider the "bed-space" impact or correctional consequences for youths confined in adult prisons, the quality or effectiveness of programs available to youths, or the relative efficacy of juvenile versus adult dispositions on recidivism (Feld 1998). In addition, even within generic legal categories, not all serious offenses are equally serious. Because of the diversity of offenses, especially assaults and robberies, prosecutors necessarily will differentiate among offenders on some bases when they charge some youths with excluded offenses. But prosecutors can achieve flexibility only by charging youths with a nonexcluded, lesser included offense and, in some instances, deprecating the normative seriousness of a youth's criminal conduct. Allowing prosecutors to manipulate charges to respond to the heterogeneity of offenses vests arbitrary and unreviewable discretion in them rather than in judges. No evidence exists that a low-visibility strategy that focuses on the seriousness of offenses rather than on characteristics of offenders and that requires legal subterfuge to achieve proper results will produce better decisions than judges make about which youths states should try as adults.

Proponents of the direct-file strategy claim that prosecutors can act as more neutral, balanced, and objective gatekeepers than either "soft" judges or "get tough" legislators (McCarthy 1994). They contend that prosecutors can provide a streamlined, flexible method to transfer the "worst" youths to criminal court, albeit with some individualized considerations (Klein 1998). Critics of the direct-file approach note that locally elected prosecutors readily succumb to political pressures, symbolically posture on crime issues just like get-tough legislators, exercise their discretion just as subjectively and idiosyncratically as do judges and without appellate courts reviewing their decisions, and introduce substantial geographic variability into the administration of justice (Bishop, Frazier, and Henretta 1989; Bishop and Frazier 1991). Young prosecutors, who typically work in juvenile court as their first assignment, often lack the experience or maturity that judges possess, and it makes little sense to have "persons barely out of law school with scant life experience and whose common sense may be an unproven asset" make such consequential sentencing decisions. *United States v. Boshell,* 728 F. Supp. 632, 637 (E.D. Wash. 1990). Moreover, the paucity of guidelines to direct prosecutors' discretion and the lack of access to personal or clinical information about juveniles make it unlikely that prosecutors will accurately and consistently identify only the "worst" youths in the pool of young offenders (Guttman 1995).

Notwithstanding the substantial problems associated with both the offense exclusion and direct-file strategies, since 1992, nearly half the states have expanded their lists of excluded offenses, lowered the ages of eligibility for exclusion from sixteen to fourteen or thirteen years of age, or granted prosecutors more authority to transfer cases to criminal court (Fritsch and Hemmens 1995; U.S. General Accounting Office 1995; Torbet et al. 1996). Despite the manifest deficiencies of these approaches, Congress's proposed federal Juvenile Crime Control Act exhorts more states to adopt these bankrupt policies.

As a result of states' statutory changes, increasing numbers of younger offenders charged with serious crimes find themselves "automatically" in criminal court. However, as legislators zealously expand lists of excluded offenses to encompass less serious crimes and lower the ages at which prosecutors may charge youths as adults, they also reduce the certainty that criminal court judges will impose significant adult sentences. Moreover, laws in about half of the direct-file and excluded-offense states allow criminal court judges to transfer back some youths for disposition in juvenile court (Snyder and Sickmund 1995). Because cases of chronological juveniles charged with excluded offenses originate in adult courts, we know virtually nothing about the numbers or subsequent sentences these youths receive in criminal courts or the numbers or dispositions of those whom criminal court judges transfer back to juvenile courts.

The number of states that endorse the direct-file strategy and authorize prosecutors to charge youths directly in criminal courts has more than doubled within the past decade (Feld 1987; Fritsch and Hemmens 1995; Snyder and Sickmund 1995). While two states' statutes use *Kent* criteria to guide prosecutors' forum selection decisions, the vast majority remit the decision to each individual prosecutor without any guidance at all. Moreover, even if prosecutors were inclined to "individualize" their forum-charging decisions, unlike judges they lack any access to clinical information or the personal background of the youth, other than the prior juvenile or criminal record. As with excluded-offense legislation, we lack extensive data on the numbers or characteristics of youths against whom prosecutors directly filed in criminal court. Research in some states indicates that they may charge as many as 10 percent of chronological juveniles in criminal court (U.S. General Accounting Office 1995). By some estimates, prosecutors in Florida alone may direct file as many juveniles into criminal courts as juvenile court judges judicially waive in the entire nation (Bishop, Frazier, and Henretta 1989; Bishop and Frazier 1991).

Because excluded-offense and direct-file laws place juveniles' cases initially in criminal courts, some states have developed screening mechanisms to remove some youths who may be suitable for treatment back to the juvenile court. In most transfer back proceedings, a criminal court judge conducts a reverse waiver hearing that replicates a *Kent*-style judicial waiver proceeding. In transfer back proceedings, however, the prosecutor's charge or the excluded offense may create a presumption of unfitness and place the burden of proof on the youth to show why return to juvenile court serves the "best interest of the youth and society." Ultimately, reverse waiver simply reallocates judicial discretion from a juvenile court judge to an already overburdened criminal court judge (Zimring 1991). The limited research on reverse waiver administration indicates that criminal court judges' decisions replicate those of juvenile court judges and exhibit the same subjectivity, idiosyncrasy, and variability. The procedural impediments engendered by *Kent* provided the impetus for a quarter-century of expanding excluded-offense legislation. In many jurisdictions, the net result of the law reform process has been to re-create the same procedural impediments in the criminal courts.

After more than two decades of struggling with many aspects of juvenile court waiver policies (e.g., Feld 1978, 1981, 1987, 1990, 1995, 1998, 1999), I now conclude that a judicial hearing conducted in juvenile court, guided by relatively objective substantive offense criteria and subject to rigorous appellate review, probably constitutes the least bad solution to the intractable sentencing problems posed by serious young offenders. Although waiver hearings are less administratively "efficient" than prosecutors' charging decision, states should not impose the "capital punishment" of the juvenile court too easily, readily, or generally (Zimring 1981). An adversarial hearing at which both the state and defense can present relevant evidence more likely will produce accurate, correct, and fair decisions than prosecutors will make in their offices without access to critical information and subject to extraneous political considerations.

Defining the substantive criteria constitutes the crucial question of any waiver process. The amorphous *Kent* criteria invite judicial subjectivity, idiosyncrasy, and disparity without any effective recourse. So which chronological juveniles should a state prosecute as adults? Earlier in this chapter, I proposed that states should waive youths for criminal prosecutions only when the seriousness of their offenses or their persistence of offending require minimum lengths of confinement substantially in excess of the maximum sanctions available in juvenile court. In order to define the presumptive outer limits of juvenile court jurisdiction, policy makers should work backward from the probable sentence that a criminal court judge likely would impose on a youth. In calculating the anticipated sentences that judges would impose on juveniles in criminal courts, "youthfulness" should constitute a formal mitigating factor that reduces the expected duration (Feld 1997). Depending upon a youth's age at the time of the offense, juvenile court judges readily may prescribe sentences for delinquents of two, three, or even five years or more. Thus, substantive waiver criteria should identify only those combinations of serious present offenses, offense histories, offender culpability and criminal participation, and other aggravating and mitigating factors that deserve "real time" sentences of substantially longer duration than those available in juvenile court (Feld 1995). Furthermore, states could use these offense criteria to create presumptions for waiver or to allocate the burdens of proof and persuasion in particular instances between the juvenile and the state to strike a proper balance and reduce the risks of errors that inevitably will occur in any process (McCarthy 1994; Feld 1995). Finally, appellate courts should closely review juvenile court judges' waiver decisions and develop general, statewide sentencing principles to define a consistent and uniform boundary of adulthood.

Excluded-offense and direct-file law reforms have done little to obviate the need for judicial discretion somewhere in the justice process. However, they do symbolize a fundamental change in juvenile justice jurisprudence and policies from rehabilitation to retribution. The overarching themes of the various legislative amendments include a shift from individualized justice to just deserts, from offender to offense, from amena-bility to treatment to public safety, and from immature delinquent to re-sponsible criminal (Feld 1987; 1995; Torbet et al. 1996). These trends in waiver policy also reflect a cultural and legal reformulation of the social construction of "youth" from innocent, immature, and dependent chil-dren to responsible, autonomous, and mature offenders. As contrasted with traditional judicial waiver proceedings that presumed immaturity and placed the burden on the prosecutor to prove criminal maturity, of-fense exclusion creates a de facto presumption of criminal responsibility and place the burden on a young offender to demonstrate that he *really* is a child, an exceedingly difficult burden. Law-and-order politicians' sound bite solutions—"adult crime, adult time" or "old enough to do the crime, old enough to do the time"—reflect criminal sentencing policies that provide no formal recognition of youthfulness as a mitigating factor. Once youths make the transition to the adult system, criminal court judges sentence them as if they are adults, impose the same sentences, send them to the same prisons, and even inflict capital punishment on them for the crimes they committed as children (Feld 1998; *Stanford v. Kentucky,* 492 U.S. 361 [1989]).

Contemporary get-tough juvenile justice policies coincide with the ma-crostructural, economic, and racial demographic changes in America's cities during the 1970s and 1980s, the emergence of the black underclass, and the rise in gun violence and youth homicides (Massey and Denton 1993; Blumstein 1995). Beginning in the 1970s, the transition from an industrial to an information and service economy reduced employment opportunities in the manufacturing sectors and bifurcated economic op-portunities based on skills and education. The migration of whites to the suburbs, the growth of information and service jobs in the suburbs, and the deindustrialization of the urban core increased racial segregation and the concentration of poverty among blacks in the major cities (Wilson 1987, 1996). In the mid-1980s, the emergence of a structural underclass, the introduction of crack cocaine into the inner cities, and the prolifera-tion of guns among youth produced a sharp escalation in black youth homicide rates (Blumstein 1995). The age-offense-race-specific increase in youth homicide provided the specific political impetus to get tough and crack down on youth crime. In this context, because of differences in rates of offending by race, "getting tough" on violence meant targeting young black men. As a result of the connection in the public and political minds between race and youth crime, juveniles have become the sym-bolic "Willie Horton" of the 1990s (Beckett 1997). It remains to be seen whether legislators can resist demagogic impulses and enact responsible youth crime policies.

Appendix 3.1
Statutory Exclusion

	Age	Capital Offense	First Degree Murder	Second Degree Murder	Murder
Alaska § 47.12.030	16+		X*	X	
Connecticut § 46b-127	14+	X			Arson, Murder
Delaware § 10-9-921	Any age		X*	X*	
District of Columbia § 16-2301	16+				X
Florida §§ 985.225,985.227	Any age	X			
	16+				
Georgia § 15-11-5	13+				X
Idaho § 20-509	Any age				X*
	14+				X*
Illinois § 805-4	Any age				
	15+		X	X	
Indiana § 31-30-1-4	16+				X
Iowa § 232.8	16+				X
Louisiana art. 305	15+		X	X	
Maryland § 3-804	14+	X			
	16+			X*	
Massachusetts 199 § 84	14+		X	X	
Minnesota § 260.125	16+		X		
Mississippi § 43-21-151	Any age	X			
Montana § 41-5-206	17+				
Nevada § 62.040	Any age				X*
	16+				
New Jersey § 2A:4A-26	14+				
New Mexico § 32A-2-3	15+		X		
New York § 1.20	13+			X	
	14+			X*	
North Carolina § 7A-608	13+				
North Dakota § 27-20-34	14+				X*
Ohio § 2151.26	14+				X*‡
	16+				X*
Oklahoma 10 § 7306-1.1	13+		X		
	16+				X
Oregon § 137.707	15+				X*
Pennsylvania 42 § 6355	Any age				X
	15+				X*
Rhode Island §§ 14-1-3, 14-1-7.2,					X*
14-1-7.4	16+				
South Dakota § 26-11-3.1	16+				
Utah § 78-3a-601	16+				X
Vermont T.33 § 5505	16+				X
Virginia § 16.1-269.1	14+	X	X	X	
Washington § 13.04.030	16+		X*	X*	
	16+				
West Virginia § 49-5-10	14+				X
	14+				
	14+				
Wisconsin § 938.183	Any age				
	10+				

Homicide	Manslaughter	Sexual Offense	Kidnapping	Arson
		X	X	X
		X*	X*	
		X		
	Voluntary	X		
		X		X
		X		X
Reckless				
		X	X	X
		X	X	
		X	X	X
		X	X	
	Voluntary	X*	X	
X*		X*	X*	X*
		X*‡		
X		X	X	X
		X	X*	X
		X*		
	X‖	X‖	X‖	X‖
	X	X	X	X
	X	X	X	X
	Voluntary†	X*†	X*†	
		X		
	X	X	X	
X		X	X	
By abuse**, Vehicular/DWI‡	X*‡	X*	X*‡	
				X‡
		X	X	X
X*				

(*continued*)

Appendix 3.1
Statutory Exclusion (*continued*)

		Aggravated Robbery	Aggravated Burglary	Firearm Offense
Alaska § 47.12.030	16+			
Connecticut § 46b-127	14+			
Delaware § 10-9-921	Any age			
District of Columbia § 16-2301	16+	X†	X	
Florida §§ 985.225; 985.227	16+			
	Any age			
Georgia § 15-11-5	13+	X†		
Idaho § 20-509	14+	X		
	Any age	X		
Illinois § 805-4	Any age			
	15+	X*†	X	
Indiana § 31-30-1-4	16+	X*†		X
Iowa § 232.8	16+	X	X	X
Louisana Art. 305	15+			
Maryland § 3-804	14+			
	16+	X*		X
Massachusetts 119 § 84	14+			
Minnesota § 260.125	16+			
Mississippi § 43-21-151	Any age			
Montana § 41-5-206	17+	X*	X*	
Nevada § 62.040	Any age			
	16+			X‡
New Jersey § 2A; 4A-26	14+	X		
New Mexico § 32A-2-3	15+			
New York § 1.20	13+			
	14+	X	X	X
North Carolina § 7A-608	13+			
North Dakota § 27-20-34	14+			
Ohio § 2151.26	14+			
	16+	X‖	X‖	
Oklahoma 10 § 7306-1.1	13+			
	16+	X†	X[5]	X
Pennsylvania 42 § 6355	15+	X*†		
	15+			
	Any age			
Rhode Island §§ 14-1-3; 14-1-7.2				
14-1-7.4	16+			
South Dakota § 26-11-3.1	16+			
Utah § 78-3a-601	16+			
Vermont T.33 § 5505	16+	X*†	X	
Virginia § 16.1-269.1	14+	X		
Washington § 13.04.030	16+	X‡	X‡	X[8]
	16+			
West Virginia § 49-5-10	14+	X*†		
	14+			
	14+			
Wisconsin § 938.183	10+			
	Any age			

Gang Offense	Drug Offense	Assault and/or Battery	Other Felony	Prior Adjudication
	X		Class A	
			Class A or B	
		X		
				X^1
			Auto theft^2	3
			Child molestation	
	X	X	Mayhem	
	X	X	Mayhem	X
	X		Treason	X^3
X	X		Carjacking	
X†	X†	X	Child endanger	
	X†	X	Carjacking	
X	X*	X*	Any felony with explosives*	
	X	X		
		X		
			Class A	
	X			
				X^4
	X	X†		
		X		
		X*†	Auto theft*†	
				X^6
			Child molestation	
	X			2
			Class A, B, 1, 2	
			Any felony^7	
		X	Maiming	
			Carjacking; poisoning	
		X*‡	Drive by; extortion‡	X
			Treason	
				X^{10}
		X^9		

(*continued*)

*Attempts.

†Committed with a firearm or weapon.

‡Prior adjudication and the present offense.

‖Prior adjudication or a firearm used.

1. Excluded if present charge is an offense of violence against a person and if the child has a previous adjudication for murder, sexual battery, armed or strong-armed robbery, carjacking, home invasion robbery, aggravated battery, or aggravated assault.

2. Excluded if offense involves stealing a motor vehicle and during the commission of the offense, a person (other than the perpetrator or a willing participant) is seriously injured or killed.

3. Excluded if there has been a prior adjudication for a felony and the present offense was committed in furtherance of criminal activity by an organized gang.

4. Excluded if either there has been a prior adjudication for murder or attempted murder, voluntary manslaughter, rape, arson, robbery, burglary, involuntary manslaughter, or felonious sexual penetration and the child was committed to the legal custody of the Department of Youth Services; or a firearm was used to commit all of the above offenses except murder or attempted murder.

5. Excluded if after three adjudications for first- or second-degree burglary.

6. Excluded if there has been a prior adjudication for rape, robbery, robbery of a motor vehicle, kidnapping, voluntary manslaughter, or attempt to commit these crimes or murder.

7. Any felony when the child has previously been committed to a secure facility.

8. Firearm used to commit first- or second-degree manslaughter, second-degree kidnapping, second-degree arson, second-degree assault, second-degree assault of a child, first-degree extortion, second-degree robbery, vehicular assault, or vehicular homicide which results from DWI.

9. Excluded when a juvenile is adjudicated delinquent and is alleged to have committed or attempted to commit a battery while in a secure detention facility, secure correction facility, or secured child-caring institution against an officer, employee, visitor, or other inmate of the facility.

10. One prior adjudication for a violent felony, two for other felonies.

Appendix 3.2
Prosecutorial Direct File

		Capital Offense	First Degree Murder	Second Degree Murder	Murder
Arkansas § 9-27-318	14+	X*	X*	X*	
	16+				
Colorado § 19-1-104	14+	X			
	16+				
Florida § 985.227	14+				
	16+				
Georgia § 15-11-5	Any age	X			
Louisiana art. 305	15+		X*	X*	
Montana § 41-5-206	12+				X*
	16+				Negligent*
Nebraska § 43-247	Any age				
Vermont T.33 § 5505	16+				X
Wyoming § 14-6-203	14+				X
	17+				

		Aggravated Robbery	Aggravated Burglary	Firearm Offense	Gang Offense
Arkansas § 9-27-318	14+	X*		X	X
	16+				
Colorado § 19-1-104	14+				
	16+				
Florida § 985.227	14+	X	X	X	
	16+				
Georgia § 15-11-5	Any age				
Louisiana art. 305	15+	X	X†		
Montana § 41-5-206	12+				
	16+	X*	X*		X
Nebraska § 43-247	Any age				
Vermont T.33 § 5505	16+	X			
Wyoming § 14-6-203	14+	X	X		
	17+				

*Second or subsequent offense.

†Prosecutor can direct file for any offense which is not already subject to statutory exclusion (arson causing death, assault and robbery with a dangerous weapon, assault and

Manslaughter	Sexual Offense	Kidnapping	Arson
	X*	X*	
	X	X	X
X	X	X	
	X		
		X*	X*
X	X	X	
X	X	X	

Drug Offense	Assault and/or Battery	Other Felony	Prior Adjudication
	X	Terroristic att; escape*	3
		Any felony	
		Class 2, 3, or unclassified‡	
	X	Stalking; child abuse; grand theft	
		Any felony	
X†	X†		
X*	X*	Any felony with explosives*	
		Any felony	
	X†	Maiming	
	X	Hijacking	2
		Any felony	

robbery causing bodily injury, aggravated assault, murder, manslaughter, kidnapping, maiming, sexual assault, aggravated sexual assault, burglary).

‡Present offense and prior adjudication.

References
Cases Cited

Bailey v. State, 269 Ark. 397, 601 S.W.2d 843 (1980).
Bordenkircher v. Hayes, 434 U.S. 557 (1978).
Breed v. Jones, 421 U.S. 519 (1975).
Chapman v. State, 259 Ga. 592, 385 S.E. 2d 661 (Ga. 1989).
Cox v. United States, 473 F.2d 334 (4th Cir.), *cert. denied,* 414 U.S. 909 (1973).
Furman v. Georgia, 408 U.S. 238 (1972).
Hansen v. State, 904 P.2d 811 (Wyo. 1995).
In re D.F.B., 430 N.W.2d 475 (Minn. Ct. App. 1988).
In re D.F.B., 433 N.W.2d 79 (Minn. 1980).
In re Gault, 387 U.S. 1, 87 S. Ct 1428, 18 L. Ed. 2d 527 (1967).
In re Ricky B., 43 Md. App. 645, 406 A.2d 690 (1979).
Jackson v. State, 311 So. 2d 658 (Miss. 1975).
Jahnke v. State, 692 P.2d 911 (Wyo. Sup. Ct. 1984).
Johnson v. State, 314 So. 2d 573 (Fla. 1975).
Jones v. State, 654 P.2d 1080 (Okla. Crim. App. 1982).
Kent v. United States, 383 U.S. 541 (1966).
Myers v. District Court, 184 Colo. 81, 518 P.2d 836 (1974).
Oyler v. Boles, 368 U.S. 448 (1962).
Pendergrast v. United States, 332 A.2d 919 (D.C. Cir. 1975).
People v. Jiles, 43 Ill. 2d 145, 251 N.E.2d 529 (Il. 1969).
People v. Sprinkle, 56 Ill. 2d 257, 307 N.E.2d 161, *cert. denied,* 417 U.S. 935 (1974).
People v. Thorpe, 641 P.2d 935 (Colo. 1982).
Russel v. Parratt, 543 F.2d 1214 (8th Cir. 1976).
Stanford v. Kentucky, 492 U.S. 361 (1989).
State v. Buelow, 587 A.2d 948 (Vt. 1990).
State v. Cain, 381 So.2d 1361 (Fla. Sup. Ct. 1975).
State v. Grayer, 191 Neb. 523, 215 N.W.2d 859 (1974).
State v. Green, 218 Kan. 438, 544 P.2d 356 (1975).
State v. Mohi, 901 P.2d 991 (Utah 1995).
State v. Sherk, 217 Kan. 726, 538 P.2d 1390 (1975).
State v. Walker, 309 Ark. 23, 827 S.W.2d 637 (Ark. 1992).
Troutman v. State, 630 So.2d 528 (Fla. 1993).
United States v. Armstrong, 517 U.S. 456 (1996).
United States v. Bland, 472 F.2d 1329 (D.C. Cir. 1972), *cert. denied,* 412 U.S. 909 (1973).
United States v. Boshell, 728 F. Supp. 632 (E.D. Wash. 1990).
United States v. Haynes, 590 F.2d 309 (9th Cir. 1979).
United States v. Quinones, 516 F.2d 1309 (1st Cir.), *cert. denied,* 423 U.S. 852 (1975).
Vega v. Bell, 47 N.Y.2d 543, 419 N.Y.S.2d 454, 393 N.E.2d 450 (1979).
Walker v. State, 304 Ark. 393, 803 S.W.2d 502 (Ark. 1991).
Wayte v. United States, 470 U.S. 598 (1985).
Woodard v. Wainwright, 556 F.2d 781 (5th Cir. 1977), *cert. denied,* 98 S. Ct. 1285 (1978).

Other References

Allen, Francis A. 1981. *The Decline of the Rehabilitative Ideal: Penal Policy and Social Purpose.* New Haven: Yale University Press.

American Friends Service Committee. 1971. *Struggle for Justice.* New York: Hill & Wang.

Beckett, Katherine. 1997. *Making Crime Pay: Law and Order in Contemporary American Politics.* New York: Oxford University Press.

Bishop, Donna M., and Charles E. Frazier. 1991. "Transfer of Juveniles to Criminal Court: A Case Study and Analysis of Prosecutorial Waiver." *Notre Dame Journal of Law, Ethics, and Public Policy* 5:281.

Bishop, Donna M., Charles E. Frazier, and John C. Henretta. 1989. "Prosecutorial Waiver: Case Study of a Questionable Reform." *Crime and Delinquency* 35:179.

Blumstein, Alfred. 1995. "Youth Violence, Guns, and the Illicit-Drug Industry." *Journal of Criminal Law and Criminology* 86:10.

Blumstein, Alfred, Jacqueline Cohen, Jeffrey A. Roth, and Christy A. Visher, eds. 1986. *Criminal Careers and "Career Criminals."* Washington: National Academy Press.

Blumstein, Alfred, and Daniel Cork. 1996. "Linking Gun Availability to Youth Gun Violence." *Law and Contemporary Problems* 59:5.

Blumstein, Alfred, David P. Farrington, and Soumyo Moitra. 1985. "Delinquency Careers: Innocents, Desisters, and Persisters." In *Crime and Justice: An Annual Review,* vol. 6. Edited by Michael Tonry and Norval Morris. Chicago: University of Chicago Press.

Bortner, M. A. 1986. "Traditional Rhetoric, Organizational Realities: Remand of Juveniles to Adult Court." *Crime and Delinquency* 32:53.

Boyce, Allison. 1994. "Choosing the Forum: Prosecutorial Discretion and *Walker v. State.*" *Arkansas Law Review* 46:986.

Buckingham, Royce S. 1993. "The Erosion of Juvenile Court Judge Discretion in the Transfer Decision Nationwide and in Oregon." *Willamette Law Review* 29:689.

Butterfield, Fox. 1995. *All God's Children: The Bosket Family and the American Tradition of Violence.* New York: Avon Books.

Chaiken, Jan, Marcia Chaiken, and William Rhodes. 1994. "Predicting Violent Behavior and Classifying Violent Offenders." In *Understanding and Preventing Violence: Consequences and Control,* vol. 4. Edited by Albert J. Reiss Jr. and Jeffrey A. Roth. Washington: National Academy Press.

Cohen, Jacqueline. 1983. "Incapacitation as a Strategy for Crime Control: Possibilities and Pitfalls." *Crime and Justice: A Review of Research* 5:1.

Cook, Philip J., and John H. Laub. 1998. "The Role of Youth in Violent Crime and Victimization." *Crime and Justice: A Review of Research* 24:27.

Cullen, Francis T., and Karen E. Gilbert. 1982. *Reaffirming Rehabilitation.* Cincinnati, Ohio: Anderson Publishing.

Dawson, Robert O. 1992. "An Empirical Study of *Kent* Style Juvenile Transfers to Criminal Court." *St. Mary's Law Journal* 23:975.

Eigen, Joel. 1981a. "The Determinants and Impact of Jurisdictional Transfer in

Philadelphia." In *Readings in Public Policy*. Edited by John Hall, Donna Hamparian, John Pettibone, and Joe White. Columbus, Ohio: Academy for Contemporary Problems.

———. 1981b. "Punishing Youth Homicide Offenders in Philadelphia." *Journal of Criminal Law and Criminology* 72:1072.

Fagan, Jeffrey. 1990. "Social and Legal Policy Dimensions of Violent Juvenile Crime." *Criminal Justice and Behavior* 17:93.

Fagan, Jeffrey, and Elizabeth Piper Deschenes. 1990. "Determinants of Judicial Waiver Decisions for Violent Juvenile Offenders." *Journal of Criminal Law and Criminology* 81:314.

Fagan, Jeffrey, Martin Forst, and Scott Vivona. 1987. "Racial Determinants of the Judicial Transfer Decision: Prosecuting Violent Youth in Criminal Court." *Crime and Delinquency* 33:259.

Fagan, Jeffrey, and Martin Guggenheim. 1996. "Preventive Detention and the Judicial Prediction of Dangerousness for Juveniles: A Natural Experiment." *Journal of Criminal Law and Criminology* 86:415.

Farrington, David P. 1986. "Age and Crime." In *Crime and Justice: An Annual Review of Research*, vol. 7. Edited by Michael Tonry and Norval Morris. Chicago: University of Chicago Press.

———. 1998. "Causes and Correlates of Male Youth Violence." *Crime and Justice: A Review of Research* 24:421.

Feld, Barry C. 1978. "Reference of Juvenile Offenders for Adult Prosecution: The Legislative Alternative to Asking Unanswerable Questions." *Minnesota Law Review* 62:515.

———. 1981. "Juvenile Court Legislative Reform and the Serious Young Offender: Dismantling the 'Rehabilitative Ideal.'" *Minnesota Law Review* 69:141.

———. 1983. "Delinquent Careers and Criminal Policy: Just Deserts and the Waiver Decision." *Criminology* 21:195.

———. 1987. "Juvenile Court Meets the Principle of Offense: Legislative Changes in Juvenile Waiver Statutes." *Journal of Criminal Law and Criminology* 78:471.

———. 1988. "Juvenile Court Meets the Principle of Offense: Punishment, Treatment, and the Difference It Makes." *Boston University Law Review* 68:821.

———. 1990. "Bad Law Makes Hard Cases: Reflections on Teen-Aged Axe-Murderers, Judicial Activism, and Legislative Default." *Law and Inequality* 8:1.

———. 1995. "Violent Youth and Public Policy: A Case Study of Juvenile Justice Law Reform." *Minnesota Law Review* 79:965.

———. 1997. "Abolish the Juvenile Court: Youthfulness, Criminal Responsibility, and Sentencing Policy." *Journal of Criminal Law and Criminology* 88:68.

———. 1998. "Juvenile and Criminal Justice Systems' Responses to Youth Violence." *Crime and Justice: An Annual Review* 24:189.

———. 1999. *Bad Kids: Race and the Transformation of the Juvenile Court*. New York: Oxford University Press.

Fox, James Alan. 1996. *Trends in Juvenile Violence: A Report to the United States Attorney General on Current and Future Rates of Juvenile Offending*. Washington: United States Department of Justice.

Frase, Richard. 1997. "Sentencing Principles in Theory and Practice." *Crime and Justice: A Review of Research* 22:363.

Fritsch, Eric, and Craig Hemmens. 1995. "Juvenile Waiver in the United States 1979–1995: A Comparison and Analysis of State Waiver Statutes," *Juvenile and Family Court Judges Journal* 46:17.

Gillespie, L. Kay, and Michael D. Norman. 1984. "Does Certification Mean Prison: Some Preliminary Findings from Utah." *Juvenile and Family Court Journal* 35:23.

Greenwood, Peter. 1986. "Differences in Criminal Behavior and Court Responses among Juvenile and Young Adult Defendants." In *Crime and Justice,* vol. 7. Edited by Michael Tonry and Norval Morris. Chicago: University of Chicago Press.

Greenwood, Peter, Joan Petersilia, and Franklin Zimring. 1980. *Age, Crime, and Sanctions: The Transition from Juvenile to Adult Court.* Santa Monica, Calif.: RAND.

Guttman, Catherine R. 1995. "Listen to the Children: The Decision to Transfer Juveniles to Adult Court." *Harvard Civil Rights–Civil Liberties Law Review* 30:507.

Hamparian, Donna M., Richard Schuster, Simon Dinitz, and John Conrad. 1978. *The Violent Few: A Study of Dangerous Juvenile Offenders.* Lexington, Mass.: Lexington Books.

Hamparian, Donna, Linda Estep, Susan Muntean, Ramon Priestino, Robert Swisher, Paul Wallace, and Joseph White. 1982. *Youth in Adult Courts: Between Two Worlds.* Washington: Office of Juvenile Justice and Delinquency Prevention.

Heuser, James Paul. 1985. *Juveniles Arrested for Serious Felony Crimes in Oregon and "Remanded" to Adult Criminal Courts: A Statistical Study.* Salem: Oregon Department of Justice Crime Analysis Center.

Howell, James C. 1996. "Juvenile Transfers to the Criminal Justice System: State of the Art." *Law and Policy* 18:17.

Klein, Eric K. 1998. "Dennis the Menace or Billy the Kid: An Analysis of the Role of Transfer to Criminal Court in Juvenile Justice." *American Criminal Law Review* 35:371.

Lab, Steven P., and John T. Whitehead. 1988. "An Analysis of Juvenile Correctional Treatment." *Crime and Delinquency* 34:60.

———. 1990. "From 'Nothing Works' to 'The Appropriate Works': The Latest Stop on the Search for the Secular Grail." *Criminology* 28:405.

Lemmon, John H., Henry Sontheimer, and Keith A. Saylor. 1991. *A Study of Pennsylvania Juveniles Transferred to Criminal Court in 1986.* Harrisburg: Pennsylvania Juvenile Court Judges' Commission.

Maguire, Kathleen, and Ann L. Pastore, eds. 1994. *Sourcebook of Criminal Justice Statistics: 1993.* Washington: Bureau of Justice Statistics.

Massey, Douglas S., and Nancy A. Denton. 1993. *American Apartheid: Segregation and the Making of the Underclass* Cambridge: Harvard University Press.

McCarthy, Francis Barry. 1994. "The Serious Offender and Juvenile Court Reform: The Case for Prosecutorial Waiver of Juvenile Court Jurisdiction," *St. Louis University Law Journal* 389:629.

Monahan, John. 1981. *Predicting Violent Behavior: An Assessment of Clinical Techniques.* Beverly Hills: Sage.

Morris, Norval. 1974. *The Future of Imprisonment.* Chicago: University of Chicago Press.

Morris, Norval, and Marc Miller. 1985. "Predictions of Dangerousness." In *Crime and Justice: A Review of Research,* vol. 6. Edited by Michael Tonry and Norval Morris. Chicago: University of Chicago Press.

Mylniec, Wallace, 1976. "Juvenile Delinquent or Adult Convict: Prosecutor's Choice." *American Criminal Law Review* 14:29.

Noon, Cynthia R. 1994. "'Waiving' Goodbye to Juvenile Defendants, Getting Smart vs. Getting Tough." *University of Miami Law Review* 49:431.

Packer, Herbert L. 1968. *The Limits of the Criminal Sanction.* Stanford: Stanford University Press.

Petersilia, Joan. 1980. "Criminal Career Research: A Review of Recent Evidence." *Crime and Justice: An Annual Review of Research,* vol. 2. Edited by Norval Morris and Michael Tonry. Chicago: University of Chicago Press.

Podkopacz, Marcy Rasmussen, and Barry C. Feld. 1995. "Judicial Waiver Policy and Practice: Persistence, Seriousness, and Race." *Law and Inequality Journal* 14:73.

———. 1996. "The End of the Line: An Empirical Study of Judicial Waiver." *Journal of Criminal Law and Criminology* 86:449.

Poulos, Tammy Meredith, and Stan Orchowsky. 1994. "Serious Juvenile Offenders: Predicting the Probability of Transfer to Criminal Court." *Crime and Delinquency* 40:3.

Rothman, David J. 1980. *Conscience and Convenience: The Asylum and Its Alternatives in Progressive America.* Boston: Little, Brown.

Roysher, Martin, and Peter Edelman. 1981. "Treating Juveniles as Adults in New York: What Does It Mean and How Is It Working?" In *Readings in Public Policy.* Edited by John C. Hall, Donna Martin Hamparian, John M. Pettibone, and Joseph L. White. Columbus, Ohio: Academy for Contemporary Problems.

Sabo, Stacey. 1996. "Rights of Passage: An Analysis of Waiver of Juvenile Court Jurisdiction." *Fordham Law Review* 64:2425.

Sanborn, Joseph B., Jr. 1996. "Policies Regarding the Prosecution of Juvenile Murderers: Which System and Who Should Decide?" *Law and Policy* 18:151.

Schlossman, Steven. 1977. *Love and the American Delinquent: The Theory and Practice of "Progressive" Juvenile Justice, 1825–1920.* Chicago: University of Chicago Press.

Sechrest, Lee B. 1987. "Classification for Treatment." In *Prediction and Classification: Criminal Justice Decision Making.* Edited by Don M. Gottfredson and Michael Tonry. Vol. 9 of *Crime and Justice: A Review of Research,* edited by Michael Tonry and Norval Morris. Chicago: University of Chicago Press.

Sheffer, Julianne P. 1995. "Serious and Habitual Juvenile Offender Statutes: Reconciling Punishment and Rehabilitation within the Juvenile Justice System." *Vanderbilt Law Review* 48:479.

Singer, Simon I. 1996. *Recriminalizing Delinquency: Violent Juvenile Crime and Juvenile Justice Reform.* New York: Cambridge University Press.

Snyder, Howard N., and Melissa Sickmund. 1995. *Juvenile Offenders and Victims: A National Report.* Washington: Office of Juvenile Justice and Delinquency Prevention.

Snyder, Howard N., Melissa Sickmund, and Eileen Poe-Yamagata. 1996. *Juvenile Offenders and Victims: 1996 Update on Violence.* Washington: Office of Juvenile Justice and Delinquency Prevention, National Center for Juvenile Justice.

Strasburg, Paul. 1978. *Violent Delinquents.* New York: Simon & Schuster.

Thomas, Charles W., and Shay Bilchik. 1985. "Prosecuting Juveniles in Criminal Courts: A Legal and Empirical Analysis." *Journal of Criminal Law and Criminology* 76:439.

Tonry, Michael. 1995. *Malign Neglect: Race, Crime, and Punishment in America.* New York: Oxford University Press.

———. 1996. *Sentencing Matters.* New York: Oxford University Press.

Torbet, Patricia, Richard Gable, Hunter Hurst IV, Imogene Montgomery, Linda Szymanski, and Douglas Thomas. 1996. *State Responses to Serious and Violent Juvenile Crime: Research Report.* Washington: Office of Juvenile Justice and Delinquency Prevention, National Center for Juvenile Justice.

Tracy, Paul E., Marvin E. Wolfgang, and Robert M. Figlio. 1990. *Delinquency Careers in Two Birth Cohorts.* New York: Plenum.

Twentieth Century Fund Task Force on Sentencing Policy toward Young Offenders. 1978. *Confronting Youth Crime.* New York: Holmes & Meier.

United States General Accounting Office. 1995. *Juvenile Justice: Juveniles Processed in Criminal Court and Case Dispositions.* Washington: U.S. General Accounting Office.

von Hirsch, Andrew. 1976. *Doing Justice.* New York: Hill & Wang.

———. 1986. *Past vs. Future Crimes.* New Brunswick, N.J.: Rutgers University Press.

Wilson, William J. 1987. *The Truly Disadvantaged.* Chicago: University of Chicago Press.

———. 1996. *When Work Disappears: The World of the New Urban Poor.* New York: Alfred A. Knopf.

Winokur, Kristin Parsons. 1996. "Juvenile Jurisdictional Transfer: An Evaluation of the Judicial and Reverse Waiver Mechanisms." Paper presented at the annual meeting of the American Society of Criminology, November 21, 1996.

Wolfgang, Marvin, Robert Figlio, and Thorsten Sellin. 1972. *Delinquency in a Birth Cohort.* Chicago: University of Chicago Press.

Zimring, Franklin E. 1979. "American Youth Violence: Issues and Trends." *Crime and Justice: An Annual Review of Research* 1:67

———. 1981. "Notes toward a Jurisprudence of Waiver." In *Major Issues in Juvenile Justice Information and Training: Readings in Public Policy.* Edited by John C. Hall, Donna Martin Hamparian, John M. Pettibone, and Joseph L. White. Columbus, Ohio: Academy for Contemporary Problems.

———. 1991. "The Treatment of Hard Cases in American Juvenile Justice: In Defense of Discretionary Waiver." *Notre Dame Journal of Law, Ethics, and Public Policy* 5:267.

————. 1996. "Kids, Guns, and Homicide: Policy Notes on an Age-Specific Epidemic." *Law and Contemporary Problems* 59:25.

————. 1998a. *American Youth Violence.* New York: Oxford University Press.

————. 1998b. "Toward Jurisprudence of Youth Violence." *Crime and Justice: A Review of Research* 24:477.

Zimring, Franklin E., and Gordon Hawkins. 1995. *Incapacitation: Penal Confinement and Restraint of Crime.* New York: Oxford University Press.

————. 1997. *Crime Is Not the Problem: Lethal Violence in America.* New York: Oxford University Press.

Notes

1. See, e.g., *Woodard v. Wainwright,* 556 F.2d 781 (5th Cir. 1977), *cert. denied,* 98 S. Ct. 1285 (1978); *Russel v. Parratt,* 543 F.2d 1214 (8th Cir. 1976); *United States v. Quinones,* 516 F.2d 1309 (1st Cir.), *cert. denied,* 423 U.S. 852 (1975); *Cox v. United States,* 473 F.2d 334 (4th Cir.), *cert. denied,* 414 U.S. 909 (1973), *United States v. Bland,* 472 F.2d 1329 (D.C. Cir. 1972), *cert. denied,* 412 U.S. 909 (1973); *Myers v. District Court,* 184 Colo. 81, 518 P.2d 836 (1974); *Johnson v. State,* 314 So. 2d 573 (Fla. 1975); *People v. Sprinkle,* 56 Ill. 2d 257, 307 N.E.2d 161, *cert. denied,* 417 U.S. 935 (1974); *State v. Sherk,* 217 Kan. 726, 538 P.2d 1390 (1975); *Jackson v. State,* 311 So. 2d 658 (Miss. 1975); *State v. Grayer,* 191 Neb. 523, 215 N.W.2d 859 (1974); *United States v. Haynes,* 590 F.2d 309 (9th Cir.1979); *Bailey v. State,* 269 Ark. 397, 601 S.W.2d 843 (1980); *People v. Thorpe,* 641 P.2d 935 (Colo. 1982); *Vega v. Bell,* 47 N.Y.2d 543, 419 N.Y.S.2d 454, 393 N.E.2d 450 (1979); *Jones v. State,* 654 P.2d 1080 (Okla. Crim. App. 1982).

2. See *Ark. Code Ann.* §9-27-318(b) (Michie 1997); *Colo. Rev. Stat. Ann.* § 19-2-518(2) (West 1997); *Fla. Stat. Ann.* § 985.226(2)(a)–(b) (West 1997); *Ga. Code Ann.* § 15-11-5(b) (1997); *La. Child Code Ann. Art.* 305(b)(3) (West Supp. 1997); *Mich. Com. Laws Ann.* § 600.606(1) (West 1997); *Neb. Rev. Stat.* § 43-247 (1997); *Vt. Stat. Ann. Tit.* 33, § 5505(c) (1997); *Wyo. Stat. Ann.* § 14-6-203 (1997).

3. *State v. Walker,* 309 Ark. 23, 827 S.W.2d 637 (Ark. 1992); *Chapman v. State,* 259 Ga. 592, 385 S.E. 2d 661 (Ga. 1989); *Hansen v. State,* 904 P.2d 811 (Wyo. 1995); *Myers v. District Court,* 518 P.2d 836 (Colo. 1974).

4. . *Ark. Code Ann.* § 9-27-318(d) (Michie 1993 & Supp. 1995); *Fla. Stat.* § 985.233 (West 1997); *Neb. Rev. Stat.* § 43-261 (1993); *Vt. Stat. Ann.* tit. 33 § 55605(c) (1991); *Wyo. Stat. Ann.* § 14-6-237(g) (Supp. 1995).

5. See, e.g., *Del. Code Ann.* tit. 10, § 1011(a)–(b) (Supp. 1994); *Ga. Code Ann.* § 15-11-5(b)(2)(B) (1994); *Ky. Rev. Stat. Ann.* § 640.0101(3) (Michie/Bobbs-Merrill 1990 & Supp. 1994); *Md. Code* art. 27 § 594A (Michie 1997); *Miss. Code Ann.* § 43-21-157(8) (Supp. 1995); *Nev. Rev. Stat. Ann.* § 62.080(3) (Michie Supp. 1995); *N.H. Rev. Stat. Ann.* § 169-B:25 (Supp. 1995); *Okla. Stat. Ann.* tit. 10, § 7306-1.1(E) (West Supp. 1996); 42 *Pa. Cons. Stat. Ann.* tit. 33, § 6322(a) (Supp. 1995); *Vt. Stat. Ann.* tit. 33 § 5505(a)–(b) (1991).

Chapter Four

Blended Sentencing in American Juvenile Courts

RICHARD E. REDDING AND JAMES C. HOWELL

Juvenile justice has come full circle in this century. With the creation of juvenile courts one hundred years ago, reformers achieved their objective of removing juveniles from the harsh, punishment-oriented criminal justice system. Now, juvenile justice is once again embracing criminal court handling of certain juvenile offenders and diminishing the role of the juvenile court. In this chapter, we discuss a relatively new legislative change aimed at enhancing sentencing authority and punishments in juvenile court: "blended sentencing," which allows juvenile courts to impose adult sentences or extend their sentencing jurisdiction into early adulthood.

In part, blended sentencing is a response to a reversal of century-old policies in juvenile justice. Three main factors account for the change. First, "extensive media coverage of violent crimes by juveniles fueled perceptions of a juvenile crime epidemic in the early 1990s" (Torbet and Szymanski 1998, 1). Legislatures across the country enacted more punitive juvenile laws that remove serious and violent offenders from juvenile court jurisdiction. Second, long before the so-called juvenile violence epidemic of the past decade, the philosophical shift from rehabilitation to punishment that had taken hold in the criminal justice system filtered down to the juvenile justice system (see Thomas and Bilchik 1985). Sweeping changes were made in juvenile delinquency laws that diminished the use of rehabilitative measures while increasing punishment. The most notable change has been states' revision of their transfer (also called "waiver" or "certification") laws to expand the types of offenses and offenders eligible for transfer for trial and sentencing in criminal court. Third, there is the view that juvenile courts fail to punish adequately and that juvenile rehabilitation programs are ineffective.

Though recent reviews have concluded otherwise (Lipsey 1995; Lipsey and Wilson 1998), this view dominated the field since the mid-1970s, when a seminal review of program evaluations in juvenile and criminal justice systems concluded that "nothing works" (Martinson 1974).

Along with the punitive trend in juvenile justice laws, policy makers continue to search for the appropriate role for the juvenile justice system in controlling serious and violent juvenile offenders. Blended sentencing (also called "blended jurisdiction") increases the sentencing options available in the juvenile court through a limited "blending" of juvenile and adult sentencing. States have adopted one of three blended sentencing options. The juvenile court may: (1) impose a juvenile or an adult sentence, (2) impose both a juvenile and adult sentence, with the adult sentence suspended under conditions, or (3) impose a sentence past the normal limit of juvenile court jurisdiction; typically, a hearing is held when the juvenile reaches eighteen to twenty-one to determine if an adult sentence will be imposed.

In this chapter, we review the structure and function of blended sentencing laws and provide an analysis of their legal and constitutional implications. We discuss their likely effects on juvenile offenders and the juvenile justice system, and a number of potential benefits and risks of blended sentencing, drawing on available outcome data of blended sentencing in two states. We conclude by discussing preferred blended sentencing schemes.

1. Why Enhance Sentencing in Juvenile Court?

What is the appeal of blended sentencing? It appears to provide a solution to the conflict between two different views on the most appropriate response to serious and violent juvenile crime. Most of the American public continues to support rehabilitation efforts (Schwartz, Guo, and Krebs 1993) while also supporting "get tough" measures with juvenile offenders. Many believe juvenile court sanctions are neither certain nor severe enough (with sanctions like probation and short periods of confinement) to deter serious delinquents from reoffending (see Regnery 1985). Over four-fifths of Americans say that juveniles convicted of a second or third crime should be punished as adults (Edmonds 1994). Still, most Americans strongly disagree with the confinement of juveniles with adults (Schiraldi and Soler 1998). Blended sentencing offers a means of resolving these disparate views because it combines rehabilitation in the juvenile justice system with the possibility of sanctions in the criminal justice system.

> There's this tug of war going on between those who believe
> we've been too soft on juveniles . . . and those that feel we treat
> juveniles differently because we believe they can be reformed
> and rehabilitated . . . [Blended sentencing is] really a marriage of
> convenience between those that want to punish more and those
> that want to give kids one more chance. (Belluck 1998, 26, quot-
> ing John Stanoch, Chief Juvenile Court Judge for Hennepin
> County, Minnesota)

In many ways, blended sentencing is an extension of the ideals of the juvenile court, allowing the court to maintain its jurisdiction over serious and violent juvenile offenders rather than having them transferred to criminal court and incarcerated in adult facilities. Blended sentencing is appealing to many juvenile justice officials, prosecutors, and defense attorneys, because it preserves juvenile court jurisdiction and discretionary control over serious and violent juvenile offenders while providing a stronger accountability sanction and greater community protection than otherwise is available in the juvenile justice system (see Belluck 1998). As Schwartz, Weiner, and Enosh (1998) point out, the juvenile court survives because it adapts to public sentiment and changing clientele. The juvenile court is criticized at once for being too soft on some offenders while too punitive with others; blended sentencing authority provides it with greater institutional flexibility and a wider range of sentencing options. Blended sentencing also provides a solution to the correctional programming problem of an influx of juveniles into adult correctional systems ill equipped to handle their special needs.

Extending juvenile court jurisdiction also allows more time to determine the likelihood that an offender will continue committing offenses into adulthood and, therefore, whether he is more appropriate for criminal justice system processing. In some states, juvenile courts can impose an adult sentence when the offender ages out of the juvenile justice system, if, after a judicial hearing, the judge determines that the suspended adult sentence should be imposed. The possible consequence of an adult sentence if the juvenile commits a new offense, violates probation, or fails to respond to rehabilitation serves to hold juveniles accountable (Torbet et al. 1996). It offers juvenile offenders a "last chance" at rehabilitation within the juvenile system, an incentive to respond to treatment in order to avoid the consequences of an adult sentence, and "the advantage of determining whether to transfer [to the adult system] at a point in the proceedings when the decision-maker has access to all relevant background information on the offense and on the offender" (Clarke 1996, 4).

2. Blended Sentencing versus Transfer to Criminal Court

The reason many juvenile justice officials favor blended sentencing laws becomes apparent by examining their relationship to transfer laws. Most states, along with the federal government,[1] have revised their transfer statutes to make it easier to transfer juveniles from juvenile court to criminal court jurisdiction, thereby permitting their incarceration into adulthood. States have lowered the minimum transfer age, expanded the number of transfer-eligible offenses, made transfer automatic for certain offenses, and/or relaxed the decisional criteria for transfer so that the juvenile's individual characteristics and treatment amenability are no longer relevant or key considerations.

Table 4.1 indicates the types of transfer provisions available in states having blended sentencing. Half of these states automatically provide for transfer for certain offenses; four allow prosecutors to file charges in criminal court ("prosecutor direct-file"); and all but two states have discretionary transfer provisions whereby the juvenile court judge (either *sua sponte* or on the prosecutor's motion) decides whether to transfer ("judicial transfer"). (Three states have "reverse transfer," with prosecution beginning in the criminal court but later transferred to the juvenile court.) In six of the nineteen blended sentencing states, juveniles aged ten to sixteen can be transferred for any criminal offense. Nine states permit transfer of fourteen- to sixteen-year-olds for drug offenses. In ten states, juveniles can be transferred for property offenses at fourteen to sixteen or younger. In the nine states having blended sentencing in the juvenile court, five have no minimum age or minimum transfer ages younger than fourteen.

Since these states' blended sentencing laws typically cover the same class of serious or violent juvenile offenders as do their various transfer provisions,[2] blended sentencing may remove transfer-eligible juveniles from the negative consequences[3] of transfer to the "permanently disfiguring" criminal justice system (see Zimring's chapter in this volume). Transfer, which Zimring (1981, 193) described as "the capital punishment of juvenile justice," has "tremendous consequences for the juvenile" (*Kent v. United States* 1966: 554). "[O]nce waiver of jurisdiction occurs, the child loses all protective and rehabilitative possibilities available" (*State v. R.G.D.*, 527 A.2d 834, 835 [N.J. Super. 1987]). (In some states, however, the criminal court can impose a juvenile sentence.) We do not know how many juveniles would be transferred to criminal court in the absence of blended sentencing, but blended sentencing may reduce the number of unnecessary transfers. As Judge Martin (1992) observed, "Much of the pressure put on the juvenile justice system by the public

Table 4.1
Types of Transfer Provisions According to State Models of Blended Sentencing

	Judicial Transfer	Prosecutor Direct-File	Automatic Transfer	Reverse Transfer
Juvenile-exclusive model:				
Massachusetts		X	X	X
Michigan[a]	X	X		
New Mexico			X	
Juvenile-inclusive model:				
Connecticut	X			X
Kansas	X			
Minnesota	X		X	
Montana	X	X	X	
Juvenile-contiguous model:				
Colorado	X	X		X
Massachusetts[b]		X	X	
Rhode Island	X			
Texas	X			
Criminal-exclusive model:				
California	X			
Colorado[a]	X	X		X
Florida	X	X	X	
Idaho	X		X	
Michigan	X	X		
Oklahoma	X	X	X	X
Virginia[c]	X	X		X
West Virginia	X			
Criminal-inclusive model:				
Arkansas	X	X		X
Iowa	X		X	X
Missouri	X			
Vermont	X	X	X	X
Virginia	X	X		

Sources: Adapted from Griffin, Torbet, and Szymanski 1998 and Torbet and Szymanski 1998.

[a]Colorado and Michigan have blended sentencing in both the criminal and juvenile courts.

[b]Massachusetts has both the exclusive and contiguous models of blended sentencing in juvenile court.

[c]Virginia has both the exclusive and contiguous models of blended sentencing in criminal court.

could be defused by extending the length of time for which a juvenile offender may be detained" (84). Massachusetts and New Mexico abolished transfer (except for homicide cases) after enactment of their blended sentencing laws (Miller 1997b). "[T]he primary justification for [transfer] is the need for minimum lengths of confinement that are substantially in excess of the maximum sanctions available in the juvenile justice court" (Feld 1987, 494); the juvenile's proximity in age to the juvenile court's jurisdictional limit is the main predictor of transfer (Dawson 1992).

Transfer to criminal court should be avoided whenever possible because it has deleterious consequences for juveniles. (Nationwide, 87 percent of serious and violent juvenile offenders transferred to criminal court are sentenced to prison. U.S. General Accounting Office 1995.) With transfer criteria increasingly based primarily on age and offense, it becomes even more important to avoid transfer to criminal court, because mentally ill or developmentally immature juveniles will be included in the widening net of criminal court jurisdiction (Bonnie and Grisso, in press). Bishop and Frazier's research (this volume) powerfully illustrates the many negative psychological and behavioral effects on juveniles of incarceration in adult correctional facilities.

There also is mounting evidence that criminal court processing increases recidivism. A review of fifty studies of juvenile transfers to the criminal justice system concluded that recidivism rates are much higher among juveniles transferred to criminal court than among those retained in the juvenile justice system (Howell 1996). Large-scale comparative studies (Bishop et al. 1996; Fagan 1996; Myers 1999; Podkopacz and Feld 1996; White 1985; Winner et al. 1997) show that transferred juveniles are more likely to reoffend more quickly and more frequently than juveniles retained in the juvenile justice system. Controlling for seven variables (race, gender, age, most serious prior offense, number of referrals to juvenile court, number of charges, and most serious charge), Bishop et al. (1996) compared the one-year recidivism rate of 2,738 juvenile offenders transferred to criminal court in Florida with a matched sample of nontransferred juveniles. Recidivism rates and time to reoffending were higher for the transferred juveniles across seven offense types (ranging from violent felonies to minor misdemeanors). Following the same offenders six years after their initial study, Winner et al. (1997) again found higher recidivism rates for those transferred to criminal court for all offenders except property felons.

Fagan (1996) suggests that criminal court processing *alone,* irrespective of whether the juvenile is incarcerated, produces higher recidivism rates. Controlling for prior record and offense severity, he examined the eight-year recidivism rate of eight hundred fifteen- and sixteen-year-old juvenile offenders charged with robbery or burglary, comparing those charged in juvenile court in New Jersey with matched offenders charged in criminal court under New York's automatic transfer law. Robbery offenders tried in criminal court reoffended faster and at a higher rate than those tried in juvenile court (81.2 percent versus 64.4 percent for juveniles receiving probation; 90.5 percent versus 73.0 percent for juveniles receiving a sentence of confinement), but there was no difference in recidivism for burglary offenders.

Blended sentencing may, however, result in longer or more punitive dispositions in juvenile court. This is not necessarily inconsistent with the court's rehabilitative mission. A developmental-rehabilitative model "recognizes the importance of lessons in accountability; slaps on the wrist fail to serve this purpose" (Scott and Grisso 1997, 187). As explained by Bonta (1996), sanctions provide the setting for service delivery, while the treatment intervention within that setting produces change in offenders. Longer sentences in juvenile court may be needed to effectuate the long-term rehabilitation efforts often necessary for serious and violent offenders, particularly those whose criminal conduct suggests persistent life-course criminality (see Redding 1997; Scott and Grisso 1997). The best treatment regimes provide intensive, multisystemic interventions while also requiring greater accountability by juveniles (Redding 1997; Tate, Reppucci, and Mulvey 1995).[4] Extended juvenile and/or suspended adult sentences may promote rehabilitation and accountability, provided the adult sentence is suspended upon continued good behavior and the sanctions are rehabilitative and community based (see Redding 1997).

Thus, blended sentencing has a number of potential advantages. But as discussed later, blended sentencing also carries a number of possible disadvantages and challenges to the juvenile justice system, including the potential for widening the net of juvenile offenders at risk of receiving adult sanctions. First, we review blended sentencing laws.

3. Blended Sentencing Laws

As of 1999, twenty states had some form of blended sentencing laws. Five basic models of blended sentencing have emerged, as table 4.2 shows. (We label these models following Torbet et al. 1996.)

Blended Sentencing in the Juvenile Court

As the focus of this volume is the juvenile court, we begin by discussing the laws of the ten states having blended sentencing in the juvenile court.

Juvenile-exclusive model. Three states (Massachusetts, Michigan, New Mexico) allow the juvenile court to impose *either* a juvenile or an adult sentence on certain repeat and/or serious offenders.[5] If a juvenile sentence is imposed, the juvenile stays in the juvenile system until age eighteen to

Table 4.2
Blended Sentencing Models

Blended Sentencing in Juvenile Court	Blended Sentencing in Criminal Court
Juvenile-exclusive model May impose juvenile *or* adult sentence	Criminal-exclusive model May impose juvenile *or* adult sentence
Juvenile-inclusive model May impose both juvenile *and* adult sentences (typically, the adult sentence is suspended unless probation is violated)	Criminal-inclusive model May impose *both* juvenile *and* adult sentences (typically, the adult sentence is suspended unless probation is violated)
Juvenile-contiguous model May impose an extended juvenile sentence until the juvenile reaches age 19–21, when procedures are triggered to transfer the juvenile or to determine whether to impose an adult sentence	

twenty-one. If an adult sentence is imposed, juvenile court jurisdiction ends and the juvenile is transferred to the custody of the adult correctional or probational system.

Juvenile-inclusive model. Four states (Connecticut, Kansas, Minnesota, Montana)[6] allow the court to impose *both* a juvenile and adult sentence, with the adult sentence conditionally suspended unless the juvenile violates the terms of the juvenile sentence or commits a new offense. The juvenile has a right to an adversarial hearing to challenge the alleged violation and litigate whether the adult sentence should be imposed. (In Connecticut, the court may impose up to the maximum adult sentence.)

Juvenile-contiguous model. In four states (Colorado, Massachusetts, Rhode Island, Texas),[7] the juvenile court may impose a juvenile sentence *extending* until age eighteen to twenty-one, when a transfer/sentencing hearing or other procedures are triggered to determine if the juvenile should be transferred to serve an adult sentence in the criminal justice system.

Blended sentencing in Massachusetts, Rhode Island, and Texas puts juveniles at risk of receiving lengthy adult sentences. In Massachusetts and Rhode Island, the juvenile court may impose the maximum adult sentence (but may suspend the balance of the sentence imposed).[8] Texas juvenile courts can impose a suspended adult sentence of up to forty years for first-degree murder and aggravated controlled substance felonies.[9] Juveniles serve the adult sentence under adult parole supervision unless paroled before age twenty-one at the discretion of the Texas Youth Commission. Many juveniles are paroled before age twenty-one and are never transferred to the criminal justice system (Dawson, personal communication).

Blended Sentencing in the Criminal Court

Twelve states have blended sentencing in the criminal court.

Criminal-exclusive model. Eight states (California, Colorado, Florida, Idaho, Michigan, Oklahoma, Virginia, West Virginia)[10] give criminal courts the authority to impose *either* an adult or a juvenile sentence (with jurisdiction continuing in the criminal court).

Criminal-inclusive model. Four states (Arkansas, Iowa, Missouri, Virginia)[11] allow the criminal court to impose *both* a juvenile and adult sentence, with the adult sentence conditionally suspended unless the juvenile violates the terms of the juvenile sentence or commits a new offense. Virginia allows the criminal court to impose a suspended adult sentence for violent felonies and a juvenile sentence for other felonies.[12]

Vermont allows for extended juvenile court jurisdiction *and* for suspended adult sentences. Vermont is unique in predicating blended sentencing on a plea of guilty or nolo contendere in criminal court (along with findings that the juvenile is amenable to treatment in the juvenile system and that family court jurisdiction will serve public safety). If these requirements are met, the court imposes the adult sentence but suspends and replaces it with a juvenile sentence, and transfers jurisdiction to the family court.[13] (This procedure is similar to reverse waiver, whereby jurisdiction originates in the criminal court, which exercises its discretion to transfer jurisdiction to the juvenile court.) Before the juvenile turns eighteen, the family court holds a hearing to determine whether to dismiss or impose the adult sentence, release the juvenile, or extend family court jurisdiction until age nineteen.[14]

Many states provide that if the criminal court imposes a juvenile disposition, the finding of guilt is not a criminal conviction but is considered an adjudication of delinquency, with none of the "civil disabilities imposed by a conviction."[15] In these states, the criminal court effectively functions as the juvenile court when it exercises discretion to impose a juvenile sentence. This is consistent with the rehabilitative philosophy underlying a juvenile sentence, since these disabilities (e.g., criminal record, loss of right to serve in the military) interfere with rehabilitation by impeding the juvenile's community reintegration, future job prospects, and life choices.

Colorado and Michigan: Blended Sentencing in Both Courts

Colorado and Michigan have blended sentencing in both the juvenile and criminal courts. In Michigan, a juvenile fourteen or older who commits serious violent felonies may be tried as a juvenile in juvenile court, as an adult in juvenile court if the prosecutor designates the case an adult case (with sentencing as a juvenile, or as an adult if *Kent*-like criteria are met), or tried and sentenced as an adult in criminal court if the prosecutor files a warrant.[16] For all other juveniles, the scheme is similar, except that *Kent*-like waiver criteria must be met for trial and sentencing in criminal court.[17] (However, for juveniles fourteen and older who commit a felony, the presumption is in favor of sentencing as an adult.)[18]

In Colorado, "youthful offenders," who are adjudicated in criminal court, are sentenced as a juvenile or adult, depending on the felony committed.[19] "Aggravated juvenile offenders" are adjudicated in juvenile court. In juvenile court, the law provides a mechanism for transferring a twenty-year-old juvenile to the adult correctional system to serve the remainder of his juvenile sentence (maximum sentence lengths are five years), or for transferring juveniles eighteen and older who are no longer benefiting from programs in the juvenile justice system (as so certified by the Department of Human Services). Otherwise, when the juvenile reaches $20\frac{1}{2}$ years of age, the Department of Human Services files a motion for the court to release the juvenile or transfer custody to the Department of Corrections.

In providing juvenile courts with the flexibility to impose adult sentences or extend jurisdiction until age twenty-one, and criminal courts with the flexibility to impose juvenile sentences, the Colorado and Michigan schemes come the closest to establishing a convergence between the juvenile and criminal courts. The effects of such convergence are uncertain. Some scholars argue for the traditional separation of juvenile and criminal court jurisdiction (e.g., Scott and Grisso 1997; Zimring 1998), others argue for greater convergence between the two systems or for exclusive criminal court jurisdiction and the abolition of juvenile courts (e.g., Ainsworth 1991; Feld 1997).

4. Legal Standards and Procedures for Blended Sentencing in Juvenile Court

Having reviewed the structure of blended sentencing laws, we now review the legal standards and procedures under blended sentencing.

Statutory criteria. Blended sentencing statutes are targeted at those juveniles who meet the criteria for transfer to criminal court under state transfer laws. Rhode Island, for example, requires the court to find that the juvenile is eligible for transfer before blended sentencing may be invoked.[20]

Moving party and burden of proof. In most states, the prosecutor initiates a petition for blended sentencing by filing a pretrial motion with the court. While many statutes do not explicitly mention which party carries the burden of proof, the burden of proving that blended sentencing is warranted generally falls with the prosecutor. The only exception appears to be Kansas, where juveniles fourteen and older who commit certain serious felony offenses bear the burden to rebut a presumption of blended sentencing (thus, operating similar to presumptive transfer laws).[21]

Standard of proof. The standard of proof for determining whether the need for blended sentencing has been shown varies across states, from the preponderance-of-evidence standard to the beyond-a-reasonable-doubt standard. Most states adhere to an intermediate standard of proof—clear and convincing evidence, or in the case of Kansas, "substantial evidence."[22] However, these are the standards for determining whether to trigger blended sentencing, not the standard for adjudication (which requires proof beyond a reasonable doubt).

Decisional criteria. If the prosecutor petitions for blended sentencing and the juvenile meets the statutory age and offense criteria, then the juvenile court judge must decide whether to proceed under blended sentencing authority. Here, statutory criteria provide the decisional standards guiding judicial discretion. In several states, the judge must first hold a probable-cause hearing (which often is part of the hearing on whether to invoke blended sentencing) to determine whether there is probable cause to believe that the juvenile committed the alleged offense(s) covered under the blended sentencing statute.

Many statutes direct the court to consider generally the same factors used in deciding whether to transfer juveniles to criminal court jurisdiction. These factors often parallel or are variants of those set forth by the U.S. Supreme Court in *Kent v. United States* (1966), with three criteria particularly significant: (1) the seriousness of the offense and need to protect the community, (2) the juvenile's maturity, and (3) the juvenile's amenability to treatment and rehabilitation through available services in the juvenile justice system.[23]

Several states require specific judicial findings beyond or in lieu of consideration of the *Kent*-type criteria. New Mexico, a state in which the juvenile court may impose an adult sentence, requires the court to find that the juvenile is not amenable to treatment available in the juvenile system (as do many state transfer laws).[24] But to invoke blended sentencing in Connecticut, the court must only find (based on clear and convincing evidence) that blended sentencing will "serve public safety."[25]

Several states have transfer/sentencing hearings when the juvenile turns age eighteen to twenty-one, to determine whether to impose an adult sentence. In Rhode Island, the court can suspend the adult sentence if it

finds by clear and convincing evidence that the juvenile has been rehabilitated and can be released into the community without endangering
public safety.[26] In Colorado, the Department of Human Services may petition the court for a hearing to release the juvenile on parole, which the
court may do only if it finds based on a preponderance of evidence that
doing so will not jeopardize public safety.[27] (However, the Colorado statute provides no evidentiary standards or decisional criteria for the transfer hearing when the juvenile turns age $20\frac{1}{2}$).

Statutes should guide but not direct courts in deciding whether to invoke blended sentencing and in deciding whether to impose a juvenile,
adult, or extended juvenile sentence. In Vermont, for example, a preponderance of evidence that the juvenile has successfully completed the
juvenile sentence creates a presumption that the juvenile has been rehabilitated, which the state can rebut by clear and convincing evidence, in
which case the court may impose extended jurisdiction or the adult sentence.[28] Kansas has rebuttable presumptions for deciding on blended
sentencing versus transfer, with the burden of proof borne either by the
prosecution or the defense, depending on the juvenile's age and offenses.
Such guidelines help reduce the arbitrary, capricious, and inconsistent
nature of judicial and prosecutorial decision making that has plagued the
juvenile court since its inception (see Allen in this volume, and Redding
1997).

Right to counsel. All states provide juveniles with the right to counsel
at the pretrial hearing on whether to trigger blended sentencing, at trial,
and (in Colorado, Massachusetts, and Rhode Island) at the subsequent
transfer/sentencing hearing on whether to impose the adult sentence.

Right to present evidence and open hearings. Juveniles have the right to
present evidence and cross-examine witnesses at the pretrial hearing on
blended sentencing, at trial, and (in Colorado, Massachusetts, and Rhode
Island) at the subsequent transfer/sentencing hearing. Many states provide for open hearings. In some states, the victim also has the right to make
a victim impact statement and submit evidence.[29]

Right to jury trial. Normally, there is no right to a jury trial in juvenile
court because only a finding of "delinquency" (rather than a criminal
conviction) is imposed. Under blended sentencing, all states provide the
right to a jury trial in juvenile court. But in Connecticut, the juvenile
must first waive the statutory right to a jury trial in juvenile court, in order
to avail himself of blended sentencing in lieu of transfer to criminal
court.[30]

Right to appeal. Since the pretrial hearing on whether to trigger
blended sentencing is neither a final adjudication of guilt nor a sentencing
disposition, it normally will not be appealable until after the juvenile has

been tried and sentenced. But several states explicitly provide the right to an interlocutory appeal of the pretrial decision on blended sentencing, thus providing juvenile defendants with leverage in plea bargaining. Of course, there always is the right to appeal adjudicatory and sentencing decisions.

5. Legal Analysis of Blended Sentencing Laws

Blended sentencing requires procedural changes to traditional juvenile court proceedings—changes that necessitate an expansion of court resources. "States must provide for jury trials, bail, and other criminal justice system rights for juveniles subject to blended sentencing or incarceration in adult correctional facilities" (National Criminal Justice Association 1997, 49). Feld (1997) notes the lack of procedural protections in typical juvenile court proceedings, but most blended sentencing laws provide the full panoply of due process rights when there is the possibility of an adult sentence, including the right to trial by jury.

However, it may be questionable whether a juvenile court adjudication does, in fact, provide the full level of due process afforded in criminal court. Juvenile courts may often follow evidentiary and procedural rules less rigorously than adult courts (Sanborn 1998), particularly in transfer or blended sentencing hearings, which are viewed as nonadjudicatory preliminary hearings (see *In re SJM* 1996). Will juvenile court judges and others in the juvenile system, unaccustomed to operating under criminal court trial procedures, be fully up to the task, or will they revert to laxer juvenile procedures? Will juries be more inclined to convict in the belief that a lengthy adult sentence is unlikely in juvenile court? These questions remain to be answered. But it is mistaken to idealize the level of due process available in the criminal court by "exaggerat[ing] the contrasts between juvenile court procedures, pictured in most glowing terms, and those of the criminal court system, viewed in a worst possible and quite inaccurate light" (Tanenhaus this volume, 39 n. 7, quoting Tappan 1949, 179–180). In fact, "[criminal court] justice is dispensed through waivers and pleas negotiated by defense attorneys who are often less than zealous and well-prepared advocates" (Rosenberg 1993, 173).

Plea bargaining: blended sentencing in lieu of transfer. In most states, the prosecutor petitions the court for blended sentencing, in lieu of charges being filed in criminal court or statutorily mandated automatic transfer to criminal court. This sets up a classic plea bargaining situation: prosecutors use the threat of criminal court transfer as leverage against juveniles to waive their right to a jury trial, plead guilty, and/or agree to a certain sentence. (Likewise, many transfer hearings are uncontested

because they are the result of plea bargains [Podkopacz and Feld 1995].)
The quality of counsel juveniles receive in the context of plea bargaining
may be problematic. Juveniles' right to a jury trial may be compromised
by attorneys' proclivity to encourage defendants to plead guilty to the
charges or accept a plea to a lesser charge, since attorneys make money
and save time when there is no trial (Mears 1998).

Right to jury trial. In Connecticut, where the juvenile court can impose
up to the maximum adult sentence (which is suspended),[31] a juvenile is
required to waive the right to a jury trial in order to avail himself of
blended sentencing in lieu of transfer to criminal court. Though the right
to a jury trial is constitutionally required if an adult sentence is imposed,
it is unlikely that a constitutional challenge would be successful here,
given that the juvenile voluntarily elects to waive the right in return for
blended sentencing in the juvenile court. On the other hand, the pressure
will be great to waive a jury trial to avoid criminal court, drawing into
question how truly voluntary any waiver will be. (Similar situations arise
in adult criminal cases where a reduced sentence is given if the defendant
pleads guilty and does not go to trial.) It is possible, but rather unlikely,
that requiring the juvenile to waive the right to a jury trial under these
circumstances will be found unconstitutional by some courts.

The lack of a jury trial does raise troubling due process concerns, however. Indeed, the denial of a jury trial is perhaps what still makes the
modern juvenile court sometimes "the worst of both worlds" for juveniles (Guggenheim and Hertz 1998, quoting *In re Gault,* 387 U.S. at 18).
The quality of judicial fact finding in juvenile court is open to question; it
appears that juvenile court judges often convict on insufficient evidence
(Guggenheim and Hertz 1998). Sanborn (1998) argues that the juvenile
court's adjudication may be influenced by concerns about whether the
juvenile needs court intervention. An adjudication of delinquency may
be based not only on criminal culpability, but also on the extent to which
the court feels that delinquency adjudication is necessary for delivering
services to juveniles from poor, dysfunctional families. Judges, however,
may be less prone to convict on insufficient evidence if an adult sentence
will be imposed and/or if juvenile adjudications can be used in future
adult prosecutions.

Adjudicative competence. When adult sentencing is possible, there
should be a hearing on the juvenile's adjudicative competence (competence to stand trial), particularly for juveniles under ages fourteen to fifteen (Bonnie and Grisso in press). There is a danger that young, incompetent juveniles will be sentenced as adults in juvenile court. While some
states have recognized that juveniles must be competent in juvenile court,
it remains very unclear exactly what this requires, with only one court to

date predicating competence on developmental maturity (Bonnie and Grisso in press). For adults, adjudicative competence entails the ability to understand legal rights and proceedings and consult with counsel, as well as rational decision-making capacity about the case (*Drope v. Missouri* 1975; *Dusky v. United States* 1960, *Godinez v. Moran* 1993). The standard for juveniles may implicitly include additional factors, such as developmental maturity, and enhanced procedural protections may be necessary. For example, Bonnie and Grisso (in press) suggest that trial courts undertake extended questioning of the juvenile to probe "the possible influence of developmental features of adolescence that can interfere with effective self-presentation and self-interested decision-making." Juveniles should not be allowed to waive their right to counsel until they have consulted court-appointed or private counsel. Enhanced protections should be afforded to ensure that waivers are fully voluntary, knowing, and intelligent (Redding 1997).

Open hearings. Many states provide for open hearings and victim comments during blended sentencing hearings. This has the potential for increasing the number of punitive adult sentences in response to victim statements and public sentiment, thus challenging the rehabilitative mission of juvenile court. As Chief Justice Rehnquist noted,[32] a lack of confidentiality in juvenile proceedings is likely to have counterrehabilitative effects. It may stigmatize the juvenile and impede his reintegration with his family and community (Laubenstein 1995). But there is another side to this question. Feld (1997, 92) argues that "[t]he closed, informal, and confidential nature of delinquency proceedings reduces the visibility and accountability of the justice process and precludes external checks on coercive interventions." For this reason, the Coalition for Juvenile Justice (1998) recommends that the adjudicatory phase of delinquency proceedings be open.

6. Constitutionality of Blended Sentencing

There are several possible constitutional challenges to blended sentencing laws. One challenge, based on the due process clause of the Fourteenth Amendment, is that due process is violated by imprisoning a person who has not been convicted of a criminal offense (Dawson 1988). A juvenile found guilty in juvenile court is only "adjudicated delinquent."[33] However, the due process claim is unlikely to succeed since the juvenile has all the legal rights (e.g., right to counsel, jury trial) as an adult in criminal court (Dawson 1988). In some states, like Texas, the juvenile actually gets *more* rights than an adult defendant since an adjudication of delinquency under blended sentencing "does not impose any civil disability ordinarily resulting from a conviction"[34] (e.g., the juvenile does not have a criminal record, retains the right to vote, etc).

The other main constitutional challenge, based on the equal protection clause of the Fourteenth Amendment, is that relatively similarly situated juveniles will be treated differently under the law depending on whether the prosecutor elects to proceed against them via delinquency proceedings, transfer, or blended sentencing jurisdiction (Dawson 1988). But as Frost and Bonnie discuss in this volume, appellate courts generally have not found transfer laws unconstitutional on this basis. It is unlikely that courts would do so with blended sentencing laws. Dawson's (1988) analysis makes clear that, as compared to a transferred juvenile, a juvenile proceeded against under blended sentencing is likely to receive a shorter sentence. In states where the adult sentence is conditionally suspended, the juvenile often is released or paroled before serving the adult sentence.

Some blended sentencing laws require a transfer hearing or other procedures when the juvenile nears the limit of juvenile court jurisdiction, to determine if an adult sentence should be imposed. A possible constitutional challenge is that the transfer/sentencing hearing (several years after the dispositional hearing following adjudication) violates the constitutional prohibition against double jeopardy. This claim would fail. The transfer hearing deals only with sentencing, not adjudication, and the juvenile never is convicted of a criminal offense.

7. Effects of Blended Sentencing Laws

Net narrowing or net widening? Does blended sentencing narrow the net of juveniles channeled into the criminal justice system, serving as an effective alternative to transfer? Or does it widen the net of juveniles subject to adult sentences, serving as a supplement to existing transfer laws? Will some blended sentencing laws do both? While blended sentencing laws are relatively new, available case outcome and sentencing data and legislative histories provide some preliminary information on these questions.

Texas. We turn first to the Texas law. Enacted in 1987, it is the oldest blended sentencing law in the nation. The legislature enacted the law in response to accounts of very serious violent offenses by juveniles. "Instead of providing for transfer of a case from the juvenile justice system to the criminal justice system, the legislature creates a new, third justice system—one that is part juvenile and part criminal—specifically for the handling of extremely violent offenses committed by juveniles" (Dawson 1988, 947). The law was enacted for two specific purposes: (1) to serve as an alternative to transfer of fifteen- and sixteen-year-old juveniles, for whom the length of confinement available in the juvenile system was insufficient, and (2) to respond to violent offenses committed by thirteen- and fourteen-year-olds, who were below states' minimum transfer age of fifteen. But the law also reaches juveniles ten and older who commit certain serious violent felonies.

The law, therefore, apparently was intended to have *both* net-narrowing (for older juveniles) and net-widening (vis-à-vis younger juveniles) effects in terms of the numbers of juveniles subject to adult punishment. As Dawson (1990) suggests, the law in Texas protects some fifteen- and sixteen-year-olds from transfer to criminal court. It also greatly expands the reach of adult sentences available in juvenile court to include juveniles as young as ten years of age. However, without such a provision, the Texas legislature surely would have lowered the minimum transfer age, perhaps to as young as thirteen (Dawson 1990). Between 1988 and late 1998, a total of 296 cases were transferred to the criminal justice system under blended sentencing but 287 cases were not transferred.

Dawson (1990) analyzes the fifty-three cases processed under the original Texas law for the first sixteen months after its enactment. These early data indicate both net widening and net narrowing, consistent with the goals of the Texas blended sentencing statute. Fifty-three percent of the blended sentencing cases were transfer eligible; in these cases, blended sentencing "saved" juveniles from criminal court. But 47 percent of blended sentencing cases were *not* transfer eligible. In these cases, blended sentencing channeled into the net of possible adult sentences younger juveniles who otherwise would not be subject to them under existing transfer laws. In addition, prosecutors took an offense-driven approach in deciding which cases to refer for blended sentencing; 60 percent of the cases had no prior offenses and only two involved juveniles previously committed to juvenile justice correctional facilities. But without the blended sentencing law, it is believed that the Texas legislature would have lowered the minimum transfer age (Dawson 1988), perhaps to include most of the younger juveniles brought into the net under the blended sentencing law. Moreover, many of the cases handled under blended sentencing do not result in the imposition of an adult sentence (Dawson 1988).

In drafting the law, Dawson says:

> I imagined that the statute would be invoked very selectively—
> that it would be reserved for only the most aggravated cases
> within the limited category of very serious offenses covered by
> the law. I also imagined that once a prosecutor sought to invoke
> the statute the case could be pursued with vigor due, in part,

to the very selectivity that marked the decision to invoke the statute. Finally, I imagined that in those cases in which the respondent was adjudicated of having committed a covered offense, the sentences imposed would be very long, again because of the selectivity in administering the law. (Dawson 1990, 1935)

But Dawson found that the practices of local prosecutors' offices varied widely across the state, that the blended sentencing law appears to have been used as a plea bargaining mechanism by prosecutors, and that judges and prosecutors often used the law merely to ensure a court-determined (rather than youth commission–determined) length of confinement. (The 1995 statutory revisions dispense with the judicial transfer hearing. The Texas Youth Commission now has discretion to parole the juvenile before age twenty-one, at which time the juvenile is automatically transferred to adult parole supervision.)

Texas prosecutors varied substantially in their use of the blended sentencing law, some using it aggressively, others cautiously. In the four largest Texas counties, eligible cases referred to the grand jury under blended sentencing ranged from 0 to 87 percent. In Dallas County, the district attorney's office had a policy of proceeding under blended sentencing in every case fitting the statutory criteria. As the chief of the Juvenile Division of the Dallas County District Attorney's Office said, "[T]he approved petition [for blended sentencing] can 'make it easier for us to dispose of a case [because] the defense attorney knows the stakes are greater'" (see Dawson 1990, 1919). Data suggest that plea bargaining often occurred in the context of blended sentencing. A jury trial was waived in 92 percent of the cases in which no adult sentence was imposed, but was waived in only 63 percent of the cases where an adult sentence was imposed, a statistically significant difference. Even in the cases where an adult sentence was imposed without a jury, it is likely that waiver of a jury trial was plea bargained by the prosecution in return for not seeking transfer of the case to criminal court (Dawson 1990). Even though the adult sentence often is not imposed, use of blended sentencing as a plea bargaining mechanism produces a net-widening effect in the numbers of juveniles brought under the umbrella of possible adult sanctions.

In addition to empirical data, how state legislatures choose to revise or expand their blended sentencing laws also speaks to the issue of net widening. Do they expand the reach of blended sentencing by increasing the types of eligible offenses or offenders?

There is a danger, for example, that blended jurisdiction will be a mechanism used by state legislatures for lowering the age at which juveniles can be subject to adult sanctions, even below the age provided for in existing transfer laws. Massachusetts and New Mexico, however, abolished transfer (except for homicide cases) after enactment of their blended sentencing laws (Miller 1997a); in these states, blended sentencing had the effect of narrowing the net of transfer laws.

Most states have not had occasion to revise substantially their blended sentencing laws since these laws have, for the most part, been enacted fairly recently. The Texas law, enacted in 1987, is a notable exception. Texas did substantially widen the net of blended sentencing. In 1995, the Texas legislature expanded the number of offenses eligible for blended sentencing from five to thirty, to include aggravated robbery, aggravated assault, aggravated controlled substance felonies, and solicitation. (Though almost all of the blended sentencing prosecutions under the new eligible offense categories are for aggravated robbery and aggravated assault, according to recent Texas Youth Commission data.) The legislature also increased the maximum sentence length from thirty to forty years. However, a significant change in the Texas blended sentencing procedures may substantially decrease the number of juveniles transferred to the criminal justice system. The 1995 statutory revisions dispense with the required transfer hearing at age $17\frac{1}{2}$. Instead, the Texas Youth Commission has discretion to parole the juvenile. If the juvenile is still serving his sentence at age twenty-one, he is automatically transferred to *adult parole supervision,* and can be sentenced to adult prison only if parole is violated and subsequently revoked.

Minnesota. An analysis of blended sentencing cases handled in Hennepin County (which adjudicates about 40 percent of Minnesota's court cases) perhaps also suggests a net-widening effect in Minnesota (Podkopacz 1998). Minnesota's blended sentencing law, enacted in 1993, was designed primarily to handle juveniles without a significant prior delinquency background who commit a serious first offense (Brummel 1998; Podkopacz personal communication). However, the 31.8 percent of juvenile arrestees for whom prosecutors filed a petition for blended sentencing had no prior record, indicating that the seriousness of the instant offense drives many blended sentencing prosecutions in Minnesota. In addition, prosecutors are petitioning the court to transfer many juveniles who commit a transfer-eligible offense. (Minnesota's law provides that a prosecutor may petition for blended sentencing in one of two ways. The prosecutor may initially file a petition for extended jurisdiction in the juvenile court. Or the prosecutor may petition for transfer to criminal court as well as blended sentencing authority, whereby the criminal court may impose a juvenile sentence and a suspended adult sentence.) About 34 percent of juveniles motioned for transfer (called "certification" in

Minnesota) had no previous out-of-home placements, and 31.9 percent had no prior delinquency adjudications or a misdemeanor adjudication only.

Sentencing. What are the dispositional outcomes under blended sentencing? Does blended sentencing tend to result in less or more punitive sentences for juveniles? How often are adult sentences imposed?

Once again, we turn to the Texas example. Because of plea bargaining, often no adult sentence or a very short one is imposed. In 35 percent of the cases in which sentencing was imposed by the judge (rather than a jury), the judge imposed a juvenile sentence followed by a brief sentence to an adult correctional facility of a few weeks or months, apparently using blended sentencing to deliver a "wake-up call" to serious offenders (Dawson 1988).

Weinmann (1995) reports the outcomes of 209 transfer hearings (under blended sentencing) between 1989 and 1994 (before the 1995 statutory revisions). The overall transfer rate was 44 percent (the rate increased from 30 percent in 1989 to 55 percent in 1994) and transfer rates varied greatly by offense type. While 78.6 percent of juveniles convicted of capital murder were transferred, only 39.4 percent of those convicted of noncapital murder were transferred. For cases in which a determinate sentence was imposed, sentence lengths varied from 1.25 to 30 years (the statutory maximum), with a mean sentence length of 15 years (Dawson 1990). (No data are available on actual time served). Thus, Texas juvenile courts were imposing adult sentences in a significant number of cases, producing substantial and reasonably certain sanctions in the juvenile court.

Judges' sentencing decisions in the Texas transfer hearings were heavily influenced by the juvenile's conduct while in juvenile facilities, which was taken as an indication of the juvenile's treatment amenability (Weinmann 1995). Judges followed the recommendation of the Texas Youth Commission in 80.8 percent of cases. In 12.5 percent of cases, judges transferred the juvenile in order to ensure an adequate sentence length, contrary to recommendations of the youth commission (Weinmann 1995). The youth commission recommended transfer in only 38 percent of cases, recommending release or an extended juvenile sentence in 62 percent of cases. Weinmann concluded that

> juvenile courts, prosecuting attorneys and the state administrative personnel all appear to be taking very responsible positions that serve the goals of the Act. The decision whether to transfer or to recommit/release the juvenile has, on the whole, been rationally related to factors which seem to be indicative of the juveniles' potential for rehabilitation. At the same time, society's

interest in retribution has not been ignored . . . the [blended sentencing act] is neither a "free ride" for juveniles nor a mere alter-ego of the adult criminal justice system. (Weinmann 1995, 29)

Dawson (personal communication) reports that judges set reasonable probation conditions and that actors in the system do not seek to impose onerous probation conditions that might readily be violated.[35]

Needed research. As the foregoing review indicates, data are sorely lacking on the efficacy of the new blended sentencing laws and no systematic evaluations have been conducted. Many questions remain unanswered. For example:

- Which cases do prosecutors and judges select for blended sentencing?
- Which cases do they exclude? What factors are relevant in their decision making, and how do decisions vary across and within jurisdictions?
- What are the procedures followed in the revocation of juvenile sentences and the imposition of adult prison sentences, including the adherence to due process requirements?
- What is the nature and quality of the decision making regarding revocation of juvenile sentences and the imposition of adult sentences?
- Does blended sentencing successfully target the intended offender groups (e.g., likely career offenders) or is there net widening?
- Which blended sentencing provisions increase or decrease the number of juveniles sentenced and incarcerated as adults?
- What are the case outcomes under various combinations of sentencing authority (e.g., juvenile court versus juvenile corrections agencies versus criminal court)?
- What is the crime reduction impact of various blended sentencing laws?

First, research must build an understanding of how blended sentencing systems operate in practice. A second research priority is to evaluate individual states' blended sentencing laws to compare the outcomes of various blended sentence models. A third research priority is to compare studies of different states' blended sentencing laws. Such studies will necessarily be limited to quasi experiments aimed at evaluating natural experiments as provided by state laws. Opportunities to conduct similarly designed evaluations of the five major blended sentencing models should be sought, with an emphasis on comparative studies in similar states having different models of blended sentencing.

Other research questions should be addressed through longitudinal studies of representative blended sentence and non–blended sentence juvenile offender samples in selected sites. For example, longitudinal studies of the crime reduction impact of various blended sentence models on criminal careers, including the maintenance and desistance of criminal careers, are needed. Evaluations are also needed to determine those juvenile justice system program interventions that work best with life-course-persistent offenders (see next section) in blended sentencing systems. Which programs work best, with various combinations of sanctions, and at different points in life-course-persistent careers? Research is needed on how progression in the pathways to life-course-persistent criminality is impeded (or not) by blended sentencing interventions. The Texas blended sentence structure provides an excellent opportunity to examine the effects of graduated sanctions within a blended sentencing system (see Tracy and Kempf-Leonard 1998).

Importantly, outcome studies are needed to determine whether blended sentencing serves as a successful alternative to transfer by narrowing the net of serious juvenile offenders processed in the criminal justice system, or whether it is a punitive supplement to transfer, only widening the net of juveniles subject to criminal sanctions. To answer this question, empirical data are needed from blended sentencing states on whether juveniles proceeded against under blended sentencing differ in important ways from those selected for transfer, the impact of blended sentencing laws on transfer rates, the percentage of juveniles transferred at the conditional transfer hearings held (in some states) when the juvenile ages out of the juvenile system, sentence lengths under blended sentencing (particularly in those states allowing the imposition of adult sentences), and legislative responses to blended sentencing. Unfortunately, to our knowledge, research on these important issues is not yet under way.

In our view, blended sentencing laws will be successful to the extent they (1) reduce the total percentage of juvenile offenders transferred to criminal court, (2) target only serious and violent juvenile offenders who have an extensive prior offending history, (3) moderate the punitive bite of adult sanctions and provide juveniles with an incentive to reform, and/or (4) provide state legislatures with a politically viable alternative to more expansive transfer laws. Outcome data of the kind listed above will help answer whether blended sentencing is a successful alternative to transfer or merely a net-widening supplement. If the latter is the case, we would expect blended sentencing to have the opposite effects of those listed above, perhaps increasing the number and type of juvenile offenders transferred to criminal court or otherwise subject to punitive adult sanctions, increasing their sentence lengths, and/or resulting in the frequent revocation of probation and the imposition of adult sentences. In addition, legislatures might use blended sentencing laws as vehicles for lowering the age and/or for expanding the offense types for which juveniles are subject to adult sanctions.

8. Effects of Blended Sentencing on the Juvenile Justice System

Blended sentencing presents many challenges to the juvenile justice system. As a fundamental matter, what Zimring in this volume calls the "Byzantine complexity" of blended sentencing laws creates confusion and uncertainty. "[C]onfusion exists about [blended sentencing] statutes and the rules and regulations governing them, especially with respect to the juvenile's status during case processing and subsequent placement" (Torbet et al. 1996, 15). The selection of sentencing options is confusing "for all system actors, including offenders, judges, prosecutors, and corrections administrators" (ibid.). In addition to procedural confusion, system ambivalence concerning what to do about serious and violent offenders is evident (Torbet et al. 1996). Arguably, blended sentencing suggests "a lack of resolve on two fronts: (1) coming to closure on (i.e., removing) certain juveniles for whom the juvenile justice system is inadequate, or (2) bolstering the resolve and resources of the juvenile justice system to adequately address the needs of these very young offenders" (Torbet et al. 1996, 15).

To the extent blended sentencing in juvenile courts produces a de facto or de jure convergence with criminal court processing, it may compromise the rehabilitative philosophy of juvenile courts, which were designed as a rehabilitative justice system apart from the retributive criminal justice system. As Zimring argues in this volume, blended sentencing has the potential to undermine the juvenile court's mission: net-widening the reach of adult sanctions imposed by juvenile courts and casting juvenile courts in the role of criminal courts that impose adult sentences—sometimes lengthy adult sentences. All this may erode the courts' rehabilitative mission, not just for juveniles under blended sentencing authority, but through the spillover effects to the juvenile court generally.

The alternative of expanded transfer provisions, however, appears to be a greater threat to the juvenile courts' ability to maintain its jurisdiction. Transfer has long been viewed as ideologically inconsistent with the mission of the juvenile court, as Tanenhaus discusses in this volume. Moreover, the very frequent result of a blended sentencing adjudication is no adult sentence or a short one. The lengthy adult sentence options available in Massachusetts and Rhode Island are disfiguring sentences providing no "room to reform," and do not take into account the diminished culpability of juvenile offenders. But there is little doubt that the very serious offenders (mainly those convicted of murder) receiving such sentences under blended sentencing authority would otherwise have been transferred to criminal court, where they may have received harsher sentences, including life imprisonment without parole (see Logan 1998) or even the death penalty (see Amnesty International 1998).

Some suggest that juvenile courts are irrelevant if they sentence like adult courts (see Ainsworth 1991). A convergence of juvenile with adult jurisdiction through blended sentencing may prevent transfers to criminal court while responding effectively to public safety concerns, preserve the juvenile court's jurisdiction and rehabilitative treatment it may offer, and avoid "the inconsistency and injustice played out in a binary either/or juvenile versus adult" transfer system (Feld 1993, 419). Moreover, juvenile court judges are far more experienced in juvenile justice, have a greater understanding of juveniles' developmental and mental health needs, are more familiar with the various community-based treatment options available for juveniles, and given the historically rehabilitative ideal of the juvenile court, are more likely to espouse a rehabilitative (or rehabilitative/punitive) philosophy of juvenile justice.[36] "[A] juvenile court can better recognize and accommodate the reduced culpability and more limited trial competence of younger offenders . . . [and] is more likely to utilize dispositional strategies, goals, and approaches that are grounded in developmental knowledge" (Scott and Grisso 1997, 188). Fifty-five percent of criminal court judges in Virginia said they had inadequate training in child development and community services to handle juvenile cases (Virginia Commission on Youth 1996).

While theoretically there is no reason why criminal courts cannot effectuate special sentencing and confinement for serious juvenile offenders (Feld 1997; Zimring 1998), rehabilitative dispositions are more consistent with juvenile court philosophy and practice. Giving juvenile courts authority to impose adult sentences "effectuate[s] the goal of assuring public confidence by imposing a proportional sanction *while also invoking the rehabilitative services available to the juvenile court*" (*State v. R.G.D.*, 527 A.2d, at 840). In addition, blended sentencing may produce a more unified juvenile justice system having greater continuity and accountability in handling the "hard cases," rather than the present system of first- and last-resort sanctions alternating between rehabilitation and punishment (see Singer 1998). "Adolescence and criminal careers develop along a continuum; the current bifurcation between the two justice systems confounds efforts to respond consistently to young career offenders" (Feld 1998).

Finally, an effect on both the juvenile and criminal justice systems is that blended sentencing will make juvenile court records readily accessible for consideration in adult sentencing decisions. Currently in many states, juvenile records are inaccessible to prosecutors and criminal courts, or they fail to make use of them (Miller 1997a). Even when such records are readily accessible to criminal courts, they are more likely to be used, understood, and updated by juvenile courts, which have experience in compiling and considering juvenile histories. Juvenile court records are critically important for making informed sentencing decisions because a juvenile's social history, particularly offending history, is the best predictor of future criminality (see Gottfredson 1997; Redding 1997; Wolfgang, Thornberry, and Figlio 1987). Delinquency adjudications in juvenile court may not have the same reliability and due process protections of a criminal conviction (Sanborn 1998), but currently it often is the case that juveniles with significant juvenile offense histories are tried in criminal court as "first-time recidivists" because the court does not have access to the juvenile record (Sanborn 1998).

9. Preferred Blended Sentencing Schemes

It is likely that blended sentencing will be adopted by an increasing number of states as a transfer alternative for handling many serious juvenile offenders.[37] What are preferred ways of structuring juvenile and criminal justice system authority over serious juvenile offenders that simultaneously moderates the punitive bite of transfer while increasing accountability and punishment in the juvenile court?

First, it is preferable to have blended sentencing in juvenile court rather than the criminal court. We should minimize the number of juveniles transferred to criminal court (Redding 1997, 1999). Criminal courts probably will be less sensitive to the immaturity and mental health problems of many juvenile offenders, who may be negatively influenced by the criminal culture of adult courts. Importantly, extant research indicates that criminal court prosecution does not deter juvenile crime, that while juveniles are more likely to receive longer and more serious sentences in criminal court they often may serve less time than they would if sentenced in juvenile court, and that criminal court processing per se produces higher recidivism rates for most offenders (Howell 1996; Redding 1999). These research findings to date argue against criminal court jurisdiction over juveniles, even if immaturity is a mitigating factor via a "youth discount" at sentencing in criminal court (see Feld 1997). Moreover, criminal court judges infrequently impose juvenile sentences when they have authority to do so (see Virginia Commission on Youth 1996; Bishop personal communication).

Second, the best blended sentencing schemes maintain jurisdiction in the juvenile court, with the adult or extended juvenile sentence conditionally suspended provided the juvenile is successfully rehabilitated and does not commit a new offense. This offers juvenile offenders a "last chance" at rehabilitation within the juvenile system and "the advantage of determining whether to transfer [to the adult system] at a point in the proceedings when the decision-maker has access to all relevant background information on the offense and on the offender" (Clarke 1996, 4). It allows flexibility in crafting sentencing dispositions responsive to the juvenile's progress in rehabilitation while maintaining the possible consequences of an adult sentence should the juvenile fail to respond to treatment. Dichotomous sentencing schemes, whereby the juvenile court imposes either a juvenile or an adult sentence, are less desirable. They do rely on the juvenile courts' expertise by maintaining the sentencing decision in juvenile court. But if an adult sentence is imposed (and not suspended), the juvenile is transferred to the adult system, losing the juvenile justice system's rehabilitative benefits and the incentive to respond to treatment in order to avoid the consequence of an adult sentence. This is particularly the case in states that may impose lengthy adult sentences once the juvenile ages out of the juvenile system.

Third, under blended sentencing, the juvenile court judge should be vested with the decision-making authority about whether to transfer a juvenile to the criminal justice system, as opposed to automatic transfer to the criminal justice system once the juvenile reaches the jurisdictional age limit of the juvenile court. Automatic transfer (with substantial adult sentences) provides no incentive or possibility for juveniles to reform. Automatic transfer provisions often are overinclusive (Howell 1996) and do not effectively target those juveniles who should be subject to adult sanctions. Studies of the three main transfer mechanisms (judicial transfer, automatic transfer, and prosecutor direct-file) suggest that juvenile court judges do the best job of selecting for transfer the truly serious, violent, and chronic offenders (Howell 1996). Historically, transfer has been used most sparingly when initiated by prosecutors (as with blended sentencing in all states) but adjudicated by juvenile court judges, as both Dawson and Zimring discuss in this volume.

Fourth, if blended sentencing systems are to serve as an alternative to transfer, then they should be structured to have maximum impact on life-course-persistent offenders, who are responsible for as much as 75 percent of the violent crimes committed by adolescents (Loeber, Farrington, and Waschbusch 1998). A good fit should be achieved between the position of delinquents along the pathways toward life-course-persistent offenders' careers (see Loeber 1996) and sanctions, which are graduated in concert with progression toward life-course persistence.[38] Life-course-persistent offenders are the most dangerous adolescent offenders and are most likely to become career criminals. These offenders should be handled in the juvenile justice system until such time as it proves ineffective in intervening in their life-course-persistent offending careers. Upon aging out of the juvenile justice system or failing in it prior to reaching the maximum age of extended juvenile court jurisdiction, life-course-persistent juvenile offenders should be transferred under blended sentencing to serve their suspended adult sentence in youthful offender programs in the criminal justice system. Unlike "adolescence-limited offenders," who limit their offenses to the adolescent period, life-course-persistent offenders begin committing offenses before the adolescent period and continue during adolescence and adulthood (Moffitt 1993; Moffitt et al. 1996; see Elliott 1994). Three criteria distinguish adolescence-limited offenders: onset of offending after age eleven to thirteen (Elliott 1994; Moffitt 1993), distance from crime by age eighteen (Moffitt 1993; Tracy and Kempf-Leonard 1996), and a lack of progression in offense seriousness (Loeber, Keenan, and Zhang 1997). Five criteria predict life-course-persistent offending: (1) early onset, (2) active offending during adolescence, (3) offense specialization, (4) offense seriousness, and (5) offense escalation (Loeber and Hay 1997; Tracy and Kempf-Leonard 1996). The percentage of juvenile offenders who are life-course-persistent offenders is relatively small and they account for a sizeable percentage of all juvenile crime (Tracy and Kempf-Leonard 1996).

Ideally, judicial transfer/sentencing decisions under blended sentencing would be informed by the use of objective, empirically based risk/needs assessment instruments, and decision-making criteria should include evidence of life-course-persistent offending. While substantial work on risk assessment remains before adolescence-limited offenders can be distinguished from life-course-persistent offenders at an acceptable level of reliability, it is likely that reliable technologies will become available within the next decade. Research results supporting the validity of risk assessments "have increased dramatically in recent years" (Andrews 1996, 43), and risk assessment instruments have been validated for juvenile probation and parole populations (see Bonta 1996; National Council on Crime and Delinquency 1996a, 1996b; Wiebush et al. 1995). These instruments are designed to estimate the likelihood of reoffending within a given time period (e.g., eighteen to twenty-four months) and are based on the statistical relationship between youth characteristics (risk factors) and recidivism rates (see Wiebush et al. 1995).

10. Conclusion

Blended sentencing carries a number of potential benefits and risks. It may provide an effective "middle ground" alternative for dealing with serious and violent juvenile offenders, serving as an alternative to transfer to criminal court, which research shows to have counterrehabilitative effects on juveniles. Effective blended sentencing laws aim to enhance community protection, hold juveniles accountable while providing an incentive to respond to rehabilitative treatment, and allow flexibility in crafting sentencing responsive to the juvenile's progress in rehabilitation. Many statutes provide the consequence of an adult sanction if a juvenile commits a new offense or does not respond to treatment in the juvenile system.

At the same time, blended sentencing carries risks, and it will present challenges to juvenile justice policy and practice. Legislatures and judges must guard against using blended sentencing as a mechanism for widening the net of adult sanctions over increasing numbers of juvenile offenders and be vigilant in ensuring that the due process protections in juvenile court are real rather than illusory. Otherwise, blended sentencing will not be an effective alternative to waiver. It will serve as a punitive supplement to the already counterrehabilitative and "permanently disfiguring" criminal justice system.

References
Cases Cited

Drope v. Missouri, 420 U.S. 162 (1975).
Dusky v. United States, 362 U.S. 402 (1960).
Godinez v. Moran, 509 U.S. 389 (1993).
In re Gault, 387 U.S. 1, 87 S. Ct 1428, 18 L. Ed. 2d 527 (1967).
In re SJM, 922 S.W.2d 241 (Tex. Civ. App. 1996).
Kent v. United States, 383 U.S. 541 (1966).
State v. R.G.D., 527 A.2d 834 (N.J. Super. 1987).

Other References

Ainsworth, Janet E. 1991. "Re-imagining Childhood and Reconstructing the Legal Order: The Case for Abolishing the Juvenile Court." *North Carolina Law Review* 69:1083.
Albert, Rodney L. 1998. *Juvenile Accountability Incentive Block Grants Program, Fact Sheet #76.* April. Washington: U.S. Dept. of Justice, Office of Juvenile Justice and Delinquency Prevention.
Amnesty International. 1998. *Betraying the Young: Human Rights Violations against Children in the U.S. Justice System.* New York: Amnesty International.

Andrews, Don A. 1996. "Criminal Recidivism Is Predictable and Can Be Influenced: An Update." *Forum on Corrections Research* 8:42.

Belluck, Pam. 1998. "Fighting Youth Crime, Some States Blend Adult and Juvenile Justice." *The New York Times,* February 11, sec. A, 1, 26.

Bishop, Donna M., Charles E. Frazier, Lonn Lanza-Kaduce, and Lawrence Winner. 1996. "The Transfer of Juveniles to Criminal Court: Does It Make a Difference?" *Crime and Delinquency* 42:171.

Bonnie, Richard J., and Thomas Grisso. In press. "Adjudicative Competence and Youthful Offenders." In *Youth on Trial.* Edited by T. Grisso and R. Schwartz. Chicago: University of Chicago Press.

Bonta, James. 1996. "Risk-Needs Assessment and Treatment." In *Choosing Correctional Options That Work.* Edited by A. T. Harland. Thousand Oaks, Calif.: Sage.

Brummel, Paula R. 1998. "Doing Adult Time for Juvenile Crime: When the Charge, Not the Conviction, Spells Prison for Kids." *Law and Inequality* 16:541.

Clarke, Elizabeth E. 1996. "A Case for Reinventing Juvenile Transfer: The Record of Transfer of Juvenile Offenders to Criminal Court in Cook County, Illinois." *Juvenile and Family Court Journal* 47:3.

Coalition for Juvenile Justice. 1998. *A Celebration or a Wake? The Juvenile Court after 100 Years.* Washington: Coalition for Juvenile Justice.

Dawson, Robert O. 1988. "The Third Justice System: The New Juvenile-Criminal System of Determinate Sentencing for the Youthful Violent Offender in Texas." *St. Mary's Law Journal* 19:943.

———. 1990. "The Violent Offender: An Empirical Study of Juvenile Determinate Sentencing Proceedings as an Alternative to Criminal Prosecution." *Texas Tech Law Review* 21:1897.

———. 1992. "An Empirical Study of *Kent* Style Juvenile Transfers to Criminal Court." *St. Mary's Law Journal* 23:975.

Edmonds, Patricia. 1994. "To Some, Ultimate Penalty Is Ageless." *USA Today,* September 28, 11A.

Elliott, Delbert S. 1994. "Serious Violent Offenders: Onset, Developmental Course, and Termination." *Criminology* 32:1.

Fagan, Jeffrey. 1996. "The Comparative Advantage of Juvenile versus Criminal Court Sanctions on Recidivism among Adolescent Felony Offenders." *Law and Policy* 18 (1 and 2):77-113.

Feld, Barry C. 1987. "The Juvenile Court Meets the Principle of the Offense: Legislative Changes in Juvenile Waiver Statutes." *Journal of Criminal Law and Criminology* 78:471.

———. 1993. "Juvenile (In)justice and the Criminal Court Alternative." *Crime and Delinquency* 39:403.

———. 1997. "Abolish the Juvenile Court: Youthfulness, Criminal Responsibility, and Sentencing Policy." *Journal of Criminal Law and Criminology* 88:68.

———. 1998. "Social Structure, Race, and the Transformation of the Juvenile Court." Presented at the annual meeting of the Society of Criminology, Washington, D.C.

Gottfredson, Michael R. 1997. "An Evaluation of the Historical Justifications for a Distinct System of Juvenile Justice: The Age, Versatility, and Stability Effects." In *National Conference on Juvenile Justice Records: Appropriate Criminal and Noncriminal Justice Uses.* Washington: U.S. Department of Justice.

Griffin, Patrick, Patricia Torbet, and Linda Szymanski. 1998. *Trying Juveniles as Adults: An Analysis of State Transfer Provisions.* Washington: U.S. Department of Justice, Office of Juvenile Justice and Delinquency Prevention.

Guggenheim, Martin, and Randy Hertz. 1998. "Reflections on Judges, Juries, and Justice: Ensuring the Fairness of Juvenile Delinquency Trials." *Wake Forest Law Review* 33:553.

Howell, James C. 1996. "Juvenile Transfers to the Criminal Justice System: State of the Art." *Law and Policy* 18:17

Krisberg, Barry, and James C. Howell. 1998. "The Impact of the Juvenile Justice System and Prospects for Graduated Sanctions in a Comprehensive Strategy." In *Serious and Violent Juvenile Offenders: Risk Factors and Successful Interventions.* Edited by R. Loeber and D. P. Farrington. Thousand Oaks, Calif.: Sage.

Laubenstein, Kathleen M. 1995. "Media Access to Juvenile Justice: Should Freedom of the Press Be Limited to Promote Rehabilitation of Youthful Offenders?" *Temple Law Review* 68:1897.

Lipsey, Mark W. 1995. "What Do We Learn from 400 Research Studies on the Effectiveness of Treatment with Juvenile Delinquents?" In *What Works? Reducing Reoffending.* Edited by J. Mcguire. New York: John Wiley.

Lipsey, Mark W., and David B. Wilson. 1998. "Effective Interventions with Serious Juvenile Offenders: A Synthesis of Research." In *Serious and Violent Juvenile Offenders: Risk Factors and Successful Interventions.* Edited by R. Loeber and D. P. Farrington. Thousand Oaks, Calif.: Sage.

Lipton, Douglas, Robert Martinson, and Judith Wilks. 1975. *The Effectiveness of Correctional Treatment: A Survey of Treatment Evaluation Studies.* New York: Praeger.

Loeber, Rolf. 1996. "Developmental Continuity, Change, and Pathways in Male Juvenile Problem Behaviors and Delinquency." In *Delinquency and Crime: Current Theories.* Edited by J. D. Hawkins. New York: Cambridge University Press.

Loeber, Rolf, David P. Farrington, and Daniel A. Waschbusch. 1998. "Serious and Violent Juvenile Offenders." In *Serious and Violent Juvenile Offenders: Risk Factors and Successful Interventions.* Edited by R. Loeber and D. P. Farrington. Thousand Oaks, Calif.: Sage.

Loeber, Rolf, and Dale F. Hay. 1997. "Key Issues in the Development of Aggression and Violence from Childhood to Early Adulthood." *Annual Review of Psychology* 48:371.

Loeber, Rolf, Kate Keenan, and Quanwu Zhang. 1997. "Boys' Experimentation and Persistence in Developmental Pathways toward Serious Delinquency." *Journal of Child and Family Studies* 6:321.

Logan, Wayne A. 1998. "Proportionality and Punishment: Imposing Life without Parole on Juveniles." *Wake Forest Law Review* 33:681.

Martin, Gordon A. 1992. "The Delinquent and the Juvenile Court: Is There Still a Place for Rehabilitation?" *Connecticut Law Review* 25:57.

Martinson, Robert. 1974. "What Works? Questions and Answers about Prison Reform." *Public Interest* 35:22–54.

Mears, Daniel P. 1998. "Theorizing and Predicting Juvenile Justice Sanctioning." Presented at the annual meeting of the American Society of Criminology, Washington.

Miller, Neal. 1997a. "National Assessment of Criminal Court Use of Defendants' Juvenile Adjudication Records." In *National Conference on Juvenile Justice Records: Appropriate Criminal and Noncriminal Justice Uses.* Washington: Department of Justice.

——. 1997b. *Understanding Juvenile Waiver: The Significance of System Resources in Case Allocation between Juvenile and Criminal Court.* Washington: Institute for Law and Justice.

Moffitt, Terry E. 1993. "Adolescence-Limited and Life-Course-Persistent Antisocial Behavior: A Developmental Taxonomy." *Psychological Review* 100:674.

Moffitt, Terry E., A. Caspi, N. Dickson, P. Silva, and W. Stanton. 1996. "Childhood-Onset versus Adolescent-Onset Antisocial Conduct Problems in Males: Natural History from Ages 3 to 18 Years." *Development and Psychopathology* 8:399.

Myers, David L. 1999. "Excluding Violent Youths from Juvenile Court: The Effectiveness of Legislative Waiver." Ph.D. diss., University of Maryland.

National Council on Crime and Delinquency. 1996a. *Nebraska Juvenile Risk Assessment Findings.* Madison, Wis.: National Council on Crime and Delinquency.

——. 1996b. *Travis County Juvenile Risk Assessment Findings.* Madison, Wis.: National Council on Crime and Delinquency.

National Criminal Justice Association. 1997. *Juvenile Justice Reform Initiatives in the States: 1994–1996.* Washington: U.S. Department of Justice, Office of Juvenile Justice and Delinquency Prevention.

Podkopacz, Marcy R. 1998. "A First Look at Blended Sentencing: Extended Juvenile Jurisdiction in Hennepin County, Minnesota." Presented at the American Society of Criminology annual meeting, November 1998, Washington.

Podkopacz, Marcy R., and Barry C. Feld. 1995. "Judicial Waiver Policy and Practice: Persistence, Seriousness, and Race." *Law and Inequality Journal* 14:73.

——. 1996. "The End of the Line: An Empirical Study of Judicial Waiver." *Journal of Criminal Law and Criminology* 86:449.

Redding, Richard E. 1997. "Juveniles Transferred to Criminal Court: Legal Reform Proposals Based on Social Science Research." *Utah Law Review* 3:709.

——. 1999. "Juvenile Offenders in Criminal Court and Adult Prison: Legal, Psychological, and Behavioral Outcomes." *Juvenile and Family Court Journal* 50:1.

Regnery, Alfred S. 1985. "Getting Away with Murder: Why the Juvenile Justice System Needs an Overhaul." *Policy Review* 34:65–68.

Rosenberg, Ira M. 1993. "Leaving Bad Enough Alone: A Response to the Juvenile Court Abolitionists." *Wisconsin Law Review* 1993:163.

Sanborn, Joseph B. 1998. "Second-Class Justice, First-Class Punishment: The Use of Juvenile Records in Sentencing Adults." *Judicature* 81:206.

Schiraldi, Vincent, and Mark Soler. 1998. "The Will of the People? The Public's Opinion of the Violent and Repeat Juvenile Offender Act of 1997." *Crime and Delinquency* 44:590.

Schwartz, Ira M., Shenyang Guo, and John J. Krebs. 1993. "The Impact of Demographic Variables on Public Opinion Regarding Juvenile Justice: Implications for Public Policy." *Crime and Delinquency* 39:5.

Schwartz, Ira M., Neil Alan Weiner, and Guy Enosh. 1998. "Nine Lives and Then Some: Why the Juvenile Court Does Not Roll Over and Die." *Wake Forest Law Review* 33:533.

Scott, Elizabeth S., and Thomas Grisso. 1997. "The Evolution of Adolescence: A Developmental Perspective on Juvenile Justice Reform." *Journal of Criminal Law and Criminology* 88:137.

Singer, Simon I. 1998. "Criminal and Teen Courts as Loosely Coupled Systems of Juvenile Justice." *Wake Forest Law Review* 33:509.

Tate, David C., N. Dickon Reppucci, and Edward P. Mulvey. 1995. "Violent Juvenile Delinquents: Treatment Effectiveness and Implications for Future Action." *American Psychologist* 50:777.

Thomas, Charles W., and Shay Bilchik. 1985. "Prosecuting Juveniles in Criminal Courts: A Legal and Empirical Analysis." *Journal of Criminal Law and Criminology* 76:439.

Torbet, Patricia, Richard Gable, Hunter Hurst IV, Imogene Montgomery, Linda Szymanski, and Douglas Thomas. 1996. *State Responses to Serious and Violent Juvenile Crime.* Washington: Office of Juvenile Justice and Delinquency Prevention.

Torbet, Patricia R., and Linda Szymanski. 1998. *State Legislative Responses to Violent Juvenile Crime: 1996–1997 Update.* Washington: U.S. Department of Justice, Office of Justice Programs, Office of Juvenile Justice and Delinquency Prevention.

Tracy, Paul E., and Kimberly Kempf-Leonard. 1996. *Continuity and Discontinuity in Criminal Careers New York.* New York: Plenum.

———. 1998. "Sanctioning Serious Juvenile Offenders: A Review of Alternative Methods." In *Advances in Criminological Theory.* Edited by F. Adler and W. Laufer. New Brunswick, N.J.: Transaction Publishers.

U.S. General Accounting Office. 1995. *Juveniles Processed in Criminal Court and Case Dispositions.* Washington: General Accounting Office.

Virginia Commission on Youth. 1996. *The Study of Juvenile Justice System Reform.* House Document No. 37. Richmond: General Assembly of Virginia.

Weinmann, Beth. 1995. "Release/Transfer Hearings under the Determinate Sentencing Act." *Texas State Bar Section Report: Juvenile Law* 9(4): 21.

White, Joseph L. 1985. *The Comparative Dispositions Study. Report to the U.S. Department of Justice.* Washington: Office of Juvenile Justice and Delinquency Prevention.

Wiebush, Richard G., Christopher Baird, Barry Krisberg, and David Onek. 1995. "Risk Assessment and Classification for Serious, Violent, and Chronic Juvenile Offenders." In *Sourcebook on Serious, Violent, and Chronic Juvenile Offenders*. Edited by J. C. Howell, B. Krisberg, J. D. Hawkins, and J. Wilson. Thousand Oaks, Calif.: Sage.

Winner, Lawrence, Donna M. Bishop, Lonn Lanza-Kaduce, and Charles E. Frazier. 1997. "The Transfer of Juveniles to Criminal Court: Reexamining Recidivism over the Long Term." *Crime and Delinquency* 43:548.

Wolfgang, Marvin E., Terence P. Thornberry, and Robert M. Figlio. 1987. *From Boy to Man, from Delinquency to Crime*. Chicago: University of Chicago Press.

Zimring, Franklin E. 1981. "Notes toward a Jurisprudence of Waiver." In *Major Issues in Juvenile Justice Information and Training: Readings in Public Policy*. Edited by J. C. Hall, D. M. Hamparian, J. M. Pettibone, and J. L. White. Columbus, Ohio: Academy for Contemporary Problems.

———. 1998. *American Youth Violence*. New York: Oxford University Press.

Notes

1. See 18 U.S.C.A. §§ 922x, 5032 and 5038(f) (West 1998) (allowing transfer for thirteen-year-olds using a firearm).

2. See *R.I. Gen. Laws* §§ 14-1-7.1–14-1-7.3 (1994) (requiring that the court first find that the juvenile is eligible for transfer to criminal court).

3. Normally, the consequences of a criminal court felony conviction are many: (1) loss of right to vote, (2) loss of right to serve in military, (3) loss of right to own firearm, (4) conviction a matter of public record, (5) requirement to report conviction on employment applications, (6) generally subject to criminal court jurisdiction for all subsequent offenses committed as a juvenile, (7) conviction generally considered in sentencing for future criminal convictions and in sentencing under "three strikes" laws, (8) possibility of receiving adult sentence, (9) possibility of incarceration in adult prison, and (10) possibility of receiving death penalty for capital offenses, if age sixteen at the time of the offense.

4. Effective programs are available for rehabilitating offenders in the juvenile justice system. Lipsey and Wilson (1998) reviewed all two hundred evaluations of treatment programs serving adjudicated serious or violent offenders. The average program reduced recidivism about 12 percent in comparison with control groups, slightly larger that the 10 percent effect found in an earlier review of programs for delinquents in general (Lipsey 1995).

5. *Mass. Gen. Laws Ann.* ch. 119, § 58 (West Cum. Supp. 1998); *Mich. Comp. Laws Ann.* §§ 712A.2–.4 (West Supp. 1999); *N.M. Stat. Ann.* §§ 32A-2-23, 32A-2-20 (Michie 1978).

6. *Conn. Gen. Stat. Ann.* § 46b-133c (West Supp. 1998); *Kan. Stat. Ann.* § 38-1636 (1998); *Minn. Stat. Ann.* § 260.126 (West 1998); *Mont. Code Ann.* § 41-5-1602 (1997).

7. *Colo. Rev. Stat. Ann.* §§ 19-2-601, 19-2-907, 19-2-908, 19-2-910 and 19-2-911 (West 1998); *Mass. Gen. Laws Ann.* ch. 119, § 72 (West 1999); *R.I. Gen. Laws* §§ 14-1-7.3 and 14-1-42 (1994); *Tex. Fam. Code Ann.* §§ 54.04 (West Cum. Supp. 1999).

8. *Mass. Gen. Laws Ann.* ch. 119, § 58 (West Cum. Supp. 1998); *R.I. Gen. Laws* § 14-1-7.3 (2) (1994).

9. *Tex. Fam. Code Ann.* § 54.04(3) (West Cum. Supp. 1999).

10. *Cal. Welf. & Inst. Code* § 707.01 (West 1998); *Colo. Rev. Stat. Ann.* § 19-2-907 (1998); *Fla. Stat. Ann.* § 985.225 (West Supp. 1999); *Idaho Code* § 20-509 (1997); *Mich. Comp. Laws Ann.* §§ 712A.2–.4 (West 1993 and Cum. Supp. 1998); *Okla. Stat. Ann.* tit. 10, § 7303-4.3 (West 1998); *Va. Code Ann.* § 16.1-272 (Michie 1996); *W. Va. Code* § 25-4-6 (1992).

11. *Ark. Code Ann.* § 9-27-318 (Lexis 1998); *Iowa Code Ann.* § 907.3A (West Supp. 1998); *Mo. Ann. Stat.* § 211.073 (West Cum. Supp. 1999).

12. *Va. Code Ann.* § 16.1-272 (Michie 1996).

13. *Vt. Stat. Ann.* tit. 33, §§ 5505(e), 5505(f) and 5529b (Cum. Supp. 1998).

14. *Vt. Stat. Ann.* tit. 33, § 5529d (Cum. Supp. 1991).

15. E.g., *Minn. Stat. Ann.* § 260.211(1)(a) (West 1998).

16. *Mich. Comp. Laws Ann.* §§ 600.606, 712A.2.

17. *Mich. Comp. Laws Ann.* §§ 712A.2–.4.

18. Ibid.

19. *Colo. Rev. Stat. Ann.* §§ 16-11-311, 19-2-601 and 19-2-517 (West 1998).

20. *R.I. Gen. Laws* § 14-1-7.3 (1994).

21. *Kan. Stat. Ann.* § 16-38-1636 (a) (3) (1993 & Supp. 1997).

22. *Kan. Stat. Ann.* § 16-38-1636(f)(2) (1993).

23. Kent was prosecuted in the District of Columbia. The waiver criteria were presented in an appendix containing the waiver policy statement of the District of Columbia's juvenile court. These criteria have since been adopted by many states and relate generally to the nature of the offense, the characteristics of the child, and the system's rehabilitative capacities:

1. The seriousness of the alleged offense to the community and whether the protection of the community requires waiver.

2. Whether the alleged offense was committed in an aggressive, violent, premeditated or willful manner.

3. Whether the alleged offense was against persons or against property, greater weight being given to offenses against persons especially if personal injury resulted.

4. The prosecutive merit of the complaint, i.e., whether there is evidence upon which a Grand Jury may be expected to return an indictment . . .

5. The desirability of trial and disposition of the entire offense in one court when the juvenile's associates in the alleged offense are adults who will be charged with a crime . . .

6. The sophistication and maturity of the juvenile as determined by a consideration of his home, environmental situation, emotional attitude and pattern of living.

7. The record and previous history of the juvenile, including previous contacts with the Youth Aid Division, other law enforcement agencies, juvenile courts and other jurisdictions, prior periods of probation to this Court, or prior commitments to juvenile institutions.

8. The prospects for adequate protection of the public and the likelihood of reasonable rehabilitation of the juvenile (if he is found to have committed the alleged offense) by the use of procedures, services and facilities currently available to the juvenile court.

24. *N.M. Stat. Ann.* § 32A-2-20(B)(1) (Michie 1978).

25. *Conn. Gen. Stat. Ann.* § 46b-133c(b) (West Supp. 1998).

26. *R.I. Gen. Laws* §§ 14-1-7.3, 14-1-42 (1994).

27. *Colo. Rev. Stat. Ann.* § 19-2-601(6) (a) (West 1998).

28. *Vt. Stat. Ann.* tit. 33, § 5529e (Lexis Cum. Supp. 1998).

29. E.g., *Vt. Stat. Ann.* tit. 33, § 5529f (Lexis Cum. Supp. 1998).

30. *Conn. Gen. Stat. Ann.* §§ 46b-133(c), (f) (West 1995).

31. *Conn. Gen. Stat. Ann.* §§ 46b-133c and 53a-28 (West Supp. 1998).

32. *Smith v. Daily Mail Publishing Co.,* 43 U.S. 97, 107–8 (1979) (Rehnquist, J., concurring).

33. See, e.g., *Tex. Fam. Code Ann.* § 51.13(a) (West 1986).

34. *Tex. Fam. Code Ann.* § 51.13(a) (West 1986).

35. However, in Minnesota, many of the juveniles sent to adult prisons under blended sentencing are transferred because of relatively minor parole violations such as missing appointments, quitting a job, smoking marijuana, or not meeting treatment goals (Belluck 1998; Podkopacz personal communication).

36. Not all agree. Feld (1997) argues that *"treating* juveniles closely resembles *punishing* adults" (86) and that "'sound discretion' simply constitutes a euphemism for idiosyncratic judicial subjectivity" (91).

37. Congress recently enacted Juvenile Accountability Incentive Block Grants for state juvenile justice programs. To be eligible, states must enact laws and policies that, inter alia, impose sanctions for every delinquent act and waive juveniles age fifteen and older who commit serious violent crimes to criminal court (see Albert 1998). States accepting the funds probably will be considering more inclusive transfer laws and/or blended sentencing.

38. The graduated sanctions approach in the Office of Juvenile Justice and Delinquency Prevention's comprehensive strategy for serious, violent, and chronic juvenile offenders involves a continuum of sanctions and treatment alternatives as a function of offending history and offense seriousness, with long-term incarceration for serious, violent, and chronic offenders only a last resort (see Krisberg and Howell 1998). Graduated sanctions have many proven benefits: reduced cost, increased accountability by the juvenile and the community, and enhanced responsiveness to the juvenile's treatment needs (Krisberg and Howell 1998).

Chapter Five

Juvenile Justice on Appeal

LYNDA E. FROST CLAUSEL AND RICHARD J. BONNIE

In the 1960s and 1970s, juvenile justice reform, including reform of the transfer process, originated in the courts. Constitutional rulings drove the engine of reform. By contrast, the locus of recent efforts to transform juvenile justice and to facilitate criminal prosecution of young offenders has been the legislatures. This chapter addresses the question of how the courts have responded to the current generation of juvenile justice reforms, specifically those relating to the transfer process. In order to accomplish the task, we have focused mainly on whether the courts have played an ameliorative role and particularly on whether legislative choices have encountered constitutional impediments.

The transfer statutes interpreted by appellate courts fall into three broad categories.[1] *Judicial waiver* statutes give the juvenile judge responsibility for determining which cases should be transferred to criminal court.[2] The statutes generally prescribe jurisdictional requirements such as a minimum age and usually list factors that should be considered by the juvenile court judge in making the transfer decision. Judges are often directed to retain jurisdiction over juveniles who are "amenable to rehabilitation" in the juvenile justice system. In contrast, *legislative exclusion* statutes remove decision-making authority from the juvenile judge by requiring that specified classes of juveniles be tried in criminal court. These statutes typically give criminal courts exclusive jurisdiction over juveniles above a specified age and/or charged with specified offenses. Residual discretion in such a system lies with prosecutors, whose decisions on which offenses to charge will determine whether a case proceeds in criminal or juvenile court. Finally, *prosecutorial election* statutes explicitly confer on prosecutors the discretion to decide whether to file charges in criminal or juvenile court for cases involving juveniles above a specified age and/or charged with specified offenses.

This chapter focuses on appellate court responses to these different types of statutes, examining the major themes emerging from recent case law and highlighting key issues and major trends.[3] Section 1 addresses the appellate review of judicial waiver. Section 2 considers the appellate response to legislative exclusion. Section 3 concerns statutes that explicitly grant discretion to prosecutors for transfer decisions.

The appellate tradition in all three modes of transfer decisions has been a passive one. With the advent of more punitive sanctions for offenders in criminal court, some appellate courts have rejected statutory provisions that fail to provide any mechanism for reviewing discretionary decisions to prosecute juvenile offenders as adults. The chapter concludes that the constitutional jurisprudence governing the transfer process has reached a critical juncture. The courts may follow a path of protective innovation, insisting on special safeguards before juveniles may be subjected to severe punishment as adults, or they may follow a well-marked path of restraint, acceding to the legislative desire for incapacitation of youthful offenders. Courts are at a crucial point, one at which they must decide whether juveniles are deserving of special protections prior to severe punishment as adults or whether legislatures may shape their systems of punishment for youthful offenders without constraint by the courts.

1. Judicial Waiver

Historically the most common statutory scheme for removing a juvenile from juvenile court for trial in criminal court,[4] judicial waiver requires a judge to assess the suitability of juvenile court jurisdiction.[5] Although judicial waiver was initially an informal process, it is now subject to constitutionally required procedures as well as additional safeguards provided under state law. Recent appellate decisions continue to explicate the scope of the juvenile judge's discretion in transfer hearings.

The U.S. Supreme Court first delineated procedural safeguards for protecting the juvenile's interests during a transfer hearing in *Kent v. United States,* 383 U.S. 541 (1966). In that case, sixteen-year-old Morris Kent found himself standing trial in the U.S. District Court for the District of Columbia for offenses including housebreaking, robbery, and rape. Although initially under the jurisdiction of the juvenile court, Kent's case was transferred to criminal court after the juvenile court judge issued an order stating only that, after "full investigation, I do hereby waive" jurisdiction (383 U.S. at 546). Following his conviction on most of the charges, Kent appealed to the Court of Appeals for the District of Columbia Circuit and subsequently the U.S. Supreme Court, challenging, among other issues, the proceedings by which his case was transferred to criminal court.

The transfer of Kent's case occurred pursuant to the District of Columbia Juvenile Court Act, which described the circumstances of permissible transfers but failed to state explicit standards other than the requirement of a "full investigation" (383 U.S. at 547). The Supreme Court, emphasizing that the transfer determination is "a 'critically important' proceeding" (383 U.S. at 560), held that in order for the waiver of jurisdiction to be valid, the juvenile is "entitled to a hearing, including access by his counsel to the social records and probation or similar reports which presumably are considered by the court, and to a statement of reasons for the Juvenile Court's decision" (383 U.S. at 557).

The *Kent* decision could be read narrowly as an interpretation of the meaning of a "full investigation" under the D.C. Juvenile Court Act. The Court was careful to specify that it based its holding on the act and appellate court decisions (383 U.S. at 556). Still, the Court emphasized the relevance of constitutional due-process requirements in interpreting the statute (383 U.S. at 557), and the decision has come to be regarded as a precursor of *In re Gault* decided the following year.

An appendix to the opinion of the Court contained a 1959 policy memorandum in which the juvenile judge of the District of Columbia's juvenile court listed determinative factors to be considered in making the transfer decision. The eight factors were:

1. The seriousness of the alleged offense to the community and whether the protection of the community requires waiver.
2. Whether the alleged offense was committed in an aggressive, violent, premeditated or willful manner.
3. Whether the alleged offense was against persons or against property, greater weight being given to offenses against persons especially if personal injury resulted.
4. The prosecutive merit of the complaint, i.e., whether there is evidence upon which a Grand Jury may be expected to return an indictment (to be determined by consultation with the United States Attorney).
5. The desirability of trial and disposition of the entire offense in one court when the juvenile's associates in the alleged offense are adults who will be charged with a crime in the U.S. District Court for the District of Columbia.
6. The sophistication and maturity of the juvenile as determined by consideration of his home, environmental situation, emotional attitude and pattern of living.
7. The record and previous history of the juvenile, including previous contacts with the Youth Aid Division, other law enforcement agencies, juvenile courts and other jurisdictions, prior periods of probation to this Court, or prior commitments to juvenile institutions.

8. The prospects for adequate protection of the public and the likelihood of reasonable rehabilitation of the juvenile (if he is found to have committed the alleged offense) by the use of procedures, services and facilities currently available to the Juvenile Court. (383 U.S. at 566–67)

Following *Kent,* most states revised their transfer statutes to comply with the Supreme Court's decision, requiring a hearing and a statement of reasons for a decision to waive jurisdiction. Some courts have interpreted *Kent* as a substantive due-process case implying specific requirements for a constitutionally valid transfer statute.[6] It must be emphasized, however, that *Kent* is better seen as a procedural due-process decision because the Supreme Court said nothing to question the fundamentally discretionary character of the decision and did not prescribe any substantive criteria. Because the Supreme Court had signaled its endorsement of the factors listed in the D.C. court's policy memorandum, now known as the *Kent* criteria, they have been incorporated into the transfer provision of many state statutes (Redding 1997, 719; Griffin, Torbet, and Szymanski 1998, 3). However, the *Kent* criteria really are not criteria at all; they do no more than list factors to be taken into account in reaching what remains a highly discretionary judgment about whether jurisdiction should be retained or transferred.

Appellate courts continue to entertain a high volume of appeals challenging juvenile court decisions to transfer jurisdiction and a small volume of cases in which the state objects to decisions retaining jurisdiction. Although decisions are occasionally reversed because the juvenile judge failed to adhere to the statutory procedures or failed to address some of the *Kent*-like criteria prescribed in the statute, appellate courts rarely reverse juvenile court judgments on substantive grounds. Appellate courts reviewing a juvenile judge's waiver decision typically examine the underlying findings of fact to see if any were clearly erroneous or lacked substantial evidence and to determine whether the trial judge abused his or her discretion.[7] Perhaps because of this deferential standard of review, the vast majority of appellate rulings in all states uphold the juvenile judge's determination (which, in most appealed cases, is to waive jurisdiction).[8]

Reversal of decisions to transfer. It can be fruitful, however, to review the relatively small number of recent appellate cases in which the juvenile judge's decision was not upheld. In a number of state court decisions favoring the juvenile offender, the juvenile judge's decision to *transfer* the juvenile has been reversed because the judge did not give sufficient consideration to the statutory factors for transfer.[9] Some opinions address both the need for an independent determination of probable cause and sufficient consideration of each of the factors relevant to the transfer decision.[10] For example, the West Virginia Supreme Court reversed a transfer decision by a juvenile judge who made no further inquiry into the charges in the juvenile petition and failed to review probation reports, psychological evaluations, and social summaries in compliance with the statutory requirement to "make a careful, detailed analysis into the child's mental and physical condition, maturity, emotional attitude, home or family environment, school experience and other similar personal factors." *State v. Sonja B.*, 395 S.E.2d 803, 807 (W. Va. 1990) (quoting *W. Va. Code* § 49-5-10[d]). Other opinions focus more narrowly on the criteria relevant to the transfer decision. For example, the Montana Supreme Court has recently reversed several transfer decisions, on the grounds that the juvenile judges failed to consider evidence on the capacity of juvenile facilities to rehabilitate the juvenile and that they had transferred the cases solely on the basis of the seriousness of the offenses. (The Montana statute required a transfer if the judge found probable cause that "the seriousness of the offense and the protection of the community require treatment of the youth beyond that afforded by juvenile facilities")[11] Many of these cases require some consideration of the various statutory factors relevant to the transfer decision, but do not provide any normative guidance regarding the evidence that must be evaluated or the weight that should be given to the various factors in making the transfer decision.[12]

A series of cases interpreting the judicial waiver provision of the federal transfer statute nicely illustrates the overall pattern of appellate decisions reviewing decisions to transfer jurisdiction—an insistence on compliance with procedural requirements and a refusal to second-guess the juvenile judge's exercise of discretion. The statute permits criminal prosecution of a juvenile upon certification by the attorney general that the case meets specified requirements and after consideration of six factors by the district court.[13] The U.S. Court of Appeals for the Eighth Circuit held that failure to comply with the statutory requirements can create a jurisdictional defect and that the attorney general's certification is necessary to confer jurisdiction and is subject to judicial review for compliance with the statutory requirements.[14] The Fifth Circuit also showed a preference for strict technical compliance in rejecting a certification signed by an assistant U.S. attorney with no personal involvement of the U.S. attorney.[15] In contrast to the strong focus on procedural correctness, the circuit courts have permitted district courts broad discretion in determining how to weigh the six substantive factors they consider.[16]

Reversal of decisions to retain jurisdiction. In recent years, state courts have occasionally reversed a juvenile judge's decision to *retain* jurisdiction over the juvenile. The Massachusetts Supreme Judicial Court found that a juvenile judge inappropriately limited testimony concerning the juvenile's amenability by rejecting a request by both sides to introduce additional psychiatric testimony.[17] The court listed evidence that had supported decisions in earlier cases to transfer a juvenile and remanded the case for a redetermination after consideration of psychiatric testimony.[18] Later, it reversed a juvenile court's decision to retain jurisdiction in another case, holding that the judge ruled incorrectly on several issues of expert testimony and erred in considering the juvenile's amenability to "treatment" rather than the statutory amenability to "rehabilitation" within the limited time that the juvenile could be within the control of the juvenile system.[19]

Several recent decisions have reversed decisions to retain jurisdiction on substantive grounds rather than procedural grounds.[20] For example, the South Dakota Supreme Court, noting that "[s]ociety must be protected from violent crime and the agony of its effects," found no substantial evidence to support a juvenile judge's finding that the juvenile could be rehabilitated, a finding upon which the decision to retain jurisdiction had been predicated.[21] A dissenting justice disagreed, noting the juvenile's successful completion of two highly structured Department of Corrections programs.[22]

The recent decision by the California Supreme Court in *People v. Superior Court (Melvin Ray Jones)*, 958 P.2d 393 (Cal. 1998), also appears to reflect a willingness to engage in more aggressive review of juvenile court decisions to retain jurisdiction. Two fifteen-year-old cousins were charged with murder after a homicide occurred during a robbery. Under California law, the juveniles were presumed unfit for juvenile court jurisdiction, although this presumption could be rebutted if the defense showed their fitness under five statutory criteria. *Cal. Welf. & Inst. Code § 707(e)*. On appeal, the court of appeals and the California Supreme Court held that the juvenile court had abused its discretion because two of the five criteria were unsupported by substantial evidence. The Supreme Court found that the offense was "sophisticated" despite the juvenile court's findings that the juveniles were ignorant of how to operate the gun, that they had selected a target in their neighborhood and had decided to wait undisguised outside the store, and that they lost the key to the apartment where they planned to hide. The court also held that the juveniles were unfit for juvenile court jurisdiction because of the circumstances and gravity of the offense, even though the juvenile court found the juveniles had been so intoxicated that they vomited several times on their way to the crime scene and they had not intended to shoot anybody. A vociferous dissent argued that the appellate courts failed to give the trial court's findings proper deference and instead were substituting their own judgment in a de novo review of the case.

In sum, appellate courts reviewing judicial waiver decisions have been willing to specify procedural requirements for judicial decision making, but generally they have not been inclined to provide much substantive constraint on the exercise of juvenile judges' discretion. In the vast majority of appealed cases, state appellate courts have rejected claims that the juvenile judge abused his or her discretion in deciding the transfer issue. Overall, the courts tend to defer to juvenile judges' discretion either to retain or transfer jurisdiction. Because the statutory criteria based on the *Kent* factors are generally viewed as broad guidelines, the appellate courts have not had the statutory leeway to provide more aggressive substantive review of judicial transfer decisions. This pattern of appellate practice could change, however, if the legislatures prescribe substantive criteria (similar to sentencing guidelines) for judicial waiver, thereby providing greater normative direction for juvenile court judges. In recent cases, the most rigorous substantive review has occurred in instances in which the juvenile court retained jurisdiction and the prosecution challenged that determination.

2. Legislative Exclusion

From the beginning of the juvenile court movement, legislatures have drawn the outer boundaries of the juvenile court's jurisdiction based on the offender's age, typically providing exclusive criminal court jurisdiction for offenders older than fifteen or seventeen at the time of the charged offense. Many states also conferred exclusive jurisdiction on the criminal court for a category of younger offenders charged with certain serious offenses (most often murder). Under recent reforms of the transfer process, many states have enlarged the category of cases for which criminal court jurisdiction is exclusive—by lowering the jurisdictional age, expanding the category of serious charges triggering criminal court jurisdiction, or supplementing age-offense criteria with criteria relating to the juvenile's prior offense history.[23] Statutory changes are not the only way to implement a new transfer mechanism. In November of 1996, Arizona voters passed Proposition 102, which added an automatic transfer provision to their constitution. The amendment provided in part "Juveniles 15 years of age or older accused of murder, forcible sexual assault, armed robbery or other violent felony offenses as defined by statute shall be prosecuted as adults. Juveniles 15 years of age or older who are chronic felony offenders as defined by statute shall be prosecuted as adults." A.R.S. Const. art. 4 pt. 2 § 22[1]. See also *Soto v. Superior Court,* 949 P.2d 539 [Ariz. 1997]".

As compared with statutes conferring discretion on juvenile court judges or prosecutors, exclusions of this type purport to reflect deliberate legislative judgments about the types of cases that should be subject to criminal prosecution. They substitute *rules* for the virtually unconstrained discretion that has been characteristic of statutes conferring authority on judges or prosecutors to decide which court should exercise jurisdiction. Of course, this determinacy is purchased at a price—all legislative categories, especially those drawn on the basis of age and offense, will be over- and underinclusive at the margin with reference to the underlying legislative judgment. From the standpoint of fairness to juvenile defendants, the main concern is that the class of juveniles transferred to criminal court is overinclusive in the sense that it encompasses offenders who are amenable to juvenile court intervention. Accordingly, the legislative exclusion statutes have routinely been challenged on the grounds that (a) they deny the juvenile automatically excluded from the juvenile court's jurisdiction an opportunity for an individualized determination of his or her suitability (a due-process violation) or (b) the lines drawn between the included and excluded classes of offenders are arbitrary (an equal-protection violation). Thus far, appellate courts have routinely rejected these challenges to legislative line drawing. They have also been unsympathetic to arguments that these legislative exclusions actually confer the ultimate discretionary authority on prosecutors, who decide whether to charge the juvenile with excludable offenses.[24]

In an early key case, Jerome Bland challenged a District of Columbia statute defining the jurisdiction of the juvenile court to exclude individuals sixteen and over who were charged with specified serious offenses. *U.S. v. Bland,* 472 F.2d 1329, 1340–41 (D.C. Cir. 1972), cert. denied, 412 U.S. 909 (1973). Bland argued that his automatic exclusion from the jurisdiction of the juvenile court denied him procedural due process because he had been given no opportunity to contest the transfer and to show at a hearing that he was amenable to rehabilitation. He also argued that it was arbitrary to exclude sixteen-year-olds charged with the excludable offenses while retaining juvenile court jurisdiction for seventeen-year-olds charged with other offenses. The trial court agreed, but on appeal the U.S. Court of Appeals for the D.C. Circuit reversed. The appellate court held that *Kent* and other cases establishing procedural requirements for judicial waivers were irrelevant because the D.C. statute left nothing to be decided, having categorically excluded certain juveniles from juvenile court jurisdiction. The court further dismissed Bland's argument that the statutory scheme denied him the presumption of innocence, opining that Bland would receive all the protections to which any adult defendant would be entitled in a criminal prosecution. Finally, the appellate court noted that legislative classifications are presumed valid and that the statute reflected a reasonable congressional judgment that juveniles who were beyond rehabilitation and who negatively influenced other juveniles should be prosecuted as adults while the juvenile court retained jurisdiction over older juveniles charged with minor offenses who might still be rehabilitated.

In an unbroken line of authority, state courts in the 1970s and 1980s also upheld legislative exclusion statutes. The Kansas Supreme Court upheld against due-process and other constitutional challenges a statute giving criminal court exclusive jurisdiction over juveniles charged with "aggravated juvenile delinquency." *State v. Sherk*, 538 P.2d 1399 (Kan. 1975).[25] The court explained that juveniles receive full procedural due-process protections in criminal court and that, as required by equal-protection doctrine, the state had a rational basis for treating juveniles who commit their offenses while confined in state juvenile facilities differently from other juveniles. The Rhode Island Supreme Court upheld a statute excluding from juvenile court jurisdiction juveniles over sixteen with records of at least two prior felony offenses who are charged with a felony offense. *State v. Berard*, 401 A.2d 448 (R.I. 1979). The court held that because juveniles have no constitutional right to special treatment, they have no due-process rights prior to the prosecutor's decision to charge them with the requisite felony. Further, the court held that because the legislature could remove all juveniles over sixteen from juvenile court jurisdiction, it could remove a rationally selected subclass without violating equal protection. The Court of Appeals of New York held that a statute prosecuting juveniles thirteen to fifteen charged with specified violent crimes in criminal court withstood a due-process challenge because all juveniles in the defined category were automatically prosecuted as adults and a "safety valve" permitted the removal of an accused juvenile to juvenile court. *Vega v. Bell*, 393 N.E.2d 450 (N.Y. 1979).[26] The Supreme Court of Louisiana upheld a statute placing under criminal court jurisdiction juveniles over fourteen charged with specified offenses and juveniles over fifteen charged with other offenses. *State v. Perique*, 439 So. 2d 1060 (Louis. 1983).[27] The court held that because the juveniles were not deprived of "important statutory rights," and because age- and offense-based classifications are not arbitrary, due process was not violated. 439 So. 2d 1064.[28]

The unfairness potentially associated with overinclusive statutory categories can be ameliorated by reintroducing an avenue of individualization into the statutory scheme of legislative exclusion. For this reason, some appellate courts have been careful to emphasize the important role played by "reverse waiver" provisions in some of the more recent statutory arrangements that enlarge the class of juveniles subject to initial criminal court jurisdiction.[29] Many of these reverse waiver proceedings give legislative exclusion statutes the effect of a judicial waiver statute with a presumption of criminal court jurisdiction and the burden of proof placed on the juvenile to rebut the presumption.[30] For example, the Vermont Supreme Court upheld a statute giving criminal courts original jurisdiction over juveniles between fourteen and sixteen who are charged with serious crimes. *State v. Buelow,* 587 A.2d 948 (Vt. 1990). The court emphasized that in such cases, Vermont law required a hearing and findings of fact to determine whether the juvenile should be transferred to juvenile court. 587 A.2d at 953.[31] In another jurisdiction, stressing the importance of a meaningful hearing, the Arkansas Supreme Court recently strengthened the prosecution's obligations in a reverse waiver hearing. *Thompson v. State,* 958 S.W.2d 1 (Ark. 1997).[32]

Recent decisions in Delaware and Washington suggest that reverse waiver may be a constitutionally required feature of statutory provisions mandating criminal court jurisdiction (and possibly severe sentences) for youthful offenders. In 1992, the Delaware Supreme Court held that the Delaware legislative exclusion statute, which provided for exclusive original jurisdiction in criminal court based solely on the seriousness of the offense, did not violate equal protection or due process. *Marine v. State,* 607 A.2d 1185, 1209 (Del. 1992), cert. dismissed, 505 U.S. 1247 (1992). The court noted that the prosecutor's charging discretion was constrained through a reverse amenability hearing and by a "proof positive" hearing examining the prima facie case against the defendant. 607 A.2d at 1209, 1211.[33] Two years later, in *Hughes v. State,* 653 A.2d 241 (Del. 1994), the court reviewed an amendment that gave the criminal court exclusive jurisdiction over juveniles who turned eighteen prior to juvenile court adjudication of felony-level delinquency charges. Because the amendment would not permit reverse waiver (the relevant juveniles had aged out of juvenile court jurisdiction), the court found the aged-based distinction in the amendment was "patently arbitrary and bears no rational relationship to a legitimate government interest," thus violating due process and equal protection. 653 A.2d at 252. Although the court recognized the broad discretion granted prosecutors in making charging decisions, the court stated that the prosecutor's good faith is not enough to protect the juvenile's rights, in part because "the State's decision to charge a child with a felony implicates constitutional rights not present in the average charging decision of an adult [because of consequences like a public trial and, if convicted, a criminal record]." 653 A.2d at 250.

In 1996, in *In re Boot,* 925 P.2d 964 (Wash. 1996), the Washington Supreme Court upheld a legislative exclusion statute against a facial challenge on a variety of constitutional grounds.[34] A concurring opinion suggested that although the statute survived a facial challenge, its lack of a reverse waiver provision might render it unconstitutionally arbitrary as applied. The concurrence noted that "there is no provision in this statute for a judicial proceeding where the prosecutor's [charging] discretion is tested" and a presumption of good faith is not sufficiently protective of the juvenile's rights. 925 P.2d at 977.

The Connecticut Supreme Court recently upheld a legislative exclusion statute that was coupled with a reverse waiver provision that permitted transfer back to juvenile court at the prosecutor's discretion. *State v. Angel C.,* 715 A.2d 652 (Conn. 1998). The juvenile defendants argued that because the juvenile court had original jurisdiction of their cases and, after automatic transfer, the prosecutor had discretion to recommend their transfer back to juvenile court, they had a vested liberty interest in that juvenile status that could not be denied without due process. 715 A.2d at 661. The defendants also argued that the lack of guidelines to structure the prosecutor's discretion exacerbated the due-process violation. 715 A.2d at 661. Finally, the defendants claimed that the prosecutor's discretion permits juveniles over thirteen charged with certain felonies to be treated disparately without a rational basis for that difference, in violation of equal protection. 715 A.2d at 670. The court rejected all these claims, holding the juveniles had no protectable liberty interest in juvenile status and the discretionary aspects of the reverse waiver provision were not discriminatory on their face or as applied.

The Delaware Supreme Court's decision in *Hughes* and the Washington Supreme Court's decision in *Boot* reveal judicial misgivings about the breadth of recent legislative action sweeping large numbers of younger adolescents into the jurisdiction of criminal courts. Under the earlier generation of juvenile justice statutes, exclusive criminal court jurisdiction was reserved for the oldest juveniles (typically sixteen or older) charged with the most serious offenses. Courts uniformly rejected constitutional challenges to those statutes, notwithstanding the absence of any mechanism to correct for the inevitable overinclusiveness of the class of offenders subjected automatically to criminal prosecution who are thereby deprived of an opportunity for an individualized determination of suitability afforded to other youthful offenders. However, in recent years, legislatures have broadened the class of youthful offenders subjected to exclusive criminal court jurisdiction, thereby increasing the risk of disproportionality and heightening the concern about widely disparate treatment of similarly situated juveniles (some of whom benefit from the rehabilitative opportunities of the juvenile court while others are subjected to lengthy criminal punishment). Though the law is only beginning to develop in this area, it appears that an opportunity for individualization through a reverse waiver hearing may be a constitutionally required safety valve in some situations. The necessity and scope of a reverse waiver provision are still unclear, though, and the Connecticut Supreme Court evidenced a willingness to define narrowly the scope of the Connecticut reverse waiver provision.

3. Prosecutorial Election

Some jurisdictions shift the locus of decision making from the juvenile judge to the prosecutor through statutes permitting the prosecutor to use his or her judgment in deciding whether to try a case in juvenile court or transfer the case to criminal court.[35] Under these statutes, prosecutors exercise discretion not only in charging a juvenile but also in selecting the forum for trial. Some of these provisions were challenged in the wake of the *Kent* holding that a juvenile is entitled to a due-process hearing prior to transfer to criminal court under a judicial waiver statute.

In *United States v. Bland* (1972), discussed above,[36] the District of Columbia Circuit Court of Appeals rejected a constitutional challenge to a District of Columbia statute excluding from juvenile court jurisdiction juveniles over fifteen charged with specified offenses. Even though this statute automatically excluded those cases from juvenile court jurisdiction, the court recognized that the prosecutor held the ultimate authority to decide which court's jurisdiction to invoke through the exercise of discretion over the offense to charge. In considering this aspect of the case, the court treated the statute as if it were functionally equivalent to a prosecutorial election statute. In so doing, the majority and dissent anticipated the arguments that have been lodged against prosecutorial election statutes over the ensuing twenty-five year period.

The court took note of the prosecutor's ultimate control over the court's jurisdiction through the charging decision, but declined to interfere. The court characterized the charging discretion as a traditional example of prosecutorial discretion exercised by an officer of the executive branch and protected from judicial interference by separation-of-powers doctrine.[37] Review would be appropriate, the court said, only if the prosecutor exercised his or her discretion on the basis of arbitrary classifica-

tions such as race or religion, but not on the age and offense classifications in the D.C. statute. *Bland,* 472 F.2d at 1336.

Judge Wright's lengthy dissent in *Bland* referred to *Kent* and concluded that a juvenile is entitled to "a hearing with counsel and a statement of reasons before he can be charged and tried as an adult." 472 F.2d
at 1339. The dissent criticized the legislature's "blatant attempt to evade
the force of the *Kent* decision" by creating a parallel waiver procedure.
472 F.2d at 1341. It concluded that because the transfer decision will be
made by a "partisan prosecutor" rather than a "neutral judge," the juvenile has a heightened need for due-process protections under the challenged procedures. 472 F.2d at 1342–43. The dissent argued that its position would not eliminate prosecutorial discretion, but would merely
ensure it is exercised in a manner consistent with procedural due-process
requirements.

Judge Wright's dissent highlights the road not taken in the constitutional law of juvenile transfer. *Kent* had subjected the judicial waiver decision to the constraints of procedural due process, requiring a hearing
and statement of reasons to make the judge's discretion rationally reviewable. As Judge Wright pointed out, however, a legislature could
evade *Kent*'s command simply by conferring the discretion on prosecutors rather than juvenile court judges, a process even more objectionable
than unregulated judicial discretion. For Judge Wright, the only acceptable response was either to require a judicial waiver procedure or to
bring prosecutorial discretion within the constraints of the rule of law
through the due-process clause. However, to do this would be incompat-
ible with a nearly unqualified tradition of noninterference with prosecutorial discretion, and this was a step that the majority of the *Bland* court
was unwilling to take.

The D.C. Circuit's reasoning in *Bland* was adopted in prosecutorial
election cases over the next few years by the Fourth and Fifth Circuits.
In 1973, the Fourth Circuit heard an appeal from a seventeen-year-old
offender prosecuted in the federal system as an adult. *Cox v. U.S.,* 473
F.2d 334 (4th Cir. 1973). Cox argued that *Kent* entitled him to a hearing
and other due-process rights prior to prosecution as an adult, a mo-
mentous step with substantially different consequences for the offender.
The Fourth Circuit, however, distinguished between a judicial or quasi-
judicial proceeding in which due-process rights traditionally are extended and decisions of a prosecutor. The court looked at traditional
treatments of prosecutorial discretion and held that the prosecutor's
decision was "beyond the reach of the due process rights of counsel
and a hearing." 473 F.2d at 335.[38] In 1977, the Fifth Circuit rejected a

Kent-based challenge to a Florida transfer statute that removed from juvenile court jurisdiction a juvenile fourteen or older charged with an offense punishable by death or life imprisonment if the grand jury returned an indictment on the charge. *Woodard v. Wainwright,* 556 F.2d 781 (5th Cir. 1977). The Fifth Circuit expressed doubt as to whether the *Kent* due-process requirement of a hearing was based on the U.S. Constitution or on the D.C. statute, which required "full investigation." Avoiding that question, the court distinguished *Kent* because it involved the judge's duty to decide issues relevant to waiver rather than a prosecutor's decision to present information to the grand jury. The court found that "the right to juvenile treatment is a legislative gift," and the legislature may determine the extent of that gift. 556 F.2d at 785. The legislature need not develop guidelines (such as the *Kent* criteria) to structure the exercise of prosecutorial discretion.

Most state supreme courts have also rejected due-process and other constitutional challenges to prosecutorial election statutes. For example, the Colorado Supreme Court upheld a statute permitting the prosecutor to decide whether to proceed against violent offenders fourteen to eighteen as adults or juveniles. *People v. Thorpe,* 641 P.2d 935, 940 (Col. 1982). The defendant argued that the lack of statutory guidelines and a hearing requirement violated due process and the potentially disparate treatment of violent juvenile offenders fourteen and older violated equal protection. The court, however, held that in the absence of suspect factors such as race, the exercise of prosecutorial discretion should not be reviewed by the courts and does not violate due process or equal protection.

The Montana Supreme Court reviewed a state statute requiring the juvenile court to grant a prosecutor's motion to transfer a case to criminal court whenever the offender was sixteen or older at the time of the offense and was charged with specified acts of homicide or attempted homicide. *In the Matter of Keith Wayne Wood,* 768 P.2d 1370 (Mont. 1989). The due-process challenge in *Wood* asserted that the Montana statute denied certain juvenile offenders a meaningful hearing prior to transfer because the statute directed the judge to grant the prosecutor's motion under specified circumstances. The Montana Supreme Court distinguished *Kent* and declared that the U.S. Supreme Court has "never attempted to prescribe criteria for, or the nature and quantum of evidence that must support, a decision to transfer a juvenile for trial in adult court." 768 P.2d at 1372, quoting *Breed v. Jones,* 421 U.S. 519, 537–38 (1975). The Montana court noted that juveniles have no inherent right to have their cases heard in juvenile court and thus the legislature may change the contours of juvenile court jurisdiction. Referring to a presumption of constitutionality, the court found that Wood failed to meet the burden of proving the statute violated due process. The court addressed the legislative intent behind the statute, but failed to examine the constitutionality of the discretion the statute gave prosecutors in determining which juveniles to try in criminal court.[39]

Other state courts have addressed and dismissed the same constitutional concerns. The Georgia Supreme Court, in a brief opinion, upheld a statute providing the juvenile and criminal courts concurrent jurisdiction in felony cases punishable by death or life imprisonment. *Chapman v. State,* 385 S.E.2d 661 (Geor. 1989). The court stated that because a juvenile's "special rights" are created by statute and not the constitution, the criminal court's exercise of jurisdiction does not violate the juvenile's due-process rights. In addition, the court rejected a separation-of-powers challenge because with concurrent jurisdiction, the litigant selects the forum for the case and therefore the prosecutor's decision does not reflect the exercise of judicial, legislative, or executive power. The prosecutor's choice of forum is "a mere consequence" of the people's decisions to create two courts and give the legislature power to determine issues of jurisdiction.

The Wyoming transfer statute, which for many offenses requires the prosecutor to determine the appropriate court for the case, has withstood several challenges. One defendant challenged the lack of appropriate guidelines to limit the discretion of the prosecutor, but the court found that in the absence of suspect factors such as race or religion, broad discretion would not violate due process or equal protection. *Jahnke v. State,* 692 P.2d 911, 929 (Wyo. 1984).[40] In rejecting another defendant's claims, the Wyoming Supreme Court stated that juveniles "have been the recipients of legislative grace by permitting them to be the object of juvenile proceedings although that grace is limited by prosecutorial discretion." *Hansen v. State,* 904 P.2d 811, 820 (Wyo. 1995). The court added, "[W]e emphasize that the prosecutor's discretion is not unfettered because of the availability of the transfer motion to an accused juvenile." 904 P.2d at 823. Such a "transfer motion," or reverse waiver provision, has become important in subsequent cases.

Several recent opinions have been more sympathetic to constitutional challenges to prosecutorial election transfer statutes. In 1995, the Utah Supreme Court found that the direct-file provisions of the Utah transfer statute violated the equal-protection provision of the state constitution. *State v. Mohi,* 901 P.2d 991 (Utah 1995).[41] The rejected portion of the transfer statute permitted prosecutors to file charges against some juveniles in criminal court and to proceed against other similarly situated juveniles in juvenile court. The defendant, Mohi, argued that the statute violated the Utah uniform-operation-of-laws provision, which required any law to treat similarly situated persons alike. The Utah Supreme Court agreed, holding that the prosecutorial election provision was not reasonably related to the state's interests in "protecting the public and addressing the needs of juveniles" because "the selection process for beneficial treatment is arbitrary and standardless." 901 P.2d at 996, 998. In contrast, the dissent argued that without a showing that the prosecutor classified individuals improperly, the statute itself was within constitutional limits and consonant with traditional notions of prosecutorial discretion.[42]

The West Virginia Supreme Court also expressed constitutional misgivings about that state's prosecutorial election statute, which required the transfer of a juvenile over thirteen meeting specific offense and criminal history criteria whenever the prosecutor chose to file a transfer motion and the court made a probable-cause determination. *State v. Robert K. McL.,* 496 S.E.2d 887 (W.V. 1997). The court noted that the prosecutor's discretion in deciding when to file a transfer motion was "statutorily unfettered" and "standardless." 496 S.E.2d at 891. Citing *Mohi,* the court expressed concern about the shift of discretion from the court to "an unreviewable, subjective decision of an executive officer" (496 S.E.2d at 891), and observed that, standing alone, such a scheme might violate equal-protection and due-process guarantees. However, the court upheld the transfer provision on the grounds that the criminal court's authority to use juvenile dispositions in fashioning an appropriate sentence represented a safety valve enabling the criminal court to consider personal factors relevant to amenability and rehabilitation "and to, in its discretion, return a child to juvenile jurisdiction" (496 S.E.2d at 893).[43]

These recent cases return to the themes raised in cases challenging legislative exclusion statutes. *Mohi* did not say why this use of prosecutorial discretion is more problematic than other routine discretionary practices in criminal justice administration. According to the traditional analysis, a state is not constitutionally required to have a juvenile court at all, and—unless the state's juvenile code creates an "entitlement" to juvenile court jurisdiction (as it might be said to accomplish in a judicial waiver arrangement)—the due process clause is not applicable to prosecutorial election.[44] Under this reasoning, a prosecutor's discretion to invoke criminal court jurisdiction would be reviewable only if a claim of discrimination based on race, national origin, etc. were alleged. Indeed, a decision to forgo criminal court jurisdiction in favor of juvenile court jurisdiction might be regarded as an exercise in discretionary leniency similar to a decision to reduce a felony charge to a misdemeanor. *Mohi* and other decisions expressing misgivings about unconstrained prosecutorial election would seem to be predicated on the idea that transfer decisions are "qualitatively different" from other prosecutorial decisions in criminal justice administration in the way that the death penalty is "qualitatively different" from imprisonment, however severe, and that this difference triggers a "heightened need for reliability" in the decision to invoke criminal court jurisdiction.[45]

From a predictive standpoint, the key question is whether *Mohi* signals a new direction in the constitutional jurisprudence of juvenile justice, or whether it will remain a rather quixotic deviation from the standard judicial line. Ultimately, the answer may turn on whether the courts are able to develop a persuasive rationale for explaining why "standardless" exercise of prosecutorial discretion in deciding whether to invoke the jurisdiction of the juvenile or criminal court is constitutionally distinguishable from all other standardless exercises of prosecutorial discretion. Consider, for example, the routine practice of deciding whether to file felony charges or to nolle prosequi such charges after they have been filed, in favor of misdemeanor charges. In some states, the legislature has explicitly authorized prosecutors to charge some offenses ("wobblers") as either felonies or misdemeanors. Similarly, prosecutors have unreviewable discretion to file or withhold habitual offender charges, a decision that can significantly extend the offender's term of imprisonment.

Unless the *Mohi* court intends to try to subject all forms of prosecutorial discretion to the rule of law, the challenge is to find a plausible reason for curtailing this practice only in juvenile transfer cases. One possible approach is to emphasize the "heightened need for reliability" in determining whether a youth should be subjected to criminal prosecution as an adult, with the attendant risk of grossly disproportionate punishment. Drawing on the body of law that has recently emerged in the analogous context of capital punishment, it can be argued that practices that are acceptable in ordinary sentencing proceedings present a constitutionally intolerable risk of arbitrariness and disproportionality in the juvenile transfer process. Thus, deciding whether a young offender should be prosecuted as an adult may not be left in the hands of prosecutors, but must instead be conferred on judges, applying rationally reviewable criteria after a full adversarial hearing. From this perspective it matters not whether the judge is a juvenile judge deciding whether to waive jurisdiction to the criminal court or a criminal court judge deciding to surrender jurisdiction to the juvenile court. This analysis, which echoes Judge Wright's *Bland* dissent, converges nicely with the principle that seems to underlie recent decisions of the Delaware Supreme Court holding that an opportunity for "reverse waiver" is a constitutionally indispensable feature of legislation subjecting youthful offenders to criminal court jurisdiction.

4. Conclusion

Kent v. United States, decided by the U.S. Supreme Court in 1966, is understood to hold that a youth under the jurisdiction of a juvenile court being considered for waiver to criminal court by a judge is entitled to procedural due process, including a hearing and a statement of reasons. On its own terms, the *Kent* ruling is uncontroversial and relatively limited. However, *Kent* was understood immediately as a harbinger of a constitutional transformation of juvenile justice. Within a year, the Supreme Court had decided *In re Gault,* 387 U.S. 1, 87 S. Ct 1428, 18 L. Ed. 2d 527 (1967), which galvanized legislatures into a sustained effort to preserve the ideals of the juvenile court while respecting constitutional norms of fairness. The wave of *Gault*-era reforms has now been superseded by another wave of reforms that have muted the aspirations of juvenile justice and curtailed juvenile court jurisdiction, subjecting large numbers of young offenders to criminal prosecution through the transfer process. Our aim in this chapter has been to describe and evaluate the appellate response to these reforms.

What can now be clearly seen is that *Kent* was more significant as a precursor of *Gault* than as an independent source of constitutional principle governing the transfer process. Indeed, according to predominant judicial understanding, *Kent* has no bearing on any transfer procedure other than judicial waiver. A youth excluded from juvenile court jurisdiction by legislative exclusion has no right to a hearing and the criteria for classification need only satisfy the rational basis formula of equal protection and due process. A youth subject to concurrent jurisdiction of juvenile and criminal courts may be prosecuted in criminal court at the sole election of the prosecutor without the hearing or statement of reasons required for judicial waiver by *Kent.* Moreover, even under judicial waiver, *Kent* requires only a statement of reasons and says nothing about what reasons are needed. Indeed, the standard approach toward judicial waiver is to confer almost unlimited discretion on judges to balance the multiple social interests at stake. Thus, the overall picture is that transfer is outside the reach of the rule of law. The decision whether a youth should be treated as a juvenile or an adult lies within the virtually unreviewable discretion of legislators (who draw unreviewable classifications based on age, offense, and perhaps offense history), prosecutors (who need give no reasons at all), or judges (who must give a reason compatible with whatever the legislature has prescribed in the statute).

Recent legislative efforts to bring more youthful offenders under criminal court jurisdiction have renewed constitutional scrutiny of the transfer process. Our review of the judicial response suggests that the courts have reached a crossroads. A handful of state supreme court decisions have begun to make a new path, arguably grounded in concerns about proportionality and the heightened need for reliability in discretionary judgments about whether young offenders should be exposed to the hard edge of the criminal justice system. The courts can reaffirm what has become the settled understanding, under which juvenile adjudication is a matter of legislative grace, not grounded in any constitutional entitlement; or they can take a new turn, reviving the promise of *Kent*, enunciating new principles aiming to bring the transfer process within reach of the rule of law.

References
Cases Cited

Anthony Lee v. State, 952 P.2d 1 (Nev. 1997).

Breed v. Jones, 421 U.S. 519 (1975).

C.C. v. State, 586 So.2d 1018 (Ala. 1991).

Chapman v. State, 385 S.E.2d 661 (Geor. 1989).

Commonwealth v. Clifford C., 610 N.E.2d 967 (Mass. 1993).

Commonwealth v. O'Brien, 673 N.E.2d 552 (Mass. 1996).

Cox v. U.S., 473 F.2d 334 (4th Cir. 1973).

Goldberg v. Kelly, 397 U.S. 254 (1970).

Hansen v. State, 904 P.2d 811 (Wyo. 1995).

Harden v. Commonwealth, 885 S.W.2d 323 (Ky. 1994).

Hughes v. State, 653 A.2d 241 (Del. 1994).

In re Boot, 925 P.2d 964 (Wash. 1996).

In re Gault, 387 U.S. 1, 87 S. Ct 1428, 18 L. Ed. 2d 527 (1967).

In the Matter of J.D.W., 881 P.2d 1324 (Mont. 1994).

In the Matter of J.K.C., 891 P.2d 1169 (Mont. 1995).

In the Matter of Keith Wayne Wood, 768 P.2d 1370 (Mont. 1989).

Jahnke v. State, 692 P.2d 911 (Wyo. 1984).

Jeremiah B. v. State, 823 P.2d 883 (Nev. 1991).

Kent v. U.S., 383 U.S. 541 (1966).

Marine v. State, 607 A.2d 1185 (Del. 1992), cert. dismissed, 505 U.S. 1247 (1992).

People in the Interest of Y. C., 581 N.W.2d 483 (S.D. 1998).

People v. Fultz, 554 N.W.2d 725 (Mich. 1996).

People v. P.H., 582 N.E.2d 700 (Ill. 1991).

People v. Parrish, 549 N.W.2d 32 (Mich. 1996).

People v. Superior Court (Melvin Ray Jones), 958 P.2d 393 (Cal. 1998).

People v. Thorpe, 641 P.2d 935 (Col. 1982).

Russell v. Parratt, 543 F.2d 1214 (8th Cir. 1976).

Soto v. Superior Court, 949 P.2d 539 (Ariz. 1997).

State v. Angel C., 715 A.2d 652 (Conn. 1998).

State v. Berard, 401 A.2d 448 (R.I. 1979).

State v. Buelow, 587 A.2d 948 (Vt. 1990).

State v. Collins, 694 So.2d 624 (La. 1997).

State v. Harris, 494 N.W.2d 619 (S.D. 1993).

State v. Mohi, 901 P.2d 991 (Utah 1995).

State v. Perique, 439 So. 2d 1060 (Louis. 1983).

State v. Robert K. McL., 496 S.E.2d 887 (W.V. 1997).

State v. Sherk, 538 P.2d 1399 (Kan. 1975).

State v. Sonja B., 395 S.E.2d 803 (W. Va. 1990).

State v. Terry, 569 N.W.2d 364 (Iowa 1997).

Thompson v. State, 958 S.W.2d 1 (Ark. 1997).

U.S. v. Angelo D., 88 F.3d 856 (10th Cir. 1996).

U.S. v. Bland, 472 F.2d 1329 (1972), cert. denied, 414 U.S. 909 (1973).

U.S. v. C.G., 736 F.2d 1474 (11th Cir. 1984).

U.S. v. Doe, 98 F.3d 459, 461 (9th Cir. 1996).

U.S. v. Juvenile Male, 923 F.2d 614 (8th Cir. 1991).

U.S. v. Male Juvenile, 148 F.3d 468 (5th Cir. 1998).

U.S. v. Vancier, 515 F.2d 1378 (2d Cir.), cert. denied, 423 U.S. 857 (1975).

U.S. v. Wilson, 14 F.3d 610 (7th Cir. 1998).

Vega v. Bell, 393 N.E.2d 450 (N.Y. 1979).

Woodard v. Wainwright, 556 F.2d 781 (5th Cir. 1977).

Other References

Griffin, Patrick, Patricia Torbet, and Linda Szymanski. 1998. *Trying Juveniles as Adults: An Analysis of State Transfer Provisions.* Washington: U.S. Department of Justice, Office of Juvenile Justice and Delinquency Prevention, National Center for Juvenile Justice.

Redding, Richard E. 1997. "Juveniles Transferred to Criminal Court: Legal Reform Proposals Based on Social Science Research." *Utah Law Review* 1997: 709.

Torbet, Patricia, Richard Gable, Hunter Hurst IV, Imogene Montgomery, Linda Szymanski, Douglas Thomas. 1996. *State Responses to Serious and Violent Juvenile Crime: Research Report.* Washington: Office of Juvenile Justice and Delinquency Prevention, National Center for Juvenile Justice.

Zimring, Franklin E. 1981. "Notes toward a Jurisprudence of Waiver." In *Major Issues in Juvenile Justice Information and Training: Readings in Public Policy.* Edited by John C. Hall, Donna Martin Hamparian, John M. Pettibone, and Joseph L. White. Columbus, Ohio: Academy for Contemporary Problems.

Notes

1. These categories of transfer statutes are not mutually exclusive and, in fact, most jurisdictions do have more than one type of transfer statute. Griffin, Torbet, and Szymanski 1998, 1.

2. To avoid confusion caused by jurisdictional variation in terminology, this chapter will use "criminal court" to refer to the trial-level court in the court system for adults, which various states may call "district court," "circuit court," or even "adult court." Similarly, it will use "juvenile court" to refer to the court that has jurisdiction over children in nondelinquency cases and some delinquency cases.

3. In preparing this chapter, the authors have reviewed hundreds of cases over the last decades decided by federal and state courts. This chapter summarizes key holdings and patterns in the case law from 1990 through mid-1998, although it touches upon earlier cases in order to put recent trends into historical perspective.

4. As of December of 1995, forty-six states and the District of Columbia had judicial waiver provisions. Torbet et al. 1996, 4. By the end of 1997, Massachusetts had repealed its judicial waiver provision, leaving forty-five states with such a statute. Griffin, Torbet, and Szymanski 1998, 2.

5. It should be noted that whether to proceed in criminal or juvenile court is not always considered a jurisdictional issue. The Illinois Supreme Court has stated that juvenile court is a division of circuit court and, therefore, "[w]hether a person is tried in juvenile or criminal court is a matter of procedure rather than jurisdiction." *People v. P.H.,* 582 N.E.2d 700, 706 (Ill. 1991). Similarly, the Connecticut Supreme Court stated that because of the state's unified court system, "the issue of juvenile 'jurisdiction' is not a question of subject matter jurisdiction, but rather more a question of venue." *State v. Angel C.,* 715 A.2d 652 (Conn. 1998), n. 17 (Conn. 1998).

6. See, e.g., *Hansen v. State,* 904 P.2d 811, 822 (Wyo. 1995) ("Those statutory factors [in the Wyoming transfer statute] manifest a clear legislative adoption of the substantive due process requirements suggested by *Kent*"). A substantive due-process case examines whether the content of legislation is fair and reasonable in relation to its restriction of an individual's life, liberty, or property. In contrast, a procedural due-process case focuses on the fairness of the procedures through which the state effectuates a deprivation of life, liberty, or property.

7. See, e.g., *People v. Fultz,* 554 N.W.2d 725, 728 (Mich. 1996); *People v. Superior Court (Melvin Ray Jones),* 958 P.2d 393 (Cal. 1998).

8. See, e.g., *Jeremiah B. v. State,* 823 P.2d 883 (Nev. 1991) (juvenile judge did not abuse discretion in deciding that vehicular homicide was sufficiently heinous crime to warrant transfer). The criteria in the Nevada judicial waiver law, as interpreted by the Nevada Supreme Court, illustrate the current trend toward a focus on the offense rather than the offender. The criteria for transfer include the nature and seriousness of the charged offenses, the persistency and seriousness of past conduct, and the personal attributes of the offender. The court stated that the attributes of the offender are less important than the first two criteria and liberally interpreted the "seriousness of the charged offenses" criteria. 823 P.2d at 884–85.

9. Some cases focus on a requirement to reference the statutory factors in the transfer order. See *C.C. v. State,* 586 So.2d 1018, 1020 (Ala. 1991) (court must specify that it considered statutory factors: "if a transferring court states that all

six factors . . . have been considered, then its order complies with the rules"); *Harden v. Commonwealth*, 885 S.W.2d 323, 325 (Ky. 1994) (reasons for transfer "must be specific enough to permit a meaningful review for the purpose of determining whether there has been compliance with the statute"); *State v. Collins*, 694 So.2d 624 (La. 1997) (transfer criteria are of constitutional magnitude and must be addressed specifically).

10. In many jurisdictions, though, the probable-cause determination is made at a separate hearing and is not addressed in reviewing a transfer decision.

11. *In the Matter of J.D.W.*, 881 P.2d 1324 (Mont. 1994); *In the Matter of J.K.C.*, 891 P.2d 1169 (Mont. 1995). In the J.K.C. case, the court ordered the juvenile court to assume jurisdiction rather than reversing and remanding to the juvenile court for a further hearing and redetermination, the usual remedy in such cases. The court justified this decision by stating "the State having had its day in court, there is no legal basis upon which to send this case back to the Youth Court on the premise that at some point the prosecution will finally get it right." *J.K.C.*, 891 P.2d at 1172. The court noted that the testimony supporting the decision to waive jurisdiction was based solely on the seriousness of the offense and that other witnesses had testified that J.K.C. could be adequately treated within the juvenile system. Ibid.

12. For example, the Nevada Supreme Court reversed a transfer decision because the juvenile court judge failed to exercise his discretion in determining whether "the child's actions were substantially the result of his substance abuse," a statutory criterion for retention of jurisdiction, because the judge concluded that criminal actions are never the result of substance abuse. *Anthony Lee v. State*, 952 P.2d 1 (Nev. 1997).

13. In the federal system, which does not have separate juvenile courts, offenders under eighteen are prosecuted in district court as juveniles if they are charged with an offense not punishable by death or life imprisonment as long as they consent to that procedure and the attorney general has not directed that the offender be prosecuted as an adult. *Federal Juvenile Delinquency Act*, 18 U.S.C. § 5032 (1994).

14. *U.S. v. Juvenile Male*, 923 F.2d 614 (8th Cir. 1991). The Eighth Circuit interpreted decisions in several other circuits, stating that the Second Circuit declined to review certification because of the lack of standards for such review and the Eleventh Circuit would not review the accuracy of statements made in the certification, but would review the certification for statutory compliance. *U.S. v. Vancier*, 515 F.2d 1378 (2d Cir.), cert. denied, 423 U.S. 857 (1975); *U.S. v. C.G.*, 736 F.2d 1474 (11th Cir. 1984).

15. *U.S. v. Male Juvenile*, 148 F.3d 468 (5th Cir. 1998). The Ninth Circuit had made a similar holding in an earlier case, observing "[t]he statutory language . . . and the regulations adopted thereunder clearly establish in whom the power to decide whether the United States will proceed against a juvenile is vested." *U.S. v. Doe*, 98 F.2d 459, 461 (9th Cir. 1996). In contrast, the Tenth Circuit upheld a certification signed by an assistant U.S. attorney where the U.S. attorney had expressly designated the assistant to serve as acting U.S. attorney in his absence. *U.S. v. Angelo D.*, 88 F.3d 856 (10th Cir. 1996).

16. See *U.S. v. Wilson,* 14 F.3d 610 (7th Cir. 1998). The *Wilson* court cites similar holdings from the Second, Third, Fifth, Sixth, Eighth, Tenth, and Eleventh Circuits. Ibid. at 614.

17. *Commonwealth v. Clifford C.,* 610 N.E.2d 967 (Mass. 1993). The Massachusetts statute required a prosecutor requesting transfer to prove the juvenile was dangerous and not amenable to rehabilitation. The statute listed a number of factors that must be considered by the court in making a transfer decision.

18. The evidence cited included: "(1) the lack of success of previous treatment efforts, . . . (2) a juvenile record involving violence to persons, . . . (3) a lack of academic effort, persistent truancy, and disciplinary problems at school, . . . (4) a history of substance abuse, . . . and (5) the absence of an intact family to support rehabilitative efforts." Ibid. at 970 (citations omitted).

19. *Commonwealth v. O'Brien,* 673 N.E.2d 552 (Mass. 1996). The court held that the juvenile judge relied on expert testimony from the bail hearing not in evidence at the transfer hearing and improperly excluded an addendum to the report of the commonwealth's expert and the testimony of an FBI special agent. The court further held that the judge erred in gauging amenability to treatment rather than rehabilitation because "while a juvenile can be treated within the juvenile justice system, transfer is still appropriate if the juvenile cannot be rehabilitated within the time that the juvenile can be kept within the juvenile justice system." Ibid. at 557.

20. In a brief order over a lengthy dissent, the Michigan Supreme Court recently reversed a trial court judgment retaining jurisdiction. The dissenting supreme court justice argued that none of the trial judge's factual findings had been found to be clearly erroneous and that the seriousness of the offense was the only statutory criterion supporting transfer. *People v. Fultz,* 554 N.W.2d 725 (Mich. 1996). In this case, the twenty-three-year-old defendant was on trial for sexual assaults recently alleged to have been committed against his seven-year-old niece when he was sixteen. No evidence was presented of any criminal activity by the defendant in the eight years since the alleged assaults. If jurisdiction had not been waived, the defendant would not have been subject to prosecution because of his age at the time of prosecution.

21. *People in the Interest of Y.C.,* 581 N.W.2d 483, 489 (S.D. 1998). The relevant statute specified that "the court shall consider only whether it is contrary to the best interest of the child and of the public to retain jurisdiction over the child" and specified seven factors that may be considered by the court. *S.D. Codified Laws* § 26-11-4. The court then cited an earlier case establishing that "[i]t is not necessary that evidence be presented on all of these factors at each transfer hearing, or that the trial court must make express findings on each factor" to support its ruling. *People in the Interest of Y.C.,* 581 N.W.2d at 485, citing *State v. Harris,* 494 N.W.2d 619, 624 (S.D. 1993).

22. This case highlights the difference between a system focused on the offender and a system focused on the offense. Recent legislative changes in many jurisdictions that expand the stated purposes of their juvenile justice system to include more punitive and incapacitative concerns have not had a dramatic impact on appellate court scrutiny of transfer decisions. Although the expanded

purposes often accompany more punitive sentencing options in juvenile court, some courts, such as the South Dakota Supreme Court, have cited these concerns to support a transfer based strongly on the offense charged rather than characteristics of the juvenile.

23. As of December of 1995, thirty-six states and the District of Columbia had statutory exclusion provisions. Torbet et al. 1996, 4; see also *State v. Angel C.,* 715 A.2d 652 (Conn. 1998) (describing legislative exclusion statutes and distinguishing whether statutes exclude certain juveniles from original juvenile court jurisdiction or mandate transfer of those juveniles). The majority of jurisdictions with legislative exclusion statutes had recently expanded the provisions. Torbet et al. 1996, 4.

24. These arguments tend to overlap arguments considered in the next section on prosecutorial election statutes and are addressed in greater depth there.

25. "Aggravated juvenile delinquency" is defined as any of six specified offenses committed by juveniles while they are confined in state reform schools or facilities under control of the department of social welfare. 538 P.2d at 1402. The defendant in this case was convicted in criminal court based on his second escape from the Boys Industrial School.

26. See supra, p. 190, for description of how reverse waiver procedures can serve as a "safety valve." The statute was challenged by a fifteen-year-old defendant charged with sodomy in the first degree.

27. The sixteen-year-old juvenile in this case had been convicted of armed robbery in criminal court.

28. The court also rejected a statistics-based equal-protection challenge. Data presented to the court showed that in the preceding three years, the four juveniles charged as adults with armed robbery were all black males. In that period, over one hundred black males, four black females, and thirteen white males had been charged as juveniles with armed robbery. 439 So. 2d at 1065.

29. As of the end of 1997, twenty-three states had reverse waiver provisions. Griffin, Torbet, and Szymanski 1998, 2.

30. See *State v. Terry,* 569 N.W.2d 364, 367 (Iowa 1997) (in reverse waiver proceeding, burden of proof on juvenile). Other reverse waiver proceedings apply after *conviction* in criminal court to permit the court to sentence the offender as a juvenile. A Michigan court found that its transfer statutes provided no significant difference in due-process protections between the juvenile waiver and legislative exclusion provisions because the "waiver-back" procedure used the same substantive criteria and flexible evidentiary standards as in a juvenile sentencing hearing. *People v. Parrish,* 549 N.W.2d 32, 35 (Mich. 1996).

31. In contrast to the Michigan statute described in note 30, the Vermont statute did not provide specific standards for reverse waiver determinations. In Buelow's case, the trial court applied the factors delineated in *Kent* and denied the defendant's motion for transfer back to juvenile court. It found that fourteen-year-old Buelow, who was charged with the murder of his seven-year-old cousin while perpetrating a sexual assault, should remain in criminal court because of the seriousness of the offense, the manner in which it was committed, the personal nature of the offense, and the merit of the charge. 587 A.2d at 953.

32. Overruling earlier cases, the Arkansas Supreme Court held that the trial court may not rely solely upon allegations in the information in finding that the offenses were of a serious and violent nature and that therefore the juvenile should be tried in criminal court. 958 S.W.2d at 3.

33. The court stated that the reverse amenability hearing "provided a judicial counterweight to any perceived prosecutorial charging excess" and "eliminate[d] the potential for arbitrary or capricious charging decisions to result in unequal treatment." 607 A.2d at 1209. Ultimately the court found that because the state had not shown a fair likelihood of convicting the defendant of first-degree murder, the case should proceed in juvenile court.

34. The challenged statute gave the criminal court original jurisdiction over juveniles over fifteen charged with a serious violent offense, or a violent offense when the juvenile has a criminal history. 925 P.2d at 964.

35. As of December of 1997, fourteen states and the District of Columbia had prosecutorial election provisions. Griffin, Torbet, and Szymanski 1998, 2.

36. See supra, p. 188–89.

37. Some defendants, without success, have turned this separation-of-powers argument on its head and argued that the prosecutorial discretion unconstitutionally permitted the legislature to restrict the courts by placing certain functions in the executive branch. See *In the Matter of Keith Wayne Wood,* 768 P.2d 1370, 1377 (Mont. 1989).

38. The Eighth Circuit applied similar reasoning in *Russell v. Parratt,* 543 F.2d 1214 (8th Cir. 1976), relying on *U.S. v. Bland,* 472 F.2d 1329 (1972), cert. denied, 414 U.S. 909 (1973).

39. Wood also raised an equal-protection challenge to the Montana statute. The relevant class, as identified in the statute, is based on age and gravity of offense. The court applied rational basis scrutiny, asking whether the classification "is rationally related to a legitimate state interest." 768 P.2d at 1375. Wood argued that strict scrutiny should apply because the statute infringed on a fundamental right, due process of law, but the court determined that procedural due process should not be considered a fundamental right. Ibid. The court then found that Wood failed to carry his burden because the legislative concern over an increase in teen homicides is rationally related to the classification, and thus the statute does not violate equal protection. Lastly, Wood argued that the Montana statute violated Montana separation-of-powers doctrine because the challenged provision permitted the legislature to restrict judicial power and place certain functions within the executive branch. The court, however, noted that the juvenile court is a creation of the legislature, not the state constitution, and therefore the legislature can adjust the contours of juvenile court jurisdiction. Ibid. at 1377.

40. Because of a failure to raise the constitutional concerns with the trial court, the Wyoming Supreme Court did not address a separation of powers argument. 692 P.2d at 928.

41. The court did not address due-process and separation-of-powers challenges because it invalidated the statute on equal-protection grounds. 901 P.2d at 1004 n. 21.

42. The *Mohi* case provided an interesting review of prosecutorial election

statutes. Tellingly, the prosecution, the defense, the majority, and the dissent differed in their computations of the number of states with direct-file statutes. Similar confusion is apparent in many judicial opinions regarding transfer, in which courts routinely cite cases involving legislative exclusion transfer statutes to support their holding on a prosecutorial election statute, and vice versa. The *Mohi* majority opinion, whose definitions coincide most closely with this chapter's analysis, found that in 1995, eight jurisdictions had prosecutorial election statutes. The eight jurisdictions are Arkansas, Colorado, Florida, Louisiana, Michigan, Nebraska, Utah, and Wyoming. 901 P.2d at 1000 n. 11. Since the *Mohi* decision, other states have passed similar provisions. See, e.g., *Va. Code* 16.1-269.1(c); *W. Va. Code* 49-5-10(d). The majority carefully distinguished traditional areas of prosecutorial discretion such as selecting which charges to bring from discretion to decide which juveniles to prosecute as adults. It found that the prosecutorial discretion in the Utah statute was far more arbitrary and uncontrolled than discretion in other statutes.

43. The court did not address the additional consequences a juvenile might face as a result of a conviction in criminal court, even if the disposition is identical to the disposition of a juvenile remaining in juvenile court.

44. Several decades ago, courts rejected arguments claiming that adjudication as a juvenile is comparable to the right to receive welfare benefits, which could not be denied without a hearing. *Woodard v. Wainwright,* 556 F.2d 781, 785 (5th Cir. 1977) (distinguishing *Goldberg v. Kelly,* 397 U.S. 254 [1970]); *State v. Berard,* 401 A.2d 448 (R.I. 1979) (same).

45. Franklin Zimring (1981, 193) has described transfer to criminal court as "the capital punishment of juvenile justice."

Chapter Six

The Punitive Necessity of Waiver

FRANKLIN E. ZIMRING

Transferring defendants still young enough for juvenile court into the criminal courts is a compound legal arrangement of a special character; it is a universal exception to a universal rule. The first universal is juvenile justice itself. In every American state, juvenile courts have been created to respond to criminal charges against offenders under a maximum age that varies from sixteen to eighteen.

The use of a juvenile court for youth crime is in fact almost universal throughout the developed nations. No major industrial democracy incorporates the processing of very young offenders into the normal operation of its criminal courts. A century after its creation, the juvenile court is the uniform major premise in policy toward youth crime in every advanced legal system.

While juvenile court is the universal rule, every American jurisdiction has provided for exceptions to it—circumstances and procedures that transfer those within the age boundaries of juvenile court to criminal court instead. The particular procedures used and the circumstances that justify their use vary, but the provision for some transfer of cases is, in the United States, just as universal as the general policy that it modifies.

Both the policy of juvenile court jurisdiction and the exception to it are puzzling American universals. Why the ubiquity of juvenile courts for trying our youngest offenders? What is the special advantage of a court for children in criminal cases? Why does such a court continue everywhere despite widespread doubts about its capacity to rehabilitate youth on the terms of the court's original philosophy? If juvenile court is a good place to process and sanction most young offenders, why not all young offenders?

My account of the answers to these questions will be delivered in four installments. Section 1 argues that the necessity of transfers must be understood in the context of the functions and limits of juvenile courts. The modern juvenile court is an institution that holds juveniles accountable for intentional wrongs but is restrained in both the kind and amount of punishment it can administer. The strong pressure to remove cases from juvenile court comes when older adolescents are accused of conduct so serious that the minimum punishment felt necessary exceeds the maximum punishment within the power of the juvenile court. It is the limited capacity of the juvenile court to punish that leads to transfers as a universal exception to juvenile court jurisdiction in the United States.

The second part of the essay examines three different structural accommodations to the need for serious punishment for a few youths: wholesale transfer of jurisdiction to criminal courts, the expansion of punishment powers available within the juvenile court so that even the most terrible crimes can meet their just deserts in a juvenile court, and the selective transfer of cases. I regard selective transfer as the obviously superior method to respond to the need for serious punishment in extraordinary cases.

But selective transfer can be achieved in many different ways. Section 3 contrasts three different mechanisms for transfer: (1) legislative standards that define both the necessary and sufficient causes for transfer, (2) a legal framework that delegates power to judges to decide whether a particular case requires transfer, and (3) a system that delegates total power to prosecutors. In practice, I show the real choice is between judicial and prosecutorial final authority.

The concluding part of this essay describes a few of the minimum conditions necessary to justice at the interface between juvenile and criminal court. Without appropriate substantive provisions for the treatment of transferred cases, no procedural restrictions on the method of transfer can rescue the system from incoherence.

One further point is necessary as an introduction to this paper. The question of transfer from juvenile to criminal court is the very opposite of an independent issue. The design of sensible provision for transfer depends on clearly understanding the functions and limits of juvenile and criminal courts, and the differences between these two institutions. Finding the appropriate methods of transfer from juvenile to criminal courts thus demands that we comprehend the entire context in which such decisions must be made.

1. The Mission and Limits of Juvenile Court

The universal popularity of juvenile court jurisdiction for very young criminals suggests a widely shared perception that the very youngest law violators are different from other criminals, as well as agreement that a special judicial institution is better suited to adjudicating cases involving the young than is a criminal court. In the original theory of the juvenile court, young law violators were considered just one class of child in need of help, and the only official reason for any legal response when children committed crimes was to help the child. On this theory, interventions in the lives of delinquent youth were no different from the responses that the legal system would choose for noncriminal children in need of supervision, and wholly different from those appropriate to adult law violators (Mack 1909). In theory, the special province of the juvenile court flowed automatically from the solely youth-serving purposes for intervention in the juvenile court.

But was there ever really a time when the legal system's response to the youthful burglar and car thief was wholly nonpunitive? Historical accounts from the earliest years suggest that help without blame was never the court's sole basis for intervention (Schlossman 1977; Platt 1969). Punitive motives seem to have been an inevitable part of juvenile court responses from the start, and by the time *In re Gault* (387 U.S. 1, 87 S. Ct 1428, 18 L. Ed. 2d 527) was decided in 1967, the punitive content of juvenile court sanctions for delinquency was the central factual premise on which modern procedural protections were based (Zimring 2000, pt. 2).

For at least a generation, then, the official jurisprudence of the juvenile court's delinquency jurisdiction has included the punishment of wrongdoing. Even with the reduction in culpability that the young may deserve because of diminished responsibility, why not administer such punishments in criminal rather than juvenile courts? Why is punishing the young in the juvenile court style so different and so much better than the sanctioning that criminal courts can deliver that every legal system chooses the juvenile court forum?

The advantages of the juvenile court are two. The first distinguishing feature of a juvenile court is expertise on youth and youth development. The court and its affiliated institutions have expertise in the special needs and special responses of young persons. In the modern understanding of juvenile justice, such special information on youth is not only relevant to a narrow band of issues concerning rehabilitation, it also informs the character of appropriate supervision, of assessments of dangerousness, and of judgments about culpability (Allen 1964, 52–53).

But more than expertise is involved in the uniform choice of a juvenile court. The second advantage of the juvenile court is restraint from the imposition of destructive punishments. Even in the post-*Gault* era of legal realism about its mission, the American juvenile court has been characterized by a qualified but very significant commitment to the welfare of all minors who come before it. The juvenile court in setting the terms of punishment must stop short of destroying the objects of its attention to preserve its legitimacy.

In other writing I have used the phrase "room to reform" to describe the objective of juvenile courts even when they punish. The policy of the juvenile court is to punish offenders without sacrificing the long-term life chances and developmental opportunities of the targets of punitive sanctions (Zimring 1998, chap. 5). The key distinction here is between punishments that hurt and those that permanently disfigure. Discomfort and restriction are elements of juvenile sanctions but permanent stigma is to be avoided at great cost, and a juvenile residential facility that did not offer schooling and life preparation to its subjects would be in irredeemable conflict with the purposes of the modern juvenile court.

This search for nondisfiguring punishments is by no means the equivalent of seeking out only the best interests of the convicted juvenile burglar. All of the customary aims of criminal punishment can be served while providing room to reform, including deterrence, short-term incapacitation, and retribution within limits. But the limits of punishment are also very important. The problem with extending secure confinement far into adulthood to punish juvenile crime is the destruction of any chance for a normal young adulthood. The typical maximum sanction in juvenile court will leave time for a young adult to emerge from confinement to enter the world of work, to mate, and to form a family. The high value placed on the future life opportunities of the delinquent is a defining aspect of the juvenile court that sets it apart from the open-ended punishment portfolio of the criminal court. The two courts may serve the same inventory of purposes of punishment, but with very different limits.

The commitment to limit punishments to preserve the juvenile's life changes is at once the singular appeal of the juvenile court and the characteristic feature of juvenile justice that inevitably produces pressure to transfer some serious cases to criminal court. The reason for this dual importance is that the mix of sanctions limited in this way is the best result for the overwhelming majority of all youth law violations, but a serious problem for a very few of the most serious of juvenile crimes. If the unwillingness of a juvenile court to disfigure is a defining characteristic of its orientation to its subjects, the very serious crime committed by a sixteen- or seventeen-year-old is exactly the kind of hard case that the juvenile court cannot easily accommodate while preserving its nondestructive mandate.

On this account, the limited range of sanctions is not an oversight or an unimportant detail of the juvenile court's organization, but rather a fundamental element of juvenile court philosophy that is the court's great strength in most cases. But there are, it seems, cases where the most severe secure confinement that the normally constituted juvenile court can permit itself falls far short of the minimum punishment that the community will tolerate. The typical worst case in a metropolitan juvenile court with a maximum jurisdiction age of eighteen will be intentional homicide (Zimring 1998, table 7.1) committed by a sixteen- or seventeen-year-old. These are visible cases where punishment responses that avoid impinging on the offender's life changes may fall short of the community's sense of minimum desert. What to do?

To ignore demands for a special punitive response is an act of will that leaves the juvenile court vulnerable to swift legislative change in a democratic government. While "worst case" events are a small part of the juvenile court's business, they are recurrent phenomena. Some accommodation to the pressure for additional punishment in serious cases has become universal in the United States. But the structural changes that have been made to account for hard cases differ, and these different systems carry very different mixes of cost and benefit, as the next section will demonstrate.

Of course, not all of the cases transferred out of juvenile court are superserious. In this regard, it is necessary to distinguish between the type of case that makes transfer necessary and the much wider variety of cases that get transferred. Once transfer out of juvenile court is institutionalized, the practice is often not restricted to the superserious cases that rendered it necessary. All manner of older, recidivist, and recalcitrant juveniles are pushed into criminal courts once the channel between the two institutions has been opened (Feld 1987; Ferguson and Douglas 1970). But my argument suggests that only one class of cases makes transfer necessary, and substantial effort should be invested in restricting the practice to cases that meet the criterion of core necessity.

If waiver is restricted to cases where the sanctions available in juvenile court are clearly inadequate, the great majority of cases close to the waiver border will be homicide charges, but not all homicide charges will be strong candidates for waiver. In my view, even murder charges are better thought of as a necessary but not a sufficient condition for transfer of juvenile defendants to criminal courts. So the number of cases where waiver might be necessary is small, but the importance of finding a principled basis for waiver is much larger than the number of cases would suggest. How juvenile and criminal courts deal with these most serious cases is one significant element of the legal framework of juvenile and criminal justice.

2. Structures of Accommodation

A very few young offenders will commit crimes that demand, at minimum, more punishment than a juvenile court that seeks to avoid debilitating injury can administer. There are three basic structural mechanisms that might change the ordinary operation of juvenile justice to meet the need for extra punishment in such extreme cases. The delinquency juris-diction of the juvenile court could be cut back or abolished to minimize the number of extremely serious cases with only limited punishment power available. Or punishment powers within the juvenile court could be expanded so that even the punishment suited to crimes of extreme seriousness would be available within the court for children. Or a safety valve procedure for transfer of some special cases could be instituted without changing either general jurisdictional boundaries or limited ju-venile court punishment powers. Of the three structural accommoda-tions, the safety valve procedure for transfer in special cases is by far the most common and also the least harmful to the appropriate functions of the Juvenile Court. Only highly selective transfer systems can avoid needless reductions in the jurisdiction of juvenile courts and gratuitous assaults on the legitimacy of the court.

Jurisdictional Cutbacks

If the juvenile court is a barrier to the just punishment of very serious cases, why not just abolish the court? Such a remedy might be regarded as overbroad, since more than 98 percent of the delinquency petitions in the United States are not transformed into adult prosecutions where the practice is discretionary. But what is the harm in dropping juvenile court jurisdiction when minors commit felonies?

The harm of adopting an overbroad reduction in juvenile court juris-diction is important only if there is special value in treating most juvenile crime in a distinctively juvenile court. For this reason, the willingness to adopt overbroad restrictions on the jurisdiction of the juvenile court is one significant indicator of continuing public commitment to the ideal of a children's court.

The broadest method of cutting back on the limited punishments of juvenile justice is to abolish the court entirely, thus ending any special restrictions on punishment tied to juvenile courts. For all its punitive sim-plicity, this has been a reform option without any constituency even in an era of great concern about lenient treatment of young criminals. Nothing speaks as powerfully to the continuing legitimacy of some ideal of juve-nile justice than the absence of credible campaigns to disestablish the juvenile court.

Short of abolishing the jurisdiction of juvenile courts, the next most effective wholesale reduction in jurisdiction would be to cut back on the court's maximum jurisdictional age. While the usual boundary between juvenile and criminal courts is the eighteenth birthday, there are many states that use the seventeenth birthday as the jurisdictional end of juvenile court and some that cut off delinquency jurisdiction at sixteen. Cutting off the oldest age groups from delinquency jurisdiction would have substantial impact on serious crimes of violence because such offenses are more common in the late teens than in younger age groups. More homicide arrests occur between the sixteenth and eighteenth birthday in the United States than in all the younger age groups combined (United States Department of Justice 1998, 232–33).

Reducing the jurisdictional age of the juvenile court is both overly broad and too narrow as a method of removing serious crimes from the protection of juvenile justice, but only its overbreadth is a decisive disadvantage. Cutting the age of juvenile court delinquency jurisdiction from eighteen to sixteen would reduce the homicide caseload by 60 percent, but that would still leave hundreds of homicides each year within the age boundaries of American juvenile justice. So reduction in age would not be a complete removal of troublesome cases and would have to be supplemented with other case reduction methods. But that is hardly a fatal defect in any legal restructuring that does not carry significant costs.

It is the overbreadth of age reduction reforms that must explain the reluctance of American states to adopt them in large numbers even during the youth crime panic years of 1991–97, when new legislative countermeasures to youth violence were an annual event. The problem with age reductions is that they indiscriminately sweep nonviolent and violent offenders alike into the ranks of criminological adulthood, flooding the criminal courts with nonserious cases. But what is the great harm in tens of thousands of adolescent thefts and house break-ins being processed in criminal courts?

The lack of recurrent efforts to lower age limits is powerful circumstantial evidence that unnecessary expulsion from the jurisdiction of juvenile courts is still widely regarded as a significant disadvantage in the late 1990s. My argument here is that general cutbacks in jurisdiction would be a natural method of responding to concern over serious cases if there were no strong preference for juvenile court jurisdiction in garden-variety delinquency cases, including many cases of juvenile violence. The prospects of this kind of cutback are worth our attention in analyzing the treatment of serious cases not because they have been a popular method of diverting troublesome cases, but precisely because they have not been embraced in the war against juvenile violence.

The failure to launch radical experiments in the reduction of delinquency jurisdiction tells us that juvenile court processing of youth crime is still a normative system. In this sense, the absence of abolition and age reduction as popular causes is the dog that did not bark in juvenile justice reform. The only explanation for no serious proposals to cut back juvenile courts is the continued legitimacy of the ideal of juvenile courts for young offenders.

There is one further respect in which the absence of any trend to reduce the maximum age of delinquency jurisdiction provides data of value on public opinion about adolescent development. The eighteenth birthday has been a consensus boundary in juvenile justice for some time, but the original subjects of delinquency jurisdiction were much younger than that (Zimring 1982, chap. 3). The age of both modal and maximum delinquency jurisdiction expanded throughout most of the twentieth century. There is no sign that the current conditions of American life carry any strong countervailing tendency. While legal reforms provide that youths accused of particular serious crimes can be transferred at earlier ages to the criminal court, the absence of any broader cutback in maximum age argues against concluding that younger offenders are being transferred because they are regarded as more mature than in previous generations. Earlier maturity would support a general reduction in jurisdictional age. The selection only of serious crimes suggests the need to punish rather than any developmental maturity of the object of punishment is the motivating factor.

So the slogan "If you are old enough to do the crime, you are old enough to do the time" is not about maturity. It is instead a denial that issues like immaturity should be relevant to the appropriate punishment for criminal offenders. The lack of consistent momentum toward lower jurisdictional age limits in the United States shows us that the shift toward punitive responses to serious youth crime is not grounded in a conception that adult levels of responsibility are acquired either earlier or more easily than in past generations. The political conflict in the United States is not about adolescent maturity but about the relevance of immaturity to the proper punishment of young offenders.

Expanding Punishments in Juvenile Courts

Once the problem presented by serious youth crimes is identified as the limited punishment powers of juvenile court, one natural remedy would be to expand the maximum punishment available in juvenile court until the gap between what the community demands and what the court can provide has been closed. For many years, the notion of expansions of penalties within juvenile courts was a road not taken in juvenile justice reform, and criticism of this strategy was a hypothetical exercise (Zimring 1981, 1991). More recently, several jurisdictions have authorized special trial procedures and expanded punishments in some branches of juvenile court under the rubric that Howell and Redding call "blended jurisdiction" in chapter 4 of this volume. The details of "blended jurisdiction" schemes vary, but most such systems share three characteristics: (1) cases are assigned to special divisions within juvenile courts where jury trials and other nonstandard procedural protections are provided; (2) very long periods of penal confinement are available after conviction, but usually the confinement extending past majority is assessed conditionally with further proceedings and findings necessary to confirm long sentences; and (3) these blended alternatives within the juvenile court are not an exclusive mechanism for extending punishment—every jurisdiction with blended jurisdiction provides for transfer to criminal court for homicide prosecutions as well.

The Byzantine complexity of the laws creating blended jurisdiction sentencing demands scrutiny. In an era where truth in sentencing is popular and hostility to indeterminacy is rampant, the Texas provisions create nominal forty-year sentences that can nonetheless result in the release of a juvenile at age eighteen unless the longer penal term is extended at a separate hearing when the offender turns eighteen. The Minnesota blended jurisdiction sentencing provisions are among the most dauntingly complicated in the history of criminal sentencing. Both the complexity and the conditional nature of typical "blended" sentences may be the result of intentional efforts to design systems that sound much tougher just after conviction than they turn out to be in the hard currency of time served in custody. There is a long tradition in the United States of creating sentencing systems that bark much louder than they bite. To some extent, both the contingency and complexity of blended sentencing may just be deliberately false advertising by drafters who want legislation to sound stringent.

But more than that must be at work to create sentencing structures distinctively inconsistent with the prevailing style of sentence determination. I would suggest that the contingency in most extended sentencing systems is an attempt to resolve the central dilemma of extended punishment power in juvenile court—any sentence long enough to satisfy the retributive demands of the community in extreme cases is too long to be consistent with the juvenile court's fundamental commitment to the life opportunities of its subjects. The only plausible escape from this dilemma is a form of doublespeak in which long prison sentences can be announced but not enforced.

I do not wish to recite in these pages the considerable litany of disadvantages associated with extended punishments in juvenile court that are mentioned in my earlier analysis (Zimring 1998, chap. 9) and discussed elsewhere in this volume. I do want to emphasize that if limiting the destructive impact of punishments on youth is a central tenet of American juvenile justice, then any juvenile court sentence of twenty years' time served turns out to be a contradiction of that central element of the juvenile court's philosophy. Criminal courts can ignore the future life chances of the defendants before them and in fact do so quite frequently. There is no violation of the criminal court's mandate in twenty-five-year-to-life sentences as long as such punishments are administered in ways consistent with penal proportionality and the offender's dignity and personhood. But when the juvenile court sacrifices its obligation to limit the destructive impact of its sanctions, it creates a crisis of mission with implications that spill over from the subunit of the court that assigns the extended punishments to the whole of the juvenile court. Once that institution gets into the business of unlimited destruction, the sincerity of its orientation to limits is open to question across the whole spectrum of delinquency jurisdiction. When the juvenile court becomes the instrument of open-ended incapacitation, the damage is to its core commitment; the court has not shot itself in the foot, it has shot itself in the heart.

One reason I believe that the complex and conditional nature of blended sentences is more denial than deception on the part of its drafters is that the false advertising of blended sentences has been totally ineffectual. In no jurisdiction where conditional sentences have been used has the new blended jurisdiction system ended transfer to criminal courts. In this important sense, extended sentences in juvenile court have been a supplement rather than a substitute for transfer. If blended sentences were too transparent to serve as a displacement of transfer to criminal court, it is plausible to search for other constituencies that might see benefit in the complex contingencies of the new provisions. One such benefit would be to reassure those who would be gravely troubled by the long shadow that "real" forty-year sentences would cast on the legitimacy of the juvenile court.

Selective Transfer

The vice of expanding punishment power in juvenile courts is that it undermines the mission of the entire juvenile system. The vice of across-the-board cutbacks in juvenile court jurisdiction is gross overbreadth, because there is still a preference for juvenile court processing of youth crimes where this does not conflict with the community's sense of minimum commensurate desert. The best outcome is to transfer only those cases where high-magnitude punishments are required over to criminal courts through a process that minimizes the transfer of juvenile court subjects where a transfer is not necessary. The optimal outcome is a system that produces selective transfer only of cases where there is direct conflict between the upper bounds of juvenile court punishment and the minimum punishment deserved by an offender if guilty of the charged offense. That highly selective transfer is a preferred result follows easily from finding positive value in the juvenile court processing of most young offenders. But who is to select the candidates for transfer and what processes should govern the transfer decision? These are the topics of the following section.

3. The Right Kind of Safety Valve

The traditional juvenile court structure in the United States developed with a discretionary system of waiver where the juvenile court judge could elect to waive his court's primary jurisdiction over an accused juvenile, and only such a waiver would allow charges to be adjudicated in the criminal court. In the post-*Gault* era of prosecutors in juvenile courts, the division of authority between prosecutor and judge in juvenile court waiver decision making is much like the division of labor in sentencing decisions. The prosecutor is the moving party who advocates the superiority of a waiver to criminal court, and the judge is an umpiral authority with wide discretion to decide the matter and very little prospect of reversal by an appellate court. This system is described in Professor Dawson's chapter in this volume. It has traditionally generated a low volume of transfers to criminal court.

An alternative or supplemental approach to discretionary waiver is legislative provision for transfer to criminal court. Two types of legislative standard setting on transfer should initially be distinguished. One type of legislation creates minimum conditions that must be met before waiver is possible. The typical legislative standard of this type will state the minimum age and list the predicate charges that can support a discretionary transfer. This sort of law provides only the necessary conditions for transfer, and usually reserves the decision in particular cases to a juvenile court judge. Such provisions narrow somewhat the discretionary power of judges and prosecutors to select candidates for transfer.

When legislative standards turn prescriptive, they attempt to set both the necessary and sufficient conditions for transfer to criminal courts. The attempt in prescriptive standards is to create binding standards for transfer based on categories of criminal offenses. As Professor Feld points out in this volume, legislation providing such prescriptive standards has been a growth industry in the 1980s and 1990s, either supplementing or replacing judicial waiver as a method of channeling juvenile defendants into criminal courts. When legislative standards are the exclusive basis for transfer to criminal court, the list of crimes that generate transfer grows rather long. Because only a minority of even homicide charges end up being waived to criminal court in discretionary systems, the impact of automatic waiver standards is to sharply expand the volume of waived cases even when the literal terms of the statute are partially nullified by prosecutorial discretions.

There are two contrasting patterns of impact that lists of automatic waiver provisions might produce. If the provisions of prescriptive transfer statutes are substantially enforced, a much larger volume of cases is transferred than under a discretionary system and the range in severity of cases transferred to criminal court will be substantial. Robbery and assault are very heterogeneous crimes. Automatic waiver of arrests for even aggravated forms of these offenses will transfer many cases into criminal court that will have relatively low prosecution priority. These are cases where the minimum levels of punishment that the community would tolerate are far lower than in the extreme cases that make transfer unavoidable. The vice of this type of wholesale prescriptive transfer is the same type of overbreadth associated with abolition of the court or reduction in jurisdictional age, though perhaps not to the same degree. The transfer of large categories of heterogeneous felony charges to criminal courts might reproduce within the criminal courts institutional arrangements for adjudicating such cases that much resemble juvenile courts. This is one take on the impact of New York's 1978 legislation and the "youth docket" that has evolved in the New York City Criminal Court (Singer 1996).

If gross overbreadth is one outcome of broad prescriptive transfer standards, subterranean discretion is a second mode of adaptation. When only 1 to 4 percent of nonlethal violent felonies were being transferred prior to prescriptive standards, laws mandating that all serious assaults and armed or injurious robberies should be transferred to criminal court might be substantially nullified by the exercise of prosecutorial discretion (see Zimring 1998, chap. 7). Few practical controls exist on the prosecutor's power to select charges and thus to avoid charging crimes that would generate automatic transfer consequences.

If automatic transfer standards merely shift discretion from juvenile court judges to prosecutors, there is little to recommend these automatic devices as a juvenile justice law reform. Prosecutors may favor such laws even if they do not intend to enforce them literally because prescriptive transfer statutes both enhance prosecutorial power and reduce the prosecutorial work effort needed to obtain transfer in judicial waiver regimes. But a juvenile court judge would seem a better umpiral authority than a prosecutor on the minimum level of punishment that would be deserved in a particular case; if waiver seems more like a sentencing than a charging decision, then maintaining judicial authority seems preferable to the concentration of all power in the prosecutor. Further, prosecutorial power is harder to observe; about the only kind of power that is less visible and reviewable than a discretionary judicial decision is an exercise of prosecutorial discretion.

Even with the manifest problems of unchecked prosecutorial discretion, a good argument can be made that aggressive prosecutorial reduction in the scope of prescriptive legislative standards is preferable to the wholesale overcriminalization that comes with the literal enforcement of broad legislative transfer categories.

Can it at least be said that prescriptive transfer statutes compensate for the tendency to be overinclusive by providing some coherent principle on which to base the transfer decision? Probably not. There is a tendency to include crimes in a prescriptive transfer list if any form of the offense appears likely to require high-magnitude sanctions. This worst-case methodology does not represent a judgment that the wide variety of different types of conduct and levels of participation that each statutory definition of a crime encompasses are all or mostly in need of exceptional punishment. The legislators will tend to provide for transfer of aggravated battery cases not if all such cases justify such a result but if any cases in the class are believed to merit transfer. This sort of legislation is often passed as a response to a well-publicized actual case.

A worst-case methodology may be appropriate when deciding on the appropriate minimum ages and crimes necessary for transfer to criminal court; the method misfires when the worst imaginable form of an offense becomes the motivation for deciding that all juveniles accused of any form of such an offense should be transferred to criminal court. The confusion in this way of necessary with sufficient causes is grounds for failing a course in elementary logic, but such confusion is also the usual foundation for using public worries about particular frightening youth crimes as the basis for wholesale reassignment of juvenile defendants to criminal courts.

So prescriptive transfer standards that move entire crime categories into criminal court are unprincipled and overbroad; the best that can befall such systems is prosecutorial discretion being exercised to select only the most serious of within-crime charges to process in the criminal courts. But even this best-case adaptation to categorical transfer legislation is inferior to the allocation of power that animates traditional judicial waiver procedures. The best we can hope for from categorical transfer edicts is high levels of prosecutorial discretion and very low-visibility decision making. In both substance and procedure, this seems clearly inferior to the judicial waiver mechanism as it has evolved over nearly a century in the American juvenile court.

The error of using broad crime categories as a conclusive presumption of particular levels of deserved punishment cannot be cured by more careful statutory drafting. If the central issue in transfer to criminal court is a matter of deserved punishment, the appropriate unit of analysis for making that punishment decision is almost always the individual case. Transferring entire crime categories on the basis of presumed desert is a repetition of the mistakes legislatures make with mandatory minimum penalties and fixed-price sentencing schemes (Tonry 1996). Only gross calculations of deserved punishment can be made without knowledge of the offender's characteristics, his particular role in the criminal event and his prior involvement with the justice system. There may be instrumental motives for punishment policies that do not vary within crime categories, but calculating deserved punishment at that level of abstraction is obviously arbitrary.

4. Justice in Criminal Courts

The processes of judicial waiver that prevailed over the first century of the American juvenile court were in many respects a well-functioning way of selecting out small numbers of cases that might otherwise create tension within the juvenile court and leave the court vulnerable to hostile outside forces. But the standard judicial waiver system I endorse as the least bad method of dealing with extremely severe cases has two major failings that should be a focus for reform efforts early in the juvenile court's second century. The first failure has been the absence of legal standards to inform and control decisions made by juvenile court judges. The second failure has been the absence of appropriate recognition of the special treatment the criminal courts owe to their very youngest defendants. The prospects for improvement soon in either of these two problem areas are not good.

The lawless character of judicial waiver decisions is as easy to explain as it is difficult to remedy. Discretionary decisions are by definition not closely connected to principles that can predict outcome, and discretionary decisions about deserved punishment have been notoriously difficult to regularize into a review procedure that assures that like cases are treated alike. Appellate review of criminal sentences is neither politically popular nor conceptually easy—because appellate judges lack clear standards of comparison (Zeisel and Diamond 1977).

These inherent difficulties have been compounded by the number and variety of criteria that judges were authorized to take into account when deciding about waiver, everything from age and offense seriousness to amenability to treatment and "sophistication." With so many different types of potentially decisive criteria available to choose from, any decision on waiver would be easy to support even if a written opinion were required (Twentieth Century Fund 1978, 55–57). Without such an opinion requirement, a reviewing body will rarely have a basis for overturning a judicial waiver decision. It should come as no surprise then that appellate courts are quite reluctant to reverse lower court decisions on waiver (Clausel and Bonnie, this volume).

Two changes in the legal environment of the waiver decision might improve the chance for meaningful appellate review, but still leave enormous discretionary power in the initial waiver decision maker. The first needed reform is a requirement for extensive written justifications of decisions to grant or to reject a waiver motion. This will make the reasons for an initial decision known, and can isolate key factual issues and assumptions for the attention of subsequent reviewers. Further, the discipline of writing such an opinion may also improve the quality of the initial decision making.

A second improvement on the current environment of waiver decisions would be to place heavy emphasis on a single criterion, the gap between available juvenile sanctions and the minimum deserved punishment if defendant is guilty. A clear focus on desert will reduce the probability that a judge will be distracted by heavy emphasis on other aspects of the case. Of course, many of the same characteristics that judges would consider in decisions about a juvenile's sophistication, attitude, or amenability to treatment will also be relevant to questions of the deserved punishment, but continual emphasis on desert can reduce to some extent the capacity for confusion and self-delusion that accompany traditional juvenile court code words like "amenability" and "sophistication," and long laundry lists of criteria for waiver.

But these interstitial efforts at reform cannot change the essentially discretionary character of judicial waiver decisions and thus will not change the substantial subjective element that will go into each waiver decision. If judges A and B differ in temperament and ideology, the discretionary character of judicial waiver means that which judge hears the waiver petition will have a substantial impact on what decision is made. Inevitably, the great majority of these subjective decisions will be upheld on appeal. If rules of eligibility only identify which cases can be considered for transfer, the actual waiver decision must be a subjective one. Only if rules identify both sufficient and necessary conditions for waiver can the selection of transfer cases be regularized, but the price of regulation by rule is extensive overbreadth. To a distressing degree, the choice in waiver decision making is between parsimony and principle. Restricting the offenses that create eligibility for waiver is one method of control that can serve both parsimony and principle. Making a criminal homicide charge a necessary condition for waiver would reduce the circumstances that allow judicial temperament to determine waiver outcome. But the general trend is to long lists of eligible charges.

The second major failure of judicial waiver systems lies beyond the boundaries of the juvenile court, but its consequences are a fundamental threat to juvenile justice as well as to the broader criminal justice system. The problem is the absence of a youth policy for waived juvenile offenders in criminal courts.

There are at least three distinct forms of youth policy in juvenile court, and a consistent legal policy would continue two of these for young offenders waived into criminal courts. First, to the extent that immaturity leads to judgments of diminished responsibility, this should reduce the level of punishment imposed on young offenders in any court (Zimring 2000, pt. 3). A second important aspect of justice policy toward young offenders is to provide age-appropriate institutions, programs, and protections (Zimring 1998, chap. 8). The third strand of policy toward youth is effort to avoid punishments that seriously impinge on the life chances of young offenders. It is this last commitment to avoid permanent harm that may be in conflict with the community's minimum needs for punishment in waiver cases, not the policies of diminished responsibility or age-appropriate institutions and programs.

In principle, a punitive theory of waiver clearly distinguishes between restraining immature offenders more because of the need for punishment in a particular case and treating young offenders as if they were not young. In practice, there is a tendency to ignore the youth of offenders once they have been transferred to criminal court as if the mandate of a waiver was to regard the offender as an adult.

Yet there are two ways in which a principled and effective juvenile justice system is a hostage to youth-oriented policies in criminal court. Arbitrary treatment of waived juveniles in the criminal courts renders the entire justice system for responding to youth crime unprincipled. Waiver in itself is not an arbitrary treatment of young offenders if it conforms to the standards of strict necessity previously discussed. But the gratuitous removal of youth-oriented protections in the criminal justice system does generate a pattern of injustice in which the juvenile justice system had a causal role.

There is a second way in which arbitrary treatment of young offenders in criminal courts threatens the quality of juvenile justice in the United States, and this is a lesson of our recent history. The experiments with "blended jurisdiction" schemes discussed in Redding and Howell's contribution to this volume expand the punishment powers of juvenile courts, risking both a crisis of mission within the court and the rejection of damage limitation as a fundamental principle of juvenile courts. Why should some of the friends of the juvenile justice system welcome this punitive Trojan horse into the court for children? To protect young offenders otherwise at risk of disappearing into the black hole of the criminal justice system. The failure of the criminal courts to offer proportional punishment and age segregation leads to unprincipled efforts to retain jurisdiction over serious young offenders at almost any risk.

While the lawless character of discretionary waiver hearings is an inherent drawback, there is no inevitable barrier to coherent policies toward waived defendants in criminal courts. The major obstacles to principled reform here are political problems, but political problems of immense proportions.

The best hope for coherent youth policy in criminal courts is elite and professional leadership in the creation of policy. But professional elite influence is out of fashion in the politics of criminal justice just now, and the network of child welfare and youth interest groups that has traditionally played a major role in juvenile justice policy has not involved itself in criminal justice policy other than age segregation in penal facilities. The coalitions that lobby for juvenile justice have often stopped at water's edge, rather than follow waived offenders into criminal courts. Recent adventures with blended jurisdiction show that the flaws of a criminal justice system in the treatment of young offenders can cast long shadows on the prospects for effective juvenile justice. But creating a youth policy in the criminal court will be no less difficult in the foreseeable future because of its importance.

References
Case Cited

In re Gault, 387 U.S. 1, 87 S. Ct 1428, 18 L. Ed. 2d 527 (1967).

Other References

Allen, Francis A. 1964. *The Borderland of Criminal Justice.* Chicago: University of Chicago Press.
Feld, Barry. 1987. "Juvenile Court Meets the Principle of the Offense: Legislative Changes in Juvenile Waiver Statutes." *Journal of Criminal Law and Criminology* 78:471.
Ferguson, Bruce, and Allan C. Douglas. 1970. "A Study of Juvenile Waiver." *San Diego Law Review* 7:39.
Mack, Julius. 1909. "The Juvenile Court." *Harvard Law Review* 23:104.

Platt, Anthony. 1969. *The Child Savers.* Chicago: University of Chicago Press.

Schlossman, Steven. 1977. *Love and the American Delinquent: The Theory and Practice of "Progressive" Juvenile Justice, 1825–1920.* Chicago: University of Chicago Press.

Singer, Simon. 1996. *Recriminalizing Delinquency.* New York: Cambridge University Press.

Tonry, Michael. 1996. *Sentencing Matters.* New York: Oxford University Press.

Twentieth Century Fund Task Force on Sentencing Policy toward Young Offenders. 1978. *Confronting Youth Crime.* New York: Twentieth Century Fund.

United States Department of Justice. 1998. *Uniform Crime Reports 1977.* Washington: Government Printing Office.

Zeisel, Hans, and Sherie Diamond. "The Search for Sentencing Equity: Sentencing Review in Massachusetts and Connecticut." *American Bar Foundation Journal* 2:883.

Zimring, Franklin E. 1981. "Notes toward a Jurisprudence of Waiver." In *Issues in Juvenile Justice Information and Training.* Edited by John Hall, Donna Hamparian, John Pettibone, and Joseph White. Columbus, Ohio: Academy for Contemporary Problems.

———. 1982. *The Changing Legal World of Adolescence.* New York: Free Press.

———. 1991. "The Treatment of Hard Cases in American Juvenile Justice: In Defense of Discretionary Waiver." *Notre Dame Journal of Law, Ethics, and Public Policy* 5:267.

———. 1998. *American Youth Violence.* New York: Oxford University Press.

———. 2000. "Penal Proportionality for the Young Offender." In *Youth on Trial.* Edited by Thomas Grisso and Robert Schwartz. Chicago: University of Chicago Press.

Part Two

The Impacts of Jurisdiction Shifts

Chapter Seven

Consequences of Transfer

DONNA BISHOP AND CHARLES FRAZIER

Transfer has traditionally been justified on the grounds that the juvenile court is ill equipped to handle two classes of offenders. In the case of seriously violent offenders, the public demands heavy penalties that have been well beyond the capacity of the juvenile justice system to provide. Whether these offenders might respond to juvenile justice intervention is irrelevant: the community simply will not tolerate mild responses to heinous crimes. The other class historically targeted for removal consists of chronic offenders who have been afforded all appropriate interventions at the juvenile court's disposal and who have not responded to those efforts. In such cases, the court reasonably concludes that they are not amenable to treatment. As a last resort, they are transferred to the criminal courts, which are better equipped to incapacitate those who present a continuing threat to the public welfare.

Historically, transfer was used sparingly precisely because it was assumed that exposing juveniles to processing and punishment in the criminal courts might do them serious harm. Resort to the criminal court was appropriate only in instances where offenders were irredeemable, either on moral grounds or in point of fact. More recently, and for a variety of reasons that are beyond the scope of this chapter, legislators and justice officials have become more sanguine about criminal punishment for young offenders. They demand more in the name of desert than the juvenile court can provide and increasingly subscribe to the idea that criminal punishment has utility as a general and specific deterrent. Consequently, transfer criteria have become inclusive of a broad range of offenders who are neither particularly serious nor particularly chronic. Legislative exclusion and prosecutorial waiver statutes frequently target a broad range of offenses and offenders. In Florida, for example, the law sanctions transfer of sixteen- and seventeen-year-old first-time offenders charged with *any* felony as well as fourteen- and fifteen-year-old first-time offenders accused of any of several felonies, some of which are property crimes. Such policies are consistent with either of two conclusions. In their zeal for retribution, policy makers are willing to ignore the jeopardy into which large numbers of adolescents are placed, or they trust that criminal punishment will ultimately prove beneficial to juvenile offenders and to society. In either event, we must be concerned about consequences.

Our purpose in this chapter is to examine the effects of transfer on a number of different levels. The ongoing debate about juvenile and criminal court line drawing must be informed by an appreciation of what is at stake for the system, for young offenders, and for society. Three broad goals define the structure of our inquiry: to identify how transfer practices and trends affect (and are likely to affect) the organization and operation of juvenile and criminal courts and correctional agencies; to review what is known about the effects on young offenders of criminal court processing and exposure to adult correctional environments; and to consider the implications of transfer for crime control.

Our discussion is divided into five parts. In section 1, we assess the reach of jurisdictional shifts, including the number and characteristics of adolescents in adult courts as well as the outcomes of criminal court processing. Section 2 explores systemic effects, inquiring into the implications of transfer for the administration of justice. Section 3 reviews the literature on the effectiveness of transfer as a method of crime control. In section 4 we assess the consequences for young people of processing and sanctioning in the adult system. With the juvenile system as a point of contrast, we take a hard look at criminal court processing and adult correctional environments, and consider the responses of youths to processing and incarceration within the two systems. Section 5 is devoted to a discussion of our major findings and their implications for transfer policy.

1. Adolescents in Adult Court

Very little information is available on juvenile offenders who are transferred to criminal court jurisdiction. It is difficult even to arrive at reasonably accurate counts of the numbers of youths transferred. Reliable national estimates of cases waived judicially have been published for many years (Sickmund et al. 1998).[1] As long as judicial waiver remained the sole method of transfer, these data were a good source of information about national transfer trends. However, beginning in the 1970s, most states enacted exclusion statutes and/or concurrent jurisdiction provisions that expedited transfer by circumventing the juvenile court. By

1995, only seven states relied exclusively on judicial waiver, and four did not use it at all.[2] Unfortunately, data collection efforts have not kept pace with these changes in practice: there is as yet no national reporting program on cases removed by exclusion or prosecutorial waiver. Even at the state level, reporting systems are often rudimentary and the data are of questionable validity.

To complicate matters further, some states have lowered the upper age of juvenile court jurisdiction. The traditional boundary dividing the juvenile and criminal courts—the eighteenth birthday—is not applicable in thirteen states. In ten states adolescent offenders become criminals at seventeen, in three at sixteen (Sickmund, Snyder, and Poe-Yamagata 1997, 30). Although not usually thought of as "transfers," these juveniles face criminal prosecution, jailing, incarceration in state prison facilities, and all of the other consequences of transfer to be discussed in this chapter. Yet we lack accurate counts and descriptions of these youths as well.

Mindful of the limitations of the data, we present what is known about transfer numbers and trends at the national level. The presentation is organized around the flow of cases through the justice system, from referral to criminal court to incarceration in adult correctional facilities.

Referral to Criminal Court

National data on judicial waivers for the ten-year period 1986–95 are reported in table 7.1. From 1986 to 1994, there was a steady increase in the *number* of cases waived (from 7,300 to 12,300) that kept pace with increases in cases processed in the juvenile court. Throughout this period, the *rate* of waiver remained stable at approximately 1.4 percent of cases formally processed. In 1995, both the number and rate of waivers declined. In all likelihood this downturn was the result of increased use of alternative transfer methods. Between 1992 and 1995, six states enacted or expanded prosecutorial transfer legislation, and an additional thirty states and the District of Columbia enacted or modified statutory exclusion provisions (Torbet et al. 1996, 6).

Judicial waiver in practice is not highly selective in targeting cases involving violence. Two of every one hundred violent offenses are waived—a rate that has remained stable for ten years—and violent offenses constitute less than half of all waivers[3] (see table 7.1). Waiver rates for drug offenses have tended to mimic the temper of the "war on drugs," and at the beginning of the decade were almost twice the rate for violent crimes. In 1995 these offenses were waived at a lower rate (1.3 percent). Property offenses and offenses against public order have traditionally

Table 7.1
Judicial Waivers to Criminal Court, 1986–95

	1986		1991		1995	
	N	%	N	%	N	%
Number of petitioned delinquency cases waived:						
Person	2,300	31	3,600	33	4,600	47
Property	4,000	54	4,600	43	3,300	34
Drugs	400	6	1,800	17	1,200	13
Public order	600	8	800	7	700	7
Total	7,300	99	10,800	100	9,700	101
Percentage of petitioned delinquency cases waived:						
Person	2.2		2.4		2.1	
Property	1.2		1.2		0.7	
Drugs	1.2		4.1		1.3	
Public order	0.7		0.7		0.4	
Total	1.3		1.5		1.0	

Source: Sickmund et al. 1998, tables 10 and 11.
Note: Percentages may not add to 100 due to rounding.

been waived at the lowest rates. Although only a very small percentage of property offenses were waived in 1995, their incidence was so high that they made up over a third of all waivers.

In 1995, most youths judicially waived to criminal court were minority males, age sixteen or seventeen. While the proportion who are male has remained stable at 96 percent, shifts have occurred in the race and age composition of the population. Juveniles are being waived at younger ages: Those under sixteen made up 6 percent of the waiver population in 1986 and 12 percent in 1995. This change may well reflect the impact of new laws that lowered the minimum age for waiver as well as those that excluded from juvenile court jurisdiction older youths charged with specified offenses (Sickmund, Snyder, and Poe-Yamagata 1997, 31). Waiver is also increasingly affecting minority youths: 43 percent of cases waived in 1986 involved minority youths, compared to 51 percent in 1995. Across all offense categories, black youths receive more severe dispositions in the juvenile court, including residential commitment and waiver to criminal court. Racial disparities in the application of waiver are most pronounced for person and drug offenses (Sickmund, Snyder, and Poe-Yamagata 1997).

At the national level, there is no information on the arrest or dispositional histories of youths subject to judicial waiver. State and local studies suggest that there is considerable variability across jurisdictions in the extent to which waived offenders have previously had access to the treatment resources of the juvenile court. Across studies, the percentage of waived youths with prior program placements ranges from 33 to 75 percent, the average being below 50 percent (Heuser 1985; Gragg 1986; Nimick, Szymanski, and Snyder 1986; Podkopacz and Feld 1996).

Transfers Prosecuted in Criminal Courts

Two recently published studies constitute the first efforts to generate national estimates of the number of transfers prosecuted in criminal courts since Hamparian et al.'s (1982) seminal research over twenty years ago.[4] As a point of historical comparison, Hamparian et al. reported that 12,600 transfer cases were processed in criminal courts in 1978 (72 percent via judicial waiver, 17 percent via prosecutorial waiver, and 11 percent via exclusion).

Officials of the U.S. General Accounting Office (1995) attempted to gather data in 1993 on prosecutorial waivers from all jurisdictions that employ this method of transfer (at that time, ten states and the District of Columbia). Data thought to be relatively complete were obtained from only four states: in the other seven jurisdictions, data were either unavailable or could be acquired in at most only a few counties. The total number of prosecutorial transfer filings reported in these very spotty data was 9,040 (U.S. General Accounting Office 1995, 15). Adding these to the number of judicial waivers in 1993 yields a total of nearly 21,000 cases. Because this figure excludes not only the balance of prosecutorial waivers but also all cases transferred by legislative exclusion, it is apparent that judicial waiver is no longer the primary method of transfer.

This conclusion is bolstered by findings from the National Survey of Prosecutors, which for the first time in 1996 included items regarding juveniles transferred by *any* method and prosecuted in criminal court (DeFrances and Steadman 1998). Surveys were sent to a nationally representative sample of felony prosecutors. Only 68 percent of those surveyed were able to provide the information requested. Based on the information submitted, DeFrances and Steadman (1998, 6) estimate that 27,000 transfer cases were prosecuted in felony criminal courts in 1996.[5] It is unknown how many of these cases culminated in either bench or jury trials.

Although there is no information at the national level by which to compare characteristics of cases transferred via exclusion, prosecutorial waiver, and judicial waiver, some information is available from state and local studies. In a study of twelve jurisdictions in 1985, Gragg (1986) reported that youths transferred via legislative exclusion tend to be younger than those transferred through other methods, and to have fewer prior arrests and prior placements. In addition, a smaller percentage of legislative exclusion cases involved blacks than transfers via other methods, but this may be changing as legislatures increasingly target for exclusion violent, weapons, and drug offenses for which minority youths are dispro-portionately arrested. Prosecutorial waiver studies, which have been con-ducted only in Florida, suggest that this method of transfer is least selec-tive. Most youths transferred via this method are property offenders, nearly 20 percent are nonfelons, and only a third have had prior commit-ments (Bishop and Frazier 1991; Bishop et al. 1998).

Convictions in Criminal Court

Information on court outcomes for transferred youths is very limited. Twenty-two states have reverse waiver provisions that permit the criminal courts to return cases to the juvenile system (Torbet et al. 1996). Unfor-tunately, there are virtually no national data on the extent to which this option is exercised, or on the characteristics of youths and cases returned to the juvenile system. Two studies of reverse waiver at the state level reveal wide variations in practice. Singer (1996) reports that in New York as many as three-fourths of the cases of youths removed to criminal court via legislative exclusion are either dismissed or reverse waived, where-upon they may be treated as delinquents in juvenile court.[6] In Florida, where over 90 percent of transfers are made via prosecutorial waiver, Bishop et al. (1998, 76) report that less than 15 percent of these cases are dismissed or returned to the juvenile system.

National data are available on the numbers of youths adjudicated as adults and convicted of felonies in state criminal courts. The Bureau of Justice Statistics (BJS) annually gathers data from a sample of three hun-dred felony courts as part of its National Judicial Reporting Program. In 1994 the program gathered data on convictions in cases transferred by *all* methods (Brown and Langan 1998). Brown and Langan (1998, 60) esti-mate that twelve thousand transferred youths were convicted of felony offenses,[7] representing 1.4 percent of all felony convictions.

There are reasons for concern that these estimates may contain con-siderable error and that they may undercount convictions by a sub-stantial margin. For 1978, Hamparian et al. (1982, 207) reported that over 90 percent of youths transferred via judicial and prosecutorial waiver were convicted (approximately nine thousand cases).[8] It is difficult to reconcile Hamparian et al.'s results with Brown and Langan's, given the substantial increase in transfers known to have taken place between 1978 and 1994.[9]

While the counts may not be accurate, there is less concern about bias in the reporting of offense distributions among those convicted. The

Table 7.2
Offense Profiles of Transferred Youths and Adults
Convicted in Felony Courts, 1994 (Percentages)

Most Serious Conviction Offense	Transferred Offenders	Offenders 18 or Over
Violent offenses:		
Murder	7	1
Rape	2	2
Robbery	28	5
Aggravated assault	16	8
Other violent	1	3
Total	53	19
Property offenses:		
Burglary	15	11
Larceny	8	13
Fraud	1	7
Total	24	31
Drug offenses:		
Possession	3	13
Trafficking	10	19
Total	13	32
Weapons offenses	4	4
Other offenses	6	14
Total	100	100

Source: Brown and Langan 1998

relevant data are presented in table 7.2, where we present profiles of transferred offenders and of offenders eighteen and over convicted in state felony courts. Examination of the table reveals that slightly more than half of the transfers were convicted of a violent felony crime. Although there are many lesser offenders in the transfer group, the transfers are a more serious group of offenders than adults convicted in felony courts. Fewer than 20 percent of the adult felons were convicted of violent crimes.

Sentencing of Transferred Offenders

National data on sentencing of transferred offenders are available for the 1994 felony court samples included in the National Judicial Reporting Program (Brown and Langan 1998). These data indicate that transferred

Table 7.3

Sentences Received by Transferred Offenders Compared to Offenders Eighteen and Over: Sentence Type and Mean Maximum Sentence Length in Months

	Transferred Youths					
	% to Prison	Prison Time	% to Jail	Jail Time	% to Probation	Probation Time
All offenses	63	111	16	8	21	51
Violent offenses:						
Murder[a]	97	287	2	10	1	46
Rape	84	200	6	3	10	54
Robbery	75	139	9	10	16	59
Aggravated assault	74	75	16	10	10	52
Other	71	130	14	4	14	unk
Total	78	139	10	10	12	57
Property offenses:						
Burglary	46	52	18	10	36	52
Larceny	36	45	28	6	36	32
Fraud	21	44	49	9	30	14
Total	42	50	23	8	36	45
Drug offenses:						
Possession	37	66	28	4	35	45
Trafficking	47	83	24	8	29	54
Total	45	80	25	7	30	52
Weapons offenses	49	66	20	9	31	47
Other offenses	67	61	24	7	9	51

Source: Brown and Langan 1998, tables 6.2, 6.3, 6.5, and 6.6
Note: Percentages may not add to 100 due to rounding.
[a] Includes nonnegligent manslaughter.

youths convicted in criminal court are very likely to be incarcerated: 79 percent of all transferred youths convicted were sentenced to terms of incarceration. Sixty-three percent were sentenced to prison, many for lengthy terms. The average maximum sentence for transferred offenders sentenced to prison was 9.25 years. Sixteen percent were sentenced to jail. The remaining 21 percent were sentenced to probation.

In table 7.3 we present data from the national felony court samples on sentences received by transferred offenders and by offenders eighteen and over, organized by offense type. Looking first at the left panel of the table, we see that most youths convicted of violent offenses receive sentences far more severe than could be imposed in the vast majority of the nation's juvenile courts. Seventy-eight percent are sentenced to prison

Offenders 18 and Over					
% to Prison	Prison Time	% to Jail	Jail Time	% to Probation	Probation Time
46	69	27	6	28	36
95	258	2	7	11	54
72	149	17	7	11	54
77	112	12	9	11	46
49	81	28	6	23	38
45	70	32	7	23	42
62	115	21	7	17	42
53	67	23	7	24	42
38	45	30	6	32	36
33	51	30	5	37	38
42	56	27	6	30	38
36	48	34	4	30	32
47	66	25	7	28	35
43	60	29	6	29	34
44	46	28	5	28	29
37	40	30	6	33	34

with an average maximum term of 11.58 years. Even assuming generous gain time provisions, most will serve far longer terms than they would have had they been retained in the juvenile courts.[10] Nearly half of those convicted of property, drug, and weapons offenses also receive prison sentences, with average maximum terms of 4.17, 6.67, and 5.50 years respectively. The remainder—a slight majority of youths transferred for property, drug, and weapons offenses—receive jail sentences or are placed on probation, sentences well within the range that may be imposed by juvenile courts. Overall, the results suggest that more than half of transferred youths who are convicted are sentenced to terms that exceed those they would have received had they been retained in the juvenile system, except in those states that have established extended jurisdiction.

Data aggregated at the national level obscure considerable variability in practice at the state and county levels. Numerous studies of state and local transfer practices and outcomes have been conducted.[11] Some report that transferred offenders receive sentences of equal or lesser severity than those imposed by the juvenile courts, while others have concluded that transferred youths are more often incarcerated and receive longer sentences than youths adjudicated in juvenile court. These apparent inconsistencies can be explained largely by jurisdictional variations both in the kinds of offenders selected for transfer as well as in sentencing practice. The effects of offense and place are perhaps best illustrated in a seven-state comparison of transfer practices and outcomes conducted by the U.S. General Accounting Office (1995). Marked differences were observed across jurisdictions in the offenses for which youths were transferred. For example, 12 percent of the transfers in Vermont involved crimes of violence, compared to nearly 40 percent in Missouri. Property offenders constituted only 21 percent of California's transfer population, compared to 84 percent of Vermont's. There was also considerable variability in conviction rates and rates of incarceration by state and by offense type. At the extreme, Vermont incarcerated fewer than one-third of juveniles convicted in criminal court of either a violent, property, or drug crime, while Minnesota incarcerated over 90 percent of youths in all three offense categories. Pennsylvania incarcerated over 90 percent of youths convicted of violent and drug offenses, but only 10 percent of those convicted of property crimes. In sum, there is much evidence of "justice by geography" in the selection, adjudication, and sentencing of transferred offenders (see also Feld 1991; Bishop, Lanza-Kaduce, and Winner 1996; Lanza-Kaduce, Bishop, and Winner 1997).

There has also been some discussion of a "leniency gap" within the criminal courts, the suggestion being that transferred offenders receive lesser punishments than comparable adults, in part because they are "first-timers" to the criminal justice system and in part because judges make allowances for their youth and immaturity. Data at the national level relevant to this issue are presented in table 7.3. If we compare the sentences imposed on transferred youths with those imposed on adults, we see that, for each of the violent offense categories and for weapons and "other" crimes, transferred youths are more often sentenced to prison, and for longer periods of time, than their older counterparts. For drug offenses, transferred youths and older offenders are about equally likely to be sentenced to prison but transferred offenders receive significantly longer sentences on average. For property crimes, transferred offenders are slightly less likely than adults to be incarcerated in either prison or jail and, when incarcerated, they are sentenced to slightly shorter terms. Overall, when the sentences of transferred youths are compared to those age eighteen and over, it appears that transferred youths are sentenced *more* harshly, both in terms of the probability of receiving a prison sentence and the length of the sentences they receive.[12] In other words, we see no evidence that criminal courts recognize a need to mitigate sentences based on considerations of age and immaturity.

Youths under Eighteen in Criminal Courts in States Where They Are Adults by Definition

In addition to youths transferred to criminal court, there are substantial numbers of offenders under eighteen who are processed in criminal courts in the eleven jurisdictions where *all* offenders age sixteen or seventeen are defined as adults under state law. Recently, Sickmund, Snyder, and Poe-Yamagata (1997, 30) estimated that 180,000 cases involving these youths were processed in the nation's criminal courts in 1994. Sickmund, Snyder, and Poe-Yamagata's estimate is based on UCR arrest data, adjusted for case processing rates in each of the jurisdictions that define the boundaries of adulthood at ages under eighteen.

Based on data from court samples, Brown and Langan (1998, 60) estimate that 12,000 youths under eighteen were convicted in criminal felony courts in 1994 in states where they were legally defined as adults. It is difficult to reconcile Sickmund, Snyder, and Poe-Yamagata's estimate of the number of prosecutions with Brown and Langan's estimate of the number of convictions. Applying a very conservative assumption that 20 percent of Sickmund, Snyder, and Poe-Yamagata's estimated prosecutions involve felonies[13] yields an estimated 36,000 felony prosecutions. Brown and Langan's estimated 12,000 convictions implies a conviction rate of only 33 percent.

The profile of conviction offenses for youths age sixteen and seventeen who are adult by state definition looks fairly similar to the offense profile of those eighteen and over. Compared to those eighteen and over, those under eighteen are somewhat more likely to be convicted of a violent crime or a weapons offense, equally likely to be convicted of a property offense, and somewhat less likely to be convicted of a drug offense. Not unexpectedly, offenders under eighteen in states where they are legally defined as adults are a much less serious group of offenders than those under eighteen who are transferred to criminal court.

Table 7.4 presents data on the sentences received by offenders under eighteen in states where they are defined as adults. Fifty-four percent were

Table 7.4
Sentences (in Months) Imposed on Convicted Felons under Eighteen in States Where
They Were Adult by Definition

	% to Prison	Prison Time	% to Jail	Jail Time	% to Probation	Probation Time
All offenses	54	87	11	8	34	44
Violent offenses:						
Murder[a]	97	279	1	12	1	60
Rape	85	117	11	12	5	53
Robbery	70	107	4	22	26	55
Aggravated assault	68	102	8	6	24	49
Other	36	124	—	—	64	40
Total	73	128	5	15	23	52
Property offenses:						
Burglary	65	68	6	11	30	48
Larceny	21	62	29	5	50	54
Fraud	22	57	9	4	70	43
Total	47	67	14	6	39	51
Drug offenses:						
Possession	31	42	9	5	60	33
Trafficking	54	62	9	10	37	40
Total	47	58	9	9	44	37
Weapons offenses	47	62	25	9	28	38
Other offenses	47	68	16	7	36	36

Source: Brown and Langan 1998, tables 6.5 and 6.6.
Note: Percentages may not add to 100 due to rounding.
[a] Includes nonnegligent manslaughter.

sentenced to prison, receiving average maximum sentences of 7.25 years.
Eleven percent were sentenced to jail, while 34 percent were placed on
probation.

Youths in Adult Correctional Institutions

In forty-two states youths transferred to criminal court may be detained
in jail prior to trial (Coalition for Juvenile Justice 1994, 17). Jurisdictions
that treat all youths age sixteen or seventeen as adults also permit them
to be detained in jail prior to trial. In addition, of course, both sets of
youths may be sentenced to jail. The jail data currently available on juvenile offenders are limited to annual one-day counts of youths under
eighteen. These counts do not differentiate between youths held prior to
adjudication and those sentenced, nor do they differentiate between

those transferred to criminal court and those jailed in states where the upper boundary of juvenile court jurisdiction is under age eighteen. BJS cautions that it is very difficult to gather accurate data on juveniles in jail, especially data that are comparable across jurisdictions. That said, they estimate that 7,000 juveniles who were being handled as adults were housed in jail at midyear 1997,[14] compared to 5,100 at midyear 1994, an increase of 37% (Gilliard and Beck 1998, 6).

With respect to youths in prison, the national sentencing reports discussed earlier indicate that approximately 14,500 offenders under eighteen were sentenced to prison in 1994.[15] In addition to these reports, data believed to include approximately 90 percent of all prison admissions are submitted to BJS by state corrections officials. They show that in 1996, 6,300 offenders under eighteen were admitted to state prisons, which was a slight increase over prior years (Allen Beck, personal communication, October 1998).[16] Given the apparent inconsistency in the information received from these two sources, we caution readers again about the reliability of the data. One possible reason the numbers are so discrepant may be that many youths sentenced to prison turn eighteen prior to admission.[17] However, it seems unlikely that this explanation can account fully for the inconsistency across data sources.

Some information on characteristics of youths admitted to prison is available through the National Corrections Reporting Program (BJS 1997). Two-thirds of the youths under eighteen admitted to state prisons in 1996 were black. In contrast, half of all offenders admitted to prison were black, showing once again the disproportionate impact of transfer policies on minority populations. The under-eighteen population also differs from other prison admissions in another crucial respect. Sixty percent of those under eighteen were admitted for violent offenses. This was true of less than a third of total admissions. This means that most of those under eighteen will serve longer sentences on average than those in other age groups. Moreover, although they represent only 1.5 percent of new admissions, because they have longer sentences their impact on prison communities will grow as they age. Over time an increasing proportion of prison populations will consist of offenders who entered during adolescence.

2. Systemic Consequences of Transfer Reform

We turn our attention now to the known and probable consequences of shifts in transfer practice on the organization and operation of the criminal and juvenile justice systems. Some of the effects are fairly obvious and predictable (e.g., those relating to increased numbers of young offenders in the adult corrections system). In addition, there are some less apparent and largely unanticipated consequences that merit consideration. Given the scope of this chapter, the discussion in this section is limited to an overview of what we see as the major systemic effects and issues.

Caseload Issues for the Criminal Justice System

The most obvious consequence of recent transfer trends is that the already strained resources of criminal courts and adult corrections agencies are and will be further taxed. Much of the increased pressure is a result of sheer numbers. As we saw in section 1, there has been a shift from relatively small numbers of transfers in the late 1970s (Hamparian et al. 1982) to potentially enormous numbers in the late 1990s.

Criminal prosecutions demand more resources than juvenile ones: they require more hearings, involve more attorney preparation, call upon more investigative resources, are more likely to result in jury trials, and take at least twice as long to process as comparable cases in juvenile court. As transfers increase, additional human and financial resources will be required. Absent new resources, if current trends continue the criminal courts will face congested dockets and greater delays. The system may slow, or more pleas may be negotiated at "bargain basement" prices, more prosecutions may be deferred, and more cases may be screened out or returned to the juvenile system to relieve the added burdens on the criminal courts.

The issues raised by the transfer trends are not only related to numbers. They also relate to the composition of the transfer population. For example, that transfer practices increasingly and disproportionately affect minority youths serves to reinforce already serious concerns about unequal justice and the appearance of equal justice. Bortner, Zatz, and Hawkins in this volume address these issues directly, so suffice it to say here that transfer reform has brought race issues into sharper relief.

The composition of the transfer population also poses special challenges for departments of corrections, for which many states are ill prepared (Torbet et al. 1996; see also Orenstein 1996). From a managerial standpoint, young offenders create problems for officials far out of proportion to their numbers in correctional populations. They are more likely to be involved in misconduct while incarcerated (Wolfgang 1961; Johnson 1966; Jensen 1977; Myers and Levy 1978; Goetting and Howsen 1986). They pose far higher risks of suicide (Memory 1989), have more medical and social needs, and will often require special precautions to protect them from harm in jail and prison facilities (McShane and Williams 1989).

A key question is whether corrections officials will recognize and respond to the special needs of young offenders, or treat them no differently from older offenders. The research to be discussed in section 4 leads us to fear that youths' needs may not receive the attention they deserve. Although corrections officials are being urged to develop programs for young offenders, Torbet et al. (1996, 33) report that this is "a population they neither want nor have the expertise to address." Transfer trends create the prospect of new and serious issues not only for prison facilities, but for detention centers and jails as well. Criminal court processing of transfer cases may take a year or more, during which time offenders remain in jail or detention facilities, neither of which have the staffing or programming to meet youths' educational or social-service needs over a protracted period.

Up to now, the influx of young offenders into prisons has resulted in some increases in funding allocations, primarily for new facilities and new beds. However, relatively little attention has been given to the need for new or additional programs (Orenstein 1996; Jepsen 1997) or to the physical limitations of existing facilities given the desirability of age segregation (Jepsen 1997; Library Information Specialists 1995). Corrections experts urge that additional teachers be hired and programming developed to meet young offenders' educational needs. These needs are atypical. Most young inmates have substantial records of school failure, many have learning disabilities (Freasier and White 1983), and traditional educational approaches simply do not work with them. In this population, learning is largely dependent upon the development of significant interpersonal relationships between teacher and student (Evans 1978), which requires specialized teacher training and low teacher:student ratios. In addition, corrections experts suggest that, at a minimum, the new wave of juvenile inmates will require staff training and/or the hiring of new staff trained in several areas, including adolescent development, risk factors in aggressive behavior, communication skills, and problem solving and crisis intervention strategies (Jepsen 1997).

Problems of Articulation between the Juvenile and Criminal Systems and Shifts in the Balance of Power

Less anticipated than the consequences associated with caseload pressures are a set of system effects that are not so easily categorized. They involve shifts in the balance of decision-making power from judges to prosecutors, legislatures, and corrections officials, and issues of articulation between the criminal and juvenile justice systems.[18] While some of these problems are not new, the introduction of extensive transfer reforms has raised them to a higher point of visibility and import.

As we saw in section 1, legislative exclusion and prosecutorial waiver have overtaken judicial waiver as the primary methods by which transfers are made. Indeed, if current trends continue, judicial waiver may well become obsolete. The appeal of prosecutorial waiver lies largely in the fact that it expedites the transfer process by circumventing the juvenile court. To politicians with a "get-tough" agenda, who perceive juvenile court judges as "too soft" on crime, prosecutorial waiver is an attractive option. Legislative exclusion has appeal also, not only because it bypasses the juvenile court, but because it permits the legislature to maintain more control over the transfer process. Legislatures may restrict prosecutorial and judicial discretion and ensure greater uniformity and consistency in practice by tying transfer to offense and prior record criteria.

It is now apparent that, despite their surface appeal, streamlined procedures generate new problems for the administration of justice. Because legislative exclusion statutes are inflexible and overinclusive (Zimring 1991; Tonry 1996) they require correctives. These have come in the form of reverse waiver or "transfer back" provisions. As we have argued elsewhere (Bishop and Frazier 1991), prosecutorial waiver statutes also tend to be too broad. In practice, they frequently require inexperienced attorneys to make quick decisions based on minimal information about offenders. Prosecutorial waiver statutes invite subjective and inconsistent decision making and thus have prompted similar counterbalancing measures.

Reverse waiver and transfer back options place the burden of correction on the criminal courts. But shifting the locus of decision making from juvenile court judges to criminal court judges makes little sense. Criminal court judges are already overworked and lack special expertise in dealing with young offenders. Moreover, criminal court judges are frequently given little guidance in exercising their discretion to return cases to the juvenile court or to impose juvenile sanctions. Are offense considerations determinative? Should offender needs be considered? Is amenability to treatment an important consideration? If so, is not familiarity with juvenile justice treatment resources essential? To the extent that offender needs, amenability to treatment, and familiarity with juvenile treatment resources matter, such decisions would presumably best be made by the juvenile courts.

Other issues relating to articulation between the juvenile and criminal justice systems arise in the corrections arena. Several states have adopted blended sentencing statutes that permit the criminal courts to impose both juvenile and adult sanctions in sequence. In many other states, when a juvenile is convicted as an adult and sentenced to a term of incarceration, it is left to corrections officials to determine whether some (or potentially all) of the sentence will be served in a juvenile or an adult facility (Torbet et al. 1996). States that adopt this practice in effect permit transfer back to take place at the corrections level. This appears to usurp judicial authority and undermines the court's purpose in sentencing youths as adults. Furthermore, there has been virtually no research on how corrections authorities determine which juveniles will return to the juvenile corrections system or how long they will remain there. Finally, such blended sentencing systems raise but do not answer questions about the clash of underlying philosophies and operating principles of the two justice systems. In one sense, blended systems statutes avoid the need to create new facilities and new layers of correctional programming because both the juvenile and the adult systems are available. But in another sense, these statutes create confusion about what philosophy of justice[19] is to be applied.

Other issues of articulation arise in the context of pretrial detention. In some jurisdictions there is confusion about where juveniles should be held pending the outcome of transfer proceedings. Do juveniles remain juveniles (to be held in a juvenile detention facility) until they are convicted as adults? Or do they become adults as soon as criminal charges are filed (which means they may spend the next several months in jail housed together with adult offenders)? Should the answer to the last question depend on whether the criminal court has the authority to waive youths back to juvenile court or to impose juvenile sanctions?

The issue of bail for transferred offenders is another matter that we do not believe has been addressed adequately. In many jurisdictions, the view that adolescent offenders are responsible criminals to be tried in adult courts makes them eligible for pretrial detention in jail, and for release on bail. Although systems of bail have long been criticized on the grounds that they discriminate against the poor, at least adults are responsible for their economic circumstances. But bail systems do not seem to be fair when applied to juveniles—especially juveniles under sixteen. Labor laws disallow full-time employment for youths under sixteen. Juveniles under sixteen are also subject to mandatory school attendance laws, which further restrict their ability to become financially independent of their parents. Moreover, bail bondsmen are unlikely to enter into contracts with juveniles. Premising bail for a transferred juvenile on parents' financial resources and on parents' willingness to permit the youth to return home makes release contingent on a youth's status as a dependent minor. There is a strange and awkward irony in the fact that a youth is in jail because he is an adult but can be released on bail only as a dependent child.

Consequences for the Juvenile Justice System

The juvenile justice system is also affected by transfer reforms. Certainly, some portion of older juveniles, juveniles charged with serious offenses, and juveniles having chronic records of offending will be less common in the juvenile justice system. It might also be expected that transfer will result in lighter caseloads for the juvenile system. This leads to the happy prospect of excess resources, which might be redirected to other areas of need within the juvenile justice system or channeled into the criminal justice system.

We are not very hopeful about either the likelihood of smaller caseloads in the juvenile system or the prospect of surplus resources. Courts (and other organizations) tend toward homeostasis. Studies of previous reform initiatives (e.g., diversion and detention) (see Blomberg 1977, 1979; Klein 1976; Frazier, Richards, and Potter 1983; Frazier and Cochran 1986) indicate that reforms designed to eliminate segments of the juvenile court's caseload generally fail because of a systemic tendency to widen the net of control. The system tends to respond to reform initiatives that would reduce its span of control over one portion of the population by increasing the number of persons brought in under other areas over which it has control.

Evidence of this tendency is already apparent. In the last few years, while referrals to the nation's juvenile courts leveled off and transfers increased, there has been a corresponding increase in the proportion of referrals to the juvenile justice system that were processed formally (Sickmund et al. 1998). In other words, the system handled formally many lesser cases that previously would have been handled informally or closed without action. In similar fashion, juvenile courts may respond to rising transfer rates by committing less serious offenders to juvenile correctional facilities. Just as barring status offenders from detention centers and training schools during the 1970s failed to reduce the populations in these facilities, we anticipate that the populations in institutions for juveniles will not decline despite the removal of serious offenders to the criminal courts. This trend is already apparent in Florida (Frazier, Bishop, and Lanza-Kaduce 1999) where commitment rates have skyrocketed despite a decline in felony referrals.[20] Not only is it unlikely that transfer reforms will reduce the size of juvenile court or correctional populations, but we must also be concerned about the potentially negative effects of increasing formal control over lesser offenders who remain in the juvenile system.

3. Consequences for Society: Implications of Transfer for Crime Control

Implicit in the strong rhetoric surrounding the criminalization of juvenile offending is a general deterrent purpose to dissuade juveniles from committing crimes through the threat of severe consequences, including lengthy terms of incarceration (Fagan 1995; Singer and McDowall 1988). The threat of transfer is the quintessence of the "scared straight" approach to crime control. In addition, as was discussed at the outset of this chapter, the expanded application of transfer to include offenders who are neither particularly serious nor particularly chronic suggests a specific deterrent purpose as well. There seems to be a general expectation that criminal punishments will motivate young offenders to reform. Unfortunately, assessments of the extent to which transfer achieves these dual aims are few and recent. Like so many other reforms, this one did not flow from or build on careful research.

General Deterrence

Only two studies to date have evaluated the general deterrent effects of transfer on juvenile crime. Singer and McDowall (1988; see also Singer 1996) conducted a very careful study of the effects of New York's Juvenile Offender Law, which lowered the age of criminal court jurisdiction to thirteen for murder and four other violent offenses. Using a time series design, they examined arrest rates for affected juveniles over a four-year period prior to enactment of the law and for six years following its implementation. Arrest rates for juveniles affected by the law were also compared with those of two control groups, including older juveniles in the same jurisdiction and juveniles of the same age in a nearby jurisdiction. Singer and McDowall report that the law had little if any measurable impact. It is important to note that the law received significant advance publicity and was well implemented. Consequently, the most plausible explanation is that the threat of criminal punishment had no general deterrent effect.

Jensen and Metsger (1994) evaluated the general deterrent effect of an Idaho mandatory transfer statute introduced in 1981. The law required transfer of juveniles as young as fourteen who were charged with murder, attempted murder, robbery, forcible rape, or mayhem. The researchers examined arrest rates for the five-year period prior to the new law and for five years following its implementation. They also examined rates of arrest in two neighboring states that were demographically and economically similar to Idaho. Both comparison states used discretionary waiver, as had Idaho prior to the change in the law. Jensen and Metsger found no evidence of general deterrent effects. Instead, arrests for the target offenses increased in Idaho following the introduction of mandatory transfer, while they decreased in the two comparison states.

Specific Deterrence

In order to assess the impact of transfer on offenders' subsequent behavior, researchers have compared rates of recidivism of transferred youths and those retained in the juvenile system. It is not enough simply to compare youths referenced for waiver with those waived to criminal court. As Podkopacz and Feld (1995, 1996) have shown, waiver decisions are frequently influenced by considerations regarding seriousness of the offense and prior record, which introduce selection bias. Consequently, it is essential that researchers take steps to ensure the equivalence of the groups under comparison. In this regard, two different methodologies have been employed in studies that have produced very similar results.

The first study was carried out by Fagan (1991, 1995, 1996), who conducted a natural experiment to evaluate the effects of juvenile versus criminal justice processing. He identified two counties in New York and two in neighboring New Jersey that were very similar on important socioeconomic, demographic, and crime indicators. New York and New Jersey also had very similar statutes for robbery and burglary. The key difference was that in New York fifteen- and sixteen-year-old robbers and burglars were automatically prosecuted in the criminal courts under that state's legislative exclusion statute while, in New Jersey, the juvenile courts retained jurisdiction over them. Fagan's samples consisted of four hundred robbery offenders and four hundred burglary offenders charged in 1981–82, who were randomly selected and evenly divided across the two states and four counties.

Postrelease recidivism was examined after a significant portion of the cohorts had completed their sentences and accumulated at least four years of time at risk. Several measures of recidivism were employed, including time to rearrest, prevalence of rearrest, prevalence of reincarceration, and frequency of rearrest adjusted for time at risk. While there were no significant differences in the effects of criminal versus juvenile court processing for burglary offenders, the findings for robbery offenders showed strong differences.

Transfer was associated with higher prevalence of rearrest: 76 percent of those processed in criminal court were rearrested, compared to 67 percent of those processed in juvenile court. An even greater effect was observed for the likelihood of reincarceration: 56 percent of the criminal court group were subsequently incarcerated, compared to 41 percent of the juvenile court group. Offenders prosecuted in criminal court also had higher rates of rearrest adjusted for time at risk (2.85 offenses) than those prosecuted in juvenile court (1.67 offenses), and they were rearrested more quickly (457 days compared to 553 days for those processed in juvenile court) (Fagan 1995, 249).

Differences across groups held up for the most part irrespective of the type of sanction imposed by the court. Those who were incarcerated were more likely to reoffend than those who were sentenced to probation, but those sentenced in criminal court to either incarceration or probation fared worse than their counterparts in juvenile court. Among those who had been incarcerated, those sentenced in criminal court were more likely to be rearrested and to be rearrested more quickly than those sentenced in the juvenile court.[21] Those placed on probation by the criminal court were more likely to be rearrested and to be arrested more often than those processed in the juvenile court.[22] In each comparison, the robbery offenders handled in the criminal court fared less well. In addition, it was determined that the effects of court type were independent of sentence length. That is, youths processed in the juvenile court had a lower probability of rearrest even after controlling for sentence length. These findings provide strong support for the utility of retaining offenders in the juvenile system.

Subsequent studies conducted by us and our colleagues (Bishop et al. 1996; Winner et al. 1997) reinforce Fagan's findings and conclusions. Our research was conducted in Florida, a state that uses prosecutorial waiver almost exclusively. In the course of other studies of prosecutorial waiver practice in the state, we had learned that, although thousands of juveniles are transferred each year, thousands of equally serious or even more serious offenders are not transferred (see, e.g., Frazier 1991). This finding provided the opportunity for a significant policy study similar to the one conducted by Fagan. Unlike Fagan's research, ours was carried out in a single state. To overcome the problem of selection bias, we used a matching procedure to pair each case transferred to criminal court with an equivalent case retained in the juvenile system. Each pair was matched on seven factors: the most serious offense charged, the number of counts charged, the number of prior delinquency referrals, the most serious prior offense, age, gender, and race. Using cases processed in 1987, we were able to generate 2,738 transfers who matched with 2,738 juveniles whose cases were retained in the juvenile system.

We assessed recidivism over the short and long terms. The short-term analysis followed cases for a maximum of twenty-four months, while the long-term follow-up tracked offenders for up to seven years. Both studies indicated that juveniles transferred to criminal court fared worse than those retained in the juvenile justice system. This was true over every comparison in the short term and over most comparisons in the long-term study.

Several measures of recidivism were employed: rearrest prevalence, incidence of rearrest, severity of the first rearrest offense, and time to failure. Over the short term, 30 percent of the transfers were rearrested, compared to 19 percent of those processed in juvenile court. Transfers were also more likely than those processed in the juvenile system to be arrested for more serious (felony) offenses. The incidence of offending was also higher in the transfer group: transfers had a rearrest rate of 0.54 offenses per person year of exposure, compared to 0.32 for those retained in the juvenile system. The transfers also reoffended more quickly (135 days) than those processed in juvenile court (227 days) (Bishop et al. 1996, 44).

Over the long term, overall differences in rearrest prevalence were no longer significant across the two groups. However, analysis by offense type indicated that transfers were more likely to reoffend in five of seven comparisons. Moreover, significant differences in rates of reoffending remained. When we calculated rearrest rates overall and for each of seven classes of offense, rates of rearrest were higher for those who had been transferred across all comparisons. Significant differences in time to failure also remained.

The Florida studies add substantively and substantially to Fagan's research. Not only do they provide a confirmation of the findings in a different jurisdiction, time frame and sociolegal context using a different transfer method, they also add new offenses to the mix. Taken together, and keeping in mind that there is no evidence of any general deterrent effect of the transfer reforms, they provide a compelling case for more limited use of transfer and more openness to the potential benefits of handling offenders within the juvenile justice system.

4. Consequences of Transfer for Juvenile Offenders

In order to interpret the findings of the comparative recidivism studies, it is essential that we develop an understanding of the impact of transfer on young offenders. No consequences of transfer are potentially more important or less frequently examined than the experiences of juveniles in the criminal justice system and the meanings they attach thereto. What is the impact on a fifteen-year-old of being tried in criminal rather than juvenile court? of being held in jail rather than juvenile detention? of serving time in prison rather than a juvenile facility? of returning to the community with a criminal rather than a juvenile record?[23]

Our search for answers takes us in three directions. There are some objective data about the juvenile and adult corrections systems from which it is possible to draw limited inferences about possible effects of transfer on incarcerated offenders. In addition, corrections research has identified special problems faced by adolescents in adult correctional settings as well as potentially important linkages between organizational goals and inmate attitudes and behaviors. Finally, most helpful are two studies that compared the experiences and reactions of adolescents processed in the juvenile system and those transferred to the criminal system. We begin the discussion in this section with these studies and interject the objective data and corrections research as appropriate.

In the early 1980s, Forst, Fagan, and Vivona (1989) interviewed 140 adolescent male offenders in four states, all of whom had been convicted of serious violent crimes. Of these, 59 had been processed in juvenile courts and confined in training schools while the rest had been transferred and incarcerated in prisons. More recently, we interviewed 95 serious and chronic adolescent male offenders in Florida (Bishop et al. 1998), of whom 49 had been transferred to criminal court and either confined in state prisons ($N = 46$) or placed on probation ($N = 3$). The balance had been prosecuted in juvenile court and were incarcerated in maximum-risk juvenile commitment facilities. Both studies inquired into youths' postdisposition experiences in correctional settings, including perceptions of staff, services, and programs. In addition, we asked youths about their experiences in the juvenile and criminal courts, about perceptions of procedural and substantive justice, and about their experiences in and reactions to preadjudicatory confinement in detention centers and jails.

These studies are valuable because they shed light on the consequences of transfer from the vantage point of offenders. It is also important to acknowledge their limitations. There are only two of them, and both employed small samples. The jurisdictions studied may be atypical. Further, we do not know whether the programs and facilities observed within the study jurisdictions are broadly representative of those found either within those jurisdictions or in other parts of the country. Consequently, we caution the reader that these studies should be viewed as exploratory and that their results may not be generalizable. With these caveats in mind, we explore adolescents' reactions to the "front end" of each system, drawing on our own research.

Processing in the Juvenile and Criminal Courts

We (Bishop et al. 1998) were particularly interested in learning what meanings juveniles attached to court hearings, and how they understood or interpreted the actions of the major players involved in the processing and disposition of their cases. From all outward appearances, Florida's juvenile courts take a "no-nonsense" approach to juvenile crime, which is reflected in high rates of detention, commitment, and transfer to criminal court.[24] Consequently, we wondered how young offenders would perceive the juvenile courts. Nearly all of them—including those who had been transferred—described the juvenile courts in favorable terms. Frequently they were impressed that judges interacted with them during court proceedings and expressed interest in their problems and concern for their well-being. Most believed that judges were trying to help them. Even those who indicated that the judge's intent was to punish them generally perceived that the punishment was well intended ("It was for my own good, to teach me a lesson"). Most recognized the purposes of the court as commendable and right. Few regarded either juvenile court processes or outcomes as unfair.

Transferred offenders most often described the criminal court in very different terms. Unlike what they had experienced in juvenile court, it appeared to most of them that criminal court judges had little interest in them or their problems. Court proceedings were described as formal and hurried, and many youths reported difficulty understanding legal terminology. Much of what they understood—or thought they understood—about court proceedings came either from brief conversations with their attorneys or fellow inmates in the jail, more often the latter than the former.

Criminal court processes were regarded as much more complex than juvenile ones, and frequently were reported to involve gamesmanship and high-stakes deal making. Many youths failed to differentiate the roles and functions of judges, prosecutors, and defense counsel, whom they perceived as one, and as adversarial to their interests. Several respondents were especially critical of public defenders,[25] whom they believed feigned advocacy in an effort to manipulate them to accept pleas that were not in their best interest. Often these interpretations were reinforced by family members and fellow jail inmates. Nearly all of the transferred youths eventually pled guilty, but because they had little basis on which to distinguish a good deal from a bad one, they almost always felt dissatisfied with the outcome.

The vast majority of transferred youths reported that the clear purpose of criminal court sentencing was to punish them. Some believed that sentencing decisions were linked to their offenses, and were designed to achieve some retributive or deterrent purpose. While these youths frequently expressed the view that their sentences were disproportionate to the gravity of their crimes, they nonetheless granted legitimacy to the idea that offense criteria guided sentencing decisions. However, many other respondents believed that sentencing decisions were based not on considerations of what they had done but, rather, on inferences about essential characteristics of their persons, including judgments that they were depraved or irredeemable. Several respondents suggested that judges vilified them and based sentencing decisions on feelings of personal animosity (e.g., "He hated me and wanted to destroy my life"), which they perceived as illegitimate. Not surprisingly, such attributions of hostility provoked feelings of anger and resentment, as well as perceptions of injustice. Attributions of hostility are common among delinquents, especially violent offenders (Crick and Dodge 1994; Dodge et al. 1990). What was unexpected is that these attributions were made frequently in discussions of the criminal, but not the juvenile, courts.

Preadjudicatory Confinement

There were many similarities in the ways that our respondents experienced preadjudicatory confinement in the juvenile and adult systems. Their general comments on juvenile detention centers and jails most often described their purposes as custodial, their staffs as indifferent, and their environments as bleak and (at least initially) threatening. In some critical respects, however, experiences in the two settings differed. For example, after repeated admissions to detention centers, many youths reported having formed significant attachments to at least one line staff member. This was not the case in jails. In addition, preadjudicatory detention stays were most often described as less stressful than stays in jail. In part this was due to the fact that the duration of detention was generally brief in comparison to time spent in jail. Pending the outcome of their criminal cases, the vast majority of transferred youths remained in jail for several months.

Other stressors associated with jail included boredom and anxieties stemming from separation from family and friends, from the unresolved nature of their cases, and from perceived dangers within the jail facilities (see also Adams 1992; Gibbs 1982). Many transferred youths had difficulty adjusting to being jailed together with adult offenders. Several mentioned that jail officials appeared not to differentiate between them and some of the chronic and violent adult offenders with whom they were housed. Most did not perceive themselves as hardened or dangerous criminals and found it very disquieting when officials viewed them in these terms. In addition, the inmate grapevine was riddled with stories of older inmates preying on young boys, which made them fearful of attack by sexual predators and "crazies." Some responded by isolating themselves as much as they could. Others reported that they formed bonds with other inmates for self protection.

In other research, the stresses of incarceration in jail have been linked to suicide. The suicide rate for juveniles in jails is estimated to greatly exceed the rate for the general youth population and to be several times higher than the rate for youths in juvenile detention centers (Memory 1989; Flaherty 1983; Library Information Specialists 1983). While none of our respondents indicated that they had contemplated suicide while in jail, many reported feeling overwhelmed, confused, and depressed.

Characteristics of Juvenile and Adult Correctional Institutions

Many transferred offenders serve sentences in adult correctional facilities. In a majority of states, they are housed together with the general adult population (thirty-one states), with youthful offenders up to age twenty-one or twenty-five (seven states), or some combination of the two (five states) (Library Information Specialists 1995, 7–8). Consequently, it is valuable to consider what we know about adult correctional settings and how they compare to juvenile ones. Unfortunately, while the corrections literature is replete with studies of juvenile and adult institutions, each system has been studied independently, rather than comparatively. Studies of institutions for juveniles have frequently uncovered problems of the same sorts as have been reported in research on adult facilities (e.g., inmate-inmate violence, staff-inmate violence, use of solitary confinement for extended periods, inadequate staffing). While we know little about how pervasive these problems are in either system, there are some dimensions along which we can compare them.

First, the populations in juvenile and adult institutions differ markedly. Obviously, the prison population is older. Nearly half of prison inmates are between the ages of twenty-five and thirty-four (BJS 1997) while over 70 percent of youths in juvenile facilities are between the ages of fifteen and seventeen (Parent et al. 1994, 30). Corollaries of age in this context include greater size and physical strength, longer criminal histories, and more experience with incarceration.[26] Adult and juvenile institutions also differ in the types of offenders they house. While 20 percent of youths confined in training schools are there for a violent offense (Parent et al. 1994, 29), nearly 50 percent of prison inmates are violent offenders (BJS 1997). Those incarcerated in juvenile institutions remain confined for much shorter periods, eight months on average (Parent et al. 1994, 39). Prison inmates have average sentences of nine years and, increasingly, they can expect to serve a major portion of that time in confinement. In sum, when juveniles are transferred to criminal court and institutionalized with adults, they are exposed to an older, stronger, more seasoned, and more violent group of offenders over an extended period of time.

Second, there are organizational differences between juvenile and adult institutions. Adult facilities tend to be much larger than juvenile ones. Over 40 percent of adult institutions house more than 500 inmates; nearly 25 percent hold more than 1,000 (BJS 1997). The average daily population in institutions for adults is 700, compared to approximately 70 in juvenile facilities. Even training schools, the largest of the juvenile facilities, have an average population of only 127 (Parent et al. 1994, 38). Overcrowding is a problem in both juvenile and adult institutions. Eleven percent of training schools in 1991 were under consent decrees for overcrowded conditions, as were 17 percent of adult correctional facilities (Parent et al. 1994, 34; BJS 1997). Institutional size and overcrowding have been linked to levels of violence and to other important behavioral and psychological consequences (Adams 1992).

Third, staffing patterns differ markedly in the two systems. Prisons accord a much higher priority to security concerns: two-thirds of all personnel in adult correctional facilities are custody or security staff. Their ratio to inmates is 1:4 (BJS 1997). The most recent census of children in custody showed that only 43 percent of training schools had at least one staff member assigned to supervise every eleven residents (the recommended standard). In most, the ratio was higher than that (Parent et al. 1994, 316). Staffing for education is also very different in adult and juvenile facilities. The teacher-to-inmate ratio in adult institutions is 1:100. A national survey of prison inmates in 1991 indicated that fewer than half received any academic instruction (Beck et al. 1993, 27). In 95 percent of training schools, there is at least one teacher for every fifteen residents. In half of these facilities all juveniles are involved in education programs, and in an additional 40 percent of these facilities, more than 75 percent are (Parent et al. 1994, 132-33).[27] There are also important differences in the numbers of counseling or treatment staff. In two-thirds of training schools there is at least one counselor for every ten juveniles; in 85 percent, the ratio is at least 1:25 (Parent et al. 1994, 149). It is difficult to determine the numbers of counseling staff in state prisons. They are included in a very broad category of "professional and technical" personnel—including but not limited to all medical and classification staff—for whom the ratio of staff to inmates is 1:25 (BJS 1997). Whether these differences in programming and staffing patterns are only nominal, or whether they translate into real differences with consequences for quality of life, emotional well-being, behavioral change, or future life chances, are matters we will discuss further below.

Young Offenders in the Juvenile and Adult Corrections Systems

Organizational settings. A substantial body of research suggests that organizational climates have important consequences for inmate attitudes and behaviors. Inmates behave differently in different settings (Adams 1992). Although inmates' backgrounds and individual characteristics clearly influence their behavior, they may be less predictive of institutional adjustment than the context in which inmates are confined. Some research suggests that inmates adapt in more positive ways to treatment-oriented institutions (Street, Vinter, and Perrow 1966; Feld 1977). Compared to inmates in custody-oriented institutions, those in treatment-oriented institutions reportedly have more favorable perspectives on staff, collaborate more with staff, and are more likely to develop egalitarian relationships with fellow inmates (Feld 1977). They are more receptive to the idea of change, develop greater personal control and problem-solving abilities, and are more optimistic about remaining law abiding following release (Street, Vinter, and Perrow 1966).

In correctional settings where custody concerns dominate, inmates tend to perceive institutions as oppressive. Staff and inmates tend to be alienated from each other and to respond to each other based on negative stereotypes, which are thereby reinforced (Street, Vinter, and Perrow 1966). Inmates in custody-oriented institutions also have more incentive to engage in deviant behavior, are more likely to resort to interpersonal violence, and are more resistant to change (Feld 1977; Poole and Regoli 1983). Moreover, there is some evidence that inmates released from custody-oriented programs are more likely to recidivate and, when they do, to commit more serious offenses than those released from treatment-oriented institutions (Feld 1977). While each of the studies just cited involved comparisons across different juvenile institutions, their findings may be applicable in a more general way to differences between juvenile and adult correctional settings. This is not to suggest that some juvenile institutions are not extremely custody oriented, or that some adult institutions are not highly treatment oriented. It is to say that, given important differences in philosophy that have traditionally characterized the two systems, juvenile institutions are likely to place greater emphasis on treatment than adult institutions.

Our findings (Bishop et al. 1998) and those of Forst, Fagan, and Vivona (1989) speak directly to this issue. Despite the punitive rhetoric of juvenile justice in Florida in 1997, the juvenile institutions we visited were clearly treatment oriented, as were the institutions observed by Forst, Fagan, and Vivona in the early 1980s. The Florida facilities were organized around a therapeutic model—most often, a cognitive-behavioral one—that provided core principles that governed staff behavior and staff-resident interactions. Residents had a full round of daily activities that included academic classes, social skills training, counseling sessions, and recreational activities. Some youths were involved in vocational training, substance abuse treatment, and other activities as well.

Staff in each of the four juvenile programs we visited were expected to model self-discipline, social skills, and strategies for problem solving and impulse control. In the juvenile institutions observed in both studies, even line staff were trained in treatment methodologies and were expected to integrate them into daily activities on a more or less ongoing basis.[28] Significant incentives—salary enhancements and promotions—were linked to therapeutic skills.

Our respondents described most juvenile program staff in very positive terms. The general sense of youths' comments was that most staff cared for them, understood what troubled them, and believed in their potential to become productive and happy adults. Staff were credited with being skilled at modeling and teaching appropriate behaviors, and providing helpful guidance about personal matters.[29] To be sure, some staff in each juvenile institution were described as "nine-to-fivers," individuals with little interest or concern for youths who were simply "working for the money." However, seldom were more than a small fraction of staff characterized in this way.

Similarly, Forst, Fagan, and Vivona (1989) found that, compared to staff in prisons, staff in juvenile facilities were perceived to be more involved in counseling, more concerned about youths' adjustment, more encouraging of their participation in programs, more helpful in assisting them to understand themselves and deal with their problems, and more facilitative of improved relationships with their families. Juvenile program staff were also rated significantly more highly than prison staff in terms of helping youths to set and achieve goals, to improve relationships with peers, to feel better about themselves, and to acquire skills that would be useful upon release.

The prisons we visited, like those observed by Forst, Fagan, and Vivona, were clearly dominated by custody concerns. In part, this was surely a function of the size of the facilities.[30] In large institutions, even in settings where the avowed purpose is to treat rather than punish, security concerns tend to become all-consuming. To ensure the safety of inmates and staff and to guard against escape, regulations must be enforced governing nearly every aspect of inmate life, and searches, segregation, counts, and restrictions on movement are routine. Quite apart from concerns about safety and prevention of escape, however, the custody orientation of today's prisons reflects the fact that the goal of incapacitation has gained such favor in policy circles (Spelman 1994; Zimring and Hawkins 1995).

Concerns about order and security were very apparent inside the prisons we observed. The vast majority of the personnel within these institutions were uniformed correctional officers. The correctional officers we observed were highly authoritarian and appeared to be focused exclusively on enforcing rules, maximizing surveillance, and demonstrating their power. They rarely spoke to inmates except to issue commands. We observed little interaction between correctional staff and inmates that was not formal and impersonal.

Because the prisons were primarily custodial facilities, most of our inmate respondents were not engaged in programs aimed at their personal or social development. Many expressed a desire to participate in rehabilitative programming, but fewer than 10 percent were engaged in any sort of counseling or treatment program.[31] Several attended remedial education classes for a portion of each day, and some reported that they were learning a trade, usually one that was related to facility maintenance. Despite these reported involvements, it was common for respondents to report that they had a great deal of idle time, which they found burdensome. There appeared to be too few work assignments to go around. This is an issue not only in Florida: Across the nation, only one-third of state prison inmates work more than thirty-four hours per week, and a third do not work at all (Beck et al. 1993, 27).

When we asked inmates about prison staff, almost all responded with reference to correctional officers. Although some inmates had contact with teachers and all had occasional appointments with classification officers and medical personnel, their contacts with correctional officers tended to color their thinking abut staff in general and, to a considerable degree, about the institution as well. Most respondents believed prison staff viewed them as "convicts," "criminals," or "nobodies" who would never change. Correctional officers were almost uniformly perceived in negative terms, as hostile and derisive. Many respondents reported feeling threatened by correctional staff, both physically and emotionally. Several gave accounts of being humiliated by correctional officers, and of being goaded or provoked into conflicts that would result in their being disciplined.[32] Many responded by trying to minimize interactions with staff. Others became confrontational and defiant: they violated rules, accumulated disciplinary reports, and, as a consequence, were punished with solitary confinement and loss of gain time.

Criminal socialization. The physical setting of the prison provided many more opportunities for private interaction among inmates than was the case in the juvenile facilities. In the juvenile programs, staff participated in activities with small groups of youths throughout the day, and at night remained in close proximity to them in their dormitories. In the prisons, for much of the day large groups of inmates congregated in the yard while correctional officers watched at a distance from the perimeter. During the evenings, inmates remained in their cells or dormitories supervised by correctional officers separated from them in glass-enclosed control rooms. Youths in prison reported that they spent much of their time talking to more skilled and experienced offenders who taught them new techniques of committing crime and methods of avoiding detection. Strained relations between inmates and staff provided additional incentive to plan unlawful behaviors surreptitiously.

Misconduct and violence. One of the most consistent findings in corrections research is that misconduct is most common among young inmates. Indeed, age is the strongest predictor of prison misconduct (see, e.g., Wolfgang 1961; Brown and Spevacek 1971; Ellis, Grasmick, and Gilman 1974; Jensen 1977; Myers and Levy 1978; Flanagan 1983, 1996; Goetting and Howsen 1986; McShane and Williams 1989; Toch and Adams 1989; Library Information Specialists 1995; Craddock 1996). In the only study to explore misconduct among juvenile inmates, McShane and Williams (1989) compared the prison adjustment of serious and violent offenders committed to Texas prisons prior to age seventeen and a matched group of offenders committed between the ages of seventeen and twenty-one. Compared to inmates in their midtwenties and above, those in the seventeen-to-twenty-one-year range have traditionally higher levels of misconduct. Yet McShane and Williams found that juvenile offenders were twice as likely as those age seventeen to twenty-one to have disciplinary incidents during the first two years of incarceration, and three times as likely to be placed in administrative segregation for aggressive behavior. Further, because work and good time were linked to good behavior, only half of the juvenile inmates had work assignments (compared to over 80 percent of the young adults) and less than 20 percent earned good-time credits at the maximum rate (compared to 40 percent of the young adults) (McShane and Williams 1989, 261).

Prisons are dangerous places where inmate norms frequently support violent behavior (see Toch 1977, 1985; Irwin 1980; Bowker 1985; Lockwood 1980). Displays of verbal and physical aggression "prove" one's toughness and masculinity and establish social position in a context in which there are few alternative means of earning status. They are also means by which gangs build cohesion and establish position in the social hierarchy. Because adolescents as a group tend to be highly sensitive to peer pressure, young offenders are especially likely to engage in violent behavior and to develop identities linked to domination and control. In the context of the prison, there is little modeling of constructive ways of building identities, satisfying affiliative needs, developing competencies, or resolving interpersonal problems.

Victimization. Forst, Fagan, and Vivona (1989) questioned their respondents about victimizations in prisons and training schools. Weapons assaults were reported by one-quarter of training school residents and one-third of juveniles confined in prisons; sexual attacks by 2 percent of training school residents and 9 percent of juveniles in prison; and beatings by staff by 5 percent of training school residents and 10 percent of juveniles in prison (Forst, Fagan, and Vivona 1989, 10). Unlike Forst, Fagan, and Vivona, we (Bishop et al. 1998) did not systematically survey respondents about victimizations. Nevertheless, in describing prison life, about one-quarter of the transferred youths reported that they had either been assaulted or witnessed an act of assault by a fellow inmate, and approximately one-third reported either being assaulted or witnessing an assault on a fellow inmate by a correctional officer. In addition, many others reported that the danger of violence was far greater in prison than in juvenile facilities (Bishop et al. 1998, 135–38).

Other corrections research consistently shows that young inmates who lack the experience to cope with the predatory environment within prisons are at greatest risk for physical and sexual assault (Fuller and Orsagh 1977; Toch 1977; Bowker 1980; Irwin 1980; Wright 1991; Cooley 1993; Gillespie n.d.). They also feel most vulnerable to physical and sexual predation, which contributes to their exploitation: fear is often interpreted as a sign of weakness. Because of their vulnerability, adolescent inmates are more likely to be placed in protective or "safekeep" custody than older inmates (McShane and Williams 1989). While this strategy is intended to protect them from harm, protective custody is not without negative consequences. Generally, inmates in protective custody are isolated from others around the clock, do not participate in educational or other programming, and have little recreation.[33]

Fear of victimization has also been linked to psychological well-being, especially among those who are unwilling or unable to retaliate against predators (Toch 1977; Maitland and Sluder 1996; McCorkle 1993a, 1993b).

Fearful inmates are frequently anxious and depressed. Thus, not only are young inmates more likely to be placed in protective custody because of their vulnerability to attack, but they are also more likely to be placed in specialized units for treatment of mental health problems (McShane and Williams 1989).

Reported effects. In our research, we asked youths about the impact of their experiences in juvenile and adult correctional facilities on their attitudes and behaviors. Nearly all of our subjects (both the transfers and the nontransfers) had been committed to at least two juvenile programs. Although critical of many juvenile programs, the vast majority of youths reported that one or more had been beneficial to them. They were most critical of programs that were impersonal and/or of insufficient duration or intensity to have a real or sustained impact (e.g., community work service, electronic monitoring, regular probation). Youths attributed the greatest benefit to intensive, long-term programs in which they had formed relationships of trust with caring adults, ones who believed in their worth and who encouraged them. While educational and vocational training were seen as important, youths tended to place greater value on programs that taught them how to exercise self-control, those that taught basic interpersonal skills, and those that focused on teaching them values and enhanced self-respect. It is noteworthy that the characteristics of the programs they nominated as most helpful are those that research suggests are most likely to produce reductions in recidivism (Cullen and Gilbert 1982; Garrett 1985; Gendreau and Ross 1987; Andrews et al. 1990; Palmer 1991, 1995; Lipsey 1992; Mulvey, Arthur, and Reppucci 1993; Lipsey and Wilson 1998).[34]

Although the transferred offenders endorsed the juvenile corrections system to the same degree as those who were still in that system, the vast majority perceived little that was positive in their experience in the adult corrections system. For most, it was at best a test of will and endurance from which they hoped to emerge intact. At worst, it was a painful and denigrating experience that they pointed to as reason or justification for becoming more angry, embittered, cynical, and defeated, and/or skilled at committing crime.

More than half of the respondents who were currently incarcerated in juvenile facilities expressed confidence that they would remain law abiding following release. Most often the optimism they expressed was attributed to shifts in attitude about themselves and others resulting from relationships with program staff and/or to new skills they had developed while in the programs. A substantial number of nontransfers (42 percent) were uncertain about their futures, but only 3 percent anticipated that they would commit further crimes. In contrast, only one-third of those in the adult system expected to remain law abiding. Those who did so attributed change to "time" or maturation, rather than to the development of personal resources or skills that rendered them better able to deal with the outside world.[35] Forty-six percent of those in the adult system were uncertain that they would remain law abiding and 18 percent expected to reoffend.

Postrelease consequences. Whether or not they are incarcerated, juvenile offenders convicted in criminal court will experience consequences associated with their involvement in the criminal justice system. Criminal conviction carries many consequences that may affect young offenders' lives in a manner that greatly impedes chances for reform long after their sentences have been served. Felony convictions commonly result in a number of civil disabilities, including loss of the right to serve in the military, to vote, to hold public office, and to sit on a jury. Perhaps the most severe consequences of conviction, however, have to do with effects on future employment and conventional associations. In many states, criminal conviction results in loss, suspension, and restriction of professional and occupational licenses as well as disqualification from obtaining some licenses in the future (Kuzma 1996). More importantly, unlike juvenile delinquency adjudications, criminal convictions must be reported on applications for employment. An adult felony conviction, especially if followed by incarceration, may have a profoundly negative effect on future labor market participation (Freeman 1992). This effect is all the more serious in light of longitudinal research on criminal career patterns that shows that entry into stable employment is a crucial factor in desistance (Sampson and Laub 1993). The informal sanction of being denied employment because of a criminal record stands as a formidable barrier to becoming a law-abiding adult, and surely places a strain on many individuals to engage in illegal behavior to support themselves and fulfill family responsibilities.

A second critical factor associated with criminal court convictions has to do with obstacles offenders encounter in becoming involved in conventional groups and activities. Development of significant bonds to conventional others has the potential to alter criminal trajectories over the life course. Research shows the importance of marriage characterized by bonds of affection and commitment in interrupting criminal careers (Sampson and Laub 1993). But the stigma of a criminal conviction limits access to conventional social networks. Ex-offenders may find themselves shunned not only by prospective employers, but by prospective friends and dating partners as well. In our own research (Bishop et al. 1998), a number of respondents recognized these problems. Most transferred youths expressed worry about finding a good job. Several anticipated that they would be turned down by prospective employers for jobs for which they were qualified. Many commented on previous or present unstable relationships, and concern about future relationships.

5. Discussion

From the studies that compared rates of recidivism among youths transferred to criminal court and youths retained in the juvenile system, there emerge three major findings. First, transfer appears to be counterproductive: transferred youths are more likely to reoffend, and to reoffend more quickly and more often, than those retained in the juvenile system. In addition, Fagan's (1991, 1995, 1996) research suggests that the differential effects of criminal and juvenile justice processing are not dependent on sentence type or sentence length. That is, the mere fact that juveniles have been convicted in criminal rather than juvenile court increases the likelihood that they will reoffend. Finally, the risk of reoffending is aggravated when a sentence of incarceration is imposed.

These findings lend themselves to several alternative explanations. It may be that processing in the criminal justice system actually promotes further offending. Alternatively, and contrary to the sentiment underlying the transfer reforms, processing in the juvenile justice system may promote law-abiding behavior. Or both of these explanations may be correct. Based on what we have learned from our interviews with young offenders and from related research, we suggest an interpretation that is consistent with both of these explanations.

We have earlier drawn upon Braithwaite's (1989) theory of shaming as a promising general theoretical perspective (Bishop et al. 1996; Winner et al. 1997). Building on social control theory, this perspective recognizes that it is through bonding or attachment to others that children learn prosocial attitudes, values, and behaviors. Children who as teens engage in serious and chronic delinquency have most often failed to develop close attachments to others. For a variety of reasons—some related to their parents, some to the children themselves—they are weakly bonded to their parents, who frequently do a poor job of monitoring and teaching appropriate behaviors (Moffitt 1999). Often the result is that these children are undersocialized, and possess traits (e.g., impulsivity, selfishness, aggressiveness) that make it more difficult for them to form positive relationships with others.[36]

We have seen that processing in juvenile court is associated with a lower probability of reoffending. We suggest that one reason this may be so is that the juvenile system communicates messages of caring—i.e., offers of attachment—to young people whose backgrounds are often replete with alienation from and rejection by conventional adults. Time and again in our interviews with young offenders we were made aware of their sensitivity to signs of interest and concern from judges, detention workers, and juvenile program staff. Where they formed significant attachments, they appeared to be positively affected by them. Although they had behaved unlawfully, and sometimes dangerously and violently, the message they heard from the juvenile courts was most often one that encouraged their sense of individual worth and potential. For many of these youths, such messages had rarely been communicated in the primary spheres of home and school. Braithwaite suggests that these messages are reintegrative. When responses to offenders are disapproving of their lawbreaking behavior but open to forgiveness and restoration, they promote the development of social bonds. Our interviews with juvenile offenders suggest that even brief positive contacts with conventional adults—say, to judges or detention workers—generally have a beneficial effect, at least in the short term. For some youths, these contacts open up the possibility of trusting enough to develop other, more enduring relationships with conventional adults—e.g., with a counselor in a long-term commitment program—that may have more long-term influences on attitudes, values, and behaviors. We think it is very significant that young offenders reported to us that most "front end" and even some of the "deep end" juvenile programs they had been in were not long enough or sufficiently intense to produce real or lasting change. These observations showed insight into the complexity of their behavior as well as into the mechanics and dynamics of behavioral change.

We suggest a second reason that processing in the juvenile system was linked to lower rates of reoffending. There is now a fairly large body of empirical research demonstrating that some programs are quite effective in reducing recidivism, even among serious and violent offenders. (For a recent and comprehensive review, see Lipsey and Wilson 1998). In our own research (Bishop et al. 1998) we learned that many of these approaches were being utilized in the juvenile programs we visited. Moreover, these were the approaches that the youths themselves identified as most beneficial to them. What is most significant to us about these approaches is that they target the deficits in socialization that inhibit the formation of social bonds. For example, many serious and violent offenders have not learned how to handle impulse in productive or at least nondestructive ways. Their inability to manage anger is a source of many of the difficulties they have experienced in past relationships and, left unaddressed, will continue to interfere with the development of future attachments. These young offenders have social deficits in many other areas as well. Many have never been taught how to make polite requests, to respond to inappropriate demands or requests without losing "face," to deal with other people's anger, to work on cooperative tasks, etc. Many have not acquired the cognitive skills to anticipate the consequences of their behavior or to take the perspective of others. Programs that enhance youths' skills in these areas facilitate conventional bonding experiences. In the juvenile programs observed in our research and that of Forst, Fagan, and Vivona (1989), young offenders had more opportunities to form attachments to conventional others (especially staff), to be reinforced in conventional beliefs (by both staff and other inmates in programs), and to make commitments to conventional lines of action (e.g., in educational and vocational programs). While not without criminal learning opportunities, these juvenile programs provided opportunities for frequent, positive staff-resident interaction and program participation that emphasized conventional values and behavior.

Regardless of whether treatment in the juvenile justice system is beneficial, the criminal justice system may actually contribute to criminal behavior. Among our interviewees, we found very negative reactions to criminal court processing. Many experienced the court process not so much as a condemnation of their behavior as a condemnation of them. Unlike the juvenile court, the criminal court failed to communicate that young offenders retain some fundamental worth. What the youths generally heard was that they were being punished not only because their behavior was bad but also because they were personifications of their behavior. If some other message was intended by the court, it failed to impress the juvenile offenders we interviewed.

It is not so much that condemnation and punishment are without value. Rather, it is more that they have value primarily when the person punished grants them legitimacy—i.e., accepts the punishment and the agents and agencies administering it as properly motivated (Matza 1964). Far from viewing the criminal court and its officers as legitimate, the juvenile offenders we interviewed saw them more often as duplicitous and manipulative, malevolent in intent, and indifferent to their needs.[37] It was common for them to experience a sense of injustice, and then to condemn the condemners (Sykes and Matza 1957; Matza 1964; Lemert 1951, 1974), reactions that are inconsistent with compliance to legal norms (Lanza-Kaduce and Radosevich 1987; Tyler 1990).

In the institutional world of the adult prison, youths were more likely to learn social rules and norms that legitimated domination, exploitation, and retaliation. They routinely observed both staff and inmate models who exhibited these behaviors, and they observed these illegitimate norms being reinforced. In addition, youths in prison were exposed to an inmate subculture that taught criminal motivations as well as techniques of committing crime and avoiding detection. Even if the pains of punishment and confinement caused most juveniles to wish to avoid returning to prison, what they learned in prison provided a destructive counterbalance to their positive intentions.

Perhaps the most harmful effects of transfer to criminal court come in the form of informal sanctions applied in the community. While most youths who engage in delinquency will desist by early adulthood as they move into jobs and marriages that give them a sense of place and purpose, many of those who enter the criminal justice system will carry the stigma of a criminal conviction. The normal transition from risk-taking adolescence to conventional adulthood will be relatively closed to them. Stigmatization and obstruction of conventional opportunities certainly make reoffending more likely.

6. Conclusion

Our analysis and discussion in this chapter began by showing that a period of extensive and rapid reform has produced large increases in the number of juvenile offenders prosecuted and convicted in criminal courts and exposed to adult sanctions. Public perceptions to the contrary notwithstanding, many of these offenders are not "extreme cases," i.e., youths accused of heinous acts or chronic, hardened criminals who have repeatedly demonstrated their resistance to intervention.

We have also seen that entry of large numbers of young offenders into the criminal justice system has important systemic consequences. It places additional burdens on already overtaxed courts and corrections systems. For corrections officials, an influx of young offenders presents significant new issues related to institutional security and programming. Whether they will respond by developing age-segregated facilities and programs designed to meet the special needs of a youth population remains to be seen. Further, we have suggested that the expansion of transfer through legislative exclusion and prosecutorial waiver has created new problems of interagency articulation and may precipitate repercussive effects in the juvenile justice system which have not been heretofore addressed.

Finally, we have argued that, as a crime control policy, transfer tends to be counterproductive. Although the empirical studies on this issue are too few in number to be definitive, they strongly suggest that transfer is more likely to aggravate recidivism than to stem it. We suggest that this effect is a product of several factors, including the sense of injustice young offenders associate with criminal court processing, the multiple criminogenic effects of incarceration in the adult system (e.g., exposure to negative shaming, opportunities for criminal socialization, modeling of violence) and the stigmatization and opportunity blockage that flow from a record of criminal conviction. Compared to the criminal justice system, the juvenile system seems to be more reintegrative in practice and effect.

In short, we conclude that current transfer policies are misguided. Transfer appears to have little deterrent value. Moreover, when applied broadly to offenders who are neither particularly serious nor particularly chronic, any incapacitative gains achieved in the short run appear to be quickly nullified. While broad transfer policies may and likely do serve retributive ends, they do so at a considerable price. The same ends might be better served through modest extensions to the upper boundary of juvenile court jurisdiction. Such a course might avoid the negative effects of criminal processing, conviction, and exposure to adult correctional environments, while possibly even enhancing the prospects of rehabilitation in intensive, long-term juvenile programs. Unless and until future research negates these conclusions, the clear implication is that transfer should be reserved for those "extreme cases" to which it has traditionally been applied, where significant retributive and incapacitative benefits can be realized.

References
Case Cited

In re Gault, 387 U.S. 1, 87 S. Ct. 1428, 18 L. Ed. 2d 527 (1967).

Other References

Adams, Kenneth. 1992. "Adjusting to Prison Life." In *Crime and Justice: A Review of Research,* vol. 16. Edited by Michael Tonry. Chicago: University of Chicago Press.

Ainsworth, Janet E. 1991. "Re-imagining Childhood and Reconstructing the Legal Order: The Case for Abolishing the Juvenile Court." *North Carolina Law Review* 69:1083.

———. 1995. "Youth Justice in a Unified Court: Response to Critics of Juvenile Court Abolition." *Boston College Law Review* 1995:927.

Andrews, Donald A., Ivan Zinger, Robert D. Hoge, James Bonta, Paul Gendreau, and Francis T. Cullen. 1990. "Does Correctional Treatment Work? A Clinically Relevant and Psychologically Informed Meta-analysis." *Criminology* 28:369.

Bartollas, Clemens, Stuart J. Miller, and Simon Dinitz. 1976. *Juvenile Victimization: The Institutional Paradox.* New York: John Wiley.

Beck, Allen, Darrell Gilliard, Lawrence Greenfield, Caroline Harlow, Thomas Hester, Louis Jankowski, Tracy Snell, James Stephan, and Danielle Morton. 1993. *Survey of State Prison Inmates, 1991.* Washington: United States Department of Justice, Bureau of Justice Statistics.

Bishop, Donna M., and Charles E. Frazier. 1991. "Transfer of Juveniles to Criminal Court: A Case Study and Analysis of Prosecutorial Waiver." *Notre Dame Journal of Law, Ethics, and Public Policy* 5:281.

Bishop, Donna M., Charles E. Frazier, and John C. Henretta. 1989. "Prosecutorial Waiver: Case Study of a Questionable Reform." *Crime and Delinquency* 35:179.

Bishop, Donna M., Charles E. Frazier, Lonn Lanza-Kaduce, and Henry George White. 1998. *Juvenile Transfers to Criminal Court Study: Phase I Final Report.* Washington: Office of Juvenile Justice and Delinquency Prevention.

Bishop, Donna M., Charles E. Frazier, Lonn Lanza-Kaduce, and Lawrence Winner. 1996. "The Transfer of Juveniles to Criminal Court: Does It Make a Difference?" *Crime and Delinquency* 42:171.

Bishop, Donna M., Lonn Lanza-Kaduce, and Lawrence Winner. 1996. *A Study of Juvenile Case Processing in Florida: Issues of Timeliness and Consistency across Jurisdictions.* Tallahassee: Juvenile Justice Advisory Board.

Blomberg, Thomas. 1977. "Diversion and Accelerated Social Control." *Journal of Criminal Law and Criminology* 68:274.

———. 1979. "Widening the Net: An Anomaly in the Evaluation of Diversion Programs." In *Handbook on Criminal Justice Evaluation.* Edited by Malcolm W. Klein and Katherine S. Teilman. Beverly Hills, Calif.: Sage.

Bowker, Lee H. 1980. *Prison Victimization.* New York: Elsevier.

———. 1985. "An Essay on Prison Violence." In *Prison Violence in America.* Edited by Michael C. Braswell, S. Dillingham, and Reid H. Montgomery. Cincinnati: Anderson.

Braithwaite, John. 1989. *Crime, Shame, and Reintegration.* New York: Cambridge University Press.

Brown, Barry S., and John D. Spevacek. 1971. "Disciplinary Offenders at Two Differing Correctional Institutions." *Correctional Psychiatry and Journal of Social Therapy* 17:48.

Brown, Jodi M., and Patrick A. Langan. 1998. *State Court Sentencing of Convicted Felons, 1994.* Washington: United States Department of Justice, Bureau of Justice Statistics.

Bureau of Justice Statistics. 1997. *Correctional Populations in the United States, 1995.* Washington: United States Department of Justice.

Coalition for Juvenile Justice. 1994. *No Easy Answers: Juvenile Justice in a Climate of Fear.* Washington: Coalition for Juvenile Justice.

Cooley, Dennis. 1993. "Criminal Victimization in Male Federal Prisons." *Canadian Journal of Criminology* 35:479.

Craddock, Amy. 1996. "A Comparative Study of Male and Female Prison Misconduct Careers." *Prison Journal* 76:60.

Crick, N., and K. Dodge. 1994. "A Review and Reformulation of Social Information-Processing Mechanisms in Children's Social Adjustment." *Psychological Bulletin* 115:74.

Cullen, Francis T., and Karen E. Gilbert. 1982. *Reaffirming Rehabilitation.* Cincinnati: Anderson.

DeComo, R., Barry Krisberg, B. Rudenstine, and D. DelRosario. 1995. *Juveniles Taken into Custody Research Program: 1994 Annual Report.* Washington: United States Department of Justice, Office of Juvenile Justice and Delinquency Prevention.

DeFrances, Carol J., and Greg W. Steadman. 1998. *Prosecutors in State Courts, 1996.* Washington: United States Department of Justice, Bureau of Justice Statistics.

DeFrances, Carol J., and Kevin J. Strom. 1997. *Juveniles Prosecuted in State Criminal Courts.* Washington: United States Department of Justice, Bureau of Justice Statistics.

Dodge, K., J. Price, J. Bachorowski, and J. Newman. 1990. "Hostile Attributional Biases in Severely Aggressive Delinquents." *Journal of Abnormal Psychology* 99:385.

Ellis, Desmond, Harold Grasmick, and Bernard Gilman. 1974. "Violence in Prison: A Sociological Analysis." *American Journal of Sociology* 80:16.

Evans, K. 1978. "Reflections on Education in the Penitentiary." In *Issues in Police and Criminal Psychology.* Edited by W. Taylor and Michael Braswell. Washington: University Press of America.

Fagan, Jeffrey A. 1991. *The Comparative Impacts of Juvenile and Criminal Court Sanctions on Adolescent Felony Offenders.* Final Report, Grant 87-IJ CX 4044, to the National Institute of Justice. Washington: U.S. Department of Justice.

———. 1995. "Separating the Men from the Boys: The Comparative Advantage of Juvenile versus Criminal Court Sanctions on Recidivism among Adolescent Felony Offenders." In *Serious, Violent, and Chronic Juvenile offenders: A Sourcebook.* Edited by James C. Howell, Barry Krisberg, J. David Hawkins, and John J. Wilson. Thousand Oaks, Calif.: Sage.

———. 1996. "The Comparative Advantage of Juvenile versus Criminal Court Sanctions on Recidivism among Adolescent Felony Offenders." *Law and Policy* 18:77.

Feld, Barry C. 1977. *Neutralizing Inmate Violence: Juvenile Offenders in Institutions.* Cambridge, Mass.: Ballinger.

———. 1988. "The Juvenile Court Meets the Principle of Offense: Punishment, Treatment, and the Difference It Makes." *Boston University Law Review* 68: 821.

———. 1991. "Justice by Geography: Urban, Suburban, and Rural Variations in Juvenile Justice Administration." *Journal of Criminal Law and Criminology* 82:156.

———. 1993. "Juvenile (In)Justice and the Criminal Court Alternative." *Crime and Delinquency* 39:403.

———. 1997. "Abolish the Juvenile Court: Youthfulness, Criminal Responsibility, and Sentencing Policy." *Journal of Criminal Law and Criminology* 88: 68.

Flaherty, Michael G. 1983. "The National Incidence of Juvenile Suicides in Adult Jails and Juvenile Detention Centers." *Suicide and Life-Threatening Behavior* 13:85.

Flanagan, Timothy J. 1980. "The Pains of Long-Term Imprisonment: A Comparison of British and American Perspectives." *British Journal of Criminology* 20:148.

———. 1983. "Correlates of Institutional Misconduct among State Prisoners: A Research Note." *Criminology* 21:29.

———. 1996. "Discipline." In *Encyclopedia of American Prisons.* Edited by Marilyn D. McShane and Frank P. Williams. New York: Garland.

Florida Department of Juvenile Justice. 1997. *Profile of Delinquency Cases and Youths Referred.* Tallahassee: Florida Department of Juvenile Justice, Bureau of Data and Research.

———. 1998. Statement of Philosophy at www.djj.state.fl.us.

Forst, Martin, Jeffrey Fagan, and T. Scott Vivona. 1989. "Youth in Prisons and Training Schools: Perceptions and Consequences of the Treatment Custody Dichotomy." *Juvenile and Family Court Journal* 39:1.

Forst, Martin, and Martha-Elin Blomquist. 1992. "Punishment, Accountability, and the New Juvenile Justice." *Juvenile and Family Court Journal* 43:1.

Fox, Vernon B., and Jeanne B. Stinchcomb. 1994. *Introduction to Corrections.*4th ed. Englewood Cliffs: Prentice Hall.

Frazier, Charles E. 1991. "Deep End Juvenile Placement or Transfer to Adult Court by Direct File?" Unpublished report prepared for the Florida Commission on Juvenile Justice.

Frazier, Charles E., and Donna M. Bishop. 1990. "Obstacles to Reform in Juvenile Corrections: A Case Study." *Journal of Contemporary Corrections* 6:157.

Frazier, Charles E., Donna M. Bishop, and Lonn Lanza-Kaduce.1999. "'Get Tough' Juvenile Justice Reforms: The Florida Experience." *Annals of the American Academy of Political and Social Science* 564:167.

Frazier, Charles E., and John C. Cochran. 1986. "Official Intervention, Diversion from the Juvenile Justice System, and the Dynamics of Human Services Work: Effects of a Reform Based on Labeling Theory." *Crime and Delinquency* 32:157.

Frazier, Charles E., Pamela Richards, and Roberto Hugh Potter. 1983. "Juvenile Diversion and Net Widening: Toward a Clarification of Assessment Strategies." *Human Organization* 42:115.

Freasier, A., and T. White. 1983. "IEP Communicators." *Journal of Correctional Education* 34:27.

Freeman, Richard B. 1992. "Crime and the Employment Status of Disadvantaged Youths." In *Urban Labor Markets and Job Opportunity.* Edited by G. E. Peterson and W. Vroman. Washington: Urban Institute Press.

Fuller, D., and T. Orsagh. 1977. "Violence and Victimization within a State Prison System." *Criminal Justice Review* 2:35.

Garrett, Carol J. 1985. "Effects of Residential Treatment on Adjudicated Delinquents: A Meta-analysis." *Journal of Research in Crime and Delinquency* 22: 287.

Gendreau, Paul, and Robert Ross. 1987. "Revivification of Rehabilitation: Evidence from the 1980's." *Justice Quarterly* 4:349.

Gibbs, Jack. 1982. "The First Cut Is the Deepest: Psychological Breakdown and

Survival in the Detention Setting." In *The Pains of Imprisonment*, edited by Robert Johnson and Hans Toch. Beverly Hills, Calif.: Sage.

Gillespie. L. Kay. N.d. "Juveniles in an Adult World: Prison Inmates under the Age of Eighteen." Unpublished paper, available through the National Institute of Justice/National Criminal Justice Reference Service, Rockville, Md.

Gilliard, Darrell F., and Allen J. Beck. 1998. *Prison and Jail Inmates at Midyear 1997*. Washington: United States Department of Justice, Bureau of Justice Statistics.

Goetting, Ann, and Roy Michael Howsen. 1986. "Correlates of Prison Misconduct." *Journal of Quantitative Criminology* 2:49.

Gragg, Frances. 1986. *Juveniles in Adult Court: A Review of Transfers at the Habitual Serious and Violent Juvenile Offender Program Sites*. Washington: Office of Justice Assistance, Research and Statistics.

Hamparian, Donna M., Linda K. Estep, Susan M. Muntean, Ramon R. Priestino, Robert G. Swisher, Paul L. Wallace, and Joseph L. White. 1982. *Major Issues in Juvenile Justice Information and Training: Youth in Adult Courts: Between Two Worlds*. Columbus, Ohio: Academy for Contemporary Problems.

Heuser, James P. 1985. *Juveniles Arrested for Serious Felony Crimes in Oregon and "Remanded" to Adult Criminal Courts: A Statistical Study*. Salem: Oregon Department of Justice Crime Analysis Center.

Hirschi, Travis. 1969. *Causes of Delinquency*. Berkeley and Los Angeles: University of California Press.

Howell, James C. 1997. *Juvenile Justice and Youth Violence*. Thousand Oaks, Calif.: Sage.

Irwin, John. 1980. *Prisons in Turmoil*. Boston: Little Brown.

Jensen, Eric L., and Linda K. Metsger. 1994. "A Test of the Deterrent Effect of Legislative Waiver on Violent Juvenile Crime." *Crime and Delinquency* 40:96.

Jensen, Gary. 1977. "Age and Rule Breaking in Prison: A Test of Sociocultural Interpretations." *Criminology* 14:555.

Jepsen, Bradette. 1997. "Supervising Youthful Offenders: Juveniles Sentenced to Adult Facilities Present Supervisory, Staffing Challenges." *Corrections Today* 59:68.

Johnson, Elmer H. 1966. "Pilot Study: Age, Race, and Recidivism as Factors in Prison Infractions." *Canadian Journal of Corrections* 8:268.

Johnson, Robert. 1987. *Hard Time: Understanding and Reforming the Prison*. Pacific Grove, Calif.: Brooks/Cole.

Klein, Malcolm W. 1976. "Issues and Realities in Police Diversion Programs." *Crime and Delinquency* 22:421.

Kuzma, Susan M. 1996. *Civil Disabilities of Convicted Felons: A State-by-State Survey*. Washington: United States Department of Justice, Office of the Pardon Attorney.

Lanza-Kaduce, Lonn, and Marcia J. Radosevich. 1987. "Negative Reactions to Processing and Substance Abuse among Young Incarcerated Males." *Deviant Behavior* 8:137.

Lanza-Kaduce, Lonn, Donna M. Bishop, and Lawrence Winner. 1997. *Juvenile Case Processing in Florida: A Comparison of Cross-Jurisdictional Variations in*

Timing Sequences and Outcomes 1993-1995. Tallahassee: Juvenile Justice Advisory Board.

Lemert, Edwin. 1951. *Social Pathology.* New York: McGraw-Hill.

———. 1974. "Beyond Mead: The Societal Reaction to Deviance." *Social Problems* 21:457.

Library Information Specialists. 1983. *Corrections Information Series: Suicides in Jails.* Boulder, Colo.: National Institute of Corrections.

———. 1995. Offenders under 18 in State Adult Correctional Systems: A National Picture. In *Special Issues in Corrections.* Longmont, Colo.: National Institute of Corrections.

Lipsey, Mark W. 1992. "Juvenile Delinquency Treatment: A Meta-analytic Inquiry into the Variability of Effects." In *Meta-analysis for Explanation.* Edited by Thomas D. Cook, Harris Cooper, David S. Cordray, Heidi Hartmann, Larry V. Hedges, Richard J. Light, Thomas A. Louis, and Frederick Mosteller. New York: Russell Sage Foundation.

Lipsey, Mark W., and David B. Wilson. 1998. "Effective Intervention for Serious Juvenile Offenders: A Synthesis of Research." In *Serious and Violent Juvenile Offenders: Risk Factors and Successful Interventions.* Edited by Rolf Loeber and David P. Farrington. Thousand Oaks, Calif.: Sage.

Lockwood, Daniel. 1980. *Prison Sexual Violence.* New York: Elsevier.

Maitland, Angela S., and Richard D. Sluder. 1996. "Victimization in Prisons: A Study of Factors Related to the General Well-Being of Youthful Inmates." *Federal Probation* 55:24.

Matza, David. 1964. *Delinquency and Drift.* New York: Wiley.

McCorkle, Richard C. 1992. "Personal Precautions to Violence in Prison." *Criminal Justice and Behavior* 19:160.

———. 1993a. "Fear of Victimization and Symptoms of Psychopathology among Prison Inmates." *Journal of Offender Rehabilitation* 9:27.

———. 1993b. "Living on the Edge: Fear in a Maximum Security Prison." *Journal of Offender Rehabilitation.* 20:73.

McShane, Marilyn, and Frank P. Williams III. 1989. "The Prison Adjustment of Juvenile Offenders." *Crime and Delinquency* 35:254.

Memory, John M. 1989. "Juvenile Suicides in Secure Detention Facilities: Correction of Published Rates." *Death Studies* 13:455.

Moffitt, Terrie E. 1999. "Pathways in the Life Course to Crime." In *Criminological Theory: Past to Present.* Edited by Francis T. Cullen and Robert Agnew. Los Angeles: Roxbury.

Mulvey, Edward P., M. W. Arthur, and N. Dickon Reppucci. 1993. "The Prevention and Treatment of Juvenile Delinquency: A Review of the Research." *Clinical Psychology Review* 13:133.

Myers, Louis B., and Girard W. Levy. 1978. "Description and Prediction of the Intractable Inmate." *Journal of Research in Crime and Delinquency* 15:214.

Nimick, Ellen H., Linda Szymanski, and Howard N. Snyder. 1986. *Juvenile Court Waiver: A Study of Juvenile Court Cases Transferred to Criminal Court.* Pittsburgh: National Center for Juvenile Justice.

Orenstein, Bruce W. 1996. "Juveniles Waived into Adult Institutions." *Corrections Today* 58:60.

Palmer, Ted B. 1991. "The Effectiveness of Intervention: Recent Trends and Current Issues." *Crime and Delinquency* 37:330.

———. 1995. "Programmatic and Non-programmatic Aspects of Successful Intervention: New Directions for Research." *Crime and Delinquency* 41:100.

Parent, Dale G., Valerie Lieter, Stephen Kennedy, Lisa Livens, Daniel Wentworth, and Sarah Wilcox. 1994. *Conditions of Confinement: Juvenile Detention and Corrections Facilities.* Washington: National Institute of Justice, Office of Juvenile Justice and Delinquency Prevention.

Podkopacz, Marcy R., and Barry C. Feld. 1995. "Judicial Waiver Policy and Practice: Persistence, Seriousness, and Race." *Law and Inequality Journal* 14:73.

———. 1996. "The End of the Line: An Empirical Study of Judicial Waiver." *Journal of Criminal Law and Criminology* 86:449.

Poole, Eric D., and Robert M. Regoli. 1983. "Violence in Juvenile Institutions." *Criminology* 21:213.

Sampson, Robert J., and John H. Laub. 1993. *Crime in the Making.* Cambridge: Harvard University Press.

Sickmund, Melissa, Anne L. Stahl, Terrence A. Finnegan, Howard N. Snyder, Rowen S. Poole, and Jeffrey A. Butts. 1998. *Juvenile Court Statistics 1995.* Pittsburgh: National Center for Juvenile Justice.

Sickmund, Melissa, Howard N. Snyder, and Eileen Poe-Yamagata. 1997. *Juvenile Offenders and Victims: 1997 Update on Violence.* Pittsburgh: National Center for Juvenile Justice.

Singer, Simon I. 1996. *Recriminalizing Delinquency: Violent Juvenile Crime and Juvenile Justice Reform.* New York: Cambridge University Press.

Singer, Simon I., and David McDowall. 1988. "Criminalizing Delinquency: The Deterrent Effects of the New York Juvenile Offender Law." *Law and Society Review* 22:521.

Spelman, William. 1994. *Criminal Incapacitation.* New York: Plenum.

Street, David, Robert D. Vinter, and Charles Perrow. 1966. *Organization for Treatment.* New York: Free Press.

Sykes, Gresham, and David Matza. 1957. "Techniques of Neutralization: A Theory of Delinquency." *American Journal of Sociology* 22:664.

Toch, Hans. 1977. *Living in Prison: The Ecology of Survival.* New York: Free Press.

———. 1985. "Social Climate and Prison Violence." In *Prison Violence in America.* Edited by Michael C. Braswell, S. Dillingham, and Reid H. Montgomery. Cincinnati: Anderson.

Toch, Hans, and Kenneth Adams. 1989. *Coping: Maladaptation in Prison.* New Brunswick, N.J.: Transaction.

Tonry, Michael. 1996. *Sentencing Matters.* New York: Oxford University Press.

Torbet, Patricia, Richard Gable, Hunter Hurst IV, Imogene Montgomery, Linda Szymanski, and Douglas Thomas. 1996. *State Responses to Serious and Violent Juvenile Crime.* Pittsburgh: National Center for Juvenile Justice.

Tyler, Tom R. 1990. *Why People Obey the Law.* New Haven: Yale University Press.

U.S. General Accounting Office. 1995. *Juvenile Justice: Juveniles Processed in Criminal Court and Case Dispositions.* Washington: U.S. Government Printing Office.

Winner, Lawrence, Lonn Lanza-Kaduce, Donna M. Bishop, and Charles E. Frazier. 1997. "The Transfer of Juveniles to Criminal Court: Reexamining Recidivism over the Long Term." *Crime and Delinquency* 43:548.

Wolfgang, Marvin E. 1961. "Quantitative Analysis of Adjustment to the Prison Community." *Journal of Criminal Law, Criminology, and Police Science.* 51: 587.

Wright, Kevin N. 1991. "The Violent and Victimized in the Male Prison." *Journal of Offender Rehabilitation* 16:1.

Zimring, Franklin E. 1991. "The Treatment of Hard Cases in American Juvenile Justice: In Defense of Discretionary Waiver." *Notre Dame Journal of Law, Ethics, and Public Policy* 5:267.

Zimring, Franklin E., and Gordon Hawkins. 1995. *Incapacitation: Penal Confinement and the Restraint of Crime.* New York: Oxford University Press.

Notes

1. The *Juvenile Court Statistics* data are generated from nonprobability samples of cases disposed in juvenile court covering approximately two-thirds of the youth population at risk. Weighted estimation procedures are used to generate national estimates. Although these procedures cannot completely overcome threats to validity associated with nonprobability samples, the estimates are believed to be reasonably accurate.

2. Currently twenty-nine states use a combination of judicial waiver and legislative exclusion, five states and the District of Columbia use a combination of judicial and prosecutorial waiver, and five states use all three. Three use legislative exclusion only and one uses prosecutorial waiver exclusively (Torbet et al. 1996). Some states that rely partly or exclusively on transfer mechanisms other than judicial waiver are known to transfer substantial numbers of juvenile offenders. For example, it is estimated that in Florida over seven thousand cases annually are transferred via prosecutorial waiver (Florida Department of Juvenile Justice 1997, 182). The trend toward legislative exclusion and prosecutorial waiver is likely to accelerate in the near future.

3. The increase over time in the proportion of violent offenders among those waived reflects an increase in the number of person offense cases filed in juvenile court, coupled with a decrease in rates of waiver for other types of offenses.

4. Their research involved a long painstaking process of gathering transfer data from each of over three thousand counties across the nation.

5. In light of the sampling and data retrieval problems encountered in the survey, the results should be viewed with caution.

6. Unlike adult offenders, for whom dismissal of charges precludes any legal

sanction, juvenile offenders whose cases are dismissed in criminal court may subsequently be treated as delinquents (Singer 1996, 117).

7. In over half the cases, only age at conviction was known. The twelve thousand figure is an estimate corrected for age misclassification based on some questionable assumptions.

8. Because information on convictions was unavailable in most of the jurisdictions that reported legislative exclusion cases, conviction rates for these cases are not included in what we have reported here.

9. The lack of fit is evident when we note that over five thousand additional cases were waived in 1994 than a decade earlier (DeFrances and Strom 1997, 1). Inconsistencies across data sources also appear if we compare the numbers of prosecutions reported for 1996 ($N = 27,000$) with the number of reported convictions in 1994 ($N = 12,000$). It is probably reasonable to assume that the number of prosecutions in 1994 was not much different than in 1996. If this assumption is correct, the conviction rate in 1994 would have been around 44 percent. This figure seems very low. By way of contrast, Hamparian et al. (1982) reported a conviction rate in 1978 of 91 percent.

10. It is estimated that serious and violent offenders incarcerated in the juvenile justice system remain confined for eight months on average (DeComo et al. 1995).

11. For the most recent and comprehensive review of this literature, see Howell 1997.

12. These comparisons do not control for prior record. Transferred offenders, especially those convicted of property crimes, often have fairly lengthy offense histories (see, e.g., Bishop, Frazier, and Henretta 1989; Bishop and Frazier 1991; Podkopacz and Feld 1995, 1996), which may exceed the prior records of the adult offenders in these comparisons. Our conclusion that transferred offenders are not treated leniently relative to their adult counterparts is thus necessarily a tentative one.

13. This estimate corresponds to the portion of UCR arrests that involve part I (index) crimes. It is conservative in that it assumes (1) that all part II offenses are nonfelonies, and (2) that nonserious cases are as likely to be prosecuted as serious ones.

14. These youths constituted approximately 1.4 percent of the jail population. An additional 2,100 youths were held in jail as juveniles.

15. This figure includes both transfers and youths under eighteen sentenced to prison in states where they were legally defined as adults.

16. More recent figures on the proportion of youths under eighteen in the total prison population are not available at the time of this writing.

17. Youths nearing the upper age limit of juvenile court jurisdiction are more likely to be transferred (see, e.g., Bishop and Frazier 1991; Podkopacz and Feld 1995, 1996).

18. States are experiencing a number of significant problems with articulation between the two systems. Even with changes in standards of confidentiality of juvenile records and the length of time records are maintained prior to expungement, criminal courts are sometimes faced with articulation difficulties. For

example, procedural issues sometimes arise when it is necessary to determine where juveniles requiring pretrial detention are to be held. Even though transfer makes a juvenile legally an adult and subject to pretrial detention in jails in many states, the decision to transfer most often requires more information than is available at the time of arrest (Torbet et al. 1996) and sometimes more than can be easily gotten from the juvenile justice system period (Frazier and Bishop 1990). Another example of situations in which articulation may be a problem is when juvenile records are to be used in applications of serious and habitual offender statutes or "three strikes and you're out" laws (Torbet et al. 1996).

19. The organization and operation of the two justice systems are intricately tied to their underlying philosophies. The criminal justice system rests on a punishment philosophy that assumes individual responsibility, culpability, and accountability. Despite recent and significant changes (Feld 1988; Forst and Blomquist 1992; Fagan 1996), the juvenile justice system still focuses to a greater degree on the malleability of young offenders and the state's responsibility to provide sanctions and programs designed to effect behavioral reform.

20. In the last five years Florida increased its commitments by 85 percent at the same time that transfers increased and felony referrals declined. It is unclear whether transfer and commitment trends are both manifestations of increasingly punitive attitudes toward juvenile offenders, or whether commitment rates increased in an effort to fill vacancies in institutional programs that otherwise would have been created as a result of transfer of more juveniles to the adult system.

21. Ninety-one percent of those incarcerated by the criminal courts were subsequently rearrested, compared to 73 percent of those incarcerated by the juvenile courts. Those incarcerated by the criminal courts reoffended much more quickly (392 days) than those incarcerated by the juvenile courts (691 days) (Fagan 1995, 250).

22. Eighty-one percent of those sentenced to adult probation were subsequently rearrested, compared to 64 percent of those sentenced to juvenile probation (Fagan 1995, 251).

23. There is an urgent need to address these questions, not only because transfer is more common, but also because there are clear signs that the juvenile justice system is becoming more like the criminal justice system (e.g., explicit endorsement of punishment, adoption of determinate sentencing, and extended jurisdiction). In addition, there have been some very serious proposals from distinguished scholars to abolish the juvenile courts and unify the two systems (see, e.g., Feld 1993, 1997; Ainsworth 1991, 1995).

24. Objective indicators of punitiveness abound. For example, the purpose clause of Florida's Juvenile Justice Act identifies protection of public safety as the primary objective. In 1994 the legislature divested the state's major social welfare agency of its authority over juvenile justice operations, and transferred it instead to a new Department of Juvenile Justice, which describes itself as a *criminal justice* agency (Florida Department of Juvenile Justice 1998). Detention is permitted for purposes of punishment and is mandated for many offenders, including some first-time misdemeanants. Until 1994, juvenile corrections

programming had been organized into a four-tier system of "restrictiveness levels." In that year, a fifth tier ("maximum risk") was added and, shortly thereafter, the state's residential commitment capacity increased by nearly 250 percent. From 1993 to 1997, while felony referrals declined, detention populations increased by 34 percent and juvenile commitments increased by 77 percent. Over the same period, an average of over seven thousand cases were transferred to criminal court annually, the highest rate in the nation (Florida Department of Juvenile Justice 1997).

25. Most drew a distinction between public defenders and "attorneys," the latter designation being reserved for retained counsel. Attorneys were generally held in high regard as advocates. Several youths' families made considerable sacrifice to hire attorneys after observing what they adjudged to be the poor performance of court-appointed public defenders. There were numerous allegations that public defenders did not visit them during many months of pretrial confinement and that they urged them, as one offender put it, to "jump on too much time."

26. Sixty percent of prison inmates have previously been incarcerated in an adult jail or prison (Beck et al. 1993, 11).

27. Of 475 incarcerated juveniles included in a recent national survey, most expressed satisfaction that staff did a "very good" job of teaching them something useful (Parent et al. 1994, 141).

28. For example, anger management might well be taught in the midst of a baseball game as well as in evening group sessions designated for that purpose.

29. The largest of the juvenile facilities we visited housed 150 residents. The smallest held 30. Although each facility was surrounded by perimeter fencing, some topped with razor wire, inside there did not appear to be a strong focus on security. There were no uniformed staff. Staff-resident contact and interaction were frequent and, most often it appeared, positive and supportive. We often observed staff offering youths praise and encouragement. It was not at all unusual to see a staff member put his hand on a boy's shoulder in a gesture of support. Although it appeared that program rules were strictly enforced through the imposition of consequences specified in behavioral contracts (e.g., loss of a weekend pass), the atmosphere was not predominantly one of control.

30. The eight prisons we visited ranged in capacity from 350 to 1,200.

31. Counseling was the responsibility of a few professional staff who met with inmates during segmental time slots. This is not surprising, since treatment often represents an "invasion" in a custody-dominated system. Even at the height of the medical model in the 1960s "those in the custodial ranks tended to view treatment personnel with varying degrees of skepticism, mistrust, or at best, grudging tolerance" (Fox and Stinchcomb 1994, 354).

32. While we had a few similar reports regarding staff in juvenile detention centers, there was no indication that juvenile detainees distrusted staff in general.

33. Inmates' preferred strategy for coping with threats of victimization (and other difficult situations) is to handle problems themselves (Flanagan 1980; Adams 1992). Reporting to officials is a sign of weakness and violates norms against "snitching" whose breach is likely to be met with violent retaliation. Some

inmates respond to threats proactively, trying to prevent victimization through "preemptive self-defense" (McCorkle 1992; Irwin 1980; Lockwood 1980; Johnson 1987). Others adopt avoidance techniques such as staying away from "risky" areas and spending as much time as possible in their cells (Bartollas, Miller, and Dinitz 1976; Lockwood 1980). These responses are age patterned: young inmates are more likely than older ones to employ aggressive responses to threats (McCorkle 1992). Thus, the manner in which young inmates tend to respond to threats amplifies problems of disruptiveness, which works to their disadvantage (e.g., loss of gain time, removal from work assignments, greater idle time and boredom) and makes it more difficult for administrators to manage them effectively (Adams 1992; McCorkle 1992).

34. The question of whether treatment in general, or specific kinds of treatment, are effective in reducing recidivism has been the subject of considerable controversy. Research reviews have reached widely different conclusions, some showing substantial positive effects, others showing insignificant or even negative effects. Frankly, we are impressed by some recent meta-analyses that represent significant improvements over earlier reviews in the comprehensiveness of their coverage of the research literature and in their ability to partition the effects of research methodology from the effects of the treatment itself (see especially Lipsey 1992; Lipsey and Wilson 1998). These efforts have produced encouraging results. For example, Lipsey and Wilson (1998, 336) report that the most effective institutional programs for serious juvenile offenders had an effect equivalent to a recidivism reduction of fifteen to twenty percentage points, from 50 to 30–35 percent. In our view, this represents a substantial reduction, especially for serious offenders in institutional settings.

35. Some of these same individuals lamented the fact that they had not previously taken better advantage of programs offered in the juvenile system. This is an interesting group of respondents. Some said the earlier juvenile programs had had a positive effect on them, but it was not enough. Others said they had simply not been open to change in the past. Personal maturation and the pain of lengthy incarceration were cited as reasons they were now ready to change.

36. When children are securely attached to parents, they have the foundation to form significant attachments in other spheres of social life (school, peer groups, religious institutions, etc.). These in turn promote investment of self in conventional lines of activity (Hirschi 1969). Children with secure attachments are more often motivated to conform to the wishes and expectations of parents, teachers, and other significant others. Consequently, they are more likely to learn and to follow conventional norms.

37. Some would argue that transfer selects offenders that are more prone to this sort of negativism, either those with serious mental health problems or other personal characteristics conducive to anger and hostility in experiences with authorities. To our knowledge, there has been no research to date addressing this issue. From our experience, it does not seem likely under prosecutorial waiver systems like Florida's, where transfer decisions are most often made with little or no information about offenders' individual characteristics.

Chapter Eight

Race and Transfer: Empirical Research and Social Context

M. A. BORTNER, MARJORIE S. ZATZ, AND DARNELL F. HAWKINS

A punitive stance toward youths is the hallmark of contemporary juvenile justice policy. Like a similar movement toward harsher penalties for adult offenders during recent decades, the most visible and well documented outcome of such policy has been a sharp rise in rates of juvenile incarceration and in the use of other forms of official social control (Krisberg et al. 1987; Snyder and Sickmund 1995). But given the unique history and distinct legal underpinnings of the juvenile justice system, greater punitiveness toward youths has also been manifested in ways not applicable to older offenders. Foremost among these is the traditional practice of permitting juvenile judges the discretion to transfer selected juvenile offenders to adult courts. Recent years have witnessed a greater willingness of judges to exercise that discretion. Perhaps more importantly, however, traditional methods of judicial waiver have been augmented or supplanted by legislative mandates that have extended the transfer process to a much wider range of offenses and to increasingly younger individuals (Snyder and Sickmund 1995; Sickmund, Snyder, and Poe-Yamagata 1997).

As with adults, the effects of public policy and legal reforms such as these have not fallen uniformly on all youths involved in the juvenile justice system. In most jurisdictions, youths of color—especially African Americans and Latinos—are the candidates most likely to be detained and confined in secure facilities (Krisberg et al. 1987; Hawkins and Jones 1989; Snyder and Sickmund 1995). Our review of the literature indicates that members of these two racial and ethnic groups are also much more likely to be refused the status of children and processed and punished as adults.

These findings of ethnic and racial differences in the handling of delinquent youths signal the continuation of a long-standing debate regarding

American juvenile justice practices. Some researchers have identified the effects of racial, ethnic, and class biases in the preoccupation of the earliest courts with immigrant and poor children and their attempts to intervene in the lives of these youths and their families. These schools of thought portray the system's disproportionate involvement with minority youths not as a realistic and humanitarian allocation of resources, but rather as a thinly veiled system of control and inequity (Krisberg and Austin 1978; Schlossman 1977; Platt 1977). On the other hand, most court personnel of that period and later have tended to view this preoccupation as the inevitable outcome of the juvenile system's mission to advance the welfare of all children. Accordingly, minority youths' diminished economic and social standing made them the "natural beneficiaries" of court attention.

Further, the special mission of the juvenile system that derives from its early history has meant that the possibility of ethnic or racial bias in the administration of justice for youths is seen by many as somewhat more problematic than evidence of similar bias in the handling of adults, who were viewed as less amenable to treatment. Such bias, it is feared, exacerbates the already diminished economic and social standing of ethnic and racial minority youths and increases the likelihood that they will be punished for juvenile offending (Krisberg et al. 1987, 200).

Unfortunately, despite decades of research, a mixture of oversimplification, selective inattention, and speculation characterizes much of the discourse on the causes of, and remedies for, the overrepresentation of ethnic and racial minorities within both the adult and juvenile justice systems. In discussions of racial disparities in the transfer of juveniles to adult courts, two contrary claims have emerged: "Minority youths are transferred in great numbers because they are the worst offenders" and "They are transferred in great numbers because the juvenile justice system is racially biased." Variations of these seemingly contradictory positions have shaped most of the literature on race, ethnicity, and criminal justice for decades. Consequently, it is inevitable that this chapter's review of current knowledge about the role of race and ethnicity in the transfer of juveniles to adult courts retraces much of this polemicized terrain. Nevertheless, we seek to reframe this decades-old debate by centering our review around the following core concerns, many of which are derived from the emerging revisionist literature on race and ethnicity published in the United States during the past decade and more.

1. The "differential criminality" versus "racial discrimination" polemic fails to capture the complexities and multidirectedness of the relationship among race, ethnicity, class, and delinquency in contemporary American society. Hence, it is incapable of provid-

ing the kind of guidance needed to frame social policies that will help achieve greater racial and ethnic equality, justice for youths, and the protection of society.

2. Any analytic framework applied to this area of research must explain why minority youths are involved in delinquency at rates higher than their numbers in the general population. Yet, in order to avoid a "decontextualizing" of the American crime problem, we must go beyond this crime and justice construction to scrutinize the multifaceted cultural and economic contexts in which *both* delinquency and the administration of juvenile justice occur. This implies that our inquiry in the present chapter must focus on the broader context in which juvenile justice policies are enacted and implemented.

3. One prominent feature of this social terrain is the marked emphasis on racial and ethnic identity and class distinctions found in American society. It is essential to explore the extent to which transfer policies and practices reflect the historical and seemingly renewed importance and influence of racial and ethnic differences within the United States. We must ask whether recent justice policies and their outcomes reflect intensified "racialization," that is, the assignment of racial meaning to behaviors, relationships, social practices, events, individuals, or groups (Cleaver 1997, 39; Omi and Winant 1986, 64). Race and ethnicity have always been extremely consequential in the United States, but increased levels of racial and ethnic disparity in punishment may signal a heightened significance.

4. We suggest that current juvenile justice policies may reflect the subtleties of entrenched, institutionalized patterns of thought and action that may eventuate in inequitable outcomes, even in the absence of race-related "intent" on the part of decision makers. This approach encourages us to examine the extent to which racial categories and racial understandings serve as the unacknowledged basis for the construction of social realities and relations, including the pursuit of justice for juveniles (Higginbotham 1992, 255; Mann and Zatz 1998).

5. Attention to the relationship between race and particular types of offenses suggests the importance of examining the potential indirect and interaction effects of race on the transfer decision. Selection biases may also distort research findings since youths who do not fit targeted images of offenders and offenses may be filtered out of the juvenile justice system prior to the transfer decision.

6. In line with this more critical and contextualized framework for the study of race/ethnicity and juvenile transfer, we propose that certain criminally sanctioned behaviors appear to have become distinctly racialized in contemporary American society. Of

particular importance to the production of racial/ethnic disparity in the juvenile justice system and the punishment of juveniles as adults is the atmosphere surrounding violence, drug use, and gang affiliation. Some social analysts suggest that these factors have become increasingly enmeshed in and associated with larger, societal-level racial and ethnic conflicts, and that *both* youths' participation in these behaviors and society's expectations and responses to them are influenced by racial divisions. In equally insidious ways, racial and ethnic identity influences youths' behavior as well as whether they will be classified and responded to as adult offenders and serious threats to public safety.

Within the context of this analytic framework and set of assumptions, the major objectives of this chapter are: to provide a thorough, accessible review of the research on transfer and race; to augment that review with an analysis of several salient controversies and complexities within which this justice system process is embedded; and to explore the ways in which social-science research can more adequately assess the nature and impact of the broader cultural context on juvenile justice policies, especially the transfer of minority youths to adult courts.

1. Major Research Questions on Race, Ethnicity, and Juvenile Transfer

As earlier chapters and our introductory comments demonstrate, the 1990s witnessed a historic shift in juvenile justice. The trend toward greater punitiveness evident during this period has resulted in two major legal and public-policy developments with potential implications for the racial and ethnic distribution of youths processed through the juvenile justice system. The first is the willingness of juvenile judges to use their traditionally permitted discretion to transfer increasingly large numbers of youths to adult criminal courts. The second is the transition in many jurisdictions away from a system whereby judges decide on an *individual* basis which cases should be waived to criminal court to a system in which the legislature or prosecutors determine which *categories* of youths or specific offenses warrant or require transfer. Both developments have profound implications for the juvenile court as an institution, for families and communities, and for our societal understanding of what it means to be a juvenile. Further, as many analysts have noted, these developments may have a significant impact on the level of racial disparity among those American adolescents who are sanctioned most severely.

The transition in the juvenile justice system away from individualized judicial discretion may be compared to the movement in criminal courts in the late 1970s and 1980s away from indeterminate sentencing and toward sentencing guidelines, determinate sentencing, and mandatory sentencing. Supporters of this movement reflected at various points an unexpected convergence of social activism among political liberals and conservatives who differed in their objectives but came together in their support of laws and policies designed to "structure" decision making in the justice system (Tonry 1988, 1992, 1993).

Given the historical legacy of racism in the administration of American justice, prisoners and their supporters alleged that judges and parole boards frequently used their substantial discretion in racially biased ways. As a result, racial and ethnic minorities, especially African Americans, were more apt than whites to receive prison terms, their sentences were longer than those handed down to whites, and they were less likely to be paroled than were whites. Other liberals and radicals of the period joined them in arguing that the arbitrary nature of indeterminate sentencing and the rhetoric of rehabilitation facilitated abridgments of prisoners' rights and was a particularly repressive form of social control. Some analysts have argued that conservative, law-and-order forces, who saw the rehabilitation model as too lenient, later used the movement to restrict judicial and parole board discretion and co-opted its liberal supporters to achieve their goals of more punitive sentencing and longer, set prison terms—now an entrenched feature of criminal justice policies in the United States (Greenberg and Humphries 1980; Irwin 1980; Reiman and Headlee 1981; Von Hirsch 1976; Zatz 1987a).

In retrospect, it is clear that few of the goals of liberal supporters of adult court reforms have been achieved. That is, the reforms they championed did not reduce the level of racial and ethnic disparity within the criminal justice system. Indeed, in some instances the level of disparity has increased (see Tonry, Tonry 1988, 1992, 1995; Miller 1996; Kennedy 1997; Russell 1998). Some suggest that one benefit of the reforms of the 1970s and 1980s may be that the most overt and blatantly unconstitutional forms of ethnic and racial discrimination were curtailed. Others suggest that the influences of race and ethnicity (and the biases they continue to elicit) are simply manifested in *less obvious* ways, for example, through interactions with legally relevant variables, making disparate treatment more intricate and harder to detect. Still others have argued that such reforms have merely shifted discretion from judges, where it was relatively public, to prosecutors, where it is much less visible and accountable. With precise sentences prescribed for each offense, plea bargaining became more important because the only way to substantially alter the sanction was to change the charge.

This brief review of developments in the juvenile and adult systems lays the groundwork for many of the issues that emerged in our investigation of race, ethnicity, and juvenile transfers. Our reading of the literature on juvenile transfer leads us to pose several interrelated sets of research questions that will guide our discussion in this chapter.

1. What is the level of racial and ethnic disproportionality among those juveniles transferred to criminal courts?
2. Are there greater racial and ethnic disparities for some offenses than for others? Which specific offenses show the highest levels of disparity?
3. To what extent do empirical studies of the transfer process reveal *direct effects* of race and ethnicity on the decision to transfer? Or are the effects of race and ethnicity on transfer and sanctioning decisions *contingent effects,* that is, produced indirectly or in interaction with other nonracial attributes of offenders, offenses, or case processing?
4. Are race and ethnicity effects absent in those jurisdictions in which legislative guidelines based on age or offense initiate the transfer process? Do racial and ethnic differences in the offenses charged fully account for racial disparities in transfer? Do age and offense type interact with race to influence discretionary components of the transfer decision?
5. How do attributions of guilt, responsibility, or blameworthiness affect transfer decisions? How do these differ for white youths and youths of color?
6. What has research demonstrated about the cumulative impact of race and ethnicity on youths' involvement in the juvenile justice system? Does race/ethnicity affect the transfer process indirectly through its impact at other processing stages of the juvenile justice system?
7. Does the level of racial and ethnic disparity vary with the method used for transfer, e.g., judicial versus legislative waiver?

To begin to address these queries, we reviewed all transfer studies published in a fifteen-year period from January 1983 through March 1998 in *Crime and Delinquency, Criminology, Journal of Criminal Law and Criminology, Justice Quarterly, Law and Inequality,* and *Law and Policy.* We extended our review through a search of the sociological, legal, and criminal justice abstracts. As the summary of our findings in table 8.1 demonstrates, the empirical literature on race/ethnicity and the transfer decision is very sparse. (See Howell 1996, for a comprehensive review of the research literature on judicial wavers *without regard to whether the authors specifically discussed race.*) To further complicate matters, most of the literature addresses judicial waivers, although by 2000 the vast majority of transfers occur through legislative exclusions. Thus, answers to

some of the questions posed above must remain at the level of speculation or as calls for future research.

Before turning to the extant literature for initial answers to the questions we have posed, we must note two serious deficiencies in the literature on race and court processing and sanctioning in both the juvenile
and adult systems. First, most of the research, including studies of the
transfer decision, is limited to comparisons between whites and African
Americans. This could result in very misleading findings about the relationship between race/ethnicity and system outcomes. Most studies use
data sets that exclude Latinos and Latinas, American Indians, and Asian
Americans. Other data sets, including national statistics, include Latinos
and Latinas, but they are coded white, thus often artificially inflating the
number of white youths, who are then compared to blacks. Moreover,
Spanish-speaking Afro-Caribbeans are sometimes coded on the basis of
Spanish surname (in which case they would be coded white) and at other
times and jurisdictions on the basis of appearance (in which case they
would be coded black). These practices would underestimate the number
of youths of color who are processed or sanctioned, making the problem
of racial/ethnic disproportionality seem smaller than it really is.

One of the central concerns of contemporary social-science research
on race and ethnicity is the attempt to "disentangle" or "unpack" the
effects of race/ethnicity versus socioeconomic status on various social
outcomes. Researchers ask whether white and minority individuals with
the same socioeconomic background exhibit the same behavior or are
treated similarly by bureaucratic institutions such as the courts. This research thrust reveals a second critical limitation of available data sets.
Currently, data come primarily from the courts and most court data do
not include reliable measures of social class. As a result, the effects of
race and class on juvenile and adult case processing and sanctioning
decisions cannot be untangled. One consequence is the inability of researchers to determine if some of the racial/ethnic differences found in
processing and sanctioning decisions may be attributable to the ways in
which class influences decision makers' perceptions of youths. Racial/
ethnic disparities may also be linked to class differences in access to resources. For example, if middle-class youths have more resources available to them than do poor youths (for example, psychiatric resources,
legal aid, ability to arrange for and afford an alternative school), then
class may explain some racial disparities (Bridges and Steen 1998; Fagan,
Slaughter, and Hartstone 1987; Bortner 1982; Emerson 1969). In the absence of reliable data to test these possibilities, researchers often resort
to the facile and implausible assumption that all youths of color are poor,
and that all white youths are middle class.

Table 8.1
Empirical Studies of Race/Ethnicity and Transfer of Youths to Adult Courts (by Date)

Author	Sample	Jurisdiction	Age	Sex
Thomas and Bilchik 1985	844 waived youths	FL, Dade County (1981)	Not stated	96.8% male
Bortner 1986	214 waived youths	AZ County (1980–81)	85.5% age 17	94.7% male
Fagan, Forst and Vivona 1987	225 chronically violent youths and 201 waiver decisions	Boston, Detroit, Newark, Phoenix (1981–84)	Not stated	Not stated
Barnes and Franz 1989	206 considered for waiver	N. CA county (1978–83)	75% age 17	92% male
Bishop, Frazier, and Henretta 1989	583 direct file proceedings	2 FL counties (1981–84)	60% age 17	93% male
Fagan and Deschenes 1990	201 waiver decisions for violent offenses	Boston, Detroit, Newark, Phoenix (1981–84)	Not stated; majority age 16–17	Not stated
Houghtalin and Mays 1991	49 juvenile probation records	NM (1981–90)	59% age 17	1 female in sample
Singer 1993	103 juvenile offender arrests	NY, NYC, Buffalo (1978–85)	Not stated	Not stated
Poulos and Orchowsky 1994	363 matched juveniles	VA (1988–90)	Mean age at arrest 16.3	97% male

Race/Ethnicity	Transfer Mechanism	Analysis Type; Dependent Variable	Findings Regarding Race Effect—Significance
67.8% nonwhite	Prosecutor's direct file, judicial waiver	Frequencies; case flow	Not stated
52.2% white, 23.7% black, 20.6% Mexican American 3.5% other	Judicial waiver	Interviews, descriptive statistics re adult sentence	Overrepresentation of blacks
Of transfers: 11% Anglo, 79% Black, 9% Chicano, 1% other	Waiver request filed by prosecutor	Discriminant analyses; waiver decision	Race not significant in multivariate analysis, but minority youths charged with homicide more likely to be transferred than similar Anglos; 27% of Anglos and 39% of minority youths petitioned were transferred
55% black or Hispanic	Judical waiver	Two-stage discriminant analysis and analysis of covariance; "fitness" for juvenile court, sentence	Minorities more likely to be found "unfit" for juvenile court
63% white	Prosecutorial waiver	Interviews, descriptive statistics re waiver decision	No significance tests conducted
Of those waived, between 20% (Boston) and 74% (Phoenix) were nonwhite	Waiver request filed by prosecutor	Discriminant analyses; waiver decision	No white youth considered for waiver in Newark; race enters model only for Detroit; higher waiver rates for minorities in Detroit and Phoenix, related to priors and participation in violent crimes
31% Anglo, 61% Hispanic, 6% American Indian, 2% Asian	Judicial waiver	Frequencies; waiver decision, sentence	Overrepresentation of Hispanics in waiver population
More than 75% nonwhite	Legislative exclusion	Multivariate logistic regression; prosecutor's decision to seek a grand jury indictment	Race not significant controlling for parents' marital status
68% nonwhite	Judicial waiver	Multivariate logistic regression; waiver decision	Race not significant controlling for offense seriousness and prior record

(continued)

Table 8.1
(*continued*)

Author	Sample	Jurisdiction	Age	Sex
Kinder, Veneziano, Fichter and Azuma 1995	All 111 males certified as adults and a random sample of 111 youths adjudicated of felonies but not certified	MO, St. Louis (1993)	74% of those sampled age 14–16; certified age 16–17; noncertified sample age 14–16	All male
Podkopacz and Feld 1995	330 waived youths	MN, Minneapolis (1985–92)	90% age 16–17	96% male
Clarke 1996	334 waived youths	IL, Cook County (November 1992–March 1994)	Unknown	96% male
McNulty 1996	472 waived youths	AZ (1994)	13–17 (75% age 17 and over)	95.5% male
Podkopacz and Feld 1996	330 waived youths	MN, Minneapolis (1985–92)	90% age 16–17 (60% age 16)	96% male
Singer 1996	9937 juvenile offender arrests	NY, NYC, Buffalo (1978–85)	Mean age at arrest, 15	92.6% male
Winner, et al. 1997[a]	3,142 waived and 2,700 matched juveniles	FL (1985–87, with recidivism data through 1994)	—	—

[a] Age, sex, and race (white/nonwhite) used as matching criteria.

Race/Ethnicity	Transfer Mechanism	Analysis Type; Dependent Variable	Findings Regarding Race Effect—Significance
90%+ black	Waiver	Frequencies; waiver decision, sentence	No race effect
28% white, 55% African American, 17% other	Judicial waiver	Interview, multivariate logistic regression; waiver decision	Overrepresentation of minority youth is explained by prosecutor's emphasis on violent crime when asking for waiver
5% white, 83% black, 11% Latino, 1% other	Automatic (legislative waiver)	Descriptive statistics re waiver decision	Overrepresentation of minorities
39% Anglo, 13% African American, 44% Hispanic, 4% Native American	Judicial waiver	Multivariate logistic regression; sentence	Blacks and Latinos have increased likelihood of incarceration
28% white, 55% African American, 17% other	Judicial waiver	Multivariate logistic regression; waiver decision, sentence	Racial differences explainable by offense type
15% white, 69% black, 16% Hispanic	Legislative exclusion	Interviews with prosecutor, multivariate logistic and OLS regression; referral to grand jury, adjudication, sentence	Race significant in analysis of adjudication severity and criminal court conviction outside NYC; significant race effect for disposition and sentence in all samples with whites getting longer sentences
—	Prosecutorial waiver	Multivariate logistic regression and survival analysis; probability of rearrest	Race and drug offense interaction; no direct race effect

Acknowledging these inadequacies, we use the studies presented in table 8.1 and other sources of information to frame our responses to the questions posed above. We begin by examining the available evidence on the level of racial and ethnic disparity in the transfer process.

Racial and Ethnic Disproportionality in Transfer

First we examine the racial composition of the transfer population seen in recent years in studies conducted at the national and state levels. What is the level of racial and ethnic disproportionality among those juveniles transferred to criminal courts? That is, to what extent is the proportion of minority youths transferred to adult courts greater than their proportion in the general population or juvenile court cases? Snyder, Sickmund, and Poe-Yamagata (1996, 28) reported that 55 percent of the youths transferred via judicial waivers in 1993 were minorities. Yet as was discussed earlier, because Latinos and Latinas were coded as white, it is likely that this figure represents an undercount of the number of minority youths. Even given the high probability of such underestimates, youths of color in the United States currently appear to be more likely than whites to be transferred to adult courts. For example, to put these transfer rates in context, the 1994 U.S. population was 80 percent white (including Latinos and Latinas) and, most importantly, white youths accounted for 64 percent of the delinquency cases processed. Yet youths of color, who are 36 percent of all delinquency cases, made up more than 50 percent of the transfers to adult courts (Butts 1996a, 2).

Further, it is widely acknowledged that aggregate national data sometimes conceal even greater racial and ethnic disparities than those found in smaller groups in local areas. Several studies conducted within particular states or counties over the last fifteen years have found considerable evidence of racial disproportionality, leading some analysts to ask whether the "threshold" for transfer is lower for minority youths (Fagan, Forst, and Vivona 1987, 272). In their study of chronically violent youths in four major cities (Boston, Detroit, Newark, and Phoenix), Fagan, Forst, and Vivona (1987) found that 27 percent of the Anglo youths for whom transfers had been requested were in fact transferred, compared to 39 percent of the nonwhite youths. Looking at *all* cases, not just violent offenses, Keiter (1973) found that in Cook County, Illinois, in 1970, 92 percent of those transferred were black, although many of the whites who were not transferred had more serious offense histories than some of the black transferees. Twenty years later, Clarke (1996) found that transfer in Cook County between 1992 and 1994 continued to affect primarily minority youths. At that time, 94.7 percent of the youths subject to automatic transfer provisions were members of racial/ethnic minorities. Similarly, Howell (1996) reports that the Ohio Department of Youth Services found that two-thirds of the youths waived in Ohio in 1992 were black, reflecting a considerable increase from 1981, when one-half of the youths transferred in the state were black (Federation for Community Planning 1983, cited in Howell 1996, 24). In all of the jurisdictions covered in the research just cited, minorities were a much smaller proportion of the overall juvenile population than of those transferred.

McNulty (1996, 68) reports that 44 percent of the youths transferred via judicial waiver in Arizona in 1994 were Hispanic, 39 percent Anglo, 13 percent African American, 4 percent Native American, and 0.002 percent Asian (one juvenile). In contrast, 29 percent of the general juvenile population (aged eight through seventeen) in Arizona at that time was Hispanic, 58 percent Anglo, 4 percent African American, 8 percent Native American, and 2 percent Asian. Finally, Howell (1996, 28–29) reports that Gragg's (1986) study of judicial waivers, prosecutorial direct files, and legislative exclusions in twelve jurisdictions during the first six months of 1985 demonstrated that about 75 percent of discretionary (judicial) transfers involved blacks, considerably higher than the figure of 57 percent for automatic (legislative) transfers.

In sum, data on the national level and for specific jurisdictions throughout the country demonstrate conclusively that youths of color are transferred to adult courts far in excess of their proportion in the youth population and in excess of their proportion of the overall cases processed by juvenile justice systems. Our subsequent questions address the available evidence about the precise nature of the relationship between race/ethnicity and transfer, including the possibility that these racial disparities may stem from factors other than race animus on the part of decision makers.

Researchers often seek to examine the extent to which racial/ethnic disparity in juvenile transfer results directly from "race differences" or, alternatively, stems from factors other than "race" per se. In the research literature these potential factors include variables that show a statistical interaction with "race" differences. Therefore we ask whether empirical studies reveal that race has direct, main effects on the transfer decision or whether racial disparities are contingent on the existence of other factors that interact with race/ethnicity and affect the transfer process.

Much research in the adult system has found that, when the main effects of race disappear, powerful and pervasive indirect and interaction effects remain. That is, the effects of race become *contingent* upon the interaction of race with legally legitimate factors, such as prior record and detention status, and other illegitimate factors, such as the gender and class of the defendant and the race, gender, and class status of the victim (see Zatz 1987a, 2000; Miethe and Moore 1985; Klepper, Nagin, and Tierney 1983; LaFree 1989; Hawkins 1987; Baldus, Pulaski, and Woodworth 1983; Mann 1993; Peterson and Hagan 1984; Petersilia 1983; Spohn, Gruhl, and Welch 1981; Hagan and Bumiller 1983; Daly 1994; Spohn 1994). We expect the statistical main effects of race to be muted and the indirect effects to be more pronounced. Which contingent factors best explain these decisions is an important concern, especially for those who seek to establish safeguards to minimize or reduce levels of racial and ethnic disparity.

Offense Type and Transfer: Obvious versus Nuanced Race/Ethnicity Effects

The possible interaction effects of race and offense type are particularly crucial when outcomes such as transfer or prison sentences are mandated for specific offenses. It is likely that such interaction also affects discretionary transfer decisions. For both the adult and juvenile systems, past research indicates that racial differences in criminal involvement vary considerably depending upon the offense type being examined. The black-white or Latino-white gap is much larger for some offense categories than for others (Blumstein 1982; Hawkins 1993). We also know that numerous determinate sentencing laws enacted during the last decades target many of the offense types characterized by the greatest racial/ethnic disparities. For example, the vast majority of mandatory sentences in criminal court are for drug and gun law violations. The small literature that addresses the question of racial disparities in the enforcement and sanctioning of gun laws in adult courts suggests that weapon-related sentence enhancements may be used more in cases involving defendants of color than whites (Lizotte and Zatz 1986). Considerably more research has focused on mandatory drug laws. The growing literature on this issue demonstrates significant racial disparities resulting from these laws, especially for African Americans and Latinos and Latinas compared to whites (Tonry 1995; Donziger 1996; Miller 1996). It would be unusual if the same drug laws that result in racial/ethnic disparities for adults do not show similar effects when black and Latino/a teens are compared to white teens. Past research on racial disproportionality in rates of imprisonment by offense type for both adults and youths lends some support to these expectations (Blumstein 1982; Hawkins 1986).

Because of the widespread attention given to violent crime by the media and politicians, even when violence rates have decreased, we are particularly interested in knowing if there are racial differences in transfer rates for violent offenses and if race interacts with violent offenses to affect the transfer decision and later sentencing decisions. Since the media have tied violence to gangs so thoroughly (see Mann and Zatz 1998), we also anticipate that the antigang legislation currently sweeping the country will target youths of color and that in the future we will see gang identification as a major intervening step in the transfer decision.

An overview of national data indicates that the type of offense is a critical factor that helps explain the relationship between race and the transfer decision. At the same time that the *numbers* of youths transferred increased, there was also a change in the *type of offense* for which waiver was requested, and a clear relationship emerged between offense type and race. By 1992, crimes against persons had surpassed property crimes as the major source of waived cases. In 1993, 42 percent of the youths transferred to adult courts across the nation were charged with violent offenses, with another 38 percent of the waivers involving property offenses (Snyder, Sickmund, and Poe-Yamagata 1996, 29). In 1995, person offenses climbed to 47 percent of the delinquency cases waived, while property offenses dropped to 34 percent (Sickmund, Snyder, and Poe-Yamagata 1997, 6). There was also a surge in waivers for drug offenses in the late 1980s and into the 1990s, with drug and public order offenses accounting for 19 percent of the waivers in 1993 (Snyder, Sickmund, and Poe-Yamagata 1996, 29). In 1994, although African Americans made up only 15 percent of the juvenile population, they were charged with 40 percent of the crimes against persons, 28 percent of property offenses, and 37 percent of drug-related offenses (Butts 1996b).

Sickmund, Snyder, and Poe-Yamagata (1997) scrutinized judicial waivers to discover if decision-making patterns varied by race/ethnicity and offense (see table 8.2). They found that waivers of black youths for drug cases surpassed waivers of black youths for offenses against persons for the period 1989–92. These statistics clearly reflect the intense effects of the war on drugs on African American communities (Tonry 1995; Miller 1996; Mann and Zatz 1998; Donziger 1996). Similarly, at least part of the increase in "white" youths waived for drug offenses in 1991 (the year when the percent was greatest for blacks, as well) probably reflects coding of Latinos and Latinas as white, since they also have been disproportionately affected by the war on drugs (Miller 1996; Donziger 1996; Diaz-Cotto 1996).

Again, as we saw with overall levels of racial disparity, when statistics are disaggregated by offense category, state and local data mirror national data. For example, 18 percent of the Ohio youths whose cases were waived to criminal court in 1992 were arrested for property offenses and 62 percent for violent offenses. Two-thirds of the youths whose cases

Table 8.2
Percentage of Petitioned Cases Judicially Waived, by Race

	White[a]		Black	
Year	Person	Drugs	Person	Drugs
1985	2.2	0.7	2.9	2.1
1986	1.8	0.8	2.9	1.9
1987	1.7	1.0	2.3	2.2
1988	1.5	1.1	2.4	2.0
1989	1.6	1.3	2.6	4.2
1990	1.3	1.0	2.8	4.1
1991	1.8	1.5	2.8	6.0
1992	2.4	1.0	3.1	3.8
1993	2.0	0.9	3.5	3.3
1994	2.2	0.9	3.4	2.8

Source: Sickmund et al. 1997, 31.
[a]"White" includes Latinos and Latinas.

were waived were African American, a substantial increase from rates a decade earlier when only one-half of the youths transferred were black. It is worth noting that 47 percent had never been incarcerated in the juvenile system prior to being waived to the adult system. The relationship between race/ethnicity and offense type is also evident in Clarke's study of Cook County, Illinois. She found that 98 percent of the juveniles who received automatic (legislative) transfers for drug and weapons violations in 1991–92 were black. Similarly, Winner et al. (1997) found an interaction effect of race and drug offenses in their Florida data set, although no main effects of race were evident. And in their study of waiver requests for chronically violent youths by prosecutors in Boston, Detroit, Newark, and Phoenix in the period 1981–84, Fagan, Forst, and Vivona (1987) found that, while race did not have significant main effects, minority youths charged with homicide were more likely to be transferred than were similar Anglos.

In summary, offense type and race do interact to produce racial disparity in transfer decisions. National and local jurisdiction studies suggest that this is particularly crucial when violent and drug offenses are involved. As we will discuss later, minority youths' involvement in these offenses is but one aspect of this matrix. The expectations and assumptions of decision makers, and the cultural context in which they are embedded, must also be scrutinized.

Obviously, racial and ethnic differences in illegal conduct will produce racial disparities in system outcomes. So will a variety of other race-related group differences. As Singer reminds us, "The significance of race is not the same across jurisdictions. Moreover, the effect of race might be explained by variables that are not contained in the available state agency data" (1996, 150). As discussed, we expect the type of offense to be the primary way in which the effects of race are mediated. Although Fagan, Forst, and Vivona's (1987) study of four major cities found substantial disparities in the percentages of Anglo and minority youths transferred, race did not have a significant influence when their multivariate discriminant analyses incorporated other factors (see similarly Fagan and Deschenes 1990, and Fagan, Slaughter, and Hartstone 1987). Further analysis of these data (Fagan and Deschenes 1990) also found higher transfer rates for minority youths charged with violent offenses in Detroit and Phoenix, and that *no* white youths were considered for transfer in Newark. These higher rates could be explained, however, by prior record and participation in violent crime.

Neither did race/ethnicity have a significant main effect when offense seriousness and prior record were held constant in multivariate studies of the transfer decision in the late 1980s and early 1990s in Virginia (Poulos and Orchowsky 1994). In Minneapolis, race/ethnicity did not have a main effect, but each year prosecutors sought transfers for higher percentages of minority youths (Podkopacz and Feld 1995, 1996). For instance, in 1986, the first year of their study, Podkopacz and Feld found that 64 percent of the youths against whom prosecutors filed transfer motions were members of racial/ethnic minorities. By 1992, this proportion had risen dramatically to 88 percent. This increase, Podkopacz and Feld (1996) suggest, is due to the prosecutor's policy of emphasizing the seriousness of the offense. Since minority youths are particularly likely to be arrested for and charged with serious violent offenses, they are also more likely to feel the ramifications of the prosecutor's transfer policy. Consistent with other research, Podkopacz and Feld also found that violent offenders received longer sentences in criminal court than did property offenders, with the end result being longer sentences for minority youths.

Barnes and Franz (1989) also found racial/ethnic minorities to be over-represented in their analysis of transfers in a northern California county in the late 1970s and early 1980s. While only 15 percent of the county's population was black or Latino/a, 55 percent of the youths involved in transfer motions were members of these racial/ethnic groups. Yet Barnes and Franz also report that the race coefficient was less than half that of the most important legal variables. They suggest that the small race effect may be due to selection biases and to the correlation of race with type of offense, which also had a significant and strong effect on the decision to waive jurisdiction.

A few studies have explored the final outcome of this transfer process—adult court sentences. McNulty's (1996) logistic analyses of the likelihood of receiving incarceration or probation in adult court indicate that minority status has a significant effect, as did previous transfers to adult court, a violent offense, and prior referrals to juvenile court. Age decreased the odds of receiving an incarcerative sentence, while prior court services did not have a significant influence. Specifically, her multi-variate study of the population of juveniles judicially waived to adult court in Arizona in 1994 demonstrated that African Americans were approximately three times as likely to be incarcerated as Anglos, and Latinos and Latinas were almost twice as likely to be incarcerated as were Anglos.

Finally, a small number of researchers are beginning to scrutinize the precise nature of racial/ethnic disparities that become evident after a state legislature has enacted provisions that remove youth from the juris-diction of the juvenile court if they commit certain offenses, but allow the exercise of considerable discretion once transfer has taken place. Most notably, Singer (1993, 1996) analyzed criminal justice processing of all youths arrested under the Juvenile Offender Law in New York State, which mandates waiver for violent offenses. During the period 1978–85, nearly ten thousand juveniles were charged with violent offenses. For the Buffalo sample, three-quarters of the juvenile offenders transferred to adult court were members of racial/ethnic minority groups. Following waiver, 54 percent of the minority juveniles were referred to grand juries, compared to 38 percent of the white youths (Singer 1993).

In a multivariate analysis of the determinants of conviction across the state, Singer found that age, gender, offense severity, and prior arrests were the major explanatory factors. Race/ethnicity was not a significant factor even though black youths were more likely to be arrested for of-fenses covered under the Juvenile Offender Law. However, when the sample was limited to courts *outside* New York City, race/ethnicity had a strong and significant effect. There, black juveniles were 1.45 times more likely to be convicted in criminal court than whites *after* controlling for offense seriousness. Hispanics were also more likely to be incarcer-ated than whites but, as we discuss below, those whites who were incar-cerated received longer sentences. Singer (1996) concludes by warning that legislative exclusion can eliminate waiver of nonviolent youths, but it achieves this goal at the expense of targeting minority youths who are disproportionately arrested for violent offenses.

Finally, we draw attention to the potential importance of the race/eth-nicity of the *victim* and of the victim-offender racial dyad to the transfer decision, particularly in cases involving violent offenses. In criminal court cases involving adults, strong evidence is accruing that the most severe sanctions are reserved for African Americans convicted of the murder or rape of whites, followed by white offenders convicted of murdering or raping white victims (Baldus, Pulaski, and Woodworth 1983; Hawkins 1987; LaFree 1989; and Spohn 1994). A key question for future research, thus, is whether the race of the victim, and the interaction of the victim's race and that of the offender, will influence the transfer decision. A related question would broaden the analysis beyond white-black comparisons to include Latino and Latina, American Indian, and Asian American victims and offenders.

The Effects of Age on Transfer

Age is a crucial factor in juvenile court, for the court is founded on the belief that children are not sufficiently mature to be fully responsible and accountable for their actions, and on the assumption that children can be rehabilitated and redeemed more readily than adults. Yet as the current debate about the handling of very young children accused of murder demonstrates, there is no magic age at which childhood ends and adulthood is reached. Aside from individual differences in maturity, there have been significant differences across states and over time in the ages at which, for example, persons may marry, vote, drive a car, and drink. Demarcations are constructed as needed. For example, during the Vietnam War the drinking age was lowered to eighteen in many states because young soldiers proclaimed the unfairness of being old enough to be conscripted into the army and die for their country, but not old enough to buy beer in the commissary.

Despite its imprecision as a measure of maturity and legal culpability, age is a deciding factor in the legislative requirements for mandatory transfer of youths. Many states have combined age and offense type in their statutes, such that youths who reach some minimum age *and* commit some category of offenses (for example, youths who are fifteen years or older and charged with felonies) are automatically transferred to the criminal court's jurisdiction. Then it is the combination of age and offense type that determines where the case will be adjudicated. To date, very little information is available about these youths and their cases, and our questions serve primarily as calls for additional research on these topics. Some preliminary findings are emerging from a few states, although they are primarily descriptive in nature. For example, Lotke and Schiraldi (1996) found that 86 percent of the fourteen-year-olds tried as adults under Virginia's 1994 legislation, which lowered the waiver age to fourteen, were African American.

As age-related guidelines for legislative transfer play a more prominent role, researchers must examine the implications. A major concern is whether race and ethnicity will directly impact transfer and sanctioning decisions in jurisdictions in which age is the deciding factor. If applied as mandated, strict age cutoffs for transfer should sweep up white middle-class youths who have never been in trouble with the law as readily as they will youths of color or those who have been identified as more troublesome based on their past interactions with the justice system. This is a presumption, however, that must be tested empirically. The question of whether age guidelines for transfer decisions will alter racial disparity is an eminently consequential issue, but it is one on which there is virtually no research. Despite its seeming neutrality in regards to race, the extension of transfer to younger juveniles may alter the complexion of the transfer population. Age-offense interactions, in particular, may have a profound effect. We will not know for certain until research probes this issue.

Decision Maker Perceptions of Youths of Color

Despite the recent passage of legislation mandating transfer for specific offenses and ages, justice officials in many jurisdictions retain considerable discretion in deciding whom to transfer. Some states have been reluctant to abandon traditional modes of judicial waiver. In addition, as many of the studies reviewed above have shown, some aspects of decision making remain discretionary even where transfer is "automatic" or required. A few researchers have attempted to identify the factors that shape these less regulated decision making junctures. There is evidence that suggests that the greatest race effects may be present in those cases involving less serious felonies, that is, cases that meet minimal offense-based criteria for transfer but are far from heinous. These gray-area cases have been shown to allow prosecutors the greatest latitude in initial charging and plea bargaining in adult courts (Albonetti 1991), and we expect to find the same pattern in juvenile court and in the borderland that transfer occupies.

Perceptions of defendants held by decision makers are extremely important in that those characteristics or personal qualities attributed to a defendant may have a major impact on the exercise of discretion. Attribution involves the assessment of intangible qualities that are interpreted as linked to an individual's motivations and actions. Decision makers routinely exercise professional judgements to decide "what defendants are *really* like" and to make prognoses for long-term behavior. For example, Albonetti (1986, 1991), Unnever and Hembroff (1988), and Spohn, Gruhl, and Welch (1981) have shown that in borderline cases the attributions that prosecutors and other social control agents (such as police, probation officers, and judges) make about adult defendants and their cases are very important in deciding what the final charge should be. Other attributional factors of significance in adult cases include evaluations of the defendant's stability of employment, family structure, marital status, ties to the community, evidence of remorse, demeanor, displays of hostility toward officials, willingness to cooperate, and estimates of the likelihood of reoffending.

The juvenile justice literature suggests that decision makers' perceptions and judgments of youths are a crucial factor in the outcomes of their cases. The process through which decision makers attribute moral character to youths may be even more salient and consequential than such judgments about adults. Assessments of attitude, demeanor, blameworthiness, school performance, family stability, psychological well-being, future dangerousness, and rehabilitative potential all play roles in the multitude of decisions made throughout youths' involvement with the juvenile system. Numerous researchers have probed the exercise of discretionary power in earlier stages of the system, including police decisions to arrest and court personnel decisions to detain prior to trial, as well as their sentence recommendations (Spencer 1983; Drass and Spencer 1987). Bridges and Steen (1998) provide an excellent example of the manner in which probation officers tend to attribute the delinquent acts of African Americans to their negative attitudinal and personality traits, while they attribute the delinquent acts of Euro-Americans to their social environment.

Few researchers have explored this less obvious dimension of transfer decisions, but extant studies lead us to believe that attributional factors also figure prominently in both judicial decisions inherent in traditional waiver and the political and prosecutorial decisions involved in legislative transfer. Singer's New York transfer research explores the way in which attributions about a youth's family impact the transfer process. In this study, children living with two parents were less likely to be transferred than those raised by single parents (Singer 1996). It is likely that decision makers attribute stability to two-parent families and, in turn, these attributions influence transfer decisions. It is also highly relevant that the impact of family stability was more statistically relevant than race/ethnicity alone. When Singer took into consideration family composition (one-parent versus two-parent households), race/ethnicity became statistically insignificant. Family composition, thus, interacts in some way with race to influence decision making. But because minority youths are more likely than white youths to be raised in one-parent families, such attributions will often lead to racial/ethnic disparity in transfer.

The initial attributions that decision makers assign to a youth shape subsequent assessments, including whether they think that individual is likely to commit future offenses and if he or she is potentially violent. Thus, we expect that racial/ethnic differences in attributions evident at other stages in juvenile justice processing would also affect the transfer decision. The effects of race-related attitudes extend far beyond the boundaries of the courtroom. In the case of legislative transfers, racialized assumptions and attributions may exert powerful influences on legislators. And finally, in prosecutorial transfers, the probation officer's and the prosecutor's attributions both come into play.

This question of whether legislators, prosecutors, probation officers, defense attorneys, and judges make race-based assumptions about young people's character, dangerousness, and likelihood of recidivating is probably one of the most important areas for future research. Studies of this type will require the collection of data on the attitudes and values of justice officials and attempts to link these values to their patterns of transfer decisions. Currently, the lack of good qualitative data on the transfer decision makes it difficult to determine whether and in what specific ways decision makers' attributions affect the level of racial disparity.

Much research is needed to scrutinize the links between decision maker attributions and a youth's racial, class, and gendered status within society. We know that the workings of race are inextricably bound with the impacts of social class and gender (Daly 1994; Chesney-Lind and Shelden 1998). Popular culture depicts crime and violence as symbolic of masculinity (Messerschmidt 1997; Messner 1995; Connell 1995) and particularly of forms of masculinity attributed to African American men. Equally important, in response to powerful cultural messages and socialization processes, as well as limited alternatives, many minority youths adopt aggression and violence as key components of their masculinity. We also know that race and ethnicity often serve as surrogates for social class because racial and ethnic minorities in the United States are disproportionately poor. The ways in which such attributional intersections influence transfer decisions are far less clear.

The findings of Singer and others suggest that some of the attributions that affect decision making and appear to be race related are actually grounded in distinctions that are related to social class and socioeconomic status (Sennett and Cobb 1973; Gans 1995). It is possible that largely middle-class justice system decision makers hold a variety of attitudes and opinions regarding the lives and social behaviors of the poor. These perceptions of the poor may include the view that they are more likely to be involved in crime and other forms of morally questionable and antisocial behavior (Tittle 1983). This may mean that justice system decision making reflects ingrained attitudes found in American society about how the poor differ from the more affluent, but we know very little about the influence of these class-related attitudes on juvenile justice decision making.

Similarly, with the increased presence of minority professionals in the working groups of the juvenile court and juvenile justice system more generally, it becomes increasingly important to assess whether the race of the decision maker makes a difference in transfer decisions. Results from adult court suggest that black and white judges view cases similarly (Spohn 1990), but no research to date has explored the effect of the race, gender, and class status of juvenile court decision makers on the transfer decision.

Similar attitudes may shape decision makers' views of how young women and their delinquent conduct differ from that of young men. Just as minorities are sometimes perceived as more predisposed to criminal behavior than whites, historically females have been perceived as *less* predisposed to criminal behavior than males. In this regard, we do know that the arrests of girls and young women for violent crimes have increased rapidly in recent years. In 1995, females were responsible for 15 percent of the total juvenile violent index offenses. From 1991 to 1995, female juvenile arrests for violent index offenses jumped 34 percent, nearly four times the male increase of 9 percent (Kelley et al. 1997, 2). Yet the waiver population remains overwhelmingly male, with only 0.3 percent of the female juvenile delinquent population transferred nationwide in 1993, compared with 1.7 percent of the male juvenile population (Poe-Yamagata and Butts 1996; see also Snyder, Sickmund, and Poe-Yamagata 1996, 29). Most studies find that over 90 percent, and more typically over 95 percent, of the youths transferred to adult court are male. This pattern may change in response to increased arrests and incarceration of girls and young women, and a greater willingness to depict young women of color as violent. Unfortunately, none of the studies we encountered explored the interactions between gender and race/ethnicity or whether and how attributes of character and future dangerousness differ for males and females. Such studies would begin to shed light on how decision makers' attributions may differ for young men and women of color and for young white men and women.

The Cumulative Impact of Race and Ethnicity

Does race affect the transfer process indirectly through its impact at other processing stages of the juvenile justice system? Transfer is the culmination of many earlier decisions, and if race/ethnicity influences any or all of them, then it will indirectly influence the transfer decision by determining which juveniles are vulnerable to transfer. One early decision point that has been shown to be linked to racial and class disparity in the juvenile justice system has been pretrial detention. At both the adult and juvenile levels, poor people and people of color are most likely to be detained pending trial, and pretrial detention often results in harsher sentencing decisions (Lizotte 1978; Bortner and Reed 1985; Zatz 1985). While there appears to be an easily traceable path from pretrial detention to subsequent negative outcomes, at other times we are looking at the cumulative effects of many earlier processing decisions, beginning with the police decision to arrest. Research has fairly consistently shown that small effects of race and class that may not be statistically significant at a given stage add up across multiple stages, with the effect that white and middle-class children are more likely to be filtered out of the system long before the transfer decision is reached than are poor youths and youths of color (Dannefer and Schutt 1982; Bishop and Frazier 1988; Bortner and Reed 1985; Fagan, Slaughter, and Hartstone 1987; Fagan, Forst, and Vivona 1987; Pope and Feyerherm 1995; Singer 1996). We expect to see cumulative effects of race such that cases involving whites, and cases involving middle-class youths, are likely to be filtered out of the system more readily than cases involving youths of color, especially if they are poor.

In his study of legislative transfers of youths charged with violent offenses in New York State, Singer (1996) found that race/ethnicity was a key factor in the incarceration decision once youths charged with violent offenses reached adult court. Fifty-one percent of white juveniles were sentenced to probation, while most black (60 percent) and Hispanic (59 percent) juveniles were incarcerated, even though the offenses involving whites tended to be more serious. Multivariate analysis showed the likelihood of incarceration for minorities to be nearly twice as great as for whites. In addition, age, race, offense severity, and prior arrests were the best predictors of sentence length. Singer explains his findings as follows:

> Black juveniles face a greater chance of being arrested, convicted, and incarcerated as juvenile offenders . . . However, when white juveniles are ultimately sentenced in criminal court to a secure facility, their sentence lengths will exceed those of black juvenile offenders. I have suggested that this is the case because of filtering at earlier stages of legal decision making. (1996, 150)

Consistent with these results, Fagan, Forst, and Vivona (1987) found that Anglos waived to criminal court were more likely to receive *jail* sentences than members of racial/ethnic minorities. However, minority youths were far more likely to be sent to *prison* than were Anglos. These differences correspond with the distinction between jails, reserved for sentences of a year or less, and prisons, commonly used for long-term sentences.

In many cases, transfer to adult court occurs after youths' prolonged interactions with the juvenile justice system. Transfer decisions are the cumulative outcome of multiple decisions and they embody whatever race-linked assumptions, biases, and actions have transpired in the past. The extensive literature on the influence of race/ethnicity on juvenile justice processing focuses on stages prior to transfer, and it is beyond the scope of this chapter to review all the steps in the process. Most pertinent for our present analysis is the recognition that, while transfer is often considered "the end of the road," it is also the culmination of all that has transpired during a youth's passage down that road called juvenile justice.

Our summary of the research findings to date suggests that the movement toward higher rates of juvenile transfers, like the determinate and mandatory sentencing movements that preceded it in adult court, have had varying and complex effects on racial disparity. On one hand, both movements *appear* to be racially neutral because they focus attention on the offense type and, in some cases, age as the determinants of decision making. Indeed, research findings have shown that, when other factors are held statistically constant, race/ethnicity does not have a significant main effect on transfers in most jurisdictions. Yet the indirect and interaction effects of race/ethnicity are evident in these preliminary studies, and the gross disparities in numbers of white youths and youths of color prompt an urgent call for attention to the multiple ways in which race/ethnicity, alongside and in interaction with gender and class, influences the decision to transfer a youth from juvenile to criminal court and the ramifications of that decision. As Howell (1996, 51–52) admonishes us:

> There are gross inequities in the transfer and incarceration of minority versus nonminority juveniles. As we saw above, almost two-thirds of the juveniles admitted to adult prisons in 1992 were black. Thus minority youths are often disproportionately selected for transfer, conviction, and incarceration in adult prisons . . . Multivariate analyses of factors related to transfer, conviction, and imprisonment usually do not uncover racial disparity because of the disproportionate representation of minorities in official records, despite the fact that national self-report data show very similar ever-prevalence rates for blacks and whites to age twenty-four.

The Racial Context of Crime and Assessments of Responsibility

The body of research discussed above illuminates both the racial context of the transfer process and, to a lesser extent, the sentencing of youths in adult courts. Yet our review also reveals a largely unfinished research agenda. We demonstrate the need for more nuanced and encompassing assessments of the influence of race and ethnicity on the juvenile justice system. For, even as research findings highlight inequities within the transfer of youths to adult courts, the intricacies and complexities of the racial dimensions of social interactions evade current research strategies. One of the greatest research challenges is to develop studies that capture the extent to which interpretations, interactions, and the exercise of power reflect preconceived, unquestioned assumptions and understandings about race and ethnicity. The racial content of juvenile justice, including transfer, is highly palpable and yet elusive, partly due to the tangled and insidious ways in which race/ethnicity drenches the entire American social fabric.

Racial inequality in American life is reflected in numerous ways that are directly tied to the transfer of youths to criminal courts. It is evident in the substandard living conditions in which many minority youths are socialized; the racialization of youth violence; the demonization of minority youth gangs; the lack of effective rehabilitation programs for minority youths; the end of the protected status of adolescence, especially for youths of color; and a great proclivity for attributing full responsibility for their actions to youths of color.

The racial component of transfer policies and practices is extremely complex, largely because it exists alongside other ideological currents that argue against its very existence. For example, transfer, like many other justice system decision points, is often seen to operate largely without regard for race/ethnicity. Youths are depicted as responsible for their behaviors and their own choices are said to account for their subsequent prosecution as adults, while justice policy is portrayed as race neutral in its "get tough" stance. Our review in this chapter suggests that this view of contemporary juvenile justice policies as race neutral and guided largely by universally applied societal norms and sanctions ignores the continuing significance of race, ethnicity, gender, and social class in American society and in the administration of justice.

The tendency to racialize violence is particularly germane to the production of racial disparity in the prosecution of youths in adult courts. The most commonly accepted justification for the disproportionate transfer of youths of color—that they are violent—ignores the fact that youths of color are also most likely to be transferred for nonviolent offenses, especially drug offenses. Although the disproportional involvement of youths of color, especially African Americans and Latinos and Latinas, in serious violence is well documented, many of the public perceptions that drive American public policy and justice decision makers represent a racialization of violence that extends far beyond familiar crime statistics. The correlation between race/ethnicity and more severe punishment, including transfer, reflects differential participation in violence, but it also reveals the extent to which youths of color and their conduct are imbued by observers with violent expectations and interpretations. Some evidence suggests that their acts of violence are more likely to be coded as violent and to be coded as *more* violent than the behavior of non-minority youths. Violence by youths of color is viewed as *real* violence and as evidence of an enduring commitment to a violent lifestyle. The cumulative effects of these expectations and interpretations, combined with fewer resources and fewer alternatives to punitive sanctions, enhance the violence quotient of the behavior of youths of color.

Numerous social analysts maintain that depictions of violence and representations of race have become so intertwined that they are virtually inseparable. For example, in the wake of recent widely publicized public school murders, some media analysts have noted that white youths involved in heinous murders have been portrayed in a markedly different manner than the common depictions of minority youths accused of violence. Media images have stressed the normality of white youths and described them as "innocent looking," "slight," "diminutive," and as "emotionally troubled." The widespread description of one fifteen-year-old broadcasts an image that would be inconceivable if he were a minority youth: "With his shy smile and slight build, 15-year-old Kip Kinkel has an innocent look that is part Huck Finn and part Alfred E. Neuman— boyish and quintessentially American" (Dowdy 1998, E1). Violence is discordant with this vision of normalcy for black youth as well as whites, and both scholars and journalists have commented on the racial bias inherent in the use of such imagery.

In contrast, a predisposition toward violence is often portrayed as the most salient characteristic of African American and Latino and Latina youths whose acts of violence are viewed as inherent in what it means to be a youth of color (Fishman 1998; Rodríguez 1998; Miller 1996; Giroux 1996; Donziger 1996; Portillos 1998). Yet, little attention is given to the pivotal role played by American culture in the generation, perpetuation, and differential punishment of youths' violence. This is especially evident in images of and responses to youth gangs. While white gangs and white gang members exist, gangs have become synonymous with poor racial-minority youths (Decker and Van Winkle 1996; Hagedorn 1991, 1998; Klein 1995; Zatz 1987b; Moore 1991; Padilla 1992; Vigil 1988). Gangs have come to be seen as a major cause of violence in our inner cities, and many youths transferred to adult courts are assumed to be gang members (Krecker and Zatz 1998). With increasing public attention to and vilification of female gang members, it is likely that transfers of African American females and Latinas will increase (Portillos, Jurik, and Zatz 1996; Curry 1998; Chesney-Lind and Hagedorn 1999).

Individualized versus Collective Responsibility

Although the contemporary era is characterized by greater willingness to assign full responsibility to children in general, the very notion of responsibility for youths varies with economic and racial standing (Bortner and Williams 1997). Looking at juvenile justice specifically, researchers observe that decision makers are especially inclined to assign criminal responsibility to African American youths, even when they are involved in less serious offenses (Singer 1996). Likewise, decision makers' race-linked perceptions of youths make them more likely to attribute the delinquency of African American youths to "negative internal attributes" and to perceive these youths as more threatening and as more likely to reoffend than white youths (Bridges and Steen 1998).

Notions of responsibility in American culture are also highly atomized and individualized. Interdependencies and connections between youths of color and *all* of society are deemphasized to the point of denial. The increased attribution of full, adult responsibility to youths of color signals the end of childhood for them (Bortner and Williams 1997). Portraying young people as equally responsible as adults is coupled with images of youths of color as singularly and uniformly violent, recalcitrant, and destined for lives of adult crime.

Race-linked notions of individual responsibility are tied to an assumption that considerable juvenile justice rehabilitation resources have been exhausted to no avail in the fight against youthful crime. In actuality, the alternative resources available to youths and the extent to which rehabilitative services are provided are also highly correlated with race and ethnicity. Members of minority communities as well as social analysts describe juvenile justice as a two-track system that sorts youths based on their socioeconomic and racial standing:

> Two tracks exist for [youths involved in the juvenile justice system]—one for those of families, largely middle- and upper-class Anglo, with means to afford private behavioral health treatment services, and a second for the children of low-income families, largely African American, Hispanic, and Native American children living in single-parent homes, perhaps surviving through public assistance, children whose parents know of no treatment options to suggest to juvenile justice decision makers. (Bortner et al. 1993, 73–74)

In one study of the disparate treatment of youths of color, individuals working at all levels of the juvenile justice system told researchers that "given the prevailing economic situations of the families and neighborhoods of youths of color, system decision makers are much more likely to view those referred to the system as 'young criminals' deserving punishment." One experienced administrator stated, "It goes again to the unwritten, unspoken word that an Anglo kid who's got in some difficulty with the law can be treated . . . and minority kids are delinquent, they're thugs, they're tough kids, and they need to be punished" (Bortner et al. 1993, 74).

When transfers were based primarily on judicial waivers, a key factor in judges' decision making was the extent to which the child was amenable to treatment and whether appropriate programs existed. Some states still emphasize judicial waiver, while others combine it with legislative and prosecutorial transfer. In all situations it is important to examine whether the programs that are available to youths are appropriate in terms of culture, gender, and maturity. Feld (1993, 408) argues, "[I]f there are no effective treatment programs for serious juvenile offenders, no valid or reliable clinical tests with which to diagnose youths' treatment potential, and no scientific bases by which accurately to predict future dangerousness, then judicial waiver statutes are simply broad grants of standardless discretion."

Sometimes no longer being amenable to treatment may reflect an unwillingness on the juvenile's part to participate in programs. Youths might also be unable to participate due to physical or psychological problems. And youths may appear to fail when it could as easily be argued that it is the treatment programs that have failed. Some programs are not appropriate for certain youths or conducive to success due to age (e.g., programs geared for preteens), gender, and culture, among other factors. The increases in the number of waivers for drug offenses and for crimes against persons suggest that traditional programs designed with adolescent property offenders in mind may not be particularly helpful for many youths today. Also, generic drug resistance programs may not be as effective as culturally specific programs (Botvin et al. 1994, 1995; Marín 1993).

As discussed above, we expect the number of Latina and African American girls and young women in the transfer population to increase markedly in the near future, given the political focus on violent and drug offenses and the growth in arrest rates for females for these offenses. Yet very few innovative programs in the juvenile or adult court systems address the needs of girls and young women (Chesney-Lind and Shelden 1998).

Ironically, the consistent lack of meaningful treatment opportunities throughout the system enhances the probability that minority youths will be deemed "no longer amenable to treatment" (Sickmund, Snyder, and Poe-Yamagata 1997). To the extent that the appropriateness of treatment programs and youths' success in those programs is related to race/ethnicity, culture, and gender, we must be particularly leery of decisions to transfer a child to adult court based on assertions that he or she is "no longer amenable to treatment."

This section has briefly reviewed concerns surrounding the racial/ethnic content of dominant U.S. cultural assumptions. These wide-ranging assessments arise from scholarly observations as well as theoretic assertions. They have clear application and implications for juvenile justice, but few have been subjected to large-scale, rigorous research related to transfer. As we will now discuss, systematic and encompassing research is imperative.

2. Urgent Need for Enhanced Research

There is an urgent need for more encompassing research adequate to probe the multitude of controversies and complexities engulfing the transfer of youths to adult courts. Within individual jurisdictions and nationwide, our understanding of transfer and its full implications will be enhanced by: (1) more comprehensive analysis of the impact on racial disparity of diverse forms of transfer; (2) increased focus on issues of class and gender, and their interactions with race and ethnicity, including nuanced analyses of specific groups of youths of color in the contexts of their unique histories and contemporary needs; (3) holistic examination of the entire juvenile and criminal justice process prior to transfer and including the fate of transferred youths within the adult system; (4) extensive qualitative research providing ethnographic accounts of decision-making processes and in-depth interviews with decision makers, families, and transferred youths in order to assess the impact of race- and class-based attributions on decision making; and (5) intensified attempts to examine the macrostructural context, especially the connections between the racialization of transfer and racial conflict and inequality in American society.

Comprehensive Analysis of Transfer

There is great need for research into legislative and prosecutorial transfers and the collective impact of all forms of transfer. The bulk of research examining the transfer of youths to adult courts has focused on judicial waiver, the most long-standing method of transfer but one that is becoming less central to the overall picture. In comparing racial disparities in judicial waiver with those in prosecutorial and legislative transfer, researchers must examine possible trends of harsher conviction and incarceration rates (Norman and Gillespie 1986). Of particular importance is the little-examined issue of potential bias in prosecutors' charging decisions (Norman and Gillespie 1986; Fagan and Deschenes 1990; Zimring 1991; Singer 1993). Although Podkopacz and Feld (1995) minimize the potential for prosecutorial bias in their analysis of prosecutorial transfer, there is little research to suggest that prosecutorial or legislative transfer results in a less racialized process. Indeed, as discussed earlier, research has demonstrated that similar efforts in the adult system have shifted the locus of discretion (i.e., from judges to prosecutors or legislators) and have rendered decision-making power less visible and accountable. They have not provided the solution to racial disparities anticipated by reformers. Especially in light of their highly politicized positions, it is dubious that transfer processes in which prosecutors and politicians dominate will provide an antidote to the abuses of discretion attributed to juvenile judges. In contrast, judges may be better able to take less popular, less politically expedient action.

Nuanced Scrutiny: Class, Gender, and Race/Ethnicity

There is an urgent need for greater attention to issues of race and ethnicity in transfer decisions, yet studies must also address issues of class and gender. Consideration of social class in transfer research is particularly difficult due to dependence upon official agency data, since these sources tend not to include good indicators of socioeconomic status.

Transfer of youths to adult courts has been a highly gendered aspect of juvenile justice policy. Virtually all youths sent to adult courts have been young men, and disproportionate numbers of them have been young men of color. Transfer thus has been primarily about perceptions of and responses to *minority masculinity*. As we have suggested, the increased presence of girls and young women in the juvenile system for violence and drug offenses and the emerging emphasis on female gangs is likely to reconfigure the gendered nature of transfer policies.

In paying attention to disparities in the transfer process, researchers need to resist the homogenization of youths of color and to probe the unique situations of specific racial and ethnic groups. Data have been more readily available for African Americans than for Latinos and Latinas, American Indians, Asians and Asian Americans, and youths of mixed heritage. Frequent coding of Latinos and Latinas as "white" in official data masks the impact of ethnicity, as does the grouping of American Indians and Asian Americans into the "other" category. Much evidence suggests that the experiences of these diverse groups are not uniform within the context of the juvenile justice system.

Our research must also transcend the white/minority dichotomy and account for multiracial identities. We must take seriously disparities between official data and youths' self-identifications. Systematic research would fill the virtual void that exists regarding American Indian youths, including patterns of policing and surveillance on and off Indian lands, problems arising from multiple jurisdictions, the tremendous lack of resources in Indian communities, and the federal system's domination of tribal justice systems (Zatz, Lujan, and Snyder-Joy 1991; Donziger 1996; Bond-Maupin, Lujan, and Bortner 1995; Melton 1998). Likewise, the specific situations of noncitizen youths, especially Mexican nationals, needs to be illuminated. In many cases language is a problem. Although translators must by law be made available for court proceedings involving non-English speakers, juvenile probation departments typically have very few officers fluent in languages other than English. If parents and grandparents cannot communicate with probation officers, they cannot work together, reducing the likelihood that court-ordered plans will succeed (Portillos 1998). Finally, distinctions between urban and rural settings may also have important ramifications for youths of color, especially the lack of resources in rural communities and the high probability of incarceration in distant adult facilities.

Holistic Examination of the Juvenile Justice Process

Decision making throughout the juvenile system must be examined in a holistic manner. Studies of transfer cannot be divorced from scrutiny of prior stages within the process, including the disproportionate arrest, pretrial detention, and imprisonment of youths of color in the juvenile system. It is crucial that researchers continue to scrutinize the cumulative effects of decision making, especially the impact of race, ethnicity, and social class early in the process. Further, we must explore how considerations of race and ethnicity are incorporated into seemingly "neutral" decision-making processes. Small effects at several junctures may accumulate as individuals traverse the system. Also, statistically observable impacts of race at early stages may become statistically unobservable at later decision points due to funneling effects or because they are highly correlated with other factors (Bortner and Reed 1985; Zatz 1987a; Donziger 1996). The implications are tremendous, even if a specific transfer process is not racially biased, for transfer decisions could reflect and exacerbate already existing disparities at other stages of the system.

The holistic approach must also include in-depth exploration of the fate of transferred youths within the adult system. When youths are in the adult system, issues that merit exploration include: the role and nature of plea bargaining as well as differential access to bargains based on race, gender, and class; examination of how and why youths' cases are dismissed after transfer and the impact of race and ethnicity on those decisions; and examination of the consequences of mandatory sentences for youths waived to adult courts. Researchers need to expose the often harsh conditions of confinement for transferred youths and the ways in which race and ethnicity affect those experiences. The vast majority of youths waived to adult court await adult trial in adult jails, where conditions are extremely restricted and punitive. Even if they are among those whose cases will eventually be dismissed or those who will be sentenced to probation, countless youths will have served time in adult jails and been subjected to isolation, depression, and abuse.

There is a tremendous need for comprehensive and systematic studies of the postconviction experiences of the thousands of youths in adult jails and prisons. Those youths sentenced to a year or less will return to abject jail conditions, while those incarcerated long-term will be subjected to state and federal prisons. Prior to reaching the age of majority (commonly eighteen), many imprisoned youths are kept in more restricted and punitive conditions than their adult counterparts, where the isolation and silence of juvenile prisons is magnified. When they are released into the general prison population, youths are acutely vulnerable to the "extra punishment" of rape, sexual domination and slavery, and suicide. Youths are more likely to need protective custody and, when their requests are granted or they are placed in protective custody against their wishes, they spend long periods virtually in solitary confinement.

Ethnographies would place a human face on transfer policies, such as that presented by columnist Bruce Shapiro in his portrayal of the life and death of one youth, Rodney Hulin Jr. of Beaumont, Texas. Sentenced at sixteen years of age to eight years in adult prison for arson, this African American child was raped shortly after arriving and his requests for protective custody were denied. After being repeatedly beaten, raped, and robbed, Rodney hanged himself and, after lying in a coma for four months, was released by death from the punishment inflicted upon him by transfer policies. Shapiro (1997, 7) concludes: "For some children, adult prison will be crime school. For others, it will be a death sentence."

Expansion of Qualitative Research

Statistical analyses alone are inadequate to explore the organizational forces and human experiences that provide in-depth explanations for the complex problem of the overrepresentation of youths of color. It is essential to examine the interactions between youths and parents, communities, and the justice system, and among personnel in the various system agencies. In-depth qualitative research, though extremely time-consuming, is crucial at those decision points where racial and ethnic identity appears to have an inordinate influence statistically, as well as at other points where racial and ethnic identity impacts the lives and experiences of minority youths and their families and communities in complex, highly nuanced ways.

Ethnographic approaches enable researchers to listen to the voices of youths, their parents and grandparents, neighbors, and teachers, as well as juvenile justice personnel responsible for working with these youths. Such research has potential to provide insight into the multifaceted implications of punishment practices, including thorough examination of alternative sentences. For example, such endeavors can explore the perceptions and experiences of youths whose cases were dismissed after long pretrial waits in adult jails, or youths whose immaturity made violation of their probation highly likely, resulting in imprisonment.

Approaching the Macrostructural Context

Perhaps the greatest challenge to researchers is the incorporation of theoretic understandings regarding the macrostructural context of juvenile justice policies into studies of the racial dimensions of transfer. Analysts often comment, however briefly, on the larger context and lament the lack of more telling information, but concerted efforts are essential to design and conduct research that uncovers and takes into account relevant data. Continued failure to contextualize statistical analyses contributes to fragmented and ineffective portraits of the transfer process. Researchers acknowledge the political and economic dimensions of the policies they study, yet they generally fail to include these dimensions in their data bases.

An encompassing analysis of the context of transfer policies would incorporate the fiscal aspects of transfer, such as the short- and long-term costs to taxpayers (Lemov 1994) and the potential impact of shifts in funding on rates of incarceration (Singer 1993). Beyond system budgets, research must articulate the extent to which serious efforts to reduce disparities in transfer decisions will require substantially increased job opportunities for poor youths, improved inner-city schools, and eliminating racial discrimination in employment, education, and housing. These structural factors limit the opportunities available to poor youths and particularly poor minority youths. They seriously impact the juvenile justice system's assessment of, interactions with, and responses to youths of color.

It is particularly crucial to research the connections between transfer policies and other social policies, for race-linked punishment reflects other contemporary policy developments (Fine and Weis 1998; Coontz 1992). Theoretic analyses capture these dynamics when, for example, Ruth Conniff (1992) speaks of the "culture of cruelty" in which there is a growing contempt for those who are impoverished, disenfranchised, or powerless. These links are likewise suggested by statements such as "The debate over child punishment is not just about jailing a few gangbangers. It's a leading edge in the campaign to further unravel social welfare and civil rights" (Shapiro 1997, 7). But these theoretic insights are rarely translated into large-scale research endeavors.

Another crucial macrostructural question is whether extensive transfer of youths to adult court is uniquely characteristic of U.S. society, characteristic of Western industrialized nations in general, or characteristic of all nations with formal juvenile justice systems. As in the past, trends in U.S. juvenile justice profoundly influence worldwide developments and, more crucially, developments within U.S. culture have global implications for youths and justice (Hackler 1991; Fornas and Bolin 1995; Cavadino 1996). To date, other nations have not enacted wide-sweeping transfer policies, but cross-cultural analysis of transfer policies and the ramifications for racial and ethnic minorities is essential.

The Political Arena

There is virtually no social-science research that articulates the highly charged political atmosphere in which the widespread transfer of youths of color to adult courts takes place. There is extensive theoretic speculation about the "political currency" gained by politicians when they promote increased punishment (Bortner 1986; Bortner and Williams 1997; West 1993), but there is a great need for research to explicate the political processes at work. Likewise, although transfer policies are frequently portrayed as the necessary response to public fears, there is a profound lack of research on the extent to which these policies provide either increased safety or symbolic solace.

Many analysts assume that major political advantages accrue to politicians who promote transfer policies but the actual outcomes have not been explicated. For example, the National Criminal Justice Commission has suggested that there has been little pragmatic, grounded discussion of the possible consequences of the "get tough" transfer provisions of the federal crime bill, "but it at least *sounded* as if something was being done about the juvenile violence problem" (Donziger 1996, 135). One writer's concerns echo numerous social analysts: "Clearly, the call to treat young criminals as adults is good politics. Is it good social policy?" (Lemov 1994, 27)

The lived and long-term consequences of sending large numbers of youths to adult courts and prisons, both for individual youths and society as a whole, are unknown. In the midst of the punitive climate, few have documented the potentially disastrous effects of large numbers of young adults with prison experiences or adult records. Few have estimated the social costs of a generation of individuals hardened by prison life and their crystallized exclusion and alienation from mainstream society. Current policies will have monumental consequences when transferred youths return to society. Researchers need to examine the degree to which, purposefully or not, our social policies are creating a "criminal generation" of excluded, angry, and uneducated individuals (Shakur 1993, 136).

The overt racialization of many aspects of juvenile justice policy in the United States requires conscious efforts aimed at deracialization. The impact of the problem of racial disparity in transfer and at other stages of the juvenile justice system extends far beyond concerns for racial equity and equal protection that are grounded in the Constitution or in civil rights law. As American business leaders have begun to acknowledge, the nation will not remain economically competitive and viable if large numbers of its youths, including its youths of color who make up a disproportionate share of the workforce of the future, are confined to juvenile and adult correctional facilities. Youths of African American, Latino/a, American Indian, and Asian American ancestry are an indispensable part of the nation's economic future.

Conclusion

The punitive nature of contemporary juvenile justice policy is evident in the transfer of youths to adult courts, and youths of color account for a highly disproportionate share of transfers. Although research on this topic has increased, much remains unknown regarding transfer processes and outcomes. Little research has captured the racialized context in which this and all aspects of juvenile justice are enmeshed. Most studies have relied upon official data and emphasized statistical analyses, while a few have provided insights gained from ethnographic observations or interviews. The research findings vary: some reveal statistically observable effects of race and ethnicity, while others conclude that the effects are indirect or linked with offense. These wide-ranging conclusions attest both to the differences among juvenile justice systems and to the difficulties of disclosing the complexities of the entrenched, institutionalized impacts of race and ethnicity, social class, and gender.

Research on transfer must extend beyond the courthouse and acknowledge the overwhelming importance of social context, including the great lack of resources within minority communities, the void in effective programming for minority youths, sweeping practices of defining and demonizing gang membership, race-based stereotypes of violence, the disenfranchisement of youths of color, and policies based on public fear and political ambition. An in-depth understanding of transfer policies and practices requires that we acknowledge the extent to which racial categories and racial meanings shape the assumptions, expectations, and responses of juvenile justice decision makers, politicians, and the public. More nuanced, encompassing research must recognize the racialization of both youthful behavior and the transfer process, and must seek to articulate how the *consequences* of racial and ethnic inequities become accepted as legitimate justifications for disparate treatment and selective punishment.

References

Albonetti, Celesta A. 1986. "Criminality, Prosecutorial Screening, and Uncertainty: Toward a Theory of Discretionary Decision Making in Felony Case Processings." *Criminology* 24:623.

———. 1991. "An Integration of Theories to Explain Judicial Discretion." *Social Problems* 38:247.

Baldus, David C., Charles Pulaski, and George Woodworth. 1983. "Comparative Review of Death Sentences: An Empirical Study of the Georgia Experience." *Journal of Criminal Law and Criminology* 74:661.

Barncs, Carole Wolff, and Randal S. Franz. 1989. "Questionably Adult: Determinants and Effects of the Juvenile Waiver Decision." *Justice Quarterly* 6:117.

Bishop, Donna M., and Charles E. Frazier. 1988. "The Influence of Race in Juvenile Justice Processing." *Journal of Research in Crime and Delinquency* 25: 242.

Bishop, Donna M., Charles E. Frazier, and John C. Henretta. 1989. "Prosecutorial Waiver: Case Study of a Questionable Reform." *Crime and Delinquency* 35:179.

Blumstein, Alfred. 1982. "On the Racial Disproportionality of the United States Prison Populations." *Journal of Criminal Law and Criminology* 73:1259.

Bond-Maupin, Lisa, Carol Chiago Lujan, and M. A. Bortner. 1995. "Jailing of American Indian Adolescents: The Legacy of Cultural Domination and Imposed Law." *Crime, Law, and Social Change* 23:1.

Bortner, M. A. 1982. *Inside a Juvenile Court: The Tarnished Ideal of Individualized Justice.* New York: New York University Press.

————. 1986. "Traditional Rhetoric, Organizational Realities: Remand of Juveniles to Adult Court." *Crime and Delinquency* 32:53.

Bortner, M. A., Carol Burgess, Anne Schneider, and Andy Hall. 1993. *Equitable Treatment of Minority Youth: A Report on the Over Representation of Minority Youth in Arizona's Juvenile Justice System.* Phoenix: Governor's Office for Children.

Bortner, M. A., and Wornie L. Reed. 1985. "The Preeminence of Process: An Example of Refocused Justice Research." *Social Science Quarterly* 66:413.

Bortner, M. A., and Linda M. Williams. 1997. *Youth in Prison: We the People of Unit Four.* New York: Routledge.

Botvin, Gilbert J., Steven P. Schinke, Jennifer A. Epstein, and Tracy Diaz. 1994. "Effectiveness of Culturally Focused and Generic Skills Training Approaches to Alcohol and Drug Abuse Prevention among Minority Youths." *Psychology of Addictive Behaviors* 8:116.

Botvin, Gilbert J., Steven P. Schinke, Jennifer A. Epstein, Tracy Diaz, and Elizabeth M. Botvin. 1995. "Effectiveness of Culturally Focused and Generic Skills Training Approaches to Alcohol and Drug Abuse Prevention among Minority Adolescents: Two-Year Follow-Up Results." *Psychology of Addictive Behaviors* 9:183.

Bridges, George S., and Sara Steen. 1998. "Racial Disparities in Official Assessments of Juvenile Offenders: Attributional Stereotypes as Mediating Mechanisms." *American Sociological Review* 63:554.

Butts, Jeffrey A. 1996a. *Offenders in Juvenile Court, 1993.* Washington: U.S. Department of Justice, Office of Justice Programs, Office of Juvenile Justice and Delinquency Prevention.

————. 1996b. *Offenders in Juvenile Courts, 1994.* Washington: U.S. Department of Justice, Office of Justice Programs, Office of Juvenile Justice and Delinquency Prevention.

Cavadino, Paul, ed. 1996. *Children Who Kill: An Examination of the Treatment of Juveniles Who Kill in Different European Countries.* Winchester, England: Waterside Press.

Chesney-Lind, Meda, and John Hagedorn, eds. 1999. *Female Gangs in America: Essays on Girls, Gangs, and Gender.* Chicago: Lake View Press.

Chesney-Lind, Meda, and Randall G. Shelden. 1998. *Girls, Delinquency, and Juvenile Justice.* 2d ed. Belmont, Calif.: West/Wadsworth.

Clarke, Elizabeth E. 1996. "A Case for Reinventing Juvenile Transfer: The Record of Transfer of Juvenile Offenders to Criminal Court in Cook County, Illinois." *Juvenile and Family Court Journal* 47:3.

Cleaver, Kathleen Neal. 1997. "Racism, Civil Rights, and Feminism." In *Critical Race Feminism: A Reader.* Edited by Adrien Katherine Wing. New York: New York University Press.

Connell, Robert W. 1995. "Masculinity, Violence, and War." In *Men's Lives,* 3d ed. Edited by Michael S. Kimmel and Michael A. Messner. Boston: Allyn & Bacon.

Conniff, Ruth. 1992. "The Culture of Cruelty." *Progressive,* September, 16.

Coontz, Stephanie. 1992. *The Way We Never Were: American Families and the Nostalgia Trap.* New York: Basic Books.

Curry, G. David. 1998. "Female Gang Involvement." *Journal of Research in Crime and Delinquency* 35:100.

Daly, Kathleen. 1994. *Gender, Crime, and Punishment.* New Haven: Yale University Press.

Dannefer, Dale, and Russell K. Schutt. 1982. "Race and Juvenile Justice Processing in Court and Police Agencies." *American Journal of Sociology* 87: 1113.

Decker, Scott H., and Barrik Van Winkle. 1996. *Life in the Gang: Family, Friends, and Violence.* New York: Cambridge University Press.

Diaz-Cotto, Juanita. 1996. *Gender, Ethnicity, and the State: Latina and Latino Prison Politics.* Albany: State University of New York Press.

Donziger, Steven R., ed. 1996. *The Real War on Crime: The Report of the National Criminal Justice Commission.* New York: HarperPerennial.

Dowdy, Zachary R. 1998. "Who Pulled the Trigger? RACE." *Boston Globe,* June 21, E1–2.

Drass, Kriss A., and J. William Spencer. 1987. "Accounting for Pre-sentencing Recommendations: Typologies and Probation Officers' Theory of Office." *Social Problems* 34:277.

Emerson, Robert M. 1969. *Judging Delinquents: Context and Process in Juvenile Court.* Chicago: Aldine.

Fagan, Jeffrey, and Elizabeth Piper Deschenes. 1990. "Determinants of Juvenile Waiver Decisions for Violent Juvenile Offenders." *Journal of Criminal Law and Criminology* 81:314.

Fagan, Jeffrey, Martin Forst, and T. Scott Vivona. 1987. "Racial Determinants of the Judicial Transfer Decision: Prosecuting Violent Youth in Criminal Court." *Crime and Delinquency* 33:259.

Fagan, Jeffrey, Ellen Slaughter, and Eliot Hartstone. 1987. "Blind Justice? The Impact of Race on the Juvenile Justice Process." *Crime and Delinquency* 33: 224.

Feld, Barry C. 1993. "Juvenile (In)Justice and the Criminal Court Alternative." *Crime and Delinquency* 39:403.

Fine, Michelle, and Lois Weis. 1998. *The Unknown City: Lives of Poor and Working-Class Young Adults.* Boston: Beacon Press.

Fishman, Laura T. 1998. "The Black Bogeyman and White Self-Righteousness." In *Images of Color, Images of Crime.* Edited by Coramae Richey Mann and Marjorie S. Zatz. Los Angeles: Roxbury.

Fornas, Johan, and Goran Bolin, eds. 1995. *Youth Culture in Late Modernity.* London: Sage.

Gans, Herbert J. 1995. *The War against the Poor: The Underclass and Antipoverty Policy.* New York: Basic Books.

Giroux, Henry A. 1996. *Fugitive Cultures: Race, Violence, and Youth.* New York: Routledge.

Gragg, Frances. 1986. *Juveniles in Adult Court: A Review of Transfers at the*

Habitual Serious and Violent Offender Program Sites. Washington: Office of Justice Assistance, Research, and Statistics.

Greenberg, David F., and Drew Humphries. 1980. "The Cooptation of Fixed Sentencing Reform." *Crime and Delinquency* 26:206.

Hackler, Jim, ed. 1991. *Official Responses to Problem Juveniles: Some International Reflections.* Onati, Italy: Onati International Institute for the Sociology of Law.

Hagan, John, and Kristin Bumiller. 1983. "Making Sense of Sentencing: A Review and Critique of Sentencing Research." In *Research on Sentencing: The Search for Reform.* Vol. 2. Edited by Alfred Blumstein, Jacqueline Cohen, Susan E. Martin, and Michael H. Tonry. Washington: National Academy Press.

Hagedorn, John M. 1991. "Gangs, Neighborhoods, and Public Policy." *Social Problems* 38:529.

Hagedorn, John M., with Peter Macon. 1998. *People and Folks: Gangs, Crime, and the Underclass in a Rustbelt City.* 2d ed. Chicago: Lake View Press.

Hawkins, Darnell F. 1983. "Crime and Ethnicity. In *The Socio-economics of Crime and Justice.* Edited by Brian Forst. Armonk, N.Y.: M. E. Sharpe.

———. 1986. "Race, Crime Type, and Imprisonment." *Justice Quarterly* 3:251.

———. 1987. "Beyond Anomalies: Rethinking the Conflict Perspective on Race and Criminal Punishment." *Social Forces* 65:719.

Hawkins, Darnell F., and Nolan E. Jones. 1989. "Black Adolescents and the Criminal Justice System." In *Black Adolescents.* Edited by R. L. Jones. Berkeley, Calif.: Cobb and Henry.

Higginbotham, Evelyn Brooks. 1992. "African American Women's History and the Metalanguage of Race." *Signs* 17:251.

Houghtalin, Marilyn, and G. Larry Mays. 1991. "Criminal Dispositions of New Mexico Juveniles Transferred to Adult Court." *Crime and Delinquency* 37:393.

Howell, James C. 1996. "Juvenile Transfers to the Criminal Justice System: State of the Art." *Law and Policy* 18:17.

Irwin, John. 1980. *Prisons in Turmoil.* Boston: Little, Brown & Company.

Keiter, Robert B. 1973. "Criminal or Delinquent? Juvenile Cases Transferred to the Criminal Court." *Crime and Delinquency* 19:528.

Kelley, Barbara T., David Huizinga, Terence P. Thornberry, and Rolf Loeber. 1997. *Epidemiology of Serious Violence.* Washington: U.S. Department of Justice, Office of Justice Programs, Office of Juvenile Justice and Delinquency Prevention.

Kennedy, Randall. 1997. *Race, Crime, and the Law.* New York: Pantheon Books.

Kinder, Kristine, Carol Veneziano, Michael Fichter, and Henry Azuma. 1995. "A Comparison of the Dispositions of Juvenile Offenders Certified as Adults with Juvenile Offenders Not Certified." *Juvenile and Family Court Journal* 46:37.

Klein, Malcolm W. 1995. *The American Street Gang: Its Nature, Prevalence, and Control.* New York: Oxford University Press.

Klepper, S., D. Nagin, and L. Tierney. 1983. "Discrimination in the Criminal Justice System: A Critical Appraisal of the Literature." In *Research in Sen-*

tencing: The Search for Reform. Vol. 2. Edited by Alfred Blumstein, Jacqueline Cohen, Susan E. Martin, and Michael H. Tonry. Washington: National Academy Press.

Krecker, Richard P., and Marjorie S. Zatz. 1998. "Anti-gang Initiatives as Racialized Policy." Presented at the Law and Society Association Meetings, Aspen.

Krisberg, Barry, and James Austin, eds. 1978. *Children of Ishmael: Critical Perspectives on Juvenile Justice.* Palo Alto, Calif.: Mayfield.

Krisberg, Barry, Ira Schwartz, Gideon Fishman, Zvi Eisikovits, Edna Guttman, and Karen Joe. 1987. "The Incarceration of Minority Youth." *Crime and Delinquency* 33:173.

LaFree, Gary D. 1989. *Rape and Criminal Justice: The Social Construction of Sexual Assault.* Belmont, Calif.: Wadsworth.

Lemov, Penelope. 1994. "Taking the 'Juvenile' Out of Justice." *Governing* 8 (December): 26.

Lizotte, Alan J. 1978. "Extra-legal Factors in Chicago's Criminal Courts: Testing the Conflict Model of Criminal Justice." *Social Problems* 25:564.

Lizotte, Alan J., and Marjorie S. Zatz. 1986. "The Use and Abuse of Sentence Enhancements for Firearms Offenses in California." *Law and Contemporary Problems* 49:1101.

Lotke, Eric, and Vincent Schiraldi. 1996. *An Analysis of Juvenile Homicides: Where They Occur and the Effectiveness of Adult Court Intervention.* Washington: National Center on Institutions and Alternatives.

Mann, Coramae Richey. 1993. *Unequal Justice: A Question of Color.* Bloomington: Indiana University Press.

Mann, Coramae Richey, and Marjorie S. Zatz, eds. 1998. *Images of Color, Images of Crime.* Los Angeles: Roxbury.

Marín, Gerardo. 1993. "Defining Culturally Appropriate Community Interventions: Hispanics as a Case Study." *Journal of Community Psychology* 21:149.

McNulty, Elizabeth W. 1996. "The Transfer of Juvenile Offenders to Adult Court: Panacea or Problem?" *Law and Policy* 18:61.

Melton, Ada Pecos. 1998. "Traditional and Contemporary Tribal Justice." In *Images of Color, Images of Crime.* Edited by Coramae Richey Mann and Marjorie S. Zatz. Los Angeles: Roxbury.

Messerschmidt, James W. 1997. *Crime as Structured Action: Gender, Race, Class, and Crime in the Making.* Thousand Oaks, Calif.: Sage.

Messner, Michael. 1995. "Boyhood, Organized Sports, and the Construction of Masculinities." In *Men's Lives.* Edited by Michael S. Kimmel and Michael A. Messner. Boston: Allyn & Bacon.

Miethe, Terance D., and Charles A. Moore. 1985. "Socioeconomic Disparities under Determinate Sentencing Systems: A Comparison of Preguideline and Postguideline Practices in Minnesota." *Criminology* 23:337.

Miller, Jerome G. 1996. *Search and Destroy: African-American Males in the Criminal Justice System.* New York: Cambridge University Press.

Moore, Joan W. 1991. *Going Down to the Barrio: Homeboys and Homegirls in Change.* Philadelphia: Temple University Press.

Norman, M., and L. Gillespie. 1986. "Changing Horses: Utah's Shift in Adjudicating Serious Juvenile Offenders." *Journal of Contemporary Law* 12:85.

Omi, Michael, and Howard Winant. 1986. *Racial Formation in the United States: From the 1960s to the 1980s.* New York: Routledge and Kegan Paul.

Padilla, Felix M. 1992. *The Gang as an American Enterprise.* New Brunswick: Rutgers University Press.

Peterson, Ruth, and John Hagan. 1984. "Changing Conceptions of Race: Towards an Account of Anomalous Findings of Sentencing Research." *American Sociological Review* 49:56.

Petersilia, Joan. 1983. *Racial Disparities in the Criminal Justice System.* Santa Monica: RAND.

Platt, Anthony M. 1977. *The Child Savers: The Invention of Delinquency.* 2d ed. Chicago: University of Chicago Press.

Podkopacz, Marcy Rasmussen, and Barry C. Feld. 1995. "Judicial Waiver Policy and Practice: Persistence, Seriousness, and Race." *Law and Inequality Journal* 14:73.

———. 1996. "The End of the Line: An Empirical Study of Judicial Waiver." *Journal of Criminal Law and Criminology* 86:449.

Poe-Yamagata, Eileen, and Jeffrey A. Butts. 1996. *Female Offenders and the Juvenile Justice System: Statistics Summary.* Washington Office of Juvenile Justice and Delinquency Prevention.

Pope, Carl E., and William H. Feyerherm. 1995. *Minorities and the Juvenile Justice System.* Washington: U.S. Department of Justice, Office of Juvenile Justice and Delinquency Prevention.

Portillos, Edwardo L. 1998. "Latinos, Gangs, and Drugs." In *Images of Color, Images of Crime.* Edited by Coramae Richey Mann and Marjorie Zatz. Los Angeles: Roxbury.

Portillos, Edwardo L., Nancy C. Jurik, and Marjorie S. Zatz. 1996. "Machismo and Chicano/a Gangs: Symbolic Resistance or Oppression?" *Free Inquiry in Creative Sociology* 24:175.

Poulos, Tammy Meredith, and Stan Orchowsky. 1994. "Serious Juvenile Offenders: Predicting the Probability of Transfer to Criminal Court." *Crime and Delinquency* 40:3.

Reiman, Jeffrey H., and Sue Headlee. 1981. "Marxism and Criminal Justice Policy." *Crime and Delinquency* 27:24.

Rodríguez, Luis J. 1998. "The Color of Skin Is the Color of Crime." In *Images of Color, Images of Crime.* Edited by Coramae Richey Mann and Marjorie S. Zatz. Los Angeles: Roxbury.

Russell, Katheryn K. 1998. *The Color of Crime: Racial Hoaxes, White Fear, Black Protectionism, Police Harassment, and Other Macroaggressions.* New York: New York University Press.

Schlossman, Steven L. 1977. *Love and the American Delinquent: The Theory and Practice of "Progressive" Juvenile Justice, 1825–1920.* Chicago: University of Chicago Press.

Sennett, Richard, and Jonathan Cobb. 1973. *The Hidden Injuries of Class.* New York: Vintage Books.

Shakur, Sanyika [Monster Kody Scott]. 1993. *Monster: The Autobiography of an L.A. Gang Member.* New York: Atlantic Monthly Press.

Shapiro, Bruce. 1997. "The Adolescent Lockup." *Nation,* 7 July, 6–7.

Sickmund, Melissa, Howard N. Snyder, and Eileen Poe-Yamagata. 1997. *Juvenile Offenders and Victims: 1997 Update on Violence: Statistics Summary.* Washington: Office of Juvenile Justice and Delinquency Prevention.

Singer, Simon I. 1993. "The Automatic Waiver of Juveniles and Substantive Justice." *Crime and Delinquency* 39:253.

———. 1996. *Recriminalizing Delinquency: Violent Juvenile Crime and Juvenile Justice Reform.* New York: Cambridge University Press.

Snyder, Howard N., and Melissa Sickmund. 1995. *Juvenile Offenders and Victims: A Focus on Violence.* Washington: Office of Juvenile Justice and Delinquency Prevention.

Snyder, Howard N., Melissa Sickmund, and Eileen Poe-Yamagata. 1996. *Juvenile Offenders and Victims: 1996 Update on Violence: Statistics Summary.* Washington: Office of Juvenile Justice and Delinquency Prevention.

Spencer, Jack William. 1983. "Accounts, Attitudes, and Solutions: Probation Officer–Defendant Negotiations of Subjective Orientations." *Social Problems* 30:570.

Spohn, Cassia. 1990. "The Sentencing Decisions of Black and White Judges: Expected and Unexpected Similarities." *Law and Society Review* 24:1197.

———. 1994. "Crime and the Social Control of Blacks: Offender/Victim Race and the Sentencing of Violent Offenders." In *Inequality, Crime, and Social Control.* Edited by George S. Bridges and Martha A. Myers. Boulder: Westview Press.

Spohn, Cassia, John Gruhl, and Susan Welch. 1981. "The Effect of Race on Sentencing: A Re-examination of an Unsettled Question." *Law and Society Review* 16:71.

Thomas, Charles W., and Shay Bilchik. 1985. "Prosecuting Juveniles in Criminal Courts: A Legal and Empirical Analysis." *Journal of Criminal Law and Criminology* 76:439.

Tittle, Charles R. 1983. "Social Class and Criminal Behavior: A Critique of the Theoretical Foundation." *Social Forces* 62:334.

Tonry, Michael. 1988. "Structuring Sentencing." *Crime and Justice: A Review of Research* 10:126.

———. 1992. "Mandatory Penalties." *Crime and Justice: A Review of Research* 16:243.

———. 1993. "Sentencing Commissions and Their Guidelines." *Crime and Justice: A Review of Research* 17:137.

———. 1995. *Malign Neglect: Race, Crime, and Punishment in America.* New York: Oxford University Press.

Unnever, James D., and Larry A. Hembroff. 1988. "The Prediction of Racial/Ethnic Sentencing Disparities: An Expectation States Approach." *Journal of Research in Crime and Delinquency* 25:53.

Vigil, James Diego. 1988. *Barrio Gangs: Street Life and Identity in Southern California.* Austin: University of Texas Press.

Von Hirsch, Andrew. 1976. *Doing Justice: The Choice of Punishments: Report of the Committee for the Study of Incarceration.* New York: Hill and Wang.

West, Cornel. 1993. *Race Matters.* Boston: Beacon Press.

Winner, Lawrence, Lonn Lanza-Kaduce, Donna M. Bishop, and Charles E. Frazier. 1997. "The Transfer of Juveniles to Criminal Court: Reexamining Recidivism over the Long Term." *Crime and Delinquency* 43:548.

Zatz, Marjorie S. 1985. "Los Cholos: Legal Processing of Chicano Gang Members." *Social Problems* 33:13.

———. 1987a. "The Changing Forms of Racial/Ethnic Biases in Sentencing." *Journal of Research in Crime and Delinquency* 24:69.

———. 1987b. "Chicano Youth Gangs and Crime: The Creation of a Moral Panic." *Contemporary Crises* 11:129.

———. 2000. "Race, Ethnicity, Gender, Class, and Court Processing and Sanctioning: Looking toward the 21st Century." In *NIJ 2000: Policies, Processes, and Decisions of the Judicial System.* Edited by Julie Horney. Washington: Department of Justice.

Zatz, Marjorie S., Carol Chiago Lujan, and Zoann K. Snyder-Joy. 1991. "American Indians and Criminal Justice: Some Conceptual and Methodological Considerations." In *Race and Criminal Justice.* Edited by Michael J. Lynch and E. Britt Patterson. Albany: Harrow and Heston.

Zimring, Franklin E. 1991. "The Treatment of Hard Cases in American Juvenile Justice: In Defense of Discretionary Waiver." *Notre Dame Journal of Law, Ethics, and Public Policy* 5:267.

Chapter Nine

Forensic Clinical Evaluations Related to Waiver of Jurisdiction

Thomas Grisso

This chapter examines the role of mental health professionals in performing clinical evaluations to assist a court in decisions about the waiver of that court's jurisdiction, allowing the youth to be tried in a different justice system. As noted elsewhere in this volume, juvenile courts since their inception have always had the option of waiving their jurisdiction over some youths, allowing their charges to be filed in criminal court. More recently, statutes have evolved that require (or allow through prosecutorial discretion) that certain offenses by youths be filed originally in criminal court (Torbet et al. 1996). Criminal courts in those instances then have the option to waive jurisdiction, allowing charges to be filed in juvenile court.

This chapter pertains to waiver of jurisdiction over youths' offenses by either juvenile or criminal courts. In this chapter, the term "upward waiver" is used to refer to juvenile courts' decisions to waive jurisdiction, allowing charges to be filed in criminal court (in some states, "transfer," "bindover," or "certification"). The term "reverse waiver" will refer to a criminal court's decision to place a youth's charges in the jurisdiction of the juvenile court.

Laws controlling waiver of court jurisdiction require hearings to address whether evidence supports the statutory criteria for waiver that judges must apply when they make waiver decisions. As described later, some of the criteria relevant for the waiver decision are certain characteristics of the youth, especially as they provide a view of the prospects for the youth's future behavior. It has become quite common, therefore, for courts, prosecutors, or defense attorneys to request clinical evaluations of youths for use as evidence in waiver hearings (Grisso 1998).

These clinical evaluations by mental health professionals are called "forensic" because they are performed specifically to assist the legal system in making a decision based on legal standards (Melton et al. 1997). They are "clinical" in the sense that in part they provide information about the youth's character and mental status. But they are unlike evaluations in general clinical practice (e.g., in hospitals or child clinics) in that they are not driven exclusively by the objective of providing necessary medical or psychological care. Indeed, in some cases they will lead to conclusions that deny to youths the benefits of treatment and rehabilitation programs. In contrast to *general* clinical evaluations, the purpose of any *forensic* clinical evaluation is to provide legally relevant information with which courts can make decisions based on legal standards—in the present context, decisions about whether the youth will be tried in juvenile court or in criminal court.

The value of examining clinical evaluations for waiver of jurisdiction is not confined to improving clinicians' evaluations nor even to educating courts on what these evaluations should provide. Clinical evaluations for waiver cases have a synergistic relation to the legal decision-making process that they inform. On the one hand, clinicians look to the law (in statutes, case precedent, and local practice) for their cues regarding the types of information that courts require for making their waiver decisions. Their knowledge and interpretations of those directives from law influence the data they collect and how they interpret them. Courts influence that clinical forensic process by providing legal guidance for clinicians—sometimes clear, sometimes vague—and often by choosing the clinicians to whom they assign the evaluation task. On the other hand, the ways that clinicians frame their opinions and reports for use by the legal decision maker—case by case and cumulatively across cases—have an effect on the way that courts structure their application of legal standards to questions of waiver. Out of this synergism evolves the meaning of legal standards that guide judicial decisions about juveniles' waiver in everyday practice.

This chapter is intended to describe primarily the clinical examiner's side of this interaction. The active reader, however, will identify within this description evidence of the inadequate guidance that law provides to clinicians in performing their evaluations, the unanswered questions within law itself regarding the definitions of standards and concepts applicable to the question of waiver, and the potential for clinical evaluations to influence the law's definition and application of waiver laws. Within this synergistic relation, clinical evaluations have the potential to contribute to injustice for youths if they function without adequate constraints imposed by courts and professional standards. They also have the potential to function reciprocally in the legal decision process out of which may evolve clearer waiver laws that are more rationally applied.

The first section of the chapter describes the scope and objectives of forensic evaluations for waiver of jurisdiction, including the process of clinical interpretation of the legal standards as well as the general nature of the evaluation task. The second section describes what we know about current practices among clinicians who perform these evaluations for courts and defense attorneys. The third and fourth sections provide a model for performing waiver-of-jurisdiction evaluations, and the fifth section offers concluding observations about their role and value.

The chapter was written for judges and attorneys, as well as for clinicians. For the former, the chapter provides insight into the structure and function of clinical evaluations for waiver of jurisdiction, what should be expected of clinicians who perform these evaluations, and standards for which those clinicians should be held accountable. For clinicians, the chapter offers a conceptual description of what waiver-of-jurisdiction evaluations should accomplish, but it does not provide details of method or interpretation that would be needed to carry out the evaluation. Those can be found in other sources (Grisso 1998; Melton et al. 1997).

1. Objectives of Evaluations for Waiver of Jurisdiction

As noted in the introduction to this chapter, the purpose of any forensic clinical evaluation is to provide information to a decision maker that is relevant for a legal decision about a case in question. This means that the forensic clinical examiner (hereinafter, "examiner" or "clinician") must know the legal standards or criteria that the legal decision maker is required to apply to reach a decision. Without this, the examiner has no basis for judging what information about a youth is relevant to obtain. Knowledge of the relevant legal standards and criteria, even when their generality may seem less than illuminating, must guide the evaluation process (Grisso 1986; Melton et al. 1997). Clinical information that is unlikely to be useful in forming an opinion about the youth in relation to the standard is irrelevant and should be inadmissible as evidence. In addition, knowledge of the appropriate legal standards will guide the way the examiner eventually communicates the results of the evaluation, making these communications most useful to the legal decision maker.

The following description of the objectives of an evaluation for waiver of jurisdiction, therefore, (a) begins with background knowledge regarding the purpose of waiver, then (b) identifies the relevant legal standards, (c) discusses how they are used to identify relevant clinical information, and (d) identifies how that information is used to address the legal standards.

Historical Purposes for Waiver of Jurisdiction

All but a few states provide for upward waiver (Heilbrun et al. 1997; Torbet et al. 1996). Virtually all states also have legal mechanisms whereby youths' charges for certain offenses at certain ages may or must be filed automatically in criminal court (without a juvenile court hearing). About one-half of those states allow for reverse waiver (Torbet et al. 1996).

Historically there have been several reasons for the juvenile court's interest in upward waiver for some juvenile offenders. First, the juvenile justice system exists in part to reform and rehabilitate delinquent youths. In cases in which there is little prospect for rehabilitation, the state has an interest in avoiding the use of scarce rehabilitation resources. This does not mean that the state can avoid its obligation by maintaining inadequate rehabilitation services, thus rendering some youths "untreatable" merely because the state will not provide a service that might rehabilitate them (e.g., see Mulvey 1984). The state also has an obligation to develop services for youths whose needs exceed the juvenile system's current capacities. But historically, waiver has been accepted as a legal mechanism for avoiding the use of resources when even the availability of the most likely mode of treatment for a given youth would be unlikely to result in rehabilitation.

Second, the juvenile justice system is responsible for the welfare of youths in its custody. One historical purpose of waiver was to avoid the inclusion of youths whose hardened criminality and potential dangerousness might detract from the rehabilitative efforts of programs that were intended to benefit youths in long-term juvenile facilities.

Third, the juvenile justice system is responsible for protecting the public. In most states, the juvenile justice system must release youths in their custody when they reach a certain maximum age; this varies from state to state, but tends to be sixteen to twenty-one, depending on laws pertaining to particular offenses. Law therefore allows juvenile courts to waive jurisdiction over juveniles for whom rehabilitation by the time of required release is considered unlikely (e.g., due to the youth's anticipated intractability), thereby potentially threatening public safety at the time of mandatory release. Of concern also is that youths who present a high risk of violence may run away from juvenile facilities, thereby presenting a threat to the community.

Identifying the Relevant Legal Standards

Many states have two levels of legal standards for waiver of jurisdiction. The first is a set of threshold fact conditions that must be met before going further. For example, often the youth must be of a certain age, charged with a certain level of offense, and/or have a specific history of prior offenses (e.g., has a prior juvenile conviction that resulted in a commitment to the state's youth commission). If those threshold matters are met, then courts in most states (Heilbrun et al. 1997) are asked to apply one or both of two standards that we will label "danger to others" and "amenability to rehabilitation." We will proceed with the presumption that both are relevant, although some states employ only one or the other.

The "danger to others" standard requires that youths cannot be waived to criminal court unless they present a serious risk of harm to others. The same standard generally would be applied in reverse waiver (requiring that the youth not present a serious risk of harm if the waiver were approved). Most states' statutes do not define the standard beyond a brief phrase that identifies it, such as "protection of the community," "danger to public," or "public safety" (Grisso, Tomkins, and Casey 1988). Sometimes statutes will include modifiers to indicate the degree of danger that must exist (e.g., significant, substantial, imminent).

The judge's task in addressing this standard is a good deal more complex than the various "danger to others" phrases imply. For example, courts often must consider the prospects of harm to others in a variety of possible contexts (Grisso 1998):

> Are other youths or staff in juvenile facilities in danger?
> What is the likelihood of escape from a juvenile facility, and of harm to others in that circumstance?
> Is the youth likely to continue to be a danger to the public when he or she must be released several years from now?

The answers to these questions might not all be the same. It follows that the examiner's task is not merely to determine whether the youth will be a "danger to others," but whether the youth is likely to present a danger in a number of different social and situational contexts that may be relevant for the waiver decision.

The "amenability to rehabilitation" standard allows the court to waive jurisdiction and remand the youth for criminal court trial only if the youth is found to be not amenable to rehabilitation within the resources of the juvenile court (e.g., *Kent v. U.S.,* 383 U.S. 541 [1966]). This standard appears in various forms in different states, including such phrases as "cannot be rehabilitated" or "is not a fit and proper subject" for juvenile custody (Grisso, Tomkins, and Casey 1988). For upward waiver, the question is not whether the youth is *more* likely to be rehabilitated in the criminal or juvenile system, but merely whether rehabilitation in the juvenile system is possible. In general, statutes regarding reverse waiver by criminal courts are not as specific as statutes regarding upward waiver concerning the amenability standards that apply.

It is important to note that the "amenability to rehabilitation" standard, as stated in most states, does not ask simply whether the youth's conduct can be modified. It asks whether it can be modified *within the resources available to the juvenile court.* Thus the amenability question is not answered merely by evaluation of the characteristics of a youth, or whether the youth is "malleable." The question also requires matching those characteristics with the options available for rehabilitation. When examiners are well aware of those options in the juvenile justice system for which they are providing evaluations, a comparison of the youth's needs to the rehabilitation options may be provided by the evaluation. (This is sometimes one of the most important roles of the evaluation, because judges often are not aware of the range of options within the juvenile justice and mental health systems in their own jurisdiction.) When clinicians don't know what resources are available, their role is to describe what the youth needs and to let others in the legal system obtain from other sources (e.g., probation officers, other mental health professionals) the information needed to identify whether there are appropriate rehabilitation services to meet those needs.

The resources available to the juvenile court are not necessarily confined to the state's existing probation programs, rehabilitation facilities, or mental health facilities run by the local juvenile justice or mental health systems. Were this so, some youths would be considered unamenable to rehabilitation (and therefore would be waived to criminal court) simply because the system was unwilling or unable to provide rehabilitation services that might be helpful for their particular psychological problems or mental disorders (e.g., see Mulvey 1984). In many states, therefore, the absence of appropriate rehabilitation programs for youths with behavior problems is not a permissible basis for finding the youth unamenable. If there is a reasonable prospect for a youth's rehabilitation with services that are not available within those states' juvenile justice or mental health systems, courts typically are required to arrange for the youth to receive those services, even if this means contracting with other states to provide them.

In addition, the question is not whether the youth could *ever* change, but whether rehabilitation efforts are likely to be effective *within the period of time* that the juvenile justice system would be authorized to have custody of the youth. The amenability-to-rehabilitation standard, therefore, requires a consideration of (a) the characteristics of the youth,

(b) the state's rehabilitation methods, and (c) the time available to accomplish rehabilitation.

It is worth noting that the danger-to-others and amenability-to-rehabilitation questions are closely related in practice. Current risk of violence can influence the course of rehabilitation, potentially increasing or decreasing the likelihood of a successful outcome. In turn, estimates of longer-range future risk of harm to others must include a judgment about the likelihood that future rehabilitative efforts will reduce the risk. Both standards exist because of a concern for risk of harm to the public; judgments about one are often (although not always) related to judgments about the other.

Identifying Legally Relevant Clinical Information

Given a knowledge of these standards, forensic examiners must determine what types of clinical information about youths will be relevant to address the questions posed by the legal standards. To do this, examiners should go to their specialized body of professional knowledge, especially relevant research, to determine what factors are known to be related to the likelihood of future violence by youths, or the likelihood of their successful rehabilitation, within the social contexts to which the standards refer. Finding how the youth stands on these factors, then, becomes the objective of the examination, and the examiner chooses methods for the evaluation (e.g., psychological testing, interview procedures, information from collateral sources) based specifically on their value for obtaining information on those factors.

Sometimes the law offers factors that courts are required to weigh when making the waiver decision. In *Kent v. U.S* (1966), for example, the U.S. Supreme Court recommended a set of eight factors, and in some states they have been incorporated into the guiding statutes or case law.

Examiners sometimes believe that they must use these legal factors as their own guide for their evaluations. Such factors should not be ignored, but generally these legal criteria are a poor guide for the examiner. The *Kent* factors are instructive in this regard. Some of them—for example, whether the case has prosecutorial merit, or the desirability of trial in criminal court because the case involved adult associates—may be important for judges, but they are not essentially clinical and they are meaningless for answering the clinical question of danger to others or amenability to rehabilitation. Other *Kent* factors, such as "previous history of the youth," are so general that they provide no guidance for examiners at all.

Therefore, by and large, examiners should look to the body of knowledge about which they are experts—scientific and clinical knowledge—for the factors that they will use to address the questions posed by the legal standards. The third and fourth sections of this chapter will review those factors, as well as examiners' methods for collecting information on them for youths who are being evaluated.

Using Clinical Information to Address the Legal Standards

Upon concluding their evaluations and arriving at opinions relevant to the questions of danger to others and amenability to rehabilitation, examiners should be able to clearly explain how they arrived at those opinions. This means showing what information from the evaluation was relevant, and what logic was used to move from the information to the clinical opinion. Courts and attorneys should always ask examiners to do this.

There is a difference between an opinion *related* to the legal standard (e.g., danger to others) and an opinion that the legal standard has been met or what the legal decision about waiver ought to be. The legal decision requires a judgment that the total weight of the relevant evidence in the case is sufficient to sustain the legal decision. Clinicians, of course, neither weigh nor ordinarily have access to all the evidence presented in a case. Moreover, as discussed later (e.g., see section titled "Assessing Danger to Others"), the best that clinicians currently can do, given the state of clinical knowledge in this area, is to provide an opinion about the *estimated likelihood* that a youth will engage in a violent behavior in the future, or that rehabilitation progress can be made with the youth. Clinicians often may be confident about that *estimate* (e.g., "I am certain that this is not a low-risk case"), but it is a rare case in which our current state of knowledge warrants a confident opinion that the youth *will* engage in violent behavior in the future.

Based on these observations, some authoritative texts on clinical forensic evaluations argue that forensic examiners should not be asked or expected to form an opinion about the legal decision itself (e.g., Grisso 1986, 1998; Melton et al. 1997). Their proper role is to form and explain clinical opinions *related* to the legal standards that apply. For example, they may describe various characteristics of the youth that they believe increase or decrease the risk of future violence, and they may decide that the risk of future violence is relatively high. But these beliefs do not constitute opinions that the legal standard has been met (e.g., "He is a danger to the public") and do not constitute a recommendation concerning the legal disposition of the case (whether the youth should or should not be waived, which depends not only on "danger to the public," but several other things, including probable cause to believe that the offense may have been committed). Once the clinician has offered an opinion about the degree of risk that the case poses, it is the job of the judge to determine whether that level of risk is sufficient to meet the legal requirements for a conclusion that the youth "is dangerous," or "should be waived to criminal court."

This argument notwithstanding, there is evidence that in other areas of forensic assessment (e.g., competence to stand trial, and questions related to the insanity defense), a majority of forensic examiners are not reluctant to express an opinion concerning whether the case satisfies the particular legal standard and/or how the case should be decided (Borum and Grisso 1996). This may also be true for examiners' assessments in waiver cases, although data are not available to inform us.

Before discussing how these objectives should be accomplished, it will be helpful to consider the contexts in which clinical forensic evaluations for waiver of jurisdiction are performed, and what is known about the current practice of examiners in this area.

2. Current Practice in Performing Waiver Evaluations
What Cases Are Referred for Waiver Evaluations?

The literature on judicial waiver of jurisdiction offers no review regarding the prevalence of referral of waiver cases for forensic evaluation. Some states' require by statute or local policy that the court must order forensic evaluations in all such cases, while no formal policies exist in other states. Moreover, referral patterns are likely to be different among courts within a given state based on differences in discretionary practice among judges. Defense attorneys often obtain such evaluations (either with private funds or through assistance to indigent defendants), but the frequency with which this occurs has not been documented.

Similarly, no statistics have been published on the types of youths for whom waiver evaluations are more or less likely to be requested. By inference (based on statutory criteria controlling who may be waived to criminal court), most youths who are evaluated in waiver cases will be between twelve and seventeen years of age and will have been charged with relatively serious offenses, and they will tend to have past records of delinquency adjudications or commitments to youth correction services. Based on offense statistics, those youths are far more likely to be males than females, and more likely to be ethnic/cultural minority youths than to be non-Hispanic white youths; but whether females or cultural minority youths are disproportionately referred (or not referred) for such evaluations is not known.

In jurisdictions in which referral for evaluation is discretionary, one might expect that the likelihood of referral for forensic evaluations would be greater for youths who are younger, who have a past history of mental or emotional disturbances, and/or who are charged with a very serious offense in the absence of past involvement with the juvenile justice system. But this conjecture is based solely on the logic that such cases are likely to produce greater uncertainty among courts or attorneys about the appropriateness of waiver, not on the basis of any known statistical evidence. It is equally plausible that in some jurisdictions, referrals are related simply to seriousness of offense because higher stakes (more severe potential dispositions) might cause attorneys to more vigorously pursue every avenue in challenging waiver.

Who Performs Waiver Evaluations?

Evaluations for waiver-of-jurisdiction cases typically are performed by psychiatrists or doctoral-level clinical psychologists with specialized knowledge of juvenile justice issues, delinquency, and adolescent mental health and development. Sometimes psychiatrists and psychologists in *general* child clinical practice accept the task of performing these evaluations without sufficient knowledge of the legal standards and forensic objectives of the evaluation. They should be required to know them if they are to be qualified as experts to provide opinions related to legal standards.

At other times, *forensic* psychiatrists and psychologists who have little or no training or experience in *child* psychiatry or *child* clinical psychology will perform the evaluations simply because they are familiar with the legal questions and experienced generally in performing evaluations for courts. These examiners should be aware that performing evaluations of adolescents without specialized training or experience in the diagnosis and evaluation of children may violate ethical standards for the practice of psychiatry or clinical psychology (e.g., see standard 1.04, American Psychological Association 1992; also Committee on Ethical Guidelines for Forensic Psychologists 1991). Attorneys who cross-examine them should challenge their qualifications, and judges should be prepared to disqualify them if they do not manifest both child specialization and adequate familiarity with the specific legal and forensic issues in waiver cases. Juvenile justice systems that provide inadequate financial compensation for forensic examiners, and systems that have not established clear standards to be met by professionals who are contracted for evaluation services, are creating conditions for substandard practice and receipt of inferior clinical forensic services.

Waiver-of-jurisdiction evaluations sometimes are performed by examiners who are full-time employees in clinical evaluation services within the juvenile court, or they may be private practitioners who are contracted by juvenile courts or who perform evaluations at the request of prosecuting or defense attorneys (Grisso 1998). Whether these various arrangements make a difference in the quality of evaluations or their professional conclusions about factors related to the waiver question is not known empirically. Professional standards recognize no difference in the way that examiners should perform forensic evaluations under these various arrangements, other than attention to differences related to confidentiality and privilege.

How Are Waiver Evaluations Typically Performed?

No studies have examined the nature and quality of waiver evaluations as they are performed in everyday practice. In fact, only a few professional articles have even discussed evaluations for waiver of jurisdiction (e.g., Barnum 1987; Kruh and Brodsky 1997; Mulvey 1984; Witt and Dyer 1997), and until recently (Grisso 1998), no professional literature offered any coherent or systematic model for performing evaluations in waiver-of-jurisdiction cases. What is probably the leading textbook in forensic child psychiatry (Schetky and Benedek 1992) offers one paragraph on conducting waiver evaluations. A similar book published by the American Psychiatric Association (Kalogerakis 1992) devotes only two pages to the process of waiver evaluations. The leading text in forensic psychology evaluations (Melton et al. 1997) offers only a discussion of the concept of amenability to rehabilitation and a sample report of an evaluation for waiver of juvenile court jurisdiction. The most recent major handbook of forensic psychology, Hess and Weiner's (1999) second edition, offers no description of waiver evaluations. (More specifically, it offers no chapter on evaluations in delinquency cases, and the terms "delinquency" and "juveniles" do not even appear in the book's subject index.)

These observations are truly astonishing. Clinicians have been performing evaluations for waiver of jurisdiction for almost one hundred years, having been an integral part of professional staff in juvenile courts since they began in 1899 (Melton et al. 1997). The extent of neglect in the development of standards in this area of clinical forensic evaluation can be appreciated by recognizing the vast literature that has evolved to assist clinicians in other forensic evaluations. Hundreds of professional journal articles, and scores of books, have described and scrutinized the finest points of law and forensic clinical practice for the evaluation of adult defendants' competence to stand trial, criminal responsibility, and risk of violence, as well as child custody evaluations and the assessment of abuse and neglect of children (see, generally, Melton et al. 1997). Seen in this light, and given the large volume of waiver evaluations in most urban courts (although, again, the literature offers us no empirical verification of their frequency), the dearth of information in the literature about any aspect of evaluations in waiver-of-jurisdiction cases is inexplicable.

In the absence of any data regarding either the accepted standard of practice or clinicians' actual practice when performing these evaluations, the following description of proper evaluations for waiver-of-jurisdiction cases must be seen as the author's own perspective. That perspective, however, is guided by well-established standards of practice for performing all types of forensic evaluations in clinical forensic psychology and psychiatry (e.g., see Melton et al. 1997, and Committee on Ethical Guidelines for Forensic Psychologists 1991), as well as empirical evidence (cited later) regarding factors that are related to the risk of violence in adolescents and the prospects for rehabilitation of youthful offenders. The discussion is offered in two sections, one for danger to others and the other for amenability to rehabilitation. Greater detail is provided in three chapters of a recent book by the author, *Forensic Evaluation of Juveniles* (Grisso 1998).

3. Assessing Danger to Others

It has long been known that clinical predictions of future violence have serious limitations in accuracy, even when they are performed to the best of our scientific and clinical abilities (Monahan 1981). Most of the evidence for this assertion comes from research on predicting violence among adults in criminal and mentally ill populations. Our abilities to do so with adolescents cannot be expected to be any better than with adults, and more likely they will not be as good, in light of the fact that youths are a "moving target" for the examiner. Adolescents are in transition, in contrast to adults, whose characteristics tend to be more stable over time. Clinical diagnosis and estimates of youths' future behavior are frustrated by the fact that data about a youth's current characteristics, collected at one point in time, may become increasingly out of date as the youth continues to develop and manifest change in his or her personality and abilities (Mash and Barkley 1996). Thus accepted information about the limits of our abilities to assess future violence derived from studies of adults is likely to be applicable to assessments of youths as well.

In that literature, clinicians are urged to follow certain principles to assure that errors in their judgments about future violence are reduced to the minimum allowed by our current state of knowledge in the field.

Those principles are examined in the following discussion, followed by a review of issues raised by limitations in applying the principles in the assessment of youths specifically, and then with a description of assessment factors and methods that examiners can use for this assessment task.

General Principles

When assessing the potential for an individual's future danger to others, several principles that have been developed in the general area of prediction of violence should be followed. (For summaries offering and supporting these principles, see Borum, Swartz, and Swanson 1996; Melton et al. 1997; Monahan 1981; Quinsey et al. 1998).

Using risk factors. First, clinicians should employ a set of risk factors that are known to have some relation to future violence among persons who are in the same general class (e.g., delinquent adolescents) as the individual being assessed. Risk factors may be static variables that, once identified, do not change (e.g., age at first arrest). Others must be assessed periodically because they represent variables that may change (e.g., current age, psychological measures of personality variables). Research has now provided considerable information regarding developmental, psychological, and situational factors that are correlated with future harmful behavior, and those factors are reviewed later in this chapter.

This does not mean, however, that the use of these factors will necessarily or reliably produce accurate predictions. Ideally, past research would have identified ways to weight and combine those risk factors in a way that would show what percentage of persons with factor characteristics like the person being examined actually engaged in violent behavior subsequent to their classification on the factors. Scientific progress recently has begun to achieve that objective for estimating the risk of violence among adults in mental health and forensic populations (e.g., Hare 1991; Hart, Cox, and Hare 1995; Quinsey et al. 1998; Webster et al. 1994). Unfortunately, research has not reached that level for purposes of predicting future violence among youths. For the time being, the best that clinicians can do is to make sure that they are attending to those factors that are known to have some *relation* to future violence, even though we do not yet have scientific guidance concerning how to combine those factors to make *predictive* statements. What factors to use will be discussed later.

Making comparative risk estimates. Second, examiners should aim to provide *comparative risk estimates,* not absolute and dichotomous predictions of violent behavior. Research and clinical experience has shown that when clinicians try to answer the question as though its answer were di-chotomous—that the individual "will" or "will not" engage in a violent behavior in the future—their predictions that an individual will engage in such behavior are more often wrong than right (Monahan 1981). This is because only a very small fraction of offenders has more than a 50 per-cent likelihood of engaging in a violent behavior in a one-year period.

In light of this, as well as the knowledge that the base rate for violence in the general population is well below 5 percent (Swanson et al. 1990), individuals who might fall in groups with only a 30 to 40 percent chance of future violence can nevertheless be considered high risk. This type of reasoning has led experts to advise clinicians to think in terms of *esti-mates* of the *degree* of risk of future violence. For some populations, cli-nicians can offer the base rate for the risk-factor group to which the in-dividual belongs, which can also be described as "high," "moderate," or "low" in *comparison* to others in the relevant, identified population.

Making conditional risk estimates. Third, examiners are now advised to think of their risk estimates as *conditional* with regard to future situa-tional contexts. This simply means that they should recognize that the likelihood of future violence is not merely a product of an individual's characteristics. It also depends on the situations and settings (conditions) in which individuals will find themselves in the future (Borum, Swartz, and Swanson 1996). For example, a particular youth with tendencies to-ward aggressive acts may be much more likely to engage in them if he is at home with inadequate parental monitoring than in the structure of a juvenile justice residential facility. Examiners should take these possibili-ties into account, and they should make risk estimates that identify the situational contexts for which the estimates are being made.

As a consequence, most cases call for more than one risk estimate— for example, an opinion about the level of risk if the youth returns home, another if the youth is sent to a secure rehabilitation program, and yet others depending on the range of placement options available (Grisso 1998). Similarly, it may be necessary to offer more than one risk estimate when a court is concerned with both immediate risks (e.g., while in cor-rectional custody during the next year) and long-range risks (e.g., were the youth to be released from custody after a year or two of rehabilitative activities). These risk estimates often are not the same.

Defining the criterion behavior. Finally, it is important to identify the type of behavior for which one is making risk estimates (Monahan 1981). Courts may be concerned with a wide range of future behaviors of youths in various delinquency proceedings, ranging from "delinquent behavior" in general to crimes committed in particular ways (e.g., with weapons). Statutes pertaining specifically to waiver of jurisdiction sometimes pro-vide no definition of the type of future behaviors to be considered in estimates of future risk of violence, often using phrases such as "harm to others" or "danger to the public" (Grisso, Tomkins, and Casey 1988). It is most likely, however, that the harm to which these phrases refer is more specific than delinquency in general, referring to behaviors that have the potential to inflict physical injury on others. The latter type of behaviors is a frequent criterion in research on the relation between risk factors and future violent behavior. Clinicians should make clear to courts that this behavior, not delinquency in general, is the focus of their risk estimates.

Limitations of Clinical Information about Future Violence

If clinicians do not have the means to combine their risk factors in ways that are empirically demonstrated to predict future violence, they cannot verify the accuracy of their conclusions about the likelihood of future violence. Might it not be argued, therefore, that their opinions on those matters pertaining to youths' future behaviors should not even be admitted as evidence in waiver cases?

This argument has been made time and again for the past three decades in reference to clinicians' estimates of future violence in adult criminal cases, both in the courts (e.g., *Barefoot v. Estelle,* 463 U.S. 880 [1983]) and in professional literature (e.g., Ennis and Litwack 1974; for reviews of the debate, see Monahan 1981 and Melton et al. 1997). The U.S. Supreme Court has consistently affirmed, in capital sentencing cases *(Barefoot v. Estelle)* and in reference to danger as a basis for the detention of juveniles *(Schall v. Martin,* 467 U.S. 253 [1984]), that the fact that assessments of future violence may often be incorrect does not mean that they should be barred from use by the courts. Litwack and Schlesinger (1999) have noted that in addition to judicial acceptance, there are many other clinical and scientific justifications for clinicians' testimony to the courts about risk of future violence: for example, that even if clinicians do not know the validity of their predictions, they do have empirically validated risk factors that provide valuable guidance to the courts; and that it is likely that clinicians are better able than laypersons to analyze and explain the factors that courts should take into consideration in weighing the risk of future violence. Moreover, when they systematically apply risk factors, clinicians are likely to arrive at somewhat better estimates of future violence than judges (e.g., see Fagan and Guggenheim 1996 concerning the questionable validity of judicial decisions about youths' potential for future violence).

This does not mean that clinicians should be given absolute free reign in their use of risk factors, nor that their estimates should be given automatic deference in reaching judicial decisions. To the contrary, professional standards (reinforced by good cross-examination) should require that clinicians clearly inform courts of the limits of their testimony. Let us examine some of those limits.

Limits of comparative estimates. Currently clinicians do not have available to them the base rates of future violence by youths associated with the combined value of the risk factors to be described later in this review. They know only that those risk factors, individually, each bear a reliable relation to future violence. Consequently, they have no factual basis for expressing their opinions about future violence in percentage base rates (e.g., "Based on the risk factors, this youth is in a group with a 37 percent likelihood of engaging in X type of violent behavior"). In evaluating youths' likelihood of future violence, the best that clinicians can do is to consider the youth's status on the various risk factors, to compare that status to cases that they have encountered in their experience in evaluating delinquent youths, and to express the degree of risk for this youth as high, low, or about average for youths who come before the court.

This approach, while it may be helpful to the courts, is not without its problems. For example, examiners with minimal experience in juvenile justice settings may not have developed a sense of the "average" among juvenile justice youths to which their present case is being compared. Moreover, inherent in this approach is the possibility that youths in a jurisdiction with less frequent violence among youths may be held to a different standard, appearing to be high risk relative to their peers while they might have been considered only moderate risk if they were being compared to the average for youths in some other geographic area. Therefore, it is important for clinicians to inform the courts that their opinions are based on experience, judgment, and empirically derived risk factors, but not on empirically verifiable base rates. Courts can then weigh the value of the clinician's opinion, based on what the court knows about the clinician's qualifications and the procedures that were employed to obtain the relevant data.

Limits of conditional estimates. We noted earlier that clinicians should attempt to make estimates of risk of violence that take into account future conditions that may inhibit or enhance the probability of violence for a given youth. One of the serious limitations in doing this pertains to the period of time for which the estimate is being made—e.g., whether it is the relatively near future or the distant future.

Long-range predictions require a consideration of the situations that a person might face in the distant future, which is far less clinically predictable on the basis of a current evaluation than are the prospects for the individual's situational contexts during the next six to twelve months. Moreover, the psychological status of an adolescent at the time of an evaluation may reasonably be expected to represent the adolescent's status during the following year. But normal development and other changes in the youth's life will make the current psychological picture of the youth less accurate as an indicator of the youth's status two or three years after the evaluation.

Estimates about the likelihood of violence two or more years beyond the clinician's evaluation, therefore, typically cannot take situational factors and changes in individual characteristics of the youth sufficiently into account, and many clinicians simply will not offer their estimates of degree of risk beyond the following year or two. Clinicians who venture such opinions should be held accountable to explain how they have arrived at their estimate, and to justify their opinion in light of the fact that very long-range estimates of risk (more than a few years) of violence are almost uniformly discouraged by the professional literature (e.g., Monahan 1981; Melton et al. 1997).

Limits Related to Gender and Race

The following discussion of risk factors related to future violence of youths is based on a large volume of research on delinquent and nondelinquent adolescents. Typically, however, studies have either employed male youths exclusively or have included only very small female samples. Thus in most cases we are far less sure that the risk factors bear a relation to future violence among girls than among boys. Moreover, the few studies that have employed female adolescent samples have produced inconsistent conclusions. Some have found that certain risk factors for adolescent violence among boys—for example, being identified as aggressive in the primary-school years—apply equally to girls, while other studies have found that the same variable bears no relation to the likelihood of violence in adolescent girls (Hawkins et al. 1998). Therefore, our ability to make meaningful estimates of the likelihood of girls' future violence is highly questionable. Clinicians must so inform the courts in such cases; only clinicians who have had substantial experience in evaluating delinquent girls should venture to form opinions about their potential for future violence.

Similarly, it is not clear that risk factors typically employed in clinical evaluations of juveniles for estimates of future violence are equally applicable to African American, Hispanic, Asian, and non-Hispanic white youths. Many studies examining risk factors among delinquent youths have employed samples in which a majority of the subjects were youths of ethnic and cultural minorities (Hawkins et al. 1998), especially African American youths. This might suggest the generalizability of the results to minority youths, but we are not sure because results typically have not been calculated separately for various ethnic/cultural subsamples. Special care should be taken, however, when applying current risk factors to Hispanic and Asian youths, because they have been represented in relatively small numbers in most studies of factors related to future violence. It is possible that differences between various ethnic/cultural groups in socio-economic characteristics, family structures, and peer relations may co-vary with risk factors for violence. If so, certain risk factors might be of greater or lesser significance for different ethnic/cultural subgroups of youths.

Risk Factors

Recent years have seen the emergence of a significant amount of research on risk factors for delinquency and future violence among adolescents, many of the studies being comprehensive and longitudinal in design. These studies, far too numerous to cite, have been reviewed by others (see Loeber and Farrington 1998, as well as Howell et al. 1995, for the most recent comprehensive reviews.)

In this research literature, the factors below have been shown with some consistency to be related to adolescents' future violence. The ex-aminer's task is to collect information about a youth on these factors, and to increase or decrease the estimate of future risk based on the strength and numbers of factors that apply for the youth in question. These risk factors and their interpretation are reviewed in greater detail elsewhere (Grisso 1998). Other lists of risk factors applicable to adolescents can be found in the literature (e.g., see Hawkins et al. 1998; Lipsey and Derzon 1998; Wiebush et al. 1995; Witt and Dyer 1997), and most of them mani-fest considerable similarities. Readers should note that the following list does not apply to the assessment of youths charged with sex offenses; a somewhat different set of factors are applicable in estimating the risk of future sex offending (e.g., see Barbaree, Hudson, and Seto 1993; Groth and Loredo 1981; Ross and Loss 1991; Weinrott 1996).

Past aggressive behavior. Examiners should identify the frequency and chronicity of youths' past aggressive behaviors. This should include not only behaviors that have been reported officially to juvenile courts in the past, but also aggressive patterns of behavior that have not been reported or that made their appearance in childhood. There is substantial evidence that delinquent adolescents whose aggressive and destructive behavior tendencies began in the preschool and elementary school years have a greater likelihood of continuing their aggression beyond adolescence, while youths whose aggressive behaviors did not appear until the ado-lescent years are less likely to manifest it as they enter early adulthood (Elliott 1994; Moffitt 1993).

It is well to keep in mind that most delinquent adolescents do not persist in delinquency (or violent behaviors) past the adolescent years. Ways to distinguish those who are likely to persist from those who are not are beginning to emerge (Moffitt 1993; Loeber and Farrington 1998). Consistent with the "conditional" principles of risk assessment, it is also important to learn the types of situations in which a youth has or has not engaged in violent behaviors in the past.

Substance use. Frequent use of drugs and/or alcohol increases the risk of violent behaviors. The effects may be direct in terms of lowering inhibitions and impairing judgment, or indirect in that obtaining drugs may require being in social contexts where violence is more likely to occur.

Peer and community factors. Past associations with gangs that have violent histories increases the risk of future violence, especially when there is reason to believe that the youth would return to gang involvement when in the community in the future. Gang association also increases the likelihood that youths will have significant amounts of unstructured time in neighborhoods with high violence base rates.

Family conflict and aggression. Studies have consistently shown an increased risk of violence by youths who have been the victims of family conflict and abuse in childhood, seen aggression modeled in family life throughout their childhood, and/or come from families who themselves have criminal lifestyles.

Social stressors and supports. To the extent that they can be anticipated, pending events that may place stress on the youth (e.g., upcoming divorces, a dying family member) may increase the risk of aggressive response to everyday events. Similarly, an assessment for risk of aggression should take into consideration the possible mitigating effects of positive social supports that the youth might have.

Personality traits. A variety of personality characteristics have been associated with an increase in the risk of future violence, including chronic anger, impulsivity, and an attitude toward others that manifests a lack of empathy or concern. While virtually no personality factors have been shown to be accurately predictive of future violence, some bear such consistent and significant relations to future violence—for example, callousness and lack of empathy typically associated with psychopathy (Hare 1991)—that failure to include them in the evaluation would be professionally negligent.

Youths, however, may show characteristics typically associated with psychopathy for many different reasons. Sometimes they are part of transitional phases of development, and are unlikely to persist. For example, most adolescents pass through a phase of development during which they manifest "egocentric" thinking, including a temporary one-sided focus on their own concerns rather than those of others and a general insensitivity to the way that others might see or experience the world (Elkind 1967; Keating 1990). Examiners are responsible for distinguishing between temporary developmental egocentrism and the more enduring lack of empathy that is a part of the construct of psychopathy. Similarly, youths who display none of the signs of remorse are not necessarily incapable of feeling guilt (for example, youths who are reacting to traumatization by temporarily suppressing their emotions). And, of course, the mere fact that a youth displays all of the signs of contrition does not necessarily mean that the youth is capable of empathy or feelings of guilt. Currently there is no empirical evidence that judges, attorneys, or clinicians can reliably determine whether or not youths feel underlying guilt or remorse.

Mental disorders. Data on the prevalence of violence among youths with mental disorders is quite incomplete. Nevertheless, the presence of some disorders does at least slightly elevate the risk of future violence for youths who have been violent in the past (Mash and Barkley 1996). Among these are affective disorders (e.g., depression), attention disorders, disorders related to trauma, and certain disorders involving neurological impairment.

Opportunity. The presence or absence of factors external to the youth that make violence more or less likely are important to consider. For example, the presence of guns in the home increases the risk of violence, while the unavailability of a person who has been the persistent object of a youth's anger (e.g., a father who has left the home) may reduce future risk.

Resiliency factors. Research is beginning to identify factors that help to distinguish why some youths from high-risk backgrounds (e.g., whose families were transient, poor, and abusive) do not conform to the odds, having manifested low rates of delinquency and aggression. For example, Smith et al. (1995) found that they were more likely to be committed to school, did well in school, intended to continue their education, were well attached to their parents, and associated with conventional peers of whom their parents approved.

Risk Assessment Methods

Examiners determine for themselves what methods to employ in order to obtain information on these factors for youths whom they evaluate. There is no standard interview schedule or battery of tests for this task. While several checklists for use in assessing risk of violence among youths have been developed (Wiebush et al. 1995), they simply allow clinicians to summarize information that they have obtained by other methods rather than offering procedures for collecting the necessary information on the factors.

Clinicians have a wealth of methods for obtaining information on violence risk factors, far too extensive to review here. Grisso (1998) discusses such methods in detail. In brief, the heart of the data collection procedure is extensive interviewing of the youth, but this must be supplemented with a complete review of records (e.g., school, delinquency, medical) and interviews with collateral informants (e.g., parents, teachers). Many clinical psychologists, and some psychiatrists, also use psychological tests to assist in collecting information about certain factors, especially relevant mental disorders and personality traits. A considerable number of such tests are available (e.g., the *Minnesota Multiphasic Personality Inventory—Adolescents:* Butcher et al. 1992; *Child Behavior Checklist:* Achenbach 1991). Many of them have norms for delinquent and nondelinquent adolescents, and research with some of the instruments has produced the empirical links that are needed to relate scores on the instruments to the risk factors described earlier (see Grisso 1998; Hoge and Andrews 1996).

As with all assessment methods, psychological test data do not produce conclusions by themselves. Scores must be interpreted, and their value is no better than the abilities of the clinician who is interpreting them. For example, an otherwise "valid" indicator on a particular test may be invalid when applied to youths who were not represented in the validating studies (e.g., to African American youths when they were not included in research relating the test scores to likelihood of aggression). Similarly, the *Hare Psychopathy Checklist* (Hare 1991), which has been very successful in identifying adults who have enduring traits of callousness and disregard for others, has recently been used to identify youths who are high on these same traits (e.g., Brandt et al. 1997; Forth, Hart, and Hare 1990; Frick et al. 1994). Yet interpreting youths' high scores as representing enduring "psychopathic personality traits" (as might be appropriate in adult cases) is not yet supported, because current research has yet to determine whether or not youths who score high on this test retain those traits as adults.

4. Assessing Amenability to Rehabilitation

Like the phrase "danger to others," "amenability to rehabilitation" does not communicate very well the nature of the issue it represents. For example, the phrase suggests that youths themselves either are or are not amenable to attempts to change their behavior. If we accepted this presumption, examiners would focus their evaluations entirely on the characteristics of the youth. Having done so, they would have misread the meaning of the concept as it applies to waiver-of-jurisdiction cases. The following are some definitions suggesting what the law wants to know when it asks clinicians about amenability to rehabilitation.

General Definitions of the Task

First, recall from the earlier discussion of legal standards for waiver of jurisdiction that courts are required to consider whether the youth is "amenable to rehabilitation within the resources of the juvenile court." For the examiner, this translates into the task of *matching a youth with the rehabilitation options that are possible* and, given the best match, forming *an opinion about its likelihood of success.* This perspective has many implications for the evaluation (some of which will be discussed later), among them that the examiner cannot possibly perform the evaluation without a thorough knowledge of the specific rehabilitation programs and resources that are available to the specific court in which the waiver-of-jurisdiction case is being heard.

Second, an opinion about the likelihood of success requires *a definition of successful rehabilitation.* Most state statutes do not provide a definition, and many judges do not express their own thoughts on the matter. Nevertheless, because examiners cannot form the requisite opinions without it, they must know their own definition and communicate it clearly to the court. One possible definition is to consider rehabilitation efforts "successful" when they produce *a substantial reduction in the likelihood of recidivism or of serious harm to others in the future* (that is, during the remainder of adolescence and early adulthood). This definition is consistent with the primary objective of the juvenile justice system, and it links the amenability concept to the danger-to-others standard. When clinicians employ such a definition, they must describe it clearly to the court, which will decide the definition's appropriateness from a legal perspective.

Third, examiners should recognize that unlike other clinical situations, rehabilitation in the juvenile justice system must be successful within a specified period of time. The maximum jurisdictional age for youth authority custody ranges from fifteen to eighteen in various states, but may reach twenty-one or twenty-five in some states under special circumstances allowing for extensions or for special sentences for certain offenses. It is quite common for youths who are less than a year away from the maximum juvenile jurisdictional age to be considered nonamenable to rehabilitation, not because they are not "treatable" given programs in the juvenile justice system, but because the youth cannot be held in the custody of the system long enough for the rehabilitative efforts to be successful. Examiners' opinions about amenability, therefore, invariably must include an estimate of the amount of time that is likely to be needed to achieve a successful outcome.

A Structure for Assessing Amenability to Rehabilitation

There is no single or established way to assess youths' amenability to rehabilitation. The nature of the questions to be addressed, however, suggests an evaluation that aims to describe four things (Grisso 1998): the youth, what needs to change, the optimal rehabilitation plan, and the probable outcome of the implementation of the plan.

Describing the youth. This objective is clinically straightforward. The examiner seeks to develop a meaningful conceptualization of the youth, providing the court with a fundamental behavioral and psychological understanding of the youth and the youth's social circumstances. Clinicians are likely to seek a wide range of clinical information relevant for this part of the task: medical and health history, family and social background, early development, academic and intellectual functioning, delinquent behaviors and legal history, personality description, an explanation of any significant psychopathology, and a description of responses to any past rehabilitation efforts.

The sources of information may be wide-ranging, including extensive interviews with the youth and family, as well as psychological testing and the review of a variety of types of past records. The examiner's model for describing the youth should derive from some theory of personality or delinquency, and might include classification of the youth according to any of a number of typologies and systems for personality description. Idiosyncratic theories without empirical support are unwarranted; the field provides a number of useful theories and typologies devised in extensive research specifically for delinquent youths (e.g., Achenbach 1991; Jesness and Wedge 1984, 1985; Quay 1987).

While the clinician's search for information may be wide-ranging, describing youths to the court requires a more selective process. All information provided in reports to the court should contain *only* information that is relevant for the questions addressed in waiver hearings and for forming clinical opinions about those questions. Providing information that is without value for the task—that is, without logical or empirical relevance to estimates of future violence or amenability to rehabilitation—runs the risk of being simply prejudicial as well as cluttering the description in ways that detract from effective communication.

Describing what needs to change. This part of the process involves the examiner's formulation of a theory about the relation between the foregoing picture of the youth and the youth's delinquency. This theory becomes the logical basis for identifying what aspects of the juvenile and/or family need to change in order to meet the juvenile justice system's objectives (to provide for the welfare of the youth and to promote public safety). What is it about this youth, and this youth's social circumstances, that best explains his or her past offenses, and therefore identifies those things that must change in order to reduce the likelihood of future offending? Examiners have a wide range of theories of delinquency from which to work in fulfilling this part of the task, based on decades of research in developmental psychology, criminology, child clinical psychology, and child psychiatry.

Describing a rehabilitation plan. Having described what needs to change, the examiner's next task involves the selection and description of interventions that make sense. The clinician seeks the best match between available intervention alternatives and the youth's characteristics and rehabilitation needs, as well as the level of security that is suggested by the assessment of risk of harm to others. The best-match interventions may be described according to placement options (e.g., home, residential treatment programs, ranches or boot camps, secure facilities) and according to types of services (e.g., educational services, psychopharmacological services, family therapy, behavior modification). The availability of the recommended placements and services should be identified. As noted earlier, courts in some states are required to purchase services out of state if necessary—that is, if the youth is considered likely to respond to those services and if they are not available within the state.

Recent research has demonstrated the value of some types of rehabilitation programs for delinquent youths in general (e.g., for reviews see Lipsey 1992; Tate, Reppucci, and Mulvey 1995), but unfortunately it has not provided much guidance in matching types of youths with types of rehabilitation programs. The examiner's reasoning about matching must be based primarily on theory, personal clinical experience, and knowledge of how existing rehabilitation programs actually work.

Describing probable outcomes. Finally, the examiner should describe the likelihood that rehabilitation objectives can be met within the time allowed for juvenile justice custody, given the interventions that have been described, the nature of the youth, and the youth's social and legal circumstances.

Courts and clinicians naturally will look to previous rehabilitative efforts with the youth for part of the answer to this question. While that information is certainly relevant, it can also be misleading. Earlier efforts may have been unsuccessful for many reasons other than inherently intractable characteristics of the youth. The youth's current developmental status or social circumstances may be different now than during the earlier intervention. Moreover, a close examination of the actual nature of the earlier rehabilitative efforts may find that they were of such poor quality that they were unlikely to provide rehabilitation for any youth. (For a more detailed description of these possibilities, see Grisso 1998.) In this light, the simple fact that a youth received rehabilitation services at an earlier time says little about the potential value of future interventions. One must also inspect closely the nature of the previous intervention itself and the actual course of the rehabilitative effort.

Estimating the probable outcomes of future rehabilitative efforts requires that the examiner take into consideration factors that have been found to be related to likelihood of change in psychotherapeutic interventions generally, including the individual's capacity to form attachments to caregivers, the individual's degree of psychological discomfort (which can be used to motivate change), and the chronicity of the condition that must be modified (Grisso 1998). Relevant considerations may range from factors borrowed from criminology (e.g., as noted earlier, the fact that youths with certain histories tend not to persist in delinquency past the adolescent years: Moffitt 1993; Loeber and Farrington 1998) to knowledge derived from psychopharmacology regarding the likely response of a youth to a proposed trial on a particular medication.

While we know the range of considerations that may be important to weigh, we have no evidence concerning the accuracy of examiners' estimates about these matters. Moreover, there are many things that examiners cannot anticipate that may eventually produce conditions that interfere with the youth's rehabilitation. For example, a local juvenile rehabilitation program that is working well today may experience insufficient funding or low staff morale sometime in the future. Unexpected stressors may arise in the youth's life. For these reasons, examiners' opinions about probable outcomes are, at best, estimates based on foreseeable circumstances. At present, the degree of trust that the courts should have in examiners' estimates of the likelihood of successful rehabilitation can be judged only by the degree to which the examiner has done a thorough job in the three preceding steps leading to this conclusion.

The Role of Amenability Opinions

While conducting and reporting the results of an assessment of a youth's amenability to rehabilitation, it is worthwhile for the examiner to keep in mind two uses for the evaluation results. One is its use by people responsible for the youth's rehabilitation, and the other is use by the legal decision maker (e.g., the judge).

Concerning the first of these, when courts decide against upward waiver or for downward waiver, examiners' reports frequently become records that accompany the youth to the juvenile rehabilitation programs that form the eventual disposition. If the examiner has done a good job of describing the youth's needs and the appropriate rehabilitation plan, this provides a helpful start for juvenile justice or mental health staff who will work with the youth. The examiner should keep this in mind when communicating the evaluation results to the court, offering enough detail to guide future clinicians yet not so much that it obscures the court's ability to understand the rehabilitation issues or contains prejudicial information in the main context (the court hearing) for which the evaluation was performed.

Concerning the second context, the examiner should recognize that although both the examiner and the judge are weighing the same standard (amenability to rehabilitation), they must reach different types of decisions. Judges will weigh the evidence regarding amenability to rehabilitation, as well as other factors that are not part of formal legal standards but that are nevertheless allowable for judicial consideration. One of these factors is the degree to which the youth, if eventually found guilty of the crime charged, deserves punishment. However that question is answered, it is wholly dependent upon one's notions of justice. As such, it is completely outside the role of the clinician. No clinical examiner should consider (as a factor for amenability) whether the youth deserves to be punished as an adult, and no examiner should testify to the question if asked.

5. The Role and Value of Waiver-of-Jurisdiction Assessments

As noted earlier, it is not known how frequently forensic clinical assessments of youths' danger to others and amenability to rehabilitation are employed in waiver-of-jurisdiction cases, whether upward or reverse. Some communities of which I am aware employ them routinely, while others do not. In my experience in juvenile murder cases in Massachusetts, waiver-of-jurisdiction evaluations have been among the most complex and extensive of any forensic evaluations I have ever performed. In some cases examinations and cross-examinations of my expert testimony have required three to four days on the witness stand. But I am aware of practices in other parts of the country in which examiners in the very same types of cases interview youths for thirty minutes and testify for five to ten minutes. In those jurisdictions, no one is served well—the courts, youths, or the communities in which they live. Assessments for waiver-of-jurisdiction cases serve many purposes that are sufficiently important for policy makers to insist on and provide the resources for adequate evaluations, and for clinicians to meet their obligations to do the job right with the resources that are provided.

First, these evaluations can be instrumental in identifying youths who are likely to desist in their delinquent behaviors as they age out of adolescence, causing society little problem thereafter. Upward waiver of such youths, if it leads to years of prison in the adult criminal justice system, wastes a life and creates an unnecessary and substantial financial cost for society.

Second, these assessments can identify youths who are developing serious mental disorders and who need psychiatric and psychological treatment that they are far less likely to obtain if they are adjudicated in the criminal justice system. For youths whose delinquency is related to their mental disorders, failing to treat the disorder is as foolish for society in the long run as ignoring the advice of one's own doctor.

Third, proper forensic clinical evaluations can contribute to the fairness of the legal process in waiver-of-jurisdiction cases. If they are designed appropriately, guided by legal standards and requirements, they assure that the court does not overlook important information, and they provide a legally relevant structure within which courts can think about the cases before them in relation to the legal standards. If they are performed carefully, guided by a scientific foundation, they protect against bias and potentially faulty presumptions, enhancing the quality of justice.

Finally, society may also be well served when evaluations for waiver of jurisdiction identify youths who are unlikely to respond to rehabilitative efforts (e.g., adolescents who have already developed well-practiced antisocial characteristics and for whom previous rehabilitative efforts have repeatedly failed). If these conclusions are accurate, juvenile justice facilities are spared fruitless efforts that may place other youths in danger while also depleting the availability of resources that could be directed toward youths for whom rehabilitation is truly possible.

These benefits, however, are possible only if evaluations of youths' danger to others and amenability to rehabilitation are performed competently. Providing competent evaluations for courts is a systemic objective requiring commitments not only by clinicians, but also by lawmakers and by other persons in authority who can influence policy and legal practice.

Concerning the legal system's potential contribution for improving waiver evaluations, we cannot expect remarkable improvements in clinicians' abilities to address the law's questions about waiver of jurisdiction when the law so poorly defines the criteria for waiver, and when it rarely provides clinicians with feedback concerning their own definitions of the criteria. This chapter has pointed out several ways in which it is unclear precisely what judges want to know in cases involving waiver of jurisdiction. For example, do courts want to know whether youths are likely to become chronic recidivists, or do they want to know whether youths are likely to engage in assaultive behavior in the near future? These questions are not the same, yet which of them is more closely related to legal criteria for waiver to criminal court has been unclear in most jurisdictions, and has been almost completely unaddressed with regard to reverse waiver. Clinicians can try to guess what judges want to know, but their efforts will continue to be dissatisfying or inconsistent until the law can provide greater clarity.

Improving evaluations for waiver cases also requires that persons in authority set appropriate standards for evaluations and provide the necessary resources to meet those standards. Standards and resources go hand in hand. Requiring that waiver evaluations meet higher standards for the data and interpretations that will fulfill the objectives described in this chapter will be of no use unless adequate resources are provided to obtain examiners who are capable of meeting those standards and who are provided the time and means to meet them. For example, earlier in this chapter I noted that clinicians who perform these evaluations should be specialized in both child psychiatry or psychology and forensic applications of that specialization. This standard simply cannot be satisfied when juvenile justice systems provide compensation for a waiver evaluation that, in some jurisdictions, would cover only about one or two hours of clinicians' time at their average hourly fee for evaluation services in general practice.

Conversely, more money will not automatically produce better evaluations if clinicians are not held to an explicit standard regarding the nature and quality of the evaluations that the court requires. Juvenile justice administrators must work with local consultants to determine specifically what those standards should be, then provide adequate resources for clinicians contingent upon meeting those standards as manifested in continuous evaluation of clinicians' performance. (For a description of a successful statewide quality control program for forensic evaluations, see Fein et al. 1991.)

Part of the answer to better waiver evaluations lies with national commitment to research. I have intended to show that it is possible to perform waiver-of-jurisdiction assessments systematically and logically, and that much of the process and clinical inference can be based on an empirical foundation. Nevertheless, the description also indicated many steps in the process for which our guidance is limited, often relying on clinical art more than is desirable and less on scientifically proven methods than we would want. The literature until recently has provided almost no guidance to clinicians in performing waiver evaluations. Fortunately, some progress is finally being made on the identification of risk factors for violence that can be used in clinical evaluations with juveniles, although a good deal more work is needed to test their combined power and accuracy. New research also is identifying more successful interventions with juvenile offenders than we have had in the past, as well as the types of youths who are most likely to respond to them. (For a review of both types of research, see Loeber and Farrington 1998).

In the meantime, judges and lawyers should consider the methods described in this chapter as aspirational. The discussion has presented what is possible, but perhaps not what one will find with consistency in everyday clinical practice. Courts and attorneys are the consumers of forensic clinical evaluations for waiver-of-jurisdiction cases. If they can hold examiners accountable for what should be expected of them, as described in this chapter, this could play a role in improving the quality of examiners' assessments for danger to others and amenability to rehabilitation.

References
Cases Cited

Barefoot v. Estelle, 463 U.S. 880 (1983).
Kent v. U.S., 383 U.S. 541 (1966).
Schall v. Martin, 467 U.S. 253 (1984).

Other References

Achenbach, T. 1991. *Manual for the Child Behavior Checklist/4-18 and 1991 Profile.* Burlington: University of Vermont, Department of Psychiatry.

American Psychological Association. 1992. "Ethical Principles of Psychologists and Code of Conduct." *American Psychologist* 47:1597.

Barbaree, H., S. Hudson, and M. Seto. 1993. *The Juvenile Sex Offender.* New York: Guilford.

Barnum, R. 1987. "Clinical Evaluation of Juvenile Delinquents Facing Transfer to Adult Court." *Journal of the American Academy of Child and Adolescent Psychiatry* 26:922.

Borum, R., and T. Grisso. 1996. "Establishing Standards for Criminal Forensic Reports." *Journal of the American Academy of Psychiatry and the Law* 24:297.

Borum, R., M. Swartz, and J. Swanson. 1996. "Assessing and Managing Violence Risk in Clinical Practice." *Journal of Practice in Psychiatry and Behavioral Health* 4:205.

Brandt, J., W. Kennedy, C. Patrick, and J. Curtin. 1997. "Assessment of Psychopathy in a Population of Incarcerated Adolescent Offenders." *Psychological Assessment* 4:429.

Butcher, J., C. Williams, J. Graham, R. Archer, R. Tellegen, Y. Ben-Porath, and H. Kaemmer. 1992. *MMPI-A: Manual for Administration and Scoring.* Minneapolis: University of Minnesota Press.

Committee on Ethical Guidelines for Forensic Psychologists. 1991. "Specialty Guidelines for Forensic Psychologists." *Law and Human Behavior* 15:655.

Elkind, D. 1967. "Egocentrism in Adolescence." *Child Development* 38:1025.

Elliott, D. 1994. "Serious Violent Offenders: Onset, Developmental Course, and Termination: American Society of Criminology Presidential Address." *Criminology* 32:1.

Ennis, B, and T. Litwack. 1974. "Psychiatry and the Presumption of Expertise: Flipping Coins in the Courtroom." *California Law Review* 62:693.

Fagan, J., and M. Guggenheim. 1996. "Preventive Detention and the Judicial Prediction of Dangerousness for Juveniles: A Natural Experiment. *Journal of Criminal Law and Criminology* 86:415.

Fein, R., K. Appelbaum, R. Barnum, P. Baxter, T. Grisso, and N. Leavitt. 1991. "The 'Designated Forensic Professional' Program: A State Government–University Partnership to Improve Forensic Mental Health Services." *Journal of Mental Health Administration* 18:223.

Forth, A., S. Hart, and R. Hare. 1990. "Assessment of Psychopathy in Male Young Offenders." *Psychological Assessment* 2:342.

Frick, P., H. O'Brien, J. Wootton, and K. McBurnett. 1994. "Psychopathy and Conduct Problems in Children." *Journal of Abnormal Psychology* 103:700.

Grisso, T. 1986. *Evaluating Competencies: Forensic Assessments and Instruments.* New York: Plenum.

———. 1998. *Forensic Evaluation of Juveniles.* Sarasota, Fla.: Professional Resource Press.

Grisso, T., A. Tomkins, and P. Casey. 1988. "Psychosocial Concepts in Juvenile Law." *Law and Human Behavior* 12:403.

Groth, A., and C. Loredo. 1981. "Juvenile Sex Offenders: Guidelines for Assessment." *International Journal of Offender Therapy and Comparative Criminology* 25:31.

Hare, R. 1991. *The Hare Psychopathy Checklist—Revised Manual.* North Tonawanda, N.Y.: Multi-Health Systems.

Hart, S., D. Cox, and R. Hare. 1995. *The Hare Psychopathy Checklist: Screening Version.* North Tonawanda, N.Y.: Multi-Health Systems.

Hawkins, J., T. Herrenkohl, D. Farrington, D. Brewer, R. Catalano, and T. Harachi. 1998. "A Review of Predictors of Youth Violence." In *Serious and Violent Juvenile Offenders: Risk Factors and Successful Interventions.* Edited by R. Loeber and D. Farrington. Thousand Oaks, Calif.: Sage.

Heilbrun, K., C. Leheny, L. Thomas, and D. Huneycutt. 1997. "A National Survey of U.S. Statutes on Juvenile Transfer: Implications for Policy and Practice." *Behavioral Sciences and the Law* 15:125.

Hess, A., and I. Weiner, eds. 1999. *The Handbook of Forensic Psychology.* 2d ed. New York: Wiley.

Hoge, R., and D. Andrews. 1996. *Assessing the Youthful Offender.* New York: Plenum.

Howell, J., H. Krisberg, J. Hawkins, and J. Wilson, eds. 1995. *A Sourcebook: Serious, Violent, and Chronic Juvenile Offenders.* Thousand Oaks, Calif.: Sage.
Jesness, C., and R. Wedge. 1984. "Validity of a Revised Jesness Inventory I-Level Classification with Delinquents." *Journal of Consulting and Clinical Psychology* 52:997.
———. 1985. *Jesness Inventory Classification System: Supplementary Manual.* Palo Alto: Consulting Psychologists Press.
Kalogerakis, M., ed. 1992. *Handbook of Psychiatric Practice in the Juvenile Court.* Washington: American Psychiatric Press.
Keating, D. 1990. "Adolescent Thinking." In *At the Threshold: The Developing Adolescent.* Edited by S. Feldman and G. Elliott. Cambridge: Harvard University Press.
Kruh, I., and S. Brodsky. 1997. "Clinical Evaluations for Transfer of Juveniles to Criminal Court: Current Practices and Future Research." *Behavioral Sciences and the Law* 15:151.
Lipsey, M. 1992. "Juvenile Delinquency Treatment: A Meta-analytic Inquiry into the Variability of Effects." In *Meta-analysis for Explanation.* Edited by T. Cook, H. Cooper, D. Cordray, H. Hartmann, L. Hedges, R. Knight, T. Louis, and F. Mosteller. New York: Russell Sage.
Lipsey, M., and J. Derzon. 1998. "Predictors of Violent or Serious Delinquency in Adolescence and Early Adulthood: A Synthesis of Longitudinal Research." In *Serious and Violent Juvenile Offenders: Risk Factors and Successful Interventions.* Edited by R. Loeber and D. Farrington. Thousand Oaks, Calif.: Sage.
Litwack, T., and L. Schlesinger. 1991. "Dangerousness Risk Assessments: Research, Legal, and Clinical Considerations." In *The Handbook of Forensic Psychology.* Edited by A. Hess and I. Weiner. New York: John Wiley.
Loeber, R., and D. Farrington, eds. 1998. *Serious and Violent Juvenile Offenders: Risk Factors and Successful Interventions.* Thousand Oaks, Calif.: Sage.
Mash, E., and R. Barkley, eds. 1996. *Child Psychopathology.* New York: Guilford.
Melton, G., J. Petrila, N. Poythress, and C. Slobogin. 1997. *Psychological Evaluations for the Courts.* 2d ed. New York: Guilford.
Moffitt, T. 1993. "Adolescence-Limited and Life-Course-Persistent Antisocial Behavior: A Developmental Taxonomy." *Psychological Review* 100:674.
Monahan, J. 1981. *The Clinical Prediction of Violent Behavior.* Rockville, Md.: National Institute of Mental Health.
Mulvey, E. 1984. "Judging Amenability to Treatment in Juvenile Offenders: Theory and Practice." In *Children, Mental Health, and the Law.* Edited by N. Reppucci, L. Weithorn, E. Mulvey, and J. Monahan. Beverly Hills, Calif.: Sage.
Quay, H. 1987. "Patterns of Delinquent Behavior." In *Handbook of Juvenile Delinquency.* Edited by H. Quay. New York: John Wiley.
Quinsey, V., G. Harris, M. Rice, and C. Cormier. 1998. *Violent Offenders: Appraising and Managing Risk.* Washington: American Psychological Association.
Ross, J., and P. Loss. 1991. "Assessment of the Juvenile Sex Offender." In *Juvenile Sexual Offending: Causes, Consequences, and Correction.* Edited by G. Ryan and S. Lane. Lexington, Mass.: Lexington Books.

Schetky, D., and E. Benedek 1992. *Clinical Handbook of Child Psychiatry and the Law.* Baltimore: Williams and Wilkins.

Smith, C., A. Lizotte, T. Thornberry, and M. Krohn. 1995. "Resilient Youth: Identifying Factors That Prevent High-Risk Youth from Engaging in Delinquency and Drug Use." In *Delinquency in the Life Course.* Edited by J. Hagan. Greenwich, Conn.: JAI.

Swanson, J., C. Holzer, V. Ganju, and R. Jono. 1990. "Violence and Psychiatric Disorder in the Community: Evidence from the Epidemiologic Catchment Area Surveys." *Hospital and Community Psychiatry* 41:761.

Tate, D., N. Reppucci, and E. Mulvey. 1995. "Violent Juvenile Delinquents: Treatment Effectiveness and Implications for Future Actions." *American Psychologist* 50:777.

Torbet, P., R. Gable, H. Hurst, I. Montgomery, L. Szymanski, and D. Thomas. 1996. *State Responses to Serious and Violent Juvenile Crime.* Washington: Office of Juvenile Justice and Delinquency Prevention.

Webster, C., G. Harris, M. Rice, C. Cormier, and V. Quinsey. 1994. *The Violence Prediction Scheme.* Toronto: Centre for Criminology, University of Toronto.

Weinrott, M. 1996. *Juvenile Sexual Aggression: A Critical Review.* Boulder: Center for the Study and Prevention of Violence, University of Colorado-Boulder.

Wiebush, R., C. Baird, B. Krisberg, and D. Onek. 1995. "Risk Assessment and Classification for Serious, Violent, and Chronic Juvenile Offenders." In *A Sourcebook: Serious, Violent, and Chronic Juvenile Offenders.* Edited by J. Howell, H. Krisberg, J. D. Hawkins, and J. Wilson. Thousand Oaks, Calif.: Sage.

Witt, P., and F. Dyer. 1997. "Juvenile Transfer Cases: Risk Assessment and Risk Management." *Journal of Psychiatry and Law* 25:581.

Chapter Ten

The Reproduction of Juvenile Justice in Criminal Court: A Case Study of New York's Juvenile Offender Law

SIMON I. SINGER, JEFFREY FAGAN, AND AKIVA LIBERMAN

> This is how the names get changed and how the people and things
> are rejigged to fit the new categories. First the people are tempted
> out of their niches by new possibilities of exercising or evading
> control. Then they make new kinds of institutions, and the institu-
> tions make new labels, and the label makes new kinds of people.
>
> *Mary Douglas, How Institutions Think*

In March 1978, Willie Bosket, a juvenile delinquent with a lengthy arrest
record, was out late at night wandering the New York City subways in
search of passengers to rob. While emptying the pockets of one sleepy
passenger, Bosket suddenly decided to shoot him in the head. Eight days
later Bosket again brutally robbed and murdered another subway passenger in a similar manner. Because he was only fifteen years of age, Bosket could not be charged in New York's criminal court. He was technically a delinquent who could be confined at most for a period of five
years. As a consequence, Bosket triggered a major crisis in New York's
system of juvenile justice.

Soon after Bosket's adjudication as a delinquent in juvenile court,[1]
New York hurriedly assembled legislation to make sure that offenders
like him would no longer be eligible for punishment as a juvenile. The
fact that Bosket could not be charged in criminal court had caused many
New Yorkers to insist that officials "do something" about violent juvenile crime. Mr. Bosket would later be referred to by those working in
the juvenile justice system as "Mr. Juvenile Offender Law" for single-
handedly causing the state of New York to change from a state without
waver legislation to a state that automatically excluded offenders like Mr.
Bosket from its juvenile jurisdiction. The Juvenile Offender Law was

quickly proposed by the then governor of New York, Hugh Carey, and immediately passed in special emergency sessions of the state legislature by near unanimous votes. The intent of this legislation, according to Carey, was to make sure juveniles such as Bosket "never walk the streets again" (*New York Times,* June 30, 1978, 12).

New York's 1978 Juvenile Offender Law came quickly on top of an earlier juvenile justice reform that was created to get tough on juvenile crime in juvenile court. After Bosket's sensational crimes, there was no time to create yet another commission to again study violent juvenile crime and to once more suggest juvenile justice reforms. Such a commission had already been created several years earlier and its get-tough recommendations had failed to prevent chronic delinquents like Bosket from repeating their violent offenses. Besides, election day was less than six months away, and the governor faced a tight race for reelection in which he was repeatedly accused by his opponent of being "soft" on crime (McGarrell 1988).[2]

New York's Juvenile Offender Law would soon become a model for other states looking to offense-based waiver legislation (Butterfield 1995, xv). It is sometimes referred to as automatic waiver, because it assumes that juveniles who commit certain violent categories of offenses are criminally responsible for their crimes in criminal court. Contrary to judicial forms of waiver, the Juvenile Offender Law does not require officials to conduct an adversarial *Kent*-like hearing in the juvenile court. There is no need to determine if a juvenile should be transferred to criminal court, because nonjudicial forms of waiver require criminal justice officials, at the point of arrest, to decide if a juvenile should be charged in criminal court.

Legislative transfer to criminal court, rather than judicial transfer, was the waiver of choice for New York's legislators, because juvenile justice officials were no longer trusted to control chronic delinquents such as Willie Bosket. Just six months prior to his murdering two subway passengers, Bosket had been released from a State Division for Youth (DFY) facility despite a record of continued violence while in residential placement.[3] The decision to release him appeared to be based more on the fact that no agency in the juvenile justice system wanted to deal with him rather than on any real progress in his treatment as a violent delinquent (Butterfield 1995, 151). It appeared that Bosket and other violent juveniles were beyond the control of a complex, confused system of juvenile justice.

In this chapter, we show that despite the stated intent of New York's Juvenile Offender Law, it did not eliminate the need for a distinctive court system very much like the juvenile court in rationale and procedure.

Rather, it reproduced juvenile justice within systems of criminal justice. The first section of this chapter traces the development of the 1978 Juvenile Offender Law in prior legislation, judicial opinions and jurisprudential rationales, and criticisms of the New York juvenile court processes. The second section examines the operation of the Juvenile Offender Law following its implementation in 1978. The final section of this paper discusses the lessons to be learned from New York's attempt to control violent juvenile crime through nonjudicial offense-based exclusion legislation.

1. Origin and Structure of the 1978 Law

The shape of the 1978 Juvenile Offender Law had multiple origins in New York State law and practice. Willie Bosket, sensational acts of juvenile violence, and political demands to be tough on juvenile crime were only some of the reasons for the 1978 law. There are other reasons that stem from a prior history of reforms, and how those reforms paved the way for future reforms, such as New York's 1978 law. With each newly created agency for juvenile justice, there are new sets of assumptions about delinquents and official ways in which to control their offensive behavior. Contemporary systems of juvenile justice can be viewed in terms of legal rules that first criminalized delinquency through a more formal juvenile court procedure and a formal judicial waiver hearing as mandated by the U.S. Supreme Court in *Kent v. United States,* 383 U.S. 541 (1966). This procedural criminalization of juvenile justice then paved the way toward recriminalization, which we will discuss in terms of New York's legal attempt to make juveniles automatically criminally responsible for certain categories of offenses.[4]

Due Process and the Criminalization of Delinquency

The Supreme Court's *Kent* and *Gault* decisions reflect part of the contemporary criminalization of delinquency. Those decisions presented the jurisprudential rationales for moving the nonadversarial civil aspects of the juvenile court closer to a due-process model of criminal justice. By mandating a more formal juvenile court, the Supreme Court presented part of the rationale for injecting adult due-process rights while maintaining the treatment-oriented objectives of the juvenile court. In commenting on Supreme Court Justice Fortas's *Gault* decision, Zimring (1982, 79) notes that "he was arguing that we could have our cake and eat it too; that procedural rights would not inhibit the child welfare mission of the juvenile court. Indeed, due process may itself be therapeutic."

Several Supreme Court decisions reinforced the division that *Gault* created among delinquents. It divided the juvenile court into a legal setting that would administer due process for serious delinquents, and continue to provide traditional forms of treatment-oriented juvenile justice for nonserious, status-offending juveniles (defined as persons in need of supervision). In a report relating the evaluation diversion from juvenile court, Cressey and McDermott (1973) predicted the current criminalization of delinquency when they stated that

> there will be a polarization of attitudes and programs: Law-breaking juveniles are likely to be processed along the lines of the adult model and hence will receive more due process and less humanistic consideration—after all, are they not merely small criminals? Juveniles who have been called "predelinquents," because they can't get along at home or in school, will be diverted. (61)

Kent criminalized the juvenile court by granting an adversarial hearing to juveniles in *serious* cases involving waiver to criminal court. But *Gault* (*In re Gault,* 387 U.S. at 36–37) also contributed to the criminalization that occurred within the juvenile court. Delinquents would be given their rights if they were identified as serious delinquents. The juvenile court would imitate a criminal court in such instances. But new legal rules soon appeared that did more than criminalize delinquency in juvenile court. There would be the recriminalization of delinquency by diverting serious delinquents before they could enter the juvenile court.

New York was a step ahead of the other states in the way it rationalized the criminalization of delinquency and ultimately its recriminalization. New York anticipated the due-process reforms that would be mandated by the Supreme Court in *Gault.* In fact, it was cited by the Supreme Court as a state that had, in its 1964 Family Court Act, instituted legal representation for juveniles in juvenile court. But it was not until 1976 that the New York Juvenile Justice Reform Act criminalized delinquency in a way that would set the stage for New York's 1978 Juvenile Offender Law.

Criminalization: The 1976 Juvenile Justice Reform Act

The 1976 Juvenile Justice Reform Act provided part of the rationale for the 1978 Juvenile Offender Law. To ignore the 1976 act is to assume mistakenly that the 1978 Juvenile Offender Law was a complete and radical shift in New York's system of juvenile justice. On the contrary, the jurisprudential rationale for the 1978 law is built on prior juvenile justice reforms, beginning with shifts in the maximum age at which juveniles could be admitted to reformatories, which may have created the precedent for New York's relatively low age of criminal responsibility. The fact that New York automatically placed all juvenile offenders over the age of sixteen in its criminal court was also part of the reason it lacked judicial waiver legislation.

The 1976 reform was created in the wake of an earlier crisis over what to do about violent juvenile crime. Governor Carey created the Cahill Commission to recommend reforms that would respond to public criticism of New York's system of juvenile justice. Based on extensive interviews with policy makers, McGarrell (1988, 104–5) reported several aspects of the deliberations of the state commission that had produced the 1976 reforms. For example, some members of the commission wanted to create waiver legislation, but Division for Youth commissioner Peter Edelman argued against it. He convinced other commission members that the juvenile justice system was the most appropriate legal setting for differentiating serious violent delinquents.

In the end a compromise was reached between those commission members who wanted to waive violent juveniles to criminal court and those who wanted to retain them in juvenile court. The commission members agreed to recommend that a separate, designated felony track be established for juveniles charged with serious violent offenses. Youths falling into the designated felony category would be subject to a wider range of minimum and maximum dispositions in New York's juvenile court.

Like other crime commissions, New York's officials attempted to strike a balance between treatment- and punishment-oriented interests. They did so by broadening the dispositional options of juvenile justice officials. By proposing the creation of separate legal labels and tracks within juvenile court, the commission attempted to satisfy political and organizational demands to produce a more punitive juvenile justice system. The majority of commission members were convinced that this was possible within the structure of the juvenile court and that there was little need for the creation of waiver legislation. By proposing to produce harsher punishments within New York's juvenile court, the commission sought to satisfy the concerns of advocates of treatment for all juveniles in a separate juvenile justice system.

The commission's recommendations produced new rules for classifying juveniles. The 1976 Juvenile Justice Reform Act moved New York's juvenile justice system closer to nonjudicial transfer by: (1) establishing a separate class of designated felony offenses; (2) allowing a publicly elected prosecutor to prosecute in juvenile court; (3) requiring determinate sentences in the form of minimum and maximum periods of incarceration in secure facilities; and (4) changing the stated purpose of juvenile justice.

First, by establishing a separate category of designated felony offenses, the Juvenile Justice Reform Act reinstituted the principle of offense-driven dispositions and emphasized that specific offense categories deserve special penalties. These penalties fit the retributory aims of criminal justice more than the stated rehabilitative purpose of the prevailing individualized models of juvenile justice. By emphasizing the principle of offense over the principle of individualized justice, the Juvenile Justice Reform Act made it possible to create separate categories of offenses that would form the basis for offense-based waiver.

Second, by allowing publicly elected prosecutors to replace the appointed county attorney (or corporation counsel in New York City), the Juvenile Justice Reform Act opened the door to case-processing decisions by criminal justice officials. The appointed county attorney differed in many significant respects from the district attorney. Appointed county attorneys were not directly responsible to the public, with its get-tough demands for punishment. The juvenile court is technically a civil court and the appointed county attorney represented the state in a diverse range of civil manners. The entrance of the public prosecutor into the juvenile court made it possible for criminal justice officials to record those serious delinquents in ways that previously were not possible.

The third feature of criminal justice procedure introduced by the 1976 act was the creation of determinate or fixed placements for juveniles convicted in juvenile court of designated felony offenses. Prior to the 1976 act, placements were for indeterminate periods of up to eighteen months. The DFY could petition the juvenile court to extend the period of placement beyond eighteen months, to a maximum age of twenty-one. In contrast, the Juvenile Justice Reform Act set limits on that discretionary authority of correctional officials by mandating minimum and maximum sentences in secure facilities. This appeared more like the sentencing in adult court with its traditional retributory objectives.

Finally, the style of New York's 1978 Juvenile Offender Law is previewed in the way the 1976 Juvenile Justice Reform Act shifted the stated purpose of juvenile justice from the best interests of the juvenile to include the interests of the state in protecting its citizens. This traditional criminal justice objective was restated so that "[i]n *any* juvenile delinquency proceeding under this article, the court shall consider the needs and best interests of the respondent *as well as the need for protection of the community*" (emphasis added) (Juvenile Justice Reform Act of 1976, N.Y. Laws chap. 878). Although the need to protect the community may have always been an implicit part of juvenile justice, the Juvenile Justice Reform Act made it an explicit reason for adjudicating delinquents.

The 1976 act made it possible for officials to distinguish types of delinquents in ways that previously were unavailable. "Restrictive juvenile delinquents" became an official category that was legally distinguished from the more general delinquent category. By increasing the possible types of adjudications and dispositions in juvenile court, the Juvenile Justice Reform Act added to the diverse set of legal labels and legal tracks in which to place juveniles. This rationalization of violent delinquency allowed for the bureaucratization of juvenile justice in ways that previously were not possible. Just as earlier status offense legislation provided for a separate track that created new administrative routines, so did the category of restrictive juvenile delinquent pave the way for the juvenile offender label.

Recriminalization: The 1978 Juvenile Offender Law

The limited reforms in the 1976 act could not survive Willie Bosket. Instead, criminalization in the 1976 act gave birth to recriminalization in the 1978 law by allowing for the further extension of offense-based waiver, and the elimination of the initial jurisdiction of the juvenile court for even relatively young juveniles. Critics of the contemporary post-*Gault* juvenile court have argued that the juvenile court failed repeatedly in its mission to provide young offenders with the controls that they needed to prevent their repeated delinquent behavior. More specifically, the juvenile court appeared incapable of controlling serious delinquents by the arbitrary manner in which it decided which juveniles are deserving of criminal punishment.

What we call the recriminalization of delinquency in the 1978 law goes a step beyond criminalization of juvenile courts because it re-creates within criminal courts some of the offense and offender divisions that existed in juvenile courts. It provides for automatic offense-based transfer to criminal court with the possibility of juvenile court as a backup for those who are seen as deserving of treatment. These offenders are "waived back" to the juvenile court. Moreover, it re-creates juvenile justice within the criminal justice system by providing officials with treatment alternatives within criminal justice, as was the case prior to the creation of juvenile courts. In other words, recriminalization via automatic transfer shifts the discretion to criminal justice officials to identify the most serious, chronic delinquents through charging and punishment decisions. The intent of automatic transfer such as New York's 1978 law is not just to let the punishment fit the crime, but to allow criminal justice officials to divide juveniles into two categories: offenders (those deserving of offense-based criminal court punishment) and delinquents (those deserving of individualized justice).

There is an intellectual history that added weight to political demands to allow criminal justice officials to make initial decisions about which juveniles should be labeled as offenders in criminal court. In 1978, the New York Commission on Management and Productivity in the Public Sector sponsored a study by Mark Moore, James Q. Wilson, and Ralph Gants (1978) to recommend policies for controlling violent juvenile crime. The report stressed the importance of identifying and tracking violent and chronic delinquents.[5]

Moore, Wilson, and Gants argued for a system of justice in which juveniles are identified not only by the seriousness of their offenses but also by their prior offensive behavior. This could not be accomplished in New York's juvenile court with its rules of confidentiality, as the authors stressed in their report. It also could not be accomplished by limiting to murder the range of offenses for which juveniles could be charged.

The Juvenile Offender Law—1978

New York's 1978 Juvenile Offender Law was structured in the form of an amendment to its 1976 Juvenile Justice Reform Act. The same set of designated felony offenses listed in the 1976 act were used to classify eligible juveniles for automatic transfer to criminal court. For juveniles charged with these offenses, the court of initial jurisdiction shifted from the juvenile court to the criminal court. Criminal justice officials instead of juvenile justice officials were required to decide which juveniles were deserving of criminal offender status. In addition to status offender, delinquent, and restrictive juvenile delinquent, legal officials now had the additional label of juvenile offender with which to classify juveniles.

The severity of sentences in the 1978 act occupies a middle ground between full criminal court sentences and the juvenile court dispositions in the 1976 act. Although the length of sentences listed for juvenile offenders is not as severe as those for adult offenders, maximum penalties are substantially greater than what juveniles could have received for the same offenses in juvenile court. For example, the Juvenile Offender Law increased the maximum length of imprisonment for murder to life in prison from a maximum of five years under the 1976 act. Moreover, the minimum period of incarceration in secure facilities for juveniles convicted in juvenile court was set at twelve to eighteen months for a designated felony offense followed by twelve months in nonsecure residential facilities. The 1978 law requires the entire length of a juvenile offender's sentence to be served in secure facilities.

Table 10.1 shows how offense severity dictates the length of sentence for juveniles convicted of designated violent felonies. The stated penalties for class A felonies are more severe than for class B and C felonies.

Table 10.1
Juvenile Offender Law: Offenses and Penalties

Designated Felony	Sentence Length (Years)	
	Minimum	Maximum
Class A:		
Murder	5–9	Life
Arson, kidnapping	4–6	12–15
Class B:		
Manslaughter 1	⅓ maximum	3–10
Rape 1		
Robbery 1		
Sodomy 1		
Burglary 1		
Arson 2		
Class C:		
Burglary 2	⅓ maximum	3–7
Robbery 2		
Assault 1		

Source: Singer 1996.

The maximum length of sentence listed for class A and B felonies under the Juvenile Offender Law is substantially greater than the five-year maximum sentence in the Juvenile Justice Reform Act. For class A felonies, juveniles as young as thirteen may be sentenced to a maximum of life in prison. Moreover, juvenile offenders sentenced to incarceration must serve their entire sentence in a maximum-security facility operated by the DFY.

By restricting institutional placement to maximum-security facilities, the 1978 law reproduced the stated penalties in the state's penal law, which significantly departed from the indeterminate, flexible placements that characterized traditional forms of juvenile justice. Instead of relying on DFY officials to decide when the most appropriate time is to bring a juvenile back into his home environment, it is the legislature that has decided, based on specific offense categories.

But the 1978 law still retains elements of traditional juvenile justice criteria and discretion. Initially, the determinate offense–based characteristics of the 1978 Juvenile Offender Law made little sense in relation to the loose way in which discretion was administered for older juveniles in criminal court. The law as originally envisioned conflicted with New York's preexisting Youthful Offender Law, which applied to offenders between sixteen and eighteen years of age and outside juvenile court jurisdiction. So in 1979, the New York State legislature modified the Juvenile Offender Law to allow for youthful offender status for *all* juveniles brought to the criminal court. Without the possibility of youthful offender status, juveniles younger than sixteen convicted in criminal court would be subject to harsher penalties than older juveniles. Making youthful offender status available to younger juveniles took some of the bite out of the Juvenile Offender Law and explicitly reproduced elements of juvenile justice within the criminal court.

By making the state's DFY facility the place where juvenile offenders must serve their sentences, the Juvenile Offender Law endorsed and reproduced aspects of juvenile-style treatment criteria and programs. The 1978 law states that "educational" and "rehabilitative" services must be provided in the DFY residential facilities. Rehabilitative services are to be provided despite the fact that sentenced juveniles are housed exclusively in the most secure facilities for the entire length of their sentence. Minors must be removed to adult corrections no later than their twenty-first birthday, although they may be transferred at any time after their sixteenth birthday.

Youthful offender status and rehabilitative treatment in secure facilities are elements of juvenile justice that make the stated automatic transfer requirements of the Juvenile Offender Law appear less than automatic. Moreover, the 1978 Juvenile Offender Law did not eliminate the harsher penalties that juveniles could receive in juvenile court; adolescents convicted under the 1978 law could still be waived back to juvenile court to be sentenced as restrictive juvenile delinquents for minimum and maximum periods of incarceration in secure juvenile facilities.

The 1978 Juvenile Offender Law gave criminal justice officials the flexibility they wanted in tracking delinquents in a variety of legal settings. Part of that flexibility is contained in the formal requirements of the Juvenile Offender Law. Eligible juveniles may be transferred to juvenile court through a process commonly known as "reverse waiver." A formal reverse waiver hearing is required if criminal justice officials think it is appropriate to prosecute a juvenile charged with murder, first-degree rape, sodomy, or armed robbery. In the reverse waiver hearing the following elements are considered:

> (i) mitigating circumstances that bear directly upon the manner in which the crime was committed; (ii) where the defendant was not the sole participant in the crime, the defendant's participation was relatively minor although not so minor as to constitute a defense to the prosecution; or (iii) possible deficiencies in the proof of the crime. (*New York State Crime Package Bill of 1978,* 1978 N.Y. Laws, chap. 481)

If the charge against an eligible juvenile involved something other than these class A designated felonies, such as robbery or assault, the legal requirements are less explicit, and the conditions allowing for transfer to juvenile court relatively vague. In determining removal, however, the law directs officials to consider "individually and collectively" all of the following factors:

> (a) the seriousness and circumstances of the offense; (b) the extent of the harm caused by the offense; (c) the evidence of guilt, whether admissible or inadmissible at trial; (d) the history, character and condition of the defendant; (e) the purpose and effect of imposing upon the defendant a sentence authorized for the offense; (f) the impact of the removal of the case to the family court on the safety and welfare of the community; (g) the impact of the removal of the case to the family court upon the confidence of the public in the criminal justice system; (h) where the court deems it appropriate, the attitude of the complainant or victim with respect to [transfer]; (i) any other relevant fact indicating that a judgment of conviction in the criminal court would serve no useful purpose. (*New York State Crime Package Bill of 1978*, 1978 N.Y. Laws, chap. 481)

If the case of an eligible juvenile is removed to juvenile court, the criminal court must "state on the record the factor or factors upon which the court's determination was based [and] give its reasons for removal in detail and not in conclusory terms." Removal can be initiated by the prosecutor and requires giving the reasons for charging the juvenile in juvenile court instead of criminal court. Those reasons are subject to interpretation, such as "the history, character and condition of the defendant" (*New York State Crime Package Bill of 1978*, 1978 N.Y. Laws, chap. 481).

There is another way in which criminal court for arrested juvenile offenders may be avoided. The charges against an arrested juvenile can be reduced by criminal justice officials from a designated felony offense to a nondesignated felony. Juveniles cannot be charged in criminal court for other than offenses for which they may be held criminally responsible. In the negotiated order of waiver, prosecutors have considerable discretion in the way they wish to formally or informally charge eligible juveniles either in the juvenile or criminal court.

Youthful Offender Status

As just shown, the classifications in the 1978 law can also be traced to earlier legislation that allowed for the reproduction of categories and concepts of juvenile justice within New York's criminal courts. This came in the form of New York's 1943 Youthful Offender Act. This act introduced elements of juvenile justice in criminal court by allowing criminal justice officials to decide whether some younger criminal court defendants deserved a "second chance." The 1943 act provided for separate treatment of sixteen- to nineteen-year-old "youthful offenders" in a variety of ways, including court parts "separate and apart from the other parts of the court which are then being held for proceedings pertaining to adults charged with crimes" (Corriero 1990, 4). The JO parts are specialized courts for youths charged in criminal courts under the 1978 law.[6] Accordingly, much the same as today, youthful offender status reproduced juvenile justice in the criminal court by exempting older juveniles from the lengthy sentences of adults and by maintaining the confidentiality of their records. Through youthful offender status juveniles are eligible for minimal periods of indeterminate sentencing and probation. The practical elements of juvenile justice are there in the form of indeterminate placements, probation, and confidentiality.

2. The 1978 Law in Action

The implementation of the Juvenile Offender Law reproduced in the criminal courts across New York State disparities in punishment that contradicted the intentions of the law's sponsors. Table 10.2 displays the frequency, rate, and mean seriousness of arrest charges and rate of conviction in criminal court for the twelve largest counties in New York State from September 1978 to May 1985. The four largest counties are located in New York City and account for 85 percent of JO arrests. Brooklyn alone produced over one-third of JO arrests. In contrast, Erie County, which includes the state's second-largest city, Buffalo, recorded little more than 1 percent of the total JO arrests, although the county's population of nearly one million is comparable to New York City–area counties where JO arrests are more common.

In addition to the frequency of arrest, the severity of arrests should be considered in evaluating how different jurisdictions respond to juveniles as offenders. Arrest seriousness was computed as a composite measure that weights the offense charges by the total severity of all arrest charges. The weights were derived from ratio scores produced in the National Crime Severity Survey (NCSS) (Wolfgang et al. 1985). The NCSS scores were based on a 1977 survey of approximately sixty thousand persons that was conducted as a supplement to the annual National Crime Survey of victimization. The average arrest seriousness by jurisdiction is related in part to the frequency of arrests. The mean offense severity rates for Erie and Monroe Counties were 24.22 and 23.20, respectively, compared to 18.70 for Kings County (Brooklyn). The substantially higher mean se-

Table 10.2
Frequency, Rate, Severity of Arrest, and Rate of Criminal Court Conviction
by Large Jurisdictions

	Frequency of Arrests	Rate[a]	Offense Severity[b]	Conviction Rate[c]
New York City counties:				
Kings	3,490	460.8	18.70	.23
Queens	1,155	205.9	18.86	.22
Manhattan	2,134	683.8	18.07	.27
Bronx	1,668	384.1	20.42	.29
Richmond	167	124.6	17.93	.19
Non–New York city counties:				
Nassau	168	33.6	18.45	.29
Suffolk	256	46.0	18.40	.23
Erie	129	35.4	24.22	.07
Westchester	185	59.4	18.45	.24
Monroe	119	47.2	23.20	.12
Onondaga	101	60.0	19.63	.32
Albany	84	92.1	16.85	.39

Source: Recriminalizing Delinquency, 1996.
[a] Arrests per 100,000 fourteen- and fifteen-year-olds in county.
[b] Mean severity of arrests.
[c] In criminal court.

riousness scores for the western part of New York State suggest greater selectivity among Erie and Monroe County officials in the arrest and the initial assignment of criminal responsibility.

In the capital county of New York State, Albany, officials seemed to follow more of the letter of the JO law by charging a larger proportion of juveniles with less serious juvenile offender offenses. Albany's mean seriousness of arrest is 16.85 compared to 24.22 for Erie County. Among New York City counties, Bronx officials charged juveniles on average with more serious arrests. Among New York City counties, Richmond and Manhattan produced the lowest mean offense seriousness scores, 17.93 and 18.07, while the Bronx recorded the highest mean severity of arrest, 20.42.

But rates of seriousness by county of jurisdiction may not be merely a product of regional variation in rates of serious violent juvenile crime.[7] These differences may also reflect jurisdictional variation in decision making on what constitutes a designated felony offense for prosecution purposes. Table 10.2 suggests that officials in Buffalo (Erie County) and Rochester (Monroe County) appeared more inclined to follow the letter of the juvenile offender law only for the most serious violent offense charges. In these western New York counties, juveniles who committed the less serious designated felony offenses were less likely to be arrested as juvenile offenders and are more often charged as delinquents. As a consequence, the cases of juveniles who commit less violent acts of crime may not even enter the criminal justice process. By being more selective initially about the kinds of juveniles arrested as juvenile offenders, western New York criminal justice officials raise the threshold of offense severity necessary for criminal justice to assign criminal responsibility to juveniles.

Variation is evident also in the relationship between offense seriousness and the frequency of arrests. In Albany County, more juveniles are arrested as juvenile offenders (92.1 per 100,000 juveniles) than in Erie County (35.4 per 100,000 juveniles). The mean seriousness scores were 16.85 in Albany County and 24.22 in Erie County, respectively. So in counties where fewer juveniles experience JO arrests, the mean seriousness of arrest was substantially greater. In other words, criminal justice officials in counties where fewer juveniles were arrested appeared more selective in their assignment of criminal responsibility to juveniles, reserving the status for more serious offenses. Table 10.2 also shows that the county's average conviction rate appears inversely related to the severity of arrest. For example, Albany County recorded the lowest mean seriousness of arrest yet the highest rate of conviction. Apparently, criminal justice officials in Albany produced a tight fit not only between arrest and adjudication, but also between adjudication and conviction.

Juvenile Courts within Criminal Courts: Specialized Youth Courts within New York City's Adult Courts

Since the 1943 YO Act, specialized court parts to handle youths have operated intermittently within New York State's criminal court system. Although the statutory requirement for separate court parts in the YO Act was removed in 1971, separate court parts for sixteen- to nineteen-year-old youths continued to operate in adult courts in New York City, until the last remaining youth part (in Queens) was abolished in 1986 (Corriero 1990; Singer 1996).

Thus, by the 1990s, adult court cases of teenagers in New York City were being handled in the all-purpose parts along with the cases of adults. At the same time, the adult court was handling the cases of even younger offenders, since the Juvenile Offender Law passed in 1978 moved initial jurisdiction for the cases of some juveniles younger than sixteen to the adult courts.

In 1992 and 1993, a specialized youth court was established in the superior (felony) court in each of New York City's four large boroughs.

These courts were created to handle the cases of thirteen- to fifteen-year-olds charged with any of the JO offenses described in table 10.1. These specialized courts began operating in Manhattan and Queens during 1992, and in Brooklyn and the Bronx about six months later. By 1995, these courts handled about two-thirds of JO cases in their boroughs (Liberman and Raleigh 1998). In contrast to the earlier youth parts that handled the cases of offenders ages sixteen to nineteen, these specialized courts handle the cases primarily of defendants under sixteen years old.

These specialized courts were established with several goals, similar to those that motivated the establishment of juvenile courts almost a century earlier, based on the recognition that juveniles have special needs and could benefit from somewhat different treatment. For example, parents generally play a more important role with juveniles, different types of alternative programs may be available, and more intensive supervision may be appropriate under probation. However, because JO cases constitute only a small percentage of the felony court (Supreme Court in New York) caseload, any special considerations are hard to apply consistently when these cases are distributed throughout the all-purpose court parts.

Upstate counties have not established separate youth courts because their population of youthful and juvenile offenders is considerably smaller. Specialized units may be unique to counties of jurisdiction where there is a large enough population of serious delinquents to justify distinct bureaucratic units. This is the case for the more densely populated counties of New York City.

Accordingly, the specialized treatment of juveniles in a youth court reproduces the progressive vision of juvenile justice within the jurisprudential framework and operational boundaries of the criminal court: treatment and rehabilitative services for those juveniles deserving of a "second chance" (Corriero 1990).[8] In an article arguing for the reestablishment of youth courts, Judge Michael Corriero drew upon the 1943 Youthful Offender Act, which dictates that hearings "may be private and shall be conducted in such parts of the court or judges' chambers as shall be separate and apart from the other parts of the court which are then being held for proceedings pertaining to adults charged with crimes" (Corriero 1990, 4). Corriero also cites New York's then Governor Dewey's memorandum supporting the Youthful Offender Act based on the savings that could subsequently be obtained through elimination of an additional probation or preinvestigation report.

> As a consequence of the shift of the determination of youthful offender treatment to the time of sentencing, only one probation report for sentencing purposes will be compiled, the delay and

cost of unnecessary probationary reports will be avoided and valuable probation resources will be conserved and more productively re-allocated. (Corriero 1991, 4)

The above quote reflects much of the bottom line in the specialized reproduction of juvenile justice. It is cheaper to implement. Convenience, as David Rothman (1980) repeatedly argues, is a significant part of the reason for juvenile justice reforms, and it is reproduced in the diverse set of ways in which criminal justice officials can label juveniles not only as juvenile offenders, but also as youthful offenders. Youthful offender status gives criminal justice officials room to negotiate by sealing the juvenile offender's conviction in criminal court, and by making probation a dispositional option.

Punishment in the New Juvenile Courts

The negotiated order of justice in specialized youth courts is different from that in general criminal courts. The stream of cases that criminal justice officials see in these courts produced rates of adjudication and disposition that are significantly different from rates in counties of jurisdiction where criminal courts are not specialized into youth courts (Singer 1996). These differences are reflected in the case processing data: after controlling for offense, prior offense, and race, the New York City counties with youth courts produced significantly higher rates of juvenile offenders convicted with youthful offender status.

Liberman, Raleigh, and Solomon (2000) examined case processing in New York City's specialized youth courts in 1994–96. During this time, the youth courts handled more than three-quarters of all JO cases in New York City. What differentiates the cases that were excluded from the specialized courts? It was not age: regardless of specialized courts, about two-thirds of JO arrestees were fifteen years old, and about a third were fourteen years old. Some charge differences on the committing case were apparent, but less than one might expect: both in specialized courts and in general courts, the most serious charges were robbery (first and second degree). In contrast, the general-purpose courts handled fewer robbery cases than the JO courts, and slightly more homicide cases and thus more serious felonies on average.

Table 10.3 shows case outcomes and sentences during this period for juvenile offenders either in specialized youth courts or in nonspecialized felony courts in two time periods: July 1994–June 1995, and July 1995–June 1996.[9] There were small differences over time within each type of court in conviction or dismissal rates. The nonspecialized parts more

Table 10.3
Case Outcomes and Sentences of JO Cases in Specialized and Regular Courts,
New York City, 1994–96[a]

	Specialized JO Courts		Nonspecialized Courts	
	1994–95	1995–96	1994–95	1995–96
Case outcome (%):				
Convicted (Pleaded or Found Guilty)	87.9	91.3	84.4	88.6
Felony Dismissed	8.8	7.2	8.9	4.3
Transferred to Family Court	2.9	1.1	6.7	7.1
N (completed cases)	306	265	90	70
Sentence (%):				
Imprisonment	47.0	56.5	52.9	48.0
Split Sentence	7.2	7.1	11.8	14.0
Probation	45.8	36.3	35.3	38.0

[a] Case Outcome and Sentence data includes only completed cases. Cases in the nonspecialized courts exclude cases where the defendant waived his or her right to a grand jury, presumably because of a plea bargain. These make up most of the cases in the nonspecialized courts, and this explains the lower volume of cases in these nonspecialized courts compared to the JO courts. See Liberman and Raleigh 1998; Liberman et al. 2000.

often waived cases back to the juvenile court. About 7 percent of the JO cases were waived back compared to about 2 percent of the cases in the specialized courts. It seems that the re-creation of a juvenile justice model of individualized justice and discretion within the criminal court reduced the incentives to return cases to the juvenile court.

Punishment was more lenient in the JO parts at the outset, but converged with regular courts over time. In their first year, youth courts more often sentenced cases to probation (46 percent compared to 35 percent in regular courts), and incarceration rates were lower (47 percent in youth court compared to 53 percent in regular parts). In addition, judges in JO parts more often granted the protection of YO status (66 percent compared to 57 percent in the regular courts). However, in their second year, this gap disappeared and in fact reversed for incarceration. Incarceration rates were higher in the youth courts (57 percent compared to 48 percent in the regular courts), and the gap in probation sentences disappeared. By the second year, split sentences of incarceration and probation were twice as likely in the nonspecialized court parts.

The New York City case study suggests that the re-creation of the juvenile court within the criminal court was a reform of degree rather than kind. That is, the introduction of the specialized courts for adolescents charged with JO crimes created a mixed system. These courts were designed to infuse probation sentences with treatment services and closer supervision. But the behavioral thresholds that provoked the use of incarceration evidently remained unchanged in the new court. By the second year, no more youths received this form of individualized justice in the specialized courts than in the regular courts. And the incarceration rate was the same for the two courts. Because of the sentencing framework for JOs (see table 10.1), it is unlikely that there were many differences in either the minimum sentences or in time served.

3. Toward a Youth Policy in Adult Court

More than twenty years after initiating the nation's first experiment in the criminalization of youth crime, New York offers two lessons in drawing and maintaining boundaries between juvenile and adult court. First, legislative exclusion does not end the influence of elements of juvenile justice either in jurisprudence or procedure. Individualization, treatment concerns, changeability, and discretion influence both the initial decision to charge a teenager in criminal court and also the allocation of punishments once transferred. Juvenile justice is reproduced in systems of criminal justice through various legal and administrative avenues for dividing eligible juveniles into categories of "offenders" to be tried as adults and "delinquents" who remain in the juvenile court.

Juvenile justice is also reproduced among criminal justice officials in the way they assess the risks that an adolescent will fall into the offender (adult) category. This is often related to parental support, or the support of some surrogate figure (Singer 1996). Courts more often applied the harsher JO label to African American adolescents. The courts were reacting ostensibly to the perception that African American youth lacked either parental support from single-parent households or community support from other social institutions, forms of support that provide adult supervision of their behavior. However, with the JO label comes a set of legal tracks that may further divide juveniles into those deserving and undeserving of youthful offender status. While these factors typically influence decision making in the juvenile court as well, the consequences in New York were far higher in terms of exposure to harsher conditions of punishment and the risk of disenfranchisement as an adult.

Whether these legal labels serve either social or legal policy goals on youth crime also is unclear. The labels are confusing to everyone except the officials directly making decisions about the status of juveniles. A simple law became quite complex in the different ways in which it conflated the stated purposes of juvenile and criminal justice. The reproduction of juvenile justice within the system of criminal justice in New York expanded the legal labels and categories to classify adolescents: status offender, juvenile delinquent, restrictive juvenile delinquent, juvenile offender with youthful offender status, and juvenile offender. Each legal label had procedural consequences that further divided juveniles into those deserving and undeserving of serious criminal punishment. For example, being convicted in New York's criminal court as a juvenile offender did not automatically mean harsher penalties than what the same juvenile might have received in juvenile court. This is reflected in the data that show a large proportion of convicted juveniles receiving sentences of probation.

Informing both the 1976 and 1978 laws is the assumption that criminal justice officials are more capable of identifying the chronic delinquent and preventing youth such as Willie Bosket from committing serious violent crimes. Accordingly, youthful offender status and a sentence of probation give criminal justice officials the ability to identify and track juveniles from the first moment they were charged with a designated felony offense. Similarly, legislative transfer, or exclusion, allows criminal justice officials to enter the business of watching over delinquents at an earlier age than what was possible prior to recriminalization. Variation in the implementation of these laws further complicates the results of the New York experiment.

The reproduction of juvenile justice in New York's criminal court suggests that the 1978 Juvenile Offender Law, as implemented in a bifurcated system of "new juvenile" and regular courts for these defendants, recreated the many patterns of decision making that gave rise to the recurring criticisms of the juvenile court. The Juvenile Offender Law contains multiple legal and organizational safety valves with which to divide juveniles into categories of offenders deserving or undeserving of treatment independent of the severity of their offensive behavior. But these are precisely the discretions that invite treating similar cases in grossly dissimilar ways. The vagueness of the sorting process that allocates some JO defendants to the specialized parts and others to the regular parts is a further illustration of the ambivalence in the criminal courts toward adolescent offenders.

In contrast to the old ideology of treatment within a singular juvenile justice system, and despite the cosmetic appearance of "specialized courts" for adolescents in the criminal court, the new ideology emphasizes managerialism and actuarial justice in systems of criminal justice (Simon 1998). It ignores the stated punishment objectives of the criminal court for the purpose of identifying youth at risk of repeated criminal behavior. How well this task is done depends not only on the knowledge that criminal justice officials accumulate of the juveniles they see in criminal court, but also on the ways in which organizational interests have emerged in classifying juveniles as offenders.

New York's Juvenile Offender Law, however, has claimed at least one success: it calmed public and official criticism of juvenile justice in New York (Singer 1996). It has satisfied a variety of professional interests in its ability to maintain the legitimacy of complex systems of juvenile and criminal justice. It stopped the rapid-fire pattern of emergency legislation that emerged in the 1970s. But new sources of injustice are emerging that will produce new grounds for a crisis in which reform will once more be advocated.

Historically, the uncontrolled discretion of the juvenile court to incarcerate juveniles for relatively minor offenses launched reforms that led to the regulation of punishment in traditional systems of juvenile justice (Bernard 1992; Zimring 1999). So too will limits be needed on the way in which criminal justice officials have unfettered discretion to decide which juveniles are deserving of criminal punishment. Youth policy and law will have to regulate the processes by which criminal justice officials identify and track juveniles as offenders, not only at the point of arrest, adjudication, and disposition, but also at the point of incarceration. To do so will require principles to animate and justify the procedures. One way to address these equity concerns is to restrict eligibility for automatic waiver to a narrow list of violent offenses. Murder is the one offense for which there is considerable jurisprudential and organizational support for letting criminal justice officials decide if criminal punishment is warranted (Zimring 1999). By restricting the discretionary decision making of criminal justice officials to capital crimes, the opportunity they currently have to introduce disparities among juveniles charged with a wide range of offenses would be eliminated. Had such discipline informed the 1976 Juvenile Justice Reform Act, the crisis created by Willie Bosket two years later would not have had the needlessly broad consequences for juvenile justice in New York that were mandated in 1978.

Acknowledgments

Andrew Pollard contributed research assistance for this chapter. Several sections of this chapter were adapted from *Recriminalizing Delinquency: Violent Juvenile Crime and Juvenile Justice Reform,* Cambridge University Press, 1996. All views, opinions, and errors in the chapter are solely those of the authors and do not reflect the opinions or policies of their institutions.

References
Cases Cited

In re Gault, 387 U.S. 1, 87 S. Ct 1428, 18 L. Ed. 2d 527 (1967).
Kent v. United States, 383 U.S. 541.

Other References

Bernard, Thomas. 1992. *The Cycle of Juvenile Justice.* New York: Oxford University Press.
Butterfield, Fox. 1995. *All God's Children: The Bosket Family and the American Tradition of Violence.* New York: Avon Books.
Corriero, Michael A. 1990. "Outside Counsel-Youth Parts: Constructive Response to the Challenge of Youth Crime." *New York Law Journal* 204:1.
Cressey, Donald, and Robert A. McDermott. 1973. *Diversion from the Juvenile Justice System.* Ann Arbor: National Assessment of Juvenile Corrections, University of Michigan.
Douglas, Mary. 1986. *How Institutions Think.* Syracuse: Syracuse University Press.
Liberman, Akiva, and William Raleigh. 1998. *Specialized Court Parts for Juvenile Offenders in New York City's Adult Felony Courts: Case Processing in 1994–1995 and 1995–1996.* Presented at the Annual Meeting of the American Society of Criminology, Washington, D.C., November.
Liberman, Akiva, William Raleigh, and Freda Solomon. 2000. *Specialized Court Parts for Juvenile Offenders in New York City's Adult Felony Courts: Case Processing in 1994–1995 and 1995–1996.* New York: New York City Criminal Justice Agency.
McGarrell, Edmund F. 1988. *Juvenile Correctional Reform: Two Decades of Policy and Procedural Change.* Albany: State University of New York Press.
Moore, Mark, James Q. Wilson, and Ralph Gants. 1978. "Violent Attacks and Chronic Offenders: A Proposal for Concentrating the Resources of New York's Criminal Justice System on the 'Hard Core' of the Crime Problem." Albany: New York State Commission on Management and Productivity in the Public Sector.
Rothman, David J. 1980. *Conscience and Convenience: The Asylum and Its Alternatives in Progressive America.* Boston: Little Brown.
Simon, Jonathan. 1998. "Ghosts of the Disciplinary Machine: Lee Harvey Oswald, Life-History, and the Truth of Crime." *Yale Journal of Law and the Humanities* 10:75
Singer, Simon I. 1996. *Recriminalizing Delinquency: Violent Juvenile Crime and Juvenile Justice Reform.* New York: Cambridge University Press
Smith, Charles P., P. S. Alexander, G. L. Kemp, and E. N. Lemert. 1980. *A National Assessment of Serious Juvenile Crime and the Juvenile Justice System: The Need for a Rational Response.* Washington: National Institute for Juvenile Justice and Delinquency Prevention.

Wolfgang, Marvin E., Robert Figlio, and Thorsten Sellin. 1972. *Delinquency in a Birth Cohort.* Chicago: University of Chicago Press.

Wolfgang, Marvin E., Robert Figlio, Paul Tracey, and Simon I. Singer. 1985. *The National Survey of Crime Severity.* Bureau of Justice Statistics. Washington: Government Printing Office.

Zimring, Franklin E. 1982. *The Changing Legal World of Adolescence.* New York: Free Press.

———. 1999. *American Youth Violence.* New York: Oxford University Press.

Notes

1. In New York, a juvenile court is technically known as a Family Court, where delinquency cases are just one part of the custody, divorce, and other civil family matters that family court judges can see. To be more consistent with the research literature that deals with delinquency and juvenile justice, we will refer to New York's Family Courts as juvenile courts.

2. Only six months earlier, he had vetoed a death penalty bill, and some believed that he wanted to act tough on crime by proposing at the time the most punitive delinquency law in the nation (Smith et al., 1980).

3. The State Division for Youth (DFY) was at that time the juvenile corrections authority for the state of New York. Today, it is known as the Office of Children and Youth Services.

4. The reasons for recriminalization in the form of nonjudicial waiver are not that far removed from the stated reasons for the juvenile court. At the beginning of the twentieth century, juvenile courts emerged in response to the perceived failure of criminal courts to control and to prevent the offensive behavior of juveniles late into adolescence. Juvenile courts made it possible to implement new ways of controlling older juveniles, particularly in the form of community treatment through probation (Rothman 1980). The juvenile court made it easier to arrest juveniles for less serious offenses. Prior to the juvenile court, criminal justice officials were limited in the kinds of adjudications and dispositions that could be granted to juveniles late into adolescence. The juvenile court provided officials with an additional legal and administrative avenue in which to label juveniles as delinquents. Thus, the Juvenile Offender Law expanded the legal ways in which juveniles in New York could be classified and labeled as either delinquents or juvenile offenders.

5. The Moore report drew on the Wolfgang, Figlio, and Sellin (1972) *Delinquency in a Birth Cohort* study to conclude that "a relatively small number of offenders account for a large proportion of all serious offenses. The implication is that if we wish to limit serious offenses there may be some advantage to concentrating on chronic offenders. Because chronic offenders account for a large fraction of serious offenses, to some extent this emphasis will occur naturally as a result of concentrating on serious offenses. However, since chronic offenders also occasionally commit lesser offenses, we may want to know something about the criminal records of even minor offenders to assist the judge in choosing a

proper disposition. In effect, we want to concentrate on both serious offenses and chronic offenders" (Moore, Wilson, and Gants 1978, 21).

6. The 1943 act mandated that cases with YO defendants be heard in specialized part. However, the 1978 law has no such provision. Youths are assigned to either JO courts or regular felony courts through a purely administrative and generally unregulated procedure.

7. There is no evidence to suggest that per capita rates of serious violent offenses by juveniles are higher in Buffalo (Erie County) or Rochester (Monroe County) than in the other urban non–New York City counties. Moreover, there is no reason to believe that citizens of Albany are so fortunate that they are victimized by only the least serious of violent juvenile offender offenses.

8. Thus, the specialized JO courts were intended to concentrate relevant institutional resources, and to facilitate timely and regular contact between the court and actors working with juvenile offenders. These include both public agencies such as the probation and police departments, as well as private agencies offering alternatives to detention and/or incarceration. It was also hoped that more individualized and meaningful interaction with the court would increase the possibility that these teenagers' initial interaction with the criminal justice system could be utilized more actively to reduce the likelihood of subsequent reoffending. These general goals, of course, are similar to the goals of other specialized courts, including drug courts and domestic violence courts.

9. This summary excludes about 15 percent of cases, in which defendants waived their rights to a grand jury, and then pleaded guilty at Supreme Court arraignment. In New York's system, this waiver occurs in criminal court, before cases are arraigned in Supreme Court. These cases are not handled in the JO courts. Because they in effect go immediately to sentencing, these cases are not useful in comparison to cases in the JO courts.

Part Three

Perspectives on Reform

Chapter Eleven

A Developmental Perspective on Jurisdictional Boundary

LAURENCE STEINBERG AND ELIZABETH CAUFFMAN

The very existence of a separate justice system within which offenders who have not yet reached the age of majority are adjudicated, sanctioned, and rehabilitated is predicated on the premise that there are significant psychological differences between adolescents and adults, and that these differences are provoked by the normal process of development, age related, and legally relevant. For the past one hundred years in the United States, the acceptance of this premise has guided juvenile justice policy and maintained a jurisdictional boundary between juvenile and criminal court. Although this boundary was never impermeable, as Tanenhaus points out in this volume, it has been historically robust and violated only in extreme cases of dangerousness or recalcitrance, and only then when the age of the offender approached the upper bound of the juvenile court's jurisdiction.

As long as transfer to criminal court remains a rare event that is reserved for the oldest, most violent, and most recalcitrant offenders, the practice does not call into question the founding principle of the juvenile justice system; one can very reasonably argue that a small number of offenders should be kept out of the juvenile system because they pose a genuine threat to the safety of other juveniles, because the severity of their offense merits a more severe punishment, or because their history of repeated offending bodes poorly for their ultimate rehabilitation. It is quite another matter, however, when the transfer to criminal court of various classes of juvenile offenders—classes defined solely by the charged offense—starts to become the rule rather than the exception. Indeed, the recent movement toward easing the transfer of large numbers of juveniles to adult criminal court, whether by legislative exclusion, prosecutorial discretion, or judicial waiver, is not simply an important change in social policy. It is a fundamental challenge to the very premise on which the juvenile court was founded: that adolescents and adults are different in ways that warrant their differential treatment under the law. It is a challenge that can be logically sustained only by arguing that the differences between adolescents and adults are illusory or insufficiently compelling to override other grounds for transfer (e.g., public safety, deterrence, retribution).

The purpose of this chapter is to add the perspective of developmental psychology to the debate about transfer policy. Generally speaking, such a perspective examines the soundness of age-based legal policies in light of scientific research and theory on psychological development. It asks whether the distinctions we draw between people of different ages under the law are sensible in light of what we know about age differences in legally relevant aspects of intellectual, emotional, or social functioning.

Our primary task in the pages that follow is to examine the evidence on the development of legally relevant competencies, capacities, and capabilities and suggest whether, on the basis of what we, as developmental psychologists, know about development, a jurisdictional boundary should be drawn between juveniles and adults, and if so, at what age it should be drawn. Although we shall indirectly address whether considerations of public safety, deterrence, and retribution are so compelling that they outweigh any claims that can be made on the basis of observed differences between adolescents and adults, a direct examination of this issue does not fall squarely within the bailiwick of developmental psychology. It is crucial to ask whether transferring juveniles to the adult criminal justice system in fact makes for more effective deterrence, community safety, or public confidence in the fairness of the legal system, and it is even more important to ask whether these goals are more worthwhile than preserving the legal distinction between juveniles and adults because of differences in their developmental status. Although a developmental perspective can inform the discussion of these moral, political, and practical questions, it cannot answer them.

Before addressing these issues further, it is only fair to ask whether or why a developmental perspective on jurisdictional boundary is even relevant to contemporary discussions of transfer policy. After all, current discussions about transfer are typically not about the characteristics of the offender, but about the seriousness and harmfulness of the offense—factors that are independent of the offender's age or maturity. Indeed, the recent shift in juvenile justice policy from an offender-based focus to an offense-based focus explicitly seeks to remove developmental considerations from the discussion. The oft-heard admonition "Adult time for adult crime" says nothing about the age of the offender, except for the fact that it ought to be considered irrelevant.

In our view, it is logically impossible to make the age of the offender irrelevant in discussions of criminal justice policy. Regardless of the different degrees of importance one attaches to the various moral, legal, political, and practical issues that enter into the transfer debate, the fact that some crimes are committed by individuals who are not yet developmentally mature cannot be ignored. A fair punishment for an adult is unfair when applied to a child who did not understand the consequences of his or her actions or who was unable to exert control over his or her behavior. The ways we interpret and apply laws should rightfully vary when the case at hand involves a defendant whose understanding of the law is limited by intellectual immaturity or whose judgment is impaired by emotional immaturity. And the implications and consequences of administering a long and harsh punishment are very different when the offender is young than when he or she is an adult.

Readers who are not convinced of the need to take the offender's age into account in adjudicating a criminal act should partake in a simple thought experiment in which they imagine the same crime—for sake of argument, a shooting—committed by a twenty-six-year-old, a sixteen-year-old, and a six-year-old, and then ask whether it is reasonable to subject individuals of these different ages to the same court proceeding and sanctions. The experiment will make clear that the issue is not *whether* the age of the offender ought to be taken into account, but *how* it ought to be taken into account. People may differ in their opinions about the extent to which, the ways in which, and the age period during which an offender's age should be considered in decisions concerning transfer, adjudication, and sentencing, but ignoring this factor entirely is like trying to ignore an elephant that has wandered into the courtroom. If one is willing to acknowledge that the age of the offender does matter, independent of the harmfulness or seriousness of the offense, a developmental perspective is needed to inform decisions about *how and at what points in the process* age ought to be taken into account.

Although this chapter is about jurisdictional boundary, it is important to recognize that maintaining separate juvenile and criminal justice systems is only one way of taking the age of the offender into account, a point of view that has been articulated by Feld (1997) and others. In theory, an offender's age could be taken into account within a single criminal justice system, in which the relevant decision makers (e.g., judges, attorneys, probation personnel) understood how juveniles and adults differed developmentally and applied this understanding at various points in the adjudication and sentencing process. In practice, however, it is unrealistic to think that widespread training to this level of enlightened expertise could be accomplished. One of the most compelling arguments in favor of a separate juvenile justice system is that doing so increases the likelihood that a young offender's case will be considered by individuals who have some special expertise in dealing with juveniles and who have developed routine ways of taking age and development into account when making decisions about adjudication, transfer, or dispositions. Our chapter starts from this premise, presumes the need for a separate juvenile justice system, and asks how a developmental perspective informs where, not whether, the jurisdictional boundary should be drawn.

Our goal in this chapter is to highlight those aspects of psychological development that are most relevant to the transfer debate and to indicate how a systematic consideration of the developmental-psychological literature might inform the discussion. We begin this endeavor with a general introduction to the science of developmental psychology, followed by a specific discussion of the nature of adolescence as a developmental period.

1. The Science of Developmental Psychology

Developmental psychology, broadly defined, concerns the scientific study of changes in physical, intellectual, emotional, and social development over the life cycle. Developmental psychologists are mainly interested in the study of "normative" development (i.e., patterns of behavior, cognition, and emotion that are regular and predictable within the vast majority of the population of individuals of a given chronological age), but they are also interested in understanding normal individual differences in development (i.e., common variations within the range of what is considered normative for a given chronological age) as well as the causes and consequences of atypical or pathological development (i.e., development that departs significantly from accepted norms). To the extent that the issues under consideration in the waiver debate are framed as part of a discussion about *policy,* the focus of a developmentally oriented discussion must be primarily on normative development, since the logic of drawing distinctions between adolescents and adults under the law must be based on age differences that characterize the population in general. As we shall make clear, differences among individuals, whether within or outside the normal range, are clearly relevant to legal practice (e.g., where a determination that an individual acted in a certain way because of mitigating circumstances or mental illness is relevant to his or her adjudication), but differences among individuals who are the same chronological age generally are not relevant to policy. From the vantage point of developmental psychology, then, one asks whether the study of normative development indicates that there are scientific reasons to warrant the differential treatment of young people and adults within the legal system.

The majority of young people who commit serious offenses are teenagers (Hirschi and Gottfredson 1983). It is important, therefore, to consider how the nature of *normative adolescent development* in particular might inform policy making and practice within the juvenile and criminal justice systems. Although delinquent and criminal acts are also committed by preadolescent children (those under twelve) and by young adults (those eighteen and older), the focus of the contemporary debate over how youthful offenders should be viewed and treated has been, and will likely continue to be, mainly on individuals between the ages of twelve and seventeen. Developmental psychology has potentially important things to say about the treatment of preadolescent children and young adults within the juvenile and criminal justice systems, but the present discussion focuses on the age period most under current political scrutiny: the years between twelve and seventeen.

With regard to public policy in general, and to the transfer debate in particular, the period from twelve to seventeen is an extremely important age range, for three interrelated reasons. The first, and most important, reason is that this age is an inherently transitional time, during which there are rapid and dramatic changes in individuals' physical, intellectual, emotional, and social capabilities. Indeed, other than infancy, there is probably no period of human development characterized by more rapid or pervasive transformations in individual competencies, capabilities, and capacities. There is therefore good reason to believe that individuals at the point of entry into adolescence are very different than are individuals who are making the transition out of adolescence. If there is a period in the life span during which one might choose to draw a line between incompetent and competent individuals, this is it.

A second feature of adolescence that makes it relevant to the transfer debate is that it is a period of potential malleability, during which experiences in the family, peer group, school, and other settings still have a chance to influence the course of development. Unlike infancy, during which much of development is dictated by biology and influenced only by extreme environmental variations, and unlike adulthood, by which time most intellectual, physical, emotional, and social development is more or less complete, adolescence, like childhood, is a period of potential plasticity in response to changes in the environment. To the extent that this plasticity is great, transferring juveniles into a criminal justice system that precludes a rehabilitative response may not be very sensible public policy. To the extent that plasticity is limited, however, transfer is less worrisome.

Finally, adolescence is an important formative period, during which many developmental trajectories become firmly established and increasingly difficult to alter. Events that occur in adolescence often cascade into adulthood, particularly in the realms of education and work, but also in the domains of mental and physical health, family formation, and interpersonal relationships. As a consequence, many adolescent experiences have a tremendous cumulative impact. The importance of this fact for the present discussion is that bad decisions or poorly formulated policies pertaining to juvenile offenders may have unforeseen and possibly iatrogenic consequences that are very hard to undo.

The transitional, malleable, and formative nature of adolescence provides a sound rationale for focusing on this age as the age period during which we might attempt to establish legally defined age-related boundaries between developmentally immature and developmentally mature individuals. Indeed, if developmental psychology were able to point to a given age at which individuals made the shift from immaturity to maturity, it would make the designation of a jurisdictional boundary that much easier. Unfortunately, adolescence does not lend itself to such a precise partitioning on the basis of chronological age, for several reasons.

First, adolescence is a period of tremendous intra-individual variability. Within any given individual, the developmental timetable of different aspects of maturation may vary markedly, such that a given teenager may be mature physically but immature emotionally, socially precocious but an intellectual late bloomer. In addition, development rarely follows a straight line during adolescence—periods of progress often alternate with periods of regression. This intra-individual variability makes it difficult, if not impossible, to make generalizations about an adolescent's level of maturity on the basis of any one indicator alone. A tall, physically mature juvenile with an adult appearance may very well have the decision-making abilities of a child. An adolescent who carries himself like an adult today may act like a child tomorrow.

Variability *among* individuals in their biological, cognitive, emotional, and social characteristics is more important still, for it means that it is difficult to draw generalizations about the psychological capabilities of individuals who share the same chronological age. Unlike infancy and most of childhood, for example, during which developmental maturity and chronological age are closely linked, most research suggests that from early adolescence on, chronological age is a very poor marker for developmental maturity—as a visit to any junior high school will surely attest. Another way to put this is that differences *within* a given age group—differences among fourteen-year-olds, for example—are likely to be greater than differences *between* this age group and the adjacent ones (i.e., differences between fourteen-year-olds and either thirteen-year-olds or fifteen-year-olds). The psychological heterogeneity of the adolescent population makes it difficult to develop policies, including transfer policies, that are based on bright-line distinctions made on the basis of age.

There is one final point about variability during adolescence that is especially relevant to the use of age in the formulation of transfer policy. Most studies of adolescent development have involved white middle-class youngsters. Although this state of affairs is changing, we still do not know whether any developmental timetables—as imprecise as they may be—apply equally well across different socioeconomic, racial, and ethnic groups. (For example, the average intellectual competencies of young- sters who have been raised in poverty lag behind those of their middle-class counterparts.) Nor do we do not know whether the developmental "trajectories" of antisocial behavior—that is, the antecedents of involve-ment in delinquent or criminal activities as well as the predictors of desis-tance—differ as a function of race, ethnicity, or socioeconomic status. Be-cause a disproportionate number of juveniles who come into contact with the legal system are neither white nor middle-class, we must exercise great caution in making age-based policy recommendations whose imple-mentation will mainly affect one group of adolescents on the basis of find-ings derived from research conducted on an entirely different population.

The highly variable nature of development during adolescence—vari-ability within individuals, among individuals, and among populations— makes it a fuzzily bounded, confusing, and moving target for policy mak-ers. It calls for caution on the part of developmental experts with regard to the sorts of generalizations one can make about adolescents of a given age. Nevertheless, an approach that focuses on age-related changes in legally relevant competencies, capacities, and capabilities can help to ar-ticulate the inherently developmental nature of the questions at the very core of the transfer debate. Even if it is not determinative, developmental evidence can provide a sensible backdrop against which various legal, policy, and pragmatic considerations can be raised, analyzed, argued, and decided upon. Our purpose in this paper thus is to set the stage, so to speak, for these analyses to take place.

2. Adjudicating Adolescents as Adults: A Developmental Perspective

Transferring a juvenile to criminal court has three sets of implications that lend themselves to a developmental analysis: those that involve the legal process, those that involve legal standards, and those that involve the possible outcomes of an adjudication. First, transfer to adult court alters the legal process by which a minor is tried. Although there are certainly exceptions to the rule, criminal court is based on an adversarial model, while juvenile court has been based, at least in theory, on a more cooperative model. This difference in the climates of juvenile versus adult courts is significant because, as we shall discuss later, it is unclear at what age individuals have sufficient understanding of the ramifications of the adversarial process and the different vested interests of prosecutors, defense attorneys, and judges.

Second, the legal standards applied in adult and juvenile courts are different in a number of ways. Although the standards for due-process protections are clearer in criminal court than in juvenile court, it is not clear whether the protections afforded in adult court are adequate for juvenile defendants. For example, competence to stand trial is presumed among adult defendants unless they suffer from a serious mental illness or substantial mental retardation. We do not know if the presumption of adjudicative competence holds for juveniles, who, even in the absence of mental retardation or mental illness, may lack sufficient competence to participate in the adjudicative process (Grisso and Schwartz 1999). Standards for judging culpability (that is, the extent to which an individual can be held accountable or blameworthy for damage or injury he or she causes) may be different in juvenile and adult courts as well. Again, in the absence of mental illness or substantial deficiency, adults are presumed to be responsible for their own behavior. We do not know the extent to which this presumption applies to juveniles, or whether the validity of this presumption differs as a function of the juvenile's age.

Finally, the choice of trying a young offender in adult versus juvenile court determines the possible outcomes of the adjudication. In adult court, the outcome of being found guilty of a serious crime is nearly always some sort of punishment. In juvenile court, the outcome of being found delinquent may be some sort of punishment, but juvenile courts typically retain the option of a rehabilitative disposition, in and of itself or in combination with some sort of punishment. The difference between possible rehabilitation and certain punishment for the minor who is waived to adult court has two significant ramifications. The first is that the stakes of the adjudication are raised substantially. Rather than face a limited amount of time in a training school, the juvenile on trial in adult court for a serious offense faces the very real possibility of a long period of incarceration in prison, with potential iatrogenic consequences and increased risk of recidivism after release (see Bishop and Frazier in this volume). Although this argument may not carry weight with those who favor harsh consequences for young offenders for purposes of retribution, from a utilitarian perspective, a punishment that ultimately results in increased offending does not make very much sense. Thus, even if one were to argue that adolescents have the competencies necessary to participate in an adversarial court proceeding and to be held culpable for their actions, one could still question the wisdom of imposing adultlike sanctions on young offenders. The second consequence concerns the presumption of amenability. In juvenile court, offenders generally are presumed amenable unless the prosecutor demonstrates otherwise. In adult court, however, amenability is not presumed, and must instead be demonstrated by the defendant's counsel.

Our argument, then, is that the significance of having a jurisdictional boundary inheres in the different *presumptions* about age and its relation to development that decision makers within the juvenile and criminal justice systems bring to the table, because different procedures and options derive from these presumptions. The juvenile court operates under the presumption that offenders are immature, in three different senses of the word: their development is incomplete, their judgment is callow, and their character is still maturing. The adult court, in contrast, presumes that defendants are mature: competent, responsible, and unlikely to change.[1] Which of these presumptions best characterizes individuals between the ages of twelve and seventeen? Is there an approximate age at which the presumptions of the criminal court become more applicable to an offender than the presumptions of the juvenile court? Because developmental psychologists have learned a great deal about the transitions that occur between childhood and adulthood in the realms of competence, responsibility, and malleability, their research may be valuable in guiding the formulation of transfer policies founded on scientifically verifiable developmental evidence.

The limitation of developmental research as far as the law is concerned is that it rarely yields the sorts of dichotomous boundaries that are customarily used to create bright-line age distinctions under the law. Instead, most developmental analyses reveal that development is gradual rather than abrupt, quantitative rather than qualitative, and, as we noted earlier, highly variable among individuals of the same chronological age. In our view, developmental research is best utilized not to establish a bright-line boundary between adolescence and adulthood, but to point to age-related trends in certain legally relevant attributes, such as the intellectual or emotional capabilities that affect decision making in court and on the street. These trends can then be used to define legal age boundaries that are reasonably consistent with the developmental evidence. This approach may be particularly useful in three pursuits relevant to transfer policy:

1. identifying the lower boundary of the age range below which a particular attribute can be safely assumed to be absent, and that therefore would preclude the treatment of younger individuals as adults;

2. identifying the upper boundary of the age range beyond which that same attribute may be safely presumed to be present, and would recommend the treatment of individuals older than this as adults; and

3. delineating the assessment tools to be used and the guidelines to be applied in making differential recommendations about individuals whose age falls between the two boundaries (this is largely a task that falls within the bailiwick of forensic psychology, but it is clear that forensic assessments of juveniles should be done against a developmental backdrop [Grisso 1998]).

This approach leads to the identification of *three,* not two, categories of individuals: *juveniles,* who should be categorically nontransferrable to criminal court; *adults,* who should automatically charged in adult court; and *youths,* whose transferability to criminal court should be determined not on the basis of the alleged offense, but through forensic evaluation (through competence testing, clinical interviews, etc.).[2] This three-way classification scheme, in our view, more appropriately recognizes the variability in development among individuals who are in the midst of adolescence and the resulting difficulty in drawing bright-line distinctions on the basis of chronological age.

3. Translating the Waiver Question into Developmental Issues

As we have suggested, the transition from adolescence to adulthood does not occur at a fixed, well-defined age. Not only do different individuals mature at different rates and times, but different abilities may develop at different times as well. Accordingly, instead of asking where to draw the line between adolescence and adulthood for the purposes of making transfer policy, we ask what ages individuals can be presumed to possess (or to not possess) the various attributes that are potentially relevant to transfer considerations, such as those listed in *Kent.* Given the aforementioned problems in using chronological age to make quantitatively precise distinctions between individuals who do versus do not demonstrate a particular capability, our approach has been to suggest approximate age ranges that best reflect the current state of knowledge in the field of developmental psychology. As we noted earlier, however, this knowledge is limited by the concentration of research on white and middle-class samples of adolescents. In the absence of systematic research on the development of these attributes in other populations, and in view of the fact that the establishment of a jurisdictional boundary cannot wait until all the relevant research is in, we have little choice other than to base our recommendations on the existing literature and to note that the conclusions must be viewed with appropriate caution.

To address the issue of transfer from a developmental perspective, we must be more specific about the aspects of development in question, and we must ask whether, how, and on what timetable these aspects of development change during the transition from adolescence to adulthood. In our view, because transfer has implications for the legal procedures, standards, and outcomes a juvenile defendant will encounter, the key developmental areas of interest can be categorized as competence, responsibility, and amenability. In the pages that follow, we examine the developmental evidence and theory relevant to these three domains. In particular we ask the following three questions:

1. *When do individuals become competent to be adjudicated in an adversarial court context?* This question is more complex than that of whether an adolescent is competent to stand trial. Adjudicative competence, broadly defined, refers to participation in a criminal proceeding and includes the ability to assist counsel in preparing a defense, to enter pleas, to retain or dismiss counsel, to consider plea agreements, and so forth. In *Gault,* it was argued that as long as one was subject to adultlike (i.e., punitive) penalties, even if administered by a juvenile court, one had the due-process rights of adults as well, an argument that can be extended to other competence-relevant issues (e.g., providing confessions, entering pleas, etc.). Given the adversarial nature of criminal court proceedings, at what age are adolescents likely to possess the skills necessary to protect their own interests in the courtroom and participate effectively in their own defense?

2. *When do individuals meet the criteria for adult blameworthiness? Put differently, is there an age before which individuals, by virtue of "normal" psychological immaturity, should be considered to be of "diminished culpability" and therefore held less accountable, and proportionately less punishable, for their actions?* The longstanding "infancy defense" holds that individuals under the age of six are incapable of forming criminal intent and are therefore not culpable for any offenses in which they are involved. Less clear is how the development of accountability progresses between the ages of six and adulthood. We know that under certain conditions—for instance, in cases in which a defendant is diagnosed as mentally ill—an individual's culpability may be viewed as inherently diminished by virtue of deficiencies in cognitive or emotional functioning. Analogous concerns have seldom been raised about deficiencies in cognitive or emotional functioning that are *developmentally normative* but that have no less an impact on an individual's behavior or decision making. Thus, it is reasonable to ask at what age one can expect a person to have the maturity and perspective to differentiate between wrong and right, foresee the consequences of his or

her decisions, and appreciate the effects of his or her decisions on other people.

3. *Is there a point in development at which individuals cease to be good candidates for rehabilitation, by virtue of the diminished likelihood of change in the psychological and behavioral characteristics thought to affect criminal behavior or because of diminished amenability to treatment?* A fundamental tenet of the juvenile justice system is that juveniles can be rehabilitated because their characters are not yet fully formed. Amenability is therefore a factor in most waiver determinations, because, if an individual is deemed to be unlikely to change or not amenable to treatment, a rehabilitative disposition will serve no useful purpose. In general, children are presumed to be more malleable than adults, but is there a predictable timetable along which individuals change from relatively changeable to relatively unchangeable?

In the following sections, we review the empirical and theoretical evidence regarding the development of competence, accountability, and amenability. Two categories of evidence are relevant. Direct evidence is derived from developmental studies of the actual legal phenomena in question—that is, studies of adjudicative competence, criminal accountability, and amenability to rehabilitation. Unfortunately, such evidence is extremely rare, because few empirical studies have examined age-related changes in these arenas. Indirect evidence is derived from studies of the intellectual and psychosocial phenomena presumed to underlie adjudicative competence, criminal accountability, and amenability to rehabilitation—phenomena such as hypothetical thinking, impulse control, or malleability. Although more research is needed to establish the links between these intellectual and psychosocial phenomena and the legal phenomena they are presumed to underlie, general trends in these domains are nevertheless informative.

4. Research and Theory on Adjudicative Competence

Two specific types of competencies are needed to be tried in criminal court; one set is well established, whereas the second set is less so. First, the individual must be competent to assist counsel. More specifically, the Supreme Court posited in *Dusky v. United States,* 362 U.S. 402 (1960), that competence to stand trial requires that a defendant have "sufficient present ability to consult with his lawyer with a reasonable degree of rational understanding" and "a rational as well as factual understanding of the proceedings against him." Second, it has been argued that the individual must also demonstrate "decisional competence": the ability to make decisions about waiving rights, entering pleas, proceeding pro se, etc.; this sort of decision-making competence is more advanced than that set out in the *Dusky* criteria (Bonnie 1992). Legal opinions on the standards for decisional competence have been mixed, however. In *Godinez v. Moran*, 509 U.S. 389 (1993), the U.S. Ninth Circuit Court of Appeals ruled that "the legal standard used to determine a defendant's competency to stand trial is different from the standard used to determine competence to waive constitutional rights. A defendant is competent to waive counsel or plead guilty only if he has the capacity for 'reasoned choice' among the alternatives available to him." The Supreme Court disagreed, however, arguing that "if the *Dusky* standard is adequate for defendants who plead not guilty, it is necessarily adequate for those who plead guilty."

Despite the Court's failure to recognize the subtle differences between choices that protect one's rights and choices that waive them, the majority opinion did allow that trial courts must ensure that waivers of constitutional rights be made knowingly and voluntarily. It has been suggested that the unwillingness of courts to consider multiple competencies may be motivated, at least in part, by the desire to avoid lengthy and complicated competency assessments (Appelbaum 1993). But while issues of competence are relevant to only a small fraction of adult criminal cases, they are at the heart of the matter for most cases involving juvenile defendants, and it is therefore vital that we have an accurate understanding of the competencies exhibited by juveniles of various ages, and that we firmly establish the specific competencies required to ensure that the integrity of the trial process is maintained when young offenders are involved.

Numerous cognitive and social-cognitive[3] competencies that change during the adolescent years likely underlie the development of adjudicative competence, among them the ability to engage in hypothetical and logical decision making (in order to weigh the costs and benefits of different pleas), demonstrate reliable episodic memory (in order to provide accurate information about the offense in question), extend thinking into the future (in order to envision the consequences of different pleas), engage in advanced social perspective taking (in order to understand the roles and motives of different participants in the adversarial process), and understand and articulate one's own motives and psychological state (in order to assist counsel in mounting a defense). Developmental research indicates that these abilities emerge at somewhat different ages, but that it would be highly unlikely that an individual would satisfy all of these criteria much before the age of twelve. At the other extreme, research suggests that the majority of individuals have these abilities by age sixteen (for analyses of these and other relevant abilities, see Grisso 1997; Scott, Reppucci, and Woolard 1995; Steinberg and Cauffman 1996).

Although direct research regarding adolescents' understanding of court proceedings is fairly limited, there is ample evidence to raise concerns regarding the competence of adolescents under age fifteen to participate in criminal trials. Much of this literature has been reviewed and summarized by Grisso (1997). Grisso cites a number of studies indicating that at or below age fifteen, scores on standardized competence measures generally fall short of the thresholds below which competence is deemed questionable by experts, and that a third or more of fifteen- and sixteen-year olds do not have accurate conceptions of what a "right" is. General knowledge regarding trials and the roles of various participants, however, appears to be fairly well developed by age thirteen, although increases in familiarity with courtroom concepts continue beyond that age. Thus, although the majority of thirteen-year-olds would likely meet the minimal *Dusky* criteria, more detailed investigations of adolescents' understanding of their rights and of the implications of courtroom decisions leave little doubt that even at age fifteen, a significant fraction of adolescents should not be assumed competent to protect their own interests in adversarial legal settings.

It is important to understand the implications of the fact that adolescents do not fully comprehend the meaning of their right to remain silent, or of a decision to accept a plea bargain. The juvenile court acknowledges this diminished competence by having lower (if any) competency standards, by attempting to function in a way that protects the interests of the youngster who may not be able to participate fully in his or her own defense, and by limiting the punitiveness of the punishments to which a less-than-competent defendant might be exposed. The adversarial system of adult criminal courts, in contrast, relies in large part on the competence of the defendant to ensure that his or her attorney has the information necessary to prepare an effective defense, and that the defense is pursued in a manner consistent with the defendant's interests. In the criminal system, it is the defendant who must ultimately make plea decisions and other critical choices throughout the course of a trial. If an adolescent does not have the understanding, appreciation, or reasoning ability necessary to make such decisions, criminal court is an inappropriate venue for determining that adolescent's disposition.

One must bear in mind that in cases involving adults who are not competent to stand trial, the defendant may be "treated" or educated to meet the competence criteria (Grisso 1997). While there is some evidence that instructional programs can increase adolescents' understanding of the roles and procedures involved in court proceedings, it is not clear whether elements of adjudicative competence that go beyond the defendant's factual knowledge, such as "the capacity for reasoned choice," can be improved through education before an individual has developed the underlying cognitive and psychosocial competencies necessary for this capacity (Grisso 1997). Additional research, not only on the abilities of juveniles to perform necessary functions in criminal proceedings, but also on their capacity for improvement in response to education designed to correct deficiencies in adjudicative competence, would clarify such issues considerably.

It is our view, therefore, that the available evidence regarding the development of capabilities relevant to adjudicative competence indicates that no youngster under the age of thirteen should be tried in adult court. On the other hand, although more research is needed, especially on samples of poor and nonwhite youth, it is likely that the majority of individuals older than sixteen would satisfy the broader criteria for adjudicative competence set out in *Godinez*. On the basis of this evidence, it seems reasonable to recommend that individuals between the ages of thirteen and sixteen should be evaluated to determine their adjudicative competence before a waiver decision is made (similar conclusions were reached by Grisso [1997]). (Note, however, that adjudicative competence is a necessary, but not sufficient, condition for waiver, since culpability and amenability issues must also be considered.)

5. Research and Theory on Culpability

The adult justice system presumes that defendants who are found guilty are responsible for their own actions and should be held accountable and punished accordingly. Historically, those who are guilty but less responsible for their actions (e.g., because of one or more mitigating factors) receive proportionately less punishment (as Zimring notes in this volume). It is therefore worth considering whether, because of the relative immaturity of minors, it may be justified to view them as being less blameworthy than adults for the very same infractions—that is, whether developmental immaturity should be viewed as a relevant mitigating factor. If, for example, adolescents below a certain age cannot foresee the consequences of their actions, or cannot control their impulses, one should not hold them as culpable for their actions as one would hold an adult.

We use the term "culpability" as a shorthand for several interrelated phenomena, including responsibility, accountability, blameworthiness, and punishability. In theory, these notions are relevant both to the adjudication of an individual's guilt or innocence, because an individual who is not responsible for his or her actions by definition cannot be guilty; and to the determination of a disposition (in juvenile court) or sentence (in criminal court), in that individuals who are found guilty but less than completely blameworthy merit proportionately less punishment than guilty individuals who are fully blameworthy.

In reality, the threshold for culpability in the context of an adjudication is so minimal—the ability to form criminal intent and the capacity to appreciate the wrongfulness of one's actions—that this is not an issue in the determination of the guilt or innocence of any normal individual older than eight or nine. Absent some sort of mental illness or retardation (which if present in a juvenile should merit the same consideration as in the case of an adult), anyone who is nine can form criminal intent and appreciate the wrongfulness of an action (Rest 1983). Diminished responsibility as a result of normative developmental immaturity is therefore not a reasonable claim in the adjudicatory phase of a juvenile's hearing. Because the criteria for taking into account diminished culpability in the context of a sentencing or dispositional decision are less clear, however, whether adolescents should receive proportionately less punishment by virtue of inherently diminished responsibility is a question best reserved for deciding how much and in what ways, not whether, a juvenile should be punished.

The extent to which culpability is relevant to the transfer issue (i.e., whether an offender is adjudicated in juvenile or criminal court) concerns the presumptions about culpability the operate within each venue and, more specifically, whether or how, during the sentencing phase of a criminal trial, a juvenile's developmental immaturity is taken into account. The rehabilitative ideal of the juvenile court argues against adjudicating a juvenile who is characterized by sufficiently diminished responsibility in a criminal court whose only response can be punitive. The argument for keeping juveniles in the juvenile system is that rehabilitation is a more reasonable disposition than punishment for a less than fully accountable juvenile. This argument hinges on two assumptions, however: (1) that juveniles are less blameworthy than adults; and (2) that the juvenile court inherently has more or better mechanisms for meting out a proportionately less severe punishment than does the criminal court. As developmental psychologists, we are interested in the first of these assumptions— that there are age differences in blameworthiness that are substantial enough to affect legal judgments about culpability.[4] Specifically, is there an age below which we can presume sufficiently diminished responsibility to argue that it is a mitigating factor, and is there an age beyond which we can presume sufficient maturity of judgment to hold an individual fully accountable?

It is important to note that culpability cannot really be researched directly, since an individual's culpability is something that is judged by someone else; it is largely in the eye of the beholder.[5] What can be studied, however, are the capabilities and characteristics of individuals that make them potentially *blameworthy,* such as their ability to behave intentionally or to know right from wrong. Some of the cognitive and social-cognitive capabilities that are potentially relevant to the assessment of blameworthiness are the same as those that are relevant to the assessment of adjudicative competence. In order to be fully accountable for an act, for example, a person must commit the act voluntarily, knowingly, and with some ability form reasonable expectations of the likely or potential consequences of the act (Scott and Grisso 1997). In this respect, logical decision making and ability to foresee the future ramifications of one's decisions are important to determinations of blameworthiness, just as they are to determinations of adjudicative competence. As we indicated in our earlier discussion of adjudicative competence, it is reasonable to assume that the average individual would be unlikely to have developed these abilities before age twelve, but that the average individual would have developed these abilities by age sixteen.

Initial studies of age differences in decision making focused on the cognitive processes involved (e.g., Fischoff 1992). (That is, they considered the mechanics of decision making in the absence of social and emotional factors that might influence the ways in which one's decision-making abilities are applied to real-world situations.) These investigations found few cognitive differences between adolescents as young as twelve or thirteen and adults, consistent with both developmental theory and research on the development of logical reasoning. Developmental theory posits that the cognitive capacity for logical reasoning emerges during early adolescence (between the ages of eleven and fourteen). According to Piaget, adolescents who have reached the stage of formal operational thinking are able to reason abstractly and deductively, and are thus cognitively equivalent to adults (Inhelder and Piaget 1958). Experimental evidence has tended to support this contention. Ward and Overton (1990) found that deductive reasoning abilities emerge during adolescence, with 80 percent of subjects exhibiting formal operational thought by grade twelve (i.e., by age seventeen), although studies also demonstrate that the *use* of these abilities varies, even among adults, in different situations (Overton 1990). Furthermore, in a review of studies concerning adolescents' abilities to make health care decisions, the Office of Technology Assessment (1991a, b, c) concluded that there were few differences in health care decision-making skills as a function of age among adolescents and young adults. A study by Belter and Grisso (1984), for example, assessed the ability of sixty males ages nine, fifteen, and twenty-one to recognize a violation of their rights as patients and take steps to protect these rights. Half of the participants at each age level received briefings on patient rights, and in a subsequent session all the subjects were shown videotaped counseling sessions and asked to identify any violation and provide recommendations for protecting the right in question. The fifteen-year-olds did not differ from the twenty-one-year-olds in the ability to recognize rights violations or in the benefit gained by briefings, but the nine-year-olds showed significantly lower recognition of (or less often asserted protection of) rights. The prevailing wisdom, then, is that cognitive differences between adolescents and adults are fewer and smaller than is customarily believed.

In addition to these cognitive and social-cognitive abilities, however, blameworthiness also presumes certain capabilities that are more interpersonal or emotional than cognitive in nature. Among these psychosocial capabilities, for example, are the ability to control one's impulses, to manage one's behavior in the face of pressure from others to violate the law, or to extricate oneself from a potentially problematic situation. Many of these capabilities have been examined in research on what we broadly refer to as "judgment," because deficiencies in these realms would likely interfere with individuals' abilities to act in ways that demonstrate mature enough decision making to qualify for adultlike accountability (e.g., Cauffman and Steinberg, in press; Scott, Reppucci, and Woolard 1995; Steinberg and Cauffman 1996). We suggest that these psychosocial factors fall into three broad categories: *responsibility* (the capacity to make a decision in an independent, self-reliant fashion), *perspective* (the capacity to place a decision within a broader temporal and interpersonal context), and *temperance* (the capacity to exercise self-restraint and control one's impulses) (Cauffman and Steinberg, in press; Steinberg and Cauffman 1996).

Although there has been some research to date on the development of various aspects of responsibility, perspective, and temperance during adolescence (for a review, see Steinberg and Cauffman 1996), few studies have compared adolescents and adults directly on these dimensions, and fewer still have attempted to examine the relations between these psychosocial elements of judgment and decision making in situations relevant to legal concerns. We recently completed a study designed to explore the relations between judgment and several aspects of psychosocial maturity within a sample of over a thousand individuals (Cauffman and Steinberg, in press). In this research, we examined age differences among twelve- to forty-eight-year olds' performance on a series of hypothetical judgment tasks designed to assess their likelihood of engaging in antisocial behavior (e.g., shoplifting, smoking marijuana, joy riding in a stolen car); performance on such tasks has been shown to be predictive of actual antisocial behavior (Brown, Clasen, and Eicher 1986).

Three overall patterns of findings from this study are relevant to the present discussion of culpability. First, we found clear and significant age differences on the measure of decision making in antisocial situations, with adults significantly less likely than adolescents to respond to the dilemmas in ways indicative of antisocial inclinations. Second, we found consistent age differences on a wide array of measures of responsibility, perspective, and temperance. Compared with adults, for example, adolescents scored lower on measures of self-restraint, consideration of future consequences, and self-reliance, three widely cited components of psychosocial maturity. Third, and most importantly, individuals who scored higher on the measures of psychosocial maturity were more likely to make socially responsible decisions in the hypothetical situations than those who were less psychosocially mature. Once the differences in responsibility, perspective, and temperance were accounted for, however, age was no longer a significant predictor of judgment. That is to say, although adults tended to make more socially responsible decisions than adolescents, this difference in decision making was due to differences in psychosocial maturity. On average, then, adolescents make poorer (more antisocial) decisions than adults because they are more psychosocially immature.

Although we did discover broad and consistent age trends in both decision making and psychosocial maturity, we could not identify a clearcut chronological age at which the increase in maturity is so dramatic that a bright-line age distinction is warranted. Nevertheless, it is clear that important progress in the development of psychosocial maturity continues to occur during late adolescence, beyond the point in development when age differences in purely logical abilities seem to disappear. Moreover, it certainly appears as if these changes in psychosocial maturity have an effect on individuals' ability to make consistently mature decisions when tempted in antisocial situations.

To the extent that judges are required to consider the "totality of circumstances" surrounding the commission of potentially illegal acts when evaluating juveniles' blameworthiness, information on the developmental timetable of these psychosocial influences on judgment is relevant to the discussion of adolescent blameworthiness. Indeed, in several previous publications (e.g., Cauffman and Steinberg 1996; Steinberg and Cauffman 1996), we have argued that these psychosocial factors may be as important in drawing inferences about juveniles' culpability as the cognitive factors mentioned earlier. Our reading of relevant rulings, moreover, suggests that when American legal opinions refer to individuals' maturity (or immaturity) of judgment, the courts have in mind something close to the psychosocial factors we have discussed. For example, in *Kent v. United States*, 383 U.S. 541 (1966), the United States Supreme Court reviewed the District of Columbia's statutory criteria for waiver to adult court, which included such factors as "the *sophistication and maturity* of the juvenile as determined by consideration of his home, environmental situation, *emotional attitude,* and pattern of living" (italics added).

Although there has been some research on the development of the various psychosocial factors potentially relevant to evaluations of blame-worthiness (for reviews, see Scott, Reppucci, and Woolard 1995; Steinberg and Cauffman 1996), few studies to date have compared adolescents and adults directly on these dimensions, and fewer still have attempted to examine the relations between these psychosocial elements of judgment and decision making in situations relevant to legal concerns. Nevertheless, it is clear from the little research that does exist (e.g., Cauffman and Steinberg, in press) that few individuals demonstrate adultlike psychosocial maturity and, consequently, adultlike judgment much before age twelve, and that many individuals do not demonstrate adultlike psychosocial maturity or judgment even at age seventeen.

The fact that many of the psychosocial capabilities that affect judgment in antisocial situations continue to develop over the course of adolescence is one reason for the difficulty we have in predicting adult offending from adolescent delinquency. Because at least some adolescent offending is likely the result of normative immaturity, rather than moral turpitude, most adolescents "age out" of antisocial behavior as they become more mature (Moffitt 1993). Although firm research evidence on the issue is lacking, antisocial behavior observed among individuals whose judgment is immature ought to be less predictive of adult offending than antisocial behavior observed among individuals who have attained the capacity for mature judgment.

It is not clear how research on the development of blameworthiness informs the transfer debate. Research on psychological development makes it quite clear that children as young as nine have the capacity for intentional behavior and know the difference between right and wrong (Rest 1983); as such, there is no reason why children of this age must unequivocally be held blameless for their conduct. At the same time, it is also clear that the vast majority of individuals below the age of thirteen lack certain intellectual and psychosocial capabilities that need to be present in order to hold someone *fully* accountable for his or her actions *under certain circumstances.* These circumstances include situations that call for logical decision making, situations in which the ultimate consequences of one's actions are not evident unless one has actually tried to foresee them, and situations in which sound judgment may be compromised by competing stimuli, such as very strong peer pressure to violate the law. Once individuals have reached a certain age—seventeen or so—

it is reasonable to expect that they possess the intellectual and psycho-social capacities that permit the exercise of good judgment, even under difficult circumstances. Thus, while pressure from one's friends to violate the law may be a reasonable mitigating factor in the case of a twelve-year-old, it is unlikely to be so in the case of a seventeen-year-old.

Research on the competencies relevant to culpability is ultimately more informative for decisions about *how* a juvenile should be treated at the sentencing or disposition phases than about *where* the juvenile ought to be treated. Both the juvenile and criminal courts have mechanisms available to take mitigating factors into account, including probation, a discounted sentence, or transfer back to the juvenile court from criminal court. Thus the relevance of research on blameworthiness to the specifics of the transfer debate is a function of the extent to which the criminal court in the particular jurisdiction is likely or able to accommodate juvenile immaturity in sentencing decisions; the less flexible the criminal court is, the more important developmental immaturity becomes as an argument to retain juvenile court jurisdiction for immature offenders.

Regardless of the venue, however, when the individual under consideration is younger than seventeen, it seems to us that developmentally normative immaturity should be added to the list of *possible* mitigating factors, along with the more typical ones of self-defense, mental state, and extenuating circumstances. Whether developmental immaturity is enough of a mitigating factor in a specific offender's case to diminish his or her blameworthiness cannot be determined without having additional information about the circumstances of the case. Nevertheless, the need for this additional information argues for a more individualized approach to both transfer and sentencing of juveniles, and argues against policies that do not permit such flexibility, such as transfer via legislative exclusion.

6. Research and Theory on Amenability

We noted earlier that one of the reasons that offenses historically have been adjudicated in juvenile court is that adolescents are presumed to be more amenable to treatment than adults and, consequently, better candidates for rehabilitation. Conversely, adults have been seen as relatively more hardened and, accordingly, less likely to profit from rehabilitation.

Amenability means something slightly different to developmental psychologists than it does under the law as it is generally practiced. In legal practice, amenability refers to the likelihood of an individual desisting from crime and/or being rehabilitated when treated with some sort of intervention that is available within the community at the time of adjudication. To developmental psychologists, however, amenability refers only to the extent to which an individual's nature has the potential to change, regardless of his or her exposure to an intervention, and regardless of the type of intervention that is applied. In other words, to developmental psychologists, amenability refers to malleability or, as it is sometimes known, plasticity.

Although these different definitions of amenability are similar, they present different standards by which to judge an individual's likelihood of desistance. An offender may be at a point in development where he or she is still malleable, but may have little likelihood of desisting from crime given the individual's life circumstances (e.g., the individual lives in a community with few opportunities for legal employment). An offender may be developmentally malleable but unlikely to desist from crime unless exposed to an intensive intervention. Research on the inherent malleability of individuals of different ages may yield different conclusions from research on the differential likelihood of desistance at different ages, which in turn may yield different conclusions from research examining whether individuals of various ages are differentially responsive to different types of interventions. As a consequence, an individual who may be judged amenable by one standard (e.g., in response to an intensive intervention of proven effectiveness) may be judged nonamenable by another (e.g., if returned to the community without any rehabilitation). As we shall see, this presents a problem for drawing clear-cut conclusions about adolescent development and transfer policy.

In theory, amenability is perhaps the most practical basis on which to make decisions about how a serious juvenile offender should be treated, because it makes little sense to invest the rehabilitative resources of the juvenile justice system in individuals who are unlikely to change and a great deal of sense to target such resources at those individuals most likely to respond to intervention or treatment. For this reason, amenability is frequently a factor in decisions regarding the transfer of juveniles to criminal court. In *Kent v. United States* (1966), the U.S. Supreme Court defined the due-process requirements for transfer hearings, listing eight criteria to be considered in making transfer decisions. Foremost among these were the seriousness of the offense and the need to protect the community, the maturity of the juvenile, and the juvenile's amenability to treatment and rehabilitation. While all states require consideration of the seriousness of the offense and community safety, not all require a consideration of the juvenile's amenability to treatment or maturity (Redding 1997).

In practice, judgments about amenability are made on an individualized basis, with decision makers taking into account a juvenile's current circumstances, psychological history, and responses to prior interventions, if any; these are forensic, or clinical, judgments about individual differences, however, and are not informed by the study of normative development. From the perspective of developmental psychology, however, the amenability question can be reframed as a question about general tendencies toward malleability rather than statements about particular individuals. In other words, developmental psychologists might ask whether there is an age below which one can presume that most individuals have the capacity to change and an age above which most people's amenability has diminished enough that they are unlikely to respond effectively to rehabilitation. If these questions could be answered definitively, at least some of the decision making about an individual's amenability to treatment could be done on the basis of age.

Unfortunately, developmental research does not provide a satisfactory answer to these questions. The bulk of the data on the stability of personality traits suggests that individuals do indeed become less changeable over the course of adolescence and adulthood, suggesting a decline in malleability over the course of development; one way to put this is that we become more like ourselves over time. But data on the over-time increase in the stability of personality characteristics do not speak to the question of whether change is *possible,* because estimates of personality stability do not inform questions about malleability. Intelligence is, for example, both a highly stable trait and a reasonably malleable one. Thus, while people who are intelligent as children tend to be intelligent as adults (the stability issue), individuals remain capable of learning throughout childhood, adolescence, and adulthood (the malleability issue). Thus, even if it were shown that antisocial tendencies were stable over time, such stability estimates may not be accurate, because they do not take into account whether the individual's environment has changed. Personality traits like aggressiveness may remain stable over time in the absence of any change in the environment, but these very traits may be unstable within a changing context. More problematically, personality and environmental factors tend to affect one another in a reciprocal fashion, so that the very individuals whose personality characteristics make them less amenable to change are likely to live in environments that are less conducive to desistance from antisocial behavior.

Because any judgment of amenability presumes not only individual malleability but at least some change in context—that is, amenability by definition under the law presumes some sort of intervention—it is impossible to evaluate an individual's amenability without considering the nature of the intervention to which the individual is going to be exposed and whether there is reason to believe that this particular intervention will be effective for this particular individual. Rather than make amenability judgments on the basis of age, therefore, developmental research would indicate that such judgments should be made on the basis of past experience. A youngster who has been exposed to certain types of interventions in the past and who has not responded to them effectively is relatively unlikely to respond to them in the future. Without such evidence, however, one would presume malleability in response to intervention.

If anything, the evidence on the development of antisocial behavior is paradoxical, at least as far as the interconnections among chronological age, amenability, and the debate over serious juvenile offenders is concerned. Despite our intuition that we can be more hopeful about individuals' potential for change when they are young than when they are older, there is fairly good evidence that the earlier a minor begins to engage in antisocial or violent behavior, the more likely it is that such behavior will persist into adulthood (Moffitt 1993). In particular, minors whose first offense occurs in preadolescence are less likely to desist than those whose first offense occurs during late adolescence. These findings seem, at first glance, to lead to the counterintuitive, if not outright peculiar, conclusion that we should view young juvenile offenders as inherently less amenable than older ones, that the best candidates for rehabilitation are older adolescents, and that the juvenile offenders who may most warrant incapacitation are the youngest, not the oldest. In essence, the inverse relationship between age of onset of criminal behavior and likelihood of desistance contradicts the conclusions one reaches from developmental analyses of the data on competence and blameworthiness, which indicate less punitive treatment for younger than for older juveniles.

There is an important caveat to this logic, however, because these findings on age of onset and patterns of reoffending describe the natural course of desistance, rather than the effectiveness of intervention programs. This is problematic, because there is a substantial literature in developmental psychology that suggests that patterns of problem behavior, if not corrected, become self-sustaining. Antisocial youngsters, for example, often are rebuffed by their prosocial peers and thus end up socializing with other antisocial youngsters, who likely encourage and reward further antisocial behavior (Cairns et al. 1988). Thus, while younger offenders may be less likely to desist on their own (as one might reasonably expect in the absence of external corrective influences), they may nevertheless be more responsive to focused rehabilitation programs when they are applied. Common sense suggests that earlier intervention with juvenile offenders is more likely to succeed than later intervention, but there is a vital need for research on this subject.

Overall, however, there is no basis in the developmental literature from which to draw generalizations about differences in amenability as a function of age. Despite our optimistic notions about the inherent malleability of young people, or our pessimistic notions about the inability of old dogs to learn new tricks, there is no research that supports either of these contentions, and some research that actually challenges them. As a consequence, we cannot recommend the implementation of age-based policies regarding the treatment of serious juvenile offenders solely on the basis of research and theory on amenability. More specifically, it is incorrect to suggest that there is an age below which individuals should remain treated as juveniles because they are especially likely to be amenable to change, or an age beyond which individuals should be categorically assumed to be too hardened to be helped. Amenability decisions should be made on a case-by-case basis and should focus on the prior history, rather than the chronological age, of the offender.

7. A Developmental Perspective on Transfer

Our analysis suggests that a developmental perspective can inform, but cannot answer, the transfer debate. Even setting aside the weighty political, practical, and moral questions that impinge on the discussion, the developmental analysis we have presented here does not point to any one age that politicians and practitioners should use in formulating transfer policies or practices. Instead, we encourage those engaged in the debate to view young offenders as falling into three broad categories: juveniles, who should not be adjudicated in adult court; adults, who should; and youths, who may or may not be developmentally appropriate candidates for transfer depending on their individual characteristics and circumstances.

In general, it appears to us appropriate to raise serious concerns based on developmental evidence about the transfer of individuals twelve and under to adult court owing to their limited adjudicative competence as well as the very real possibility that most individuals this young will not prove to be sufficiently blameworthy to warrant exposure to the harsh consequences of a criminal court adjudication; individuals twelve and under should continue to be viewed as juveniles, regardless of the nature of their offense. At the other end of the continuum, it appears, from a developmental perspective, appropriate to conclude that the vast majority of individuals older than sixteen are not appreciably different from adults in ways that would prohibit their fair adjudication within the criminal justice system. Our sense is that variability among individuals older than twelve but younger than sixteen requires that some sort of individualized assessment of an offender's competence to stand trial, blameworthiness, and likely amenability to treatment be made before reaching a transfer decision.

The framework we propose argues strongly against transfer policies that are solely offense-based and argues instead for a return to offender-based policies that permit the relevant decision makers (e.g., judges, prosecutors, defense attorneys) to exercise judgment about individual offenders' maturity and eligibility for transfer. This approach would be workable both within a system that employed judicial waiver and within one that relied on prosecutorial discretion, so long as retribution was not the sole motivating force behind prosecutors' charging decisions (e.g., in cases in which the interests of the community may be better served by retaining the adolescent offender within the juvenile justice system). To the extent that transfer via legislative exclusion is solely offense based, however, it is a bad policy from a developmental perspective.

The irony of employing a developmental perspective in the analysis of transfer policy is that the exercise reveals the inherent inadequacy of policies that draw bright-line distinctions between adolescence and adulthood. Indeed, an analysis of the developmental literature indicates that variability among adolescents of a given chronological age is the rule, not the exception. In order to be true to what we know about development, a fair transfer policy must be able to accommodate this variability.

References
Cases Cited

Dusky v. United States, 362 U.S. 402 (1960).
Godinez v. Moran, 509 U.S. 389 (1993).
Kent v. United States, 383 U.S. 541 (1966).

Other References

Appelbaum, P. 1993. "*Godinez v. Moran:* The U.S. Supreme Court Considers Competence to Stand Trial." *Hospital and Community Psychiatry* 44:929.
Belter, R., and T. Grisso. 1984. "Children's Recognition of Rights Violations in Counseling." *Professional Psychology: Research and Practice* 15:899.
Bonnie, R. 1992. "The Competence of Criminal Defendants: A Theoretical Reformulation." *Behavioral Sciences and the Law* 10:291.
Brown, B. B., D. R. Clasen, and S. A. Eicher. 1986. "Perceptions of Peer Pres-

sure, Peer Conformity Dispositions, and Self-Reported Behavior among Adolescents." *Developmental Psychology* 22:521.

Cairns, R., B. Cairns, H. Neckerman, S. Gest, and J. Gariepy. 1988. "Social Networks and Aggressive Behavior: Peer Support or Peer Rejection?" *Developmental Psychology* 24:815.

Cauffman, E., and L. Steinberg. In press. "(Im)Maturity of Judgment in Adolescence: Why Adolescents May Be Less Culpable Than Adults." *Behavioral Sciences and the Law.*.

Feld, B. 1997. "Abolish the Juvenile Court: Youthfulness, Criminal Responsibility, and Sentencing Policy." *Journal of Criminal Justice and Criminology* 88:68.

Fischoff, B. 1992. "Risk Taking: A Developmental Perspective." In *Risk-Taking Behavior.* Edited by J. Yates. New York: Wiley.

Grisso, T. 1997. "The Competence of Adolescents as Trial Defendants." *Psychology, Public Policy, and Law* 3:3.

———. 1998. *Forensic Evaluation of Juveniles.* Sarasota, Fla.: Professional Resource Press.

Grisso, T., and B. Schwartz, eds. 1999. *Adolescent Development and Juvenile Justice: The Competence and Culpability of Youth.* Chicago: University of Chicago Press.

Hirschi, T., and G. Gottfredson. 1983. "Age and the Explanation of Crime." *American Journal of Sociology* 89:552.

Inhelder, B., and J. Piaget. 1958. *The Growth of Logical Thinking from Childhood to Adolescence.* New York: Basic Books.

Keniston, K. 1970. "Youth: A 'New' Stage of Life." *American Scholar* 39:631.

Moffitt, T. 1993. "Adolescence-Limited and Life-Course-Persistent Antisocial Behavior: A Developmental Taxonomy." *Psychological Review* 100:674.

Office of Technology Assessment. 1991a. *Adolescent Health.* Vol. 1, *Summary and Policy Options.* Washington: U.S. Government Printing Office.

———. 1991b. *Adolescent Health.* Vol. 2, *Background and the Effectiveness of Selected Prevention and Treatment Services.* Washington: U.S. Government Printing Office.

———. 1991c. *Adolescent Health.* Vol. 3, *Cross-Cutting Issues in the Delivery of Health and Related Services.* Washington: U.S. Government Printing Office.

Overton, W. 1990. "Competence and Procedures: Constraints on the Development of Logical Reasoning." In *Reasoning, Necessity, and Logic: Developmental Perspectives.* Edited by W. F. Overton. Hillsdale, N.J.: Erlbaum.

Redding, R. 1997. "Juveniles Transferred to Criminal Court: Legal Reform Proposals Based on Social Science Research." *Utah Law Review* 3:709.

Rest, J. 1983. "Morality." In *Handbook of Child Psychology.* Vol. 3, *Cognitive Development.* Edited by J. Flavell and E. Markman. New York: Wiley.

Scott, E., and T. Grisso. 1997. "The Evolution of Adolescence: A Developmental Perspective on Juvenile Justice Reform." *Journal of Criminal Law and Criminology* 88:137.

Scott, E., N. Reppucci, and J. Woolard. 1995. "Evaluating Adolescent Decision Making in Legal Contexts." *Law and Human Behavior* 19:221.

Steinberg, L., and E. Cauffman. 1996. "Maturity of Judgment in Adolescence: Psychosocial Factors in Adolescent Decision-Making." *Law and Human Behavior* 20:249.

Ward, S., and W. Overton. 1990. "Semantic Familiarity, Relevance, and the Development of Deductive Reasoning." *Developmental Psychology* 26:488.

Notes

1. To be sure, the criminal court recognizes that *some* adults are incompetent, incapable of behaving responsibly, or excellent candidates for rehabilitation, and it even has options available for accommodating these special circumstances, but it historically has defined these cases as exceptional. Demonstrating that there exist adults who are as immature as juveniles may certainly warrant the maintenance of options for dealing with these special cases, but it does not necessarily follow that such evidence challenges the logic of having a standing age-based boundary between juveniles and adults, any more than this logic would be challenged by demonstrating that there are juveniles who are exceptionally mature for their age. That is, it is perfectly reasonable to erect age-based legal boundaries that are based on population averages while being cognizant of the fact that some individuals may end up being treated unfairly because their competencies are not typical for people of their chronological age. The issue is not whether age-based legal boundaries should exist, but whether the presumptions behind a particular boundary are reasonable ones.

2. Our choice of the word *youth* for this middle category is consistent with the use of the term in contemporary developmental psychology to refer to individuals who are between adolescence and adulthood (e.g., Keniston 1970).

3. *Social-cognitive competencies* are the particular cognitive competencies that are used in social situations, such as the ability to see a situation from someone else's point of view.

4. It is worth noting that some legal scholars have argued that criminal court is perfectly capable of taking into account juveniles' diminished culpability by punishing juveniles less severely or in a qualitatively different fashion. This is, in fact, what Feld (1997) has argued in his writings on what he has called the "youth discount," or what others believe can be accomplished through "blended sentencing" or through other administrative structures, such as New York City's "youth part" of the criminal court (see chapters by Redding and Howell and by Singer, Fagan, and Liberman in this volume).

5. In this sense, we draw the distinction between "blameworthiness," which we use to refer to the psychological and social factors that affect individual accountability, and "culpability," which is a legal construct, the determination of which is based on an assessment not only of the individual's blameworthiness, but of the totality of circumstances surrounding the offense. Our interest here, technically speaking, is in the development of blameworthiness, although we recognize that the terms are used interchangeably in many legal writings.

Chapter Twelve

Transfer Policy and Law Reform

FRANKLIN E. ZIMRING AND JEFFREY FAGAN

The purpose of this concluding note is to suggest some of the policy lessons that emerge from this volume. Of course, this book is not a unified treatment that spans its subjects with a single authorial voice. The preceding chapters represent a diversity of views on several questions. Imposing a grand synthesis on them is a task beyond difficulty. But the diversity of perspectives of our authors makes all the more credible the two important respects in which the studies in this volume do cumulate to a series of shared perspectives on a quarter century of debate and legislation about transfer to criminal courts and law reform.

In the first place, there is much common ground in the preceding chapters on how various transfer systems work. In the second place, there is substantial agreement among our contributors on the character of the choices that legislatures, prosecutors, and judges will be facing in the hybrid systems and political contexts of juvenile justice in the proximate American future.

We hope to explore these common themes by proposing eight conclusions about the current debate on transfer policy and by illustrating these themes with materials assembled from earlier chapters. The portrait we paint of transfer policy choices is a composite of many analyses that produce some surprisingly consistent conclusions. The examples of the phenomena we posit come from the contributions to this volume.

Here then are our eight lessons about transfer as a topic of law reform:

1. The history of unprincipled debate about transfer policy.
2. The inevitability of hard youth welfare choices in contemporary transfer decision making.
3. The complex outcomes produced by mixed systems of transfer decision making.
4. The danger of redundant reforms in transfer policy.
5. The inherent problem of overbreadth in categorical exclusions from juvenile court.

6. The necessity of regulatory perspective on transfer systems.
7. The limits of developmental psychology as a decisional tool for transfer policy.
8. The necessity of appropriate legal standards in criminal courts to fairness in transfer policy.

1. The History of Unprincipled Transfer Debate

What purposes of punishment should be considered when making decisions about transfer from juvenile to criminal court? Desert? If so, how defined? Deterrence? Incapacitation? Why should a minimum age be imposed for transfer if a juvenile meets minimum standards of competence for standing criminal trial? Should the need for incapacitation be considered in making transfer decisions? If deterrence and incapacitation can inform transfer decisions, should these considerations also influence dispositional decisions for juveniles?

At the heart of such questions is this: What are, and what should be, the differences between juvenile and criminal courts? Why should those still under the maximum age for juvenile court ever be at risk of transfer? There has been very little attention to these matters in debates about transfer policy.

Indeed, transfer of juveniles to criminal court is a fascinating and complex process that has produced almost no principled debate and sustained analysis. Why is this? Transfer of persons under maximum age for delinquency to the criminal courts has been an important issue for a century, yet there has been almost no thoughtful analysis of the transfer problem during this time. We suspect the reason for this is that all parties to the issue come with strong result preferences that have discouraged them from any interest in the principles that might inform transfer decisions.

Those who strongly support juvenile courts have approached the waiver issue by believing that youth welfare is always better served in juvenile courts than in criminal courts, so that the task of drafting standards or laws is to hold the practice to an absolute minimum level. Under such circumstances, it might not have been considered a profitable enterprise to inquire about the appropriate principles to decide when transfer to criminal court should be chosen, because many youth advocates believed there were no such appropriate cases. With this standing point, the standard-setting process should create as many cumulative obstacles to transfer as possible, and never mind the overall rationale of the criteria. This is our reading of the process that produced the Institute for Judicial Administration–American Bar Association standards on waiver (Institute for Judicial Administration 1977). Any standards that minimize transfer outcomes are preferable for that reason. A set of neutral principles to guide the selection of transfer cases is literally beside the point.

For at least twenty years, there has been strong interest group support for substantial increases in the number of juveniles sent to criminal court. Has the arrival of protransfer interest groups led to a principled dialogue on what sorts of cases justify criminal court treatment? No, it has not; and one reason for the lack of principled analysis in recent years is that the protransfer groups are just as result oriented as their opponents.

The major premise of such legislative proposals as the U.S. House and Senate attempts to encourage transfer since 1996 is that more severe punishments for serious juvenile crimes are a good thing, and the minor premise is that transfer to criminal courts will achieve these harsher punishments. Rather than producing a set of principles for when transfer is justified, the proposals assume that an increase in transfers will be a policy benefit, the more the merrier.

The general hostility of these proposals to juvenile court processing of serious cases is principle enough for the new federal proposals. The objective of these proposals is increasing the punishment for serious youth crime. This version of result orientation is the mirror image of those antitransfer stalwarts who sought to minimize the number of criminal court cases in any event. The debate that is the product of these two preferences is only an exchange of preferred outcomes, with those who sought a minimum number of transfers being opposed by those who wish to encourage a maximum number of serious punishments. The difference of opinion is really just about the desirability of serious punishment for adolescent offenders, not about reasons for such outcomes. So the different preferences do not produce different principles for decision; instead, these two camps assume the correctness of their contrasting assumptions toward getting tough on juveniles and make any debate on waiver or legislative transfer into nothing more than a referendum on toughness. The prospects that such a shouting match will provide jurisprudential insights are pretty slight. There has been little or no reasoned elaboration about transfer policy in the legislative process.

We do not mean to suggest that single-minded result orientations are never right. If it were actually true that transfer to criminal court never made sense, then seeking a principled basis for transfer would be a waste of time, and perhaps a dangerous waste of time. But is it obvious that this universal American practice has no value? If not, we avoid principled debate at our peril.

Recent history teaches that there is also great cost generated by the failure to conduct analysis of juvenile court transfer questions on a principled basis. Two decades of debate and legislative activity on transfer have left almost no legacy of analysis and empirical data to inform future debate: the transfer question has generated no intellectual capital for all its years of high public importance. And that means that efforts like the studies in this book must start from scratch in sorting out the values at stake in transfer standards and the likely effects of policy changes.

Unprincipled debate is a hard habit to break when both sides in a policy conflict are locked into positions that assign no importance to theory, facts, or analysis. It does not stretch matters much to suggest that this is the current condition of juvenile court transfer as an issue of political contention in the United States.

One objective that all of the contributors to this volume share is to bring principle to the transfer debate and to provide a foundation on which further efforts toward principled analysis can be built. Principled debate is anything but value free on topics like transfer from juvenile court. But good choices in considering alternative changes in the legal borders between juvenile and criminal courts will require much more than good intentions.

2. The Inevitability of Hard Choices

There may be some easy choices between alternative transfer policies but not many. Even assuming that the best choice for those accused of delinquency is always to minimize the number of transferred cases, it will often be quite difficult to determine which of a number of policy options will lead to the smallest number of transfers. A second problem is that there are other youth welfare values to be served by a transfer policy, such as principles of nondiscrimination that might conflict with transfer policies that produce the smallest numbers. A third problem is that a minimum transfer preference is based on an assumption that any outcome in juvenile court is superior to any outcome in criminal court for the same cases. But what if reformers change the rules in juvenile court to ward off the prospect of more transfers, but allow for much longer juvenile court sentences? By changing the nature of the juvenile justice system, the reformers may have altered the calculus of benefit and harm that was the basis of the preference for minimizing transfers. Consider two of the many case studies in hard child welfare choice that are confronted in earlier chapters.

The first case study concerns the choice between legislative exclusion and judicial waiver as it affects two important policy dimensions, the number of African American juveniles transferred to criminal court and the degree to which a transfer system puts African American delinquents at disproportionate risk of transfer. Assume a simple choice between a system dominated by legislative exclusions and a system dominated by discretionary judicial waivers. The data presented by Bortner, Zatz, and Hawkins in chapter 8 are consistent with a conclusion that judicial waiver will result in the smallest number of total delinquents transferred and the smallest number of African American juveniles transferred. But while legislative exclusions transfer more kids, including more African American kids, to criminal court, this process appears to reduce the disproportionate concentrations of African Americans found in judicial waiver systems. The legislative exclusion system transfers more African American kids, but also transfers many more white kids than judicial waiver. The number and proportion of African American kids transferred goes up, but the percentage of all transferred kids who are African American goes down.

The advantage of the legislative system is that racial concentration of transfers is lower, but the number of youths is far higher. The advantage of judicial waiver is that fewer kids and fewer African American kids are transferred, but the percentage of African American kids is far higher. Singer, Fagan, and Liberman show a similar pattern in New York, where the post-1978 Juvenile Offender Law brought high percentages of white adolescents into the criminal courts in the non–New York City counties. Knowing you want to make a choice based on youth welfare in such trade-offs may not make selecting an outcome between these alternatives much easier.

A second case study in the complexity of child welfare choices in transfer policy concerns some of the systems that Redding and Howell refer to as blended jurisdiction. The strategic idea of blended jurisdiction is to make juvenile court processing of serious delinquents less unpopular with the public and prosecutors by expanding the amount of punishment that one branch of the juvenile court can administer. In Texas, blended jurisdiction juvenile courts can give prison sentences of up to forty years, subject to a second hearing, to be held at the delinquent's eighteenth birthday, at which either the defendant can be released or his or her sentence can be confirmed. Confirmation results in transfer to the adult penal system to serve the remaining time.

Putting aside equity and procedural considerations in the contingent phase of blended sentencing, why should we assume that a forty-year-maximum blended sentence in juvenile court is preferable to transfer for any juvenile? If we cannot make that assumption, then how can we identify the kids who benefit and those who suffer from blended jurisdiction?

Can we determine whether new schemes such as blended jurisdiction keep rates of transfer to criminal court low? If there is some reduction in transfer rates under blended statutes, and time served is somewhat lower in marginal cases when kept in blended jurisdiction juvenile courts, it well may be that those delinquents promoted to blended jurisdiction *who otherwise would have been sanctioned in a conventional juvenile court* are the losers when blended jurisdiction is introduced, while those juveniles sentenced in blended systems *who otherwise would have been transferred to adult court in its absence* are better off for the reform. If these turn out to be the realities of blended jurisdiction, the new system is a shift that improves prospects for some kids and makes things worse for others.

If the observer's basic commitment is to the welfare of delinquent kids, how should he or she decide about blended jurisdiction in these circumstances? Compare the number of kids disadvantaged with the number of kids better off and favor the blended system if it benefits more kids than it hurts? Or weigh the extent of harm and benefit so that the search is for the greatest good for the greatest number. Jeremy Bentham here we go!

Three points need be underlined in considering the race and blended jurisdiction case studies. The first is that even when all the facts are known about the impact of various transfer-relevant policies, finding the policy path to maximize youth welfare is not an easy task. Is it better to reduce the number of African American juveniles transferred or to reduce the size of the disadvantage suffered by African American defendants even if more of them get transferred to criminal court as a result? Should we give many more juveniles longer sentences in juvenile court to avoid even worse fates for some of this number if transferred? These are hard questions even under conditions of full information.

But the second headline of these examples is that full information is a dream world. A decade into a variety of blended jurisdiction experiments, we know next to nothing of the impact of these policies on the systems where they function. Operating numbers have been generated by state systems, but policy impact is unknown. Is Texas waiving fewer kids because it has been giving blended sentences for twelve years? We do not know. Indeed, the near void of data on the policy impact that Redding and Howell report seems to us one major scandal in the recent history of United States juvenile justice. It is not merely stupid to conduct such experiments in a factual vacuum, it is immoral as well. What is most necessary is not fancy behavioral research but basic factual data.

The third fundamental point about child welfare criteria for transfer policy is that calling such matters the search for the "best interest" of juveniles mislabels the texture of the decisions that must be made. The best interests of serious delinquents might be better served by not allowing transfer at all. Even if youth welfare is the important tiebreaker in choosing between politically possible transfer regimes, the search is really much more a damage control operation than an unfettered pursuit of Johnny's best interest. A quarter century ago, Joseph Goldstein, Anna Freud, and Albert Solnit suggested relabeling a child custody test that had previously been called "the best interests of the child" as "the least detrimental alternative" placement available for the same child. The argument was that the new label would better represent the factual reality (Goldstein, Freud, and Solnit 1972). This is even more true in the transfer debate of the 1990s—the best that can be hoped for is the least detrimental alternative for adolescent offenders given the considerable list of other interests and constituencies that will be served in making decisions about transfer from juvenile court.

3. The Complexity of Mixed Systems

Dawson's chapter on judicial waiver notes that the introduction of legislative exclusion statutes has an important influence on the type of cases judges see in judicial hearings and probably also on the standards the judges are likely to apply to the cases that come before them. This may be because a different sample of cases with the most serious individual crimes now excluded by legislation will invite greater emphasis on the chronicity of offenders with less serious current charges. In addition, the political reminder of legislative exclusion might loosen the standards that might be required for judicial approval of transfer. In either case, what might seem like a separate legislative process for generating transfer has important implications for the residual of cases that are routed through the juvenile court.

The interaction that Dawson warns us about in the judicial and legislative transfer analysis has more general applicability. Even though legislative innovations are designed and passed one at a time, new layers of practice interact with existing rules and practices in complicated and often unpredictable ways.

With respect to transfer of juveniles to criminal court, a legislative scheme that provides two different ways to transfer is more complex than a system with a single channel. Adding intermediate courts in the style of blended jurisdiction complicates matters still more. If we are correct in assuming that mixed systems of transfer and heightened punishment are more complex than single-channel processes, the recent history of juvenile justice reform suggests an overwhelming trend toward complexity in the rules and systems that govern transfer. By 1999, the appropriate generalization is that most if not all systems for determining transfer or creating transfer-like sanction outcomes are now mixed systems (Griffin, Torbet, and Szymanski 1998). Indeed, the trend over time toward complexity is as pronounced as the increased provision for transfer in the legislative output of the 1990s. Complexity may not have been the objective of 1990s-style juvenile justice reform, but complexity has been the inevitable outcome of the multichannel mechanisms established.

What policy implication should this pattern of increasing complexity carry? The more difficult it becomes to predict the nature and magnitude of a law's impact before the fact, the greater the necessity to carefully measure the impact of legal change after the fact. As systems in the states become multilayered and complex, the hope would be that careful empirical curiosity would document the impact of the clusters of new laws on court processes and on sanctions. But neither the curiosity nor the counting has yet developed over the decade during which mixed systems became the norm. The complexity of mixed systems makes guessing the outcomes of changing rules in such a system a risky business. But the absence of close observation over a decade of increased complexity means that guess and assertion will remain the dominant discourse about mixed juvenile justice systems for some time.

4. The Problem of Redundant Reform

The typical reason for public pressure to increase the sanctions that can happen when fifteen-year-olds commit serious offenses is either a notorious case or a free-floating public fear about serious youth crime (see Tanenhaus, chapter 1 in this volume). This type of stimulus is not specific to any particular legal reform—one can imagine the same public fear producing harsher punishments in juvenile court or special extended punishment systems in a blended jurisdiction section of the juvenile court, or easier standards for allowing judicial waiver, or legislative exclusion rules that bypass the juvenile court entirely. Each of these outcomes might fit the felt need to expand punishment options in an atmosphere of citizen anxiety.

But if that public mood fits any of the four responses outlined in the last paragraph, why not pass all four simultaneously? The same public anxieties might support legislative exclusions from juvenile court *and* easier standards for judicial waiver, *and* expanded punishments in special blended proceedings in juvenile court *and* higher sanctions in standard delinquency proceedings. The political energy generated by fear and anger may provoke the phenomenon of redundant reforms, where several different ways of coping with the same problem are put in place at about the same time.

The problem with this understandable phenomenon is overkill. If one assumes that the punishments of young offenders should be restricted to the minimum levels necessary, such redundant reforms create much more punitive pressure in the system than is necessary. Of course, if one views any additional punishment for young offenders as an unqualified good, then redundant punitive reforms are a wonderful political opportunity to use public concern to achieve maximum punitive effect. So whether redundant punitive changes in juvenile justice are abhorrent or positive is to a large extent dependant on the values of the observer.

But even in the hard-line view that animated the redundant 1996 congressional proposals, these multifaced changes are not necessary to respond to the particular problems of drive-by shootings or midadolescent homicide epidemics. It is just that the public fear provides an opportunity to pile on. The effect is to push further in the direction the proponent desires than the particular problem would require. In that sense, redundant reforms are gratuitously punitive, even from a hard-line perspective.

Examples of this phenomenon are spread throughout this book, but the specific issue of redundancy has not been addressed. Can the tendency to legislate redundant responses to public alarm be brought under control? The best hope for limiting redundancy is to impose a specific problem-oriented perspective on all proposals made to change practices in juvenile justice. Instead of general concerns about youth violence, participants in the legislative process should be required to specify a particular problem, estimate its frequency, outline alternative methods to respond to the problem and their impacts, and choose their version of the best alternative available. If that kind of discipline can be imposed on legislative debate, great strides can be made in reducing the frequency and scope of redundant punitive reforms.

But how to impose such discipline on juvenile justice reform? The best hope is for juvenile justice system professionals to play important expert roles in the legislative process. Judges, probation staff, and defense lawyers should join prosecutors in actively monitoring the shaping and consideration of legislative reform proposals. Prosecutors should fight the temptation to accept any proposed changes in the system that increase prosecutorial power and instead make common cause with juvenile court judges and others in creating quality control for juvenile justice reform.

Often, the best state-level mechanism available for this type of professional influence will be blue-ribbon commissions or permanent advisory groups that cut across narrowly parochial interest groups like prosecutors and defenders. The extent to which these processes can protect against redundantly punitive change is not known. But the more important the role played by coalitions of system professionals, the better the prospects.

5. Rule, Discretion, and the Specter of Overbreadth

The debate about transfer standards from juvenile to criminal court involves a choice between discretionary decisions by judges or prosecutors and rule-based legislative standards that announce in advance the circumstances that should require transfer. One corollary of a commitment to the rule of law is that, all other things being equal, observers should prefer a system based on preannounced rules and standards to a system that puts the final power of decision in the hands of a governmental official with discretionary power. So if the other costs and benefits of rule-based verses discretionary systems were quite close, the preference should go to the rule-based system.

But all other things are not equal in the competition between rule and discretion in structuring transfer decisions. The inevitable cost that comes with a rule-based system is overbreadth—the tendency for a formal rule to transfer all cases in a class if some cases require the transfer. Discretionary waiver decisions result in the transfer of very small fractions of juveniles charged with robbery and sex crimes (Dawson 1992). But if a legislature had to draft a rule that either required or prohibited the transfer of sex crime defendants, for example, the pressure would be to transfer all cases rather than live with a system that could not achieve transfers in the very worst cases imaginable of juvenile sex offenses. Feld has documented examples of this worst-case mentality in chapter 3.

The general phenomenon that lies behind the rule-versus-discretion competition for waiver is that using general standards will require transfer in many cases where a frankly discretionary approach would often result in retention in the juvenile court. The particular cost of requiring binding rules is that many more young offenders get transferred than if a juvenile court judge could make a decision without any binding rules to force his or her decision. Rules tend strongly to be overbroad because they place emphasis on the worst-case scenario of a very serious young offender who cannot be effectively treated or long restrained. This is an inherent problem and probably an insoluble one as well.

But the choice in transfer policy is not between overbreadth and lawlessness. The right kind of standards for transfer are those that create the necessary conditions for transfer eligibility—for example, the combination of age and offense seriousness that need be present before transfer can be considered. A rule orientation can provide the *necessary* conditions for transfer to criminal court without generating needless expulsion from juvenile court, but rules cannot provide the *sufficient* conditions for transfer without overbroad transfers as an inevitable result.

If the legislative process is best restricted to generating the necessary conditions for transfer, legislation must delegate the power to decide in individual cases either to judges or prosecutors. We believe an explicit delegation of authority is superior to formal statements that prescribe transfer but leave practical authority with prosecutors. As between prosecutors and judges, our preference would rest with the judiciary. But the need for discretion and to restrict legislative standards to necessary conditions is independent of the discretionary agency one chooses to carry out this vital function.

6. Compared to What? The Need for Regulatory Perspective in Juvenile Justice Reform

We use the term "regulatory perspective" here to describe a style of policy analysis that (1) emphasizes the way reforms work in practice in juvenile and criminal courts and (2) judges the benefits and drawbacks of particular policies against alternative regimes that states are likely to adopt. This brand of empirically oriented pragmatism is the best hope for transfer policy analysis. Yet neither policy analysis nor reform in contemporary juvenile justice is based in such pragmatism. We already have mentioned that youth advocates often avoid choosing between the unpalatable alternatives of current events by declaring that all transfer policies are bad. While that is a firm statement of principle, it will not serve youth protection unless it also happens to be the case that all transfer policies and systems are equally bad. This seems to us unlikely.

There are also policy proponents who take permanent comfort in factual assumptions that are far from factual truth. We count among this number persons who continue to view blended sentences as alternatives to waiver and automatic transfer when there are in fact no systems that use blended tribunals as the exclusive method of increasing punishment for juveniles.

A regulatory perspective judges the operational virtues and vices of particular rules against their probable alternatives. In this spirit, one of the common threads in many chapters in this volume is the rehabilitation of judicial waiver as the lesser of two evils in transfer policy. Feld's analysis of legislative exclusion in chapter 3 is only one example of this phenomenon. Bishop and Frazier present data very much to this effect in chapter 7.

A further example is less obvious. Thomas Grisso outlines the considerable limits of clinical assessments of waiver candidates in chapter 9. That might be a pretty good argument against all forms of transfer, except for the fact that American juvenile courts cannot extend their delinquency jurisdiction very far into adolescence without some transfer safety valve. When comparing individualized waiver based on clinical assessment to legislative exclusion systems, the big question becomes whether clinical assessment in judicial waiver decisions is better than no assessment at all of the individual targeted for transfer by the legislature.

Clausel and Bonnie's analysis of the appellate process yields a particular type of regulatory insight worthy of note. All-but-standardless discretionary decisions like the judicial waiver process are notoriously bad candidates for meaningful appellate review. Sure enough, the authors show that appellate review of judicial decisions is toothless. But by substituting broad rules for judgment, legislative exclusion and prosecutorial choice systems are also very poor candidates for meaningful appellate review. So when the judicial waiver system is judged on one of its most disturbing faults, it doesn't lose points to alternative systems currently in use. Indeed, nothing has contributed more to the partial rehabilitation of judicial waiver in this volume than the conspicuous vices of legislative exclusion systems.

If waiver and legislative exclusion are the field of choice in the United States in the near future, we think that a pragmatic lesser-of-evils approach is exactly right. But it is an empirically based pragmatism that is not easy to practice. Ongoing evaluations of transfer law in action are necessary conditions to good judgments about the choice of alternative policies.

However necessary a regulatory perspective is to the law reform process, the informational and human resources it requires are rarely available to state legislatures in current circumstances. State bar associations, the executive branch of state government, and blue-ribbon nongovernmental organizations will be the best hope to provide the panoramic perspective that can create quality control in the law reform process. More federal support for research on the impact of legislative initiatives would also help build the infrastructure of information that is now missing from the discussion of alternative paths to juvenile justice reform.

7. The Limits of Data on Human Development as a Source of Transfer Policy

Developmental psychology has learned a great deal about the timing and content of adolescent maturity, and the prospects for further advances are good. Yet it seems to us unlikely that the insights from developmental psychology will often translate directly into policy about transfer from the juvenile to the adult court. These insights fit better as paradigm than policy.

There are three reasons why the policy significance of developmental findings will be attenuated. The first reason is that the most clear-cut developmental findings are also easy cases for sociocultural reasons. The developmental psychologist can tell us many reasons why nine- and ten-year-olds are inappropriate targets for full criminal responsibility. But children younger than thirteen commit a tiny fraction of serious youth crime, and the culture already excludes the most obvious candidates for developmental exclusion from criminal legal liability. While the mass media pay copious attention to reports of eight-year-old killers, there is no strong movement toward putting very young children at significant legal risk. Some of the minimum ages in transfer statutes are very young but there is no evidence that the systems will deliver on the threat of ten-year-old adulthood. Americans still know young children when they see them. So the developmental data on very young children is clear but not critically important to the law. It is, instead, the adolescent years that are the high-risk period for punitive legal liability.

And that produces the second limit on the policy applications of developmental findings. What psychology tells us is that adolescent development is an incremental process with very few step function transitions of the kind legal boundary makers would wish to see. Moreover, any measurable group differences exhibit wide variances around uncertain means, further weakening the predictions inherent in developmental classifications. Since there is no single cognitive, social, or behavioral boundary in the developmental findings on criminal responsibility of adolescent offenders, the incremental differences between ascending age groups do not easily translate into binary distinctions like juvenile or adult, or full versus partial culpability. Findings of incremental processes of responsibility or maturity do not fit well with the yes-or-no texture of legal decisions about penal responsibility. The empirical truth of developmental data is thus more a critique of the binary legal systems than a basis for locating at a particular age the type of bright-line distinctions that current law requires. And that limits the potential influence of the developmental data.

The third limit of the developmental data on adolescence as a direct measure of penal responsibility is that assessments of responsibility are essentially moral judgments that can be informed by but not decided behavioral data. Many of the attributes of maturity are attained as much by social experience as they are by cognitive growth. Accordingly, the judgment about when an adolescent has not had enough practice in the tasks of peer management to be fully accountable for harmful acts requires a moral decision more than a finding about cognitive development. Even when developmental data offer clear evidence of maturational deficit, the translation of these deficits as signs of immaturity versus risk for purposes of legal decision making requires a moral judgment of developmental status.[1]

To say that the boundaries of penal adulthood are moral rather than cognitive issues is neither a license for arbitrary choices nor a rejection of behavioral data as a basis for making the moral choices that the issue requires. But legal policy can very rarely be derived from behavioral data, it can only be influenced by our emerging knowledge.

One of the most constructive influences of the kind of data that Steinberg and Cauffman describe in chapter 11 would be to shift the law's application from binary "all or nothing" categories to a system of assessing penal liability that reflected the more incremental nature of maturity. There would still be moral and social judgments about the timing and consequences of immaturity, but there would be a better fit between how kids grow up and how we make decisions about the punishments they deserve for criminal wrongdoing.

8. The Necessity of Criminal Court Youth Policies

There is no such thing as substantive justice or utilitarian success in transfer policy because transfer to criminal court is not a final substantive outcome. Other decisions follow that will determine the justness and effectiveness of a criminal court case outcome.

What are the punishment choices in the criminal courts and what policies about youth and diminished responsibility inform the choice of punishments? If the principles and practices of criminal courts toward young offenders are consistent with the principles of the juvenile courts, the system as a whole can be coherent even if the sanctions delivered differ. But if criminal courts ignore factors important in juvenile courts, or if different behavioral assumptions are made about the same situations, then the system that is formed when the two courts interact must be incoherent.

So the achievement of justice in transfer cases depends on the quality of justice in the criminal courts, as it always has. The multiple avenues of transfer between juvenile and criminal court have simply made evident a substantive interdependence that has existed all along. And the tendency of recent legislation to encourage the transfer of more and younger adolescent offenders means that explicit policies toward youths must now evolve in criminal courts, or the entire system is rendered arbitrary.

In this sense, the criminal courts have inherited some of the most difficult cases that juvenile courts ever had to face but the legacy has not come with any legal framework attached. Hard-line advocates who have been pushing for wider transfer boundaries and policies would want to see a criminal court with no explicit youth policy to reduce the severity of its punishment. The larger the case flow into criminal court of adolescent offenders, however, the less likely it will be that no youth policy will evolve. In this regard, Singer, Fagan, and Liberman show that the impact of New York's 1978 "dirty dozen" law is an instructive case study of how form follows function in criminal court processing of young offenders.

There is, however, one contrast between juvenile and criminal court policy that creates discontinuity in youth sanctions. Over the past quarter century, the criminal courts have greatly increased the magnitude of incarceration they deliver during a period when the juvenile courts have not (Zimring, forthcoming). Pushing young defendants over the line is thus a rational way to increase the chances of incarceration and its length.

In the near future, one of the most important domains for what we used to call "juvenile justice reform" will be the criminal courts and state penal codes. Interest groups that have long operated in a more limited legislative environment will have to follow the young offenders into the criminal courts or lose influence over what happens to them.

Perhaps the new emphasis on criminal court processes for serious young offenders will create positive pressure to fill an extraordinary void in American criminal sentencing law. The English, the German, and other European systems have long had special doctrines and sentencing provisions for the youngest defendants in their criminal courts. In the United States, the federal Youth Corrections Act of 1948 created one such system oriented to the indeterminate sentencing of offenders under twenty-one years of age. It was supplanted in 1984 by a federal criminal code that is as silent on the question of youths as are most state codes. If the New York experience is a guide, the existence of fourteen- and fifteen-year-old defendants in criminal court may produce a reexamination of youth in punishment policies that extends to much older age groups as well as to those who provoked the reexamination. Indeed, we are likely to create an institution much like the current juvenile court within the procedural boundaries of the criminal court.

Nothing could have been further from the intention of those who have mobilized the political campaign to substitute criminal for juvenile courts. But the first century of juvenile court history has often witnessed such triumphs of latent over manifest functions when the systemic changes of legislation are assessed.

There is a historical puzzle to address when considering the extraordinary amount of legislative concern about transfer policy concentrated in the last decade of the twentieth century. As Tanenhaus shows in chapter 1, the conflicts and pressures present when younger adolescents commit serious offenses are as old as the juvenile court. Yet the breadth and intensity of the push to increase transfer in the 1990s was unprecedented. Why?

The consensus answer to that question in current debate is that rates of serious youth violence were increasing rapidly and threatened to continue increasing as the adolescent population increased from its 1990 low. Adolescent homicide arrests did increase quite dramatically in the late 1980s and early 1990s but fell back very quickly after 1993. By 1997, homicide arrest rates for youths under age eighteen were close to their 1980 levels while youth arrests for robbery and rape were lower than in 1980 (Zimring 1998, chap. 3). While rates of youth violence rose and fell, the pressure for generating more transfer to criminal court and for relocating the transfer decision from judge to prosecutor was relentless. Something more than youth crime trends was pushing on transfer policy.

In part, the effort to push serious cases out of juvenile court in the 1990s was an attempt to bypass the one set of judicial institutions that had not greatly increased levels of incarceration during the 1970s and 1980s. The rate at which adults (including young adults) were incarcerated by the criminal courts more than doubled during the two decades after 1970, while the rate at which persons under eighteen were incarcerated after committing criminal offenses stayed quite stable. Transferring from juvenile to criminal court was attractive in the 1990s because it meant removing cases from the only courts that had not joined the incarceration boom into a criminal court system that more accurately reflected the punitive temper of the times.

The debate about transfer policy in the 1990s involved two sharply contrasting visions of the role of transfer from juvenile to criminal court. At one pole are those who imagine that transfer into criminal courts is a method of resolving the difficult conflicts that arise when young people commit serious crimes. It is helpful to think of this as a "conflict resolution" theory of transfer to criminal court. The contrasting view—which is also the organizing principle of this volume—is that transfers relocate but do not automatically resolve the tensions that high punishment for young offenders generates. The "conflict resolution" view of court transfer is that it confers an all-purpose adult status on the young person transferred so that the need to worry about diminished responsibility and youth protection disappears. Move the case to criminal court and the mixed motives and conflicts that make such cases difficult will have disappeared. From this perspective, the automatic transfer of large numbers of juveniles will solve problems rather than create them.

The second model of transfer to criminal court can be called a "conflict continuation" theory. It regards the doubt and ambivalence about transfer as inevitable and not susceptible to solution by merely shifting the type of court that will hear the case. The supporters of legislative expansions of transfer in the 1990s often embraced the image of transfer as a device that resolves the inconsistencies and mixed feelings about punishing youth. The notion that transfer creates adult levels of maturity and responsibility was one of the great myths and appeals of transfer as a response to youth crime.

The central problem with a "conflict resolution" model of transfer is its manifest untruth. Transferring a fourteen-year-old defendant from one court to another does not add to his or her age or maturity. There is no evidence that the commission of terrible crimes is an indicator that the offender is more mature or sophisticated than his or her age peers. A "conflict resolution" model of transfer is persuasive under these circumstances only if there is no real conflict to resolve—if the unqualified punishment of young adolescents does not present any substantial problems of proportionality or inconsistency with other governmental theories about childhood.

These two competing theories of transfer connect to two contrasting notions of the impact of the transfer legislation that have recently proliferated. To view the transfer process as a way of resolving conflicts is to imagine the decisions made in transfer statutes as the last act in a morality play. In this view, basic moral and social decisions about the treatment of serious young offenders have been made. The important work has been done.

A "conflict continuation" model of transfer regards the legal changes of recent years as a part of a large and complex process that has pushed unresolved and serious problems into new jurisdictional rubrics. In this view, the important work of seeking just outcomes in difficult cases has only just begun. And the legacy of the changes in the 1990s is a justice system where the transfer of young adolescents to criminal court is a more important and more problematic part of the criminal justice system than ever before.

References

Dawson, Robert O. 1992. "An Empirical Study of *Kent* Style Juvenile Transfers to Criminal Court." *St. Mary's Law Journal* 23:975.

Goldstein, Joseph, Anna Freud, and Albert J. Solnit. 1972. *Beyond the Best Interests of the Child.* New York: Free Press.

Griffin, Patrick, Patricia Torbet, and Linda Szymanski. 1998. *Trying Juveniles in Adult Court: An Analysis of State Transfer Provisions.* Washington: Office of Juvenile Justice and Delinquency Prevention, Office of Justice Programs, U.S. Department of Justice.

Institute for Judicial Administration. 1977. *Standards for Juvenile Justice.* 27. vols. New York: Institute for Judicial Administration.

Zimring, Franklin E. 1982. *The Changing Legal World of Adolescence.* New York: Viking.
———. 1998. *American Youth Violence.* New York: Oxford University Press.
———. Forthcoming. "The Common Thread: Diversion in the Jurisprudence of the Juvenile Courts." In *A Century of Juvenile Justice.* Edited by Margaret Rosenheim, Bernadine Dohrn, David Tanenhaus, and Franklin E. Zimring.

Notes

1. The ambiguity in developmental outcomes also leads to decisions with ambiguous principles. The impulsive and immature teenager, for example, may benefit from "room to reform" (Zimring 1982) in the long run, but may be a public safety risk in the near future while catching up developmentally.

CONTRIBUTORS

FRANCIS A. ALLEN
Emeritus professor, College of Law, University of Florida; emeritus professor, College of Law, University of Michigan

DONNA BISHOP
Associate professor, College of Criminal Justice, Northeastern University

RICHARD J. BONNIE
John S. Battle Professor and director, Institute of Law, Psychiatry, and Public Policy, University of Virginia

M. A. BORTNER
Associate professor, School of Justice Studies, Arizona State University

ELIZABETH CAUFFMAN
Assistant professor, Western Psychiatric Institute and Clinic, University of Pittsburgh

CHARLES FRAZIER
Professor, Department of Sociology, University of Florida

LYNDA E. FROST CLAUSEL
Assistant professor, Institute of Law, Psychiatry, and Public Policy, University of Virginia

ROBERT O. DAWSON
Bryant Smith Chair in Law, University of Texas, School of Law

JEFFREY FAGAN
Professor, School of Public Health, Columbia University

BARRY C. FELD
Professor, University of Minnesota School of Law

CHARLES FRAZIER
Center for Studies in Criminology and Law, University of Florida

THOMAS GRISSO
Professor, University of Massachusetts Medical School

DARNELL HAWKINS
Professor, Department of African American Studies, University of Illinois-Chicago

JAMES C. HOWELL
Criminologist, Pinehurst, N.C.

AKIVA LIBERMAN
Social science analyst, National Institute of Justice

RICHARD E. REDDING
Assistant professor, Institute of Law, Psychiatry, and Public Policy, University of Virginia School of Law

SIMON SINGER
Professor, Department of Sociology, The University at Buffalo

Laurence Steinberg
Professor, Department of Psychology, Temple University

David S. Tanenhaus
Assistant professor, History Department, University of Nevada, Las Vegas

Marjorie S. Zatz
Professor, School of Justice Studies, Arizona State University

Franklin E. Zimring
Professor, University of California— Berkeley School of Law

CASE INDEX

Estelle; Barefoot v., 463 U.S. 880 (1983), 335

Fitzgerald; People v., 322 Ill. 54 (1926), 27
Fultz; People v., 554 N.W.2d 725 (Mich. 1996), 201n7, 203n20
Furman v. Georgia, 408 U.S. 238 (1972), 90

Gault, In re, 387 U.S. 1, 87 S.Ct. 1428, 18 L.Ed.2d 527 (1967), x, 15, 38n3, 39n5, 40n13, 87, 157, 183, 198, 209, 355, 356
Georgia; Furman v., 408 U.S. 238 (1972), 90
Godinez v. Moran, 509 U.S. 389 (1993), 159, 391, 393
Goldberg v. Kelly, 397 U.S. 254 (1970), 206n44
Grayer; State v., 191 Neb. 523, 215 N.W.2d 859 (1974), 144n1
Green v. United States, 308 F.2d 303 (D.C. Cir 1962), 32
Green; State v., 218 Kan. 438, 544 P.2d 356 (1975), 96

Hansen v. State, 904 P.2d 811 (Wyo. 1995), 144n3, 195, 201n6
Harden v. Commonwealth, 885 S.W.2d 323 (Ky. 1994), 202n9
Harris; State v., 494 N.W.2d 619 (S.D. 1993), 203n21
Hayes; Bordenkircher v., 434 U.S. 557 (1978), 94
Haynes; United States v., 590 F.2d 309 (9th Cir. 1979), 144n1
Hicks v. Superior Court, 36 Cal. App. 4th 1649, 43 Cal. Rptr.2d 269 (Cal. App. 1995), 57
Hughes v. State, 653 A.2d 241 (Del. 1994), 47, 190

In the Matter of. See name of party

J.D.W., In the Matter of, 881 P.2d 1324 (Mont. 1994), 202n11
J.K.C., In the Matter of, 891 P.2d 1169 (Mont. 1995), 202n11
J.R.C., In the Matter of, 551 S.W.2d 748 (Tex. Civ. App.-Texarkana 1977), 57
Jackson v. State, 311 So.2d 658 (Miss. 1975), 144n1

Jahnke v. State, 692 P.2d 911 (Wyo. Sup. Ct. 1984), 99–100, 195
Jeremiah B. v. State, 823 P.2d 883 (Nev. 1991), 201n8
Jiles; People v., 43 Ill.2d 145, 251 N.E.2d 529 (Il. 1969), 96
Johnson v. State, 314 So.2d 573 (Fla. 1975), 144n1
Jones v. State, 654 P.2d 1080 (Okla. Crim. App. 1982), 144n1
Jones; Breed v., 421 U.S. 519 (1975), 87, 194
Juvenile Male; U.S. v., 923 F.2d 614 (8th Cir. 1991), 202n14

Keith Wayne Wood, In the Matter of, 768 P.2d 1370 (Mont. 1989), 194, 205n37
Kelly; Goldberg v., 397 U.S. 254 (1970), 206n44
Kent v. United States 383 U.S. 541 (1966), xv, 14, 32–33, 52, 56, 86, 87, 88, 89, 90, 91, 93, 95–96, 113, 118, 121, 148, 155, 178n23, 182–184, 188–189, 193, 198, 327, 355, 356, 400
Kentucky; Stanford v., 492 U.S. 361 (1989), 129

L.J.S. and J.T.K., In the Matter of, 539 N.W.2d 408 (Minn. App. 1995), 57
Lattimore; People v., 362 Ill. 206, 199 N.E. 275 (1935), 27–28, 30, 42n29

Male Juvenile; U.S. v., 148 F.3d 468 (5th Cir. 1998), 202n15
Marine v. State, 607 A.2d 1185 (De. 1992), *cert. dismissed,* 505 U.S. 1247 (1992), 190
Mei, Ex parte, 122 N.J. Eq. 125, 192 Atl. 81 (1937), 28–29
Mohi; State v., 901 P.2d 991 (Utah 1995), 100–102, 195–196, 205n42
Moran; Godinez v., 509 U.S. 389 (1993), 159, 391, 393
Myers v. District Court, 184 Colo. 81, 518 P.2d 836 (1974), 144n1, 144n3

O'Brien; Commonwealth v., 673 N.E.2d 552 (Mass. 1996), 203n19
Oyler v. Boles, 368 U.S. 448 (1962), 94

NAME INDEX